WHAT'S NEW ?

When the first edition c [barcode: MW01124982] ιat it would make people excited, . ique and historic underwater world of the inland seas. It was a massive undertaking, but the book met with immediate success! It became, and continues to be, the best selling book by prolific Great Lakes author Cris Kohl. From the hundreds of positive messages he has received from scuba divers in several countries (mostly, logically enough, from the USA and Canada), Cris feels that, with this book, he achieved his goal.

Now, this new, immensely enlarged second edition completes and updates the information about shipwrecks and scuba diving in the region of the freshwater seas.

...AND WHAT AN UPDATED EDITION IT IS! It has become ENCYCLOPEDIC!

Nearly 200 pages have been added, interspersed, to the 416-page first edition -- for a total of 608 pages! New or additional information about shipwrecks and scuba diving in the Great Lakes region has been added to every one of the 50 chapters in this book.

Over 100 shipwrecks, mostly new discoveries, have been added to this second edition -- including each shipwreck's history and present-day condition.

This edition offers several hundred more photographs than appeared in the previous edition, many of them showcasing the talents of other Great Lakes photographers.

This edition offers many shipwreck drawings by new and established artists.

A totally new and exciting chapter about *The Importance of Scuba Dive Clubs* -- including how to start one and keep it operating with members excited to participate in its activities -- has been added to this edition.

Arguably the BEST new addition: 30 highlights of the Great Lakes are shown in dramatic style. These significant sidebars of Great Lakes information (see complete list on page 10) include the ten worst maritime disasters in the inland seas; the mysterious story of the *Griffon*, the first shipwreck on the upper Great Lakes; the raising of the 121-year-old sailing ship named the *Alvin Clark* from Green Bay in 1969; the tragic tale of the schooner *Rouse Simmons*, the Great Lakes' famous Christmas Tree Ship; the tale of the *Edmund Fitzgerald*, the most famous of all shipwrecks in the freshwater seas.

We hope that you will enjoy these many additions to *The Great Lakes Diving Guide*.

Praise for
The Great Lakes Diving Guide

"The Great Lakes have some fantastic diving, and Cris Kohl would know. He's been diving here for most of his life. His passion for shipwrecks and the stories behind them have inspired him to write *The Great Lakes Diving Guide*.... I don't think anybody who would be coming to dive the Great Lakes could go wrong having this [book] as part of their dive kit."

--- Richie Kohler, co-subject of the bestselling book, *Shadow Divers,* co-host of the "Deep Sea Detectives" series on the History Channel, and co-producer of *Dive Portal DVD Magazine*; taken from his interview with Cris Kohl on *Dive Portal DVD Magazine, Issue 2*, November, 2006.

Continued on next page...

THE
GREAT LAKES
DIVING
GUIDE

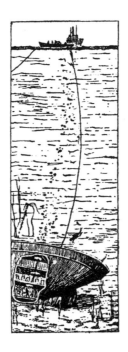

Second Edition

BOOKS BY CRIS KOHL:

Dive Southwestern Ontario! (1985)
Shipwreck Tales: The St. Clair River (to 1900) (1987)
DIVE ONTARIO! The Guide to Shipwrecks and Scuba Diving (1990)
DIVE ONTARIO TWO! More Ontario Shipwreck Stories (1994)
Treacherous Waters: Kingston's Shipwrecks (1997)
The 100 Best Great Lakes Shipwrecks, Volume I (1998; revised 2005)
The 100 Best Great Lakes Shipwrecks, Volume II (1998; revised 2005)
TITANIC, The Great Lakes Connections (2000)
The Great Lakes Diving Guide (2001; revised 2nd edition 2008)
Shipwreck Tales of the Great Lakes (2004)

WITH JOAN FORSBERG:

Shipwrecks at Death's Door (2007)

THE GREAT LAKES DIVING GUIDE

SECOND EDITION

CRIS KOHL

DEDICATION:

TO THOSE WHO EXPLORE, APPRECIATE, RESPECT AND PROTECT
THE BEAUTIFUL, INCREDIBLE AND UNIQUE GREAT LAKES
AND TO MY FRIEND
JOYCE HAYWARD
WHO DOES IT ALL.

THE GREAT LAKES DIVING GUIDE
BY CRIS KOHL

COPYRIGHT © 2008 SEAWOLF COMMUNICATIONS, INC.

ALL RIGHTS RESERVED

ISBN 10: 0-9679976-9-0

ISBN 13: 978-0-9679976-9-8

LIBRARY OF CONGRESS CARD NUMBER: 2007934528

SEAWOLF COMMUNICATIONS, INC.
PO BOX 66
WEST CHICAGO, IL 60186
USA

E-mail: SeawolfRex@aol.com
www.seawolfcommunications.com

NOTE: Photo credits are shown in terms of the author's source for the photograph rather than a specific photographer who might have taken it, except where the photographer is known and specifically named. All maps are by Cris Kohl, unless otherwise indicated, and are © Seawolf Communications, Inc. Artwork © artists as indicated. Underwater photos © photographers as indicated, excluding Cris Kohl, whose photos are © Seawolf Communications, Inc.

Printed and bound in the United States of America

FIRST EDITION: 2001
SECOND EDITION: 2008

5   4   3   2   1

FRONT COVER PHOTO: Diver Joan Forsberg glides past the anchor chains from the tragic wooden steamer, *Myron*, as they drape off the wreck's bow into the undulating sands of Lake Superior off Whitefish Point, Michigan. For more information about this site, see page 499. PHOTO BY CRIS KOHL

BACK COVER PHOTOS, *clockwise from upper left*: Poor navigation for the *George M. Cox* (see page 545); diver Joan Forsberg gazes at the *Sandusky's* figurehead (see page 356); wreckwatchers in 1900 view the *Fontana* (see page 210); diver Barb Marshall explores the upright paddlewheel of the *Comet* (see page 94); the steamer, *Algoma*, broke in half at Isle Royale (see page 547); diver Steve Radovan views skeletal remains of Christmas trees in the wreck of the *Rouse Simmons* (see page 462); diver Joyce Hayward approaches a trio of deadeyes on the Chicago wreck of the *Wells Burt* (see page 418); background photo: Joan Forsberg swims over the boiler of the *Columbus* in Gargantua Harbor (see page 565). UNDERWATER PHOTOS BY CRIS KOHL. ARCHIVAL PHOTOS FROM THE CRIS KOHL COLLECTION

INTRODUCTION

Once again, I have tightened my margins and crammed as much information as I can onto every single page of this book (I'm not a strong believer of selling blank pages.)

The growing interest in scuba diving as a recreational activity has produced large numbers of scuba-certified people searching for new dive sites. This book provides them with over 1,000 places to go diving in the Great Lakes.

I wrote my first book about scuba diving in the Great Lakes 22 years ago out of frustration at what I was seeing: men and women taking scuba courses in the Great Lakes region, then using their certification cards only for their annual winter trip down to warm tropical waters. They were totally missing out on what we have in our own back yard! I also saw "old pros" make the claim that they had seen and done everything when it came to Great Lakes scuba diving. It was a shame to see them hang up their fins because they had run out of dive sites or because they felt that the Great Lakes offered no more challenges.

To all of those people, I say, "READ MY BOOKS."

I have written eleven books (with more to come) about scuba diving and/or shipwrecks and the Great Lakes. Obviously, I still wasn't satisfied that I had done everything I could to let the world know that what we have here in our freshwater seas is unique and worthy of aquatic exploration. Even I have ventured considerably into tropical waters all around the world. Each place has its notable attributes. However, with all that I have experienced, I maintain that the best shipwreck diving lies in our five Great Lakes. And we also have other types of excellent freshwater diving as well: caverns, quarries, inland lakes, rivers, old docks, etc.

Right here in the middle of the continent, straddling the two great nations of the United States and Canada, lie the massive and scuba-underrated bodies of water which store the best preserved shipwrecks in the world. Unlike that incorrectly labeled "Shipwreck Capital of the World" over in Asia, Truk Lagoon, which offers only one type of shipwreck (steel war machines) from only one point in history (the year 1944) in one small quantity (50 shipwrecks), the varied types of, and eras represented by, the approximately 1,200 Great Lakes shipwrecks located to date, take one's breath away in their epic and substantial scope.

This book offers suggestions and descriptions of where to go scuba diving in the Great Lakes region, and is also a clearinghouse for scuba or scuba-related businesses. Divers and non-divers can find providers of Great Lakes services through information in this guide.

Since no book is perfect (I like to say that my books provide something for everyone --- and some people are always looking for mistakes!), I welcome your comments, corrections, additions, and suggestions. For example, if I missed mentioning someone who located a shipwreck, please send me your information (photocopied newspaper articles, or whatever, no matter how old), so I can give credit where credit is due. I can be contacted at: Cris Kohl, c/o Seawolf Communications, P.O. Box 66, West Chicago, IL 60186, USA, or e-mail me at SeawolfRex@aol.com or CrisKohl@aol.com, or check out our website at www.seawolf communications.com.

This book invites people (back) into the exciting waters and incredible shipwrecks of Great Lakes scuba diving.

Cris Kohl,
High Lake, Illinois
September, 2007

ACKNOWLEDGEMENTS

No book is the product of a single writer without access to human resources and/or material research facilities. The author's sincere THANK YOU goes out to the following for their help in the massive undertaking of this book's production:

Artwork and underwater photographs: Many artists have applied their talents to drawing Great Lakes shipwrecks, and there are also many gifted underwater photographers in the Great Lakes. This book is a showcase for some of their work. Heartfelt thanks go to the artists and photographers listed on page 11 for the use of their excellent work.

For underwater modeling: Alan Armbruster, Bill Atkins, Joe Corsaro, Ron DeBoer, Karen Della-Mattia, Sharon Dickson, Joe Drummond, the late Don Edwards, Jennifer Elcomb, Gary Elliott, Joan Forsberg, Joyce Hayward, Tony Kiefer, Christoff Kohl, Nathan Kroll, Ryan LeBlanc, Kathy Mahoney, Barb Marshall, Marcy McElmon, Sean Moore, Tom Pakenas, Dan Perry, Doug Pettingill, Tim Philp, Roy Pickering, Steve Radovan, Brian Roffel, Greg Schieman, Winston Smith, Jim and Pat Stayer, James Taylor, Frank Troxell, Art Vermette, and Steve Whitman.

For providing information or other assistance: the former Institute for Great Lakes Research, Bowling Green State University, Bowling Green, Ohio (now absorbed into the Archival Collections of Bowling Green State University, which I also thank wholeheartedly), Robert Graham of the Center for Archival Collections, Bowling Green State University, Bowling Green, Ohio, the Ontario Archives in Toronto, the Public Archives of Canada in Ottawa, the Great Lakes branch (in Chicago) of the National Archives, the Great Lakes Marine Collection of the Milwaukee Public Library/Wisconsin Marine Historical Society and its excellent staff, the Great Lakes Historical Society, Vermilion, OH, and its superb staff, the Marine Museum of the Great Lakes, Kingston, ON, the Metropolitan Toronto Public Library, the Underwater Archaeological Society of Chicago, Kent Divers Association (Chatham, ON), the Great Lakes Aquanauts of Greater Detroit (MI), the Bay Area Divers (Sandusky, OH), the Neptune's Nimrods (Green Bay, WI), Kent Bellrichard, George Bommarito, Jim Brotz, Gerry Buchanan, Jean Edwards, Paul Ehorn, Ed Fabok, Tom Farnquist, Chuck and Jeri Feltner, Doug Gossage, Jerry Guyer, Dennis Hale, John Halsey (Michigan State Historian), Joyce Hayward, Jim Herbert, Jim Herbert, Jr., Brian Jackson, Jim Kennard, Geoff Kohl, Joe Lark, Ryan LeBlanc, Frank Mays, Ken Merryman, Greg Millinger and Aqua Vision Research, Jeff Omstead, Doug Pettingill, Roy Pickering, Steve Radovan, Peter Rijnieks, Ralph Roberts, Kimm Stabelfeldt, John Steele, Stan Stock, David Trotter, Gene Turner, the late Rev. Peter Van der Linden, Jon Paul Van Harpen, Valerie van Heest, Peter Venoutsos, George West, Erika Wetzel, Hugh Wyatt, Susan Yankoo and George Wheeler, Dean Ziegler, and Lara Hernandez Corkrey, Ph.D., my hardworking stepdaughter who will someday be a famous writer.

To the advertisers in this edition: THANK YOU for believing in this book and in its author, and for supporting his goal of getting as many scuba divers as possible actively engaged in the great adventure of exploring the best preserved shipwrecks in the world.

An intensely heartfelt THANK YOU to Jim and Pat Stayer for their assistance, artwork, modeling, underwater images, computer training sessions and patience. Without them, a book of this caliber would simply not have been possible.

My apologies to anyone I may have inadvertently overlooked.

The largest THANK YOU goes to my patient wife, Joan Forsberg, who, besides tolerating long days of my absence and seclusion necessitated by this work and providing me with strong coffee and the world's best meals, worked enthusiastically as my proofreader, editor, research assistant, underwater model, travel buddy and believer. She's the best.

CONTENTS

FEATURES

30 Significant
Great Lakes Events

ARTISTS

Sincere thanks go to these remarkable artists and their organizations, listed alphabetically, who very generously allowed their work to be used in this edition of *The Great Lakes Diving Guide*:

UNDERWATER PHOTOGRAPHERS

Although the vast majority of the underwater photographs in this book were taken by author Cris Kohl, we thank the following talented photographers, listed alphabetically, who contributed to this edition, and we are pleased to have been able to provide a showcase for their exceptional work:

HOW TO USE
THIS BOOK

These 608 pages, a "where to" rather than a "how to" book on scuba diving in the Great Lakes, are divided into 50 chapters, each covering one, small geographical area of the vast Great Lakes system. Basically, the chapters begin at the extreme eastern end of this region, and head west, concluding in the Lake Superior area.

I have attempted as often as possible to divide this book into geographic areas rather than political ones, and in large part I been able to avoid those human delineations in favor of the natural ones. It makes no sense to divide Lake Michigan, for example, into four areas, each under the jurisdiction of Michigan, Indiana, Illinois, and Wisconsin, and to ignore the natural divisions and subdivisions provided by nature. Lake Michigan is Lake Michigan; one simply has to look at it to see what its real boundaries happen to be. The state lines of Michigan, Indiana, Illinois and Wisconsin, even extending out over the waters, are manmade and, theoretically, alterable at the stroke of a pen. Writers in the past, myself included with my *Dive Ontario!* books, have been guilty of this "political limitation" which implies that the waters they are writing about end in the middle of the lake where that invisible boundary line has been set. I shake my head over "Great Lakes" travel books (and there are many) which exclude New York and Pennsylvania because they are considered Atlantic Ocean, East Coast states, in spite of the fact that those two states have many miles of Great Lakes shoreline. Is the vast Ontario portion of the Great Lakes non-existent simply because it's on the other side of that political line which separates Canada from the United States? A few so-called "Great Lakes" travel books would have you believe that. It makes no sense to me (but then again, I have long felt that the Great Lakes and the land 100 miles around them, all the way east to the Atlantic Ocean, should be their own single country, the "Empire of the Great Lakes," if you will. I am not holding my breath for that to happen any time soon). For this book, think more in terms of geography than politics.

This book is mostly about shipwrecks because shipwrecks are the mainstay of scuba diving in the Great Lakes. Remove the shipwrecks, or the access to them, and you kill the scuba industry here. The **names of shipwrecks** appear in *italic type*. If the ship was named after a human being, I have indexed it under its surname (to quote what the late Dr. Richard Wright of the Institute for Great Lakes Research at Bowling Green State University in Ohio told me in early 1986, "Do we call that famous, big ship the *'Fitzgerald'* or the *'Edmund'*?" Take it from there.)

The site coordinates are given, if known or required to find the site, in both the gradually outgoing LORAN-C system and in the latitude and longitude of the newer GPS (Global Positioning System). A few latitude/longitude locations are given in the old, traditional system of having only 60 seconds in a minute and, of course, 60 minutes in a degree. Today's electronic method of showing latitude/longitude eliminates "seconds" completely in favor of three decimal places following the minute number.

For example,

LAT 45° 02′ 59″   LON 074° 37′ 18″

is the old, traditional method of giving latitude/longitude. The last two numbers in each set indicate "seconds," of which there could never be more than 59 before the "minute" number ahead of it moved up to the next one.

Today's GPS latitude/longitude for the same destination as above reads like this:

GPS: 45° 02.986′/074° 37.302′

where the last three numbers are a decimal point fraction in thousandths of a whole minute.

Some LORAN-C units can convert their TD (Time Differential) numbers to latitude/longitude, but these are rarely the same as the latitude/longitude reading you would get from a GPS unit at the same location. However, my experience has been that there is a difference of usually no more than 400 feet in the distances given by two such readings. If the coordinates in this book place you within 400 feet of a shipwreck, and you still can't find it, then you shouldn't be out there on your own boat. Take a charter.

The dive site **depth** is usually given as its deepest point, but sometimes there is a range, indicating the distance which the shipwreck rises off the lake bottom (e.g. "59 to 74 feet" for the *Admiral* on page 176), or the depth range of an underwater slope (e.g. "25 to 115 feet" for the *Keystorm* on pages 76-77).

The **level** of diver experience is explained in the section called "Some Notes on Diving Safety" on pages 25 and 26.

The **dimensions** of a ship before it became a shipwreck are given as a set of three numbers, in feet and inches, in parentheses after the vessel's name in the body of the description, for example

(343′4″ x 43′8″ x 22′8″)

where the first measurement is the ship's length of 343 feet and 4 inches, the second is the ship's beam, or width, of 43 feet and 8 inches, and the third is the ship's draft, or depth from the waterline, namely 22 feet and 8 inches. If only two sets of numbers are given, then the ship's draft was unknown. If a ship was rebuilt during its career and its dimensions changed, the vessel's dimensions at the time of loss are given. A metric conversion chart is on the right; this chart can also be applied to dive site depths, which are also given in feet.

METRIC CONVERSION CHART

FEET	METERS
1	0.3
2	0.6
3	0.9
4	1.2
5	1.5
6	1.8
7	2.1
8	2.4
9	2.7
10	3
20	6
30	9
40	12
50	15
60	18
70	21
80	24
90	27
100	30
200	60
300	90
400	120
500	150
1000	300

The **maps** in this book, most of which were drawn by Cris Kohl and are © Seawolf Communications, Inc., are not to be used for navigation, as they omit information which is vital to the safe operation of a boat. Regulations require vessels operating in Great Lakes waters to carry the latest, best scale, corrected charts for their area of operation. The maps in this book do not meet those requirements.

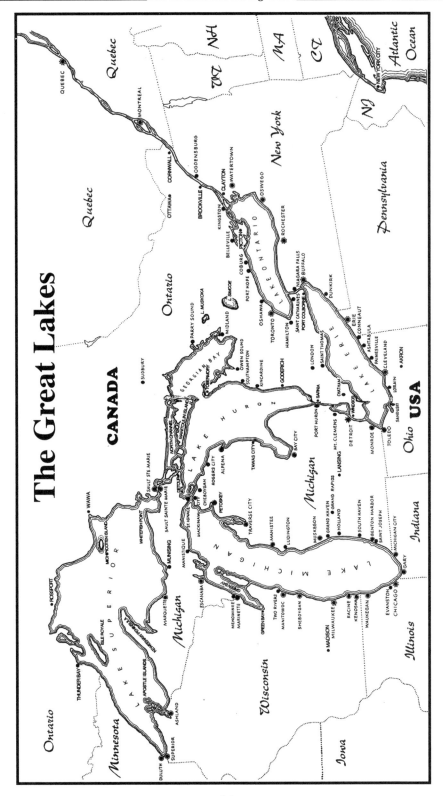

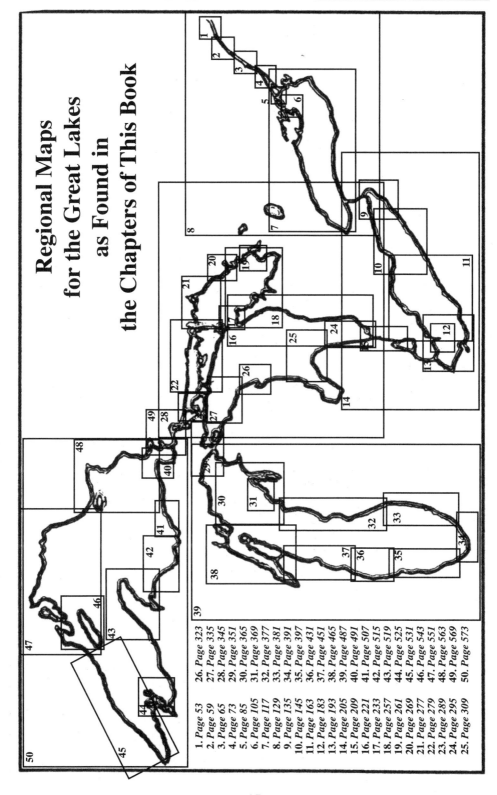

Regional Maps
for the Great Lakes
as Found in
the Chapters of This Book

GREAT LAKES DISTANCE CHART

Road distances, in miles, are calculated by the shortest or quickest routes from town or city center to center. Factors such as weather, road conditions, construction, detours and traffic may affect the time in which any given distance may be traversed.

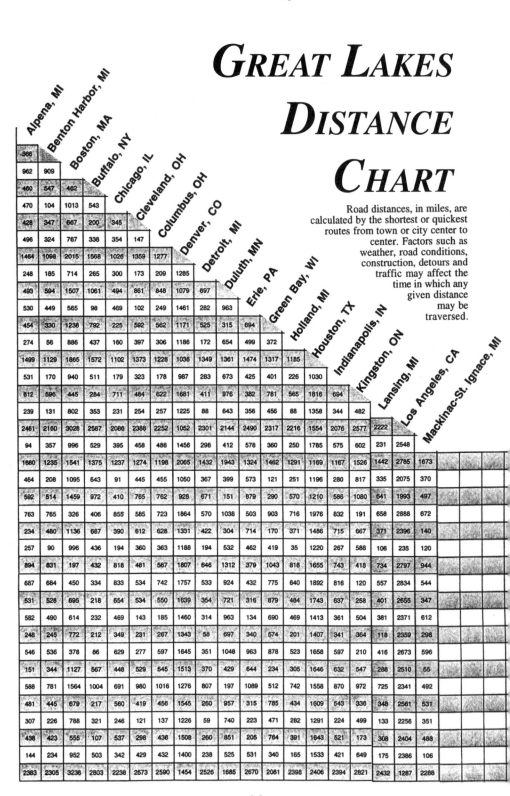

Quick Glance Map of the Great Lakes

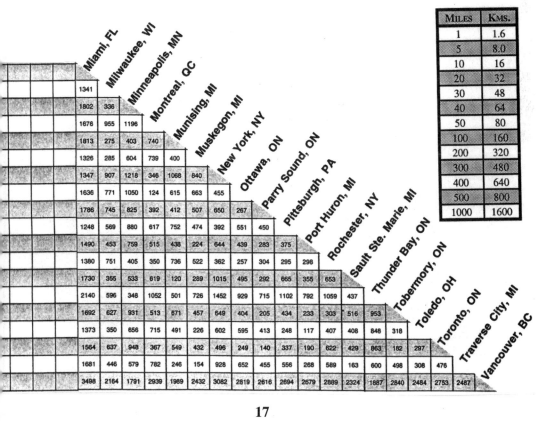

Miles	Kms.
1	1.6
5	8.0
10	16
20	32
30	48
40	64
50	80
100	160
200	320
300	480
400	640
500	800
1000	1600

Distance chart (miles) between: Miami, FL; Milwaukee, WI; Minneapolis, MN; Montreal, QC; Munising, MI; Muskegon, MI; New York, NY; Ottawa, ON; Parry Sound, ON; Pittsburgh, PA; Port Huron, MI; Rochester, NY; Sault Ste. Marie, MI; Thunder Bay, ON; Tobermory, ON; Toledo, OH; Toronto, ON; Traverse City, MI; Vancouver, BC

| 1341 |
1802	336
1676	955	1196
1813	275	403	740
1326	285	604	739	400
1347	907	1218	346	1068	840
1636	771	1050	124	615	663	455
1786	745	825	392	412	507	650	267
1248	569	880	617	752	474	392	551	450
1490	453	759	515	438	224	644	439	283	375
1380	751	405	350	736	522	362	257	304	295	298
1730	355	533	619	120	289	1015	495	292	665	355	653
2140	596	348	1052	501	726	1452	929	715	1102	792	1059	437
1692	627	931	513	671	457	649	404	205	434	233	303	516	953
1373	350	656	715	491	226	602	595	413	248	117	407	408	848	318
1564	637	948	367	549	432	496	249	140	337	190	622	429	863	182	297
1681	446	579	782	246	154	928	652	455	556	268	589	163	600	498	308	476
3498	2164	1791	2939	1969	2432	3082	2819	2616	2694	2679	2889	2324	1887	2840	2484	2753	2487

BORDER CROSSING

INFORMATION

Thousands of scuba divers from both the United States and Canada have found visits to their neighbor's Great Lakes dive sites to be interesting and fun, and it's a nice experience to be able to visit a foreign country once in a while and still be close to home.

To make the border crossings easier, for both leaving and returning, do this:

1. If you are taking your scuba gear with you, as you likely would be if you are driving across the border, make certain that, for every item of gear that has a serial number on it (tanks, regulators, dive computers, B.C.'s, etc.) you either have a receipt for it to prove that it was purchased in your country (and any receipts have to bear that item's serial number to be recognized as legitimate), or you need to register your equipment by taking it to any Customs Office in your country prior to your departure. (Don't forget your C cards, either.)

2. Be prepared to state politely to the Customs Officer of the country that you are visiting what your citizenship is (and have proof of citizenship handy if asked to see it), exactly how long and where you will be staying in that country, what goods you are bringing into the country, and what goods will be staying in that country. One concern is that you are crossing the border with scuba equipment which you intend to sell or give as a gift, which is illegal unless you explicitly state that you are taking goods into that country for resale or as gifts, and go through the necessary paperwork and pay any taxes, duties or fees applicable.

3. Remember that it is virtually impossible to enter Canada with any type of firearm or dangerous weapon. Leave the spearguns and shark knives at home. Do take your passport.

DISCLAIMERS

Firstly, the maps in this book are not suitable for navigation. To locate the majority of the sites in this book, you will need a boat and you must have the most up-to-date navigation charts available issued by the proper authorities.

Secondly, every effort has been made to make this book accurate, informative, and useful. However, the information presented in *The Great Lakes Diving Guide* is not infallible. There may be errors, but we are certainly not aware of them.

Thirdly, boating to these Great Lakes destinations is not always a simple task. Readers must be confident that they have the skills required to safely enjoy their exploration of these waterways, or at least they must be travelling with someone who does. When going to these sites, you do so at your own risk.

Lastly, and most importantly, scuba diving is a potentially dangerous activity. The author and publisher do not endorse or encourage specific practices, nor is this book meant to be a substitute for proper training, education, and personal dive site and self-skills evaluation. The author and publisher accept no liability for the diving practices or judgments of the readers of this book. You're on your own.

Introduction
to Great Lakes Diving

First, the lay of the land (or the water).

The Great Lakes, lying between the United States and Canada in nearly the middle of the North American continent, form the largest group of lakes in the world. The Great Lakes proper, extending from east to west, are Lakes Ontario, Erie, Huron, Michigan and Superior. The lakes are all connected to form a single drainage system which discharges down the St. Lawrence River into the Atlantic Ocean. The combined shorelines of the five lakes are an enormous 7,870 miles long and enclose a water surface of 95,170 square miles, of which 60,960 square miles are in the United States and 34,210 square miles are in Canada. The shallowest Great Lake is Lake Erie (maximum depth, 210 feet) and the deepest is Lake Superior (maximum depth, 1,333 feet). Lake Superior, at the head of this vast system, stands at an altitude of 600 feet above sea level, and it's downhill from there all the way to the Atlantic Ocean 2,340 miles away.

The Great Lakes are so vast that one could spend a lifetime scuba diving in them and not see the same site twice.

◆　　◆　　◆　　◆　　◆　　◆　　◆　　◆　　◆

The Great Lakes hold more than 6,000 shipwrecks, a staggering number unknown even to many longtime residents of the region. Because of their location near the middle of a continent which is a producer of heavy commodities, the Great Lakes have historically provided the transportation system for enormous quantities of bulk freight, such as iron ore, lumber, coal and grain. Florida and other tropical areas had the gold-laden galleons; the Great Lakes swarmed with the workhorses.

The shipwrecks in the Great Lakes are, as I explained earlier, the best preserved shipwrecks in the world. Some of the elements which promote this preservation are the same which add challenges to scuba diving:

1. Cold water was invented in the Great Lakes.

The water in the Great Lakes, below a depth of 100 feet, remains almost steady at about 39 degrees fahrenheit (surface temperatures generally warm up to the high 50's or as high as the low 70's in the southern areas by summer's end). Usually it is the shipwrecks which lie in deeper water that have remained in the most pristine condition, enjoying the preserving powers of this ice water, as well as being situated too deep to suffer from the damaging effects of ice, waves and wind.

Scuba diving in the Great Lakes is quite gear-intensive compared to warm-water locations. PHOTO BY CRIS KOHL

Scuba divers in the Great Lakes require some sort of thermal protection, such as good wetsuits or, even better, drysuits accompanied by thick, woolen underwear. Regardless of your choice, it is still a shock when that cold water hits one's face!

2. The Great Lakes are freshwater lakes. Called the "sweetwater seas" by early explorers, these bodies of water lack the saltwater organisms which destroy wood almost instantly. This fresh water, with its low temperature and lack of oxygen, preserves our shipwrecks.

3. The deeper you go, the darker it gets. This darkness also helps preserve the shipwrecks in the Great Lakes, and it sells a lot of dive lights. However, a couple of the best-preserved and most frequently visited Great Lakes shipwrecks, the *Bermuda* and the *Sweepstakes*, lie in only 20 to 30 feet of water and are blessed with an abundance of natural light. If you dive near the middle of the day, when the sun is at its highest point, even the deeper sites will receive a fair amount of ambient light available to help you see all the wonderful sights.

4. The visibility in the Great Lakes can range from 70 feet on a good day in Lake Superior down to one foot in the St. Clair River after a heavy rainfall. Generally, poor visibility results from millions of suspended particles in the water, usually caused by strong weather churning up the lake bottom. It usually requires at least a couple of days for heavily disturbed water to settle.

In 1988 I was fortunate enough to be scuba diving in New Zealand. While our dive charter boat headed out to the Poor Knight's Islands, the divemaster on our charterboat, a robust, young Australian named Mark, chatted up each of the 16 divers who were going to

be under his care once our large boat reached the island of our destination. Mark got to me and casually asked, "And where do you do most of your diving, mate?"

"In the Great Lakes," I replied.

"Well, we won't have to worry about you then," was his immediate response before turning to the next diver. He was evidently aware of the fact that scuba diving in the Great Lakes is tougher than diving in the tropics.

Scores of charter boats take divers to many of the best-preserved shipwrecks in the world. PHOTO BY CRIS KOHL

That's a trade-off that thousands of scuba divers who explore the Great Lakes are willing to make, as evidenced by the fact that there are over 300 scuba dive shops, as well as over 100 charter boats and over 170 dive clubs, all around the Great Lakes, all of them promoting local diving.

While not exactly the waters of Bonaire or Key Largo, the Great Lakes offer many opportunities for underwater exploration and enjoyment, similar to diving conditions in the waters of New England, the Pacific Northwest, British Columbia, and the British Isles (except for the fact that our waters are fresh).

Besides seeing shipwrecks the likes of which are not available anywhere else on the planet, visitors to Great Lakes waters are indulging in an even more adventurous form of an already exciting activity.

ELEVEN FISH A SCUBA DIVER MIGHT ENCOUNTER IN THE GREAT LAKES

(In alphabetical order. Sizes are not to comparative scale.)

BASS -- This popular game fish is often seen by divers in streams, ponds, rocky lake areas and shallow water shipwrecks.

BLUEGILL -- This fish is commonly seen by scuba divers on shallow shipwrecks and especially in quarries. They are usually no longer than 8 inches and weigh 0.5 pound.

BURBOT -- Also called ling, lingcod, or "lawyer fish," the burbot is seen on most Great Lakes shipwrecks, even deeper ones, and is easily recognized by the barbel at the tip of the jaw and its "eel-like" tail. Shunned as a food-fish due to its appearance and texture, it predaciously feeds upon smaller fish and may reach 4 feet in length.

CARP -- Viewed as a delicacy by some who know how to prepare it, and as a junk fish by others, the carp is a bottom feeder which can grow to a maximum length of 3 feet and a weight of 50 pounds.

CATFISH -- Considered an active game fish and, by some, fine eating, in spite of the fact that they are bottom feeders, catfish can reach a maximum length of four feet and a maximum weight of 55 pounds, but they are usually much smaller.

MUSKY (MUSKELLONGE) -- This fierce game fish, which has teeth like a small barracuda and sometimes the temper to match, is rarely seen or caught today. Large ones could reach 6 feet in length and weigh 90 pounds.

PERCH -- Its white flesh is valued as one of the best food fish in the Great Lakes, and many people enjoy it as a sport fish. Although the record perch weighed over 4 pounds, most are just under one pound, with an average length of 10 inches.

PIKE -- Although usually found in the northern Great Lakes regions, pike, a fighting game fish, are occasionally seen and caught in the southern portions as well. They reach a length of 3.5 feet.

SMELT -- Smelt runs along shorelines in the spring (usually late April) were very popular with net fishermen wearing waders, but smelt numbers have decreased alarmingly in recent years. The average length of this small fish is 6 to 9 inches.

STURGEON -- This migratory fish has occasionally been caught by sportsfishermen; in the 1980's, a five-footer was "captured" by a young man when he saw it basking near the

surface of the St. Clair River. He jumped in and dragged it, alive and kicking, ashore. Their once-vast numbers have been so decimated that they now need our help to replenish.

WALLEYE (also called PICKEREL) -- This fish, like the perch, is one of the most important game and food fish in the Great Lakes. The large ones will be 2 feet in length and weigh as much as 14 pounds.

Freshwater Versus Saltwater Scuba Diving

My scuba dive buddies have come in many varieties, ranging from the weather-beaten, long-time Great Lakes diver clad in thick, wooly underwear and a dry suit that requires 30 pounds of lead weight for proper buoyancy (why not just strap an old transmission to your stomach?), to those bikinied novice divers in the tropics who are unknowingly (or knowingly) imitating Jacqueline Bissette in "The Deep" (am I giving away my age with that reference?). There must be a reason that I wrote this book about the Great Lakes instead of applying my research and writing abilities to an easier, smaller, more managable, more laid back, warmer and, one would think, more enjoyable subject like scuba diving in Bonaire or the Florida Keys or Fiji.

Here are the reasons I prefer scuba diving in the Great Lakes:

Firstly, the Great Lakes are freshwater and the tropics are saltwater. If you have ever accidentally swallowed a mouthful of saltwater while you were diving, you may have cut your dive short because it made you sick. Great Lakes divers, on the other hand, often take their regulators out of their mouths and suck in a bit of cool fresh water to rinse off their dry tongues (this is generally not done in the waters off Cleveland or Toronto, and don't even think about Detroit).

Of course, post-diving activities in the tropics include the mandatory and completely thorough rinsing of all dive equipment in fresh water to remove that nasty salt. Any hurried diver who has ended up throwing his gear into his dive bag and forgetting about it for a few days will know, from the cloud of salt dust that he kicks up when he yanks his gritty equipment out of that white bag that used to be blue, that his last dive was definitely not done in Lake Superior.

In the Great Lakes after a dive, we get out of our wetsuits or drysuits and jump overboard for a refreshing swim. The only salt we have to wash off is the sweat we worked up from the surface swim back to the boat (that distance varies with one's ability to find the anchor line at the end of the dive.) In the tropics, taking a dip off the back of the boat to rinse off the salt isn't going to work, no matter how many times you make the jump.

If salt corrodes your scuba equipment like that, can you imagine what it does to your hair, your skin, your fingernails and other parts we don't dare mention?

Secondly, I like diving in the Great Lakes because no matter how long I stay in the water, there is nothing in there that can eat me. The same can't be said for the tropics. I remember Easter Sunday, 1988. I was in Tahiti, the French divemaster was my dive buddy, we were the last ones left in the water and we were making an extra-long safety stop because this was our second deep dive of the day. We hung off, back-to-back, while a half dozen black-tipped sharks steadily circled us. On the first dive that day, a huge moray eel had tried to eat my camera. I was glad to get back to the Great Lakes, where we're not afraid to turn out backs on burbots, and zebra mussel shell cuts are the closest we'll come to losing life or limb to some critter.

Thirdly, no matter where I do my scuba diving, I prefer to photograph shipwrecks. However, that is often a difficult thing to do in the tropics because I have to kick all those fish out of the way so I can get my picture! I don't have that problem in the Great Lakes.

Reason number four for loving the Great Lakes: when the weather kicks up, the waves rarely exceed the height of your boat, and it's over in a few hours. No matter how wet I get on board, it's always freshwater wet. In the tropics, when the weather kicks up, it lasts for four months (they call it the hurricane season) and the wind and the waves yank out palm trees and flatten houses. When I get wet in the tropics, it's saltwater wet (review reason number one above).

Fifthly, I prefer our more adventurous Great Lakes scuba diving to that easy stuff in the tropics. I enjoy being in that no-man's-land zone between the surface and the bottom and not being able to see either one. I welcome all those opportunities to practice my underwater navigation, and I thrill at that rush of adrenalin when I wonder exactly where the heck my boat is. In the tropics, all I have to do is look up and I can see the bottom of my dive boat, even when I'm in 100 feet of water. Now what fun is that?

Lastly, I dive the Great Lakes for their shipwrecks, which, regardless of age, are fabulously preserved in our cold, fresh waters. Saltwater does nasty things to wood, metal, in fact, almost everything (review reason number one above). Scuba divers enjoy shipwreck diving a lot more when the wrecks still resemble ships. It's hard to imagine a pile of ballast stones as a ship, and it's impossible to convince people back home that that pile of rocks in tropical waters once conveyed people and cargoes across oceans. It really stretches the imagination. Not so in the Great Lakes (have you been on the *Cornelia B. Windiate* yet? Or the *Annie Falconer*? Have you seen the *George A. Marsh*? Or the hundreds of others?)

But things are not perfect in our Great Lakes paradise. We don't have everything here. I understand that the tropics have some exotic beaches frequented by scuba divers, mostly Europeans, with a proclivity for eliminating tan lines and being transformed into bronze gods and goddesses. Perhaps it would be worthwhile to investigate the possibility of importing that custom and attitude and physical transformation capability to our inland seas.

But then again, it wouldn't work. We palefaces would just end up having to kick those people out of our way as we, in our full drysuits, schlepp our small mountain of dive gear down to the beach to do a shore dive. But at least it's in fresh water.

Some Notes on Diving Safety

Scuba diving is a potentially dangerous activity. The author and publisher do not endorse or encourage specific practices, nor is this book meant to be a substitute for proper training, education, and personal dive site and self-skills evaluation. The author and publisher accept no liability for the diving practices or judgments of the readers of this book. You're on your own.

This is not a "how to" book about scuba diving, but rather a "where to" guide to dive sites in the Great Lakes.

Regarding scuba safety, these statistics might offer some insight: in the U.S.A. in one recent year, the following activities had these death rates per 100,000 people participating in that activity -- mountain climbing, 599; hang gliding, 114; parachuting, 24; snowmobiling, 13; mountain hiking, 6.4; scuba diving, 2.9.

Scuba diving is one of the safest adventures a human being can enjoy.

◆   ◆   ◆   ◆   ◆   ◆   ◆   ◆   ◆

I have identified each of the dive sites as suitable for novice, intermediate, advanced or technical divers, or midway points in between each of these designations. I thank Joyce Hayward and the Bay Area Divers of Ohio for their assistance:

A novice dive:
a) is less than 6o feet in depth.
b) is suitable for a newly-certified or infrequent diver.
c) has no or very little current.
d) has good visibility.
e) may include wreck diving with no penetration.

An intermediate dive:
a) is suitable for more experienced divers.
b) may reach depths between 60 and 100 feet.
c) may include wreck diving with no penetration.
d) may involve some current or waves.
e) may involve open water sites with boat entries.
f) has good to moderate visibility.
g) may have other conditions that may warrant more experience.

An advanced dive:
a) may reach depths between 100 and 130 feet.
b) is suitable for very experienced divers.
c) may involve limited wreck penetration where there are multiple, visible exits, or swift or variable current diving, or very cold water diving.
d) may have extremely limited or zero visibility.
e) may require special skills such as navigation, rescue, cavern diving, or special equipment.

A technical dive:
  a) may reach depths in excess of 130 feet.
  b) may do deep shipwreck penetration, or cave diving, or ice diving, or any type of diving where there is an overhead environment blocking direct and immediate access to the surface.
  c) may involve the use of any gas that is not compressed air, including nitrox.

Regarding safety during scuba diving: use common sense and neither forget nor neglect nor ignore your training. Keep these pointers in mind:

When using a diveboat, keep a lookout aboard at all times. Fly both the swallowtail, blue-and-white alpha flag (it means that the boat has limited maneuverability) and the red-and-white dive flag from your boat when divers are actually in the water. The passing boater who may fail to recognize one flag may respond to the other.

Use a dive flag any time you are scuba diving, whether from a boat or from shore.

Never dive with your diveboat unattended. Should an emergency occur below, or should the exhausted divers be unable to climb back on board the boat, an assistant who stays on the boat is always helpful.

An obvious bit of advice, yet on occasion ignored, is to avoid diving in front of freighters which require great distances to make even slight turns. If you do end up with one passing immediately over you, hug the bottom of the river or the lake. If necessary, sink your dive knife into the bottom to act as a holding post. Don't do anything that may force you to make an emergency ascent. While you're on the bottom, with the water, sand, silt and other debris swirling madly all around you from the freighter's propeller, ask yourself how you got into that situation in the first place. Then, don't do it again.

Current, or swiftwater, diving requires special training and practice; begin with a mild current before you take on one of the "rush" dives in the St. Lawrence River or at the mouth of the St. Clair River.

Make sure that you have a sharp dive knife with you just in case you get caught in some of the old fishing nets on shipwrecks, or in the miles of monofilament fishing lines around docks and in river debris.

Never, ever dive alone.

Beware of concrete buoy anchors and submerged cribs or posts which may suddenly appear from the edge of visibility in any current. These things could frighten a novice diver. Obviously, divers should not hit these obstructions or snag any of their gear on them.

Don't scuba dive in a busy harbor or in or near canals. Harbormasters, boaters and lockmasters would find scuba divers to be a potentially dangerous (mostly to the person of the diver) nuisance.

Dive only when weather and water conditions permit. For example, the *City of Superior* shipwreck at Copper Harbor, Michigan, from shore on a calm day will create fond memories, but when the waves are pounding, you might end up remembering this site from a hospital bed.

Lastly, don't forget that there is a list of emergency telephone numbers on the last page of this book.

Safe diving!

The Importance of Scuba Dive Clubs

If it hadn't been for a scuba dive club, I might have hung up my fins and tucked away my certification card for my annual trip down south, as I witnessed so many of my Great Lakes dive buddies do. This scuba dive club became so important to me that the dedication at the beginning of my first shipwreck book back in 1985 read

> This book is dedicated to a Windsor friend who first sparked my interest in diving, and to Kent Divers Association, who rekindled the embers and turned them into a bonfire.

The words I wrote in my first book in 1985, in a section called "On Dive Clubs" praising their merits, bear repeating here:

Sometimes divers lack buddies. The best recommendation I can make is that they join a club.

A club definitely takes up where the diving instructor leaves off -- and I assure you, without intending to criticize diving instructors, that your scuba education is nowhere near "graduation" level, regardless of what your certification card might indicate, unless you log up a variety of diving experiences. A good dive club will safely give you a vast array of delightful dives and a long telephone list of potential dive partners.

My own experiences perhaps show this best.

When my basic scuba class was certified many years ago, it was understood, with almost religious devotion, that we would transfer our dive partnerships from warm, clean swimming pool and cold but protected open-water quarry training dives to the most challenging depths of Tobermory and the deep, mysterious oceans of the world.

Welcome to reality. We did make it to 60-foot depths together at Tobermory that first season, somehow, basically on our own. However, we were timid about it, and we gave one another looks of quiet apprehension before each dive. After all, we were subconsciously aware that we knew exactly as much, or as little, about diving as did our dive buddy.

It wasn't long before it became harder to find former classmates who felt exuberant about going diving. I was averaging about seven local dives a year. Things looked bad.

A decision had to be made. I did not want to forsake scuba diving because, between those moments of novice terror, I really did enjoy this activity.

So I joined a club.

In my first year with that club, a more experienced diver guided me skillfully onto a 90-foot-deep wreck in the Atlantic Ocean [the relatively new wreck of the *Chester A. Poling*], and shortly thereafter, another advanced diver patiently took me into the "100 Club" when I reached a depth of 100 feet for my first time ever at Flowerpot Island near Tobermory. The hesitations in dives gave way to the experience of control. Other club members taught me ice diving in a pond, speedy current diving in the St. Clair River, bottle diving in low visibility and at night, as well as pig-roasting, sign-painting, float-making, equipment-repairing, treasure-hunting, scallop-cleaning, deely-bopping, picture-taking, and insights on friendships.

But don't get your hopes up just yet -- a club is only as good as its members. Some clubs could make you feel as insignificant as a floppy disk amidst a sea of hard drives. Perhaps that's why large cities like Toronto, Detroit and Chicago foster several scuba clubs each. Regardless of its size, join a club and be active. Your nearest scuba dive shop can certainly give you information about a local club.

Speaking of your nearest scuba dive shop, it is wise for any dive club to form a close friendship with the local dive shop. When one supports the other, both sides win.

If there is no club in your area, start one. Kent Divers Association started in 1976 with eight people who were interested in diving and forming a club; despite membership fluctuations ranging from 8 to 80 and back to a variety of high and low points in between over the years, they maintain an active profile in their community -- and they have lots of fun doing it!

♦   ♦   ♦   ♦   ♦   ♦   ♦   ♦   ♦

Starting and Organizing a Scuba Dive Club

Here is an example of a scuba dive club's Constitution. Organization is vital for any group of people, including scuba divers. Some individuals are far more political than others, and they are the ones who will run with this information. For the sake of your dive club's future, keep the politics light and the actual scuba diving heavy. Although the following is based upon the Constitution of the first dive club to which I belonged, Kent Divers Association, we will give our club the fictional name of the ABC Dive Club.

What follows can be used as a template for organizing any scuba dive club in the Great Lakes or beyond, and, of course, any of these components can be altered, modified, or removed. Each group is different, so the following information will not necessarily apply to, or be approved by, every diving group -- but it can be a starting point. Go from there. And no, I will not defend or renounce or debate any of the following items with anyone. I prefer to go diving.

CONSTITUTION

Article 1: PURPOSE

The purpose of ABC Dive Club shall be

a) to encourage safe diving practices,
b) to encourage educational and social activities,
c) to act as a liaison between the resident diving body of our community and diving-related agencies.

Article 2: HEAD OFFICE

The head office of the ABC Dive Club shall be in the County of _____ in the (state or province) of _____, at such place therein as the Executive Board may, from time to time, decide.

Article 3: EXECUTIVE BOARD

The affairs of the ABC Dive club shall be managed by an Executive Board consisting of

> President,
> Vice President,
> Treasurer,
> Secretary,
> Dive Coordinator

The Executive Board shall ensure that an annual financial statement is published.

Article 4: DUTIES

a) The PRESIDENT shall
--be the general manager and coordinator of the ABC Dive Club.
--preside over meetings when present.

b) The VICE PRESIDENT shall
--assist the Executive Board in the discharge of its duties.
--officiate in the temporary absence of any Executive Board member or in the event of Presidential succession.
--record membership attendance at meetings.

c) The TREASURER shall
--keep full and accurate records of all receipts and disbursements of ABC Dive Club in proper books of account ready for presentation at any time.
--deposit all funds received in the name and to the credit of ABC Dive Club into any recognized financial institution as directed by the Executive Board.
--be directed by the Executive Board in the financial transactions of the ABC Dive Club.
--sign all checks drawn on the funds of the ABC Dive Club together with any other Executive Board member with signing authority.
--prepare an annual financial statement for publication when requested by the Executive Board.

d) The SECRETARY shall
--keep the minutes of all general meetings of ABC Dive Club in a book provided for that purpose.
--have custody of all literature pertaining to the ABC Dive Club by the end of the calendar year.
--prepare and distribute, by May of each year, a list of members, their addresses, and telephone numbers.
--direct the production of the ABC Dive Club's newsletter.

e) The DIVE COORDINATOR shall
--organize and arrange all ABC Dive Club dives according to dates, methods, and costs agreed upon by a majority of a membership quorum.

Article 5: MEMBERSHIP

a) There will be two types of membership in the ABC Dive Club:

--<u>Full</u> <u>Membership</u> in ABC Dive Club shall be open to any certified scuba diver and their mates.

--<u>Associate</u> <u>Membership</u> in ABC Dive Club shall be open to individuals wishing to participate in ABC Dive Club activities, but not dive as full members or have voting privileges.

b) Resignation from the ABC Dive Club must be in writing and addressed to the ABC Dive Club. Failure to pay dues by the February meeting shall be considered a resignation from the ABC Dive Club. In case of resignation, a member shall remain liable for payment of any assessment or other sum levied or which became payable by him to the ABC Dive Club prior to acceptance of his resignation.

c) Any member shall be expelled from the Association by a two-thirds vote of the membership for conduct detrimental to the ABC Dive Club.

d) Termination of membership in the ABC Dive Club shall terminate the right or interest of such a member in the assets and operations of the ABC Dive Club, or to the right or interest or claim that he, as a member, may have had.

Article 6: DUES AND FEES

a) Membership dues and fees shall be determined by the Executive Board or a majority vote of a membership quorum.

b) Annual membership dues shall become due and payable at the first general meeting of each calendar year.

c) Non-members wishing to participate in club events must pay a fee decided by the Executive Board.

Article 7: MEETINGS

a) General meetings shall be held at a designated time and place as decided by the Executive Board.

b) Notice of general meetings shall be given to all members prior to the meeting.

c) A quorum shall consist of 20% of those paid as "FULL MEMBERS" and include a majority of the Executive Board.

d) Executive Board meetings:
--the Executive Board shall hold meetings as required.
--a quorum of the Executive Board shall consist of a majority of its members.

Article 8: ELECTIONS

a) Elections shall be held annually for all Executive Board positions at the November general meeting.

b) All candidates for office shall be determined prior to the November elections.

c) All candidates for office shall be members of the ABC Dive Club in good standing during the six months preceding the November general meeting, must retain this status throughout the following year, and be elected by a majority of the "FULL MEMBERS" at that meeting.

d) Only "FULL MEMBERS" shall have voting privileges for the ABC Dive Club Executive Board.

e) All Executive Board offices shall be held for a period of one year commencing on January 1st and concluding on December 31st.

f) Executive Board members have no executive privileges or benefits other than those needed for the execution of their offices.

Article 9: COMMITTEES

All committees and committee members shall be appointed by the Executive Board.

Article 10: LIABILITY

Every member of the ABC Dive Club and his heirs, executors, and administrators, and estates and effects, respectively, shall from time to time and at all times, be indemnified and saved harmless out of the funds of the Association, from and against:

all costs, charges, and expenses whatsoever which such member sustains or incurs in or about any action, suit, or proceeding which is brought, commenced, or prosecuted against him for or in respect of any act, deed, matter, or thing whatsoever, made, done, or permitted by him, in or about the execution of the duties of his office if he holds one.

Article 11: AMENDMENTS AND RATIFICATION

a) To amend the Constitution, the proposed amendment shall be submitted in writing to the Executive Board and signed by five members.

b) Notice of this proposed amendment shall be made in writing to the membership.

c) It shall require two-thirds majority of a quorum at the next general meeting to adopt such an amendment.

Article 12: SPECIAL BY-LAWS

Special by-laws shall exist as voted upon annually by the membership (See By-Laws section).

RATIFIED _____   _____   _____
                    (day)   (month)   (year)

_____
                    (signature)

_____
                    (signature)

_____
                    (signature)

By-Laws: These are easily changeable club operating items which should be voted upon annually, either at the very end of the calendar year, or at the very beginning of the new calendar year. These are taken, once again, from the Kent Divers Association By-Laws, and generalized.

2008 By-Laws of our imaginary scuba dive club, the ABC Dive Club. Of course, the dollar amounts will vary with group, year, and location:

1. All certified divers of the ABC Dive Club must be members of the (state or province) Underwater Council (or whatever name that council goes by).

2. FULL MEMBERSHIP fee for a first diver in the family is $15.00 plus the (state or province) Underwater Council membership fee of $10.00. The second diver in that family is subject to the (state or province) Underwater Council membership fee of $10.00 only, as are any additional divers in that family.

3. Non-diving mates are included in the first full membership.

4. ASSOCIATE MEMBERSHIP fee for non-voting members will be available for 50% of the FULL ABC Dive Club membership fee.

5. Membership cards are issued only to certified diving FULL MEMBERS.

6. ·a) The DIVER-OF-THE-YEAR AWARD will be presented to the member who has contributed outstanding time and talent for the betterment of the club.
    b) This is not necessarily a yearly presentation, but a "special" award given at the discretion of the current Executive Board.

7. a) The ROOKIE-DIVER-OF-THE-YEAR AWARD will be presented to a person who is in his first full year of diving and is a member of ABC Dive Club, and who, in the estimation of the Executive Board, has made an outstanding effort as a new diver with the club.
    b) This is not necessarily a yearly presentation, but a "special" award given at the discretion of the current Executive Board.

8. ABC Dive Club members shall uphold and follow the (state or province) Underwater Council club diving standards.

9. ABC Dive Club members shall follow club Divemaster standards.

10. The ABC Dive Club Divemaster Kit shall be available at every club dive.

11. Any person participating in a club dive shall be required to sign an ABC Dive Club waiver form.

NOTE: For this particular dive club from which these by-laws are taken, safe diving standards are spelled out in the Ontario Underwater Council's club diving standards (see item #8 above). Your club may wish to add something like this to your club by-laws in absence of uniform safety standards established by a state body:

A Safety Diver must be designated for all club dives and this Safety Diver has the ultimate authority to call off the dive or to disqualify a member from a dive.

Regular Scuba Dive Club Activities

The Club Diving -- The main activity of a scuba dive club should be scuba diving. But no matter how much scuba diving is planned or even carried out, there will be very little time actually spent in the water compared to doing all the other things that scuba dive clubs do.

However, I will address the actual scuba diving activities first.

I joined a club for diving companionship, and my first club dive was under the ice -- alone, with my "dive buddy" outside the hole holding the other end of this rope to which I was tethered. But it was only the first of many interesting diving experiences. PHOTO SET-UP BY CRIS KOHL

As a member of a local scuba dive club, you will be in contact with other scuba divers, many of whom will share your interest in doing local scuba diving on weekends or even on a weekday evening right after work. I was very fortunate in that, where I lived when I started scuba diving, Lake Erie was only a one-half hour drive away to the south, the St. Clair River was only a one-half hour drive away to the north, Lake Huron was a one-hour drive away a bit further north, and the Detroit River was also a one-hour drive away to the west. By comparison, the nearest quarry where we could scuba dive (legally) was nearly a two-hour drive away. But Lake Erie, the St. Clair River, Lake Huron, and the Detroit River all offered shore diving possibilities, meaning we did not need a boat to go scuba diving. This made it possible to explore many local areas and to fill up numerous dive log books with detailed descriptions of each dive.

Of course, as a club, we also had the numbers to charter a dive boat to take us out to shipwreck locations in either Lake Erie or Lake Huron. It's a good feeling knowing that the club Dive Coordinator can book a charter boat for a certain date or dates and there are enough club members anxious to go on that charter to make it a success.

It was this local scuba diving -- mostly drifting down rivers or exploring shipwrecks in the lakes -- which gained great enthusiasm from our club members.

Once a year, our club did a major trip to a more distant location. Since everybody had day jobs, we would plan a four-day weekend getaway at least eight months in advance and fill up several vans with divers and dive gear and do an all-night drive to Boston's Cape Ann or to New Jersey or North Carolina and

Dive club members help launch a number and variety of boats to take divers to a site [in this case, Hidden Lake on an island in the Detroit River.]   PHOTO BY CRIS KOHL

Inflatable boats reach Hidden Lake and divers suit up.   PHOTO BY CRIS KOHL

get in two or three days of great diving. We didn't fly to those locations because we didn't want to lose a day of diving -- and besides, we were too cheap. We pulled another all-nighter driving back home with everybody getting to work dead tired, but on time. On trips like this, all of the group expenses were kept minimal and divided up evenly among the participants -- the club purposely did not make money on club dives or charters.

Annual club trips to more distant locations have also been popular. Some of those included *(left to right)* Boston's Cape Ann, New Jersey, and North Carolina. PHOTOS OR PHOTO SET-UP BY CRIS KOHL

"You can take the diver out of the Great Lakes, but...." OK, so we ALL thought the fresh-water gear-rinsing tubs were for bathing. This was, after all, our club's first trip east! PHOTO BY CRIS KOHL

Once or twice a year, we would organize a joint dive with a dive club across the border which was our "sister club in Michigan" -- the Great Lakes Aquanauts of Greater Detroit. One of the really nice things about living close to an international border was getting to know where and how they do things on the other side. This sharing of dive site information was of great benefit to both clubs. The areas where we got together for some shared diving were usually close to the border -- the St. Clair River forms the border between Canada and the USA for about 30 miles, with both sides of that river being rich in places to go shore diving. We alternated on whose side of the river we would dive; one year, it was at the northern tip of Canada's Walpole Island, while the next joint dive would be in the river from the municipal park in Port Huron, Michigan. Sometimes our two clubs even ran joint charters out of places like Port Burwell, Ontario, to some of the shipwrecks in Lake Erie.

Any dive club which does not seriously promote scuba diving

Members of the Great Lakes Aquanauts of Greater Detroit (Michigan) and Kent Divers Association (Ontario) share diving, lunch, relaxation, and dive site/dive club information at Highbanks Park on the northern tip of Canada's Walpole Island in the St. Clair River during a joint clubs (GLA-KDA) diving event. PHOTOS BY CRIS KOHL

"in its own back yard," so to speak, much more so than dive trips to faraway places, becomes little more than a scuba travel agency -- and there are plenty of those around already. What we have in the Great Lakes is unique, and we should promote it because it's where we live!

It's not particularly easy scuba diving (compared to being waited upon hand and foot as you dive off the back of a large, open boat which took ten minutes of motoring across smooth water to reach its warm, clear-water, coral reef destination in Grand Cayman, for example), but our Great Lakes shipwrecks -- the best preserved shipwrecks in the world, and hundreds of them are explorable by sport divers -- are fascinating and worthwhile.

One club's rules state that you must participate in at least one of the club's diving trips per year to remain a member in good standing. Now that's a club that wants active members!

The Club Meetings -- Scuba dive club meetings are a wonderful experience -- a chance to socialize with people who share very similar interests. Most dive clubs meet once a month. They pick a day, say the second Monday evening of the month, or the last Wednesday evening of the month, and that becomes established on individuals' calendars as club night.

The question of WHERE to hold club meetings is an important one. I have attended (or been a presenter at) club meetings which were held in noisy restaurants, where waiters or waitresses constantly milled about delivering food and drinks, or picked up empty plates and bottles with impressive clatter, or where suffering restaurant customers who were not members of the dive club became noisy (or noisier as they resented a club's intrusion upon THEIR meal). Sometimes the restaurant's usual background music could, or would, not be turned off or at least down. Some restaurants can provide a separate side room where a dive club can hold its meeting, which can be nice, and perhaps that intrusive background music can even be turned off. But those are few and far between. The food could be the least of the potential problems, because alcohol has a way of sometimes becoming a stumbling block in

Many dive clubs use a local school's classroom for their meetings. The desks may be a bit uncomfortable, but the lighting is good, the AV equipment is available, the parking is free, and the use cost is usually low. Here, Darryl Ertel and Matt Turchi share their deep wreck survey tales with Kent Divers Association.   Photo by Cris Kohl

the progress of any dive club meeting. It's best to save that for the Post-Meeting Meeting (see page 37).

There are better places to hold meetings than restaurants or bars. Kent Divers Association holds meetings in a high school classroom. The desks are not the most comfortable, but there are at least 30 of them in the room, and the school has always allowed the group to use its AV equipment -- a very important consideration. There is free parking next to the school. And the price was always low (about $50.00 for nine meetings throughout the school year). The main drawback is that the school is closed in July and August, so the club usually held one meeting during those months at the residence of one of its members -- preferably someone with a swimming pool! The club's December meeting was replaced by its Christmas/Awards Banquet at about the same time. Meetings were scheduled from 7:30 PM until 10:00 PM -- and with that generous 2 1/2-hour time slot, the club rarely runs a meeting past ten o'clock.

The Great Lakes Aquanauts of Greater Detroit hold their meetings in a conference room of a local library -- a large, modern building with an enormous lot with free parking. The main drawback is that the library closes at 9 PM. At least two clubs I know hold their monthly meetings in large rooms at their local YMCA. Some clubs rent a small conference room at a local motel or hotel, like a Holiday Inn. Some use an education room at a local college, or at a dive shop, or a storage room of a museum, while others use members' homes on a rotating basis. All of these have their advantages and disadvantages.

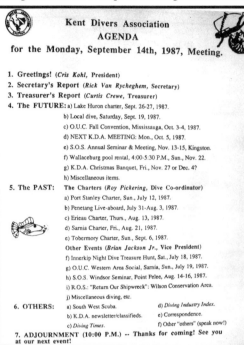

Kent Divers Association

AGENDA

for the Monday, September 14th, 1987, Meeting.

1. Greetings! (*Cris Kohl*, President)
2. Secretary's Report (*Rick Van Rycheghem*, Secretary)
3. Treasurer's Report (*Curtis Crewe*, Treasurer)
4. The FUTURE: a) Lake Huron charter, Sept. 26-27, 1987.
   b) Local dive, Saturday, Sept. 19, 1987.
   c) O.U.C. Fall Convention, Mississauga, Oct. 3-4, 1987.
   d) NEXT K.D.A. MEETING: Mon., Oct. 5, 1987.
   e) S.O.S. Annual Seminar & Meeting, Nov. 13-15, Kingston.
   f) Wallaceburg pool rental, 4:00-5:30 P.M., Sun., Nov. 22.
   g) K.D.A. Christmas Banquet, Fri., Nov. 27 or Dec. 4?
   h) Miscellaneous items.
5. The PAST: The Charters (*Roy Pickering*, Dive Co-ordinator)
   a) Port Stanley Charter, Sun., July 12, 1987.
   b) Penetang Live-aboard, July 31-Aug. 3, 1987.
   c) Erieau Charter, Thurs., Aug. 13, 1987.
   d) Sarnia Charter, Fri., Aug. 21, 1987.
   e) Tobermory Charter, Sun., Sept. 6, 1987.
   Other Events (*Brian Jackson Jr.*, Vice President)
   f) Innerkip Night Dive Treasure Hunt, Sat., July 18, 1987.
   g) O.U.C. Western Area Social, Sarnia, Sun., July 19, 1987.
   h) S.O.S. Windsor Seminar, Point Pelee, Aug. 14-16, 1987.
   i) R.O.S.: "Return Our Shipwreck": Wilson Conservation Area.
   j) Miscellaneous diving, etc.
6. OTHERS: a) South West Scuba.   d) *Diving Industry Index.*
   b) K.D.A. newsletter/classifieds.   e) Correspondence.
   c) *Diving Times.*   f) Other "others" (speak now!)
7. ADJOURNMENT (10:00 P.M.) -- Thanks for coming! See you at our next event!

A meeting <u>AGENDA</u> is absolutely necessary to give any guests or new members (or potential members) the idea that this club is not only active, but also organized. The club President usually produces the <u>AGENDA</u>, running off enough copies for everyone at the meeting, plus a copy for the club archives. A copy of an informative <u>AGENDA</u> will often help a diver determine if he is going to return for a future meeting or not. Have the date of the next meeting on the agenda, plus the dates of near-future club activities. Contact information should appear in the club newsletter, copies of which should be available at the meeting. Contact information will spur members on to action!

Obviously, any meeting's time needs must be carefully considered and a place which can accommodate the desired time slot must be located.

It should be clear that only one person is running the meeting, and that person should be the club President (see Constitution). Chaotic meetings will not attract new members, or keep old ones.

Some clubs arrange to have a guest speaker for every meeting they have, while others have certain months where they would prefer NOT to have a guest speaker. September was always the "end of the summer" meeting, where members were eager to share stories of their recent diving adventures, so we rarely scheduled a guest speaker for that month. November is usually the month when clubs hold their elections for next year's Executive Board -- and this is sometimes a painstaking and/or boring event, if willing candidates are not established prior to the actual meeting. Some club members plan to miss the November meeting because of those elections, so perhaps that would be a good month to arrange to have an absolutely fantastic guest speaker! (Ensure that the election process takes very little time!) Be responsive of the AV needs of any guest speaker you arrange for a meeting, prior to the meeting. Screens are awkward to transport, so definitely provide one -- as well as any other needed electronic equipment. Gas

The September, 2004, meeting of the Underwater Archaeological Society of Chicago, normally held in one of the Shedd Aquarium's education classrooms, had to be moved to the auditorium because of the large turnout for guest speaker Robert Kurson, whose bestselling *Shadow Divers* book had just come out three months earlier.

PHOTO BY CRIS KOHL

City helicopter pilot hoping to join Cousteau in January

Guest speakers for dive club meetings offer many topics. Bill Humphries, author of the 1975 book, *Great Fury*, and the man who reportedly found the wreck of the *Wexford* in 73 feet of water in the mid-1970's, awed members of Kent Divers Association in the mid-1980's. Speakers could include specialists in antique bottles (many people took up scuba diving just so they could locate antique bottles!), or Great Lakes Maritime History antique postcard collectors. They all offer fascinating subjects! PHOTOS BY CRIS KOHL. The local newspaper reported the event when we had area pilot Jim Standard, who worked as Jacques Cousteau's helicopter pilot for the Amazon River Expedition and presented 8mm movie film of his experiences, at a Kent Divers Association meeting in 1986.

money, perhaps in the form of an "honorarium" (a check), is not out of order nowadays. Give guest speakers who produce books or DVD's a chance to sell them without the club asking for a cut. Nowadays, many speakers have a set fee for their services, usually based upon time and distance. At the Underwater Archaeological Society of Chicago, we also often take our guest speaker out for dinner prior to the meeting, and sometimes to the post-meeting meeting as well (at club expense for his food and drink, of course).

The Post-Meeting Meeting -- Much of the REAL work of running a dive club gets accomplished at the "post-meeting meeting." Due to time limitations at the regular meeting, or the consideration of giving the guest speaker as much time as possible, some club business may be postponed. But it does not have to wait until next month's meeting because often the vital people involved with the club's decision-making are present at the post-meeting meeting.

It is wise to get most of the club's business done, and enjoy the guest speaker, at the regular meeting; select a location for the post-meeting meeting where people can be more relaxed and socialize with a beer or some other favored beverage or treat. Kent Divers Association has long used the Montreal House Tavern as their location, while the Great Lakes Aquanauts of Greater Detroit retreat to a wonderful ice cream parlor down the road.

The Post-Meeting Meeting place varies with each dive club. *From left to right:* The Underwater Archaeological Society of Chicago gets together after its regular meetings at a 1946 restaurant (which retains its original atmosphere!), while between May and August, that same group has been known to step outdoors along Lake Michigan near the Shedd Aquarium after their meeting and, while watching the Wednesday night fireworks from nearby Navy Pier, indulge in pizzas and a cooler full of soda pop, water and other refreshments procured by a zealous member who knows the value of sustenance. The Three Rivers Dive Club of Fort Wayne, Indiana, meets at a neighborhood pub across the street from their regular meeting place. PHOTOS OR PHOTO SET-UP BY CRIS KOHL

ATTENTION
KENT COUNTY SCUBA DIVERS

need a buddy or some new places to dive ?
why not join the

KENT
DIVERS
ASSOCIATION

WE OFFER
* LOCAL DIVES
* CHARTER DIVES
* CAMP/DIVE WEEKENDS
* QUALIFIED EXPERIENCED
   DIVE BUDDIES
* SOCIAL AND DIVE ACTIVITIES
* CLUB MOVIES

NEXT MEETING

Advertising the Dive Club -- Simple things can work well to let your community know that it has an active scuba dive club. Flyers such as the one on the left help by being posted EVERYWHERE -- bulletin boards in dive shops, libraries, grocery stores, any place where real people congregate -- announcing the time and place of the next meeting.

Have a talented, artistic member produce a scuba dive club logo to use on patches, T-shirts, polo shirts, hooded sweatshirts -- anything! In this way, that logo acts like a bumper sticker advertising your club. We also learned the fine art of silk screening onto cloth so we could make up table banners, which accompanied us on every club event and clearly identified our club in a unique, classy way.

Every club will have its internet wizards who can set up a club website, but the biggest human turn-off is for a new or potential member to be told to "Go to our web site" for any information about the club. Always have descriptive paper flyers handy.

The best club advertising you can get will be (free) promotional or human interest photos and/or stories in your local newspaper; that's where clubs in towns and small cities have an advantage over big city newspapers, which often feel they are above such trivial items.

The Club's Newsletter -- The dive club's newsletter is its official voice to its members, to potential members, to other dive clubs, to scuba businesses, and to the rest of the world. However, it is not easy producing a club newsletter regularly with uniform quality. Whoever does the club newsletter is doing the most difficult and the most important job of anyone in the club. If a club finally finds a person willing and capable of regularly producing a good newsletter, they should offer as much assistance as possible (by contributing articles, photos

and artwork, or by getting someone else to do the folding and the mailing out of the newsletters; etc.). Do not be cheap and run off only enough copies for your members. If you've got it, flaunt it! Mail out paper copies (and paper copies are taken far more seriously, especially by collectors, than are electronic transmissions. I am frequently told, "But the internet is FREE!" which is exactly why it is looked down upon by most message recipients.) Mail your newsletter to your local museum(s) and dive shop(s). They don't have time to visit your website. Ask them if you can leave some free newsletters sitting on their counters for their customers. Incorporate the price of some

Did you miss the boat?

What's that? You haven't participated in too many Kent Divers Association activities yet this year? And you're really sorry that you missed the boats that took KDA members out of Leamington, Sarnia, and Mackinac City? And you waited too long to make up your mind about the Peterborough Ice Floe Race in March, the Bonne Terre Mines, Missouri, Trip in May, the Tobermory Trip in July, the Spouse Appreciation Day in August, and the Scuba Olympics on Oct. 5th, and those many excellent, exciting GUEST SPEAKERS at our meetings, so you missed them all?! There are still a few activities left in this ...

Use humor in your newsletter every chance you get. Through my newspaper connections (I taught journalism from 1974 to 1985), I was given discarded or unused advertising artwork which I put to good use in our dive club newsletter. Similar artwork is available as electronic clip-art today. CRIS KOHL COLLECTION

photocopied pages and a few postage stamps per member into your annual dues, and don't be cheap about running extra copies. Take them to all club events and give them away there to new people. The Chicago Aquanauts Scuba Association produces its large newsletter electronically, and sends it out that way to its members, but it also prints quite a few paper copies and brings them to their club meetings for distribution, mainly to new people and guest speakers. Do not underestimate the importance of paper copies of your club's newsletter. They are readily hand-out-able, readily readable (a computer is not needed), and the paper copies will probably be around a lot longer than those stored electronically. Your latest newsletter will act as a fancy club business card. Clubs can be, and often are, judged by their newsletter. Produce a good one. It will be well worth it!

A newsletter can be either monthly, bi-monthly or quarterly, but it should be regular. How many pages? I have seen large newsletters over ten pages per issue, but those are difficult to maintain on a regular basis. Small ones also serve the purpose. Wisconsin's oldest dive club, the Neptune's Nimrods, mail out a one-sheet, two-sided newsletter without fail each and every month. It's short but wonderful, and it maintains that all-important physical contact with club members -- 12 times a year! Also, make the newsletter practical: provide precise times and dates and locations (maybe with maps) of club events, and provide a contact name and telephone number for each club event in case anyone has any questions. In describing past club events, don't hesitate to NAME NAMES (members love to see their name in print!) and get some photos of club activities in there as well.

Someone in the club, possibly the Secretary, should be responsible for filing all club paperwork, including newsletters, mail received, copies of mail sent out, etc. -- in other words, doing the job of Club Archivist. That material will be priceless 10 or 20 years down the road. Or at least worth a good laugh then!

As with the diving, the newsletter should "Keep it fun!" Once it's not fun any more, it may be time to say goodbye to it. A good dive club will be enthusiastic about what it does. A wise man once said that nothing great was ever accomplished without enthusiasm. And the really good news is that enthusiasm is contagious!

Special Scuba Dive Club Events

Besides its regular activities, a scuba dive club can organize the following events. They appear here as close as possible in annual chronological order.

The New Year's Day Dip-- This activity can quickly become your community's first BIG public event of the calendar year. Do this two or three years straight, and you'll have created a tradition! Where to take your club dip? Ideally in a body of water close to a member's warm house, or where your club can rent a motel room, to offer a "warm-up headquarters"

PHOTOS OR PHOTO SET-UPS BY CRIS KOHL

providing hot soup and a place to change clothes, and ideally close to where you can get a crowd of people to watch what they refer to as "bizarre behaviour." If a river flows through the middle of your town, that's ideal. In mild weather, you might have no ice, making the dip less dramatic. Do it anyway! If it's really cold, you'll need somebody with a good chain-saw to cut a hole through the ice. Mark the hole afterwards with evergreen trees or posts and orange tape, or snowmobilers will go into the drink before the hole refreezes. Announce your club's "jump!" time to the press and television stations in advance; they'll have camera crews there. This is a great way to welcome in the New Year, as well as give your club some publicity for craziness (most people think divers are crazy to begin with! This will prove it.)

Winter Pool Rentals -- Rent a local, indoor pool for two hours on a Sunday afternoon, once a month in the winter during diving's off-season. Invite all members, neighbors and friends for the swim, and organize a game or two for adults and kids. Charge a really reasonable rate (e.g. $3 per adult member, $5 per adult non-member, and all children are free) and have the club treasury pay for the rest. Divers can practice their scuba skills, try

PHOTOS BY CRIS KOHL

Scuba divers really stick out at mall displays; these really raise a community's awareness of its dive club! High schools and colleges welcome ideas to put their marketing classes to work creating displays in the school.

out new equipment, or get into a wild game of underwater hockey.

Mall Display, and Elsewhere -- Most indoor shopping malls have arrangements for community groups to set up weekend exhibits for a modest fee. Schedule club members at the booth for all hours that the mall is open on that weekend. Offer displays of club activity photos, videos, equipment exhibits and demonstrations, free brochures and newsletters -- whatever it takes to get people interested! Invite them to learn scuba; invite non-member divers to the next club meeting!

Museum/Freighter Tours -- Winter is a good time to arrange for your dive club to tour a museum or, with a bit of inside help or daring-do, an actual freighter in winter layup. Both are great experiences!

The Algoma steel freighter, *Agawa Canyon*, wintered at Sarnia, ON, giving our dive club a chance to tour it.

Education -- Learning is more fun when you're doing it in a scuba dive club group, whether it's CPR, First Aid, O2, any specialty courses, or the Scuba Bronze course from the Royal Lifesaving Society!

PHOTOS OR PHOTO SET-UPS, ABOVE AND BELOW, BY CRIS KOHL

Environment -- The Saturday before Earth Day at the end of April each year is the perfect day to schedule a scuba dive clean-up of some body of water which has been abused. The one which leaps to my mind immediately is Crystal Bay in the Detroit River. All summer long, boaters raft off together, six at a time, and party, party, party all weekend long. Some divers make it a point to dive there each Monday to find the good stuff, like wallets and outboard motors. The rest of the garbage -- many beer and soda cans and bottles, much plastic wrapping from food, numerous odd running shoes and many pairs of undergarments -- are left for environmentally-conscious divers to clean up. The Windsor Skin and Scuba Club has organized this annual clean-up with great effect, even turning it into a competition some years when many dive clubs participate. The garbage is sorted into categories, including recyclable trash, and all of it is hauled away. This is the type of event which really gives a dive club a high profile in the press -- and in the community.

Crystal Bay, on the downstream side of the Detroit River, offers water filtered clean by the island nearly wrapped around it. The Windsor Skin and Scuba Club has run a very successful bay clean-up annually for many years around Earth Day. PHOTOS BY CRIS KOHL

Competition -- A dive club can set up an internal competition, e.g. a Tube Push Race, where, in the spring when there's some current, club members compete by pushing an inner tube upstream in a river and back for the fastest time. Underwater Olympics can offer a variety of competitions in a pool -- be imaginative! Or the dive club can compete against other dive clubs in a number of possible fun events, including those pictured below.

It's so easy even a cave man can do it!

The annual Ice Floe Race at Peterborough, ON, held every March by the Trident Underwater Club, offers themes, costumes, innovative ways in which a dive club can move a large piece of ice down a fast-moving river in the shortest time, and awards for a variety of achievements. Often 20+ dive clubs participate in this weekend event and its accompanying parties. Sorry -- not available in Florida! PHOTOS BY CRIS KOHL

KENT DIVERS

After a River Tube Push, keep the safety boat handy for the "Michelin Man" diver.

Right: A night dive treasure hunt at a local quarry attracts members of several different dive clubs. PHOTOS OR PHOTO SET-UPS BY CRIS KOHL

The dive club's parade "float" can be basic, like an inflatable boat filled with ice and a couple of suited up divers sitting in it, or a tin man in dive gear towed on a boat. Always have signs with your club's name on the float, and at least two divers in scuba gear! We got lucky one year and had the use of a fine pirate ship float -- a definite attention-grabber, even in the local newspaper!   PHOTOS BY CRIS KOHL

Parades -- It's true that everybody loves a parade! Every community holds at least one parade each year. Get your scuba dive club into it! Make the application early and get some ideas on the board for a unique and memorable float. A fully suited diver, clomping along in old fins next to the float, can wander over to the spectators and let kids try on his mask -- something they think is really cool! Create club signs for use on the float, and make sure you have at least two (four is better) fully suited scuba divers on the float during the parade.

The Local Fair -- Local fairs draw lots of local people, and all of them would be amazed to see a large, glass-sided tank of water with a couple of scuba divers in it. The drawback is that such tanks are few and far between. To construct one properly would require engineering know-how, because that much water, plus the pressure of two divers, could cause major problems if it's not built right. But it sure is a crowd magnet, and it would give a high profile to any local dive club that set up "scuba demonstration" times, say, every half an hour for ten to fifteen minutes, using such a tank!

A scuba exhibition tank attracts large crowds at fairs or other public events.
PHOTO BY KENT DIVERS ASSOCIATION

Open House for the Dive Club -- Setting up an evening where the scuba dive club has an "Open House," inviting all members of the community to see what they're all about, creates good will and often even gets a few new members. This can be held in the cafeteria of a local school from, say, 6:30 to 9 PM. Make sure there are lots of photos, posters, videos, and equipment demonstrations going on throughout the evening. An interesting guest speaker helps attract the general public. Advertise this event at least a couple of weeks in advance, especially in the community newspaper. Local fast food restaurants have generously donated items such as a large barrel of soda pop, along with cups and napkins. Have free coffee and sweets available for the public. And lots of free flyers and club newsletters!

Advertise your club's Open House in every possible way!

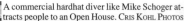
A commercial hardhat diver like Mike Schoger attracts people to an Open House. CRIS KOHL PHOTOS

Pig Roasts/Turknics/Camping/Moteling -- Dive clubs enjoy pig roasts as much as the next group, and with a bit of organizing, club members can enjoy a weekend of camping or motelling and pig roasting during the summer. You will need an experienced person here, along with a metal roaster and, of course, a pig, and get it roasting many hours ahead of the planned meal time. This gives divers lots of time to get caught up on tall diving tales. One club member was fabulous at roasting turkeys, so we combined "turkeys" and "picnic" to form the work "turknic" for what was usually an entire camping weekend along the shores of the St. Clair River. These were always fabulous fun times.

The roasted pig lands on the picnic table -- just in time for dinner!
PHOTO BY CRIS KOHL

Christmas/Awards Banquet -- At the end of the year, many dive clubs honor one or two of their members who contributed much to the club. They may have awards for the "Diver of the Year" and a "Rookie Diver of the Year" (see sample By-Laws, page 32). One club offers a "President's Award," given to the club member chosen by the President for the work he or she has done for the club (that group's Diver of the Year Award automatically goes to the diver who accumulates the most bottom time on club dives).

Often this Awards Banquet is combined with the club's Christmas Banquet. There are various methods of having a Christmas gift exchange, but the one I feel is the most fun (and

Left: Don't forget that underwater pumpkin carving contest in October!
Below: Dive club awards come in all shapes and sizes. PHOTOS BY CRIS KOHL

The club's Christmas Gift Exchange can be hilarious -- and even cut-throat (if desirable, quality gifts are brought into the exchange)! *Clockwise from above left:* The ladies may fight over a gift which includes a Chippendale calendar displaying manly men wearing Speedo's (you know -- typical male diver types); two male gift recipients may compare risqué shirts or aprons; one desirable gift may be taken away by a new "owner" several times before it ends up permanently in someone's hands; a club sweatshirt can be a favored gift which might end up being "exchanged" several times; novelty gifts can be fun, like a shovel with the words written on it, "For the diver who likes to go deeper." PHOTOS BY CRIS KOHL

which can be the most cutthroat!) goes like this (NOTE: this is a bit different from a "White Elephant" gift exchange):

Each diver is requested to bring a brand new, wrapped gift worth (put a recommended maximum price -- not "value" -- on it, say either $15.00 or $20.00). Guys bring a gift for a guy. Gals bring a gift for a gal. Label the gift correctly as "Guy" or "Gal." Place all the gifts under the Christmas tree, the "Guys" on one side and the "Gals" on the other. During the dinner, all the guys who brought a gift will draw a number from a hat; the gals will then do the same. (We use blue and pink paper for the numbers respectively). After dinner, when the gift exchange begins, the guy who drew #1 selects a "Guy" gift from under the tree, opens it, shows everyone what it is, and sits down. The guy who drew #2 selects a "Guy" gift from under the tree, but before opening it, he must decide if he wants that unopened gift or the open one that #1 has. This can get pretty dramatic. If he selects #1's gift, then he hands #1 the unopened gift he selected, and that gift becomes #1's new gift. #1 opens it and shows everyone. #3 then picks an unopened gift from under the tree and decides if he wants it, or one of the two that has been previously opened....and so on down the line. Obviously, the person with the highest number gets the best selection of opened gifts to choose from, or he can gamble on the one, final unopened gift under the tree. When the Guys are done, the Gals start from scratch with their gifts and their set of numbers (they cannot take any of the guys' opened gifts). The nicer, serious gifts exchange hands often, while the plain or the risqué gifts generally remain with the person who opened them. But it's all good fun, and anyone who brought a gift will go home with a gift.

Sometimes donated raffle prizes add to the fun and excitement of this banquet. At least one club I know of, the Aquanauts Scuba Association of Chicago, gives its members each a DVD of highlights of many of the club's activities during the past year -- a great idea! -- after they show it at their year's end banquet.

Organizing a Local Dive Show

This takes a fair amount of work for a dive club, but offers great rewards. The Bay Area Divers of Toledo, OH, have run the annual day-and-evening-long "Shipwrecks and Scuba" Show for well over 20 years now; the Niagara Divers Association in Ontario has organized the annual "Shipwrecks!" Show since 1995, held in a large high school auditorium; the full-day, 9-5 festival includes an excellent catered lunch.

Here are some basic suggestions for setting up a successful dive show:

Establish a core group of reliable volunteers to organize the show. Assign certain jobs to these individuals, including: programs, publicity, ticket sales and distribution, and AV (audio/visual). Find a large auditorium with a good sound (PA) system, comfortable seats, a large screen, and free, close parking. This is truly challenging. You might be surprised at how important this "free, close parking" is. I have seen shows where people had to pay $10 or $12 to park their cars, then they had to walk a quarter of a mile to where the show was taking place. This makes for very frazzled attendees by the time they arrive! Choose your venue carefully. A good choice can make your show a success for years to come!

Establish your presenters early, and get the correct spelling of their names and the correct titles of their presentations. Make sure their presentations are good. A good presenter, besides having excellent images, should be able to speak well in terms of enunciation, volume and pace.

Do not expect to get volunteers or presenters for free if they have to drive more than an hour to get there. We live in an era of increasing gasoline prices, making our mobility, to which we have become so accustomed, indeed, even spoiled, in the past few decades, costlier than ever before. More and more established presenters are finding that they have to charge a fee, either as blunt payment or in the form of an "honorarium," to cover their time, their presentation, and the expense of getting to the show. You may have to fly in a special speaker; arrange for travel from and back to the airport.

Find out, and possibly arrange for, your presenters' AV needs. You should automatically provide a large screen, a podium and a microphone/PA system. The major AV problem is that not all laptop computers are compatible with all digital projectors. In fact, most are not. Time-consuming crises can occur just before show time, and these are frustrating experiences for both the organizers and the audience, and a true nightmare for the presenter. A well-organized show can solve AV problems quickly, but it is best if the presenter brings his own computer and projector which he knows will work.

Arrange accommodations for your volunteers and presenters, if necessary.

Arrange meals or places to eat for a day-long show. Seriously consider having a venue catered, or run the show in a place which has a large restaurant, so that your crowd won't have to leave the building to get fed. If they leave, they may return late, or, even worse, not at all. For a day-long show, provide food and a place to eat for your volunteers and your presenters. You definitely don't want those people to leave!

Allow speakers opportunities to sell their books, DVD's or whatever they have. This helps keep down their expenses for doing these presentations, and they truly appreciate it. The ideal time for a presenter to make some sales is *immediately* after his talk, and as close by as possible, as well as later in the exhibit area. Set up a sales table in the back of the room or in the hall for immediate post-presentation product sales.

Seriously consider the idea of offering booth space for a nominal fee to dive shops, charter boat operators, and anyone else involved in the local scuba, scuba-related, and/ or boating activities. These businesses often set up very interesting exhibits, and ideally they should be allowed to sell their wares at their exhibit booth. Their paying for booth space will help you offset the cost of the show.

Arrange for an "after glow" party for the volunteers, any exhibitors, and the speakers. This could be held in a small meeting room of a hotel -- with a few tables and a couple dozen chairs, with the organizers supplying late-night finger food and several portable coolers filled with refreshments. This is a considerate and valuable opportunity, after a show, for volunteers and exhibitors to personally meet the speakers, and vice versa, as well as for speakers to chat informally with one another, all in a very relaxing atmosphere. Ideally, have the after glow party at the same location as the day's presentations; that makes it very convenient, and people won't get lost driving around searching for some different place.

Price show tickets reasonably. Compare what other shows of similar duration are charging.

Work with dive shops to distribute flyers and to sell tickets.

Go to other dive clubs' meetings and advertise the show.

Most importantly: advertise the daylights out of the show in detail at least four months in advance with flyers, small posters, electronic notices, etc. It takes several months of leeway time to get news of your show placed in the "Calendar" section of a major scuba magazine, so do that as early as possible. Get your local newspaper excited about the show, and persuade them to do a promotional article at least a week in advance of the show. Arrange for at least one of your presenters to be interviewed by the local newspaper, by telephone if necessary, with that presenter providing the interviewer with an underwater image or two, sent electronically, for use in that newspaper article.

Arrange to take credit card ticket orders over the phone, and arrange to use several phone numbers. This could be difficult, but you will make far more sales than if you rely on people mailing you checks or showing up at the door on the day of the show.

Print an informative program which gives the attendee a good idea of what each presentation is about, and some biographical information about each presenter, as well as information about the exhibits and about your club and how to join. These programs have souvenir value to many attendees; some get their programs signed by the presenters!

On the day of the show, have good signage with proper arrows, not only inside the building, but also along roadways to make it easier for attendees to find their way. Small dive flag signs with the words "Dive Show" under the flag, plus an arrow pointing in the correct direction, help drivers get there. Also, make sure you put a good map in your advertising flyers.

Make up classy volunteer and speaker badges.

Arrange for an emcee to introduce and thank each speaker. This should be someone with a clear, enthusiastic voice, someone who can ad-lib in any emergency should it arise. The show should move smoothly between presentations, with no awkward pauses; a good emcee can keep things flowing. He will also know where the light switch is!

Develop a mailing list to make next year's show easier, and start planning that show at least six months in advance by arranging presentations that you can publicize as early as possible. Good luck!

Great Lakes Highlight No. 1

TEN MARITIME "FIRSTS"

① *The First European to See the Great Lakes*

The first white man to see the Great Lakes was 18-year-old French explorer Étiénne Brulé, who reached Lake Huron's Georgian Bay in the year 1610. Five years later, he became the first European to see Lake Ontario. In 1629, he fell out of grace with the French for selling his services to the English (who promptly captured Quebec City a a result), and in 1632, Brulé was killed in a drunken brawl over an Indian woman and eaten by his Indian associates.

Explorer Brulé could not keep away from the Great Lakes...or booze...or women.... CRIS KOHL COLLECTION

② **Frontenac:** *The First Shipwreck in the Great Lakes*

In the 1670's, French explorer Sieur de La Salle built four small sailing ships on Lake Ontario, and the largest of these, the 30-ton *Frontenac*, carried men and construction materials for the *Griffon* to the western end of the lake. There, on January 8, 1679, due to his pilot's carelessness, the ship sank just off shore near presentday Thirty Mile Point, NY, with many supplies, causing a major setback for La Salle.

The *Frontenac*. ART BY GEORGE CUTHBERTSON, CANADA STEAMSHIP LINES COLLECTION

③ **Griffon:** *The First Shipwreck in the Upper Great Lakes*

La Salle's men built the 45-ton *Griffon*, with a keel length of 50′ and an overall 70′ length, near the Lake Erie end of the Niagara River, in early 1679. In August, the *Griffon* sailed to Lake Michigan's Green Bay, loaded a valuable fur cargo there, and headed back towards the Niagara River, but was never seen again, disappearing on the return leg of her maiden voyage and thus creating the greatest mystery of the Great Lakes.

Detail of the *Griffon's* construction in 1679. CRIS KOHL COLLECTION

④ **Frontenac** *and* **Ontario:** *First Steamers on the Lakes*

The peaceful era following the War of 1812 saw the first steamships built on the lakes. Launched near Kingston, Ontario, on September 7, 1816, the 150-foot-long, 740-ton *Frontenac* was larger than the 110-foot-long, 240-ton *Ontario*, launched in March, 1817, at Sackets Harbor, NY. Both were scrapped a dozen years later.

Left: The *Frontenac*. ART BY GEORGE CUTHBERTSON, CANADA STEAMSHIP LINES COLLECTION. *Right*: The *Ontario*. ART BY ERIC HEYL, CRIS KOHL COLLECTION

5   Walk-in-the-Water: *First Upper Great Lakes Steamer*

The sidewheel steamer, *Walk-in-the-Water* (135'6" x 32'2" x 8'7"), built at Buffalo, NY, in 1818, cruised across Lakes Erie, Huron and Michigan, but lasted only three years, being storm-wrecked at Lake Erie's Point Abino, Canada, on October 31, 1821, with no lives lost. Her steam engine was recovered and placed in another ship, but her hull was pounded to pieces.

The *Walk-in-the-Water*. ART BY SAMUEL WARD STANTON, CRIS KOHL COLLECTION

6   Vandalia: *First Propeller on the Great Lakes*

Steam-powered ships on the Great Lakes were all propelled by large paddlewheels until the *Vandalia* (127' x 20' x 8'), utilizing a new invention named a screw propeller, was built at Oswego, NY, on Lake Ontario, in 1841. This ship reportedly sank off Lake Erie's Point Pelee on Oct. 27, 1851.

The *Vandalia*. ART BY CAPT. VAN CLEVE, CRIS KOHL COLLECTION

7   R. J. Hackett: *First Great Lakes Freighter Design*

The *R. J. Hackett*.
CRIS KOHL COLLECTION

The wooden *R. J. Hackett* (211'2" x 32'5" x 19'2"), built at Cleveland in 1869, revolutionized bulk freight carrier design by moving the pilothouse to the extreme bow, and the engine to the extreme aft, with unhampered cargo space in between. This ship was wrecked in Green Bay in 1905 (see p. 480).

8   Barge 101: *First Whaleback Ship*

Whalebacks, nicknamed "cigar boats" and "pigboats" because of their appearance, were a unique Great Lakes ship design, with over 40 of them built from 1888 to 1898. Several ended their careers on the East Coast. See pages 534-535 for more details about whalebacks.

The launch of whaleback barge 101. CRIS KOHL COLLECTION

9   *First Non-Commercial Mixed Gas Scuba Diving*

In 1979, Jerry Buchanan of Duluth, MN, became the first scuba diver to experiment with, and develop information about, trimix diving, along with his doctor colleagues, Robert Horton and Joe Schneeweis. In 1980, they presented their findings at Chicago's "Our World--Underwater" and Toronto's "Underwater Canada." They were also the first to advocate post-dive oxygen use. This team, which included Ryan LeBlanc, explored the deep (257') wreck of the fabled yacht, *Gunilda* (see p. 560), using experimental gasses. This was in the early 1980's, when other divers in the Great Lakes -- and in the rest of the world -- riskily did deep dives on air.

10   Wolfe Islander II: *First Ship Sunk in Great Lakes to Create a Scuba Dive Site*

On September 21, 1985, the mothballed car-and-passenger ferry, *Wolfe Islander II* (144'3" x 43'1" x 8'), was purposely sunk off Kingston, Ontario, for the express purpose of creating a new shipwreck as a scuba dive site. See pages 88-89 for more information. More ships have been scuttled since then (see page 52).

Great Lakes Highlight No. 2

THE TEN WORST
MARITIME DISASTERS

1 *Eastland* **(July 24, 1915)**

A ship which didn't even leave port became the Great Lakes' worst maritime disaster! The steamer, *Eastland* (265' x 38'2" x 19'5"), with over 2,500 excursionists, tipped over in the Chicago River. Over 800 people died. The hated vessel, returned to service for military use as the USS *Wilmette,* was scrapped in 1948.

The capsized *Eastland*. CRIS KOHL COLLECTION

2 *Lady Elgin* **(Sept. 8, 1860)**

The wooden sidewheel steamer, *Lady Elgin* (251' x 31'8" x 11'1") sank in Lake Michigan off Winnetka, IL, during a storm after a collision with the schooner *Augusta*. At least 300 people perished.

The *Lady Elgin*. CRIS KOHL COLLECTION

3 *G. P. Griffith* **(June 17, 1850)**

Approximately 275 people died on Lake Erie when the wooden paddlewheel steamer, *G. P. Griffith* (193'3" x 28' x 11'3"), caught on fire at night, while the mostly immigrant passengers slept, and sank about 18 miles northeast of Cleveland.

The *G. P. Griffith* in flames. CRIS KOHL COLLECTION

4 *Victoria* **(May 24, 1881)**

The double-decked sternwheel steamer, *Victoria* (80' x 22'6" x 3'6"), overloaded with more than 600 excursionists celebrating Queen Victoria's birthday, capsized in the Thames River at London, Ontario, with 182 people perishing. This tragedy has been largely overlooked by Great Lakes maritime historians.

The capsized *Victoria*. CRIS KOHL COLLECTION

5 *Phoenix* (November 21, 1847)

Fire at night destroyed the steamer, *Phoenix* (144' x 26' x 11'), off Sheboygan, WI, killing about 160 people, mostly Dutch immigrants; 46 survived. The burned hulk was towed to Sheboygan and abandoned.

The *Phoenix* in flames. CRIS KOHL COLLECTION

6 *Atlantic* (August 20, 1852)

The palatial sidewheel passenger steamer, *Atlantic* (265'7" x 33' x 14'6"), sank in Lake Erie off Long Point, Ontario, after being rammed at night by the *Ogdensburg*. About 150 people perished. She became a controversial "treasure" ship in the 1990's.

The doomed *Atlantic*. CRIS KOHL COLLECTION

7 *Erie* (August 9, 1841)

The wooden paddlewheel steamer, *Erie* (176' x 27' x 10'), caught on fire off Silver Creek, NY, on Lake Erie, and sank. Many well-to-do northern European immigrants perished among the approximately 140 lost.

The *Erie*. GREAT LAKES HISTORICAL SOCIETY

8 *Asia* (September 14, 1882)

Only two, a young man and a young woman, survived from the 125 people on board the wooden steamer, *Asia* (136' x 23'4" x 11'), when it foundered in a violent storm on Georgian Bay near Lonely Island.

The ill-fated *Asia*. CRIS KOHL COLLECTION

9 *Noronic* (September 17, 1949)

The popular cruise ship, *Noronic* (385' x 52' x 29'8"), launched in 1913, burned to a total loss in Toronto harbor while passengers slept; 119 of them perished. The charred hull was raised, towed away, and scrapped.

The burning *Noronic*. CRIS KOHL COLLECTION

10 *Pewabic* (August 9, 1865)

The steamer, *Pewabic* (200'3" x 31'1" x 12'5"), sank in Lake Huron off Alpena, MI, after a collision with her sister ship, the *Meteor*; about 90 people lost their lives, and the valuable cargo of copper ingots inspired many salvage attempts.

The *Pewabic*. CRIS KOHL COLLECTION

Great Lakes Highlight No. 3

MAKING NEW SHIPWRECKS

I sometimes begin a shipwreck presentation at scuba shows with the tongue-in-cheek comment that, "They're just not making shipwrecks like they used to!" Modern aids to navigation have reduced natural shipwrecks from about one a week to perhaps one a decade. This is, of course, a good thing in terms of lives and property saved, but not so good for scuba divers in search of shipwrecks to explore. So, to make up for the rarity of real shipwrecks nowadays, and to reduce the risk of overvisitation of our historic, natural shipwrecks, and to create artificial reefs, many places have purposely sunk obsolete vessels in the past 30+ years.

Purposely created shipwrecks sunk beyond the Great Lakes to attract scuba divers include *(clockwise from lower left)*: The *Eagle*, sunk in the Florida Keys, December, 1985; the *Mahi*, sunk off Oahu, Hawaii, in 1982; the *Indra*, sunk off North Carolina in 1992; the *YO-257* off Waikiki, Hawaii, sunk in 1989; and the *Duane*, sunk in the Florida Keys in November, 1987. PHOTOS BY CRIS KOHL

The Great Lakes have their share of created shipwrecks. While those in other areas are, for the most part, decommissioned military ships, we most frequently sink commercial vessels from our merchant marine in the inland seas:

1. ***Wolfe Islander II*** (Lake Ontario, Sept. 21, 1985.) First commercial ship to be sunk in the Great Lakes to create a new dive site. See p. 88-89.

2. ***Caroline Rose*** (Lake Huron, late August, 1990.) This East Coast schooner was sunk near Tobermory, Ontario, to attract scuba divers. See p. 250.

3. **USCG Cutter *Mesquite*** (Lake Superior, July, 1990.) Naturally wrecked on Dec. 4, 1989; donated and moved to deeper water. See p. 521-522.

4. ***Effie Mae*** (Lake Ontario, Oct. 17, 1993.) This former dive boat was placed next to a natural wreck near Kingston, Ontario. See p. 92-93.

5. ***Steven M. Selvick*** (Lake Superior, June 1, 1996.) This historic tugboat was sunk near Munising, Michigan, to attract more divers. See p. 510.

6. ***Niagara II*** (Lake Huron, May 15, 1999.) Built in England in 1930, this historic vessel was scuttled near Tobermory, Ontario. See p. 254.

7. **"Holly barge"** (Lake Michigan, May 6, 2000.) This barge became a new dive training area; sunk near a natural wreck off Chicago. See p. 404.

8. ***The Straits of Mackinac*** (Lake Michigan, April 10, 2003.) Largest commercial ship sunk to date, it lies off Chicago, IL. See p. 416.

St. Lawrence River: Area 1

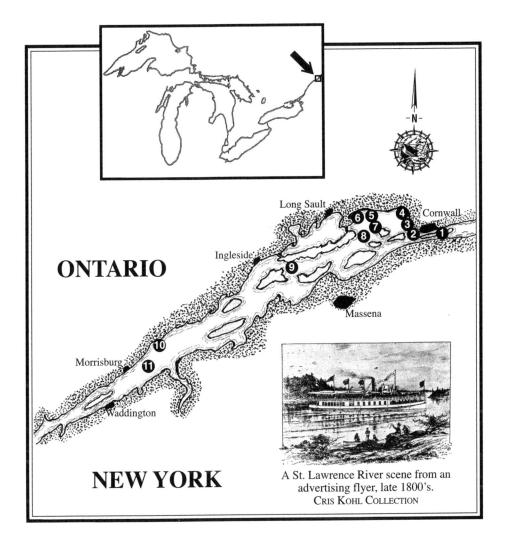

A St. Lawrence River scene from an advertising flyer, late 1800's.
CRIS KOHL COLLECTION

ONTARIO

NEW YORK

1. *Fred Mercur*
2. Aultsville
3. Dickinson's Landing
4. *Cornwall*
5. Mille Roches Power House
6. Sheik Island dam
7. "Belly Dumper" wreck
8. Swing bridge
9. Lock 21
10. Chrysler Park wreck
11. *Eastcliffe Hall*

1. FRED MERCUR

LORAN:	GPS: 45° 02.050'/074° 37.315'
DEPTH: 3 to 45 feet	LEVEL: Novice-Intermediate

LOCATION: You'll need a boat to take you over to the west side of Stanley Island in the St. Lawrence River near Cornwall, Ontario.

The wooden propeller, *Fred Mercur,* (232' x 35'5" x 18'2"), burned to a total loss after she was beached in a bed of rushes off Stanley Island on July 3, 1925. A nearby cottager saved the entire crew in six round-trips with his rowboat. Built at Buffalo in 1882, the *Mercur* sailed under U.S. registry until being sold to Canadian interests in 1919.

The bow reaches to within a few feet of the surface and is often marked with a jug by local divers. Numerous fish and American eels inhabit this site, with most of the hull intact and on a slope to 45'. Coal cargo can be seen inside the hull, while a rudder and propeller

The steamer, *Fred Mercur,* was destroyed by fire in the St. Lawrence River in 1925.
CRIS KOHL COLLECTION

grace the stern. A tractor that went through the ice rests in about 25' just off the bow. Beware of a moderate current and the silt bottom, which is quick to stir up and affect visibility.

2. AULTSVILLE

LORAN:	GPS:
DEPTH: To 70 feet	LEVEL: Novice-Intermediate

LOCATION: Off Cornwall, Ontario. Accessible from shore, but a boat is needed to reach the more distant and more interesting parts of this site.

This village was totally flooded during the construction of the St. Lawrence Seaway in the 1950's. One of the oldest pottery works in Ontario was located at this site, and, in 1987, a crock was recovered from the 60' depth by government divers for analysis in Ottawa.

When water levels drop late in the year, parts of this submerged village can be explored without getting wet. Reportedly the best areas for diving are along the old shoreline by the former town pier and ferry landing, because bottles are common there.

3. DICKINSON'S LANDING

LORAN:	GPS:
DEPTH: To 65 feet	LEVEL: Novice-Intermediate

LOCATION: Near Cornwall, Ontario.

Dickinson's Landing was formerly a small village which existed mainly to service the locks of the old St. Lawrence River canal system. The village, like most of the old locks in this region, is now totally submerged as part of the St. Lawrence Seaway project connecting the Great Lakes with the Atlantic Ocean and the rest of the world. Local divers placed ropes on the underwater locks as guides for visiting scuba divers. Use wise judgment with the variable visibility at this site, and beware of depth/time limitations.

4. CORNWALL

LORAN:	GPS:
DEPTH: 60 feet	LEVEL: Advanced

LOCATION: This site is off the south side of Machinette Island (Island 17) near Cornwall, Ontario. A boat is necessary.

The old schooner-barge, *Cornwall,* rests upright in 60′ of water, with the bow fairly intact, but the stern somewhat disintegrated. Be cautious of the boating traffic here, as well as variable visibility, depth/time limitations, and the 2-3 knot current.

5. MILLE ROCHES POWER HOUSE

LORAN:	GPS: 45° 01.30′/074° 49.86′
DEPTH: 35, 55, and 75 feet	LEVEL: Intermediate-Advanced

Art © Save Ontario Shipwrecks

LOCATION: From Highway 401's exit #778 (Moulinette Road), head east on Moulinette Rd. towards Cornwall for about three miles until you reach Guindon Park. The park offers a boat launch ramp, changing and restroom facilities, and picnic tables for meals and post-diving festivities. The site, usually buoyed in season, is 0.5 nautical mile away on a heading of 183° magnetic from the tip of Guindon Park.

Drawing by Nick Baets for Save Ontario Shipwrecks

The Mille Roches Power House, built in 1900-1901 by the St. Lawrence Power Company, was part of the former town, now submerged, named Mille Roches. The plant operated until 1955, and in 1958, the roof and walls of the building were removed in preparation for the St. Lawrence Seaway flooding.

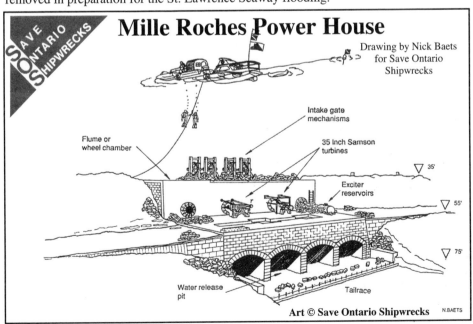

Mille Roches Power House

Drawing by Nick Baets for Save Ontario Shipwrecks

Intake gate mechanisms

Flume or wheel chamber

35 Inch Samson turbines

Exciter reservoirs

▽ 35′

▽ 55′

▽ 75′

Water release pit

Tailrace

Art © Save Ontario Shipwrecks

N.BAETS

Although the roof, walls and generators were removed, two 35-inch Samson water turbines remain intact, as well as a wheel chamber, exciter reservoirs, and other items of interest. The intake gate mechanisms lie at a depth of 35', while the power house floor is situated at 55', and the water release pits and tailrace are at 75'. Bring a dive light for viewing the deepest remains, but penetration is only for the trained and prepared.

Boating traffic here can be a problem, especially on summer weekends; use a dive flag as one precaution. The one-to-two-knot current is not usually a problem, and is noticeable only during your descent and ascent. On the deepest level, beware of time/depth limitations.

6. SHEIK ISLAND DAM

LORAN:	GPS:
DEPTH: 30 to 65 feet	LEVEL: Advanced

LOCATION: Near Long Sault, Ontario, St. Lawrence River.

The flooding of the St. Lawrence River lowlands in the late 1950's for the Seaway project created numerous submerged sites that scuba divers are exploring to this day.

A boat is necessary to reach the Sheik Island Dam, which is similar to another nearby site, Lock 21 (see site #9 in this section). Boating traffic, current, dark waters, and depth can make this a challenging divesite.

7. "BELLY DUMPER" WRECK

LORAN:	GPS:
DEPTH: 65 to 92 feet	LEVEL: Advanced

LOCATION: In the Long Sault area, near the Mille Roches Power House.

This unidentified steel barge, used in the St. Lawrence Seaway construction in the late 1950's, was located by Bob Dumond in 1991. This shallow vessel rests on an incline and has three compartments which were used for gravel or other bulk materials. One door is fully open on the bottom of one compartment, while the other two are only half so.

Beware of boating traffic, some current, and depth/time limitations.

8. SWING BRIDGE (MOULINETTE)

LORAN:	GPS:
DEPTH: 30 to 65 feet	LEVEL: Advanced

LOCATION: Just west of the Mille Roches site (see site #5 in this section).

The small farming town of Moulinette disappeared completely in the flooding which was necessary for the creation of the St. Lawrence Seaway. The swing bridge itself is no longer there, but its old stone pillars remain submerged. There are six pillars total, with the swivel mechanism still in place on the center one. For this dive, you should have some experience in current diving. Besides the current, there is some boating traffic, depth/time limitations, and occasional low visibility.

9. LOCK 21

LORAN: Shore dive	GPS:
DEPTH: 40 to 60 feet	LEVEL: Advanced

LOCATION: From either Ingleside or Long Sault, Ontario, take Highway 2 to the Long Sault Parkway (entrance fee) to Macdonell Island. Past picnic areas, restrooms and snackbars, at the southwestern end of the island, you will find ropes that run from shore to the site.

Lock 21, which was built in 1885-86 as part of the second enlargement of the old St. Lawrence River canal system, is 270' long between the gates, 45' wide, and has 14' of

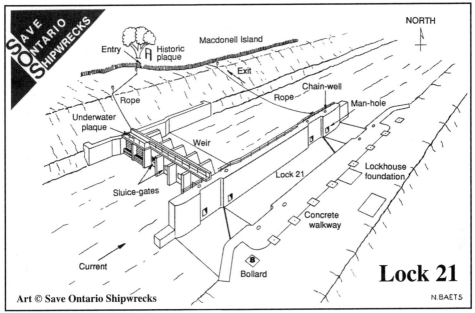

Lock 21

Art © Save Ontario Shipwrecks

N.BAETS

clearance over the sill. It was flooded as part of the St. Lawrence Seaway system in 1958.

From shore, the upstream rope takes the diver to the site and the downstream one leads back to shore. Following the rope system, the diver will see the weir and sluice gates, as well as concrete walkways, a bollard, and chain-wells. The current is fairly strong (2-3 knots), the visibility can be low, and the bottom is 60' down. On land, watch your step. Canada geese and their droppings abound.

10. CHRYSLER PARK WRECK

LORAN:	LAT 44° 56' 03" LON 075° 03' 43"
DEPTH: 65 feet	LEVEL: Advanced

LOCATION: Northeast of Morrisburg, Ontario, off Chrysler Memorial Park. From the park, you can look across the waters of the St. Lawrence River to Wilson Hill Island, which is part of the USA. Between these two points, and just inside the Canadian side of the international boundary, is this shipwreck.

This small wooden propeller is a mystery wreck, but some people believe it is the *Chippewa,* which sank in this area on August 12, 1920. It is approximately 65' in length and rises off the bottom about 18'. Boating traffic is heavy since this site lies right in the middle of the main shipping channel, meaning that huge freighters traverse these waters. A strong current flows through this site as well. For these reasons, this site is not very popular and little survey work has been done in an effort to identify the shipwreck.

11. *EASTCLIFFE HALL*

LORAN:	GPS: 44° 55.48'/075° 06.07'
DEPTH: 40 to 65 feet	LEVEL: Advanced

LOCATION: Near Morrisburg, Ontario, with relatively easy boat launch and access from Chrysler Marina, just east of Upper Canada Village. The wreck lies just inside the Canadian border in the busy St. Lawrence River shipping channel. Beware of boating traffic!

The *Eastcliffe Hall* (343'4" x 43'8" x 22'8"), a bulk freight motor vessel built in Montreal in 1954, struck a shoal and the concrete buoy abutment at Chrysler Shoal at 3:00 AM on

July 14, 1970, and sank on a slope with the tragic loss of nine lives. She carried pig iron.

The shallow bow points into the current. Even with her superstructure dynamited off due to being a hazard to navigation, this is an interesting site. Her bow cabins and open holds are inviting, but wreck penetration is for the ultra-experienced only! The stern is a labyrinth of tangled steel ideally avoided (both props were salvaged). With the current stronger than usual (3 to 6 knots), this is a challenging dive, and, at times, poor visibility causes disorientation. Use an anchor line to descend, and remember where it is for your return!

The *Eastcliffe Hall*. CRIS KOHL COLLECTION

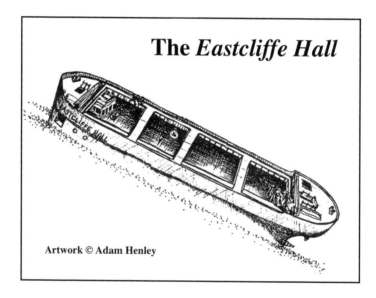

The *Eastcliffe Hall*

Artwork © Adam Henley

St. Lawrence River: Area 2

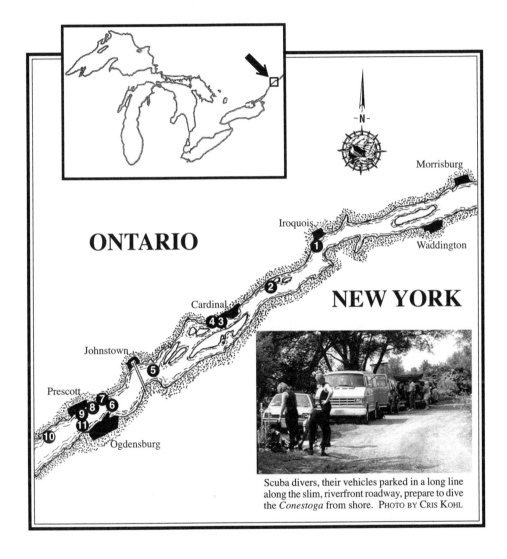

ONTARIO

NEW YORK

Morrisburg

Iroquois

Waddington

Cardinal

Johnstown

Prescott

Ogdensburg

Scuba divers, their vehicles parked in a long line along the slim, riverfront roadway, prepare to dive the *Conestoga* from shore. PHOTO BY CRIS KOHL

1. Iroquois Beach
2. Seaway barge graveyard
3. *Conestoga*
4. *Wee Hawk* and Lock 28
5. Channel barge
6. *Fleur Marie*

7. Windmill site and wreck
8. Prescott ferry docks
9. Prescott underwater park
10. *Rothesay*
11. "Loblaw's" wreck

1. IROQUOIS BEACH

LORAN: Shore dive	GPS:
DEPTH: To 40 feet	LEVEL: Novice-Intermediate

LOCATION: At the village of Iroquois, Ontario, near the Iroquois Locks, along the St. Lawrence River.

This site, accessible from shore just west of the actual beach, has a sandy bottom, some submerged cribs (rocks inside square timber frames used as bases for docks), an old anchor and a wooden-hulled sailboat about 15' in length.

Stay aware of your underwater location so that you don't drift out into the shipping channel. The backwash current can make returning to shore confusing, so take a compass along to find your way back.

2. SEAWAY BARGE GRAVEYARD

LORAN:	GPS:
DEPTH: To 30 feet	LEVEL: Novice-Intermediate

LOCATION: A boat is required to take you to the old canal wall just a few miles downstream from Cardinal, Ontario. One abandoned wooden barge rests alongside the wall, while the remains of two more lie inside the old canal. These sites offer "Kodak moments" for the underwater photographer as well as opportunities to view fish life.

3. CONESTOGA

LORAN: Shore or boat dive	LAT 44° 46' 46" LON 075° 23' 36"
DEPTH: 28 feet	LEVEL: Novice-Intermediate

LOCATION: From the intersection of Highway 2 and Road No. 22 in Cardinal, Ontario, proceed along Road No. 22 towards the river. At the bottom of the hill, turn right and follow the unserviced (bumpy) dirt road along the narrow causeway for about 0.6 mile. The large upper portion of the vessel's 1878 Cuyahoga Iron Works steeple compound engine seems

STEAMER BURNS NEAR CARDINAL

Conestoga, Grain Laden For Montreal, Totally Destroyed on Sunday.

Prescott, May 22.—The steamer Conestoga, loaded with

Above: The steamer, *Conestoga,* worked on the Great Lakes for over 40 years before burning in 1922. CRIS KOHL COLLECTION.   *Below:* The top of the *Conestoga's* engine reveals the wreck's location. PHOTO BY CRIS KOHL

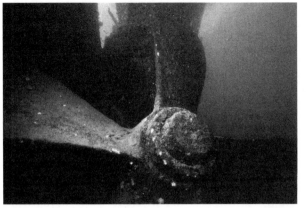

Above: The *Conestoga's* propeller. PHOTO BY CRIS KOHL. *Right:* The
engine towers above the surface. ART BY MICHAEL ANGELO GAGLIARDI

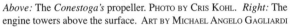

intent on exhibitionism as it flashes out from the river and reveals the underwater resting place of the rest of this ship about 80′ from shore. There is a small, narrow parking area at the site.

The wooden combination passenger and package steam freighter, *Conestoga* (253′ x 36′ x 16′3″), launched at Cleveland on July 6, 1878, caught fire and sank with 30,000 bushels of wheat outside Lock 28 of the Galop Canal on May 22, 1922. No lives were lost, and much of the cargo was salvaged, but the ship was a total loss.

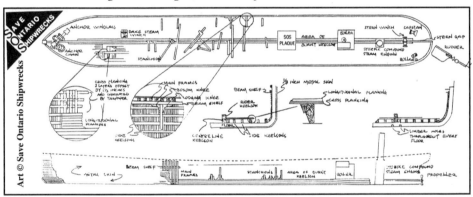

Art © Save Ontario Shipwrecks

The wooden hull, pointing upstream, is still in very good condition, although the fire (and ice in subsequent winters) took their toll on the superstructure. A windlass and anchor chain adorn the bow, near a Dake steam winch. The enormous, upright engine makes for fascinating exploration, while the rudder lies flat off the stern. The usually mild current is strongest at the bow. Fly the divers down flag because of the boating traffic.

4. *WEE HAWK* AND LOCK 28

LORAN: Shore dive	GPS:
DEPTH: 18 feet	LEVEL: Novice-Intermediate

LOCATION: The abandoned hull of the old steel ferry, *Wee Hawk*, lies about one-quarter mile upstream (that is, to the west) of the *Conestoga* site. Lock 28 has gained popularity in recent years as a picnic site. The best diver access is to the east of the wreck at the closed lock gate. A popular drift dive takes divers through the old gates, ending up just upstream of the *Conestoga*. Warning: Do not penetrate this old, steel hull unless properly trained and prepared, as the silt reduces visibility to zero easily.

5. CHANNEL BARGE

LORAN: Shore dive	**GPS:**
DEPTH: 50 feet	**LEVEL: Advanced**

LOCATION: Access to this site is by boat from Johnstown, Ontario. A wooden barge approximately 60′ long with a beam of 20′ was located in 1995 in front of Chimney Island at the head of the Galop Rapids.

Because of the fast current, this is an exhilarating dive for experienced divers only

6. *FLEUR MARIE*

LORAN:	**GPS: 44° 42.987′/075° 28.578′**
DEPTH: 52 feet	**LEVEL: Intermediate-Advanced**

LOCATION: Taking a boat from Ogdensburg, NY, or Prescott, ON, will get you to this site just inside the US border near the middle of the river.

Originally constructed as a brigantine at Lanoraie, Quebec, in 1850, the *Fleur Marie* (92′5″ x 20′1″ x 8′7″) aged gradually into a decrepit hulk and was scuttled in 1884.

A strong current flows above this shipwreck, but

The wreck of the *Fleur Marie*. PHOTOS BY CRIS KOHL

diminishes considerably at the bottom, so the challenging part of the dive is at the beginning getting down and at the end getting up. Visibility in recent years has been up to 35′ because of filter-feeding zebra mussels, and the water temperature has reached 70 degrees by the end of summer.

Most of the ship's framing, beams and conterboard box remain explorable, with an ornate stern undercut by the current. The rudder, unfortunately, is missing, perhaps carried downstream by these fast waters long ago when the ship sank. The river bottom consists mainly of clean sand and millions of tiny, white seashells, offering a soft bottom for this ship and its artifacts. You'll find fish galore! Numerous bass, sunfish, pickerel and the odd carp greet visiting divers. Boating traffic can be hectic on summer weekends; use caution.

7. WINDMILL SITE AND WRECK

LORAN: Shore or boat dive	**GPS:**
DEPTH: 0 to 30 feet	**LEVEL: Novice-Intermediate**

LOCATION: East of Prescott, Ontario.

This windmill played a significant role in the Upper Canada Rebellion of 1838 when Canadian refugees and American sympathizers launched an attack on Prescott from the

U.S. side. After a seven-day fiasco, most of the 300 invaders were captured.

Dive directly below the old windmill. To the left (east) of the windmill, a set of wooden stairs and a path lead to a picnic table positioned on a flat rock at the water's edge. It's an ideal place to suit up. Enjoy the underwater sights of rubble from the old mill and American eels. In about 60' of water near the red buoy on the Canadian side lie the remains of a small, unidentified wooden vessel, only about 35' long and consisting mainly of ribs and planks.

The windmill. PHOTO BY CRIS KOHL

8. PRESCOTT FERRY DOCKS

LORAN: Shore dive	GPS:
DEPTH: To 55 feet	LEVEL: Intermediate-Advanced

LOCATION: Just to the east of the town of Prescott, Ontario.

Long a favorite location for drift diving the St. Lawrence River, this site also offers small, unidentified shipwrecks. Two lifeboats, in very poor shape, lie at a depth of about 55' approximately 300' and 350' off shore.

9. PRESCOTT UNDERWATER PARK

LORAN: Shore dive	GPS:
DEPTH: To 40 feet	LEVEL: Novice-Intermediate

LOCATION: This popular site is located off the town docks right in the heart of downtown Prescott, Ontario.

Used frequently as a training site by scuba instructors and their students, a large parking lot right next to the river helps make parking and suiting up as easy as the access. Reportedly ice boom anchors lie scattered on the bottom in front of the Coast Guard Station.

10. *ROTHESAY*

LORAN: Shore dive	LAT 44° 41' 58" LON 075° 31' 40"
DEPTH: 20 to 30 feet	LEVEL: Novice-Intermediate

LOCATION: An historic marker commemorating Loyalist Justus Sherwood stands just southwest of Prescott, Ontario. Park your car on the grass strip there, carry your dive gear down the convenient wooden stairs to the water's edge and suit up at the picnic tables.

Launched in 1868 at St. John, New Brunswick, the wooden sidewheel passenger steamer, *Rothesay* (193' x 28'8" x 7'9"), sank in a collision with the tug *Myra* on September 12, 1889, killing two of the latter's crew. Ottawa scuba divers located the wreck in 1964.

The best visibility is found in the spring; sometimes the early fall can also be good. Two buoys mark the route to the wreck: one about 100' off shore and the other placed right on the wreck about 300' out. A rope strung along the river's bottom from shore can be used as a guideline. Impressive sights include the smokestack, boilers, walking beam, paddlewheels, and rudder. The wreck was dynamited for target practice in 1901, so not much of the middle remains intact.

The paddlewheeler, *Rothesay,* before and after the collision. CRIS KOHL COLLECTION.

63

Concrete block for rope trail to
the *Rothesay*. Only bare planking remains where a porthole
once hung, and massive bow-
wood dwarfs a diver.

PHOTOS BY CRIS KOHL

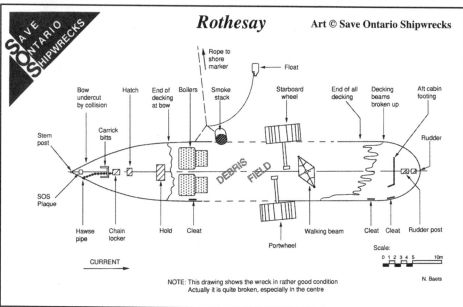

11. "LOBLAW'S" WRECK

LORAN:	GPS:
DEPTH: 52 feet	LEVEL: Intermediate

LOCATION: If you take a boat halfway between the wreck site of the *Rothesay* and the Canadian Coast Guard Station, and line up directly in front of a huge brick chimney over in Ogdensburg, this unidentified wreck lies south of the downstream channel.

This wooden ship sits upright in the firm clay, rising about eight feet off the bottom. The vessel's dimensions appear to be approximately 130' x 24' x 8', and there is evidence that the vessel burned to the waterline. It is usually buoyed with some sort of marker.

St. Lawrence River: Area 3

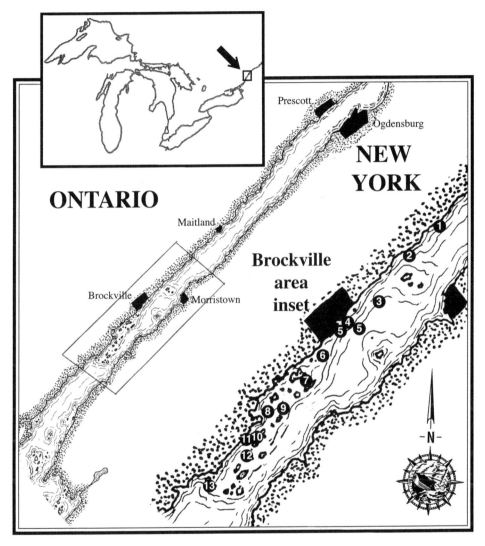

1. *Muscallonge*
2. Brockville wall dive
3. *Robert Gaskin*
4. Mahogany launch
5. Two unidentified hulls
6. Unidentified motor vessel
7. Narrows current "rush"
8. MacDonald's Point
9. *John B. King*
10. *Lillie Parsons*
11. Needle's Eye "rush"
12. *Sam Cooke*
13. 3 Molly's Gut wrecks

1. MUSCALLONGE

LORAN:	GPS: 44° 36.288'/075° 39.199'
DEPTH: 99 feet	LEVEL: Advanced

The huge tug, *Muscallonge,* worked on inland waters for 40 years.   CRIS KOHL COLLECTION

LOCATION: Three miles east of Brockville, Ontario; 1.5 miles downstream from Blockhouse Island.

The wooden tug, *Muscallonge* (128' x 24'5" x 12'), launched as the *Vigilant* at Port Huron, Michigan, on April 23, 1896, received her name change when Canadian owners purchased the ship in 1913. On August 15, 1936, while towing a barge to Toronto, the *Muscallonge* caught fire near Brockville. Captain F. Ahern ran his doomed ship aground, where it broke in two as it slid into deep water. No lives were lost in this mishap.

In spite of its land proximity (it's about 300' off shore), the *Muscallonge* is a boat dive. The main portion of the ship sits in 90' to 100' of water, with much to see for the visiting scuba diver: winches, the scotch boiler, the engine, the starboard side and numerous other ship's parts. The stern and props have reportedly been located across the channel on the U.S. side. How they got there is anyone's guess. Local divers try to keep this main site buoyed throughout the dive season. It is well away from the main shipping channel, but small boat traffic can be heavy during summer.

2. BROCKVILLE WALL DIVE

LORAN:	GPS:
DEPTH: To 100 feet	LEVEL: To Advanced

LOCATION: Three-quarters of a mile downstream from Blockhouse Island, these underwater walls are halfway between the wrecks of the *Muscallonge* and the *Robert Gaskin*.

The advantage of this site is that it provides varying levels of difficulty (or "challenges") for any scuba diver, and the diver can stay shallow or go deep within a very short distance from shore. Absolutely use a dive flag on a float above you as you drift downstream. Keep track of where you are heading, as the current varies in places and can provide casual slow drifting or a thrilling, fast ride downstream. Things to look for as you drift along are sturgeon (apparently increasing numbers have made this unusual type of fish a regular sight for divers), milk cans, and old vehicles on the river bottom. Reportedly illicit booze from the Prohibition days of the 1920's can also be encountered here. Good luck!

3. ROBERT GASKIN

LORAN:	GPS: 44° 35.359'/075° 40.625'
DEPTH: 55 to 70 feet	LEVEL: Intermediate-Advanced

LOCATION: This is a boat dive about 2,500' downstream from the pier at Brockville.

The *Robert Gaskin* (132'6" x 26'3" x 11'3"), launched as a triple-masted, iron-rigged, wooden barque on April 21, 1863, at Kingston, Ontario, but later altered to a work barge, had an impressive carrying capacity of 20,000 bushels. However, that did not save her from sinking not once, but a total of three times in late 1889 while salvaging the train ferry *William Armstrong*. First, on September 18, 1889, a salvage pontoon broke loose and put a

The Robert Gaskin

Artwork © Adam Henley

hole into the *Gaskin*. She ended up sinking on top of the vessel she was trying to salvage! On November 11, 1889, when the *Gaskin* was nearly raised, she dropped to the bottom again when a hose coupling broke. Twelve days later, the *Gaskin* was again raised and towed about 600′ before sinking for the third and final time after a rear pontoon tore her stern away. Ironically, the *William Armstrong* was successfully raised and returned to service.

Long a favorite divesite, the *Robert Gaskin* sits with her bow in 55′ of water, while what is left of her stern rests in 70′. Her bow faces downriver, parallel to the shore. Many interesting items appear on the deck, such as chains and a kingpost, while cargo holds can be cautiously penetrated for those trained and prepared for such diving. Do not destroy your visibility by disturbing the silt in the holds, one of which contains two steel barrels full of rivets and chain links. A large anchor sits about 40′ off the bow towards shore. Local divers usually keep this site buoyed.

4. MAHOGANY LAUNCH

LORAN:	GPS:
DEPTH: 70 feet	LEVEL: Advanced

LOCATION: Brockville, just off the "Sabre Jet" memorial on Blockhouse Island.

A motor vessel, 22′ in length, complete with engine and wheel still in place, reportedly sits in the midst of this busy (boatwise) waterfront. Do not do this as a shore dive; use boat access. This little wreck, supposedly sunk after a collision with a yacht, rests in about 70′ of water on a clay bottom. Make sure you utilize a divers down flag here.

5. TWO UNIDENTIFIED HULLS

LORAN:	GPS:
DEPTH: 32 feet and 82 feet	LEVEL: Intermediate/Advanced

LOCATION: In front of the bandshell, Hardy Park, Brockville, Ontario.

The ribs of two old, wooden vessels, a small one (approximately 40′ x 15′) in 32′ of water, the other larger one (estimated at 130′ x 25′) in 82′ of water, remain a mystery.

6. UNIDENTIFIED MOTOR VESSEL

LORAN:	GPS:
DEPTH: 60 feet	LEVEL: Intermediate-Advanced

LOCATION: Smith Island (drifting from the southeast corner), near Brockville.

Besides a wooden vessel about 35' long sitting upright at a depth of 55'-60', this fun drift dive in good visibility shows the visitor a couple of old garbage dump sites from back in the environmentally worry-free days when people got rid of their garbage the easy and most immediate way. Today, the occasional old bottle can still be found. It is possible to explore all around this small island on a single dive. Use a dive boat and a divers down flag in this high boating traffic area.

7. NARROWS CURRENT "RUSH"

LORAN:	GPS:
DEPTH: 100 feet	LEVEL: Advanced

LOCATION: Upstream of the Brockville waterfront.

This site is only for divers experienced in swiftwater diving! Similar to the speedy mouth of the St. Clair River at the Bluewater Bridge in Sarnia/Port Huron, this site whisks the diver along an "express current" producing quite a "rush." Slower speeds can be found along the wall or at the bottom at a depth of 100'. A boat is necessary to take you out there; good island access points are off the west end of McCoy or Conran/Refuge Islands. You'll need a boat to pick you up. Avoid drifting downstream from Royal Island, as the very strong current will push you out into the open shipping channel through a narrow cut at Heathers Point. Having been in a strong current which seems to press the diver down and away from shore, I can vouch that there are better ways of having fun. Some "rushes" you don't need.

8. MACDONALD'S POINT

LORAN:	GPS:
DEPTH: 30 to 100 feet	LEVEL: Intermediate-Advanced

LOCATION: Southwest of Brockville. Launch your boat at Brockville; MacDonald's Point is privately owned and there is no place to park unless you know a cottage owner.

An old dump site is located about 200' west of the end of MacDonald's Point, right against the shore, which drops off steeply. Ten feet out, the diver will be in 30' of water; 20' out and the water is 60' deep, while 30' from shore, the diver will be in 100' of water. Old bottles and even a model T automobile have been located here.

Be cautious with depth and the rather strong current. If done properly, the current will take the divers round the point into calm water, but if they attempt to surface earlier, they will likely encounter a strong downdraft current from the slight whirlpool effect at the end of the point, a frightening encounter if unprepared for it. Save plenty of air for surfacing.

9. *JOHN B. KING*

LORAN:	GPS: 44° 33.747'/075° 42.693'
DEPTH: 90 feet	LEVEL: Advanced

LOCATION: Upstream from Brockville, Ontario, about 80' downstream from the number "143 A" flashing green light buoy, just west of Cockburn Island.

One of the St. Lawrence River's worse loss-of-life marine accidents occurred off the northeast point of Cockburn Island on June 26, 1930. The 140' wooden drill scow, *John B. King*, with a large crew of 41 men on board, was busily placing underwater charges while at anchor in the main shipping channel. A summer thunderstorm suddenly developed, and

The tragic drill barge, *John B. King*. EVERRIT SNYDER COLLECTION

lighting struck just as the vessel was pulling away from the dynamite-laden site. All the submerged charges, as well as the dynamite still on board, detonated. The massive explosion rocketed wreckage a couple of hundred feet into the air, and a few seconds later, when the miniature atomic-like mushroom cloud began to dissipate, the ship was gone, along with 30 of the crew. The U.S. Coast Guard cutter, *Succor,* almost a mile upstream, responded to the frightening sound and was able to rescue eleven survivors at the tragic site.

The wreck site consists of heavily twisted metal lying scattered on the deep bottom. This is a very challenging (read "dangerous") dive. The St. Lawrence River currents are strong at this point, and the depth of 90′ makes it a deep, dark dive. The strong current could sweep you off this site into the deeper channel (155′ deep). Maintaining a boat anchorage near this site is also difficult.

10. *LILLIE PARSONS*

LORAN:	GPS: 44° 33.333′/075° 43.125′
DEPTH: 42 to 83 feet	LEVEL: Advanced

Art © Save Ontario Shipwrecks

LOCATION: Along Sparrow Island, southwest of Brockville, Ontario.

Launched on September 5, 1868, at Tonawanda, NY, the two-masted, fore-and-after, centerboard schooner, *Lillie Parsons* (131′ x 26′ x 12′), was loaded with 500 tons of coal when she encountered disaster. Sailing from Black Rock, NY, to Brockville, ON, on August 5, 1877, the *Lillie Parsons* plowed headlong into a violent squall which heeled her onto her beam ends and shifted her cargo. Just after the crew escaped to safety, the ship struck a rock, filled with water, and sank on a relatively shallow shoal. The swift current in

the treacherous Brockville Narrows gradually worked the *Lillie Parsons* into deeper water.

This shipwreck lies just off the northwest corner of Sparrow Island, which is about two miles southwest of Brockville, Ontario. The Brockville Parks Department operates this island's facilities: with prior permission and fee payment, one may camp upon the island, which offers docks, outhouses, picnic tables, and firewood.

The anchor and chain from the *Lillie Parsons* are

Hardware such as a double-sheave block remains attached to the *Lillie Parson's* main boom. PHOTO BY CRIS KOHL

on land display on Sparrow Island, with the anchor chain trailing down into the water and extending to the wreck itself, thus making it easy for divers to locate this site. The chain ends at the intact hull, which lies upside-down, enabling divers to explore the hull and keel areas. Other interesting parts of this wreck are the rudderhead, stern deadwood, bowsprit, and the keelson with stanchions still attached. The masts jut out from beneath the overturned hull, and a huge rudder can be viewed at the ship's square stern.

The ever-present and variable current runs between 2.3 and 3.6 knots, so this site is recommended only for very experienced swiftwater divers. Totally deflate your BCD and maintain as low a profile as possible while hugging the rocks. Penetration of the wreck is possible, although not recommended because of the potential difficulties or problems. Cave

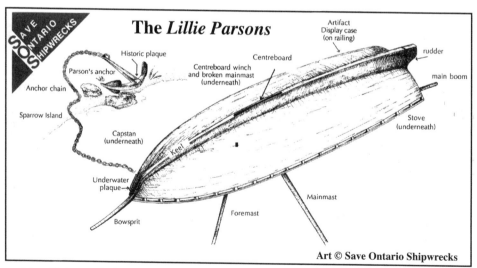

The *Lillie Parsons*

Art © Save Ontario Shipwrecks

and ice diving techniques prevail when shipwreck penetration is done. There is boating traffic above, so the use of a divers down flag is recommended. The wreck is gradually slipping off the ledge where she currently rests, so make certain that you are not inside or under her when she finally does slide off.

11. NEEDLE'S EYE "RUSH"

LORAN:	GPS:
DEPTH:From 30 to 100 feet	LEVEL: All levels

LOCATION: Between the mainland of Ontario and Needle's Eye Island, just across the channel from the *Lillie Parsons* wreck site.

Drop from the dive boat into the current at the west entrance and enjoy the ride (the south side of the island seems to provide the zestiest run). Going further west along the shoreline will take divers deeper (50' to 100'), yet keep them close to shore. Divers down flags are vital.

12. SAM COOKE

LORAN:	LAT 44° 33' 11" LON 075° 43' 34"
DEPTH: To 60 feet	LEVEL: Advanced

LOCATION: On the west side of Battersby Island, which lies between Black Charlie Island and Picnic Island.

Divers have long been aware of the remains of a wooden vessel, seemingly constructed in the mid-nineteenth century, and, it appears, at least partially salvaged, which have rested in the strong currents at the upstream side of Battersby Island for some time.

Still referred to occasionally as the "Battersby Island Wreck," these remains may be those of the three-masted schooner, *Sam Cooke*. Constructed at Oswego, New York, in 1873, the *Sam Cooke's* anchor failed to catch during a sudden strong breeze out of the north on July 6, 1882, and she was blown onto Battersby Island. The ship and her iron ore cargo sank, but no lives were lost. Subsequent salvage removed most of the cargo and virtually all of the ship's fittings and rigging.

The very strong currents at this site demand that only properly trained and fully prepared scuba divers attempt to explore this area.

13. THREE MOLLY'S GUT WRECKS

LORAN:	GPS:
DEPTH: To 20 feet	LEVEL: Novice-Intermediate

LOCATION: On the west side of Molly's Gut, southwest of Brockville, Ontario.

Three abandoned wooden hulls lie in shallow water in this quiet backwater area, accessible by boat. This is a good place to go snorkeling or shallow water scuba diving, or to capture impressive underwater images on film or videotape.

One of the hulks is possibly the small steamer, *Roosevelt,* built in 1906 and burned to a total loss on October 7, 1936, at Edgewood Park, Alexandria Bay, New York. The other two hulls remain unidentified.

St. Lawrence River: Area 4

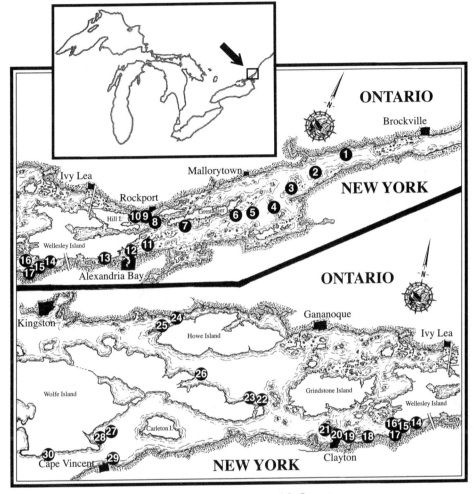

1. *Henry C. Daryaw*
2. *"Eel City"*
3. **Indian Chief Island and Shoal**
4. *America*
5. *Keystorm*
6. **S E Grenadier Island wrecks**
7. *Clara White*
8. *Kingshorn*
9. **Rockport wall**
10. *Sophia* (?)
11. *Catherine*
12. *Islander*
13. *Roy A. Jodrey*
14. *Sir Robert Peel*
15. *Iroquois*

16. *Oconto*
17. *A. E. Vickery*
18. *Raymond*
19. *Dauntless*
20. *Squaw*
21. *Maggie L.*
22. **Gas launch**
23. *Julia*
24. **Bateau Channel wreck**
25. **Howe Island wrecks**
26. **Holliday Point wreck**
27. *Lewiston*
28. *Harvey J. Kendall*
29. *St. Louis* (?)
30. *Arizona*

1. HENRY C. DARYAW

LORAN:	GPS: 44° 31.567'/075° 45.754'
DEPTH: 55 to 85 feet	LEVEL: Advanced

LOCATION: About six miles west of Brockville, Ontario, at Buoy Shoal (the wreck is marked on C.H.S. Chart #1418) about one-quarter mile off shore.

The *Henry C. Daryaw* -- afloat and a wreck. PUBLIC ARCHIVES OF CANADA

The *Henry C. Daryaw*

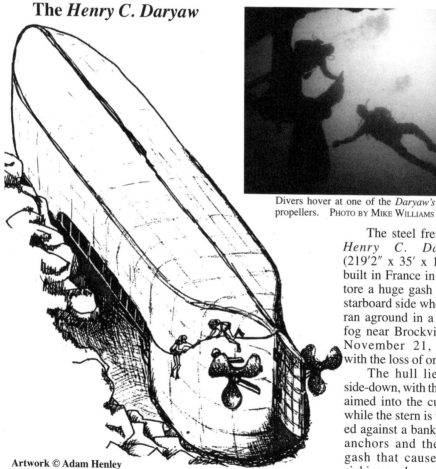

Divers hover at one of the *Daryaw's* propellers. PHOTO BY MIKE WILLIAMS

Artwork © Adam Henley

The steel freighter, *Henry C. Daryaw* (219'2" x 35' x 13'2"), built in France in 1919, tore a huge gash in her starboard side when she ran aground in a dense fog near Brockville on November 21, 1941 with the loss of one life.

The hull lies up-side-down, with the bow aimed into the current, while the stern is wedged against a bank. Bow anchors and the hull gash that caused her sinking can be seen. The

74

current is strong, so use a solid anchor line for the descent and ascent. The current poses another problem as there are no handholds on the smooth hull. It often gets dark beyond the hull, so bring a light. Avoid getting wedged between the ship's stern and the bank.

2. "EEL CITY"

LORAN:	GPS:
DEPTH: To 40 feet	LEVEL: Novice-Intermediate

LOCATION: Off the shores of Crossover Island.

A boat is required to reach Crossover Island, where, in recent years, scuba divers have noticed an unusually large number of American eels thriving in these waters. If it's Great Lakes sub-aquatic wildlife you wish to see and possibly photograph, this site is for you.

3. INDIAN CHIEF ISLAND AND SHOAL

LORAN:	GPS:
DEPTH: To 60 feet	LEVEL: Intermediate

LOCATION: This island and shoal lie across the main channel and Chippewa Point.

Scuba divers have reported locating pieces of a shipwreck off Indian Chief Shoal (possibly portions of the *Persia,* which hit a rock, lost her rudder, and was carried by the current to this shoal, where she broke up), but nothing large enough to be identifiable.

Relaxing scuba diving can be enjoyed off Indian Chief Island, and further downstream from Bilberry Island, Big Island, Robinson Island and Ingal Island, as well as at Blind Bay. Beware of small craft boating, as there are marinas in this region.

4. *AMERICA*

LORAN:	GPS: 44° 27.018'/075° 48.590'
DEPTH: 78 feet	LEVEL: Advanced

LOCATION: Between Brockville and Mallorytown, Ontario, a few hundred yards off the southwest side of Singer Castle Island. Sometimes a buoy line is established just east of black buoy #167 on the shipping lane's downstream side. The wreck lies just inside Canada near the international boundary in the busy shipping channel, and therefore makes access dangerous for divers and

The barge, *America.*
CRIS KOHL COLLECTION

Artwork © Adam
Henley

The *America*

boaters. Never leave a boat unattended! Check for oncoming ships!

The steel drill barge, *America* (sometimes also referred to as *American*), worked at dynamiting shoals when an explosion on board sank the vessel on June 20, 1932.

She lies upside-down, with the four bracing posts, or retractable legs, which kept her anchored at a site, now helplessly aimed upwards. Experienced divers can view the twin propellers at a depth of 55', as well as the twin rudders. Trained and experienced divers exploring underneath the wreck will see winches, a brick oven or kiln, and a jumble of wire rigging. Don't get lost inside! The deck cabin appears on the stern end, but inside it, too, is a tangled clutter of equipment (remember that this wreck is upside-down). A small, wooden barge which accompanied the *America* lies off her stern.

5. KEYSTORM

LORAN:	GPS: 44° 25.785'/075° 49.390'
DEPTH: 25 to 115 feet	LEVEL: Advanced

LOCATION: East of Mallorytown, Ontario, and south of the shipping channel, at Outer Scow Island Shoal.

The *Keystorm*. CRIS KOHL COLLECTION

Scuba divers explore the bridge of the *Keystorm*. PHOTO BY MIKE WILLIAMS.

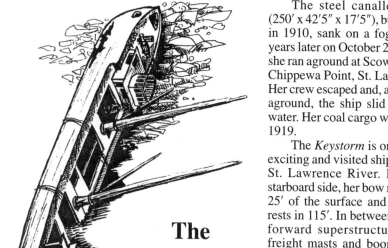

The Keystorm

Artwork © Adam Henley

The steel canaller, *Keystorm* (250' x 42'5" x 17'5"), built in England in 1910, sank on a foggy night two years later on October 26, 1912, when she ran aground at Scow Island Shoal, Chippewa Point, St. Lawrence River. Her crew escaped and, after five hours aground, the ship slid off into deep water. Her coal cargo was salvaged in 1919.

The *Keystorm* is one of the most exciting and visited shipwrecks in the St. Lawrence River. Lying on her starboard side, her bow reaches within 25' of the surface and her propeller rests in 115'. In between are an intact forward superstructure, a pair of freight masts and booms, and huge cargo holds. Four-inch cable double-wrapped at 20' intervals are remnants of failed salvage efforts (a blessing for today's scuba divers!). The gash in the ship's port bow area is quite evident. Swimming a bit off-site at midship will often reveal an impressive

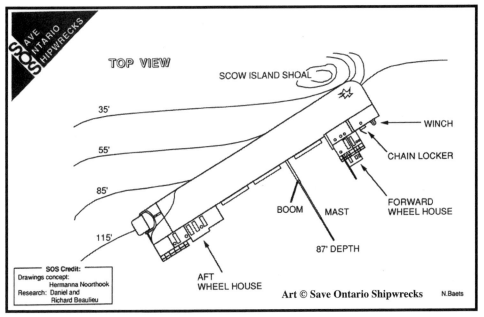

TOP VIEW

SCOW ISLAND SHOAL

35'

55'

85'

115'

WINCH

CHAIN LOCKER

FORWARD WHEEL HOUSE

BOOM MAST

87' DEPTH

AFT WHEEL HOUSE

SOS Credit:
Drawings concept:
          Hermanna Noorthook
Research: Daniel and
          Richard Beaulieu

Art © Save Ontario Shipwrecks   N.Baets

panoramic view of the entire shipwreck.

Usually local charter operators maintain a buoy at the bow and another at midship. Beware of boating traffic, which can be heavy, and use precaution in the usually moderate current at this site. Penetration requires special training and preparation.

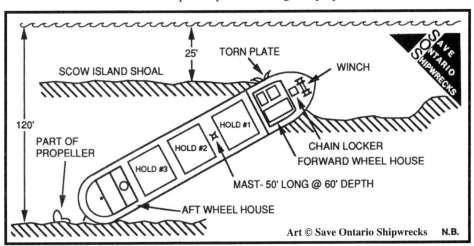

25' TORN PLATE

SCOW ISLAND SHOAL

WINCH

120'

PART OF PROPELLER

HOLD #1

HOLD #2

HOLD #3

CHAIN LOCKER
FORWARD WHEEL HOUSE

MAST- 50' LONG @ 60' DEPTH

AFT WHEEL HOUSE

Art © Save Ontario Shipwrecks   N.B.

6. SOUTHEAST GRENADIER ISLAND WRECKS

LORAN:	LAT 44° 24' 14" LON 075° 53' 13"
DEPTH: To 18 feet	LEVEL: Novice-Intermediate

LOCATION: Grenadier Island, near Mallorytown, Ontario. The locations of these shipwrecks are marked on Canadian Hydrographic Service chart #1418 off the southeast part of Grenadier Island.

This unidentified wooden wreck was likely abandoned for age at a spot along Grenadier Island where it would be out of the way and not interfere with navigation. The wreck lies broken and scattered on a sandy bottom in about 18' of protected water, offering a refuge for fish, usually found in large numbers at this site. Two other shallower and less interesting wrecks lie at **LAT 44° 24' 57"   LON 075° 53' 00".**

7. CLARA WHITE

LORAN:	GPS:
DEPTH: To 25 feet	LEVEL: Novice

LOCATION: Off the north side of Bloomfield Island, south end of Grenadier Island.

Built in 1871, the small, two-masted, 63-ton, carvel style schooner, *Clara White* (79' x 18'5" x 6'), caught fire (a cook stove accident) on November 11, 1889, while moored for the night. She burned to a total loss with her bow in close to shore and the stern in slightly deeper water. Early divers called her the "Clay Pipe Wreck" because of the many clay pipes found at the site.

8. KINGSHORN

LORAN:	GPS: 44° 22.606'/075° 55.838'
DEPTH: 92 feet	LEVEL: Advanced

LOCATION: Rockport, Ontario, directly in front of the Customs Office and the marina.

The *Kingshorn's* wheel. PHOTO BY MIKE WILLIAMS.

Located in 1995 by Ron McDonald with research assistance from Deb Ring, this schooner-barge, about 130' long, sits upright and incredibly intact in a busy small boat shipping channel. Plates found on the wreck were manufactured only during a six-year period in the 1890's; this fact helped establish the probable identity of the wreck as the *Kingshorn*, one of seven wheat-laden schooner-barges being towed by the powerful tug, *Hiram A. Walker,* on April 27, 1897, bound for Montreal. A storm sank three of the barges, with the *Kingshorn* leaking so badly that she eventually sank just before the tug captain could reach Rockport.

This fascinating shipwreck sports a rarity: a ship's wheel! Also at the stern, the broken-off rudder lies flat while a windlass adorns the bow area. Three bilge pumps, one mounted just forward of each of the three cargo holds, add to the unique nature of this shipwreck. Anchor chain lies on the forward deck, and authorities are still searching for the divers who removed the anchor in 1997.

9. ROCKPORT WALL

LORAN: Shore dive	GPS:
DEPTH: To 90 feet	LEVEL: Advanced

LOCATION: Off the town of Rockport, Ontario.

Ask permission at the restaurant along the river to dive off their huge dock. Just downstream (east) of the dock is a large rock. Divers have customarily suited up at the dock and swum over to the rock to make their descent along the Rockport wall there.

This wall dive is a popular checkout site for advanced courses because of its shore proximity and good visibility. Boating traffic can be heavy during summer, so use a divers down flag. Don't forget to account for the current and the depth. Go only as deep as your experience and training will allow.

10. SOPHIA (?)

LORAN: Shore dive	GPS:
DEPTH: 65 feet	LEVEL: Advanced

LOCATION: Off the government dock at Rockport, Ontario, across the bay on the west wall of the harbor.

This shipwreck, in poor condition, may be that of the *Sophia* (82' x 18' x 8'), a two-masted schooner built in Kingston, Ontario, in 1844. The site lies in a busy pleasure craft channel which must not be blocked. Use care and discretion about diving here.

11. CATHERINE

LORAN:	GPS:
DEPTH: 60 feet	LEVEL: Advanced

LOCATION: This schooner lies downstream from Alexandria Bay, New York, between Sunken Rock Island and Sunken Rock Shoal.

12. ISLANDER

LORAN:	GPS:
DEPTH: 15 to 60 feet	LEVEL: Novice-Intermediate

LOCATION: On the shoreline of Alexandria Bay, New York, north of the hospital.

Built in Rochester, New York, in 1871, and originally named the *James H. Kelly,* the 118-gross-ton sidewheel steamer, *Islander* (125' x 20' x 7'), operated as a mail boat between Clayton and Alexandria Bay, New York, as well as an island and river excursion ship, until she burned to a total loss at Alexandria Bay on September 16, 1909.

The popular Thousand Islands ship, *Islander.* CRIS KOHL COLLECTION

Divers park in the town lot in front of the pavilion in Alexandria Bay to the west of the hospital, where they suit up before walking across to the east end of the pavilion and down the hill to the dock, the entry point. The wreck site is between 100' and 150' downstream of this dock. The wreck's downstream starboard side is a bit lower than the port side, offering an unecessary shield from the slight current. The stern sits in 15' of water, while the intact bow is settled deeper in 60'. The considerable boating traffic warrants using a dive flag.

13. ROY A. JODREY

LORAN:	GPS: 44° 36.245'/075° 39.213'
DEPTH: 140 to 242 feet	LEVEL: Technical

The _Roy A. Jodrey._ REV. PETER VAN DER LINDEN COLLECTION

LOCATION: Off the Coast Guard Station on the south shoreline of Wellesley Island.

The freighter, _Roy A. Jodrey,_ is a very deep shipwreck site for technically-trained divers only. This site is deeper than the recommended sport diving limit.

The Algoma Central Railway motor vessel, _Roy A. Jodrey_ (640'6" x 72' x 40'), carried over 20,000 tons of iron ore pellets towards Detroit when she struck Pullman Shoal near Wellesley Island and sank at 3:00 A.M., November 21, 1974, with no loss of life. The nine-year-old freighter, named after one of Algoma's directors (who lived from 1888 until 1973), was almost 90' shorter than the famous _Edmund Fitzgerald,_ the Great Lakes system's largest shipwreck, which sank in Lake Superior with the loss of 29 lives a year after the _Jodrey_ went down. The _Fitzgerald_ also carried iron ore pellets when she sank. Perhaps these resemblances to the _Edmund Fitzgerald,_ which lies virtually unreachable in 529' of water, make the _Jodrey_ a symbolic, acceptable, and attainable substitute among technical divers.

The _Jodrey's_ bow lies in about 140' of water, her wheelhouse is in about 155', and her stern rests in 242'. The extreme depth, the fast current, and the high volume of boating traffic make this an extremely formidable site, well beyond the realm of sport diving.

14. SIR ROBERT PEEL

LORAN:	GPS: 44° 18.040'/075° 59.175'
DEPTH: 80 to 135 feet	LEVEL: Advanced

LOCATION: Just upstream from the 1000 Islands Bridge.

The small sidewheel passenger steamer, _Sir Robert Peel,_ built at Brockville, Upper Canada (today Ontario) in 1837, had a short life. On May 29, 1838, during the tumultuous Upper Canada Rebellion, a rebel named "Pirate" Bill Johnston and his followers, some dressed as Indians, decided to steal the _Sir Robert Peel._ After removing the crew and the 60 passengers when the ship stopped at the Wellesley Island refueling station, Johnston and his men, unable to start the ship which they had appropriated, set it on fire.

Today the burned out remains of this historic vessel rest with her stern in 135', the bow in 95', and the boiler in 80'. Beware of the current, depth and boating traffic at this site.

15 . IROQUOIS/ANSON

LORAN:	GPS: 44° 17.238'/076° 00.324'
DEPTH: 65 to 80 feet	LEVEL: Advanced

LOCATION: Near the foot of Niagara Shoal, 150' south of green buoy number 211.

Built in 1759 by the French and named _L'Iroquoise,_ but was captured by the British and renamed HMS _Anson,_ this ship sank after striking a shoal off tiny Susan Island in 1763. Only the fragile ribs remain of the oldest known wreck site in the Great Lakes. Please do not disturb the remains. Three cannons and two anchors were removed in the 1960's and 1970's. Beware: access is tricky, the river current is fast, and it drops to 180′ just beyond the wreck.

16. OCONTO

LORAN:	GPS: 44° 17.005′/076° 00.972′
DEPTH: 175 to 200 feet	LEVEL: Technical

LOCATION: Across the channel from the *A.E. Vickery* (see site #17), at light #214 south of Thousand Islands Park on Wellesley Island and west of the Thousand Islands Bridge.

In July, 1886, the steamer, *Oconto,* struck a boulder in mid-channel and sank with her bow out of the water. During salvage operations several weeks later, the ship suddenly slid

Oconto, at dock and after sinking, but before she slid deep. CRIS KOHL COLLECTION

down the embankment into deep water. Today, the wreck lies beyond sport diving range in a dangerously swift current in 175′ to 200′ of water. Technical divers usually reach this site by anchoring their boat in shallow water next to the concrete light abutment (#214) and descending along the drop-off to 175′.

17. A. E. VICKERY

LORAN:	GPS: 44° 16.820′/076° 01.183′
DEPTH: From 65 to 118 feet	LEVEL: Advanced

LOCATION: Off Rock Island Shoal, about four miles southwest of Alexandria Bay, New York, west-south-west of the Ivy Lea Bridge.

In 1994, I printed details of this story because, as I wrote then, "I don't think the interesting story of this shipwreck has yet been told...." The details bear repeating here:

The schooner, *A. E. Vickery* (136'2" x 26'2" x 10'8"), launched as the *J. B. Penfield* in July, 1861, and renamed in 1884, struck a shoal on August 16, 1889, and sank. Her entire crew escaped uninjured, but the old river pilot was almost murdered by the angry Captain Massey. The *Chicago Inter Ocean* of August 21, 1889, reported the dramatic incident:

MARINE INTELLIGENCE.

Captain Massey Becomes Excited and Attacks His Pilot with a Revolver.

———

A Duplicate of the Steel Steamer America to Be Con-structed.

———

Rates Unchanged, with an Ur-gent : Demand for Vessels.

———

CAPTAIN MASSEY WAS ANGRY.
KINGSTON, Ontario, Aug. 20.—*Special Tele-gram.*—The sinking of Chicago schooner Vickery near Alexandria Bay came near being the cause of a tragedy. Captain Massey, though

CRIS KOHL COLLECTION

...The captain got excited and attacked the pilot with a revolver, using violent language and pointing the weapon at him. The mate, a brother of the captain, instantly sprang for Massey's arm, discharging the revolver and sending the bullet into the deck. The revolver fell on the hatch and was picked up by the mate and thrown overboard. Captain Massey states that he would have certainly shot Webber, but now that he is cooled off is glad the thing happened the way it did. Pilot Webber made himself scarce....

Like the *Oconto*, the *A. E. Vickery* slipped off the shoal and into deep water before she could be salvaged.

This popular site, usually buoyed, has a strong surface current. Once the upright wreck is reached at 65', the angled bow, which sports a photogenic windlass, shields the diver from most of the current. In the hold, a huge centerboard box can be studied by careful divers experienced in wreck penetration. The rudder is in place at a depth of 118'.

Incidentally, has any scuba diver found a revolver near this site?

18. *RAYMOND*

LORAN:	GPS:
DEPTH: 25 feet	LEVEL: Novice-Intermediate

LOCATION: This wreck lies midway between the east end of Round Island and Irwin Point on the mainland.

The *Raymond* was a 40', two-masted sailing yacht which burned to the waterline.

19. *DAUNTLESS*

LORAN:	GPS:
DEPTH: 50 feet	LEVEL: Intermediate

LOCATION: Midway between Washington Island (near Clayton) and Round Island.

This double-ender wreck, with scroll work near the bow, much decking, and hatches still in place, shows evidence of a fire. With the engine missing, she may have been scuttled.

20. *SQUAW*

LORAN:	GPS:
DEPTH: 60 feet	LEVEL: Intermediate

LOCATION: About halfway between the public docks at Clayton, New York, and the wreck of the *Maggie L*. This motorized workboat, about 35' in length, sits on a hard sand bottom. The wheel, deck hardware (e.g. cleats), and the engine are still in place on this boat.

82

21. MAGGIE L.

LORAN:	GPS:
DEPTH: 75 feet	LEVEL: Advanced

LOCATION: In the shipping channel between the public docks at Clayton, New York, and Governors Island. A steel freighter plowed into the small schooner, *Maggie L.*, as the latter was heading for Clayton in June, 1927. The stern portion is located in 75' of water, while divers are still searching for the bow section.

22. GAS LAUNCH

LORAN:	GPS:
DEPTH: 30 feet	LEVEL: Novice-Intermediate

LOCATION: Just north of Quebec Head on the eastern tip of Wolfe Island.
Reputedly this 30' long motor launch utilized the first gas-powered engine on the St. Lawrence River. The small boat burned to a total loss in 1912.

23. JULIA

LORAN:	GPS:
DEPTH: 20 feet	LEVEL: Novice-Intermediate

LOCATION: On the east tip of Wolfe Island halfway between Brakey Bay and Quebec Head. The 108-ton schooner, *Julia,* burned to a complete loss on February 25, 1895.

24. BATEAU CHANNEL WRECK

LORAN:	LAT 44° 15' 53" LON 076° 20' 23"
DEPTH: To 18 feet	LEVEL: Novice-Intermediate

LOCATION: Just off the north side of Howe Island. About 60' long, this wreck may be the ferry vessel, *Amherst Islander I.* You will find mild current and abundant fish life here.

25. HOWE ISLAND WRECKS

LORAN:	GPS:
DEPTH: To 12 feet	LEVEL: Novice-Intermediate

LOCATION: In shallow water on the northwest end of Howe Island.
The westernmost wreck has considerable chain strewn about the limestone and sand bottom, but the two wrecks in the eastern corner of the bay are more lackluster.

26. HOLLIDAY POINT WRECK

LORAN:	GPS:
DEPTH: 17 to 46 feet	LEVEL: Novice-Intermediate

LOCATION: Just off Holliday Point on eastern Wolfe Island, Ontario.
This unidentified wooden sailing vessel, because of her position in the shallows, is broken up except for the relatively intact bow section.

27. LEWISTON

LORAN:	GPS:
DEPTH: To 20 feet	LEVEL: Novice-Intermediate

LOCATION: In the Hinckley Flats off the south side of Wolfe Island.

The *Lewiston,* a wooden propeller barge built in 1864, lies abandoned in shallow water at the entrance to Button Bay. This broken-up wreck is marked on the chart.

28. HARVEY J. KENDALL

LORAN:	GPS:
DEPTH: 7 to 18 feet	LEVEL: Novice-Intermediate

LOCATION: In Button Bay, on the southwest side of Wolfe Island.

The wooden steam barge and bulk freighter, *Harvey J. Kendall* (141'7" x 31' x 9'2"), was launched at Marine City, Michigan, on April 10, 1892. The vessel was converted to a self-unloading bulk freighter at Ogdensburg in 1917. The *Kendall* was abandoned for age in 1932.

The *Harvey J. Kendall.* CRIS KOHL COLLECTION

29. ST. LOUIS (?)

LORAN:	GPS:
DEPTH: 40 feet	LEVEL: Novice-Intermediate

LOCATION: Close to shore at the east end of Cape Vincent, New York.

The large barge, the *St. Louis,* built in 1864, sank on February 18, 1914. Reports, however, suggest that the *St. Louis* was raised from its location near Cape Vincent in 1923, and scuttled off Amherst Island. Today, this wreck site, whatever vessel it was, is popular as a dive training site.

30. ARIZONA

LORAN:	GPS: 44° 06.55'/076° 24.38'
DEPTH: 25 feet	LEVEL: Novice-Intermediate

LOCATION: Southwest of the ferry landing on the south shore of Wolfe Island near the red buoy. The oak-built wooden steamer, *Arizona* (201' x 32'6" x 14'3"), launched at Cleveland in 1868, caught fire at Cape Vincent, New York, on December 1, 1922. Since no adequate firefighting equipment was available, the blazing ship was towed 1.5 miles upstream,

The *Arizona* loaded with lumber. CRIS KOHL COLLECTION

where she was scuttled. She carried no cargo at the time of her loss.

Divers can explore the hull (which rises 12' off the bottom) and framing, the shaft, a portion of the propeller and the fallen rudder at the stern, plus a huge winch and considerable chain at the bow.

5. Kingston

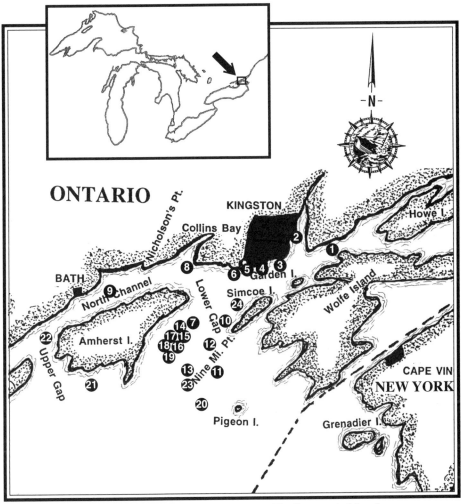

ONTARIO

KINGSTON

Howe I.

Nicholson's Pt.

Collins Bay

BATH

North Channel

Lower Gap

Amherst I.

Upper Gap

Simcoe I.

Nine Mi. Pt.

Garden I.

Wolfe Island

CAPE VIN
NEW YORK

Pigeon I.

Grenadier I.

1. *Wolfe Islander II*
2. *Prince Regent* and *Psyche*
3. Marine Museum dock
4. *St. Lawrence*
5. Anchors and stacked hulls
6. "The K.P.H. wreck"
7. *"Titanic"*
8. *Munson*
9. *William Jamieson*
10. *Aloha* and *Effie Mae*
11. *George T. Davie*
12. *Comet*

13. *George A. Marsh*
14. *Cornwall*
15. *Mapleglen*
16. *"Glendora"*
17. *Simla*
18. *Varuna*
19. *"Ricky's Tug"*
20. *Frontenac*
21. *City of Sheboygan*
22. Scuttled deep hulls
23. *S. M. Douglas*
24. *William Johnston*

Kingston and Lake Ontario

Kingston, Ontario, nestled nicely in the northeast corner of Lake Ontario at the point where the lake tries to empty itself into the St. Lawrence River, is rich in history, particularly maritime history. The Kingston site is the location that was chosen by the explorer La Salle for an important meeting between the Governor of New France, Frontenac, and the Iroquois chiefs in 1673, as well as for the construction of a fort in 1675 named Fort Frontenac. In the 1700's, the site served as a defended port of trans-shipment, handling supplies heading to the western forts and furs brought up in canoes and lake schooners from the frontier regions. In 1783, the site was settled by United Empire Loyalists from New York State, who renamed it Kingston in honor of King George III. By 1793, Kingston was chosen as the chief naval base for Lake Ontario, the establishment of which was crucial later during the War of 1812 with the United States. The Kingston stockyard became furiously engaged in a shipbuilding race with the American Lake Ontario base at Sackets Harbor. Ships the size of those which were sailing across the oceans of the world at that time were constructed at Kingston.The fort which had been built at Point Henry during the War of 1812 to protect the dockyard was rebuilt on a larger scale in 1823-36 (this is the present Fort Henry which serves as a public attraction). Shipping traffic from the west increased steadily, and the harbor at Kingston enjoyed boom times until the rise of the railways. The last regularly-scheduled passenger steamer called at Kingston in 1951.

What all of this means to the average scuba diver is that this area has a high concentration of shipwrecks! Kingston is considered by many to be one of the top three scuba diving destinations in the huge province of Ontario. The shipwrecks at Kingston range from sailing vessels to sidewheelers, from War of 1812 naval ships to 20th century ferryboats.

Non-shipwreck shore dives can also be done; in the mid-1980's, we explored the area along the Marine Museum's waterfront, and found charred remains of a ship, chain twisted by the flames' heat, old embossed bottles located beyond elbow depth in the muck, and a lawn chair in superb condition!

The area around old Fort Henry still, on occasion, yields items of historical interest, and in late November, 1985, two divers doing routine maintenance on the 139-year-old Martello tower in Kingston's Confederation Basin found fifteen 32-pound cannonballs, which Parks Canada refurbished for display at historic sites across Canada.

I have seen the number of scuba charter boats at Kingston triple in number since the early 1980's; that should give any aquatic visitor a good idea of the dramatically increasing popularity of Kingston as a Great Lakes scuba diving destination! Enjoy!

1. *WOLFE ISLANDER II* -- SEE PAGES **88-89.**

2. *PRINCE REGENT* AND *PSYCHE*

LORAN: Shore dive	LAT 44° 13′ 00″ LON 076° 27′ 13″
DEPTH: 12 to 20 feet	LEVEL: Novice-Intermediate

LOCATION: In Deadman Bay, east of Fort Henry, Kingston.

The 1,294-ton *Prince Regent,* built completely at Kingston in 1813-14, carried 58 cannons and was heavily involved in the War of 1812 in its final year. After the war and several years of inactivity, the huge ship sank in the bay. The *Psyche*, transported in pieces from England and assembled at Kingston, was completed right when the war ended, and was eventually abandoned in the bay.

The *Prince Regent* is located in about 20′ to 25′ of water about 300′ from the shore opposite Cartright Point. The *Psyche* is located in shallower water (about 12′) at the end, or the head, of the bay. The wrecks can be done as a shore dive from Arrowhead Point. The

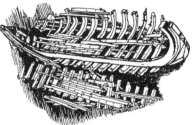

keels and ribs are virtually all that remain of these two old, historic shipwrecks lying in a shallow, sand-and-silt-bottom bay.

Left: The War of 1812 ship, *Prince Regent.* PUBLIC ARCHIVES OF CANADA

The *Prince Regent*

Artwork © Adam Henley

3. MARINE MUSEUM DOCK

LORAN: Shore dive   GPS:
DEPTH: To 50 feet far off shore   LEVEL: Novice-Intermediate

LOCATION: Behind the Marine Museum of the Great Lakes, Kingston, Ontario.

This local favorite offers sights common to the waters off old shipbuilding yards: ship timbers, old bottles, and fish. Scuba instructors take their students here for checkouts, and sometimes night dives, with perch, pike, burbot, and salamanders, attract other divers.

4. ST. LAWRENCE

LORAN: Shore dive   GPS:
DEPTH: 5 to 20 feet   LEVEL: Novice-Intermediate

LOCATION: The *St. Lawrence* is marked on Canadian Hydrographic Service chart #1459 as lying just east of the Kingston Penitentiary, in a little bay at the foot of Morton Street. A city-owned park is adjacent to this site, and divers can suit up and wade in there.

The *St. Lawrence* is considered the mightiest sailing war vessel ever seen on the Great Lakes. Constructed at Kingston for use in the War of 1812, the ship ironically took most of the war to construct. When she finally did sail across Lake Ontario to do battle, no enemy ship was sighted! Canadian historian Pierre Berton described the *St. Lawrence* as a ship "too precious to be risked in battle and too grand to be used as transport." Although the vessel never faced a human enemy, she came close to being destroyed during her first voyage on Lake Ontario. Lightning violently struck one

The mighty *St. Lawrence.*
METROPOLITAN TORONTO LIBRARY

of her tall masts, killing seven men and wounding 22 others, narrowly missing the cache of gunpowder on board. The war ended two months after her maiden voyage, and this 2,304-ton vessel was stripped of her cannons and masts and towed to Morton's distillery, where, as a storage vessel, she decayed over the years. The few remaining planks of the *St. Lawrence* are scattered along the bottom of this shallow bay quite close to shore. Silt is easily stirred and visibility is usually poor.

Lightning did the only killing on the *St. Lawrence.* ARTWORK © PETER RINDLISBACHER, USED WITH PERMISSION. FOR INFORMATION ABOUT MR. RINDLISBACHER'S ART, CONTACT THE CANADIAN SOCIETY OF MARINE ARTISTS, OR GO TO WWW.ULTRAMARINE.CA

Great Lakes Highlight No. 4

THE *WOLFE ISLANDER II*:
OUR FIRST CREATED DIVE SITE

LORAN: 15639.2/60051.06   LAT 44° 13′ 55″ LON 076° 24′ 98″
DEPTH: 40 to 85 feet   LEVEL: Intermediate-Advanced

LOCATION: Three miles east of Kingston, Ontario.

Built at Collingwood, Ontario, 1946, the *Wolfe Islander II* (144′3″ x 43′1″ x 8′) plied the waters between Wolfe Island and Kingston for almost 30 years, carrying tourists, cars, trucks, and future divebook writers. After sitting idle for ten years, she became the very first commercial vessel to be scuttled in the Great Lakes (on September 21, 1985) for the express purpose of creating a scuba dive site. The ship was sunk in a protected "all weather" area three miles east of Kingston. Since 1985, the *Wolfe Islander II* has become the most visited shipwreck in Lake Ontario!

The ship sits upright in 85′ of water, with the superstructure starting just 40′ below the surface. Visiting divers can explore her open deck area, complete with davits, bitts, dorades, smokestack, railings galore, a motorcycle and other items too numerous to mention. Divers trained in shipwreck penetration can also explore her interior, including the engine room. But don't get lost below deck! All doors and hatches have been removed for diver safety, but she's a big ship. Keep track of your depth and bottom time, since a diver can get carried away while exploring the many wonderful nooks and crannies at this site. It takes at least two scuba dives at this site to become comfortably familiar with the vessel.

Below: Piping inside the engine room appears almost decorative! PHOTO BY CRIS KOHL

Above: A plaque mounted on the bridge names those who arranged the scuttling. PHOTO BY CRIS KOHL

Above: Scuba instructor Marcie McElmon explores the ship's interior rooms. PHOTO BY CRIS KOHL

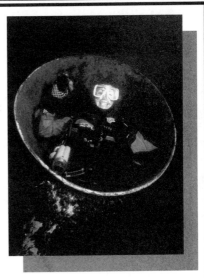

Left: Marcie McElmon poses at the propeller, and later *(right)*, in a dorade (air vent). PHOTOS BY CRIS KOHL

The *Wolfe Islander II*

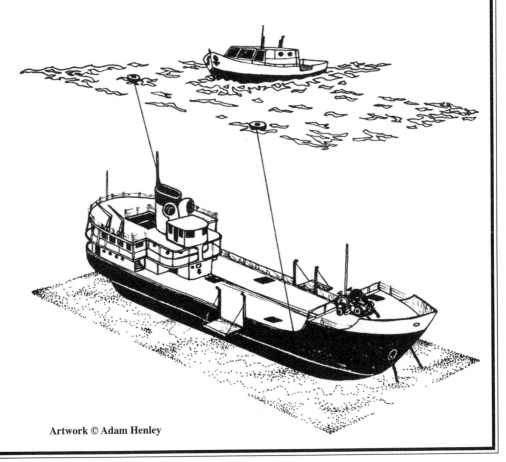

Artwork © Adam Henley

5. ANCHORS AND STACKED HULLS

LORAN: Shore dive	GPS:
DEPTH: To 50 feet	LEVEL: Novice-Intermediate

LOCATION: Portsmouth Olympic Harbour, near the Coast Guard Station at the corner of the government dock.

There is a line (rope) starting from shore to the site of the anchors. From there, a second line runs out about 600' to the remains of a couple of stacked ship's hulls. Although it is a long swim, the scenery is well worth it. Use a divers down flag to let boaters know that you are there, and keep an eye on your air supply. Respect the rights of local private residence owners.

6. "THE K. P. H. WRECK"

LORAN:	GPS: 44° 12.42'/076° 31.46'
DEPTH: 65 feet	LEVEL: Intermediate-Advanced

LOCATION: This unknown wreck is situated off Olympic Harbour in front of the Kingston Psychiatric Hospital (the K. P. H., from which the site takes its name).

This unidentified flat barge, 135' long, is steel-framed, wood-sheathed, wood-decked, and has 6'-8' of height when exploring below deck (use caution!). There are two boilers inside this wreck, as well as other numerous internal details like coal chutes, piping and machinery. The stern is completely broken open, with loose boards littering the area. Steel beams supporting the decking make penetration safer than one might expect it to be. The rudder appears to be missing, but a four-bladed propeller is still intact. Right at the stern, the steering post, resembling a funnel or smokestack, stands upright off the bottom. The heavy amount of silt at this site makes it too easy to destroy your visibility, especially inside the wreck. Use cave diving swimming techniques and plenty of caution! This site is usually buoyed.

Inside the K. P. H. wreck.
PHOTO BY CRIS KOHL

The *Water Lily* at Collins Bay, ON, in 1910. Is this the K. P. H. wreck? CRIS KOHL COLLECTION

An old captain claimed that this wreck is that of the 138-ton steamer, *Water Lily* (106'9" x 18'4" x 5'7"), which was built at Brewer's Mills (Picton), Ontario in 1879, and disposed of due to age shortly after 1920. That is certainly possible, but definite proof is still forthcoming.

The K. P. H. wreck

Artwork ©
Adam Henley

7. *"TITANIC"*

LORAN: 15740.4/60027.1	GPS: 44° 08.33'/076° 37.20'
DEPTH: 75 feet	LEVEL: Intermediate-Advanced

LOCATION: To the west of Kingston, Ontario.

This unidentified vessel, so huge it was nicknamed *"Titanic,"* is an intact barge with two large boilers and enormous anchor chain. This wreck may be penetrated by more experienced and trained divers. This site is usually buoyed by local divers in the spring.

8. *MUNSON*

LORAN: 15701.4/60016.0	GPS:
DEPTH: 93 to 111 feet	LEVEL: Advanced

LOCATION: About six miles west of Kingston, just off Lemoine Point, near Kingston Airport.

On the last day of April, 1890, the dredge, *Munson,* having completed the most significant dredging job of its career (that of ensuring that the largest sailing ship ever built on the Canadian side of the Great Lakes, the *Minnedosa,* would have adequate depth for its upcoming

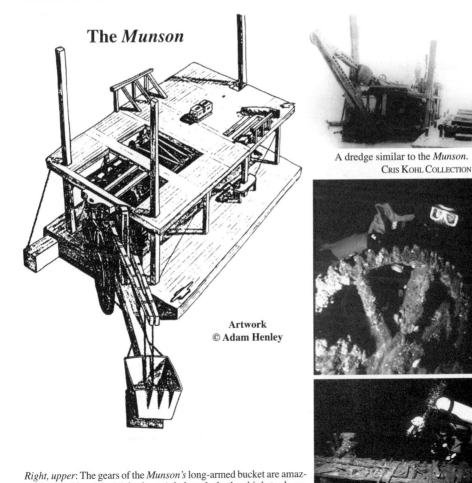

The *Munson*

A dredge similar to the *Munson.*
CRIS KOHL COLLECTION

Artwork
© Adam Henley

Right, upper: The gears of the *Munson's* long-armed bucket are amazing to behold, while *(right, lower)*, below deck, the ship's tools are carefully laid out on a workbench.   PHOTOS BY CRIS KOHL

launch at Kingston), was being towed back to Rossmore, Ontario, when it leaned to one side and, within a few minutes, vanished beneath the waves. The three *Munson* crew were saved. A hardhat diver later inspected the dredge and proclaimed the vessel to be unrecoverable.

The dredge, *Munson,* sits upright in 111' of water, and experienced scuba divers can penetrate her basic, skeletal layout, and appreciate the distinctive crane and bucket features. On the upper deck, divers have placed an interesting collection of plates, bottles and other artifacts in one area for easy viewing. Below deck, on a workbench, are laid out many of the original 1890 ship's tools. Please do not remove any of these items. Besides their removal being illegal, they mean much more at the shipwreck site than they do as souvenirs to you. Sometimes the site is dark, even at midday; take a light with you!

9. *WILLIAM JAMIESON*

LORAN: 15781.55/59986.62	GPS:
DEPTH: 80 feet	LEVEL: Advanced

LOCATION: Off the north shore of Amherst Island, west of Emerald, Ontario.

The two-masted schooner, *William Jamieson* (100' x 25'4" x 8'6"), built by Mr. William Jamieson at Mill Point (Deseronto), Ontario, and named after himself, was launched on July 3, 1878. On May 15, 1923, the 45-year-old ship showed her age when she opened her seams during a severe storm. The crew abandoned the doomed vessel just before she hit the bottom with her hard anthracite coal cargo. Much silt rests on this site, but, with a bit of buoyancy skill and con-

sideration, the visibility can remain quite good. The wreck is intact with some of her rigging and bow pumps still in their original positions. This wreck was found by a team of divers led by Lloyd Shales and Barbara Carson on July 31, 1963.

Above: The aging schooner, *William Jamieson.* INSTITUTE FOR GREAT LAKES RESEARCH, BOWLING GREEN STATE UNIVERSITY, BOWLING GREEN, OHIO.
Right: A diver closely examines a fallen *Jamieson* deadeye. PHOTO BY CRIS KOHL

10. *ALOHA* AND *EFFIE MAE*

LORAN: 15715.2/60034.3	LAT 44° 09' 00" LON 076° 34' 07"
DEPTH: 55 feet	LEVEL: Novice-Intermediate

LOCATION: Off Nine Mile Point, Simcoe Island, west of Kingston, Ontario.

The schooner-barge, *Aloha* (128'5" x 24'5" x 12'5"), built in Mt. Clemens, Michigan, in 1888, began to leak in a gale on October 29, 1917, and foundered with her aging captain and her load of coal several hours later. The rest of the crew survived the sinking.

Most of the hull is intact, although she was divested of the majority of her small artifacts years ago. Anchor chain sits on the bow attached to a windlass, and divers can see the original coal cargo by carefully descending into the holds. At the stern, a capstan, steering quadrant, and rudder post lie in the sand. Roman numeral depth markings can be seen on the bow. The *Aloha* was found by Lloyd Shales and Barbara Carson in August, 1964.

In the early 1990's, when owners of the popular, old scuba charter boat, *Effie Mae* (39'10" x 13' x 3'3"), could find no buyer for her, they donated their vessel to a local marine conservation group, consisting mostly of divers, who cleaned her up and decided that the old *Aloha* needed some company. They scuttled the *Effie Mae* right next to the old schooner-

Clockwise from upper left: The schooner-barge, *Aloha* (1888-1917). CRIS KOHL COLLECTION. Diver Marcie McElmon examines Roman numeral draught markings at the bow. A diver explores *Effie Mae's* cabin. *Effie Mae* afloat in the mid-1980's. PHOTOS BY CRIS KOHL

barge on October 17, 1993, and they lie within easy underwater swimming distance of each other. Yes, it does feel strange to be exploring, underwater, the dive boat that used to take me (and thousands of other scuba divers over the years) to so many wonderful shipwrecks. The former dive boat, ever faithful, continues to practice her calling (in a slightly different way) of providing a service to visiting scuba divers.

11. *GEORGE T. DAVIE*

LORAN:	GPS: 44° 06.815'/076° 34.804'
DEPTH: 105 feet	LEVEL: Advanced

LOCATION: Approximately three miles southwest of Nine Mile Point, Simcoe Island, less than two miles south of the *Comet* (see site #12) and almost one-and-a-half miles southeast of the *George A. Marsh* (see site #13).

The composite bulk freight barge, *George T. Davie* (186' x 35' x 12'5"), built in Levis, Quebec in 1898 by the George T. Davie & Sons Company, worked on fresh water for 47 years before foundering in heavy seas on April 18, 1945. All four men who had been on board were rescued, but the ship and more than 1,000 tons of hard coal cargo were lost.

The *George T. Davie* rests on her starboard side with most of her coal cargo spilled out of her five hatches. The ship's wheel, a type utilizing steam-powered assistance, remains at the stern, while the crane (which had been salvaged from the wreck of the *Henry C. Daryaw* in the St. Lawrence River in 1941 -- see page 74) lies parallel to the starboard side, with a photogenic lifeboat lying between the hull and the crane's arm. A windlass adorns the bow, while an anchor hangs off the bow's port side.

The *George T. Davie*.
PUBLIC ARCHIVES OF CANADA

12. COMET

LORAN: 15732.7/60036.2	GPS: 44° 08.350'/076° 35.070'
DEPTH: 90 feet	LEVEL: Advanced

LOCATION: The wreck lies two miles off Nine Mile Point on Simcoe Island.
The elegant sidewheel steamer, *Comet* (174'8" x 23'5"--or 45' with sidewheels--x 10'),

Art courtesy of the Metropolitan Toronto Library.

was built at Kingston in 1848, but sank 13 unlucky years later after a collision with the American schooner, *Exchange,* on May 15, 1861, with the loss of three lives. Kingston scuba divers located this shipwreck in October, 1967.

As with about 20 other shipwrecks in the Kingston area, the *Comet* is buoyed annually by a marine conservation group named Preserve Our Wrecks (P.O.W.). The vessel's bow and stern have collapsed, but her distinctive sidewheels are still intact and tower about 25' off the lake bed. The rocker arms and walking beam are also clearly visible. Remnants of her railing, doors and smokestacks can be seen along the east side, and portions of her farm implements cargo are scattered around the site. Experienced divers may penetrate below deck and study the ship's boiler. Beware of depth/time limitations and of disturbing the silt.

Above: Exploring between paddlewheel spokes. *Right:* The *Comet* sports tall, breathtaking structures, such as the engine and paddlewheels. *Below:* A pair of 1840's procelain doorknobs lie among the wreckage.   PHOTOS BY CRIS KOHL

13. GEORGE A. MARSH -- SEE PAGES 96-97.

14. CORNWALL

LORAN: 15742.2/60028.5	**GPS:** 44° 08.02'/076° 37.05'
DEPTH: 73 feet	**LEVEL:** Advanced

LOCATION: About seven miles west of Kingston, Ontario.

This iron-hulled sidewheeler, launched in 1855 at Montreal, worked for more than 70 years on the Great Lakes under a variety of names: *Kingston* (1855-1873), *Bavarian* (1873-1895), *Algerian* (1895-1906), and finally, *Cornwall* (1906-1928). The *Cornwall* (176'6" x 27'1" x 9'9") was a wrecking tug, outfitted with an A-frame derrick, clamshell outfit, steam pumps, air compressor and other equipment used in the

The wrecking tug, *Cornwall.* CRIS KOHL COLLECTION

salvage business. In 1928, the vessel had outlived its usefulness, and was towed to the ship graveyard off Amherst Island and dynamited.

The wreck sits upright in 73' of water. Her engine was removed before scuttling, but the two large boilers are in place, as are the ten-bladed, 20-foot-diameter paddlewheels. Scattered around the site are woodwork, a windlass, a ladder, barrels, pipes and tools.

The author thanks Josephine Donnelly Cole of Kingston for information which she mailed to him about the *Cornwall* (her family had owned it) and its discovery in 1989.

See *Cornwall* art and photo on page 98...

Great Lakes Highlight No. 5

TRAGIC MYSTERIES

OF THE *GEORGE A. MARSH*

> **LORAN: 15744.2/60034.8**   **GPS: 44° 07.690'/076° 36.260'**
> **DEPTH: 70 to 85 feet**   **LEVEL: Advanced**

LOCATION: About three miles off Nine Mile Point, Simcoe island.

The three-masted schooner, *George A. Marsh* (135'x 27' x 9'3"), named after a Great Lakes lumber magnate from Chicago when the ship was launched in 1882 at Muskegon, Michigan, foundered in a furious summer storm with a cargo of coal from Oswego, New York, on August 8, 1917. Reportedly 12 of the 14 people on board drowned, including Captain John Smith, his new wife, their new baby, five of his children from a previous marriage, plus family friends.

The *George A. Marsh* was located by Barbara Carson and her team of divers on October 7, 1967. The wreck sits deep in silt that is easily disturbed. Be aware that there are probably divers coming down the line not too far behind you, and they, too, will want to be impressed by this beautiful shipwreck site. Don't muck it up for them. Learn and use buoyancy control!

This shipwreck is almost 100% intact! Besides the many deadeyes, blocks and belaying pins, there is the ship's wheel and a stove, complete with cooking utensils in place, on the deck. Also look at and appreciate the ship's rigging, lifeboat, bowsprit and pottery artifacts. It is easy to see why Kingston divers are proud and protective of this, and the other, shipwrecks. Charter boat operators, whose livelihoods depend upon the continued integrity of these incredibly preserved shipwreck sites, will hand over to the police any diver who removes anything from any of the area's shipwrecks.

My dive buddy, local historian Doug Pettingill, first brought one of the mysteries of the *Marsh* to my attention in the early 1990's: Did the captain actually survive the sinking?

Left, top to bottom: The schooner, *George A. Marsh*. The tragic loss of life made front page news in every Kingston area newspaper. One even published photos of the mast portions seen above water.   CRIS KOHL COLLECTION

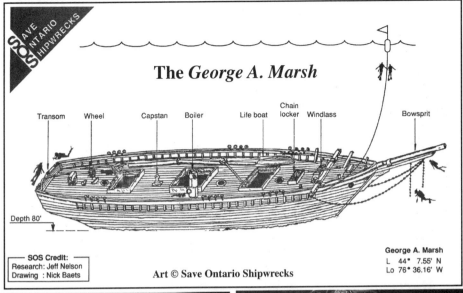

The *George A. Marsh*

Transom Wheel Capstan Boiler Life boat Chain locker Windlass Bowsprit

Depth 80'

SOS Credit:
Research: Jeff Nelson
Drawing : Nick Baets

Art © Save Ontario Shipwrecks

George A. Marsh
L 44° 7.55' N
Lo 76° 36.16' W

A diver is silhouetted with the *Marsh's* magnificent bowsprit, while another diver takes a close look at a pair of deadeyes along the port rail.   PHOTOS BY CRIS KOHL

My wife, Joan, and I drove to Harrah, Oklahoma, to investigate the rumor that the captain, John Smith, had secretly survived the sinking of the *George A. Marsh* and, in his grief and shame, fled as far away from water as possible to begin life anew. Exactly how he accomplished this -- and why he went to Harrah -- are part of the *Marsh's* mysteries. We found much information; see the book, *Shipwreck Tales of the Great Lakes*, for details. Smith died ten years later, finally revealing his story on his death bed.

Left: These railroad tracks brought Capt. John Smith (*below,* CRIS KOHL COLLECTION) into Harrah, Oklahoma, shortly after the sinking of the *George A. Marsh*. *Below, right:* Smith was buried in Harrah in 1927.   PHOTOS BY CRIS KOHL

The *Cornwall*

Artwork © Adam Henley

Diver Doug Pettingill examines the secondary boiler mounted atop one of the larger ones on the scuttled tug, *Cornwall*.   PHOTO BY CRIS KOHL

15. *MAPLEGLEN*

LORAN:	GPS:
DEPTH: 78 feet	LEVEL: Advanced

LOCATION: In the Amherst Island ships' graveyard, about seven miles west of Kingston.

The wooden package freighter, *Mapleglen* (241' x 39'9" x 14'6"), built in Buffalo, New York, in 1887 and launched as the *Wyoming,* had outlived her usefulness by 1920 and was sold inexpensively to Canadian interests, who renamed her *Mapleglen.* On June 19, 1925, the old and, by now, unreliable, ship was towed out into Lake Ontario and scuttled.

This vessel sits upright on a muddy bottom. The decking and hull have collapsed and are in great disarray, with frames, planking, hanging knees and other wood aiming in all directions. It is possible to explore under portions of the decking. The boilers and the four-bladed propeller are definitely the highlights. Bass, perch, burbot (ling cod) and American eels can be seen, particularly around the boilers. The intact bow area is worth viewing, but plan your bottom time well. This is a big wreck!

The *Mapleglen*, still named the *Wyoming*.
CRIS KOHL COLLLECTION

The *Mapleglen*

A diver explores the upper portion of one of the *Mapleglen's* boilers. PHOTO BY CRIS KOHL

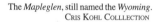

Artwork © Adam Henley

16. *"Glendora"* (Unidentified, Scuttled Ship)

LORAN:	LAT 44° 08' 50" LON 076° 37' 00"
DEPTH: 75 feet	LEVEL: Advanced

LOCATION: In the ships' graveyard about seven miles west of Kingston.

This shipwreck was given the nickname *"Glendora"* (supposedly the name of a "treasure ship" which allegedly sank in this area) to get divers excited. Hopefully the excitement among divers is still there for this wreck, despite no treasure! And no identification! This hull is one of several abandoned vessels scuttled off Amherst Island in 1925 by the Donnelly Wrecking Company. The ship was stripped of any useful machinery before she went to the ships' graveyard. All of her fittings and machinery, except for the 12' high rudder and four-bladed propeller, were removed. The bow was extensively damaged in the scuttling. A couple of large holds allow easy access for divers to the below deck area. A dive light is necessary for exploring the holds. Try not to stir up the silt. Have fun!

The unidentified *"Glendora"*

Artwork © Adam Henley

17. SIMLA

> LORAN: 15745.9/60046.1   GPS:
> DEPTH: 90 feet   LEVEL: Advanced

The *Simla* was one of the last wooden steamers built on the Great Lakes. CRIS KOHL COLLECTION

LOCATION: In the ships' graveyard about seven miles east of Kingston, Ontario.

The oak-hulled, propeller-driven bulk freighter, *Simla* (225'6" x 34'8" x 15'), launched at Garden Island just off Kingston, Ontario, on May 9, 1903, was one of the last steamers built of wood on the Great Lakes. The ship sat idle at Kingston for years before finally burning and sinking in 1926. These sunken remains were raised and towed out into Lake Ontario to be scuttled on September 6, 1927. The large propeller is the most impressive part of this site. Take an underwater light along, as this location is frequently dark.

18. VARUNA

> LORAN: GPS:
> DEPTH: 67 feet   LEVEL: Advanced

LOCATION: In the ships' graveyard about seven miles west of Kingston, Ontario.

This small, 72-ton, steam-powered passenger and freight ferry was built in Picton, Ontario, in 1880 and, after more than 40 years of service, the old ship was scuttled off Amherst Island in the 1920's. Several hatches on this wreck offer divers huge points of entry for shipwreck penetration, but

The *Varuna*. CRIS KOHL COLLECTION

with the amount of silt in the hold, this may not be advisable.

The Varuna

Artwork © Adam Henley

19. "RICKY'S TUG"

> LORAN: GPS:
> DEPTH: 70 feet   LEVEL: Advanced

Artwork © Adam Henley

LOCATION: The wreck lies about 7 miles west of Kingston.

The background of this large, 80-foot-long tugboat is unknown. It was nicknamed after Rick Nielson, a local diver-historian who found the wreck, which sits upright with a damaged stern, and which was probably scuttled.

20. *FRONTENAC*

LORAN:	**GPS: 44° 01.128'/076° 36.164'**
DEPTH: 100 to 115 feet	**LEVEL: Advanced**

LOCATION: The wreck lies to the west-northwest of Pigeon Island.
The wooden tugboat, *Frontenac* (89' x 22'), launched at Garden Island immediately

Left: The tug, *Frontenac,* in drydock. MARINE MUSEUM OF THE GREAT LAKES AT KINGSTON
Right: Braided steel cable is still coiled around the *Frontenac's* winch. PHOTO BY CRIS KOHL

opposite the city of Kingston, Ontario, in 1901, was returning from a wrecking job on December 11, 1929, when she began taking on water. She sank within ten minutes, with her crew escaping to another tugboat just in time. Spencer Shoniker, acting on a fisherman's tip, located the *Frontenac* in September, 1995.

This site offers many visual treats: porcelain plates, cups and saucers still sit in their

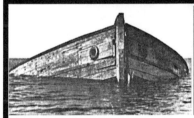

Left: The *Frontenac's* bow rises majestically from the lake bottom. *Right:* numerous items like wooden crates intrigue visiting divers. PHOTOS BY CRIS KOHL

boxes. The large four-bladed propeller and the rudder are still upright and in place. There are also the ship's anchors, a huge winch fully loaded with braided steel cable, fallen dorades, chain running down the bow, the ship's wheel and, at last report, the ship's compass. As with all Great Lakes shipwrecks, please leave every item in place for the next divers to see.

21. CITY OF SHEBOYGAN

LORAN: 15805.2/60016.6	LAT 44° 04′ 56″ LON 076° 44′ 04″
DEPTH: 90 to 105 feet	LEVEL: Advanced

LOCATION: Southwest of Amherst Island, near Nut Island, west of Kingston.

The three-masted schooner, *City of Sheboygan* (135′2″ x 27′4″ x 10′), was launched at Sheboygan, Wisconsin, on July 5, 1871. The ship's career spanned almost 45 years on the Great Lakes until she foundered in a violent storm on September 25, 1915. Helpless fishermen on Amherst Island gazed in silent horror as the captain and the crew of four drowned. The wreck is deep, and hence well-preserved and mostly intact. The wreck of the *City of Sheboygan* was located by a team of divers led by Lloyd Shales and Barbara Carson in the early

Left: The schooner, *City of Sheboygan.* CRIS KOHL COLLECTION.
Right: A diver swims over the bow of the *City of Sheboygan.* IMAGE BY DAN LINDSAY OF SEA-VIEW DIVING (SEE PAGE 156 FOR THE AD)

SCHOONER WENT DOWN

CITY OF CHEYBOYGAN SANK ON SUNDAY MORNING

Near Amherst Island—It Left Kingston on Saturday With Feldspar For Buffalo.

Above: A local newspaper misspelled the *City of Sheboygan's* name, but it reported the tragic details of the sinking accurately. CRIS KOHL COLLECTION

Left: The *City of Sheboygan* sports a Save Ontario Shipwrecks plaque relating the vessel's history. PHOTO BY CRIS KOHL

Right: Diver Doug Pettingill takes a close look at a deadeye along the *City of Sheboygan's* starboard rail. PHOTO BY CRIS KOHL

The *City of Sheboygan*

Artwork © Adam Henley

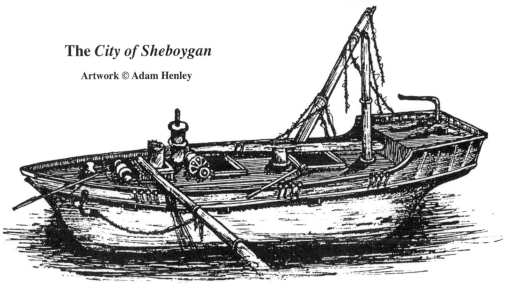

summer of 1963. The ship's wheel and an anchor are the only items that have been removed, and they are on exhibit at a local museum. Her masts, rigging and most other items, including deadeyes, are present. The depth, the cold and the dark (take along a light) are inhibiting factors at this site.

22. SCUTTLED DEEP HULLS

LOCATION: In the Upper Gap off the northwest corner of Amherst Island.

Two (and possibly three) scuttled hulls have been located in about 260' of water in an oddly deep section of one of the relatively narrow passages between the islands and the mainland. These wrecks are being developed as an attraction for technical divers.

Two deep hulls in the Upper Gap off Amherst Island. *Left:* The *Hilda* (164′ x 30′ x 12′3″), built in Toronto in 1898, was scuttled on November 7, 1967, in 260′ of water (**GPS: 44° 08.102′/076° 49.595′**). *Right:* The *Londonderry* (215′ x 40′ x 14′6″), built in Levis, Quebec, in 1901 as the schooner-barge named *Quebec*, and renamed in 1930 before conversion to a crane-equipped barge. She was sunk in 1969 in 260′. (**GPS: 44° 08.158′/076° 49.157′**). BOTH CRIS KOHL COLLECTION

23. S. M. DOUGLAS

LORAN:	GPS: 44° 01.010′/076° 36.227′
DEPTH: 110 feet	LEVEL: Advanced

Built at Montreal in 1897, this iron-hulled, sidewheel steamer was named *White Star*, but in 1949, the ship was purchased by the Simpson Sand Company of Brockville, Ontario, converted into a sandsucker with a diesel engine, and renamed *S. M. Douglas* (160′6″ x 25′4″ x 8′1″), after one of the company's three owners. This aging vessel was considered for use as a Kingston breakwater, and also as an additional scuba site after the successful sinking of the *Wolfe Islander II* in 1985, but those plans fell through. The ship was scuttled in 1986 in 110′ of water off Pigeon Island.

The *S. M. Douglas* as a sandsucker. CRIS KOHL COLLECTION

24. WILLIAM JOHNSTON

LORAN:	GPS:
DEPTH: 90 feet	LEVEL: Advanced

Built as a sidewheel steam tug named the *Raftsman* in 1840 at Garden Island, ON, this ship spent the 1840's towing log rafts between Montreal and Quebec City. The tug returned to Kingston in 1851 and in 1878 was converted to propeller-power and renamed *William Johnston* (73′ x 20′ x 6′6″). From 1912 to 1929, it worked for the Donnelly Wrecking Company of Kingston, and from 1929 to 1941, was owned by the Sin Mac Tug Lines. The *Johnston* was scuttled in 90′ of water off Simcoe Island in 1941 when it was 101 years of age!

The wrecking tug, *William Johnston,* at dock. CRIS KOHL COLLECTION

STILL MORE SCUTTLED HULLS -- WITH MORE TO COME!

More old hulls from the several ships' graveyard sites off Kingston have been discovered in recent years, but few have been identified, including: two 200′ steamers off Wolfe Island in 80′ and 90′; a scuttled tug in 90′ off Brothers Island, nicknamed "Terry's Tug" (**GPS: 44° 12.777′/076° 38.078′**); and several hulks off Snake Island and Amherst Island.

6. Point Traverse

Doug Pettingill and James Taylor head to a Point Traverse shipwreck site.   PHOTO BY CRIS KOHL

1. **Cabin cruiser and habitat**
2. *Echo*
3. *Banshee*
4. *Florence*
5. *Annie Falconer*
6. *Katie Eccles*
7. *China*
8. *Alberta*
9. *Fabiola*
10. *Manola*
11. *Olive Branch*
12. *Oliver Mowat*
13. *John Randall*
14. *Atlasco*
15. *Condor*
16. *R. H. Rae*
17. *Ocean Wave*
18. *"Bluff-Nosed Wreck"*
19. *"Two-Masted Wreck"*

A dive boat carefully passes through the narrow opening of Point Traverse harbor. PHOTO BY CRIS KOHL

1. CABIN CRUISER AND HABITAT

> **LORAN:** Shore dive   **GPS:**
> **DEPTH:** To 30 feet   **LEVEL:** Novice-Intermediate

LOCATION: Behind Ducks Dive Shop at Point Traverse.
The purposely sunk 30-foot-long wooden Owen cabin
cruiser just off shore is usually marked with a buoy, as is the
underwater habitat, which is the original "Sublimnos" built in
the late 1960's by Dr. Joseph McGinnis for experiments in
Georgian Bay near Tobermory.

Simply enter the water from the beach and surface swim
to the left (northern) marker; this is the cabin cruiser, which
sits upright and is intact and penetrable. You can certainly get
to the underwater habitat from the surface, but you're good if
you can do it underwater from the cabin cruiser. Both sites
can easily be done on a single tank of air.

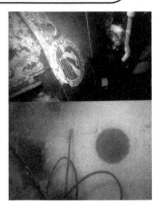

The underwater habitat. PHOTOS BY CRIS KOHL

2. *ECHO*

> **LORAN:**   **LAT 43° 56' 19" LON 076° 49' 54"**
> **DEPTH:** 22 feet   **LEVEL:** Novice-Intermediate

LOCATION: One-half mile off Gull Bar near False Duck Island.
This Canadian "fore-and-after" (meaning it was a two-masted schooner; a "three-and-after" was marine slang for a three-masted schooner) sank on October 11, 1861, with a load of barley. The entire crew was saved. This broken up shipwreck in shallow water was located on September 17, 1967 by members of the Quinte Aqua Divers of Belleville, Ontario.

3. *BANSHEE*

> **LORAN:** 15904.2/60020.4   **LAT 43° 56' 14" LON 076° 50' 04"**
> **DEPTH:** 18 feet   **LEVEL:** Novice-Intermediate

LOCATION: The wreck lies between Timber Island and the Duck Islands, not very far from the wreck of the *Echo*.
The 400-ton wooden propeller, *Banshee* (119' x 18' x 8'), carried a cargo of 6,000 bushels of wheat, 250 barrels of flour and 300 kegs of butter from Port Stanley on Lake Erie towards Montreal when she sank in a nefarious storm on August 21, 1861, after her engine expired and she drifted into the shallow waters of Gull Shoal. One life was lost from the 18 that were on board. Members of the Quinte Aqua Divers of Belleville, Ontario, located these badly broken up shipwreck remains in late 1967.

The sidewheel steamer, *Banshee*. CRIS KOHL COLLECTION

4. *FLORENCE*

LORAN: 15892.7/60019.4	LAT 43° 57' 49" LON 076° 49' 00"
DEPTH: 40 to 50 feet	LEVEL: Novice-Intermediate

LOCATION: About 300 feet off Timber Island, off Point Traverse.

The wooden tugboat, *Florence* (91' x 19'8" x 9'), built at Levis, Quebec, in 1885, worked in Quebec, New Brunswick and the Windsor, Ontario, area before springing a leak and sinking at this site on November 14, 1933, with no loss of life. Salvage attempts moved the ship from her original depth of 80' to shallower water, and her engine and propeller were salvaged. The bow and boiler, plus a hatch ladder and several other items, are intact, but much of the vessel is broken up from the salvage efforts plus the shallow water conditions.

Above, left: The tugboat, *Florence*, plied both fresh and salt waters for nearly half a century.
CRIS KOHL COLLECTION

Above, right: Dramatic 1933 newspaper headlines used the area's longtime label: "Graveyard of Lake Ontario." CRIS KOHL COLLECTION

Left: A diver takes a close look at chain and the upper portion of the boiler on the *Florence*.
PHOTO BY CRIS KOHL

107

Left: The schooner, *Annie Falconer,* from a painting by Gibbons. CRIS KOHL COLLECTION. *Right:* The *Annie Fal-coner* at a dock in Cobourg, Ontario. CRIS KOHL COLLECTION. *Middle left:* Doug Pettingill, one of the three co-discoverers of the *Annie Falconer,* takes a turn at "steering the *Annie.*" The wheel is a ship's usual focal point. *Bottom, left:* Diver and marine historian/artist Pat Stayer approaches the precariously-perched port bow anchor to get a closer look at it; two weeks later, the anchor fell off the rail to the lake bottom. Pat claims she didn't do it. PHOTOS BY CRIS KOHL.   *Below, right:* Adam Henley's detailed drawing points out the *Falconer's* highlights.

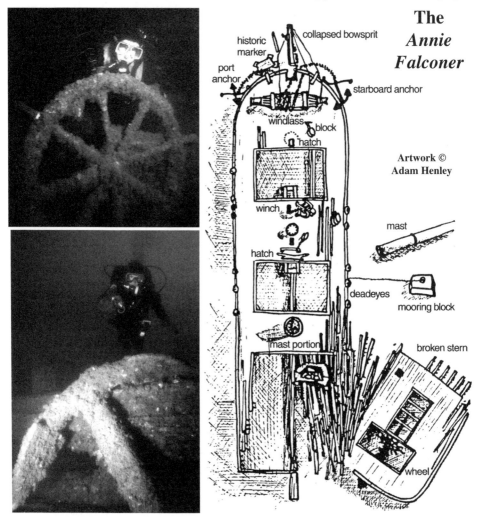

The
Annie
Falconer

historic marker
collapsed bowsprit
port anchor
starboard anchor
windlass
block
hatch

Artwork ©
Adam Henley

winch

mast

hatch

deadeyes

mooring block

mast portion

broken stern

wheel

5. *ANNIE FALCONER* -- see also page 108.

LORAN: 15882.20/60015.06	LAT 43° 58' 10" LON 076° 48' 28"
DEPTH: 67 to 78 feet	LEVEL: Intermediate-Advanced

LOCATION: The wreck lies 1.5 miles north of the False Duck Island lighthouse.

The two-masted schooner, *Annie Falconer* (108' x 24' x 9'), named after the first owner's wife who had died seven years before her namesake vessel was built, is one of the best and most popular shipwreck dives in the area. The vessel, built at Kingston and launched on May 22, 1867 (just a few weeks before Canada became a country!) foundered in a violent storm on November 12, 1904, with a cargo of soft coal. The crew of seven reached Amherst Island in the ship's yawl boat "after hours of suffering and hardship"

PERISHED FROM EXPOSURE

MATE OF SCHOONER FALCONER, WHICH FOUNDERED IN GALE.

Picton, Ont., November 14.—The schooner Annie Falconer, with coal from Sodus Point to Picton, foundered near Timber Island in the furious gale last Saturday. .

Capt. Ackerman and his crew took to the life-boats. After great suffering

Newspapers reported the tragedy of the lost mate and ship. CRIS KOHL COLLECTION

(*The Daily British Whig*, Kingston, November 14, 1904), but the first mate, James Sullivan, died of exposure shortly thereafter when he wandered away from the rest of the crew.

Barbara Carson, Audrey Rushbrook and Doug Pettingill located the wreck of the *Annie Falconer* in 1975. The wreck sits upright on a mud bottom, and is well-preserved, with deadeyes, anchors, blocks, chain and the ship's wheel in place. Her stern broke off, but it lies within visible range at an angle to the main hull. Limited shipwreck penetration is possible in the forward portion. There's lots to see at this incredible site!

6. *KATIE ECCLES*

LORAN: 15843.18/60028.99	GPS:
DEPTH: 102 feet	LEVEL: Advanced

LOCATION: The wreck lies to the northeast of Timber Island.

The small, graceful 122-ton schooner, *Katie Eccles* (95' x 24'6" x 9'6"), was built in 1877 by William Jamieson (see page 92) at Mill Point (now Deseronto), Ontario. On November 26, 1922, the ship left Oswego, New York, with 300 tons of hard coal and made it to Timber Island without her rudder, which she had lost outside Oswego. After dropping anchor, the crew rowed to Timber Island, but that night, the anchor chain cut through the vessel's planking, and she foundered in deep water. The wreck is upright and intact.

A small, modest schooner, the *Katie Eccles (left:* Cris Kohl Collection) appears much larger underwater. Photo by John Veber

7. CHINA

LORAN:	GPS: 43° 58.331'/076° 46.342'
DEPTH: 104 feet	LEVEL: Advanced

LOCATION: The wreck lies northeast of False Duck Island.

The propeller-driven steamer, *China*, was accidentally located in the 1970's by divers seeking the schooner, *Annie Falconer* (see pages 108-109). This is a badly-burned, quiet wreck sitting in deep, dark waters. This 130-foot-long, 333-ton ship burned to a complete loss in October, 1872, the same year she was launched at Kingston. She carried a load of pig iron and general merchandise, and her explorable remains include a steeple compound engine, a boiler, and a four-bladed propeller. Take a dive light along, as it gets dark down there.

8. ALBERTA

LORAN: 15828.6/59974.6	GPS: 44° 05.822'/076° 53.054'
DEPTH: 106 feet	LEVEL: Advanced

LOCATION: This wreck lies opposite Prinyer's Cove, east of Picton, Ontario.

The flat barge, *Alberta* (not to be confused with the wooden steamer, *Alberta,* which burned to a complete loss at nearby Trenton, Ontario, on October 8, 1902) was a 62-ton, 65-foot-long paddlewheeler built at Deseronto, Ontario, in 1888. She sank on July 21, 1899.

This flat barge-type boat with a single paddlewheel in the middle of it lies upside-down. The bay waters here are quite dark, so take along a dive light and do your dive only if you feel secure about it. This is a deep dive, so watch your depth and time.

9. FABIOLA

LORAN: 15889.8/60031.3	LAT 43° 56' 52" LON 076° 47' 38"
DEPTH: 55 feet	LEVEL: Novice-Intermediate

The *Fabiola* resembled this vessel, *the C. Michelson.* Cris Kohl Collection

LOCATION: Off the southeast corner of False Duck Island.

The two-masted schooner, *Fabiola* (95' x 22'4" x 9'), was launched at Oakville, Ontario, under the name *Red Oak* in 1852 (her name was changed to *Fabiola* in 1876). She was an old, twice-rebuilt vessel when she was lost on October 23, 1900, while downbound from Oswego, New York, with a cargo of coal. The bow, with its windlass and capstan, is quite intact, but the stern has collapsed. This is usually a relaxing dive in good visibility, a sandy bottom, and no current.

Doug Pettingill explores the bow of the *Fabiola* and later stops at a local museum to see the ship's wheel. Bass are often found on Great Lakes shipwrecks; notice the freshwater sponges growing on the *Fabiola's* railing in the background.   PHOTOS BY CRIS KOHL

10. *MANOLA*

LORAN: 15907.5/60046.7	GPS:
DEPTH: 45 to 82 feet	LEVEL: Intermediate-Advanced

LOCATION: Southeast off False Duck Island, eastern Lake Ontario.

The steel steamer, *Manola* (282'4" x 40'3" x 21'2"), launched on January 21, 1890 at Cleveland, Ohio, was needed for overseas service during World War I. However, to get such a long ship out of the upper Great Lakes through the Welland Canal required cutting her in half. The stern half was towed safely across Lake Ontario, while the bow half sank during a snowstorm on December 3, 1918, taking the lives of all 11 men who were on her. Ironically, World War I had just ended, and the ship was no longer needed to win the war.

ELEVEN ARE DROWNED WHEN VESSEL SINKS

The Bow Section of the Minola Went Down at Duck Island.

Watertown, N.Y., Dec. 4.—Eleven men, comprising the crew of the bow section of the freighter Minola, are believed to have been drowned when that section of the boat went down in Lake Ontario, near Duck Island, Monday night, in a terrific gale and blizzard.

News of the disaster was brought into Cape Vincent yesterday, by the Government tug Michigan, which was towing the Minola. The captain of the Michigan reports that within five minutes after the lines parted, the Minola foundered. The sea was

The wreck was located in 1976 by Barbara Carson and Doug Pettingill. Diving on this enormous bow half of a ship is exhilarating, even though it lies upside-down. Both bow anchors hang down impressively, while a spare anchor can be seen below the wreck. Brass portholes are situated along the bottom portion of

The tragic news of the *Manola*. CRIS KOHL COLLECTION

the vessel. The wooden bulkhead where the ship was torched in two is of interest. A variety of pulleys and other marine parts litter the lake bottom. Penetration is possible, but confusing due to the upside-down nature of the wreck and the many corridors; this should be left to the trained and prepared experts!

The orphaned stern half was given a new bow half and renamed the *Mapledawn,* which sank in Lake Huron five years later (that story and site description are also in this book).

The *Manola* very early in her career.
ARTIST UNKNOWN. CRIS KOHL COLLECTION

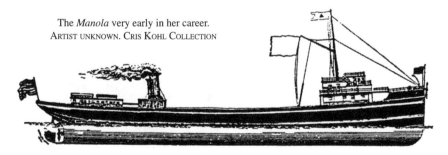

STEEL SHIP MANOLA, ON HER MAIDEN TRIP

111

The large steel freighter, *Manola*.
CRIS KOHL COLLECTION

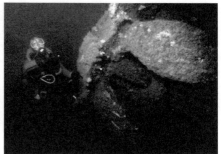

The *Manola's* co-discoverer, Doug Pettingill, approaches the upside-down wreck's port anchor.
PHOTO BY CRIS KOHL

11. OLIVE BRANCH

> **LORAN: 15885.11/60047.79**   **LAT 43° 55' 00" LON 076° 44' 37"**
> **DEPTH: 90 to 101 feet**   **LEVEL: Advanced**

LOCATION: Southeast off False Duck Island.

The *J. H. Stevens* (102'6" x 21' x 7'), built at Milan, Ohio, in 1859, was similar to the *Olive Branch*. CRIS KOHL COLLECTION

The schooner, Olive Branch

The small schooner, *Olive Branch* (92' x 22' x 8'), sank in a storm on September 30, 1880, with the loss of all five people on board. The uninsured ship (her insurance had expired just two weeks earlier!) had been constructed in 1871 in nearby Picton, Ontario. The wreck is intact, resting upright at the base of a shoal down which she seems to have slid (the original account put the wreck in 70' of water, but she now sits in about 100'). Most of her original equipment remains on board, including a windlass, deadeyes, blocks, a standing capstan, a pump, hinged catheads (the starboard one holds a steel-stock fluke anchor), a Quebec stove, a fallen mast with wire rigging, a collapsed bowsprit, and the ship's wheel. The depth and occasional low visibility can make this a challenging dive.

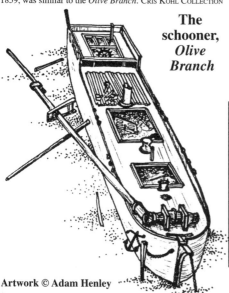

Artwork © Adam Henley

The *Olive Branch's* wheel. PHOTO BY CRIS KOHL

12. OLIVER MOWAT

LORAN:	LAT 43° 55' 40" LON 076° 44' 05"
DEPTH: 105 feet	LEVEL: Advanced

The schooner, *Oliver Mowat*. INSTITUTE FOR GREAT LAKES RESEARCH, BOWLING GREEN STATE UNIVERSITY, OHIO

LOCATION: To the southeast of False Duck Island.

The 295-ton schooner, *Oliver Mowat* (116' x 23'8" x 9'8"), sank after the steel freighter, *Keywest,* struck it midship on September 1, 1921, with the loss of three of the five lives on board the schooner. The *Oliver Mowat* had been built in 1873 at Mill Haven, near Kingston. Her masts were dynamited, as they presented a menace to navigation. This wreck was located in the early 1960's and many of her artifacts were removed by divers, as was the accepted practice in those early days. The damage which sank her can clearly be seen on her hull.

13. JOHN RANDALL

LORAN:	GPS:
DEPTH: 20 feet	LEVEL: Novice-Intermediate

LOCATION: This shipwreck lies in School House Bay at Main Duck Island.

The wooden steamer, *John Randall* (104'4" x 22'5" x 7'7"), built in Kingston in 1905, encountered a severe storm on November 16, 1920, while hauling a cargo of coal from Oswego, New York, towards Belleville, Ontario. Captain Harry Randall (John was his father) steered his ship towards shelter at School House Bay at Main Duck Island, where the vessel sank. The entire crew safely reached the island and stayed as guests of the lighthouse keeper for eight days before word of their survival reached the outside world. A year later, Capt. Harry Randall perished when the ill-fated steamer, *City of New York,* sank on Lake Ontario with all eight hands.

CAPT. RANDALL AND HIS CREW EIGHT DAYS ON DUCK ISLAND

Steambarge John Randall Foundered Half a Mile From Island At 1:30 a.m. of 17th—Crew Swam to Shore—Stormy Weather Held Them on Island With Lighthouse Keeper—Reached Kingston on Friday.

For eight, long days, even though it was 1920 and the modern era had begun, the friends and family, and the rest of the world, did not know what had happened to the *John Randall* and her crew. CRIS KOHL COLLECTION. *Right:* School House Bay at Main Duck Island is shallow enough to be snorkeled. *Left:* Jim Stayer videotapes the remains of the *John Randall.*

PHOTOS BY CRIS KOHL

The *John Randall* lies broken and scattered around the waters of the bay, and is an excellent site for novice scuba divers and for snorkelers.

14. ATLASCO

LORAN: 15968.0/59996.9   GPS: 43° 52.76'/076° 58.90'
DEPTH: 43 feet   LEVEL: Intermediate

LOCATION: South of Ostrander Point, near Point Traverse, eastern Lake Ontario.
The wooden steamer, *Atlasco* (218'5" x 32'8" x 13'4"), launched as the *Russell Sage* on May 21, 1881, at Buffalo, New York, sank in a violent storm on August 7, 1921. No lives were lost, but her cohort, the schooner-barge, *Condor,* was also destroyed.

Above: The *Atlasco*. CRIS KOHL COLLECTION. *Right:* The many bales of wire from the *Atlasco's* cargo remain impressive. *Below, right:* Doug Pettingill peers through the spokes of the *Atlasco's* wheel. PHOTOS BY CRIS KOHL

On a tip from commercial fisherman Doug Harrison in the summer of 1990, Doug Pettingill was the first diver to see the wreck of the *Atlasco,* initially called "the wire wreck" because of her cargo, until her identity was established. Items to see here include the "valley of wire," the huge coils that lay rusting in the forward half of the vessel, four (!) anchors, a winch, bitts, rudder and ship's wheel.

Left: Commercial diver James Taylor glides through the "valley of wire."
PHOTO BY CRIS KOHL

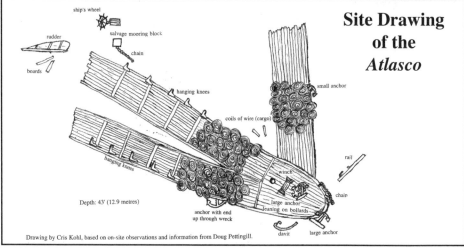

Site Drawing of the *Atlasco*

ship's wheel
rudder
salvage mooring block
chain
boards
hanging knees
small anchor
coils of wire (cargo)
hanging knees
rail
winch
Depth: 43' (12.9 metres)
chain
large anchor leaning on bollards
anchor with end up through wreck
davit
large anchor

Drawing by Cris Kohl, based on on-site observations and information from Doug Pettingill.

15. CONDOR

LOCATION: Along the shoreline, east of Ostrander Point, eastern Lake Ontario.

The barge *Condor* (180'7" x 34'5" x 11'6"), which was being towed by the *Atlasco* (see site #14), was also wrecked, but stranded and broke up along the shoreline. The ship had been built in Montreal in 1888. As with the *Atlasco*, no lives were lost.

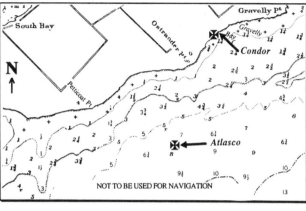

Left: The ribs and framing of the barge, *Condor,* embedded in the shoreline, are examined by Cris Kohl. PHOTO BY KATHY MAHONEY. *Above:* This map shows the relative positions of the *Condor* and the *Atlasco.*

16. R. H. RAE

LORAN: 15932.2/60032.8	GPS: 43° 53.136'/076° 50.340'
DEPTH: 105 feet	LEVEL: Advanced

LOCATION: South of Point Traverse, eastern Lake Ontario.

The 137-foot-long, three-masted bark, *R. H. Rae*, built in St. Catharines, Ontario (then Canada West) in 1857 by famous shipbuilder Louis Shickluna, capsized and sank during a white squall on August 4, 1858, during her first full season afloat, with the crew barely escaping with their lives. Located by Barbara Carson in 1976, the *R. H. Rae* was offered for exploration to the 1980 Jacques Cousteau expedition, the only time they ever visited the Great Lakes. They recovered many artifacts, including the ship's wheel, all of which are presently held at the marine museum in Kingston. Unfortunately, the Cousteau expedition also lost a diver at this site. The wreck location returned to secrecy, known but to a few divers unwilling to "open" this

Marcy McElmon views the *R. H. Rae's* unusual bilge pump pipes.   PHOTO BY CRIS KOHL

site. This shipwreck was relocated by a group of Great Lakes divers (including the author) on July 25, 1996, and opened to the diving public.

The wreck's huge, wooden rudder rests on a twisted angle, and most of the ship's decking has collapsed, except at the bow. Interesting items include an ornately-carved bow stem, a large windlass, copper cappings on the bow, samson and windlass posts, a pump, a deck winch, blocks, deadeyes, and an 1857 toilet.

17. Ocean Wave

LORAN:	GPs: 43° 50.753'/076° 54.139'
DEPTH: 153 feet	LEVEL: Technical

The paddlewheel steamer, *Ocean Wave* (174'2" x 26' x 11'6"), built in Montreal in 1852, burned and sank with great loss of life (28) on April 30, 1853. The wreck lies upside-down in deep, dark, usually silty water. Her engine stands upright almost half a mile from the hull. Barbara Carson and Doug Pettingill found this deep wreck in 1991.

The *Ocean Wave* ablaze. Nineteenth-century artist unknown.   CRIS KOHL COLLECTION

18. The "Bluff-Nosed Wreck"

LORAN:	GPS: 43° 49.05'/077° 02.04'
DEPTH: 165 feet	LEVEL: Technical

This old wreck could date from the War of 1812 era: its ornately curved, massive beak head style of bow (which may have supported a figurehead!) just below the bowsprit (which was pushed back when the ship hit bottom bow-first) is of that style. Both masts lie to starboard leaning on the rail. A stove sits inside the roofless wheelhouse; the wheel is damaged.

NOTE: These two shipwrecks in deep water (#18 and #19) approximately ten miles east-southeast of Point Traverse are extremely fragile. Do NOT drag an anchor into them in an attempt to snag them! (In fact, don't do that with ANY shipwreck!) Experienced charter boat operators Susan Yankoo and George Wheeler drop their anchor a safe distance off the wreck, and divers descending on the anchor line swim over to the wreck when it is sighted.

19. The "Two-Masted Wreck"

LORAN:	GPS: 43° 48.29'/077° 03.38'
DEPTH: 178 feet	LEVEL: Technical

Both masts on this small, but pristine, shipwreck remain standing, the main mast rising to a depth of about 110'. The 30'+ bowsprit remains upright. An anchor is stowed on the port bow inside the railing, while a windlass with anchor chain decorates the bow. The ship's wheel is mounted to the roof of the very low stern cabin. The mizzen topmast and crow's nest lie off the starboard bow. The ship's yawl boat is missing, but may lie nearby.

The "Two-Masted Wreck" near Picton, Ontario, is a deep diver's delight! IMAGES BY DAN LINDSAY OF SEA-VIEW DIVING (SEE PAGE 156 FOR THE AD)

7. Other Lake Ontario Sites

Oswego, NY, lighthouse on a rough day. PHOTO BY CRIS KOHL

Hundreds of divers take part in the Treasure Hunt at Presqu'ile Provincial Park near Trenton, Ontario, every June. PHOTO BY CRIS KOHL

1. QUINTE

LORAN:	GPS: 44° 10.583'/077° 02.500'
DEPTH: 5 to 10 feet	LEVEL: Novice

Built at Montreal in 1871 and launched as the *Beauharnois*, the sidewheel steamer, *Quinte* (138' x 22'5" x 7'5"), received that name in 1882 as the flagship of the Deseronto Navigation Company. On Oct. 23, 1889, the vessel, with 24 passengers on board, caught on fire just off Grassy Point, three miles southwest of Deseronto, ON. She was fully ablaze when she grounded, and five people died.

Only that portion of the vessel below the waterline exists on a sandy bottom with negligible current; visibility is usually good. Years ago, boys swimming around the wreck found coins. Boating traffic can get heavy, so fly a divers down flag.

The steamer, *Quinte*.
CRIS KOHL COLLECTION

2. BELLE SHERIDAN

LORAN:	GPS:
DEPTH: 12 feet	LEVEL: Novice

LOCATION: Outside Weller's Bay, near Beecroft Point, south of Trenton, Ontario.

A captain and three of his four sons perished when the two-masted schooner, *Belle Sheridan* (123' x 22'8" x 10'2"), grounded during the Great Gale of November, 1880, while

WHERE THE "BELLE SHERIDAN" POUNDED TO PIECES

LAKE ONTARIO

From *The Toronto Telegram*, November 7, 1928. CRIS KOHL COLLECTION

running a load of coal to Toronto. Captain McSherry and his sons, John (21), Thomas (17) and Edward (13), plus two other crewmembers, died 100 yards from shore while their ship was pounded to pieces. The sole survivor was the captain's 18-year-old son, James, who clung tightly to a timber, jumped into the raging waters, and swam madly, finally reaching shore more dead than alive. This schooner was built in Oswego, New York, in 1852. In 1933, portions of the *Belle Sheridan's* deck and ribbing were raised and returned to Toronto. This wreck lies badly broken up and scattered, with portions of it buried in the sandy bottom.

3. IDA WALKER

LORAN:	LAT 44° 00' 57" LON 077° 36' 22"
DEPTH: 10 to 12 feet	LEVEL: Novice

LOCATION: At the mouth of Weller's Bay, near Presqu'ile Point, Ontario.

The two-masted schooner, *Ida Walker,* sought storm shelter on November 19, 1886, while loading at the nearby unprotected port of Wellington. The sweeping seas forced her, half-loaded with barley and dragging her anchor, onto the shoal at the mouth of Weller's Bay. The Wellington lifesaving station rescued the entire crew before the vessel broke up.

Today, the wreck lies broken and scattered and partially buried in the sandy bottom at a depth of about 12′ of water. Caution: boating traffic can be heavy here during summer.

4. JOHN A. MacDONALD

LORAN:	LAT 44° 00′ 36″ LON 077° 40′ 30″
DEPTH: 6 to 8 feet	LEVEL: Novice

LOCATION: Off the east shore, at the mouth of Presqu'ile Bay, Ontario.

Launched as the *John A. Torrance* in 1841 at Burlington, Ontario, the two-masted schooner, *John A. MacDonald* (112′ x 19′9″ x 9′), received her name change in 1860. On November 17, 1872, while enroute from Hamilton to Kingston with a coal cargo, she began to leak badly and was run ashore at the mouth of Presqu'ile Bay, where she broke up with no loss of life. While most of the wreck is broken up and buried in the sand, decking, with its planks and spiking, is visible. Use a dive flag; boating traffic can get heavy.

5. SPEEDY

LOCATION: Off Presqu'ile Point, Ontario.

The two-masted schooner, *Speedy* (128′ x 24′ x 8′), constructed in 1798 at Kingston, Ontario (Ontario was actually called Upper Canada then), sank with all hands, estimated to be from 20 to 27 persons, in a storm about four miles off Presqu'ile on October 8, 1804, with the loss of prominent politicians and an Indian, accused of murdering a white trader, in chains below deck. Conjectured: the ship struck a rock pinnacle, or the desperate prisoner scraped a hole through the hull. Scattered wreckage was found two decades ago, but proof that it came from the historic *Speedy* is not 100% definitive.

The *Speedy,* as seen in this 1913 depiction by Canadian maritime historian C. H. J. Snider.
CRIS KOHL COLLECTION

6. JUNO

LORAN:	LAT 43° 53′ 01″ LON 078° 80′ 02″
DEPTH: 6 to 12 feet	LEVEL: Novice

LOCATION: Just off shore, south of Bowmanville, Ontario.

Built in Wallaceburg, Ontario, in 1885, the oak-hulled propeller, *Juno* (139′7″ x 26′8″ x 8′8″) was stripped of her machinery in 1914 and used as a breakwall and loading pier for a shoreline quarry. A few years later, her commercial use ended when her hull broke up.

Lying about 200′ from shore, the wreck site is 42 miles east of Toronto, south of Highway 401, near Waverly Road. The site is usually marked with jugs early in the season. The badly broken up bow, with a half-buried windlass, rests in the shallows; the slightly deeper stern offers the 8′ upright propeller. The wreck sits on a hard sand bottom in a current-free location. Use a dive flag, as passing boaters can pose a problem.

The steamer, *Juno.*
CRIS KOHL COLLECTION

7. ALEXANDRIA

LORAN:	GPS:
DEPTH: 5 to 10 feet	LEVEL: Intermediate

LOCATION: Below the Scarborough Bluffs, off Markham Road, in suburban Toronto.

WARNING: Divers require permission from the Metropolitan Toronto Police Marine

The paddlewheel steamer, *Alexandria; left:* old postcard view; *right:* wrecked. CRIS KOHL COLLECTION

Unit to dive this area, and they must sign liability release forms.

The sidewheel steamer, *Alexandria* (161'7" x 25'2" x 8'1"), built in Montreal in 1866, stranded during severe weather on August 3, 1915 and broke up with no loss of life. Locals quickly picked this shallow shipwreck clean. The boiler remains visible from the surface, and bits and pieces of wreckage lie scattered widely. The usually poor visibility and the busy boating traffic make this site unpopular among scuba divers.

8. *LYMAN M. DAVIS*

LORAN:	GPS: 43° 36.165'/079° 24.973'
DEPTH: 148 feet	LEVEL: Technical

LOCATION: Off Toronto.

The *Lyman M. Davis* early in her career. ARTIST UNKNOWN. CRIS KOHL COLLECTION

The ship, *Lyman M. Davis* (123' x 27'2" x 9'4"), built in Muskegon, Michigan in 1873, was one of the last working schooners on the Great Lakes. However, she was a remnant of a bygone era in an unappreciative time, so she was sacrificed for the mindless entertainment of the masses in a flaming spectacle off Toronto's Sunnyside Park on June 29, 1934. Her charred hull lies half buried in the lake's soft bottom in deep water notorious for poor visibility.

9. *JULIA B. MERRILL*

LORAN:	GPS: 43° 37.054'/079° 26.801'
DEPTH: 60 feet	LEVEL: Intermediate-Advanced

LOCATION: Off Toronto, near the mouth of the Humber River.

A mob's fondness for Viking-funeral-style spectacle doomed the classic schooner, *Julia B. Merrill* (125'5" x 26'5" x 8'2"), to be purposely engulfed by flames at Sunnyside Park in Toronto in July, 1931. Built in 1872 at Wenona, Michigan, the ship had maintained her original purpose of working under sail right up to the time of her demise.

The superstructure of this wreck is totally burned away, but her keel, rudder and posts are intact. Again, this is a silty area of poor visibility. Metropolitan Toronto Police Marine Unit permission and a signed waiver are required to dive this site.

The elegant schooner, *Julia B. Merrill.* CRIS KOHL COLLECTION

10. SLIGO

LORAN:	GPS: 43° 36.640'/079° 27.275'
DEPTH: 67 feet	LEVEL: Advanced

LOCATION: Off Toronto, near the mouth of the Humber River.

Launched as the three-masted bark, *Prince of Wales,* in 1860 at St. Catharines, Ontario, and rebuilt as a schooner renamed the *Sligo* (138' x 23' x 11'8") in 1874, this ship worked on the Great Lakes for many years, mainly as a schooner-barge. But a fierce gale parted her towline on September 5, 1918, and she foundered with her 90 tons of limestone cargo. Located by Toronto diver Don MacIntyre in the early 1980's, this wreck features an anchor, a windlass, and her wheel. The site is usually buoyed. Unfortunately, this is an area of low visibility. Use caution when diving here. Metropolitan Toronto Police Marine Unit permission and waiver are needed to dive here.

Artwork © Adam Henley

Left: Jan Miller and Kimberley Monk study a photomosaic of the *Sligo* at the annual conference of the Association for Great Lakes Maritime History. PHOTO BY CRIS KOHL. *Right:* The impressive *Sligo* docked in Kincardine, Ontario, harbor in the late 1800's. CRIS KOHL COLLECTION

11. HAMILTON AND SCOURGE

DEPTH: 275 to 289 feet	LEVEL: Legally off limits

LOCATION: Off St. Catharines, Ontario, in Canadian waters of Lake Ontario.

The two vintage schooners, *Hamilton* (built in Oswego, New York, in 1809 as the 112-ton *Diana*) and *Scourge* (built at Fort George, Ontario, in 1811 as the 110-ton *Lord Nelson*) are extremely historic, War of 1812, figureheaded shipwrecks laden with cannons, swords and human remains. Both ships were caught in a squall and sank on August 8, 1813, with 53 of their 72 sailors perishing. Reportedly, a large number of technical divers visited these extremely fragile shipwrecks before the province of Ontario declared them legally off limits (along with the famous *Edmund Fitzgerald* in Lake Superior; see pages 568-569) in 2006.

The War of 1812 ships, the *Hamilton* and the *Scourge,* resembled this vessel. ARTWORK © PETER RINDLISBACHER, USED WITH PERMISSION. FOR INFORMATION ABOUT MR. RINDLISBACHER'S ART, CONTACT THE CANADIAN SOCIETY OF MARINE ARTISTS, OR GO TO WWW.ULTRAMARINE.CA

12. "TILLER WRECK" (*HENRY CLAY?*)

LORAN:	GPS: 43° 14.755'/079° 17.072'
DEPTH: 116 feet	LEVEL: Advanced

LOCATION: This wreck lies 2.3 nautical miles off Port Dalhousie, Ontario.

Located by Canadian diver Jim Garrington and first explored by him in 1996, this small (94' x 21') but significant, unidentified, two-masted schooner appears to be of considerably early vintage. Initial research suggested that it could be the (then) new Oswego schooner, *Henry Clay,* which sank after capsizing in a gale on July 19, 1831, during its first season, but definite evidence as to this vessel's identity has not been found yet.

Underwater images of the beautiful "tiller wreck" off Port Dalhousie, Ontario, show the vessel to have a 38-degree starboard list, but much of the railing, the bowsprit, and the entire tiller after which it was nicknamed remain intact. This is one of the many shipwrecks which has been moored annually (this one to a mooring block off the wreck) as part of the Mooring Project of Ontario's Niagara Divers Association.

PHOTOS BY JOHN VEBER

13. ONTARIO

LOCATION: Off Niagara County, NY, near the town of Olcott, NY .

This early, two-masted, 226-ton, 22-gun brig, the *Ontario* (64′8″ x 25′4″ x 9′)) was constructed by the British Navy at Carleton Island (Upper Canada) and launched on May 10, 1780. Later that year, on Oct. 31, 1780, the ship sank in a storm; all 80-89 people on board, mostly soldiers, perished. This vitally historic wreck was reportedly located by scuba divers in July, 1995, off the New York state coast between Olcott and the Niagara River.

14. UNDINE AND JAMES A. SHRIGLEY

LORAN:	GPS: 43° 21.131′/077° 47.750′
DEPTH: 20 to 30 feet	LEVEL: Novice

LOCATION: Wautoma Shoals off Braddock's Point, NY, 10 miles west of Rochester.

Two shipwrecks are intermingled at this site. The first is the two-masted schooner, *Undine* (108′0″ x 23′0″ x 12′0″), built in 1868 at Hamilton, Ontario, which stranded and sank on Nov. 1, 1890, with only the ship and the 800 tons of coal cargo lost. The second is the wooden steamer, *James A. Shrigley* (171′ x 31′2″ x 11′5″), built at Milwaukee in 1881, also coal-laden and which also stranded in a storm on Aug. 18, 1920. The Coast Guard rescued her crew. The *Shrigley* had survived the Great Storm of 1913 while on lower Lake Huron; she was sold to Canadian owners in 1915. Both wrecks are broken and scattered, with the steamer's boiler being the most recognizable item.

The steamer, *James A. Shrigley.*
CRIS KOHL COLLECTION

15. LAURA GRACE

LORAN:	GPS: 43° 17.609′/077° 40.188′
DEPTH: 15 feet	LEVEL: Novice

LOCATION: Just west of Rochester, New York.

The *Laura Grace* was a steam-powered, wooden tugboat which sank in Lake Ontario close to shore in 1920. The site is directly off Long Pond Road, but a boat is required because all of the shoreline is private residences. Sitting on a soft, sandy lake bottom are some of the site's highlights: the winch, anchor chain, boiler, rudder and propeller. Boaters use caution: the boiler sits within four feet of the surface.

16. HENRY RONEY

LORAN:	GPS: 43° 15.792′/077° 33.430′
DEPTH: 70 feet	LEVEL: Advanced

LOCATION: Straight out from Durhand Eastman Park, Rochester, NY.

The schooner, *Henry Roney,* carrying limestone and lath, sprang a leak in strong winds while trying to reach the harbor of Charlotte (Rochester), NY, on Oct. 22, 1879. The cook perished. Contemporary salvage did damage; only the bow and stern remain visible today.

17. USCG BOAT *56022*

LORAN:	GPS: 43° 17.800′/077° 19.547′
DEPTH: 70 feet	LEVEL: Advanced

LOCATION: A little over one mile north of Ontario-on-the-Lake, New York.

This 56-foot US Coast Guard cable boat sank in a storm on Dec. 1, 1977 while enroute from Oswego to Niagara. Another CG boat took this one in tow after removing its 3-man

Above: USCG boat *56022* underway. JIM KENNARD COLLECTION
Right: USCG boat *56022* underwater. FREEZE-FRAMES BY DAN SCOVILLE

crew, but the tow line parted and the cable boat sank. Its stern has sunk 12 feet into the lake at a 45-degree angle out of the lake bottom! Many fish, mostly bass, congregate at this site. Noted wreck hunter Jim Kennard and cave diver Dan Scoville located this shipwreck.

18. *ETTA BELLE*

LORAN:	GPS:
DEPTH: About 180 feet	LEVEL: Technical

LOCATION: Several miles off Sodus Point, New York.

The two-masted schooner, *Etta Belle* (93' x 19'), was rebuilt in 1871 on the recovered hull of the wrecked schooner *Champion*, originally built at Oakville, Canada West, in 1852. The *Etta Belle* left Little Sodus, NY, for Toronto on Sept. 3, 1873, but developed a serious leak which sank the ship! No lives were lost, as the crew escaped in the yawlboat. This wreck was located in the fall of 2003 by wreck hunters Jim Kennard and Dan Scoville.

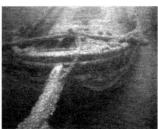

Left: The Canadian schooner, *Etta Belle,* under full sail. JIM KENNARD COLLECTION

Right and below: The beauty and the details of this shipwreck (ship's bow and bowsprit, rails, bilge pump, and wheel) are captured in these exciting images. DIGITAL FREEZE-FRAMES BY DAN SCOVILLE

19. MILAN

> LORAN: GPS:
> DEPTH: About 200 feet LEVEL: Technical

LOCATION: About 5 miles off Point Breeze, New York.

The twin-masted, 147-ton schooner, *Milan* (93' x 19'8"), built at Three-Mile Bay, NY, in 1845, was, on Oct. 13, 1849, bound from Cleveland, OH, to Oswego, NY, with 1,000 barrels of salt. The *Milan* sank, reportedly in 750' of water, after springing a leak. All 9 crewmembers and their dog were rescued by a passing ship. This fascinating wreck was located by Jim Kennard and Dan Scoville in 2005.

Artwork © Roland "Chip" Stevens

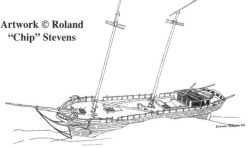

Above left: The schooner *Milan,* as it appears on the lake floor today.
ART BY ROLAND "CHIP" STEVENS.

Underwater images: The *Milan* sits upright and very intact, with the main items of interest including the two, upright masts, the windlass, the bow anchors, a bilge pump, a beak head style bow, the tiller, and the ornate transom.
VIDEO FREEZE-FRAMES BY DAN SCOVILLE

20. ORCADIAN

> DEPTH: 200+ feet LEVEL: Technical

LOCATION: Several miles off Sodus Point NY.

The two-masted brig, *Orcadian* (94' x 20' x 9'), launched in 1854 at St. Ours, Quebec, carrying a full cargo of wheat, sank after colliding with the schooner, *Lucy J. Latham*, on May 8, 1858. No lives were lost, but the sinking ship's rigging became so snagged on the *Latham's* bowsprit that the schooner was nearly pulled to the bottom with the *Orcadian*! This deep wreck was located in 2007 by Jim Kennard, Dan Scoville, and Roland "Chip" Stevens.

Artwork © Roland "Chip" Stevens

21. HOMER WARREN

LORAN:	GPS:
DEPTH: 130+ feet	LEVEL: Advanced-Technical

LOCATION: Several miles off Pultneyville, New York.

The wooden steamer, *Homer Warren* (176'5" x 30' x 12'), launched in 1863 at Cleveland, OH, as the *Atlantic*, had her name changed to *Homer Warren* in 1901, was sold to Canadian owners in 1914, and foundered off Pultneyville, NY, on Oct. 28, 1919, with the loss of all nine people on board. The ship was bound from Oswego, NY, to Toronto with a cargo of coal. This wreck was found on June 25, 2003, by Jim Kennard and Dan Scoville.

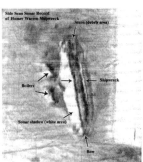

Left: The steamer, *Homer Warren.* CRIS KOHL COLLECTION.

Right: Sidescan sonar image of the wreck of the *Homer Warren.* IMAGE COURTESY OF JIM KENNARD

22. ST. PETER

LORAN:	GPS: 43° 18.321'/077° 07.707'
DEPTH: 98 to 120 feet	LEVEL: Advanced

LOCATION: Five miles northwest of Sodus, New York.

The sister schooner to the *St. Peter*, the *John Wesley.* ART BY SETH ARCA WHIPPLE, 1880. CRIS KOHL COLLECTION

This three-masted schooner (135'7" x 26' x 12'1"), launched in Toledo, Ohio, on Saturday, May 24, 1873, foundered on October 27, 1898, with a load of coal plus six of the seven people who were on board. The ship's master, Captain Griffin, clinging to a spar, was rescued by the tug, *Proctor.*

The wreck of the *St. Peter* was located in 1971 by Robert Bristol and his team of divers. Sitting upright and impressively intact, and rising a fair distance off the lake bottom, this schooner offers visiting divers views of a winch and pump sitting on the bow, both anchor catheads still in place, deadeyes lining the railings, and much more.

23. ROBERVAL

GPS:
DEPTH: 600+ feet LEVEL: Technical

LOCATION: About 12 miles off Oswego, NY.

The steel bulk freight steamer, *Roberval* (128' x 24' x 8'), built in Toronto in 1907, sank in a storm on Sept. 25, 1916. Because of the extreme depth, no diver has yet visited this shipwreck.

Right: The steamer, *Roberval.* CRIS KOHL COLLECTION

127

24. DAVID W. MILLS

GPS: 43° 26.628'/076° 35.095'
DEPTH: 25 feet   LEVEL: Novice

LOCATION: On Ford Shoal about 3.5 miles west-southwest of Oswego, New York.

The wooden steamer, *David W. Mills* (220' x 34' x 15'), stranded on August 11, 1919, because of smoke from forest fires in Canada disorienting the navigator. The ship, built in Cleveland in 1874 as the *Sparta*, broke up in later storms. The wreck lies broken and scattered.

The *David W. Mills*. CRIS KOHL COLLECTION

25. MARY KAY

LORAN: 16094.77/28669.81   GPS: 43° 27.705'/076° 33.198'
DEPTH: 42 feet   LEVEL: Novice-Intermediate

This 1957, 55-foot-long tug foundered on September 21, 1988, just west of Oswego, NY, with no loss of life. It is in excellent condition considering how shallow it sits.

26. CORMORANT

LORAN: GPS:
DEPTH: 135 feet   LEVEL: Advanced-Technical

This 1941 tug sank three miles north of Oswego, NY, on October 17, 1958, and remains very much intact, complete with a spotlight, a penetrable engine room, and the ship's wheel.

8. Sites near Lake Ontario

PHOTO ABOVE: The long-running **Peterborough Ice Floe Race** each March in Peterborough, Ontario, grandstands imaginative, unique, colorful, absurd and eccentric participants and inventions, all used to propel a block of ice down a fast-moving river in the quickest time. This non-scuba-diving event for divers offers competition, camaraderie and individuality, as bag-piping Todd Shannon attests while he musically encourages his wild team to victory. PHOTO BY CRIS KOHL

1. *Minnie*
2. *Otter*
3. **The Mint site**
4. *Ivy*
5. *Bruce*
6. *William King*
7. *Mansfield*
8. *Resolute*
9. *Quinte Queen*
10. **Braeside: Sand Point lighthouse**
11. **Red Pine Bay Wreck**

12. **Calabogie**
13. *Mayflower*
14. **Mazinaw Lake's highway signs**
15. **Bon Echo Provincial Park**
16. **Marmora's Crowe River**
17. **Fenelon Falls**
18. **Kirkfield Quarry**
19. **Lake Simcoe Sites**
20. **Seneca Lake State Park**
21. **Coal Barge in Seneca Lake**
22. **Keuka Lake: "Tanglewood barge"**

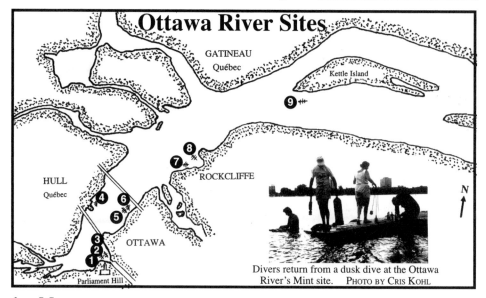

Divers return from a dusk dive at the Ottawa River's Mint site.   PHOTO BY CRIS KOHL

1. MINNIE

LOCATION: The Ottawa River, below Parliament Hill, just off the western end of Stirling's Wharf (also called the Ottawa Locks Wharfage). The 109-gross-ton rectangular barge, *Minnie* (95'5" long), constructed in 1873, sprang a leak and sank in 22' of water in 1930 next to the *Otter*. Beware of low visibility and boating traffic.

2. OTTER

LOCATION: The Ottawa River, below Parliament Hill, just off the western end of Stirling's Wharf (also called the Ottawa Locks Wharfage). On November 5, 1870, the 99-gross-ton tug, *Otter* (102'5" x 23'5"), built in 1840, burned to the waterline and sank in 22' of water while her captain socialized (i.e. drank) at the lockmaster's house. Beware of low visibility and boating traffic.

3. THE MINT SITE

LOCATION: The Ottawa River, in downtown Ottawa, just behind and a bit downstream from the Royal Canadian Mint. Head out of Ottawa on Sussex Drive. Just past the Mint, turn left at the first set of lights. This is Lady Grey Drive. From the parking lot just off Sussex, when you are facing the river, turn left down a short, rough road, or park in the lot and carry your gear down.

This intermediate-advanced shore dive will take the diver from 0' to 60' in the dark, tea-colored (take a dive light with you) waters along the river drop-off. Beware of some current and boating traffic. Use a divers down flag. In spite of this site's proximity to the place where Canada's money is made, it is not likely that you will find any here. Instead, you'll see old bottles, perhaps a clay pipe or two, lots of sunken logs and trees, and, if you're lucky, the 7-foot-long sturgeon which resembles a log -- until he swims away! His name is Oliver. Don't hurt him.

4. IVY

LOCATION: The Ottawa River, at the southeastern end of Hull Wharf at Hull. This is an intermediate-advanced dive in 18' to 22' of water in usually poor visibility (1' to 3'). The 100'-long sidewheeler, *Ivy,* built in 1871, exploded on September 21, 1890, while at dock.

5. *Bruce*

LOCATION: From the Mint site, drive downstream along that road off Lady Grey Drive to the Rideau Rowing Club. The 87-ton, 100-long wooden paddlewheel steamer, *Bruce*, built at Goderich, Ontario, in 1862, mysteriously burned to the waterline in March of 1875 and sank in 20 to 30 of water at the foot of the Rideau Canal Locks close to shore. This is an intermediate-advanced dive. Sometimes a rope is tied between the dock and the wreck to help overcome the low visibility. Boating traffic can be heavy, beware of en-

This postcard, circa 1906, shows the Rideau Canal Locks on the Ottawa River. Two shipwrecks lie close to where the tug is docked.   CRIS KOHL COLLECTION

tanglement in old fishing line (carry a knife or two), and there is a bit of a current (about one-and-a-half knots) which is usually no problem.

6. *William King*

LOCATION: The Ottawa River, next to the site of the *Bruce*. This is an advanced dive to 45' of water about 35' from shore in usually zero visibility. Launched as the *William Annesty* in Montreal in 1826, this 95'-long sidewheeler was abandoned in 1841.

7. *Mansfield*

LOCATION: The Ottawa River, near the Prime Minister's wharf. This is an inter-mediate-advanced dive to 25' of depth about 80' from shore in usually poor visibility. The steam-powered ferry, *Mansfield*, operated between Ottawa and Gatineau Point from 1888 to 1896 when, on May 7, she caught fire and burned to a complete loss with no lives lost.

8. *Resolute*

LOCATION: Rockcliffe Point at the northeastern end of Governor's Bay. This is an intermediate-advanced dive to 35' of water about 50' from shore in very limited visibility. This small (54' long) propeller-driven steam tug, built in 1875, caught fire on the evening of July 29, 1890 and was cast adrift to save the dock from damage. Beware of boating traffic.

9. *Quinte Queen*

LOCATION: The Ottawa River, southwest end of Kettle Island. This is an intermediate-advanced dive in 20' of poor visibility water about 260' from shore. Built in 1902 and launched as the *Salaberry* in Valleyfield, Quebec, the *Quinte Queen* ran as a pleasure ferry carrying picnickers to and from Kettle Island. In about 1920, the ship struck a sandbar and sank at its present location.

10. BRAESIDE: SAND POINT LIGHTHOUSE

LOCATION: About 40 miles west of Ottawa along the Ottawa River. This is an intermediate level shore dive to 60' of dark water (take along a dive light). The old cross-river ferry ran from here, and the lighthouse's base is the old 1910 wharf. About 300' downstream are the submerged remains of an older wharf which run out from shore. Old bottles have been found. Some current, plus boating and fishing traffic, are possible problems.

Sand Point lighthouse is used for divers' entries and exits.
PHOTO BY CRIS KOHL

11. RED PINE BAY WRECK

LOCATION: In the Ottawa River near Braeside, ON, just west of the Tembec Inc. facility. The remains of a small steamer about 77' long and 18' wide with a port list, bow pointing south, stern damaged, superstructure missing, rest in 20 to 30 of water. The wreck retains its engine, boiler, tiller, rudder, 4-bladed propeller, and, off the port side, the smokestack. There is evidence of a fire. Save Ontario Shipwrecks surveyed the site and found that the wreck may be that of the 75-ton *Levi Young* (84' x 19'), built at Sand Point, ON, in 1882 and burned in 1887. A picnic area with outhouses, launch ramp, and ample parking is at the site.

12. CALABOGIE

LOCATION: The town of Calabogie is about 50 miles west of Ottawa. From town, follow signs to Black Donald Lake. At this unusual divesite are the foundations of a small town (once the site of Ontario's richest graphite deposit) which was flooded by Ontario

Left: Warning signs try to keep careless divers out of the underwater mine. *Right:* The small bay area holds the main objects of interest for divers: the house foundations and the remains of an old car.
PHOTOS BY CRIS KOHL

Hydro in 1967. This is an intermediate dive to 30'. An old Packard and plenty of snails can also be seen here, but stay out of the old mineshaft nearby. Respect the rights of adjacent homeowners. Nearby Green Lake offers intermediate rock wall dives to a depth of 50' with plenty of smallmouth bass, perch, lake trout, sunfish and pike and usually good visibility.

13. *MAYFLOWER*

LOCATION: Lake Kamaniskeg, near Barry's Bay, Ontario. This wreck lies about 500' off the eastern shore of the lake, with a public boat launch at Combermere. A compass bearing of 040 degrees magnetic to the southern end of Mayflower Island and a bearing of 135 degrees magnetic to Sand Beach

The
Mayflower

Artwork © Adam Henley

The 59-ton sternwheeler, *Mayflower,* was built at Combermere in 1904.
PUBLIC ARCHIVES OF CANADA

will pinpoint the wreck site. The depth of this novice-intermediate dive is about 20'.

The wooden steamer, *Mayflower* (77' x 18' x 4'), sank in a storm on November 12, 1912, while underway from Barry's Bay to Combermere with 12 people and a corpse in a coffin. The floating coffin saved three people, but the other nine died. On the lake's sandy bottom, the *Mayflower's* hull, boiler, engine and paddlewheel, as well as resident bass and sunfish, may be seen. Save Ontario Shipwrecks has surveyed and placed a plaque on this wreck. Use a dive flag and respect the rights of cottage owners when diving here.

14. MAZINAW LAKE'S HIGHWAY SIGNS

LOCATION: Exactly 2.2 miles north of the Bon Echo Provincial Park entrance, turn right (east) on the Mazinaw Heights North Road (just before Bon Echo Villa). Drive for 1.1 miles and park along the

roadway just before the public boat ramp. This novice-intermediate shore dive will take you to 50' and beyond in tea-colored water. Between 20' and 40', you will find dozens of old, dumped Ministry of Transportation "King's Highway" signs indicating the highway number, curves and speed limits (don't swim too fast!). The water is dark and beware of submerged trees.

Scene of the old highway signs site in Mazinaw Lake.
PHOTO BY CRIS KOHL

Some of the old highway signs in Mazinaw Lake.
PHOTO BY CRIS KOHL

15. BON ECHO PROVINCIAL PARK

LOCATION: About 70 miles northwest of Kingston and about 100 miles from Ottawa. This intermediate-advanced shore or boat (preferred) dive offers variable depth along the best wall dive in Ontario. In this park, drive to the large parking lot at the Visitor Centre. From here, it is a brief hike to "The Narrows," a popular area for diving. Sometimes the local pontoon boat ferry is hired to take scuba divers to the cliff face to the northwest of "The Narrows."

Mazinaw Lake cliffs, Bon Echo Provincial Park, at sunset.
PHOTO BY CRIS KOHL

Cascading rocks and jagged cliffs slope down the rock face to a depth of about 50'. Beyond that is a sheer, straight wall plunging into the black abyss (the lake is 473' deep!). There is considerable fish life here. Above water, impressive cliffs rise 373' above the lake. Bring your camera.

16. MARMORA'S CROWE RIVER

LOCATION: At the town of Marmora, 28 miles north of Trenton, Ontario. Dive below the dam near the "Marmora Ironworks" historic marker to the west of town. Besides tea-colored water to a depth of 30', the novice-intermediate diver can see bass, lots of crayfish, bottles, cans and submerged trees. Beware of these trees and seasonal strong currents.

17. FENELON FALLS

LOCATION: This town sits 20 miles east of Lake Simcoe. It is a long swim across the river from the Ontario Hydro right-of-way to reach this advanced divesite. How railway cars ended up here, scattered and broken at a depth of 40' to 65', is a mystery. Huge iron wheels adorn the cars. Visibility is good, but the water is dark and cold, and the current can be strong. Beware also of the underwater overhangs which can create an overhead environment.

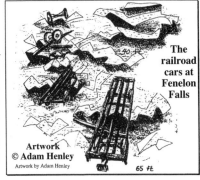

The railroad cars at Fenelon Falls

Artwork © Adam Henley
Artwork by Adam Henley
65 ft

18. KIRKFIELD QUARRY

LOCATION: Northeast of Toronto, just to the east of Lake Simcoe. The popular Kirkfield Quarry contains the usual quarry formations, rocks and sunfish. Depth is variable.

19. LAKE SIMCOE SITES

This is a large, inland lake north of Toronto. It has much boating traffic (use a diver down flag and caution), variable visibility from 3′ to 20′, and many dive sites, including:

Cook's Bay, depth from 10′ to 40′, with old bottles commonly found here.

"Four Friends Reef," north of the town of Keswick, in 30′, a manmade reef of rocks in 10′ by 10′ wooden crates, commemorating four fishermen who died in a boating accident.

Roches Point dock, to 30′, a lightly-grassed area rich with fish life (bass and pike).

Willow Beach, a shore dive to 25′, with ice-fishing remnants littering the bottom.

Jackson's Point, with the remains of the original wooden dock in 8′ to 20′.

Pefferlaw dock, a scrounge dive to a maximum of 30′, but low vis in river run-off.

Beaverton dock to 30′, again a good place to scrounge for things accidentally dropped.

Orillia and Barrie docks, to 28′, with a wide range of underwater debris.

Big Bay Point dock at Kempenfelt Bay, to a depth over 100′ close to shore. Use caution!

The *J. C. Morrison*

The wooden excursion steamer, *J. C. Morrison*. ARTIST UNKNOWN. CRIS KOHL COLLECTION

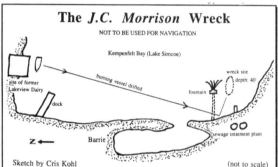

The *J.C. Morrison* Wreck
NOT TO BE USED FOR NAVIGATION

Sketch by Cris Kohl (not to scale)

The wreck of the sidewheel steamer, *J. C. Morrison,* lies in Lake Simcoe's Kempenfelt Bay at Barrie, ON. This ship, launched in 1854 and used as an excursion steamer on Lake Simcoe, caught fire on Aug. 4, 1857 while docked. Cut loose, the vessel drifted to the opposite shore, burned to the waterline and sank. Barrie diver Ron Marshall found the wreck in 1975. Remains include parts of the large paddlewheels and axles, bow, anchor, smokestack, boiler, plus small artifacts. The wreck lies 420′ from shore (so strong swimmers can do it as a shore dive) in 40′ between the fountain and the mini-golf course. Visibility is often poor.

20. SENECA LAKE STATE PARK

LOCATION: About 42 miles east-southeast of Rochester, New York. Highlights include good bottle diving and easy entrance and exit shoreline for novice-intermediate scuba divers and a depth of 15′, but avoid the swim area.

21. COAL BARGE IN SENECA LAKE

LOCATION: Off the center west side of Seneca Lake, at Severn Point at the end of Severn Road. This large coal barge lies in 70′ of water, and a boat is necessary as it is illegal to dive from the New York state boat launch.

22. KEUKA LAKE: "TANGLEWOOD BARGE"

LOCATION: On the east side of southern Keuka Lake, 40 miles southwest of Rochester, NY. A boat is needed to reach the "Tanglewood Barge" in 20′ to 65′ off 431 East Lake Road.

9. Eastern Lake Erie

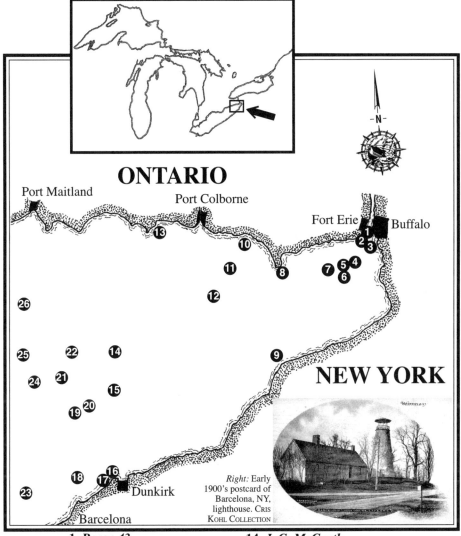

ONTARIO

Port Maitland

Port Colborne

Fort Erie

Buffalo

NEW YORK

Dunkirk

Barcelona

Right: Early 1900's postcard of Barcelona, NY, lighthouse. CRIS KOHL COLLECTION

1. *Barge 43*
2. *Alabama*
3. *W. C. Richardson*
4. *Acme* (tug)
5. *Finch*
6. *Tonawanda*
7. *O. W. Cheney*
8. *Briton*
9. *Dacotah*
10. *Raleigh*
11. *Dupuis No. 10*
12. *C. B. Benson*
13. *Marengo*
14. *J. G. McGrath*
15. *Brunswick*
16. *Annabell Wilson*
17. *Canadaway Creek*
18. *Passaic*
19. *Washington Irving*
20. *"Schooner C"*
21. *Acme* (propeller)
22. *Carlingford*
23. *Betty Hedger*
24. *"Schooner G" ("Admiralty Wreck")*
25. *George C. Finney*
26. *Niagara* (propeller)

1. BARGE 43

LORAN: 44933.28/59237.85	GPS: 42° 52.435'/078°54.098'
DEPTH: 30 feet	LEVEL: Intermediate

LOCATION: About one-quarter of a mile off Buffalo, New York, at the east harbor entrance just inside the western breakwater.

The old, beamy, steel *Barge 43* (150' x 36' x 12'1"), built at Manitowoc, Wisconsin, in 1911, sprang a leak 50 years later on May 24, 1961, while being used as a floating wood-burner when Buffalo's north harbor entrance was relocated and all the ancient wooden cribs were yanked up and had to be disposed of somehow. The sinking barge was moved from her workplace to her present location. She sits upright and shallow, with much boating traffic and fish life, as well as occasional current. For trained and experienced wreck penetration divers, there are several openings on the deck offering access below.

2. ALABAMA

LORAN:	GPS: 42° 52.399'/078° 54.720'
DEPTH: 35 feet	LEVEL: Intermediate

LOCATION: About 3/4 of a mile off Buffalo, New York, north harbor entrance.

The very old, 799-ton, wooden sidewheel steamer, *Alabama* (234' x 29' x 12'), was built, apparently poorly, at Detroit in 1848 and sank in a waterlogged condition only six years later on August 29, 1854. Realizing that the ship needed a major overhaul, and being told that the Buffalo drydock could not be tied up for that long, the *Alabama's* owners tried to take her to another drydock (at Huron, Ohio), but did not get very far. Arranging salvage took too long, and within a week, parts of the ship floated down the Niagara River. The engine was ultimately salvaged from the site in 1855.

The wreck is broken up and scattered in a busy boating area, with the identifiable portions including iron paddlewheel parts, the keel and a capstan.

3. W. C. RICHARDSON

LORAN: 44923.18/59228.87	GPS:
DEPTH: 40 feet	LEVEL: Intermediate

LOCATION: About 1.5 miles off Buffalo, New York, east harbor entrance.

Built at Cleveland, Ohio, in 1902, the flax-laden steel freighter, *W. C. Richardson* (374' x 48' x 28'), foundered off Waverly Shoal during the December 8, 1909, storm (which also sank the *Clarion* and the *Marquette & Bessemer #2* in Lake Erie) with the loss of five lives; the 14 other crewmembers were rescued by another ship. The dynamiting of this wreck four years later left it leveled to a height of eight feet off the bottom,

W. C. Richardson. CRIS KOHL COLLECTION

with considerable debris to the east of the main site in this area of heavy boating traffic.

4. ACME (TUG)

LORAN: 44922.12/59222.68	GPS: 42° 50.698'/078° 57.837'
DEPTH: 36 feet	LEVEL: Intermediate

LOCATION: Three and a half miles off Buffalo, New York, north harbor entrance.

The wooden tug, *Acme* (66'8" x 17' x 9'6"), built at Buffalo in 1893, sank on April 15, 1902, after a collision with the vessel she was towing through ice. The boiler, hull frames, rudder and steering mechanism remain identifiable at this busy boating traffic site.

5. *FINCH*

> **LORAN: 44940.85/59191.87**   **GPS: 42° 50.944'/078° 59.011'**
> **DEPTH: 45 feet**   **LEVEL: Intermediate**

LOCATION: This wreck lies about six miles west of Buffalo, New York, harbor.

The wooden barge, *Finch* (105' x 22'6" x 7'9"), began leaking in heavy seas and sank on August 2, 1883, with no loss of life. The relatively broken up site features chain, a capstan, the stove at the starboard quarter and the rudder about 100' to the northwest.

6. *TONAWANDA*

> **LORAN: 44902.17/59191.68**   **GPS: 42° 50.734'/078° 58.998'**
> **DEPTH: 47 feet**   **LEVEL: Intermediate**

LOCATION: Almost five miles off Buffalo, New York, harbor.

The wooden package steamer, *Tonawanda* (202'3" x 32'3" x 13'3"), was lost on October 18, 1870, in a severe storm which sank three other ships with great loss of life. Heavily loaded with a huge cargo of corn, flour and lead, she foundered with no loss of life. The ship had been built in 1856 at Buffalo, New York. One boiler was removed in 1875, and salvage efforts to raise the hull succeeded only in damaging it. In this immense collection of timbers, one hogging arch lies broken at midship starboard, while the stern offers views of the propeller and engine. Beware of the boating traffic around this site.

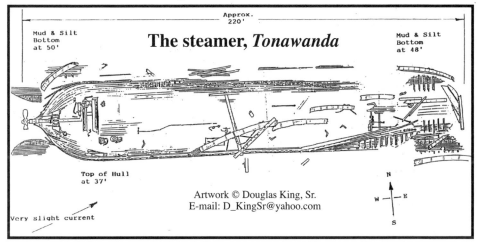

The steamer, *Tonawanda*

Artwork © Douglas King, Sr.
E-mail: D_KingSr@yahoo.com

7. *O. W. CHENEY*

> **LORAN:**   **GPS: 42° 50.282'/079° 00.457'**
> **DEPTH: 47 feet**   **LEVEL: Intermediate**

LOCATION: The wreck lies about six miles off Buffalo, New York, harbor.

Built in Buffalo, New York, in 1881, the wooden tug, *O. W. Cheney* (66' x 16' x 9'8"), sank on June 23, 1903, after having raced out to the steamer, *Chemung,* in hopes of contracting their business and towing their ship into Buffalo harbor. Instead, the *O. W. Cheney,* in its enthusiasm, accidentally crossed the path of the *Chemung* and was almost sliced in two in the subsequent collision. Two firemen below deck on the tug were killed.

Scuba divers found this shipwreck in 1991. The bow section of the hull has broken up completely, but the stern still holds the propeller and its shaft. The rudder lies about 100' to the west, while her boiler lies about 100' to the southwest. In between these recognizable parts is a large debris field of the tug's pieces and contents.

8. BRITON

LORAN:	**GPS: 42° 49.934'/079° 06.014'**
DEPTH: 21 feet	**LEVEL: Novice**

LOCATION: This site is about one-quarter mile southwest of the Point Abino Light.

A brand new captain, an aging ship which had twice been cut in two, some heavy seas with strong winds and a malfunctioning foghorn combined forces to create an embarassing situation. The steel freighter, *Briton* (296'2" x 40'4" x 21'), ran ashore at Point Abino, Ontario, on November 13, 1929, only a dozen miles out of Buffalo where she had just taken on a full cargo of grain. This ship, which had survived very active saltwater duty during World War I, for which she needed to be cut in half to pass her through the short locks of the old Welland Canal and then welded back together again, twice over, was now pounded to a total loss within two days by the Great Lakes' notorious gales of November. Fortunately, her entire crew was rescued by the Buffalo Coast Guard.

The steamer, *Briton*. CRIS KOHL COLLECTION

The wreckage from the steamer, *Briton*, which had been built in Cleveland in 1891, is widely scattered, as she was flattened by dynamite in the early 1930's, and her steel pieces lie jumbled among the large boulders off this part of Point Abino.

9. DACOTAH

LORAN: 44813.22/59119.24	**GPS:**
DEPTH: 20 to 25 feet	**LEVEL: Novice**

LOCATION: Off Sturgeon Point, New York.

The *Dacotah* (193'4" x 30'3" x 12'5") was a 698-ton wooden steamer which survived on the Great Lakes for only three years after she was launched at Cleveland in 1857. On November 24, 1860, this vessel (as well as two others) was pounded to pieces in a fierce storm with the loss of all 24 people on board.

This pre-Civil War ship's pieces (like the capstan and rudder) and general cargo (which included everything from pottery to horseshoes) lie strewn across a broad debris field.

10. RALEIGH

LORAN: 44868.88/59104.18	**GPS: 42° 51.890'/079° 09.260'**
DEPTH: 33 feet	**LEVEL: Novice-Intermediate**

LOCATION: The wreck lies about five miles off Port Colborne, Ontario.

On November 30 (yes, those nasty gales of November once again), 1911, the wooden freighter, *Raleigh* (235' x 34' x 23'9"), damaged her rudder in severe winds, ran aground and foundered in the heavy seas. Three people, the chief engineer, the male cook and the cook's wife, lost their lives. The *Raleigh* was an old vessel, having been built at Cleveland in 1871.

The ship's boiler, engine room machinery, propeller, rudder, bow winch and anchor chain with an anchor remain at this site.

The steamer, *Raleigh*. CRIS KOHL COLLECTION

11. DUPUIS NO. 10

LORAN:	GPS: 42° 49.090'/079° 13.295'
DEPTH: 60 feet	LEVEL: Intermediate

LOCATION: Four miles to the south-southeast off Port Colborne, Ontario.

The 316-ton, bulk freight, steel barge, *Dupuis No. 10* (143' x 32'3" x 6'), built in 1915 by Nicholson at Ecorse, Michigan, was already leaking when she was being towed towards Toronto for repairs on Dec. 24, 1997. Her generator ran out of gas, so the pumps failed, and the ship sank. The pumps were recovered and the barge sits deep in the lake bottom.

12. C. B. BENSON

LORAN:	GPS: 42° 46.260'/079° 14.612'
DEPTH: 87 feet	LEVEL: Advanced

LOCATION: The wreck lies approximately six miles south of Port Colborne, Ontario.

The sturdily-built three-masted barquentine, *C.B. Benson* (136'5" x 26' x 13'), constructed in 1873 at Port Clinton, Ohio, had wanderlust. A year after her launch, she crossed the Atlantic Ocean to Ireland with a heavy load of corn, and then spent seven years plying the trade routes between the British Isles and South America. She returned to the Great Lakes for a dozen years before being overpowered by the fury of a shallow freshwater

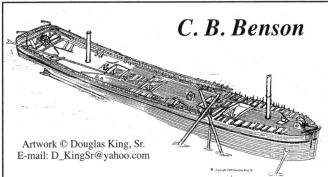

Left: The *C. B. Benson*. CRIS KOHL COLLECTION

C. B. Benson

Artwork © Douglas King, Sr.
E-mail: D_KingSr@yahoo.com

sea named Erie. The same storm which sank the *Dean Richmond* also claimed the coal-laden *C. B. Benson*, with the loss of all seven people on board.

The wreck of the *C. B. Benson* sits upright and is very intact. Wonderful nautical sights assist visiting divers in overcoming the tragedy of this site: belaying pins in the fife rail, deadeyes, blocks, a bilge pump, an anchor, the lifeboat davits and the ship's wheel still in place. To assist divers/boaters and to help protect this fabulous wreck, the site has had mooring blocks installed at both bow and stern.

13. MARENGO

GPS: 42° 51.122'/079° 20.589'
DEPTH: 23 feet   LEVEL: Novice

LOCATION: The wreck lies near Morgan's Point, west of Port Colborne, Ontario.

Built in 1873 at Milwaukee, Wisconsin, the huge schooner-barge, *Marengo* (195'6" x 32' x 15'5"), was driven ashore at Morgan's Point in a severe Lake Erie

The schooner-barge, *Marengo*.
CRIS KOHL COLLECTION

storm on October 12, 1912, which also sank the wooden steamer, *S.K. Martin*, off Erie, Pennsylvania. The steamer, *Lloyd S. Porter,* was towing the *Marengo,* loaded with a cargo of coal, when the powerful winds forced both ships ashore. The steamer, however, had the propulsion to free herself, while the helpless *Marengo* was only impaled further on the rocks until she broke up.

At such a shallow depth, the *Marengo* is broken up badly, with the wood of her frames, planks and decking intermingling with the vast debris area of her coal cargo.

14. *J. G. McGrath*

LORAN: 44739.69/58949.82	GPS: 42° 40.080'/079° 23.761'
DEPTH: 90 feet	LEVEL: Advanced

LOCATION: About 12 miles slightly west of due north of Dunkirk, New York.

Built in 1870 in St. Catharines, Ontario, by famed shipbuilder Louis Shickluna, the two-masted schooner, *J. G. McGrath* (104' x 26' x 12'), foundered in a severe storm on October 28, 1878, with her crew barely surviving by rowing 16 miles to the Canadian shore. The ship's heavy stone cargo caused great damage to the vessel when she hit the lake bottom, but her working gear (such as windlass and capstan) and other artifacts seem to be in place.

15. *Brunswick*

LORAN: 44706.72/58931.12	GPS: 42° 35.431'/079° 24.558'
DEPTH: 85 to 105 feet	LEVEL: Advanced

LOCATION: The wreck lies about 7.5 miles west-northwest of Dunkirk, New York.

The four-masted iron steamer, *Brunswick* (236'9" x 36'4" x 14'), sank during her first season afloat. On November 12, 1881, she collided with the smaller wooden schooner, *Carlingford* (see page 143), and both ships sank within the hour with loss of life. Three of the 15 people on board the *Brunswick* perished as the captain tried in vain to steam his ship to Dunkirk. The *Brunswick* had been launched on May 21, 1881, at Wyandotte, Michigan.

Although portions of the *Brunswick* have deteriorated (all four masts are down, for

The four-masted iron steamer, *Brunswick,* in 1881.
Cris Kohl Collection

Left to right: A shovel from the *Brunswick* appears welded into a strange position. A wooden double block lies on the deck. A heavy, concrete mooring block was accidentally placed in the middle of the ship. *Above:* Joyce Hayward takes a closer look at a *Brunswick* pump.   Photos by Cris Kohl

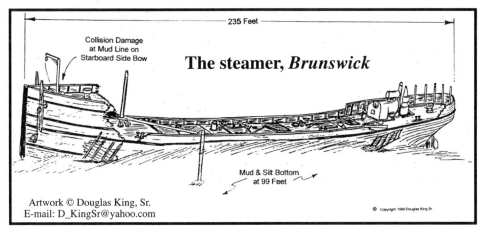

Collision Damage
at Mud Line on
Starboard Side Bow

235 Feet

The steamer, *Brunswick*

Mud & Silt Bottom
at 99 Feet

Artwork © Douglas King, Sr.
E-mail: D_KingSr@yahoo.com

© Copyright 1999 Douglas King Sr

example), the engine and boiler are in place at the stern, as are two capstans and the windlass on deck, as well as both bow anchors. The hole from the collision is on her starboard side.

16. ANNABELL WILSON

> **LORAN: 44682.77/58945.33**   **GPS: 42° 29.915'/079° 21.120'**
> **DEPTH: 52 feet**   **LEVEL: Intermediate**

LOCATION: About half a mile northwest of Dunkirk, New York, harbor.

Built in 1887 at Mount Clemens, Michigan, the three-masted schooner, *Annabell Wilson* (180' x 32'2" x 12'), foundered in heavy seas just as she and the tug that was towing her almost reached the safety of Dunkirk harbor on July 12, 1913. The schooner sank with her captain and his wife (the three crewmembers were rescued) and her cargo of coal. Beware of all the boating traffic so close to the harbor entrance.

17. CANADAWAY CREEK

LOCATION: About two miles west of Dunkirk, New York, harbor, following the shoreline past Point Gratiot Light. Avoid the shallow water across the bay at Van Buren Point. In depths of 20' to 25' can be found everything from tree stumps to a propeller, a couple of rudders and a water intake pipe.

The three-masted schooner, *Annabell Wilson*.   CRIS KOHL COLLECTION

18. PASSAIC

> **LORAN: 44648.45/58883.16**   **GPS: 42° 28.733'/079° 27.776'**
> **DEPTH: 74 to 84 feet**   **LEVEL: Advanced**

LOCATION: This wreck lies about six miles due west of Dunkirk, New York.

The wooden steamer, *Passaic* (198'3" x 27'7" x 11'4"), launched on May 24, 1862, at Buffalo, foundered on November 1, 1891, with a load of lumber. No lives were lost.

The remains of the *Passaic* were dynamited about 30 years ago by a "salvager" who thought he had the wreck of the *Dean Richmond*! The wreck's sides have collapsed outwardly, revealing the large boiler and the entire steam engine, including the crankcase and connecting rods, right to the keel. At the stern are the rudder, a four-bladed propeller and propeller shaft. The bow displays an anchor and an anchor windlass. The site is usually buoyed.

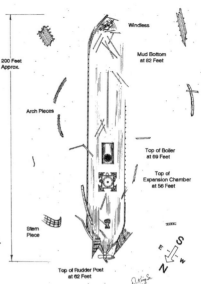

Above: The wooden steamer, *Passaic.* CRIS KOHL COLLECTION
Right: The *Passaic* shipwreck site. Artwork © Douglas King, Sr.
E-mail: D_KingSr@yahoo.

19. WASHINGTON IRVING

LORAN:	GPS: 42° 32.365'/079° 27.641'
DEPTH: 120 feet	LEVEL: Advanced

LOCATION: This wreck lies almost seven miles northwest of Dunkirk, NY.

The small, two-masted schooner, *Washington Irving* (81'1" x 20'1" x 7'7"), disappeared mysteriously one weekend (July 7 or 8, 1860) with all six people who were on board. Built in 1845 at Cleveland, the *Washington Irving* carried a load of pig iron and coal on her final voyage. The weather was calm and there were no reports of fire or collision on the lake, so her complete disappearance is a mystery. Today, her upright masts and intact bowsprit make her look like she's ready to sail once more. A windlass and the starboard anchor and chain adorn the bow. The port quarter, however, is partially buried.

20. "SCHOONER C"

LORAN:	GPS: 42° 33.232'/079° 27.186'
DEPTH: 115 feet	LEVEL: Advanced

LOCATION: The wreck lies about seven miles north-northwest of Dunkirk, NY.

This unidentified schooner (or possibly a brigantine) lies nearly covered in silt, with the stern castle offering the highest relief of 10' off the bottom. The bow retains both wooden stock anchors, one in place and the other lying in the mud off the wreck. There appear to be eight square windows at the stern, with empty lifeboat davits hanging overhead. This wreck was located by Garry Kozak in 1977 during his quest to find the *Dean Richmond.*

21. ACME (PROPELLER)

LORAN:	GPS: 42° 36.598'/079° 29.848'
DEPTH: 130 feet	LEVEL: Advanced

LOCATION: The wreck lies about 11 miles north-northwest of Dunkirk, New York.

A wooden steamer propeller-driven and hog-arched, the *Acme* (190'10" x 33'3" x 12'9"), carrying a cargo of general farm products (corn, flour, beef, cowhides), sprang a leak and sank with no lives lost on November 4, 1867. The ship had been built at Buffalo in 1856.

The *Acme's* steam engine sits exposed on the open hull, while her hogging arches rise about 12 feet off the floor of the lake. Her windlass and other items provide diver interest.

The wreck of the wooden steamer, *Acme,* makes an interesting site, with its hog arching braces clearly in view.   PHOTOS BY JON VEBER

22. *CARLINGFORD*

LORAN:	GPS: 42° 39.274'/079° 28.596'
DEPTH: 90 to 105 feet	LEVEL: Advanced

LOCATION: The *Carlingford* lies about 13 miles north-northwest of Dunkirk, NY.

The 12-year-old three-masted schooner, *Carlingford* (154'7" x 31'1" x 12'3"), loaded with wheat, sank in the middle of Lake Erie after a collision with the iron bulk freight steamer, *Brunswick* (see page 140) on November 12, 1881. Built at Port Huron, Michigan, in 1869, the *Carlingford* lost one life from the seven on board in this tragic sinking, and the *Brunswick,* which also sank, lost several.

The *Carlingford*, one of many shipwrecks located by Garry Kozak in the early 1980's in his quest for the legendary *Dean Richmond,* sits upright in water slightly shallower than the *Brunswick*. The deepest point is found inside the hull at the bow, a location requiring special penetration diving training, experience, preparation and attitude. The hole in the schooner's side offers sufficient proof of the collision. The stern is somewhat broken up. Of diver interest are an anchor, rudder, masts and numerous blocks.

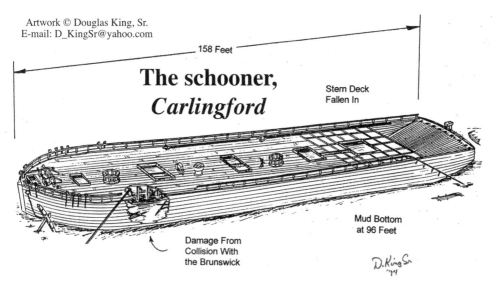

Artwork © Douglas King, Sr.
E-mail: D_KingSr@yahoo.com

158 Feet

The schooner, *Carlingford*

Stern Deck Fallen In

Mud Bottom at 96 Feet

Damage From Collision With the Brunswick

D. King Sr. '94

Left: A mast rail on the schooner, *Carlingford.*

Right: A row of hanging knees below deck on the *Carlingford.*

PHOTOS BY
CRIS KOHL

23. BETTY HEDGER

LORAN:	GPS: 42° 25.118'/079° 36.535'
DEPTH: 115 feet	LEVEL: Advanced

LOCATION: The wreck lies about 12 miles due west of Dunkirk, NY.

This 113' barge, built in 1927 at Kingston, NY, was sulfur-laden and in tow of the tug, *Ballenas,* on Nov. 2, 1937, when a powerful storm struck and the *Hedger* sank. Massive framing rests exposed, with mounds of sulfur in place. The wreck, found by Garry Kozak in 1975, features a small pilot house, portholes, an anchor, a small winch, among other items.

24. "SCHOONER G" (ALSO CALLED "ADMIRALTY WRECK")

LORAN:	GPS:
DEPTH: 110-170 feet	LEVEL: Technical

LOCATION: The wreck lies about 12 miles northwest of Dunkirk, NY.

This unidentified schooner, about 90' long with a beam of 20', sits upright in 170' of water, with both masts rising to a depth of 110'. The deck level rests at about 15' off the lake bottom, providing excellent relief. Several features suggest that this is an old wreck: she has a tiller instead of a wheel for steering, a detachable or hinged bowsprit (to enable passage in tight quarters such as small canal locks), and a carved "fiddle" figurehead. The stern offers the rudder, two large open windows, and an intact cabin. An anchor sits on the port bow next to the windlass, while two open hatches and a bilge pump grace the deck.

25. GEORGE C. FINNEY

LORAN:	GPS: 42° 40.087'/079° 36.250'
DEPTH: 100 feet	LEVEL: Advanced

LOCATION: The wreck lies about 15 miles south of Port Maitland, Ontario.

The three-masted schooner, *George C. Finney* (130' x 26'5" x 10'), built in 1866 at Oswego, NY, departed Toledo for Buffalo with wheat on Nov. 14, 1891. Sunk by a storm, all 7 crew were lost. Her masts stuck out of the water a week later. Today the masts are down and most decking is gone, but the site sports a windlass, anchors, winch, and bilge pump.

26. NIAGARA

LORAN:	GPS: 42° 44.315'/079° 36.261'
DEPTH: 90 feet	LEVEL: Advanced

Lying about ten miles south of Port Maitland, Ontario, the wooden steamer, *Niagara* (135'6" x 26'3" x 12'2"), built at St. Catharines, Ontario, in 1875, foundered in a storm with all 16 hands and a lumber cargo on Dec. 5, 1899. Stern broken and sides collapsed, she features an exposed engine, a winch, and a windlass.

The *Niagara.* CRIS KOHL COLLECTION

144

10. Lake Erie's Long Point

Long Point is a long, slender, sandy spit of land which juts halfway across Lake Erie from the north shore. Hundreds of ships met with calamity as a result of this obstacle to navigation and aberration of nature. This chapter covers many of those shipwrecks plus others in this general area.

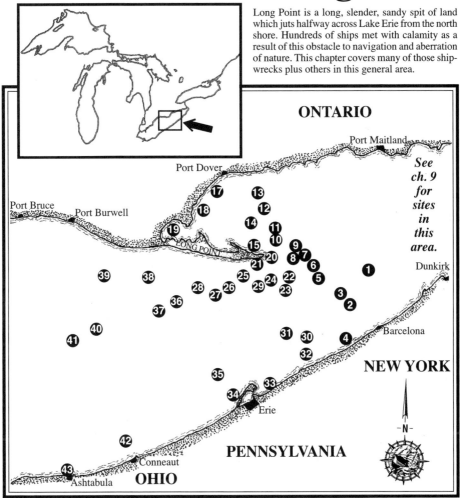

1. "Barge F"	15. *Pascal P. Pratt*	29. *Andrew B.*
2. *John J. Boland*	16. *Siberia*	30. *Dean Richmond*
3. *George Whelan*	17. *Cecil J.*	31. *Indiana*
4. *City of Rome*	18. Tire reef	32. *S. K. Martin*
5. *Oxford*	19. *Ontario?*	33. *Canobie*
6. "Cracker Wreck"	20. *Henry Clay*	34. *Philip D. Armour*
7. *Persian*	21. *C. W. Elphicke*	35. *Charles Foster*
8. *Straubenzie*	22. *Smith*	36. *Aycliffe Hall*
9. *Swallow*	23. "Arches"/*Oneida?*	37. Drill rig
10. "T-8" schooner	24. "Stern Castle"	38. *Majestic*
11. *Brown Brothers*	25. *Atlantic*	39. *Barge No. 3 or No. 4*
12. *Wilma*	26. *St. James*	40. *William H. Stevens*
13. Nanticoke Shoal	27. *Trade Wind*	41. *James H. Reed*
14. "17-Fathom Wreck"	28. "Crystal Wreck"	42. *John B. Lyon*
		43. Harbor wrecks

1. "BARGE F"

GPS: 42° 30.105'/079° 41.005'
DEPTH: 145 feet   LEVEL: Technical

LOCATION: The wreck lies about 12 miles north of Barcelona, NY.

This unidentified barge was given the name "Barge F" by Garry Kozak when he found her during his long quest to locate the legendary *Dean Richmond*. In fact, he located 32 shipwrecks in Lake Erie between 1976 and 1983 before he finally found the *Richmond*!

This barge rises 8' off the lake bottom, and features many nautical items of interest, e.g. two anchors lying flat on the bow, a windlass, a deck winch, the rudder, two pumps, and the ship's wheel!

Right: There is much to see on the unidentified "Barge F." ART BY CLUE (CLEVELAND UNDERWATER EXPLORERS) WHICH SURVEYED THIS WRECK SITE, COURTESY OF CLUE AND KEVIN MAGEE

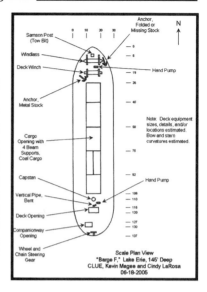

2. *JOHN J. BOLAND, JR.*

LORAN: 44545.48/58721.09   GPS: 42° 22.794'/079° 44.000'
DEPTH: 95 to 136 feet   LEVEL: Advanced-Technical

LOCATION: The wreck lies just over seven miles northwest of Barcelona, NY.

Built as the *Tyneville* in England in 1928, the steel freighter, *John J. Boland, Jr.* (252'9" x 43'4" x 17'8"), foundered in a storm on October 5, 1932, because of a hatch left open to accommodate a pile of 400 excess tons of coal that would not fit below deck. Eventually the hold filled with enough water to capsize the ship, and she sank in four minutes, taking four

Above: The steel steamer, *John J. Boland, Jr.* CRIS KOHL COLLECTION
Right and below: The *Boland's* railing and propeller offer dramatic views.   PHOTOS BY CRIS KOHL

lives with her.

The *John J. Boland, Jr.* lies on her starboard side, with her four-bladed propeller and rudder the highlights at the stern. One anchor is in the hull, while the other one lies on the lake bottom just off the wreck. Railings, ladders, portholes and the huge cargo holds are still intact. Penetration at this silt-covered site should be done only by the best-trained, most-experienced and utterly-prepared divers.

3. GEORGE WHELAN

LORAN:	GPS: 42° 25.560′/079° 44.991′
DEPTH: 150 feet	LEVEL: Technical

LOCATION: This steel wreck lies about eight miles northwest of Barcelona, NY .

Built at Toledo, Ohio, as the *Erwin L. Fisher* in 1910, this ship underwent several name changes: to *Port De Caen* in 1915, to *Bayersher* in 1922, to *Claremont* in 1923, and finally to *George J. Whelan*, (220′ x 40′ x 15′3″) in 1930 just before its loss. Her final namesake was the President of a quarry company on Kelley's Island who lived from 1872 until 1945. This ship sank earlier in the Detroit River (May 4, 1911), and after it hit a mine in the English Channel in World War I (1918), but was repaired each time. Finally, the vessel swamped and sank in Lake Erie with 15 lives and a limestone cargo on July 29, 1930. There were only six survivors. Garry Kozak and Jim Herbert located this shipwreck on Oct. 13, 2005. The wreck, 3/4 over on her port side, offers views of the propeller, rudder, lanterns, life rings, port holes, anchor, life boat, doors, hatches, stairs, and railings.

Left: The steel steamer, *George J. Whelan,* when it was still named the *Erwin L. Fisher.*

Right: Even the far-away *New York Times* newspaper gave the tragic loss of the *George J.Whelan* considerable ink and space.

CRIS KOHL COLLECTION

SAND BOAT CAPSIZES; 15 LOST IN LAKE ERIE

All But Six of Crew Are Caught Asleep or in Fire Hold When Craft Sinks.

SURVIVORS IN LAKE 2 HOURS

Picked Up by Buffalo Collier—Federal Inspectors Order an Inquiry Into Overloading.

Special to The New York Times.
ERIE, Pa., July 29.—Fifteen of the crew of the sandsucker George J. Whelan were drowned when the dredge capsized in Lake Erie near Dunkirk, N. Y., early this morning

4. CITY OF ROME

LORAN: 44507.82/58710.48	**GPS: 42° 17.167'/079° 43.075'**
DEPTH: 15 feet	**LEVEL: Novice**

LOCATION: The wreck lies about one-half mile off Ripley, NY, west of Barcelona.

The wooden steamer, *City of Rome*, (268'2" x 40'2" x 20'3"), built at Cleveland in 1881, burned to a complete loss after being purposely grounded on May 7, 1914. No lives were lost. The wooden hull and some machinery remain at this site, with the propeller lying where "salvage divers" had abandoned it at the base of the cliff 750' from the main wreckage. This is a boat dive, since the property adjacent to the wreck is private.

The steamer, *City of Rome*. CRIS KOHL COLLECTION

5. OXFORD

LORAN: 44558.67/58671.69	**GPS: 42° 28.852'/079° 51.839'**
DEPTH: 164 feet	**LEVEL: Technical**

LOCATION: The wreck lies about 25 miles north-northeast of Erie, Pennsylvania.

This early Great Lakes two-masted, 114-foot-long brig, built in 1842 at Three Mile Bay, New York, sank in a collision with the steamer, *Cataract,* on May 30, 1856, with five of the eight people on board the doomed vessel perishing, including Captain John Lee, his wife and his daughter. The *Cataract* continued her journey to Buffalo.

Also nicknamed the "Tiller Wreck" and the "Crowsnest Wreck" (because those items comprise very noticable parts of this shipwreck's character), the *Oxford* makes a unique subject for study. Besides having a tiller (instead of a wheel) and a crowsnest, the vessel displays a windlass, a winch, a bilge pump, two bow anchors and an offset centerboard. Collision damage can be seen in the starboard bow.

Left: The *Oxford's* crowsnest and its tiller are its two most distinguishing features. *Below:* The *Oxford's* unusual bilge pump. *Below right:* A burbot's tail remains unhidden in the *Oxford's* winch. PHOTOS BY CRIS KOHL

6. "CRACKER WRECK"

LORAN: 44590.46/58687.11	**GPS: 42° 33.492'/079° 51.652'**
DEPTH: 190 feet	**LEVEL: Technical**

LOCATION: The wreck lies almost ten miles east of Long Point Light.

This unidentified, three-masted schooner, approximately 120 feet in length, appears to have been built in an early (pre-Civil War) style, and sank so slowly that the usual air pressure build-up from water entering the hull did not blow off the weaker superstructure items, such as the vessel's cabin. Attesting to the ship's intactness are her anchors, a bilge pump, and an ornately carved bow. A mast lies along the port side.

7. PERSIAN

LORAN: 44581.27/58661.33	**GPS: 42° 33.777'/079° 54.703'**
DEPTH: 195 feet	**LEVEL: Technical**

LOCATION: The wreck lies seven miles east of Long Point Light.

The wooden steamer, *Persian* (243' x 40' x 19'), sank on August 26, 1875, while enroute with a grain cargo from Chicago to Buffalo. A fire which started in the coalbunker spread quickly. The crew became so involved in fighting the flames that they failed to notice that their lifeboats were being destroyed. As a measure of desperation, floating hatch covers saved all 19 people on board, who were picked up by ships that were attracted by the smoke.

The *Persian* (her charred remains include the engine, boiler, and propeller) and the *Van Straubenzie* (#8) are closest among known sites to sitting in Lake Erie's deepest part (215').

8. SIR C. T. VAN STRAUBENZIE

LORAN:	**GPS: 42° 32.599'/079° 55.432'**
DEPTH: 200 feet	**LEVEL: Technical**

The wreck lies seven miles southeast of the Long Point Light. The three-masted schooner named after a British military man, the *Sir C. T. Van Straubenzie* (127'7" x 26'2" x 12'2"), built by the famous Louis Shickluna at St. Catharines, ON, in 1875, sank on Sept. 27, 1909, after a fatal collision with the steamer, *City of Erie*, in which 3 lives were lost. On site are the ship's windlass, yawl boat, wheel, bell (no name), anchors, and upright forward mast. This wreck was found by Garry Kozak on July 9, 1982, during his quest for the *D. Richmond*.

Left: The *Sir C. T. Van Straubenzie*. CRIS KOHL COLLECTION

9. SWALLOW

LORAN: 44572.08/58645.31	**GPS: 42° 34.899'/079° 56.451'**
DEPTH: 190 feet	**LEVEL: Technical**

LOCATION: The wreck lies about five and a half miles east of Long Point Light.

The wooden steamer, *Swallow* (133'8" x 25'8" x 10'8"), built at Trenton, Michigan, in 1873, was caught in a severe storm which swamped and sank the ship on October 18, 1901, but not before she caught on fire. Fortunately, no lives were lost, as the crew transferred safely to the barge which they were towing. The wreck today displays fire damage. Her engine, boiler and bow anchor are still in place. Beware of commercial fishing nets.

The steamer, *Swallow*. CRIS KOHL COLLECTION

10. THE "T-8" SCHOONER (THE "22 1/2 FATHOM WRECK")

> LORAN: GPS: 42° 35.222'/080° 01.333'
> DEPTH: 145 feet   LEVEL: Technical

LOCATION: Approximately three miles north-northeast of Long Point Light.

This unidentified two-masted schooner, discovered in the 1960's and nicknamed the "22 1/2 Fathom Wreck" (renamed "T-8" when she was the eighth target in a 1995 sidescan survey) sank in a collision, as evidenced by hull damage. Her centerboard and surprisingly intact wooden railings offer interesting exploration for the specially trained and experienced.

11. *BROWN BROTHERS*

> LORAN: 44583.77/58618.08   GPS: 42° 37.644'/080°005.905'
> DEPTH: 120 feet   LEVEL: Advanced

LOCATION: This site is located almost six miles off Long Point Light.

The wooden fishing tug, *Brown Brothers* (75'2" x 16'5" x 7'7"), is a relatively modern shipwreck, having gone to the bottom of Lake Erie on October 28, 1959. This aging, low-freeboard ship foundered in a storm while being towed by another tug. No lives were lost. Built in 1915, her original steam propulsion system was replaced with diesel in the early 1950's. She sits upright, with her wheel lying flat near the bow. Fish life is abundant.

The fishing tug, *Brown Brothers*.
CRIS KOHL COLLECTION

12. *WILMA*

> LORAN: 44607.4/58620.1   GPS: 42° 42.151'/080° 02.065'
> DEPTH: 74 feet   LEVEL: Intermediate-Advanced

LOCATION: The wreck lies ten miles off Port Dover, Ontario.

Built at Collingwood, Ontario, in 1911, the steam-powered fishing tug, *Wilma* (67'9" x 16' x 6'7"), was a bit early in trying to reach the fishing grounds. Ice punctured her hull on April 14, 1936, and she sank with no lives lost.

The main attractions at this popular site are the forward hatch and ladder, the boiler, the smokestack lying along the port side, portholes still in place at the bow, and the rudder and propeller at the stern. All in all, this is very much a fun dive, but beware of commercial fishing nets around this wreck; not all of the netting may be lying flat due to zebra mussel attachment, and it's no fun finding oneself entangled in it. Take along a dive knife or two just in case.

13. NANTICOKE (FIVE-MILE) SHOAL

> LORAN: GPS: 42° 44.238'/080° 04.002'
> DEPTH: To 30 feet   LEVEL: Novice

LOCATION: This shoal is about six miles east-southeast from Port Dover, Ontario.
The attraction of exploring this natural reef rests with the abundance of fish.

14. "17-FATHOM WRECK"

> LORAN: 44585.02/58602.77   GPS: 42° 39.101'/080° 03.142'
> DEPTH: 106 feet   LEVEL: Advanced

LOCATION: The wreck is located almost 12 miles off Port Dover, Ontario.

151

This unidentified shipwreck was a small (about 75' long) two-masted schooner. There is evidence of fire damage. Sitting upright on the silty lake bottom, with a slight starboard list, this wreck's main attractions are the windlass and chain locker at the bow, plus hatches near the stern. A mast lies across the starboard rail, close to the concrete mooring block.

15. *PASCAL P. PRATT*

LORAN:	GPS: 42° 33.665'/080° 05.558'
DEPTH: 24 feet	LEVEL: Novice

LOCATION: This wreck lies about one mile off Gravelly Bay, three miles from the tip of Long Point.

The wooden bulk freighter, *Pascal P. Pratt* (272'4" x 40'5" x 21'5"), caught on fire while hauling a coal cargo from Buffalo to Milwaukee. Her captain grounded her on Long

The wooden steamer, *Pascal P. Pratt*.
CRIS KOHL COLLECTION

Point, where the ship burned to a total loss on November 16, 1908, with no lives lost. The vessel had been constructed in Cleveland in 1888.

The *Pascal P. Pratt* is fairly broken up due to the ravages of ice,

STEAMER BURNS
TO WATER'S EDGE
___

Pascal Pratt is Total Loss in Lake Erie—Crew Safe in Port Dover.

Special to The Free Press.
Cleveland, Ohio, November 19. — The wooden steamer Pascal P. Pratt is on the beach near Long Point, Lake Erie, burned to the water's edge.

The crew of the steamer reached Port Dover, on the Canadian shore,

News of the *Pascal Pratt's* fiery demise.
CRIS KOHL COLLECTION

wind and waves over the years. The wreck sits on a sand bottom, and the boiler is about 50' away from the main wreckage, surrounded by coal. The boilers and the huge propeller are the site's highlights. Bass and perch abound at this site.

16. *SIBERIA*

LORAN: 44538.57/58555.02	GPS:
DEPTH: 19 feet	LEVEL: Novice

LOCATION: The wreck lies on Bluff Bar near the north side of Long Point, about 15 miles from Port Dover, Ontario.

The wooden bulk freight steamer, *Siberia* (272' x 39' x 18'), was built at West Bay City, Michigan, in 1882. More than two decades later, this ship was one of the victims (along with the schooner-barge, *Tasmania,* the schooner, *Mautenee*, and the steamer, *Sarah E. Sheldon*) of the massively violent storm of October 20, 1905. Heading for Buffalo with a cargo of barley, the *Siberia* stranded in the storm and broke apart after her crew had been rescued.

For some strange reason, "salvagers" used dynamite to blow this wreck apart in the early 1960's. What remains today is scattered far and wide, with the boiler and keelson remaining the highlights of this site. Shifting sands cover and uncover parts of this wreck.

The steamer, *Siberia*. CRIS KOHL COLLECTION

17. Cecil J.

> **LORAN: 44589.27/58529.88**   **GPS: 42° 45.777'/080° 13.702'**
> **DEPTH: 17 feet**   **LEVEL: Novice**

LOCATION: The wreck lies about two miles southwest of Port Dover, Ontario.

Built at Erie, Pennsylvania, in 1915, and launched as the steamboat, *Rambler,* the 14-gross-ton, (later) gasoline-powered fishing tug, *Cecil J.* (47'5" x 12'5" x 3'9"), was set ablaze and scuttled by her owner in 1943 after she had provided years of sinkings, a collision and other misfortunes. The scattered remains attract considerable fish life.

18. Tire reef

> **GPS: 42° 41.039'/080° 08.496'**
> **DEPTH: 23 feet   LEVEL: Novice**

LOCATION: About one mile off Turkey Point, Ontario.

An artificial reef of over 1,000 old, rubber tires was created in 1992 for the creation of a fish habitat, which has attracted large numbers of fish, mainly bass, since then.

In the mid-1980's, a similar tire reef project took place on Rondeau Bay.
PHOTO SET-UP BY CRIS KOHL

19. Ontario?

> **LORAN: 44511.85/58436.63**   **GPS: 42° 38.107'/080° 22.016'**
> **DEPTH: 9 feet**   **LEVEL: Novice**

LOCATION: The wreck lies off Port Rowan in Long Point's inner bay.

General opinion is that what little remains of this shipwreck (keel, framing, some planking, two centerboard boxes and mast steps) came from the three-masted schooner, *Ontario* (130' x 23'), which sank in a storm on August 27, 1858, with the crew barely escaping with their lives. The ship had been built in Quebec City in 1851. Many artifacts, such as both centerboards, an anchor, and many smaller items, were removed from this site. Bass abound here, but beware of entanglement in weeds later in the dive season.

20. Henry Clay (The "lighthouse wreck")

> **LORAN: 44547.69/58589.12**   **GPS: 42° 33.072'/080° 02.717'**
> **DEPTH: 15 feet**   **LEVEL: Novice**

LOCATION: The wreck lies about a quarter of a mile off Long Point Light.

The wooden steamer, *Henry Clay* (134'4" x 22'8" x 11'), was named after a political figure and popular orator (Mansfield listed six Great Lakes vessels with that name!). But this vessel had a particularly tragic demise. During a violent gale on October 25, 1851, the steamer's cargo shifted and smashed the engine, putting the ship, crew and passengers at the mercy of the weather. Of the 17 people on board, only one sailor survived by clinging to an overturned yawl and reaching shore. The ship's cargo of baled wool washed ashore for weeks after the sinking. Keelson, framing timbers, and fish remain at this site.

21. C. W. Elphicke

> **LORAN:**   **GPS:**
> **DEPTH: 22 feet**   **LEVEL: Novice**

LOCATION: About one-and-a-quarter miles west from Long Point Light.

The wooden bulk freighter, *C. W. Elphicke* (273' x 41'3" x 23'), built at Trenton, Michigan, in 1889, sprang a leak on October 19, 1913, and was purposely run aground at Long Point to prevent her from sinking in deep water. The crew was rescued, but the ship

Great Lakes Highlight No. 6

BATTLE FOR THE *ATLANTIC*

LORAN: 44522.68/58561.09   GPS: 42° 30.616'/080° 05.091'
DEPTH: 135 to 160 feet   LEVEL: Technical

LOCATION: The wreck lies about three miles south-southwest of Long Point Light. The luxurious sidewheel steamer, *Atlantic* (265'7" x 33' x 14'6"), built at Newport (now Marine City), Michigan, in 1849, sank with enormous loss of life (about 150-200 people perished) after a night-time collision with the steamer, *Ogdensburg,* on August 20, 1852. Both vessels continued on their separate ways, but the *Ogdensburg* turned around when her captain heard the screams of the *Atlantic's* panicked passengers when

The luxurious paddlewheel steamer, *Atlantic.* CRIS KOHL COLLECTION

Left: The luxurious paddlewheel steamer, *Atlantic.*
Above: Hardhat divers competed to bring up the original "treasure" of the *Atlantic* in the 1850's.   CRIS KOHL COLLECTION

they became aware that their ship was sinking. Subsequent salvage descriptions, such as the competition between hardhat divers Johnny Green and Elliot Harrington in the 1850's, and, much later, the *Atlantic's* 1984 discoverer, Mike Fletcher of Port Dover, Ontario, fighting California pirates in the 1990's who claimed that they had just discovered this "treasure wreck" in Canadian waters and had the rights to salvage everything on it (eventually, the courts ruled against them), make for fascinating stories.

The famous/infamous *Atlantic's* giant paddlewheels rise dramatically from the lake bottom, where she sits upright but is slowly collapsing. The intact holds contain everything from farm implements to books. Penetration diving, particularly at this depth, is only for the highly trained, experienced and prepared. A double ship's wheel lies flat in the silty bottom.

Left: When California pirates claimed ownership of the "treasure" wreck, *Atlantic,* in Canadian waters, Mike Fletcher fought back in a highly publicized conflict. CRIS KOHL COLLECTION. *Right:* Mike Fletcher, David Barrington study Bob McGreevy's original artwork of the *Atlantic.* PHOTO BY CRIS KOHL

The steamer, *C. W. Elphicke.*
CRIS KOHL COLLECTION

The *Elphicke,* wrecked off Long Point, Ontario.
CRIS KOHL COLLECTION

broke in two and, along with her huge cargo of wheat, became a total loss. This broken up shipwreck "comes and goes" in Long Point's shifting sands; a south wind will uncover her.

22. SMITH

LORAN: 44530.12/58607.09	GPS: 42° 28.481'/079° 59.064'
DEPTH: 165 feet	LEVEL: Technical

LOCATION: This wreck lies about six miles southeast of Long Point Light.

The aging tug, *Smith* (120' x 22' x 10'), built in 1881 at Buffalo, foundered while in tow on October 25, 1930. Her wheelhouse remains intact, with her wheel, a chadburn (telegraph), her whistle on top of the wheelhouse, and a mushroom anchor on the port bow.

The tug, *Smith.* CRIS KOHL COLLECTION

23. "ARCHES"/ONEIDA?

LORAN: 44516.03/58586.86	GPS: 42° 27.471'/080° 01.017'
DEPTH: 129 to 160 feet	LEVEL: Technical

LOCATION: This wreck lies about 6.5 miles south-southwest of Long Point Light, or about 21 miles north of Erie, Pennsylvania.

The length of this shipwreck, the upright hogging arches rising about 30' off the bottom and the fact that the wreck has many very visible barrels in its holds, all lead one to believe that it is indeed the package steamer, *Oneida* (138'3" x 24'1" x 11'). On November 11, 1852, the *Oneida,* loaded with 3,500 barrels of flour, left Cleveland for Buffalo, but fell victim to an extremely destructive storm. The ship was lost with all hands (about 20). Except for the decking being mostly missing, the shipwreck is intact, displaying rudder, propeller, boilers, engine, bow anchors, upright hogging arches and barrels viewable from her open hatches.

24. "STERN CASTLE"

LORAN: 44529.98/58583.37	GPS: 42° 30.301′/080° 02.383′
DEPTH: 185 feet	LEVEL: Technical

LOCATION: About three miles west of Long Point Light, 24 miles north of Erie, PA.

The stern of this unidentified two-masted schooner rises sharply off the lake bottom (hence the nickname). Her bow also rises, with the vessel's midsection being mostly buried in the lake bottom. Her masts and ship's wheel are still in place.

25. *ATLANTIC* -- SEE PAGE 154.

26. *ST. JAMES*

The deck of the *St. James* exhibits many interesting items. DIGITAL IMAGE BY DAN LINDSAY OF SEA-VIEW DIVING (SEE PAGE 156 FOR THE AD)

The ship's wheel from the *St. James* still remains in place in its original position. DIGITAL IMAGE BY DAN LINDSAY OF SEA-VIEW DIVING (SEE PAGE 156 FOR THE AD)

The ornately carved scroll figurehead on the schooner *St. James* suggested that the wreck was an older vessel.
PHOTO BY JOHN VEBER

> **LORAN: 44491.03/58530.38**   **GPS: 42° 27.100′/080° 07.328′**
> **DEPTH: 164 feet**   **LEVEL: Technical**

LOCATION: The wreck lies about 7.5 miles southwest of the Long Point Light.

For years, this incredibly preserved but unidentified shipwreck, first located in 1984, was referred to as "Schooner X." Dan Lindsay and dive team members, John Veber and Ray Stewart, were instrumental in the investigation and discovery of the identity of the schooner, *St. James*. Thanks to them, Toronto marine historian, Art Amos, ascertained, from the tonnage numbers stamped into the main beam, that the vessel was the two-masted schooner, *St. James* (118′ x 25′), built in Milan, Ohio, in 1856, and lost mysteriously with all hands in late October, 1870. Both masts are upright and rise to a depth of 81′. The ship's anchors are in place, and this magnificent shipwreck is complete with bow chains, deadeyes, rigging, the ship's wheel, a wooden and an iron bilge pump, and a figurehead. Art Amos and Dan Lindsay were co-authors of the report, "The Discovery of the Schooner *St. James*." This report won the "Henry N. Barkhausen Award for Original Research in Great Lakes Maritime History" for the year 2001, sponsored by the Association for Great Lakes Maritime History.

Although half buried in sand, the ship's wheel makes a dramatic picture. DIGITAL IMAGE BY DAN LINDSAY OF SEA-VIEW DIVING (SEE PAGE 156 FOR THE AD)

Identification as the *St. James* occurred when these tonnage numbers were found. DIGITAL IMAGE BY DAN LINDSAY OF SEA-VIEW DIVING (SEE PAGE 156 FOR THE AD)

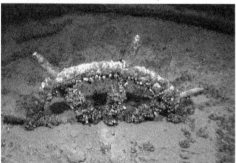

27. TRADE WIND

LORAN: 44463.48/58483.81	GPS: 42° 25.512'/080° 12.061'
DEPTH: 120 feet	LEVEL: Advanced

LOCATION: The wreck lies about 11.5 miles southwest of the Long Point Light.

This 140-foot-long, three-masted bark, constructed at Buffalo in 1853, sank after a collision in a blinding blizzard with the bark, *Charles Napier,* on December 1, 1854. The *Trade Wind's* cargo was railroad iron, 1,000 stoves and two U.S. government lifeboats bound for Chicago. After the collision, the crew rescued themselves using the two government lifeboats. The wreck's masts lie on the mud bottom off the port side, while the site contains her capstan, ship's wheel, and many scattered stove parts and railroad iron.

Catheads in place and its hull listing to port, the *Trade Wind*, including its partially embedded rudder *(right)*, is very photogenic.

PHOTOS BY JON VEBER

28. "CRYSTAL WRECK"

LORAN:	GPS: 42° 27.153'/080° 16.522
DEPTH: 119 feet	LEVEL: Advanced

LOCATION: The wreck lies about 13 miles west-southwest of the Long Point Light.

This unidentified grain-carrying, twin-masted, 117-foot-long schooner offers visiting divers much to see, including a hinged bowsprit, wheel, stove, rail, and many small artifacts. Snagged commercial fish nets abound. Note: The Crystal wreck received its nickname from the first divers to explore her -- because they drank Crystal brand beer after their great dive!

29. ANDREW B.

LORAN:	GPS: 42° 28.474'/080° 04.153'
DEPTH: 155 to 186 feet	LEVEL: Technical

LOCATION: The wreck lies about four miles south of the end of Long Point, Ontario.

The modern derrick scow, or dredge barge, *Andrew B.* (120' x 50' x 8'), built in 1958 by the Canadian Dredge and Dock Company at Port Weller, Ontario, was being towed when it sank in a storm on Nov. 8, 1995. The towline to the tug had broken, and the unstable barge quickly capsized. No lives were lost. The wreck lies on its side with the crane still attached.

30. DEAN RICHMOND

LORAN: 44471.03/58602.82	GPS: 42° 18.436'/079° 55.857'
DEPTH: 100 to 120 feet	LEVEL: Advanced

LOCATION: This shipwreck lies about 11.5 miles northeast of Erie, Pennsylvania.

The wooden, arch-type, twin-propeller-driven freighter, *Dean Richmond* (238' x 35' x 13'5"), loaded with flour and zinc, disappeared with all hands (18 lives) in a severe storm on October 14, 1893. She was the largest package freighter on the Great Lakes when she was

The *Dean Richmond.*
CRIS KOHL COLLECTION

The *Dean Richmond* wreck: dynamite damage, *above,* and the remaining propeller, *right. Lower left:* Garry Kozak at home with some *Richmond* memorabilia. PHOTOS BY CRIS KOHL

launched at Cleveland in 1864.

Located by Garry Kozak in 1983 after spending eight summers sidescanning various parts of Lake Erie (and finding 31 shipwrecks before finally attaining his goal!), the *Dean Richmond* lies upside-down and, at one point, dynamited open. One of her twin propellers is still in place. Penetration is possible, but only by trained, experienced, prepared divers.

31. *INDIANA*

LORAN: 44451.66/58564.82	GPS: 42° 17.762'/079° 59.902'
DEPTH: 90 feet	LEVEL: Advanced

LOCATION: The wreck lies a bit over ten miles north-northeast of Erie, Pennsylvania.

The barkentine, *Indiana* (136'9" x 25'2" x 11'), built at Oswego, New York, in 1852, sank shortly after she began to leak on September 24, 1870. Her cargo of stone was also lost, but her crew survived. This wreck is adorned with a windlass, capstan, winch, deadeyes, her collapsed bowsprit, two bow anchors, and a fallen rudder.

32. *S. K. MARTIN*

LORAN: 44441.76/58587.29	GPS: 42° 14.551'/079° 56.001'
DEPTH: 57 feet	LEVEL: Intermediate

LOCATION: The wreck lies about nine miles northeast of Erie, Pennsylvania.

The wooden steamer, *S.K. Martin* (152'5" x 28' x 11'), built at Benton Harbor, Michigan, in 1883, began to leak during a storm on October 12, 1912. The crew escaped in the ship's yawl.

159

The wooden steamer, *S. K. Martin*.
CRIS KOHL COLLECTION

The wooden steamer, *Canobie*.
CRIS KOHL COLLECTION

The wreck lies upright, with her large boilers and propeller in place. Other items lie just off the wreck site: a capstan, the smokestack, and two sets of bitts off the port stern side, and an anchor off the starboard bow. The rudder lies flat at the stern.

33. CANOBIE

GPS: 42° 10.328'/080° 00.898'
DEPTH: 15 feet   LEVEL: Novice

LOCATION: The wreck lies three miles east-northeast of Erie, Pennsylvania.

The wooden steamer, *Canobie* (259'3" x 37'4" x 19'8"), launched as the *Iron King* at Detroit in 1887, sailed in a dilapidated condition into a violent storm on November 1, 1921. She barely survived to reach Erie harbor, where her owners knew they could no longer risk this ship on open water. So they towed her east of Erie, where they burned and scuttled her. Her hull timbers, huge propeller and boiler lie next to a buoy. **LORAN: 44394.82/58533.88**.

34. PHILIP D. ARMOUR

LORAN: 44339.22/58434.48   GPS: 42° 07.680'/080° 10.701'
DEPTH: 30 feet   LEVEL: Novice

The *Philip D. Armour* as a steamer.
INSTITUTE FOR GREAT LAKES RESEARCH

LOCATION: The wreck lies about five miles west-southwest of Erie, Pennsylvania.

The wooden barge, ex-steamer *Philip D. Armour* (280'6" x 40' x 23'), stranded in a storm on November 13, 1915, and was abandoned in place. A four-bladed propeller, rudder lying flat, two boilers, engine, piping and bitts adorn this large hull.

35. CHARLES FOSTER

GPS: 42° 10.444'/080° 15.001'
DEPTH: 75 feet   LEVEL: Advanced

LOCATION: The wreck lies about nine miles west of Erie, Pennsylvania. **LORAN: 44345.18/58406.16**

The oak-hulled, schooner-barge, *Charles Foster* (233'x 36' x 16'), built for the iron ore trade at Milan, Ohio, in 1877, became waterlogged and sank with all eight hands on December 9, 1900. Anchor and chain sit on the bow, along with a pump, a windlass and a metal tank. Two capstans stand in place on deck; the ship's wheel lies off the broken stern.

The *Charles Foster*.
CRIS KOHL COLLECTION

36. AYCLIFFE HALL

LORAN: 44410.42/58393.17   GPS: 42° 22.526'/080° 21.231'
DEPTH: 70 feet   LEVEL: Advanced

LOCATION: The wreck lies about 20 miles southwest of Long Point Light.
The steel freighter, *Aycliffe Hall* (253' x 43'6" x 20'6"), constructed in England in 1928,

The steel freighter, *Aycliffe Hall.*
CRIS KOHL COLLECTION

sank after being rammed on the port stern by the steel freighter, *Edward J. Berwind,* in the dense early morning fog of June 11, 1936. Fortunately, no lives were lost, and the *Berwind* proceeded to Buffalo with both crews.

The hull lies upside-down, with cracks and tears in the steel, likely caused by a failed salvage attempt. The large propeller and rudder remain impressive.

37. DRILL RIG

LORAN: 44396.98/58359.42   GPS: 42° 22.467'/080° 25.111'
DEPTH: 80 feet   LEVEL: Advanced

LOCATION: This wreckage lies about 23 miles west of Long Point Light.

A storm destroyed this 40' by 40' oil drill rig on November 5, 1958, with the loss of all five men on it. Many scattered pipes form the highlight of this site.

38. MAJESTIC

LORAN: 44418.13/58325.82   GPS:
DEPTH: 55 feet   LEVEL: Intermediate-Advanced

LOCATION: The wreck lies about 18.5 miles off Port Burwell, Ontario.

The wooden steamer, *Majestic* (291' x 40' x 21'1"), built at West Bay City, Michigan, in 1889, burned to the water's edge on September 10, 1907. The crew was rescued by a passing steamer. Highlights include the huge double boiler and propeller.

The *Majestic* as she appeared on a postcard dated July 13, 1908. CRIS KOHL COLLECTION

Right: Manard Goette of the Hamilton Sea Devils explores a boiler and works a large wrench on the *Majestic* in May, 1986. PHOTOS BY CRIS KOHL

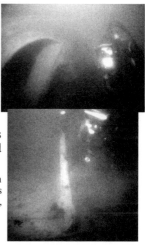

39. BARGE NO. 3 OR NO. 4

LORAN: 44388.39/58238.21   GPS:
DEPTH: 60 feet   LEVEL: Intermediate-Advanced

LOCATION: The wreck lies about ten miles south-southeast of Port Burwell, Ontario.

Identical *Barge No. 3* and *Barge No. 4* (335' x 44' x 11'), both built at Toledo, Ohio, in 1895, both sank carrying pulpwood on November 13, 1900, in a storm, with the towing tug rescuing both crews. This located wreck (is it *No. 3* or *No. 4*?) sits upright; her sister may be 1/4 mile away.

Right: Barge No. 4 underway. CRIS KOHL COLLECTION

40. WILLIAM H. STEVENS

> **GPS: 42° 19.503'/080° 40.498'**
> **DEPTH: 70 feet   LEVEL: Advanced**

LOCATION: This wreck lies in mid-Lake Erie closer to Port Burwell, ON, than to Erie, PA.

The wooden steamer, *William H. Stevens* (212'4" x 37'2" x 13'7"), built at West Bay City, Michigan, in 1886, caught on fire and sank on Sept. 8, 1902, with no lives lost. Most of the copper cargo was salvaged in 1904. The wreck lies split open with netting and other hazards.

The steamer, *William H. Stevens.*
CRIS KOHL COLLECTION

41. JAMES H. REED

> **LORAN: 44277.78/58138.89   GPS: 42° 16.172'/080° 47.777'**
> **DEPTH: 76 feet   LEVEL: Advanced**

LOCATION: The wreck lies about halfway between Ashtabula and Port Burwell.

The steel freighter, *James H. Reed* (128'5" x 24'5" x 12'5"), built in 1903 at Wyandotte, Michigan, sank after colliding with the steamer, *Ashcroft*, in dense fog on April 27, 1944. Twelve lives were lost in this mishap. The *Reed* was hauling iron ore for the war effort. The wreck was dynamited, so the twisted, broken steel remains are considerably scattered.

Left: The *James H. Reed.* CRIS KOHL COLLECTION

42. JOHN B. LYON

> **LORAN: 44222.42/58212.02   GPS: 42° 02.369'/080° 33.757'**
> **DEPTH: 52 feet   LEVEL: Intermediate-Advanced**

LOCATION: This wreck lies about four miles north of Conneaut, Ohio.

The wooden steamer, *John B. Lyon* (255'9" x 38'8" x 20'), was caught in the tail end of the hurricane which destroyed Galveston, Texas, and sank with the loss of nine of the 15 crew. This shipwreck's highlights are two boilers, chain and a large four-bladed propeller.

Right: The oak-hulled steamer, *John B. Lyon,* was built in 1881 at Cleveland. CRIS KOHL COLLECTION

43. HARBOR WRECKS

In about 12' of water in Ashtabula harbor, lie the remains of three ships, the schooner *James F. Joy*, the schooner *Gulnair*, and the wooden sandsucker, *Wonder.*

The *James F. Joy* (175'9" x 24'8" x 11'), stranded with an iron ore cargo during a storm on October 24, 1887, was built at Detroit in 1866. Her crew, retreating to the rigging, was saved. Posing a hazard to navigation, the wreck was dynamited in 1889. She sits at a depth of 13' about 100' east of the channel's east bank. The *Joy's* rudder was removed in 1974.

The three-masted *Gulnair* (142'9" x 24'8" x 11') stranded during a storm on July 15, 1892, forcing her crew to spend several hours in the rigging before being rescued. Built at Port Robinson, Ontario, in 1873, the *Gulnair* carried a coal cargo.

The wooden steamer, *Wonder* (95'9" x 19'8" x 5'), used as a sandsucker, was built in 1889 at New London, Wisconsin, and stranded in a storm on July 13, 1908, with none of her four lives lost.

11. Middle Lake Erie

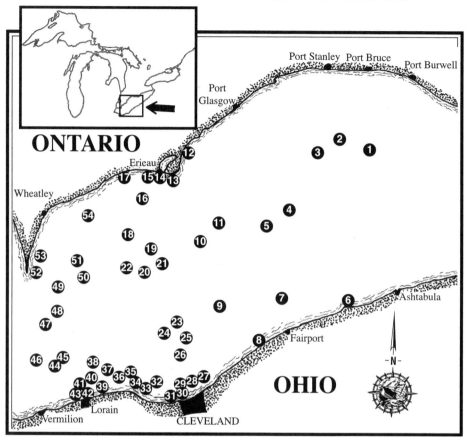

1. *Nimrod*
2. *Louis O'Neil*
3. *Dawn*
4. *Merida*
5. *H. A. Barr*
6. *Charles B. Hill*
7. *Queen of the West*
8. *North Carolina*
9. *Cleveco*
10. *James B. Colgate*
11. *"Sternless schooner"*
12. *"Morpeth schooner"*
13. *Lycoming*
14. *"Brians' Wreck"*
15. *Erieau Dock*
16. *Robert*
17. *Colonial*
18. *"Light Wreck"*
19. *Frank E. Vigor*
20. *Little Wissahickon*
21. *Valentine*
22. *F. A. Meyer*
23. *Steven F. Gale*
24. *Duke Luedtke*
25. *Dundee*
26. *Admiral*
27. *Algeria*
28. *Charles H. Davis*
29. *Fannie L. Jones*
30. *Mabel Wilson*
31. *"117th St. Wreck"*
32. *H. G. Cleveland*
33. *John B. Griffin*
34. *Mecosta*
35. *Two Fannies*
36. *"Bay coal schooner"*
37. *Sand Merchant*
38. *John Pridgeon, Jr.*
39. *Craftsman*
40. *Ivanhoe*
41. *Hickory Stick*
42. *Sarah E. Sheldon*
43. *St. Lawrence & Quito*
44. *Cortland*
45. *Morning Star*
46. *Gen. Anthony Wayne*
47. *Marshall F. Butters*
48. *"Civil War Wreck"*
49. *"Jackie's Wreck"*
50. *"Net Wreck"*
51. *"Bow cabin schooner"*
52. *Wend the Wave*
53. *Jorge B.*
54. *New Brunswick*

1. NIMROD

LORAN: 44279.7/58053.2	**GPS: 42° 22.649'/081° 00.309'**
DEPTH: 56 to 72 feet	**LEVEL: Advanced**

LOCATION: The wreck lies about 22 miles southeast of Port Stanley, Ontario.

The three-masted schooner, *Nimrod* (184' x 31'7" x 13'4"), built in 1873 at Toledo, Ohio, sank with a cargo of corn after a collision with the schooner, *Michigan,* on November 8, 1874, in dense fog. No lives were lost, but the new ship was a total loss.

A windlass and much anchor chain adorn the bow, which faces southwest. An impressive

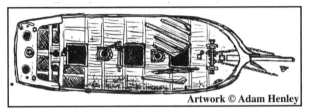

Artwork © Adam Henley

Former U.S. Navy diver, Frank Troxell, studies a *Nimrod* double sheave block. PHOTO BY CRIS KOHL

bowsprit was in place until the weight of zebra mussels collapsed it in the late 1990's; now it lies next to the remaining large anchor (the first 3,000-pound bow anchor was raised in 1979 and is on exhibit next to the Port Burwell lighthouse). The stern offers the fallen rudder post, a davit, and bitts. Three dark holes indicate where the masts used to be. Much of the wooden railing remains intact.

2. LOUIS O'NEIL

LORAN: 44269.2/57975.8	**GPS: 42° 25.444'/081° 10.312'**
DEPTH: 72 feet	**LEVEL: Advanced**

LOCATION: The wreck lies 13.6 miles off Port Stanley, Ontario.

Nicknamed the "Coal Schooner Wreck" when local fishermen, who had snagged their nets on it, first told scuba charter boat operator Wayne Weingarden about it in 1987, this shipwreck was later identified as the schooner-barge, *Louis O'Neil* (196' x 31' x 13'). Launched in 1862 at Cleveland, the coal-laden *Louis O'Neil* was being towed along with four other schooner-barges by the tug, *Swain,* when they encountered severe gales on April 29, 1887. One tow, the *Thomas L. Parker,* collided with the *Louis O'Neil,* sinking the latter. As the Port Huron newspaper succinctly put it on Monday, May 2, 1887: "...The crew went 70 miles in a rowboat but were saved...." when they landed near Conneaut, Ohio.

This shipwreck is loaded with sights: a huge pile of chain at the bow, a capstan, double blocks, hatches, pump, rudder, an enormous rudder post, the coal cargo, and an anchor partially buried at the bow. Beware of fishnets at various parts of this wreck.

The *Louis O'Neil's* chain pile and blocks. PHOTOS BY CRIS KOHL

Artwork © Adam Henley

Great Lakes Highlight No. 7

LAKE ERIE'S
BLACK FRIDAY STORM, 1916

An intensely violent storm sank four ships and claimed the lives of 51 people on western Lake Erie on Friday, October 20, 1916, a tragic event which became known as the Black Friday Storm of 1916.

The schooner-barge, *D. L. Filer*, became waterlogged and sank near the mouth of the Detroit river with the loss of six of her seven lives -- her captain clutched tightly to a protruding mast until rescued by a passing ship.

The wooden steamer, *Marshall F. Butters*, fared better, losing none of her sailors when she sank off Point Pelee near the midpoint between Canada and the USA.

The *D. L. Filer*. See p. 200.
CRIS KOHL COLLECTION

An unusually designed ship, the steel whaleback, *James B. Colgate*, foundered in the middle of Lake Erie off Rondeau Point, with only her captain surviving by clinging to a makeshift raft for over 30

The *Marshall F. Butters*. See p. 181.
CRIS KOHL COLLECTION

hours before being rescued by a passing steamer.

The powerful steamer, *Merida*, at one time in her career

The *James B. Colgate*. See p. 168.
CRIS KOHL COLLECTION

the largest ship on the Great Lakes, sank with all hands in the middle of the lake.

The *Merida*. See pages 166-167.
CRIS KOHL COLLECTION

Right: Newspapers across the Great Lakes were generous and up-to-date in their coverage of the worst storm in recorded history to hit Lake Erie, with its resulting loss of ships and sailors. *Far right:* William Livingstone, the President of the Lake Carriers Association in Cleveland, Ohio, offered a reward for the recovery of sailors' bodies from the crews of the *Merida* and the *Colgate*. CRIS KOHL COLLECTION

DEATH TOLL IN "BLACK FRIDAY" BLAST MOUNTS TO FIFTY-ONE SOULS

Ten Goderich Men Lost When Merida and Crew of 23 Went Down

Four Ships Lost in Gale—Loss Placed at Half Million Dollars

Admit Merida Gone.

The Cleveland managers of the steamer Merida conceded yesterday that the ship had gone down. The admission was made following the finding of seven bodies of the crew in mistake by passing steamers. The total dead is now placed at 51. Four ships were lost with their cargoes, valued at $500,000.

3. DAWN

LORAN: 44233.4/57878.3	GPS: 42° 25.251'/081° 21.502'
DEPTH: 67 feet	LEVEL: Advanced

LOCATION: This wreck lies about 18 miles south-southwest of Port Stanley, Ontario.

This shipwreck sits upright with a slight starboard list. Its deck exhibits a windlass, two bilge pumps, a rudder post, two open hatches and parts of both masts, plus mid-hull collision damage. This is the schooner, *Dawn* (105' x 20'4" x 8'11"), which sank within ten minutes of being rammed by the steamer, *New York*, on October 21, 1859. Fortunately, no lives were lost. The *Dawn* had been built in 1847 at Milan, Ohio.

4. MERIDA

LORAN: 44160.0/57843.9	GPS: 42° 13.951'/081° 20.786'
DEPTH: 65 to 83 feet	LEVEL: Advanced

LOCATION: The wreck lies 24.6 miles east of Erieau, Ontario.

The steel freighter, *Merida* (360' x 45' x 25'8"), was one of four ships which sank on Lake Erie in the "Black Friday" Storm of October 20, 1916 (see page 165), but she was the only one lost with all hands (23 sailors). The *Merida* was the largest ship of her kind on the Great Lakes when she was launched at Bay City, Michigan, in 1892.

Above: The steel steamer, *Merida.* CRIS KOHL COLLECTION. *Left:* A large school of burbots congregates on the *Merida. Right:* Roy Pickering studies a bow capstan on the *Merida.* PHOTOS BY CRIS KOHL

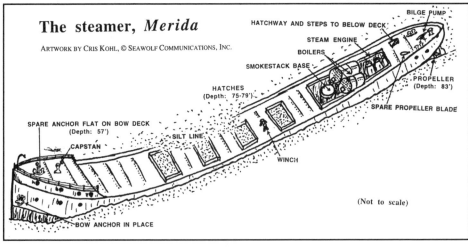

The steamer, *Merida*

ARTWORK BY CRIS KOHL, © SEAWOLF COMMUNICATIONS, INC.

BILGE PUMP

HATCHWAY AND STEPS TO BELOW DECK

STEAM ENGINE

BOILERS

SMOKESTACK BASE

PROPELLER (Depth: 83')

HATCHES (Depth: 75-79')

SPARE PROPELLER BLADE

SPARE ANCHOR FLAT ON BOW DECK (Depth: 57')

SILT LINE

CAPSTAN

WINCH

(Not to scale)

BOW ANCHOR IN PLACE

Local fishermen discovered the wreck in 1975. She sits upright and intact, but her back seems to be broken as her midsection virtually disappears into the lake bottom. The bow, rising from the lake bottom at a sharp angle, is adorned with a hinged fluke anchor lying flat on the deck, a capstan, a second anchor and chain in place, stanchions and railings. A few brass portholes still remain at the lower levels of the bow. The stern's engine room is penetrable, but silty; this is for very trained, experienced and prepared divers only.

5. *H. A. Barr*

LORAN: 44118.3/57803.2	GPS: 42° 09.112'/081° 23.412'
DEPTH: 84 feet	LEVEL: Advanced

LOCATION: The wreck lies about 22 miles east-southeast of Erieau, Ontario.

The schooner-barge, *H. A. Barr* (225' x 35' x 17'), built in 1893 at West Bay City, Michigan, foundered in a storm off Rondeau, Ontario, on August 24, 1902. No lives were lost.

The bow section of this large wreck sits upright, but the stern is completely broken up and encased by dangerous commercial fishnets which snagged onto the obstructions. A long line of deadeyes grace the port rail. A windlass has recently collapsed into the hold at the bow, but a capstan, fife rail, winch and belaying pins enhance the rest of the deck.

Left: Diver Joe Corsaro exchanges stares with a deadeye along the port rail of the schooner-barge, *H. A. Barr.* Deadeyes, so-named due to their resemblance to human skulls, were part of a ship's running rigging. Rope, passed through each hole, ran to the top of a mast.   PHOTO BY CRIS KOHL

6. *Charles B. Hill*

LORAN:	GPS: 41° 50.455'/081° 03.081'
DEPTH: 18 feet	LEVEL: Novice

LOCATION: This wreck lies about 1/2 mile off Madison, Ohio.

The wooden steamer, *Charles B. Hill* (261' x 36' x 23'), began to leak seriously during a storm and was driven ashore. All were rescued. The site is comprised of huge, wooden timbers, steam pipes and other metal pieces, including a large and a small boiler. Fish abound.

7. *Queen of the West*

LORAN: 43986.0/57735,1	GPS: 41° 50.769'/082° 23.133'
DEPTH: 71 feet	LEVEL: Advanced

LOCATION: This shipwreck lies about eight miles north of Fairport, Ohio.

The wooden steamer, *Queen of the West* (215' x 32'6" x 16'4"), sprang a leak and foundered on August 20, 1903. The entire crew was rescued by a passing steamer.

The bow is the most intact area, with a windlass, some chain and a winch. The stern offers the engine and a huge boiler. The wreck's mid-section is mostly open hull.

The steamer, *Queen of the West.*
CRIS KOHL COLLECTION

8. *North Carolina*

LORAN: 43934.28/57709.32	GPS: 41° 43.810'/081° 22.888'
DEPTH: 40 feet	LEVEL: Novice-Intermediate

LOCATION: This wrecked tug lies about 3/4 mile off Mentor-on-the-Lake, Ohio.
Built at Cleveland in 1908 as the *L. C. Sabin* and in 1941 renamed the *North Carolina*

(74'8" x 19'9" x 11'6"), this is a modern wreck of an old ship. She foundered with no lives lost on December 9, 1968. The site, with the tug's hull facing south, includes the ship's rudder, propeller, smokestack and boiler.

9. CLEVECO

LORAN: 43926.18/57609.49	GPS: 41° 47.468'/081° 36.006'
DEPTH: 63 to 78 feet	LEVEL: Advanced

LOCATION: This wreck lies about 14 miles north of Euclid, Ohio.

The steel tanker barge, *Cleveco.*
CRIS KOHL COLLECTION

Lost with all hands (18) when she foundered on December 3, 1942, the steel tanker barge, *Cleveco* (260' x 43' x 25'1"), was being towed by the tug, *Admiral,* which also sank with all hands (and is also in this book). Originally launched at Lorain, Ohio, in 1913 as the *S.O. Co. #85,* she was renamed three times before given her final name in 1940. Unfortunately, that was the name she held for the shortest period of time.

The wreck lies upside-down, rising about 14 feet off the lake bottom. Salvage in 1961 and 1995 removed most of her 1,000,000 gallons of fuel oil. Half a dozen sealed valves on the keel act as a reminder of the first salvage.

10. JAMES B. COLGATE

LORAN: 44032.52/57607.72	GPS: 42° 05.378'/081° 44.281'
DEPTH: 85 feet	LEVEL: Advanced

LOCATION: The wreck lies about twelve miles southeast of Erieau, Ontario.

The steel whaleback ship, *James B. Colgate* (308' x 38' x 24'), disappeared with almost all hands in the "Black Friday" Storm of October 20, 1916. Only her captain survived by clinging to a raft for over 30 hours before being picked up by a passing railroad car ferry. Built in 1892 at West Superior, Wisconsin, the *Colgate* was one of only 43 whalebacks ever constructed.

Len Cabral, a commercial fisherman, located the *James B. Colgate* in the summer of 1991. The wreck lies upside-down, with the rudder and propeller being the site's highlights. Penetration is possible, but only

The unique whaleback steamer, *James B. Colgate.*
CRIS KOHL COLLECTION

for the trained, experienced and prepared. Silt thrives here. An interesting debris field, which includes the smokestack, lies off the stern.

11. "STERNLESS SCHOONER"

LORAN: 44071.09/57673.82	GPS: 42° 08.380'/081° 37.939'
DEPTH: 84 feet	LEVEL: Advanced

LOCATION: The wreck lies about 16 miles southeast of Erieau, Ontario.

This unidentified, three-masted schooner, measuring about 125 feet long with a 25 foot beam, has a stern so severely damaged and collapsed that the first divers at this site thought it was missing. This site, facing west, sports a port bow anchor, a windlass, chain on the deck, intact railing, part of a fife rail at the first mast hole, a capstan near midship, a pump near the stern, and the remnants of a rudder post. A capstan plate hints at 1850's construction.

12. "MORPETH SCHOONER"

> **LORAN:** 44133.02/57629.09   **GPS:** 42° 22.444'/081° 49.278'
> **DEPTH:** 15 feet   **LEVEL:** Novice

LOCATION: The wreck lies about 200' off the concrete steps along the shoreline south of Morpeth. Ask permission first of the property owner if you plan to do this as a shore dive.

This unidentified schooner, measuring about 123 feet long and 24 feet wide, rises only about four feet off the lake bottom. For that reason, it gets covered and uncovered in sand at the whim of Lake Erie. An unusual feature is her iron hanging knees, which supported the horizontal deck on the vertical hull; usually the hanging knees were made of wood. The hull, filled with wood and stone debris, also has trees snagged into it. The wreck is possibly that of the schooner, *Phalarope* (137' x 26'3" x 11'1"), built at Cleveland in 1854 and stranded near Rondeau on September 29, 1872.

13. *LYCOMING*

> **LORAN:** 44073.0/57566.4   **GPS:** 42° 15.080'/081° 53.386'
> **DEPTH:** 28 feet   **LEVEL:** Novice-Intermediate

LOCATION: This shipwreck lies about four miles east of Erieau, Ontario.

This wooden steamer, discovered by commercial gas divers in 1977, was called the "Erieau Wreck" until research on its engine by members of Kent Divers Association identified it as the *Lycoming* (251' x 36' x 15'3"), which burned to the waterline on October 21, 1910, while docked at Erieau. The floating inferno was cut loose to save the dock. The site today includes a large four-bladed propeller, a recently restored and returned capstan, a steam engine and a boiler. The *Lycoming's* sister ship, the *Conemaugh,* lies off Point Pelee.

Left: The wooden steamer, *Lycoming*. CRIS KOHL COLLECTION. *Right:* Sidescan sonar image of the *Lycoming*. Compare this to the.site drawing on the next page, made years earlier. COURTESY OF MIKE & GEORGANN WACHTER

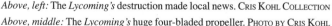

**Steam Barge
Burned at Erieau.**

Steamer Lycoming of Tonawanda Burned to Water's Edge and Sunk—Is Now a Complete Wreck.

The steam barge Lycoming, of Tona-wanda, N. Y. was burned to the water's edge at Rondeau, early Saturday morn-ing.
The Lycoming, with the schooner Emma C. Hutchison in tow, appeared off Rondeau harbor Friday afternoon during the storm and whistled for a tug to come and tow them in. Mr. Bir-

Above, left: The *Lycoming's* destruction made local news. CRIS KOHL COLLECTION

Above, middle: The *Lycoming's* huge four-bladed propeller. PHOTO BY CRIS KOHL

Right: Roy Pickering and members of Kent Divers Association pose with the *Lycoming* capstan which they restored and returned to the site in 1996.

PHOTO BY CRIS KOHL

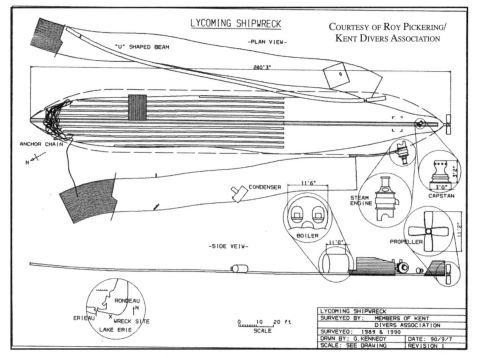

LYCOMING SHIPWRECK

COURTESY OF ROY PICKERING/
KENT DIVERS ASSOCIATION

14. "BRIANS' WRECK"

LORAN: 44072.59/57559.28	GPS: 42° 15.415'/081° 54.338'
DEPTH: 16 feet	LEVEL: Novice-Intermediate

LOCATION: This site lies just east of the East Erieau Channel breakwall.

Brian Jackson and Brian Roffel were diving with Roy Pickering (all Past Presidents of Kent Divers Association, like ye author) to explore this site. Brian R. came up and said he saw lots of quarry-cut stones. Brian J. came up and said that he saw a wooden shipwreck under the stones. Hence we have "Brians' (the apostrophe is in the right place because there was more than one Brian) Wreck" (it's a simple story, but one that had to be chronicled).

15. ERIEAU PIER

LOCATION: This site consists of the West Erieau Channel breakwall. Hug the wall and beware of boats.

Items accidentally dropped off this cement pier (mostly fishing equipment, but also everything from lighters to bicycles and lawn chairs) can be found in depths to 22'. Dive around the dock's end on rough days only if you can handle the churning wave action of the "washing machine" effect: an underwater thrill!

The west dock at Erieau, Ontario.
PHOTO BY CRIS KOHL

16. ROBERT

LORAN: 44044.0/57510.6	GPS: 42° 13.100'/081° 58.941'
DEPTH: 48 feet	LEVEL: Novice-Intermediate

LOCATION: The wreck lies about five miles southwest of Erieau, Ontario.

The commercial fishing tug, *Robert* (38'3" x 13'1" x 4'8"), built at Vermilion, Ohio, in 1948, sank in a collision with another fishing tug on September 26, 1982. Fortunately, the

Robert's crew escaped uninjured, picked up by the other boat. When I first explored this new wreck in 1983, it still had everything, from the ship's wheel and all the electronics to the fire extinguishers and propeller. Today, all that remains is some netting, a radar unit, the autopilot, and fish boxes.

The tug, *Robert*. ARTIST UNKNOWN.
CRIS KOHL COLLECTION

17. COLONIAL

LORAN: 44042.5/57472.3	GPS: 42° 15.065'/082° 04.292'
DEPTH: 13 to 22 feet	LEVEL: Advanced

LOCATION: The wreck lies about 1/4 mile off shore, seven miles west of Erieau.

The wooden steamer, *Colonial* (244'5" x 36'3" x 22'9"), built at Cleveland in 1882, sprang a leak and stranded on November 12, 1914. The crew abandoned ship in the lifeboat and used the lights of the newly-constructed church on shore to guide them in to the rural community of Pardoville, where they received hospitality, food and shelter from the Pardo family. The ship broke up within two days.

Roy Pickering and Tim Roberts researched and located the remains of the *Colonial* in 1991. The wreck is broken up and scattered over a wide area in the shallows, with highlights including the ship's brass bell (newly anchored to a concrete base), the boiler, engine, anchor chain, winch, bilge pump, bollards, the rudder post and many smaller items such as blocks, sinks and tools.

Left: The wooden steamer, *Colonial*. CRIS KOHL COLLECTION. *Right:* The *Colonial* cruising on the inland seas. ARTWORK © PETER RINDLISBACHER, USED WITH PERMISSION. FOR INFORMATION ABOUT MR. RINDLISBACHER'S ART, CONTACT THE CANADIAN SOCIETY OF MARINE ARTISTS, OR GO TO WWW.ULTRAMARINE.CA

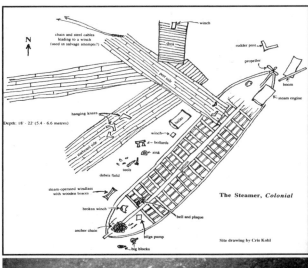

STEAM BARGE BLOWN UP ON THE SHORE OF LAKE ERIE DURING STORM

The "Colonial" was on Her way to Port Huron with a Cargo of Coal—The Wind Blew Her out of Her Course—The Captain Tried to Make Rondeau Harbor But Failed—The Crew was Saved

The steam barge "Colonial" of Port Huron come to grief in the severe storm on Lake Erie last night, and is was found impossible to keep her to her course. When the crew realized their danger

The Steamer, *Colonial*

Site drawing by Cris Kohl

Above: Roy Pickering explores the *Colonial's* propeller. *Above right:* The ship's bell was restored, secured in a concrete base (Roy Pickering poses with Geoffrey Kohl, the author's son), and returned by divers to the wreck site on September 21, 1991.

PHOTOS BY CRIS KOHL

18. "LIGHT WRECK"

LORAN: 43942.0/57414.4	GPS: 42° 00.185'/082° 04.220'
DEPTH: 76 feet	LEVEL: Advanced

LOCATION: The wreck lies about 20 miles southwest of Erieau, Ontario.
This unidentified wooden steamer, named the "Light Wreck" by Canadians because

Below, left: On the unidentified "Light Wreck," fish nets are snagged on burned frames. *Middle:* Roy Pickering and Winston Smith study the steering post. *Right:* Roy Pickering searches under charred planking for a diver's light while carefully holding on to his.   PHOTOS BY CRIS KOHL

the first divers on her lost a light (and referred to as the "Brick Wreck" by U.S. divers, in reference to the bricks in her firebox), was stripped and burned, as was the fate of many aging ships in the 1920's and 1930's. It has been conjectured that these remains are those of the steamer, *Fleetwood* (265'5" x 40'6" x 19'4"), and that the towing captain discreetly scuttled her rather than deliver her all the way to Buffalo (but how discreet can you be when you torch a 265-foot-long ship in the middle of Lake Erie? Dozens of ships, upon seeing the smoke, would have rushed to the "rescue!") Her machinery is gone, but a large rudder post and steering quadrant remain in place. The vast planking of this wooden ship is impressive.

19. *Frank E. Vigor*

LORAN: 43941.9/57464.44	GPS: 41° 57.549'/081° 57.238'
DEPTH: 92 feet	LEVEL: Advanced

LOCATION: In the shipping lane in mid-lake.

Upside-down and facing north, the steel freighter, *Frank E. Vigor* (418'3" x 48'2" x 23'9"), sank in a collision with the steel steamer, *Philip Minch,* on April 27, 1944, the same night of dense fog that sank the *James H. Reed* (also in

REV. PETER VAN DER LINDEN COLLECTION

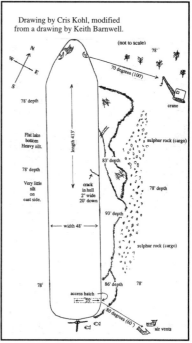

this book) in another collision just down the lake. Fortunately, the *Vigor's* crewmembers were all rescued by the *Minch.* The *Vigor* had been launched in 1896 at Cleveland as the *Sir William Siemens,* and, like the *Reed,* was carrying raw war materials (sulphur) at the time of loss.

Diver Joe Corsaro poses with the lower gudgeon of the large, wooden, steel-encased rudder on the *Frank E. Vigor.*   PHOTO BY CRIS KOHL

The rudder and propeller are most interesting. In the late 1980's, Ohio divers dynamited a small opening in the stern area, but penetration diving, especially at that depth, is for those specially trained, experienced and prepared. The crane lies about 100' off the port bow.

20. *Little Wissahickon*

LORAN: 43919.3/57454.8	GPS: 41° 54.222'/081° 56.786'
DEPTH: 68 to 80 feet	LEVEL: Advanced

LOCATION: The wreck lies in the middle of Lake Erie between Erieau and Cleveland.

The three-masted schooner, *Little Wissahickon* (148' x 28'), launched in 1869 at Marine City, Michigan, sprang a leak as she was being towed across Lake Erie with a cargo of coal and foundered on July 10, 1896, with three lives lost.

The wreck sits upright and intact, with the ship's wheel at the stern and two anchors

Examining the *Little Wissahickon's* wheel.
PHOTO BY CRIS KOHL

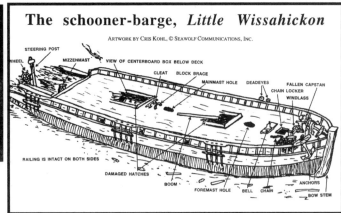

The schooner-barge, *Little Wissahickon*

ARTWORK BY CRIS KOHL, © SEAWOLF COMMUNICATIONS, INC.

STEERING POST
WHEEL   MIZZENMAST   VIEW OF CENTERBOARD BOX BELOW DECK
CLEAT   BLOCK BRACE
MAINMAST HOLE   DEADEYES   FALLEN CAPSTAN
CHAIN LOCKER
WINDLASS
RAILING IS INTACT ON BOTH SIDES
DAMAGED HATCHES   ANCHORS
BOOM   FOREMAST HOLE   BELL   CHAIN   BOW STEM

and a windlass at the bow. The ship's bell, originally removed by Ohio divers and exhibited in a dive shop there, was returned to the wreck bolted to a concrete block (Canadian authorities, upset at the removal of the bell from a shipwreck in Canadian waters, encouraged its return).

21. VALENTINE

LORAN: 43931.37/57476.32	GPS: 41° 55.122'/081° 54.786'
DEPTH: 80 feet	LEVEL: Advanced

LOCATION: This schooner lies 23.6 miles off Erieau, ON.
Built in 1867 at Conneaut, Ohio, the three-masted schooner, *Valentine* (128' x 25'8" x 10'), foundered on October 10, 1877, with no lives lost. This silty site features a windlass with chain, two pumps, a winch, rudder post and a capstan. The coal cargo is visible in the open holds. The anchors and wheel are missing. Beware of snagged fishnets.

Left: Diver Sharon Dickson studies a broken mast and a fife rail, with belaying pins in it, on the wreck of the *Valentine*. PHOTO BY CRIS KOHL.

22. F. A. MEYER

LORAN:43912.03/57406.42	GPS: 41° 55.441'/082° 02.952'
DEPTH: 68 to 78 feet	LEVEL: Advanced

LOCATION: This wreck lies in the middle of Lake Erie between Erieau, Ontario, and Avon Point, Ohio.

Punctured by ice on December 18, 1909, the wooden steamer, *F. A. Meyer* (256'4" x 38'5" x 19'8"), sank with a load of lumber and no lives lost; a passing steamer rescued the crew. The ship had been launched in 1888 at Detroit as the *J. Emory Owen*.

The site exhibits a huge triple expansion engine and two enormous boilers, as well as a

Left: The steamer, *F. A. Meyer*, as the *J. Emory Owen*. CRIS KOHL COLLECTION

Right: Diver Roy Pickering cautiously approaches a snagged fishing net on the *F. A. Meyer*. PHOTO BY CRIS KOHL.

capstan and a beautiful, rounded rail at the stern, where careful penetration is possible. The wreck is intact and upright, but the bow is in collapsed disarray. Beware of freighter traffic (you're in the shipping channel) and snagged fishnets at this site.

23. STEVEN F. GALE

LORAN: 43858.57/57449.42	GPS: 41° 44.451'/081° 52.919'
DEPTH: 70 to 79 feet	LEVEL: Intermediate-Advanced

LOCATION: This wreck lies 17.8 miles northwest of Cleveland, Ohio.

The two-masted schooner, *Steven F. Gale* (122'6" x 24' x 9'9"), built at Chicago in 1847, foundered with a cargo of stone, all hands and a cat on November 28, 1876.

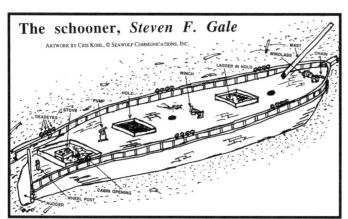

The schooner, *Steven F. Gale*

ARTWORK BY CRIS KOHL, © SEAWOLF COMMUNICATIONS, INC.

An old stove sits in the open (the cabin floated to Fairport) below-deck area near the stern, the forward mast lies atop the port bow area, the railings are lined with deadeyes, a pump rests on the deck near the stern, a winch sits midship, chain and windlass repose on the bow, and the forward hatch contains a ladder. This is a great Cleveland-area shipwreck!

24. DUKE LUEDTKE

LORAN: 43825.54/57396.29	GPS: 41° 41.628'/081° 57.651'
DEPTH: 65 to 71 feet	LEVEL: Intermediate-Advanced

LOCATION: The wreck lies 13 miles north of Avon Point, Ohio.

The tug, *Duke Luedtke* (68'7" x 17' x 11'), launched at Cleveland in 1917 as the *Alpena* and used in the attempted salvage of the *Prins Willem V* (also in this book) in Lake Michigan in the mid-1960's, sprang a leak and suddenly rolled and sank on September 21, 1993, with one life lost (a sailor trapped in the engine room). The wreck sits upright in mud listing to port, with rubber tires and hoses lying around the hull. Much silt sits inside.

25. DUNDEE

LORAN: 43841.0/57456.5	GPS: 41° 41.333'/081° 50.629'
DEPTH: 60 to 77 feet	LEVEL: Intermediate-Advanced

LOCATION: This wreck lies 13.8 miles north of Rocky River, Ohio.

Built in 1893 at West Bay City, Michigan, the large schooner-barge, *Dundee* (211' x 35' x 16'5"), lasted only seven years before foundering in a fierce storm with a load of iron ore on September 12, 1900, with the loss of one life (the female cook was washed overboard) from the seven on board. This storm, the tail end of the infamous "Galveston (Texas) Hurricane," also sank the *John B. Lyon* (which is also in this book).

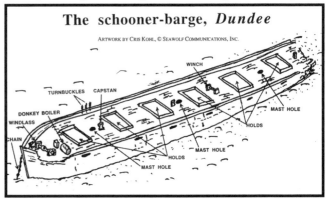

The schooner-barge, *Dundee*

ARTWORK BY CRIS KOHL, © SEAWOLF COMMUNICATIONS, INC.

Six holds make penetration possible into this wreck, but the silt inside makes this very dangerous. Outside, the stern has collapsed, and the bow is beginning to collapse from the weight of the donkey steam boiler, a windlass and chain. A *Dundee* anchor sits in Vermilion, Ohio, outside the Cargo Warehouse.

26. ADMIRAL

LORAN: 43808.88/57412.71	GPS: 41° 38.243'/081° 54.198'
DEPTH: 59 to 74 feet	LEVEL: Intermediate-Advanced

LOCATION: This wreck lies eight miles northwest of Cleveland, Ohio.

The tragic tug, *Admiral*. CRIS KOHL COLLECTION

The tug, *Admiral* (93'3" x 22'1" x 11'7"), foundered with all hands (14) in severe weather while towing the tanker, *Cleveco* (which also sank and is described in this book), on December 2, 1942. The tug had been built at Manitowoc, Wisconsin, in 1922, and launched as the *W. H. Meyer* (she received the name, *Admiral,* for only the final 89 days of her life).

The *Admiral* was located by diver George Walton in October, 1969. The wreck's bow points towards Cleveland. The pilot house and the engine room may be entered only by divers specially trained, experienced and prepared for penetration diving. The smokestack lies along the port side.

27. ALGERIA

LORAN: 43783.62/57482.18	GPS: 41° 31.222'/081° 42.940'
DEPTH: 40 feet	LEVEL: Novice-Intermediate

LOCATION: The wreck lies about one mile north of Cleveland harbor.

The schooner-barge, *Algeria* (288'7" x 44'6" x 19'1"), built at West Bay City, Michigan, in 1896, foundered in a storm on May 9, 1906, with one life lost. Lying east-to-west, this shallow site is broken up, with much wood and many cables. Beware of boating traffic!

28. CHARLES H. DAVIS

> LORAN: 43778.57/57475.69   GPS: 41° 30.777'/081° 43.515'
> DEPTH: 38 to 42 feet   LEVEL: Novice-Intermediate

LOCATION: The wreck lies about a mile north of Cleveland, Ohio.

The small wooden steamer, *Charles H. Davis* (145' x 31' x 9'), foundered in a storm on June 13, 1903, with the loss of her captain (the six remaining crewmembers were rescued). The ship's boiler and pony boiler sit surrounded by wooden wreckage at this busy site.

29. FANNIE L. JONES

> LORAN: 43777.03/57473.11   GPS: 41° 30.636'/081° 43.747'
> DEPTH: 37 feet   LEVEL: Novice-Intermediate

LOCATION: The wreck lies almost a mile northwest of Cleveland, Ohio.

The scow-schooner, *Fannie L. Jones* (92'8" x 22'6" x 7'4"), built in 1867 at Lorain, Ohio, foundered in a storm (the same one which claimed the schooner, *Two Fannies,* also in this book) on August 10, 1890. The captain went down with his ship, which carried a cargo of stone for the new Ashtabula breakwall. The wreck lies scattered in a busy boating area.

30. MABEL WILSON

> LORAN: 43774.24/57470.48   GPS: 41° 30.333'/081° 43.913'
> DEPTH: 38 feet   LEVEL: Novice-Intermediate

LOCATION: The wreck lies about 1/2 mile west of the Cleveland lighthouse.

The huge, four-masted schooner, *Mabel Wilson* (242'9" x 39'2" x 16'2"), built in 1886 at West Bay City, Michigan, sprang a leak and foundered outside Cleveland on May 28, 1906, with the loss of one sailor and her iron ore cargo. The wreck was dynamited, leaving only the stern somewhat intact and the rest scattered in a busy boating area of low visibility.

31. "117TH STREET WRECK"

> LORAN: 43771.88/57452.58   GPS: 41° 30.780'/081° 46.151'
> DEPTH: 40 feet   LEVEL: Novice-Intermediate

LOCATION: This site is almost three miles west of Cleveland's main harbor entrance.

This unidentified tugboat is possibly one of the vessels scuttled due to their age by the Great Lakes Towing Company about 100 years ago. The bow is somewhat intact, but the rest is broken and scattered, with her boiler lying a fair distance from the main wreckage.

32. H. G. CLEVELAND

LORAN: 43775.55/57436.12   GPS: 41° 32.048'/081° 48.607'
DEPTH: 55 feet   LEVEL: Intermediate

LOCATION: The wreck lies about four miles off Lakewood, Ohio.
The three-masted schooner, *H. G. Cleveland* (137'2" x 25'8" x 10'4"), built at Lorain, Ohio, in 1867, sprang a leak and foundered with a load of quarry stone from Kelley's Island on August 4, 1899, with no lives lost. At this site, the cargo is far more evident than the shipwreck; however, the centerboard box and a capstan are among the wreck sights.

33. JOHN B. GRIFFIN

LORAN: 43767.15/57427.39   GPS: 41° 31.100'/081° 49.172'
DEPTH: 46 to 53 feet   LEVEL: Novice-Intermediate

LOCATION: The wreck lies about two miles off Lakewood, Ohio.
The tug, *John B. Griffin* (57'4" x 14'6" x 6'8"), burned to the waterline on July 12, 1892, with no loss of life. The ship had been built in 1874 at Buffalo, New York. Very evident at this east-facing site are the tug's rudder, smokestack and boiler.

34. MECOSTA

LORAN: 43763.32/57397.34   GPS: 41° 31.854'/081° 52.997'
DEPTH: 50 feet   LEVEL: Novice-Intermediate

LOCATION: The wreck lies three miles north of Bay Village, Ohio.
The wooden steamer, *Mecosta* (281'7" x 40'6" x 20'), built at West Bay City, Michigan, in 1888, was stripped of her machinery and scuttled on October 29, 1922. An interesting aspect of this otherwise lackluster site is a Victorian bathtub. This is an area of heavy boating.

35. TWO FANNIES

LORAN: 43773.1/57385.2   GPS: 41° 33.850'/081° 55.280'
DEPTH: 52 to 61 feet   LEVEL: Intermediate

LOCATION: This wreck lies 4.8 miles north of Bay Village, Ohio.
Built in 1862 at Peshtigo, Wisconsin, the three-masted bark, *Two Fannies* (152' x 33' x 12'), foundered with a load of iron ore and no lives lost on August 10, 1890. The wreck sits upright, with her rudder and rudder post dominating the stern, a capstan, windlass and chain at the bow, plus another capstan and a winch at midship; this is a visually exciting dive!

36. "BAY COAL SCHOONER"

LORAN: 43764.47/57374.79   GPS: 41° 33.007'/081° 56.080'
DEPTH: 55 feet   LEVEL: Intermediate

LOCATION: This unidentified wreck lies about four miles off Bay Village, Ohio.
Measuring about 75 feet in length and 20 in beam, this coal-carrying scow sits upright in mud with her bow facing north. Decking is absent, but there are support posts in the hull.

37. SAND MERCHANT

LORAN: 43771.77/57368.32   GPS: 41° 34.431'/082° 57.520'
DEPTH: 65 feet   LEVEL: Advanced

LOCATION: The wreck lies four miles northeast of Avon Point, Ohio.
The steel sandsucker built at Collingwood, Ontario, in 1927, *Sand Merchant* (252' x

43'6" x 17'5"), tragically foundered on October 17, 1936, with the loss of 19 lives. She had just scooped up a load of sand from Point Pelee and was heading to Cleveland with it when the wind picked up heavily and the ship capsized. The wreck lies upside-down, bow southeast, with a crane lying off the starboard side and another one lying to the west in an interesting debris field which also contains a spotlight and a whistle. Do not penetrate this wreck at the mud banks.

Sand Merchant. Cris Kohl Collection

38. *John Pridgeon, Jr.*

LORAN: 43775.71/57362.29   GPS: 41° 35.316'/081° 58.597'
DEPTH: 55 to 62 feet   LEVEL: Intermediate-Advanced

LOCATION: The wreck lies five miles northeast of Avon Point, Ohio.

Constructed in 1875 at Detroit, the wooden steamer, *John Pridgeon, Jr.* (221'5" x 36'3" x 14'), sprang a leak and foundered on September 18, 1909. All 14 on board were rescued. The wreck lies on its port side, with the stern almost upside-down. Features include the huge propeller and engine, plus much of the ship's lumber cargo. Be careful in low visibility.

39. *Craftsman*

LORAN: 43745.64/57332.59   GPS: 41° 31.938'/082° 00.370'
DEPTH: 42 feet   LEVEL: Novice-Intermediate

LOCATION: The wreck lies about one mile north of Avon Lake, Ohio.

The wooden derrick barge, *Craftsman* (90'1" x 28'1" x 8'3"), built in 1921 at Lorain,

Ohio, foundered while in tow on June 3, 1958, with both crewmen surviving.

The wreck lies along an east-west line, with the crane lying about 100' to the southeast. The upright barge displays winches and hatches on its flat deck, but it's silt city down there, so penetration is not advised. Beware of fishermen trying to hook some of the resident fish.

40. IVANHOE

LORAN: 43750.09/57316.93	GPS: 41° 33.315'/082° 02.830'
DEPTH: 58 feet	LEVEL: Intermediate

LOCATION: This wrecked schooner lies about three miles off Avon Lake, Ohio.

Built in 1849, the Buffalo schooner, *Ivanhoe* (110' x 25'9" x 9'3"), sank with her coal cargo after a collision with the schooner, *Arab,* on October 4, 1855. Called the "Jug Wreck" by early divers, the vessel sits upright with a slight port list. The windlass and starboard railing are intact, while the stern, with its rudder upright, is mostly collapsed.

41. HICKORY STICK

LORAN: 43733.88/57282.82	GPS: 41° 32.299'/082° 06.241'
DEPTH: 52 to 57 feet	LEVEL: Intermediate

LOCATION: The wreck lies about three miles north of Sheffield Lake, Ohio.

The 1944 dredge barge, *Hickory Stick* (110' x 30' x 8'), sank with no lives lost during a storm on November 29, 1958, while being towed by the tug, *Black Marlin*. Both tug and tow sank after the towline parted; the tug has yet to be found. The dredge's crane, boiler and hull form the most conspicuous items at this scattered site.

42. SARAH E. SHELDON

LORAN: 43713.77/57268.59	GPS: 41° 29.737'/082° 06.676'
DEPTH: 20 feet	LEVEL: Novice

LOCATION: The wreck lies about 1/2 mile off Sheffield Lake, Ohio.

The wooden steamer, *Sarah E. Sheldon* (184'1" x 32'4" x 13'8"), was one of several ships lost on Lake Erie in an extremely violent storm on October 20, 1905 (two others, the *Siberia* and the *Tasmania,* are also described in this book). The *Sheldon,* built at Lorain, Ohio, in 1872, ran aground in the storm and began to break up. Two crewmen were washed overboard, while the other five clung to the mast before being rescued by a tug. The wreck lies scattered, with the broken propeller and two capstans forming the highlights. The boiler lies on shore. Boat traffic is very heavy here; use boating and diving caution.

43. ST. LAWRENCE AND QUITO

LORAN: 43696.9/57233.9	GPS:
DEPTH: 10 to 22 feet	LEVEL: Novice

LOCATION: These two wrecks lie intermingled about 3/4 mile east of Lorain harbor.

The schooner, *St. Lawrence* (137'1" x 26' x 11'5"), built in 1863 at Cleveland, stranded on November 21, 1900, and broke up with no lives lost. The wooden steamer, *Quito* (204' x 36'2" x 21'7"), constructed at Bangor, Michigan, in 1873, grounded and broke up on November 25, 1902, also with no lives lost. The scattered wreckage from both vessels includes an anchor and a vast debris area of wood and metal.

44. CORTLAND

LOCATION: This wreck lies 3/4 mile southwest of the *Morning Star* shipwreck.

The massive, three-masted, 676-ton bark, *Cortland* (173'6" x 34'4" x 13'8"), built in

1867 at Sheboygan, WI, was only one year old when it was run down on June 21, 1868, a dark and stormy night, by the sidewheel steamer, *Morning Star,* which also sank (see site #45). Ten lives were lost from the *Cortland,* and many more from the *Morning Star.* This tragic wreck, lying in 61 feet of water, was located on July 30, 2005 by David VanZandt and Kevin Magee, based upon research done by Jim Paskert, all members of the Cleveland Underwater Explorers (CLUE). The wreck is very intact, with its figurehead, blocks, and other significant items in place. The bell was recovered from the mud in August, 2006, by archaeologists; it will be properly conserved and displayed in a local museum.

45. MORNING STAR

> **LORAN: 43752.7/57246.5**   **GPS: 41° 36.812'/082° 12.530'**
> **DEPTH: 59 to 68 feet**   **LEVEL: Intermediate-Advanced**

LOCATION: This tragic wreck lies about eight miles north of Lorain, Ohio.

The sidewheel steamer, *Morning Star* (248'2" x 34' x 14'7"), built at Trenton, Michigan, in 1862, sank in a collision with the bark, *Cortland*, on June 21, 1868, with the loss of 31 lives from the 90 that were on board. The *Cortland* also sank and lies nearby (see site #44). While much of the vessel has sunk into the soft lake bottom, the *Morning Star's* engine, boiler, walking beam and parts of a paddlewheel are intact. Fish abound at this site.

46. GEN. ANTHONY WAYNE

LOCATION: The wreck lies in about 50' of water about 8 miles off Vermilion, Ohio.

The paddlewheel steamer, *Anthony Wayne* (sometimes called *Gen. Anthony Wayne*) (156'6" x 25'9" x 10'3"), exploded her boiler and killed 22 people before sinking on April 27, 1850. This ship was built in 1837 at Perrysburg, Ohio. Relocated by Tom Kowalczk in 2006, the wreck was surveyed by members of the Cleveland Underwater Explorers (CLUE).

47. MARSHALL F. BUTTERS

> **LORAN: 43791.13/57233.05**   **GPS: 41° 43.639'/082° 17.368'**
> **DEPTH: 62 to 70 feet**   **LEVEL: Intermediate-Advanced**

LOCATION: The wreck lies in Canadian waters about 15 miles north of Lorain, Ohio.

When the wooden lumber hooker, *Marshall F. Butters* (164' x 30'4" x 10'5"), succumbed to the "Black Friday" Storm of October 20, 1916, no lives were lost, unlike the tragic losses on the other three wrecks from the same storm: the *Merida*, the *James B. Colgate*, and the *D.L. Filer* (all are described in this book). The *Marshall F. Butters* had been built in 1882 at Milwaukee, Wisconsin. With her bow pointing north, she sits upright with a slight starboard list. Both bow and stern have collapsed, with a bow anchor off to starboard and the windlass in place. The midship section, the boiler and the engine remain intact.

48. "Civil War Wreck"

> LORAN: 43817.48/57274.31   GPS: 41° 46.070'/082° 13.750'
> DEPTH: 65 feet   LEVEL: Intermediate-Advanced

This two-masted sailing vessel, about 72' long and 16' wide, with a stone cargo, appears to be from the 1860's and is fire damaged. It lies about 20 miles north of Lorain, Ohio.

49. "Jackie's Wreck"

> LORAN: 43839.42/57233.69   GPS: 41° 51.710'/082° 21.083'
> DEPTH: 50 feet   LEVEL: Intermediate

Lying eight miles southeast of Point Pelee, the unidentified "Jackie's Wreck," a two-masted schooner about 120' long, lies flat with her centerboard just off the wreck.

50. "Net Wreck"

> LORAN: 43889.22/57307.59   GPS: 41° 56.561'/082° 14.869'
> DEPTH: 70 feet   LEVEL: Intermediate-Advanced

This unidentified coal-laden schooner, about 90' by 18', lying 14 miles east of Point Pelee, features pumps, a windlass, an anchor, a winch, deadeyes, blocks and lots of fishnets.

51. "Bow cabin schooner" (*E. K. Gilbert?*)

> LORAN: 43892.62/57315.02   GPS: 41° 56.807'/082° 14.110'
> DEPTH: 70 feet   LEVEL: Intermediate-Advanced

With her bow facing west and lying 13 miles northeast of Point Pelee, this two-masted schooner (possibly the *E.K. Gilbert,* 92'6" x 23'6" x 8'4", which leaked and sank on November 11, 1868) rises only 4' off the bottom. Artifacts include a winch, a capstan, a bilge pump, a windlass, a stove, an anchor, some chain, plus blocks and deadeyes.

52. *Wend the Wave*

> LORAN: 43829.21/57174.29   GPS: 41° 52.915'/082° 28.530'
> DEPTH: 30 feet   LEVEL: Novice

The schooner-barge, *Wend the Wave* (128' x 28' x 10') lay at anchor with a coal cargo during a storm on October 6, 1889, when she sank in a collision. One life was lost. This wreck is buried in the sand, with only some of the flattened hull and a windlass showing.

53. *Jorge B.*

> LORAN: 43851.19/57184.02   GPS: 41° 56.307'/082° 29.058'
> DEPTH: 38 feet   LEVEL: Advanced

This commercial fishing tug, about 50' long, capsized and sank in a storm on September 16, 1983, taking all three crew to the bottom almost one mile east of Point Pelee. The many fishnets from the tug, plus usually poor visibility, make this a hazardous dive.

54. *New Brunswick*

> LORAN: 43950.88/57321.22   GPS: 42° 06.777'/082° 18.120'
> DEPTH: 48 to 54 feet   LEVEL: Intermediate-Advanced

The three-masted bark, *New Brunswick* (128'8" x 22'), built at St. Catharines, Ontario, in 1847, foundered four miles south of Port Alma, ON, with five lives lost on August 26, 1858. Located in 1980 by Jim Kennard hired by Mike Diltz, and salvaged extensively, only bare hull and deadeyes remain.

12. *ErieQuest*
Western Lake Erie

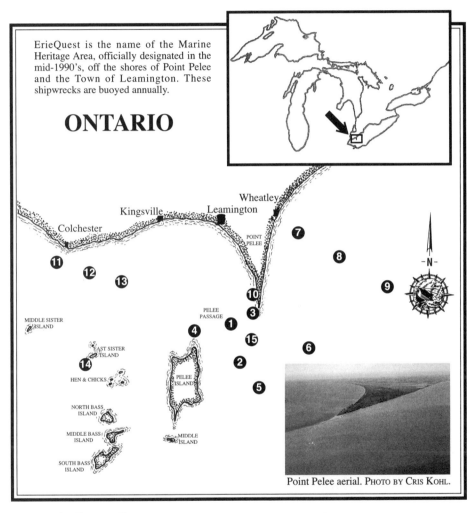

ErieQuest is the name of the Marine Heritage Area, officially designated in the mid-1990's, off the shores of Point Pelee and the Town of Leamington. These shipwrecks are buoyed annually.

ONTARIO

Wheatley

Leamington

Kingsville

Colchester

POINT PELEE

PELEE PASSAGE

MIDDLE SISTER ISLAND

EAST SISTER ISLAND

HEN & CHICKS

NORTH BASS ISLAND

MIDDLE BASS ISLAND

MIDDLE ISLAND

SOUTH BASS ISLAND

PELEE ISLAND

-N-

Point Pelee aerial. PHOTO BY CRIS KOHL.

1. *George Stone*
2. *Specular*
3. *Northern Indiana*
4. *Tioga*
5. *Tasmania*
6. *Jay Gould*
7. *Dominion*
8. *Clarion*

9. *Willis*
10. *Conemaugh*
11. *M. I. Wilcox*
12. *Grand Traverse*
13. *George Worthington*
14. *Case*
15. "Capstan Wreck"
    (Charger?)

1. GEORGE STONE

LORAN: 43820.3/57135.3	GPS: 41° 53.247'/082° 33.246'
DEPTH: 32 to 42 feet	LEVEL: Novice-Intermediate

LOCATION: The southern edge of Grubb's Reef, four miles southwest of Point Pelee.
The wooden steamer, *George Stone* (270' x 40' x 9'1"), built at West Bay City, Michigan, in 1893, stranded and caught on fire on Grubb's Reef while loaded with a coal cargo on

Left: The steamer, *George Stone.* CRIS KOHL COLLECTION

Right: Examining the *George Stone's* hull. PHOTO BY CRIS KOHL

October 13, 1909. Six lives were lost during the rescue efforts in heavy weather conditions.

The site contains a huge, wooden hull, complete with a boiler, anchor, anchor chain, propeller, steam engine and boiler cradle. There is plenty of lumber and piles of burned wood. The rudder lies flat on the reef in shallower water. Other machinery (e.g. windlass, capstans) is missing because the wreck was partially salvaged. In 1999, a small, steel boat was scuttled next to the wreck.

2. SPECULAR

LORAN: 43795.3/57128.4	GPS: 41° 49.371'/082° 32.170'
DEPTH: 37 feet	LEVEL: Novice-Intermediate

LOCATION: Southwest of Point Pelee, 5 miles east of the northern tip of Pelee Island.

Left The steamer, *Specular,* underway. CRIS KOHL COLLECTION

Right: Diver Jennifer Elcomb approaches the fluke of the *Specular's* anchor. PHOTO BY CRIS KOHL

Sidescan sonar image of the steamer, *Specular*. Note the two boilers at the stern. © AQUA VISION RESEARCH

A collision with the steamer, *Denver,* sank the iron-ore-laden, wooden steamer, *Specular* (263'7" x 38'4" x 20'1"), on August 22, 1900, with no lives lost. Launched on September 7, 1882, at Cleveland as a schooner, the *Specular* (named after a high grade of iron ore) was converted to a steamer in 1888. The wreck was dynamited as a hazard to navigation on October 23, 1900. Although the site is scattered over a wide area, her engine, boilers, anchor and propeller form interesting highlights for the visiting diver.

3. NORTHERN INDIANA

Below: The paddlewheel steamer, *Northern Indiana,* as she appeared in a contemporary drawing.   CRIS KOHL COLLECTION

LORAN: 43830.6/57160.5	GPS: 41° 53.879'/082° 30.599'
DEPTH: 20 to 25 feet	LEVEL: Novice-Intermediate

LOCATION: This wreck lies just southwest of Point Pelee's very tip.

Built in 1852 at Buffalo, New York, the passenger paddlewheel steamer, *Northern Indiana* (300'6" x 36'10" x 13'8"), owned by the Michigan Southern and Northern Indiana Railroad, dramatically burned to a tragic loss with about 28 people

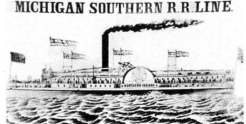

MICHIGAN SOUTHERN R.R. LINE.

Below: The paddlewheel steamer, *Northern Indiana,* as she appeared in Peter Rindlisbacher's modern watercolor. ART © COPYRIGHT AND COURTESY OF PETER RINDLISBACHER, AND COURTESY OF ROY PICKERING, ORIGINAL ART OWNER. FOR INFORMATION ABOUT MR. RINDLISBACHER'S ART, CONTACT THE CANADIAN SOCIETY OF MARINE ARTISTS, OR GO TO WWW.ULTRAMARINE.CA. *Right:* A grill lies in the vast debris field where diver Brian Roffel located this railroad tag in 1996 which positively identified this shipwreck. PHOTOS BY CRIS KOHL

perishing on July 17, 1856. The vessel is broken up and scattered, and the huge, shallow debris field includes a capstan, boiler, and much wood and piping. Beware of the Point's occasional strong currents.

4. TIOGA

LORAN: 43813.5/57115.9	GPS: 41° 53.058'/082° 35.339'
DEPTH: 40 feet	LEVEL: Novice-Intermediate

LOCATION: This wreck lies five miles west of Point Pelee and north of Pelee Island.
The wooden steamer, *Tioga* (177'4" x 24'7" x 11'2"), built at Cleveland in 1862, caught on fire and sank on October 5, 1877, with no loss of life. Sitting on the combination sand and mud bottom are the ship's capstan, windlass, rudder, four-bladed propeller and boiler.

5. TASMANIA

LORAN: 43786.8/57140.1	GPS: 41° 47.302'/082° 29.799'
DEPTH: 38 to 40 feet	LEVEL: Novice-Intermediate

LOCATION: Southwest of Point Pelee, about seven miles east of Pelee Island.

Left: The immense schooner, *Tasmania.* CRIS KOHL COLLECTION. *Above:* The media were out in full force on June 3, 1989, when the *Tasmania's* stolen anchor was returned to the shipwreck. Minutes after its placement, diver Art Vermette read the historic plaque next to the anchor. PHOTOS BY CRIS KOHL

Launched on April 22, 1871, at Port Huron, Michigan as the *James Couch,* the large, wooden, four-masted schooner, *Tasmania* (221' x 35' x 16'), foundered in a severe storm with all hands (8) and an iron ore cargo on October 20, 1905 (the *Siberia* and the *Sarah E. Sheldon,* also in this book, sank in the same storm). Part of the *Tasmania* wreck was dynamited on July 13, 1906, to remove her as a hazard to navigation.

The large wreck site includes a capstan, a winch, a cargo donkey boiler, vast amounts of iron ore and two anchors, one of which was removed by Ohio divers in 1987. Crossing an

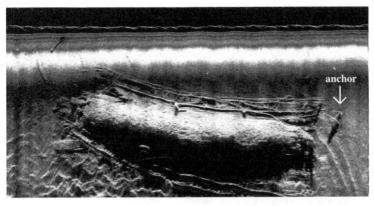

Sidescan sonar image of the *Tasmania.* Note the anchor at the wreck's upper right.
© AQUA VISION RESEARCH

international boundary line with stolen archival property caused problems galore for those divers (including confiscation of their boats!) Federal agents seized the anchor and it was returned to the wreck site by the Canadian Coast Guard ship, *Kenoki,* on June 3, 1989, due in large part to the efforts of the Windsor chapter of Save Ontario Shipwrecks, as well as other agencies and individuals. This enormous anchor is probably the highlight of this site.

6. JAY GOULD

LORAN: 43829.2/57202.6	GPS: 41° 51.530'/082° 24.608'
DEPTH: 36 to 44 feet	LEVEL: Novice-Intermediate

LOCATION: This wreck lies about five miles southeast of Point Pelee.

Constructed at Buffalo, New York, in 1869, the 840-gross-ton wooden steamer, *Jay Gould* (213'8" x 33'9" x 11'5"), foundered with a cargo of coal on June 17, 1918. The entire crew was rescued by a passing steamer. The highlight of this wreck site is the tall, early (which makes it a rare one) steeple compound steam engine, in which even the Smithsonian Institute has expressed an interest. Although dynamited as a threat to navigation, this wreck still displays her huge, four-bladed propeller, stern capstan and many scattered artifacts.

Far left: The steamer, *Jay Gould*. CRIS KOHL COLLECTION. *Left and below:* The steam engine towers high above the lake bottom; a diver examines the *Gould's* propeller. PHOTOS BY CRIS KOHL

Above: Sidescan sonar image of the *Jay Gould*. © AQUA VISION RESEARCH. *Below:* Valerie Olson van Heest of the Underwater Archaeological Society of Chicago worked with Save Ontario Shipwrecks to produce this site plan.

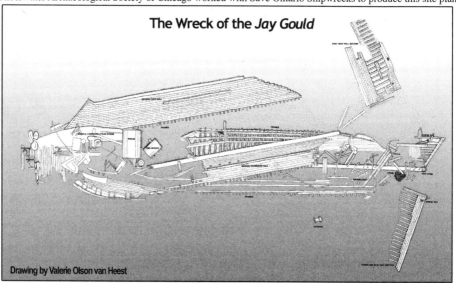

The Wreck of the *Jay Gould*

Drawing by Valerie Olson van Heest

7. DOMINION

LORAN: 43880.5/57218.3	**GPS: 41° 59.751'/082° 26.719'**
DEPTH: 45 feet	**LEVEL: Novice-Intermediate**

LOCATION: This site lies a bit over five miles south of Wheatley, Ontario, harbor.

The flat, steam-powered dredge barge, *Dominion,* about 75 feet long and 25 feet wide, capsized while under tow on October 28, 1892. Once hoped to be the long-lost steamer, *Kent,* these shipwreck remains do offer the visiting diver views of a huge boiler, a winch with chain, and a variety of tools and artifacts.

Right: A scuba diver descends to the boiler of the barge, *Dominion.*   PHOTO BY CRIS KOHL

8. CLARION

LORAN: 43890.1/57298.2	**GPS: 41° 57.262'/082° 16.308'**
DEPTH: 58 to 77 feet	**LEVEL: Advanced**

LOCATION: This wreck lies about 13 miles northeast of Point Pelee.

The composite (iron and wood) package freight steamer, *Clarion* (240'9" x 36'1" x 15'5"), launched at Wyandotte, Michigan, on July 27, 1881, burned to a total loss during a storm on December 8, 1909, off Point Pelee. Tragically, 15 of the 21 men on board the *Clarion* perished. The rescue of the 6 survivors is a fascinating tale of heroism. This storm also sank the *W. C. Richardson* (also in this book) at the other end of Lake Erie, and the train car ferry, *Marquette & Bessemer #2,* a long-sought Great Lakes shipwreck.

This upright wreck offers a very intact stern section which is penetrable by trained, experienced and prepared divers (beware of much silt!) In contrast, most of the bow burned off or is buried. The first divers at this site called this the "Stern Wreck" because they could find no bow at all. Items of interest at this site include a mushroom anchor and windlass and chain at the bow, a propeller, rudder, steam engine and boiler at the stern, and, in between, a capstan, bitts, and locomotive wheels in the holds.

The *Clarion.* CRIS KOHL COLLECTION

Left: The steamer, *L. C. Hanna,* in a daring, nighttime rescue of some crewmembers from the stern of the burning steamer, *Clarion.* ARTIST UNKNOWN. THE MARINE REVIEW, JANUARY, 1910. CRIS KOHL COLLECTION

9. WILLIS

LORAN: 43897.2/57349.5	GPS: 41° 55.879'/082° 09.669'
DEPTH: 60 to 73 feet	LEVEL: Intermediate-Advanced

LOCATION: This wreck lies about 15 miles east-northeast of Point Pelee.

The three-masted schooner, *Willis* (131'7" x 27'9" x 9'), sank in her first year afloat on November 11, 1872, after a collision with the bark, *Elizabeth Jones.* Built at Manitowoc, Wisconsin, the short-lived *Willis* was downbound with grain from Escanaba, Michigan, at the time of loss. Although no lives were lost in the sinking, a long court case ensued.

Originally located by Canadian gas-well-working hardhat diver, Michael Schoger, in about 1960, and finally identified when Cleveland diver, James Paskert, found the tonnage numbers on the rear hatch combing in the late 1980's, the *Willis* is an impressive shipwreck. The steering gear is interesting, even though the wheel was removed. Several deadeyes and blocks remain, as well as a capstan, a bilge pump and a long portion of the bowsprit.. The smallest of the spars straddling the starboard rail could be the bowsprit of the *Elizabeth Jones,* torn off in the impact of the collision.

Top: The *Willis*: under sail and under water. ART © COPYRIGHT AND COURTESY OF PETER RINDLISBACHER, AND COURTESY OF ROY PICKERING, ORIGINAL ART OWNER. FOR INFORMATION ABOUT MR. RINDLISBACHER'S ART, CONTACT THE CANADIAN SOCIETY OF MARINE ARTISTS, OR GO TO WWW.ULTRAMARINE.CA. *Above:* Sidescan sonar image of the *Willis*. Note such details as the bowsprit, rails, posts and hatches. © AQUA VISION RESEARCH. *Bottom, right:* Diver Sharon Dickson follows steel rigging to a cleat on the *Willis. Top, right:* A missing *Willis* stern porthole.   PHOTOS BY CRIS KOHL

10. CONEMAUGH

LORAN: 43835.2/57162.8	GPS: 41° 54.568'/082° 30.660'
DEPTH: 16 to 20 feet	LEVEL: Novice-Intermediate

LOCATION: This wreck lies about 400' off shore on the west side of Point Pelee right where the forest ends at the point. But make it a boat dive; you can't drive up to it on shore.

The wooden freighter, *Conemaugh* (251'3" x 36' x 15'2"), sister ship to the *Lycoming* (which is also in this book), was built at Bay City, Michigan, in 1880. On November 24,

Left: The *Conemaugh*. CRIS KOHL COLLECTION. *Right:* A park sign visually depicts the *Conemaugh's* loss. *Below:* Joyce Hayward prepares to dive the *Conemaugh* (where the boats are), and inspects the wreck's machinery. PHOTOS BY CRIS KOHL.

1906, a violent storm beached the *Conemaugh* just off Point Pelee with such smashing force that three of her four propeller blades broke off on the sandbar. Fortunately, the entire crew was rescued by the men at the nearby Lifesaving Station.

The sand covers and uncovers the timbers, the boiler and the broken propeller that comprise the main items left of this ship. Years ago, a local scuba diver salvaged the capstan and donated it to Point Pelee National Park, which put it on outdoor display. Unfortunately, it was not properly conserved and it soon became a broken pile of rust, especially after vandals rolled it around the concession stand.

11. *M. I. WILCOX*

LORAN: 43802.2/56959.8	GPS: 41° 58.832'/082° 56.455'
DEPTH: 20 to 26 feet	LEVEL: Novice-Intermediate

LOCATION: About 1/3 mile south of the Colchester, Ontario, dock.

The three-masted schooner, *M. I. Wilcox* (137' x 27'5" x 12'7"), built at Toledo in 1868, sprang a leak and sank on May 8, 1906, with no lives lost. Site sights include a windlass, donkey boiler, capstan, anchor, wheel, deadeyes and sometimes low visibility. This wreck was found on July 2, 1990 by Ed Fabok, Joe Drummond, & Lloyd & Betty Kerr.

The schooner, *M. I. Wilcox*, full sail, but little wind. CRIS KOHL COLLECTION

Drawing by Cris Kohl, based on on-site observations and information from Ed Fabok.

191

12. GRAND TRAVERSE

LORAN: 43796.0/56975.1	GPS: 41° 56.902'/082° 53.688'
DEPTH: 35 to 40 feet	LEVEL: Novice-Intermediate

The *Grand Traverse*. CRIS KOHL COLLECTION

LOCATION: This wreck lies off Colchester Reef, three miles southeast of Colchester.

Now broken and scattered on a silty bottom, the wooden steamer, *Grand Traverse* (181' x 33' x 14'1"; launched as the *Morley* in 1879 at Marine City, MI), sank in a collision with the steamer, *Livingstone*, on October 19, 1896. Considerable machinery salvage took place after the sinking, but the hull remains.

13. GEORGE WORTHINGTON

LORAN: 43800.1/56994.4	GPS: 41° 56.687'/082° 51.319'
DEPTH: 32 to 40 feet	LEVEL: Novice-Intermediate

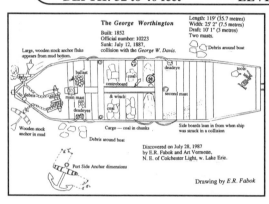

LOCATION: This wreck lies off Colchester Reef.

The twin-masted schooner, *George Worthington* (119'9" x 25'2" x 10'1"), built in 1852 at Euclid Creek, Ohio, sank after a collision with the schooner, *George W. Davis,* on July 12, 1887. No lives were lost. This intact, upright wreck sports twin bow anchors, windlass, deadeyes, centerboard, tools on deck and a coal cargo. The wreck was discovered on July 28, 1987, by Ed Fabok and Art Vermette.

14. CASE

LORAN: 43744.3/56956.9	GPS: 41° 48.586'/082° 51.660'
DEPTH: 18 to 20 feet	LEVEL: Novice

LOCATION: This wreck lies about 600' off the southwest side of East Sister Island.

The large, wooden steamer, *Case* (286' x 42'5" x 22'), loaded with coal (which was later salvaged, along with some machinery), stranded, caught on fire and broke up in a storm on May 1, 1917. No lives were lost. Built at Cleveland in 1889, wood and metal parts of the *Case* lie scattered over a wide area on a rocky bottom.

The *Case*. CRIS KOHL COLLECTION

15. CAPSTAN WRECK (*CHARGER?*)

LORAN: 43812.7/57141.2	GPS: 41° 51.659'/082° 31.769'
DEPTH: 30 to 36 feet	LEVEL: Novice-Intermediate

LOCATION: This wreck lies in the Pelee Passage, west of Point Pelee.

This unidentified sailing vessel may be the remains of the schooner, *Charger* (136' x 25' x 10'), which sank in a collision with the steambarge, *City of Cleveland,* on July 31, 1890. The *Charger* sank within ten minutes, the crew barely escaping with their lives.

As the nickname implies, this site on a silty bottom has a capstan, as well as a windlass, wheel and deadeyes.

192

13. Other Western Lake Erie Sites

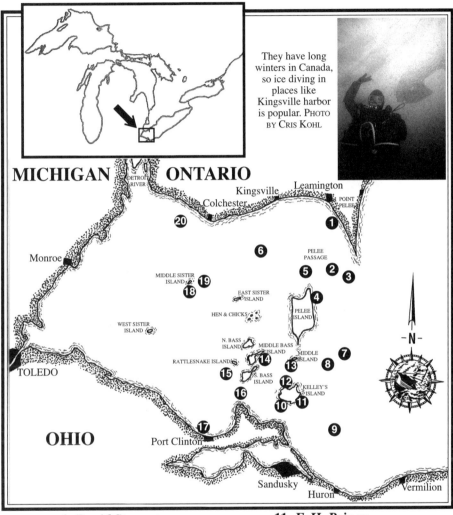

They have long winters in Canada, so ice diving in places like Kingsville harbor is popular. PHOTO BY CRIS KOHL

MICHIGAN   ONTARIO

DETROIT RIVER

Kingsville   Leamington
Colchester   POINT PELEE

20   1

Monroe   6   PELEE PASSAGE

MIDDLE SISTER ISLAND   19   5   2   3
18   EAST SISTER ISLAND   4
HEN & CHICKS   PELEE ISLAND

WEST SISTER ISLAND

N. BASS ISLAND   MIDDLE BASS ISLAND   MIDDLE ISLAND   7
RATTLESNAKE ISLAND   14   13   8
15   S. BASS ISLAND   12   KELLEY'S ISLAND   -N-
16   10   11
9

TOLEDO   17

OHIO   Port Clinton

Sandusky   Huron   Vermilion

1. *David Stewart*
2. *Isaac W. Nicholas*
3. *David Vance*
4. *America*
5. *Armenia*
6. *Charles B. Packard*
7. *Philip Minch*
8. *George Dunbar*
9. *City of Concord*
10. *Exchange*

11. *F. H. Prince*
12. *Adventure*
13. *Keepsake*
14. *Isabella J. Boyce*
15. *Toledo*
16. *Charles Spademan*
17. *Success*
18. *Wesee*
19. *Magnet*
20. *D. L. Filer*

1. DAVID STEWART

LORAN: 43858.0/57160.2	GPS: 41° 58.695'/082° 32.939'
DEPTH: 25 to 32 feet	LEVEL: Novice

LOCATION: 700' off the western shore of Point Pelee, two miles from Leamington.

The 545-ton merchant schooner, *David Stewart* (171' x 31' x 13'), launched at Cleveland in 1867, stranded and broke up in a storm on October 6, 1893. The six men and one woman on board were daringly rescued from the sunken ship's masts by the fishing tug, *Louise*. Weather conditions were so odd and powerful that the *Louise* could not make headway into Leamington harbor two miles away, and instead steamed all the way across the lake to Sandusky with the rescued crew. Ice, wind and waves have flattened this wreck, but the stern is upright and belaying pins and a hawse pipe are on the bow. Beware of silt and nets.

2. ISAAC W. NICHOLAS

LORAN: 43819.39/57138.69	GPS: 41° 52.932'/082° 32.701'
DEPTH: 30 to 36 feet	LEVEL: Novice-Intermediate

LOCATION: This wreck lies at Grubb's Reef to the southwest of Point Pelee.

Built at Vermilion, Ohio, in 1862 by Isaac W. Nicholas and named after himself, this three-masted schooner (137'8" x 26'2" x 12'2"), attempting to ride out a tempestuous storm on October 20, 1873, dragged her anchor and stranded on what was later named Grubb's Reef (after the Point Pelee light keeper who reported the shoal to officials). The crew took to the rigging, from which they were rescued the next day by the schooner, *Denmark*.

This wreck, in surprisingly very good condition, features a rudder, steering gear, blocks, deadeyes, belaying pins, windlass, anchor and wheel! Beware of fishnets and boating traffic.

3. DAVID VANCE

LORAN: 43813.82/57144.29	GPS: 41° 51.724'/082° 31.440'
DEPTH: 42 feet	LEVEL: Novice-Intermediate

LOCATION: This wreck lies to the south-southwest of Point Pelee.

The three-masted schooner, *David Vance* (206'6" x 33'7" x 14'4"), built at Manitowoc, Wisconsin, in 1874, sank in a collision on July 20, 1873, with the schooner-barge, *Lizzie A. Law*, which was, like the *David Vance,* being towed by a steamer at the time. Both the *David Vance* and the *Lizzie A. Law* sank, but the latter was salvaged and returned to service.

Flattened by nature, the wreck of the *David Vance*, with the bow facing south on a sand bottom, exhibits a rudder post, centerboard, wheel and deadeyes. It lies within a few hundred feet of the wreck of the *Charger* (which is also in this book).

4. AMERICA

LORAN: 43783.49/57078.39	GPS: 41° 49.679'/082° 38.069'
DEPTH: 15 feet	LEVEL: Novice

The *America,* based on a drawing by Heyl.

LOCATION: This wreck lies 175' off the northeast tip of Pelee Island, 1/2 mile south of the abandoned lighthouse.

The sidewheel steamer, *America* (240'2" x 34'2" x 13'8"), ran aground on April 5, 1854, with no lives lost. Spring storms quickly broke up the ship. A tall boiler, planking, and other remains are scattered in a large debris field.

5. ARMENIA

LORAN: 43806.62/57091.06	GPS: 41° 52.948'/082° 38.503'
DEPTH: 35 to 39 feet	LEVEL: Novice-Intermediate

LOCATION: This wreck lies off Colchester Reef.

The schooner-barge, *Armenia* (288'6" x 44'6" x 19'1"), with a cargo of iron ore, foundered in a storm on May 9, 1906, with no lives lost. Built at West Bay City, Michigan, in 1896 by James Davidson, the *Armenia* was eventually dynamited, but not before she caused another shipwreck, the *Charles B. Packard* (which is the next wreck in this book). The *Armenia's* wood, rudder and machinery lie scattered, and in a silt-heavy area where one good fin-kick an arm's length above the shipwreck will destroy the visibility in that area for the rest of the day. Beware of fishnets.

Left, the schooner-barge, *Armenia,* which caused the steamer, *Charles B. Packard, right,* to sink.

CRIS KOHL COLLECTION

6. CHARLES B. PACKARD

LORAN: 43808.49/57053.82	GPS: 41° 55.222'/082° 43.661'
DEPTH: 37 to 40 feet	LEVEL: Novice-Intermediate

LOCATION: This wreck lies near the *Armenia* off Colchester Reef.

Sunk after colliding with the wreck of the *Armenia* on September 16, 1906, with no lives lost, the wooden steamer, *Charles B. Packard* (180'5" x 35'7" x 13'3"), had been built in 1887 and launched as the *Elfin-Mere* (the name was changed in 1902), also at West Bay City, Michigan, but by James Davidson's competition, F. W. Wheeler & Company. How the jokes must have flown in Bay City about a wrecked Davidson boat sinking a Wheeler steamer! This site, in much silt, consists of a huge boiler sitting in a broken hull surrounded by a large debris field.

7. PHILIP MINCH

LORAN: 43741.93/57106.21	GPS: 41° 41.301'/082° 30.813'
DEPTH: 42 to 48 feet	LEVEL: Intermediate

LOCATION: This wreck lies about eight miles east of Middle Island.

Built at Cleveland in 1888, the wooden steamer, *Philip Minch* (275' x 40'8" x 22'), caught on fire and sank with no lives lost on November 20, 1904. Machinery and seemingly endless collapsed hull sections make up most of this site, with the huge (but recently toppled over) steeple compound steam engine at the stern. Beware of snagged fish nets.

Left: The steamer, *Philip Minch.*
CRIS KOHL COLLECTION

195

At the *Philip Minch's* bow.
PHOTO BY CRIS KOHL

Sidescan sonar image of the *Philip Minch*. The engine and boiler are evident at the left. © AQUA VISION RESEARCH

8. GEORGE DUNBAR

LORAN: 43729.63/57076.39	GPS: 41° 40.627'/082° 33.891'
DEPTH: 42 to 45 feet	LEVEL: Intermediate

LOCATION: This wreck lies about six miles southeast of Fish Point, Pelee Island.

The small steamer, *George Dunbar* (133'5" x 25'3" x 9'1"), sprang a leak and foundered on June 29, 1902, with a coal cargo and all seven crewmembers who did not survive their lifeboats capsizing. The captain, his wife and their daughter, the only ones wearing lifejackets, were rescued by islanders in a small boat. The wreck sits in mud, with a boiler, windlass and upright support posts the dominant features.

Sidescan sonar image of the *George Dunbar*. Note the central support post shadows. © AQUA VISION RESEARCH

9. CITY OF CONCORD

LORAN: 43675.02/57052.68	GPS: 41° 32.730'/082° 32.808'
DEPTH: 45 feet	LEVEL: Intermediate

LOCATION: About ten miles north of Huron, Ohio.

The wooden steamer, *City of Concord* (135'2" x 25'8" x 11'), constructed in 1868 at Cleveland, took on water during a storm and foundered on September 29, 1906, with the loss of two lives. One crewman was rescued by a passsing vessel, while the rest of the crew reached land near Cedar Point in a yawlboat. Sitting upright in mud, this wreck site features a

Left: The *City of Concord*. CRIS KOHL COLLECTION

rudder, engine, boiler, windlass, chain, decking and the relatively intact hull.

10. EXCHANGE

LORAN: 43672.22/56974.02	GPS: 41° 35.644'/082° 43.229'
DEPTH: 15 feet	LEVEL: Novice

LOCATION: 200' off the south side of Kelley's Island, east of the ferry dock.

The schooner, *Exchange* (138' x 26' x 11'8"), stranded with a load of stone on November 21, 1874, and was abandoned. Planking, ribs and chain remain at the site.

11. F. H. PRINCE

LORAN: 43683.02/57000.38	GPS: 41° 36.242'/082° 40.518'
DEPTH: 18 feet	LEVEL: Novice

LOCATION: This wreck lies about 1/2 mile off the east side of Kelley's Island.

Launched at Detroit in 1890, the wooden steamer, *F. H. Prince* (240' x 42' x 23'4"), caught on fire in the lake on August 8, 1911, and was beached and extinguished. On Aug. 14th, the fire re-ignited, and she burned to a total loss. Large timbers and machinery rest on a rock bottom, but the engine/boiler were salvaged. Beware of heavy boating traffic!

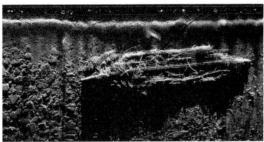

The steamer, *F. H. Prince* (CRIS KOHL COLLECTION) and sidescan sonar image of it today. © AQUA VISION RESEARCH

12. ADVENTURE

LORAN: 43688.09/57000.92	GPS: 41° 37.088'/082° 40.871'
DEPTH: 10 feet	LEVEL: Novice

LOCATION: This wreck lies in North Bay, Kelley's Island. The wooden steamer, *Adventure* (108' x 24' x 8'3"), built originally as a schooner at Detroit in 1875 and converted to a steamer in 1897, burned on October 7, 1903. Hull timbers and machinery remain.

Great Lakes Highlight No. 8

THE *SUCCESS*:

AUSTRALIAN CONVICT SHIP WRECK

LOCATION: 1/2 mile off Port Clinton, Ohio.

LORAN: 43616.38/56855.91   GPS: 41° 31.319'/082° 54.703'
DEPTH: 15 feet   LEVEL: Novice

This historic teak barquentine (135' x 30' x 14'), built in Burma in 1840 but passed off as being much older, toured the world as a notorious "Prison Ship" which allegedly had conveyed convicts to Australia (in reality, it had served as a women's prison there for a few years). The *Success* sailed from Australia to England in the 1890's, and left England for America on the same day in 1912 that *Titanic* did, only *Success* made it (even though it took more than 90 days!). The ship toured many North American ports, attracting enormous crowds. Contests were held in each port to see who could spend the longest time in the dark "brig," and many couples were married on board. After nearly two decades, the ship fell victim to the Great Depression and spent more time sitting idle than touring. She aged poorly, and was in a sad state when vandals set fire to her in Lake Erie on July 4, 1946. Keel, ribs, planking, metal parts and fish are plentiful, but good visibility is rare at this shallow site. For more details about this ship and its unique history, read the chapter called "Flaunting '*Success*'" in the book, *Shipwreck Tales of the Great Lakes* by Cris Kohl.

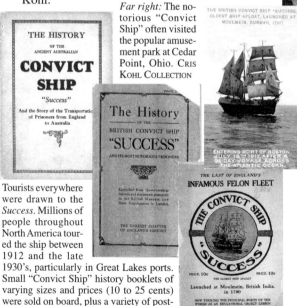

Far right: The notorious "Convict Ship" often visited the popular amusement park at Cedar Point, Ohio. CRIS KOHL COLLECTION

Tourists everywhere were drawn to the *Success*. Millions of people throughout North America toured the ship between 1912 and the late 1930's, particularly in Great Lakes ports. Small "Convict Ship" history booklets of varying sizes and prices (10 to 25 cents) were sold on board, plus a variety of postcards depicting real and staged scenes of "convict ship life." CRIS KOHL COLLECTION

13. KEEPSAKE

LORAN:	LAT 41° 40' 55" LON 082° 41' 16"
DEPTH: 10 feet	LEVEL: Novice

LOCATION: 125' off the southwest side of Middle Island. The small scow schooner, *Keepsake* (72'6" x 19'9" x 3'7"), built in 1880 at Puce River, Ontario (just east of Windsor), stranded on August 11, 1911. Parts and artifacts lie scattered on rocks.

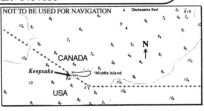

14. ISABELLA J. BOYCE

LORAN: 56972.21/43708.99	GPS: 41° 41.831'/082° 46.507'
DEPTH: 5 to 10 feet	LEVEL: Novice

LOCATION: East Point Reef off Middle Bass Island. The wooden sandsucker, *Isabella J. Boyce* (138' x 29'6" x 11'), stranded and burned on June 6, 1917. This wreck is very broken and widely scattered among rocks in VERY SHALLOW WATER! See archival photograph on next page.

15. TOLEDO

LORAN: 43690.68/56916.60	GPS: 41° 41.141'/082° 52.601'
DEPTH: 35 feet	LEVEL: Novice-Intermediate

LOCATION: One mile west of Rattlesnake Island. The barge, *Toledo*, foundered on November 19, 1924, with all 7 men surviving. She is broken and scattered on a rock bottom. See archival photograph on next page.

16. CHARLES SPADEMAN

LORAN: 28853.28/56920.12   GPS:
DEPTH: 32 feet   LEVEL: Novice-Intermediate

LOCATION: About 2/3 mile 160° from South Bass Island Lighthouse. The schooner, *Charles Spademan* (134'2" x 25'9" x 10'8"), sank after her hull was punctured by ice on Dec. 10, 1909. Her coal cargo was salvaged and the wreck was dynamited, so little remains.

The steamer, *Isabella J. Boyce,* the barge, *Toledo,* and the schooner, *Charles Spademan.*   CRIS KOHL COLLECTION

17. SUCCESS -- SEE PAGE 198.

18. WESEE

LORAN: 43739.3/56895.1   GPS: 41° 50.597'/082° 59.565'
DEPTH: 22 feet   LEVEL: Novice

LOCATION: This wreck lies off Middle Sister Island. The wooden steamer, *Wesee* (265'5" x 42' x 22'7"), built in 1901 at Green Bay, WI, burned to a total loss on November 12, 1923. The crew, plus two starving fishermen who had been marooned on the island, were rescued. Although engine and boiler were salvaged, much of this ship remains scattered.

The wooden steamer, *Wesee,* burned in 1923.   CRIS KOHL COLLECTION

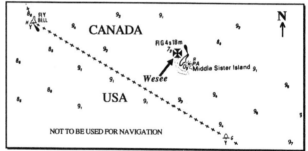

NOT TO BE USED FOR NAVIGATION

19. MAGNET

LORAN: 43757.82/56926.73   GPS: 41° 52.866'/082° 57.406'
DEPTH: 35 feet   LEVEL: Novice-Intermediate

LOCATION: The two-masted schooner, *Magnet* (141'8" x 24' x 7'4"), built in 1856 at Saginaw, Michigan, as a sidewheel tug and converted in 1888, foundered in a storm east of Middle Sister Island on Sept. 12, 1900. Her crew was rescued. This shipwreck and its coal cargo lie scattered.

20. D. L. FILER

LORAN: 43787.81/56925.78   GPS:
DEPTH: 20 feet   LEVEL: Novice-Intermediate

The *D. L. Filer.* CRIS KOHL COLLECTION

The schooner-barge, *D. L. Filer* (156'6" x 30' x 10'), built in 1871 at Manistee, Michigan, sank in the Black Friday Storm of Oct. 20, 1916, with only the captain surviving. Silty conditions abound at this site!

The Zebra Mussel Invasion of the Great Lakes

My home town of Windsor, Ontario, is located about five miles from where the zebra mussel invasion was first noticed in shallow Lake St. Clair. I wrote my first article on the zebra mussel invasion of the Great Lakes in the spring of 1989, and it appeared in *Diving Times* (Royal Oak, Michigan) that summer under the heading, "Shipwrecks Threatened by Freshwater Barnacles" (their identification as zebra mussels was made later that summer by two University of Windsor biology students).

I gave a presentation on this topic, focusing primarily on how these uninvited guests were affecting shipwrecks and, hence, scuba diving, at the annual meeting of the Ontario Archaeological Society in October, 1989 (held that year in London, Ontario), at the annual Save Ontario Shipwrecks Forum in November, 1989 (held that year in Windsor, Ontario), and at the annual Great Lakes Shipwreck Festival, Dearborn, Michigan, in February, 1990. Since then, I have kept updating that presentation, which I have given dozens of times to a wide variety of audiences mostly in the Great Lakes region but also as distant as New York City.

The next four pages give the essence of my presentation about the zebra mussel invasion.

◆   ◆   ◆   ◆   ◆   ◆   ◆   ◆   ◆

In the spring of 1988, I received a letter from Graeme Henderson, author of the book, *Maritime Archaeology in Australia* and curator, Department of Maritime Archaeology, at the Western Australian Maritime Museum in Fremantle near Perth. He stated, among other things, that "I have of course read about your amazingly well-preserved Great Lakes shipwrecks...."

He was naturally comparing them to saltwater shipwrecks, with their fast-forming coral encrustations, such as the steel vessel, *Denton Holmes,* off Rottnest Island near Perth in the Indian Ocean, or the purposely sunk World War II minesweeper, the *Mahi,* off the coast of Oahu, Hawaii.

The shipwrecks in our own Great Lakes area are now being threatened by the saltwater invader known as the zebra mussel (or by its Latin name: dreissena polymorpha). Present in the ballast water of ocean-going freighters, these zebra mussels somehow adapted to

Left: Denton Holmes wreckage in the Indian Ocean. *Middle:* The *Mahi* off Oahu in 1988 after 6 years of submergence. *Right:* Joan Forsberg examines coral encrustation on the *Mahi* in 2001 when the ship had been submerged for 19 years. We expect saltwater shipwrecks to look like this, but our freshwater shipwrecks in the Great Lakes looked comparatively pristine! PHOTOS BY CRIS KOHL

freshwater conditions when this ballast water was dumped in Lake St. Clair in about 1986. The unknown ship(s) which did the dumping probably filled its ballast tanks in coastal Europe and, instead of dumping and replenishing in mid-Atlantic Ocean (where the saltwater is devoid of zebra mussel larvae) as was the custom, it waited until it was in the Great Lakes system before it dumped and replenished.

Laws were recently passed prohibiting the dumping of ballast water from ocean-going freighters in the Great Lakes, but that's like closing the gate after the horses have escaped.

The opening of the St. Lawrence Seaway system more than 40 years ago paved the way for greater wealth in the Great Lakes region, but now we who live, work and play there are paying a potentially severe price for that participation in world trade.

There are several biological hitchhikers now in our Great Lakes, including the River Ruffe fish and European water fleas, but the zebra mussel seems destined to be the most destructive in overall terms.

Physically, zebra mussels are small and unimposing. Averaging the size of a ten-cent coin, they individually look quite harmless and perhaps even "cute," as one of my scuba diving colleagues described them. However, they attach themselves by the millions to anything that is solid in the lakes, and their reproduction abilities make rabbits seem celibate.

Originating in the salt-water Caspian Sea between Russia and Iran, the zebra mussels started spreading to western Europe's coasts in the mid-1800's, at about the same time that steam-powered ships developed Caspian Sea trade with the rest of Europe along the River Volga and the Baltic Sea and Black Sea routes.

Mature zebra mussels' size compared to a dime.
PHOTO BY CRIS KOHL

By the late 1800's, coastal Europe, with its combination of salt and fresh water areas (from its freshwater rivers flowing into the saltwater ocean), was inundated by zebra mussels. To date, the Europeans have found no effective method of eliminating this problem.

In late 1988, these "vile crustaceans" (as one newspaper article at that time described them) were clogging water intake pipes along southeastern Lake St. Clair and the northwestern shore of Lake Erie. By February, 1989, the mussels had spread along Lake Erie's north shore as far east as Port Burwell. They reached Dunkirk, New York, by October 16, 1989, and by year's end, western Lake Ontario. Carried upstream by freighters to which they had attached themselves in Lake Erie, the first zebra mussels were identified in Green Bay harbor, Wisconsin, Lake Michigan, in late October, 1989. The harbors of Duluth, Minnesota, and Thunder Bay, Ontario, both on Lake Superior, were also soon colonized. Generally, the largest and coldest of our five Great Lakes contains too little calcium which zebra mussels need to form their shells, as well as the wrong amount of Ph (acidity) which zebra mussels in the southern, heavily-populated half of the Great Lakes find so nourishing.

Each zebra mussel female can produce 30,000 to 40,000 offspring in one season. Zebra mussel larvae resemble fine grains of sand as they drift along with the current encased in an invisible jelly-like blob. As they grow larger, they seek anything solid to which they can attach themselves by means of a hair-like thread called a byssal thread. This makes them different from their bivalve relatives called clams. Mussels attach themselves to objects, while clams just sit freely on the bottom.

The first dramatic incident of scuba divers being awed and dazed by the surprising presence of zebra mussels occurred in late February, 1989, when Roy Pickering and Jeff Bliss, members of Kent Divers Association, Kent County, Ontario, were exploring the Erieau channel on Lake Erie. In about 18 feet of water, they unexpectedly came upon an automobile. However, it seemed to be almost totally encrusted with what the divers, not knowing what they were dealing with, termed "barnacles." One of the local media profiled the police retrieval of this vehicle, which had been stolen the previous August and likely had been submerged for those preceding six months. The zebra mussels had attached themselves to virtually every part of the vehicle, not just to the metal body, chrome bumpers and rubber tires, but also to the vinyl interior.

As more water intake pipes started clogging because of gradual zebra mussel build-up inside them, more media attention in that central Great Lakes area was paid to this new problem. At about this time (May, 1989), I began reshooting underwater photos of some of the shipwrecks in the western Lake Erie area. At that early stage, the shipwrecks lying in less than 40 feet of water were almost totally covered by zebra mussels. I noticed that portions where there were no mussels were parts of the shipwreck where the silt or sand covering was too thick for mussel attachment. They need something solid, such as steel, iron, or wood. We could no longer discern what we were looking at because a lump of coal or a chunk of limestone cargo from a shipwreck resembled exactly an indigenous lake-bottom rock or a ship's compass when it was covered in several layers of zebra mussels (they do attach themselves to each other and, like in a coral reef system, the lower layer dies once it is covered by another layer). I have even seen clustered balls of zebra mussels attached to each other rolling around the sandy lake bottom off Rondeau Point in their desperation to attach themselves to anything solid. A biologist in Wheatley, Ontario, declared that the zebra mussels are mildly caustic, which means that they damage their roosts. At least one archaeologist has argued that the zebra mussels will help preserve our Great Lakes shipwrecks for future generations, but he is grasping at straws. The weight of thousands upon thousands of zebra mussels, for another thing, has not only caused Coast Guard buoys to sink, but also parts of shipwrecks to collapse, such as the once-impressive bowsprit of the schooner, *Nimrod*.

BEFORE **AFTER**

Diver Joyce Hayward with the propeller hub of the steamer, *Conemaugh,* western Lake Erie, in June, 1988, just before the zebra mussel invasion. PHOTO BY CRIS KOHL

That same propeller hub photographed from the same angle in July, 1989, a mere 13 months later. It is totally unrecognizable. PHOTO BY CRIS KOHL

These two photos were published in the *Washington* (D.C.) *Post* newspaper in the summer of 2000 to illustrate a zebra mussel article.

One potential effect of dubious benefit is that illegal shipwreck-stripping is made more difficult, since the identification of choice shipwreck souvenirs is made more difficult. A chadburn, or telegraph, sitting on the lake floor coated with five layers of zebra mussels could well be shrugged off by the passing scuba diver as being merely a rock.

I photographed the Colchester Reef wreck of the schooner, *George Worthington,* in western Lake Erie, and it was totally covered in multi-layers of zebra mussels -- except for one unusual item. It was a light-colored pipe which we, at first, suspected was made of lead. It turned out to be copper. Initially, zebra mussels avoided attaching themselves to anything made of copper, brass or bronze, but within two years, they had acclimatized to those metals as well.The readily-adaptible zebra mussels rolled on like the plague.

By September, 1989, biologists were predicting the probable destruction of our large freshwater clams because the smaller zebra mussels are attaching themselves to them in such vast numbers until the native clams can no longer open their shells, and thus they starve to death. Zebra mussels even attached themselves to freshwater crayfish. Ropes left dangling in the water from docks soon became home to thick clusters of zebra mussels.

A questionable benefit of the zebra mussel invasion has been a cleansing of our Great Lakes waters. Zebra mussels are filter feeders, each tiny individual filtering about one liter of water each day. Since they remove the floating particles in the water, increased visibility has been a boon to scuba diving in Lakes Erie, Ontario and the St. Lawrence River in recent years. But at what a price! Besides the aesthetic destruction of our shipwrecks, the cleaner water is allowing more sunlight to reach greater depths -- forcing fish, such as pickerel, or

The *Merida's* bow anchor, August, 1987. PHOTO BY CRIS KOHL   The same, August, 1992. PHOTO BY CRIS KOHL   The *Merida's* starboard bow anchor chain, April, 1990. PHOTO BY CRIS KOHL   The same, August, 1992. PHOTO BY CRIS KOHL

walleye, which prefer darker, colder water, to seek deeper spawning grounds. In the shallows, the increased clarity and sunlight have caused incredible growth of aquatic plants, which, when they die, wash ashore. The shoreline of Lake St. Clair was inundated by foul-smelling, decaying seaweed, and the aerial photographs I took of Lake St. Clair in 1991 showed enormous beds of weeds in multihued green and blue shallow water, like in the Bahamas!

Of course, once the zebra mussels have depleted their food supply in their area, when the water is really clean, they starve to death. In June, 2002, we explored the wreck of the *Wells Burt* off Chicago in 36' of water -- and had 55' of horizontal visibility! And most of the zebra mussels had died and fallen off the wreck! Just five years earlier, the wreck was totally covered in multiple layers of mussels; by the summer of 2007, the wreck was again nearly totally covered, suggesting that when particle-rich waters (low visibility) return, zebra mussels thrive again. The trick is to learn when the zebra mussels have died and most of them have fallen off the wrecks in any given area, and the water retains its excellent visibility -- THAT's when to explore and photograph those shipwrecks! I refer to that year or two as the desirable "slack tide" period in the zebra mussel cycle, excellent for scuba diving.

Scientists in Europe have observed zebra mussels thriving in cycles which recur about every six or seven years, and that seems to be the case for the Great Lakes' zebra mussels, and their larger cousin, the quagga mussel.

Scientists have also found zebra mussels in Europe's cold inland lakes (carried there by waterfowl in all likelihood) at depths of 300 feet, so the hope that the cold will eliminate them from certain Great Lakes regions or depths was dashed. In March, 2000, Capt. Jerry Guyer showed videotape at Milwaukee's Ghost Ships Festival of zebra mussels attached to a new shipwreck discovery in 300 feet of Lake Michigan water.

As far as marine archaeology is concerned, Great Lakes interests may have to accept and learn saltwater methods of conducting their business. Many well-traveled scuba divers have observed that the Great Lakes possess, without question, the best preserved shipwrecks in the world. For now, we can only hope that these shipwrecks, Great Lakes scuba diving and freshwater marine archaeology will continue to have a future.

14. Sites near Lake Erie

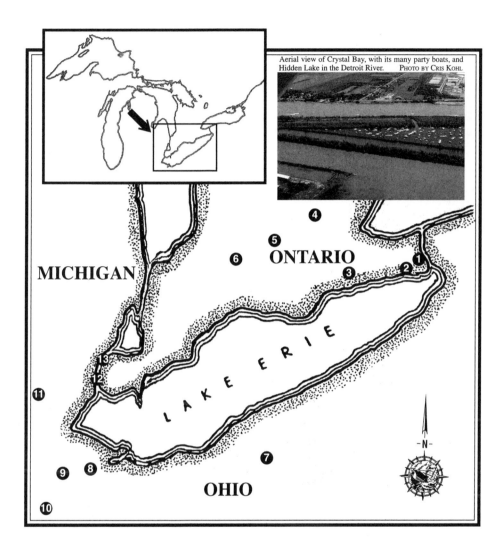

Aerial view of Crystal Bay, with its many party boats, and Hidden Lake in the Detroit River. Photo by Cris Kohl

1. Chippawa Creek
2. Sherkston Quarry
3. Hagersville Quarry
4. Elora Gorge Quarry
5. Trout Lake (Innerkip) Quarry
6. St. Marys Quarry
7. Nelson's Ledges Quarry
8. White Star Quarry
9. Portage Quarry
10. Gilboa Quarry
11. Baw Beese Lake
12. Crystal Bay/ Hidden Lake
13. Unidentified schooner

1. CHIPPAWA CREEK

Near the town of Chippawa, Ontario, along the Niagara River, this site is a popular drift dive in swift water (so it's not for novices) for old bottles and other discarded items. There are many public exit and entry points along this short creek. The depth reaches 35 feet.

2. SHERKSTON QUARRY

Located five miles east of Port Colborne, Ontario, this quarry, to a depth of 35 feet, still contains old locomotives and railway tracks from its active quarry days. There is also an underwater pumphouse and lots of fish life to enjoy. Fee. Camping is available.

3. HAGERSVILLE QUARRY

Located 1.5 miles outside the town of Hagersville, Ontario, this spring-fed quarry, also called "Sunspot Quarry," has an average depth of 25 feet, with one 80-foot-deep hole with a 30-foot sailboat at the bottom of it (this is for more experienced divers only). Fee. Facilities.

4. ELORA GORGE QUARRY

Located between the towns of Elora and Fergus, Ontario, north of Kitchener, this popular quarry has very limited hours for scuba diving (10 AM to noon daily in season) and divers must sign a waiver at the gate. Fee. Sandy beach, camping and facilities are available.

5. TROUT LAKE (INNERKIP) QUARRY

Located at the town of Innerkip, Ontario, near the city of Woodstock, this quarry offers submerged airplanes, boats, a car, a schoolbus, and a mineshaft for the specially trained. Maximum depth is 28 feet, but the mineshaft goes down to 54 feet. Fee.

Right: This rare photograph shows Innerkip Quarry in the 1930's, with the mine shaft at the lower right. CRIS KOHL COLLECTION

6. ST. MARYS QUARRY

Located just south of the town of St. Marys, Ontario, this old limestone quarry reaches a depth of 60 feet and is a day-use only park. May to September. Fee.

The St. Marys Quarry, originally named the Thames Quarry because the Thames River flows by a short distance to one side, is so old that horses and wagons were used here in its early days.   ST MARYS DISTRICT MUSEUM

7. NELSON'S LEDGES QUARRY

Located halfway between Cleveland and Youngstown, Ohio, at the town of Nelson, this 30-acre park offers two sunken boats, several cars, large boilers, old machinery and fish (bluegill, catfish and bass) in a maximum depth of 40 feet. Fee. Camping is available.

8. WHITE STAR QUARRY

The 15-acre White Star Quarry Park is located between the towns of Gibsonburg and Helena, Ohio, southeast of Toledo. It offers rocky drop-offs, an underwater forest, and a spiral staircase to a stone-crushing room. Depths reach 70 feet. Fee. Limited facilites.

9. PORTAGE QUARRY

Located one mile south of Bowling Green, OH, south of Toledo, this 22-acre quarry has an underwater silo, dynamite hut, school bus, cars, telephone booth and six boats. Fee.

10. GILBOA QUARRY

This 14-acre quarry, 20 miles west of Findlay, Ohio, features a sunken forest, a van, bus and boat, and averages 40-foot depths, but gets deeper than 120 feet at one end. Fee.

11. BAW BEESE LAKE

Located one mile southeast of Hillsdale, which is about 25 miles south of Jackson, MI, this lake reaches 70-foot depths, with a cabin cruiser in 55 feet and two others shallower.

12. CRYSTAL BAY/HIDDEN LAKE

Located just upstream from Amherstburg, Ontario, on the downstream side of a Detroit River island, the bay is a popular party place for Detroit area boaters who drop a lot of things overboard. Hidden Lake is a manmade cut 30' feet deep just off the bay. A boat is needed to get there. The clear water here has been filtered naturally through the island's limestone.

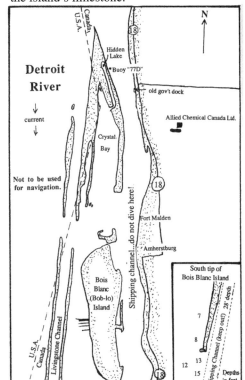

Diver Winston Smith and other members of Kent Divers Association enjoy a relaxing spring dive in Hidden Lake, a manmade cut, originally planned for use as a marina during the construction of the St. Lawrence Seaway in the 1950's. Scuba divers can easily locate the "bar" in the cut's bottom *(below)*. PHOTOS BY CRIS KOHL

207

The late Jack McKenney, former editor of *Skin Diver* magazine and famous underwater filmmaker, was born and raised in Windsor, Ontario, and began his illustrious diving career here. He once wrote, "Visibility in the Detroit River never got above one foot, but in Crystal Bay, you could see 40 to 50 feet...."

Hidden Lake also has an underwater habitat made of steel, although no longer airtight and sometimes toppled over.

PHOTOS BY CRIS KOHL

13. UNIDENTIFIED SCHOONER -- Downtown Windsor, Ontario, is very cosmo-

Drift Diving in the
Detroit River at Windsor, Ontario

Map by Cris Kohl, based on information from Brian Roffel.

politanized, with walkways, parks, and parking along the Detroit River. The waterfront just at the end, and to the east, of Ouellette Ave (Windsor's main street) is where passenger ferry vessels docked until the 1930's. Many old bottles and crocks have been found here, plus an unidentified wooden shipwreck with one deadeye on it in 8' to 27'. The low visibility, variable current, boating traffic, and the challenging exit points limit this demanding divesite to experienced divers with good plans.

15. St. Clair River

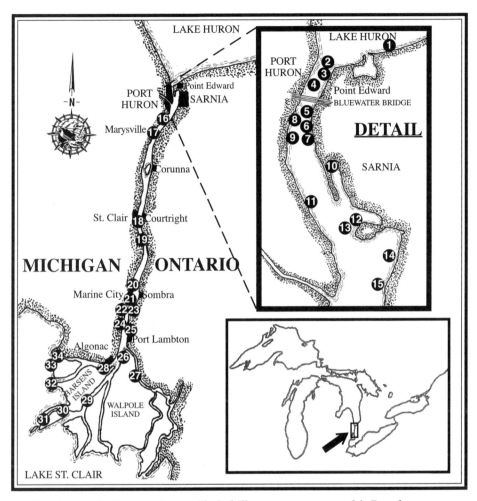

1. *Gladstone* and other wrecks
2. *Fontana*
3. *Charles H. Weeks*
4. *John B. Martin*
5. Dump scow ("The Barge")
6. *Monarch*
7. C. S. L. Docks
8. *Sidney E. Smith, Jr.* boom
9. *M. E. Tremble* and two salvage boats
10. Fishing boat
11. *A. R. Colborn* and crane
12. *Sidney E. Smith, Jr.* dock
13. *Saltillo*
14. Unknown wreckage
15. Ferry Dock Hill
16. *James Beard*
17. *Mineral Rock*
18. *Erin*
19. *Nelson Mills*
20. *Tokio*
21. *John Francomb/ Dashing Wave*
22. *William Dickinson*
23. *William H. Wolf*
24. *Penobscot*
25. Unidentified wreck
26. Highbanks Park
27. Snye Channel
28. *Badger State*
29. *Joseph Duvall*
30. *N. C. West*
31. *Bothnia*
32. *Harlow*
33. *H. Houghton*
34. *Nellie Lyon*

1. GLADSTONE AND OTHER WRECKS

DEPTH: 10 to 15 feet   **LEVEL: Novice-Intermediate**

LOCATION: The wreck of the wooden steamer, *Gladstone* (282' x 40'3" x 23'), lies intermingled with the remains of the old schooners, *Arrow* and *A.W. Wright*. All three of

The steamer, *Gladstone*. CRIS KOHL COLLECTION

them were used as the foundation for a dock in 1923; in 1936, the dock burned.

The *Gladstone,* built in 1888 at Cleveland, lies 200' offshore from the western end of Canatara Park. Leave your car in the lot north of the traffic circle at the park's western entrance. Enter Lake Huron about 200' east of the old boat ramp at the end of the parking lot. Look for pieces of the hull, piping and other metal items. Boating traffic is heavy, so use a divers down flag. Compensate for the mild current before it takes you into the swift mouth of the St. Clair River.

2. FONTANA

LORAN: **GPS: 43° 00.091'/082° 25.359'**
DEPTH: 70 feet   **LEVEL: Very Advanced**

LOCATION: This wreck lies a fair distance upstream of the Bluewater Bridge.

The *Fontana* (241'3" x 39'1" x 17') was a graceful, huge schooner built at St. Clair, Michigan, on the shores of the St. Clair River, in 1888. Originally sailing under four masts, she was cut down to two when she was demoted to a towbarge.On the hot night of August 3, 1900, the *Fontana,* with over 2,500 tons of iron ore, sank in a collision with the schooner-barge, *Santiago.* One life was lost, a sailor named John McGregor who was sleeping below deck on the *Fontana.* While Canada and the U.S. bickered over which country the wreck was in (and who was

The dramatic shipwreck, *Fontana*. ONTARIO ARCHIVES

responsible for removing her), the dangerously positioned *Fontana* caused the *John B. Martin* (which is also in this book) to sink with 4 lives lost. The *Fontana* was later dynamited. This is a challenging shore or boat dive. The current is extremely fast and the river bottom zooms by quickly. Enter from shore upstream of the wreck, or pull yourself upstream in the shallows before descending. It is difficult to stop and study the wreck if you are lucky enough to be carried onto it. If you missed it, follow the bottom back to shore. Never surface anywhere but at the shore! The boating traffic is horrendous.

3. CHARLES H. WEEKS

LORAN: **GPS: 43° 00.052'/082° 25.337'**
DEPTH: 68 feet   **LEVEL: Very Advanced**

LOCATION: This wreck, just downstream from the *Fontana,* is often mistaken for her.

The schooner, *Charles H. Weeks* (134'2" x 26' x 11'), built at Marine City, Michigan, in 1873, was stranded at Point Edward, Ontario, in the very damaging gale of October 6, 1889, and slid off into deep water at the mouth of the St. Clair River. The mate of the *Charles H. Weeks* died the next day from injuries he had received at the ship's wheel when the vessel struck the beach. Both bow anchors were removed in the early 1960's, with one of them sold to a Wisconsin collector for $1,000. The capstan was also removed, restored and placed in front of a local restaurant, but it disappeared when the building burned down in 1986, This very challenging dive should be handled the same way as a dive to the *Fontana*.

4. JOHN B. MARTIN

LORAN:	GPS: 43° 00.050'/082° 25.352'
DEPTH: 65 to 80 feet	LEVEL: Very Advanced

LOCATION: 500' off the Michigan shore, just upstream of the Bluewater Bridge.

The three-masted schooner, *John B. Martin* (220'2" x 34'2" x 14'2"), was forced to

pass in a narrow part of the St. Clair River on September 21, 1900, because of the wrecked *Fontana* (also in this book), thereby, indirectly because of the wreck, becoming a wreck herself after she collided in such close quarters with the steel steambarge, *Yuma*. Four lives were lost from the *John B. Martin*. Government and shipping representatives hastily met and worked out plans for the removal of two wrecks as obstructions to navigation.

Longtime local divers describe the *John B. Martin* as the most dangerous wreck in the entire

The *John B. Martin*. CRIS KOHL COLLECTION

Left: In the Port Huron park just beneath the Bluewater Bridge which connects the USA and Canada, an anchor from the *John B. Martin* attracts considerable attention to the river's maritime history, as does the ship's bell *(right)* on display in the Port Huron Museum.
PHOTOS BY CRIS KOHL

St. Clair River to dive. She sits in one of the deepest depressions in the river bottom, adding depth challenges to those already evident in the extremely strong 5-10 knot current which reportedly plays direction games in that depression. The boating traffic here in the shipping channel is heavy. Diving from shore, locals enter at the foot of Riverview Street, where there is a small, public beach, and they exit on the large, flat rocks just beneath the Bluewater Bridge. In between, they hope to reach the wreck of the *John B. Martin* and do some exploring. The wreck's anchor, on display in the park below the bridge, was raised by Bill Patterson, his sons and some friends in early 1981.

5. DUMP SCOW ("THE BARGE")

LORAN:	GPS: 42° 59.808'/082° 25.475'
DEPTH: 40 feet	LEVEL: Advanced

LOCATION: This wreck lies off the Canadian shore just south of the Bluewater Bridge.

This unnamed barge is the dump scow which sank on May 7, 1948, about 250' south of the bridge and 100' from shore. A tug was towing her, laden with mud, into the lake, when she suddenly nose-dived and sank. One man on the scow swam to shore. A cable from the north corner of the cement retaining wall runs to the wreck from shore. The scow's trap door, chains and three holds can be studied. Beware of strong current, boating traffic, and fishing lines here. Experienced divers with plenty of air can drift down to the *Monarch*.

6. *MONARCH*

LORAN:	GPS: 42° 59.700'/082° 25.360'
DEPTH: 58 feet	LEVEL: Advanced

LOCATION: This wreck lies 500' south of the Bluewater Bridge in Canadian waters.
This is one of the most popular St. Clair River shore dives for experienced divers.
Entry point is a convenient set of steel stairs to the river in the cement wall, remnants of the
Canada Steamship Line's glory days. Parking is a few feet away. The wreck of the tug,
Monarch (63'3" x 19'1" x 7'7"), lies about 200' off shore. Just follow the submerged cable
that runs across the sand bottom to the site. The *Monarch,* built at Sheboygan, Wisconsin, in
1889 as the *W. H. Simpson,* swung out of control while towing the old steamer, *C. F. Bielman*
(also in this book) on July 6, 1934, and sank with the loss of four lives. The deck is missing,
but penetration is possible at the bow. The strong 4-8 knot current makes this a challenging
dive. If you get blown off the wreck, follow the bottom back to shore (the <u>Canadian</u> shore!).
Also, beware of boating traffic and fishing lines.

Left: The tug, *Monarch,* when it was still named the *W. H. Simpson. Above:* This tragic 1934 sinking made front-page headlines in Port Huron.　　CRIS KOHL COLLECTION

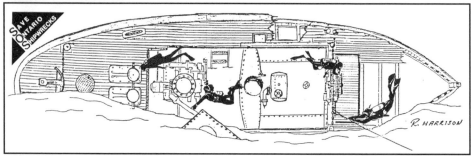

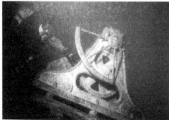

Left: Tim Philp studies the *Monarch's* steering machinery

Right: Alan Armbruster pulls himself upstream on the port railing.

PHOTO BY CRIS KOHL

7. C. S. L. Docks

DEPTH: 20 feet   LEVEL: Novice-Intermediate

LOCATION: This shore dive is just downstream of the *Monarch* shore entry.

Tour submerged posts (from the old Canada Steamship Lines docks) and find everything from bottles and cans to fishing rods, lures and bicycles. Good for current dive beginners. Don't go out too far, and exit at the same point where you entered.

Left: Divers at the C.S.L. docks. *Above:* Fast water rushes past the wrecks in the mouth of the St. Clair River.   PHOTOS BY CRIS KOHL

8. *SIDNEY E. SMITH, JR.*, BOOM

DEPTH: 50 to 55 feet   LEVEL: Advanced

LOCATION: About 100 feet off Whipple Street, Port Huron.

On June 6, 1972, the 66-year-old steel freighter, *Sidney E. Smith, Jr.* (489' x 52'2" x 26'5"), sank near the mouth of the St. Clair River after a collision with another steel freighter, the *Parker Evans* (which remained afloat, although damaged). Over the next 6 months, the *Smith* was salvaged (the bow was removed and the stern became a dock across the river in Canada). Part of the self-unloader boom broke off at the site. It helps to dive with someone who knows precisely where this boom is located. Launched as the

Part of the *Sidney E. Smith, Jr.'s* boom remains in the river.   PUBLIC ARCHIVES OF CANADA

W. K. Bixby in 1906 at Wyandotte, Michigan, this ship was renamed the *J. L. Reiss* in 1920, and finally the *Sidney E. Smith, Jr.* in the spring of 1972. Her new name's paint was barely dry when she sank. In 1997, I had the unique honor of doing a 25th anniversary presentation about this shipwreck in Port Huron with Sidney E. Smith, Jr., in the audience. Also present was Robert Campbell, who had rescued the crew in his boat that night. The *Sidney E. Smith, Jr.* remains one of the best-remembered maritime disasters in the Bluewater region.

9. *M. E. TREMBLE* AND TWO SALVAGE BOATS

DEPTH: 50 to 70 feet   LEVEL: Advanced

LOCATION: This wreck lies off the U.S. side just below the Bluewater Bridges.

The large, three-masted schooner, *M. E. Tremble* (198' x 34'5" x 13'4"), was under tow of the steamer, *B. W. Blanchard,* on the night of September 7, 1890, when the downbound steamer, *W. L. Wetmore* (which is also in this book) crashed into her port side. The crew hastily launched the yawl boat and left the sinking ship, realizing too late that one of their number had been left behind and was struggling for survival in the doomed ship's rigging. Unfortunately, he perished. Recovery of the coal cargo resulted in the accidental sinking of the salvage schooner, *Ben Hur,* when it was struck by a passing schooner-barge, the *Superior*, in tow of the *Passaic*, along with a small lighter which tended its cables, on November 8,

The schooner, *M. E. Tremble,* has long played visual roles in St. Clair River maritime history. *Left:* An exquisitely detailed ship model is on display at the Port Huron Museum, while *(right)* the Marysville Historical Museum displayed, on its front lawn, a *Tremble* anchor, donated by Wayne Brusate, and the ship's windlass, donated by Bill Patterson. PHOTOS BY CRIS KOHL

1890. The *Ben Hur* (314 tons, built in 1874 at Dunnville, Ontario) today lies upside down, upstream of, but alongside the wreck of the *M. E. Tremble,* which lies across the current, while the lighter sits broken up just downstream from the *Tremble.* With the installation of a long, steel breakwall here in the late 1980's, it has become more challenging to reach this wreck and then exit the water. Divers often suit up and jump in right beneath the Bluewater Bridges and let the current swiftly take them to the wrecks. This could be tricky in low visibility and is not recommended, as the strong current could pin a diver against the wreck. Use of a dive flag is mandatory in Michigan waters, although some divers tie one off where they enter the water and have another one anchored where they intend to surface. You have to be good to do this, because the law states that you must surface within 50′ of your flag.

10. FISHING BOAT

DEPTH: 22 feet	LEVEL: Novice

LOCATION: This unidentified fishing tug lies abandoned at the northwest end of the channel leading from the St. Clair River to Bridgeview Marina in Sarnia, Ontario.

11. *A. R. COLBORN* AND CRANE

LORAN:	GPS: 42° 59.126′/082° 25.359′
DEPTH: 35 feet	LEVEL: Novice-Intermediate

LOCATION: This wreck lies just north of the YMCA Building in Port Huron, Michigan.

The wooden steamer, *A. R. Colborn* (129′9″ x 27′7″ x 9′5″), launched at Saugatuck, Michigan, on April 18, 1882, was, after a long career in the lumber industry, formally abandoned at this location on April 28, 1922, with her final enrollment surrendered and endorsed as "abandoned as unfit for service." The boiler, engine and hull remain at the site, while the propeller graces a college lawn in Port Huron. Miller's crane, which was lost here in about 1953, also lies at this site.

The *A. R. Colborn.*
CRIS KOHL COLLECTION

In 1980, members of the St. Clair County Community College Scuba Club salvaged the *Colborn's* propeller. PHOTO BY CRIS KOHL

12. *SIDNEY E. SMITH, JR.* DOCK

DEPTH: 30 feet	LEVEL: Novice-Intermediate

LOCATION: The remains of half of the steel freighter, *Sidney E. Smith, Jr.,* were raised from the bottom of the St. Clair River in late 1972 (see site # 8 in this chapter) and moved to the Canadian side for use as a dock. When you dive here, it may be hard to imagine that this was once a large vessel. Many fish congregate around the broken end. Take Exmouth Road in Sarnia towards the river, turn left (south) at Harbour Road, and swing west on that road to the government dock. The *Sidney E. Smith, Jr.* is part of that dock.

214

13. SALTILLO

| LORAN: | GPS: 42° 58.832'/082° 25.022' |
| DEPTH: 35 to 45 feet | LEVEL: Advanced |

LOCATION: This wreck lies straight out into the river from the Canadian government dock in Sarnia. Diving from a boat is the best way. The schooner, *Saltillo,* is the oldest known shipwreck in the St. Clair River, having gone there after a collision with another schooner on November 25, 1853. She carried a cargo of coal and railroad iron. Her holds are mostly filled with sand and silt, but her hatches, blocks and deadeyes are intact. Her anchors were removed by early divers. Beware of the current and much boating traffic.

14. UNKNOWN WRECKAGE

| DEPTH: To 15 feet | LEVEL: Novice-Intermediate |

LOCATION: The remains of unidentified, abandoned shipwrecks lie scattered in the southern section of Sarnia Bay, just to the north and west of the entry channel. That's not surprising, since Sarnia Bay was the dumping ground for wrecked or abandoned vessels from both sides of the border around the turn of the last century. Vessels that were taken here to get them out of the way included the *City of Genoa, Yakima, Aztec, Province* and at least a dozen others, most of which were removed in the 1920's and 1930's by raising them or their pieces and scuttling them out in Lake Huron about 11 miles from Sarnia.

15. FERRY DOCK HILL

| DEPTH: To 20 feet | LEVEL: Novice-Intermediate |

LOCATION: Just off Front Street, along the southern portion of Sarnia Bay.

This site is the location of the Canadian side of the Sarnia-Port Huron ferry service which was put out of business in the late 1930's with the construction of the Bluewater Bridge. Beware of boating traffic and fishing lines from active anglers.

16. JAMES BEARD

| LORAN: | GPS: 42° 57.670'/082° 25.466' |
| DEPTH: 15 to 30 feet | LEVEL: Novice-Intermediate |

LOCATION: The wreck lies along the southeast edge of Port Huron, Michigan.

The 86-ton ferry, *James Beard* (73'5" x 17'2" x 6'3"), built at Au Sable, Michigan, in 1873, as the *Wesley Hawkins*, was renamed in 1882 when she was rebuilt. For 40+ years, she worked as a ferry between Port Huron and Sarnia, but was abandoned in 1927.

The ferry, *James Beard.* CRIS KOHL COLLECTION

17. MINERAL ROCK

| LORAN: | GPS: 42° 55.189'/082° 27.620' |
| DEPTH: 25 feet | LEVEL: Novice-Intermediate |

The *Mineral Rock.*
CRIS KOHL COLLECTION

LOCATION: The wreck lies off Marysville, MI.

Built in 1856 at Buffalo, NY, with the original steam engine from the *Monticello* (1848), the wooden, 428-ton steamer, *Mineral Rock* (167'5" x 27'5" x 13'3"), hauled copper ore from Lake Superior (hence her appropriate name), her arched supports giving her strength, until 1880, when she was cut down to a lumber carrier. She was formally abandoned after half a century in Dec., 1896.

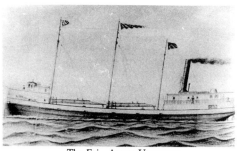

The *Erin*. ARTIST UNKNOWN.
CRIS KOHL COLLECTION

THIS U.S. CHART REPRODUCTION IS NOT FOR USE IN NAVIGATION.

18. *ERIN*

LORAN:	GPS: 42° 48.399'/082° 28.919'
DEPTH: 33 to 36 feet	LEVEL: Advanced

LOCATION: Opposite the Courtright (Ontario) Light.

The wooden, Canadian steamer, *Erin* (174' x 26' x 12'6"), sank after a collision with the huge, steel freighter, *John B. Cowle*, on May 31, 1906, taking to the bottom her cargo of coal and five of her crew sleeping below deck at the time. The *Cowle* continued on her downbound course. The remains of the *Erin* lie right across the middle of the river. Technically, her bow is in the USA, while her stern is in Canada (take your birth certificate with you on this dive!) The hull is badly twisted, and the middle part of the vessel was dynamited. Much of the wreck is buried in sand, but she rises about ten feet off the bottom. Her large four-bladed propeller, engine and boiler are the highlights. Beware of freighters!

19. *N. (NELSON) MILLS*

LORAN:	GPS: 42° 47.730'/082° 28.669'
DEPTH: 33 to 40 feet	LEVEL: Intermediate-Advanced

LOCATION: About one-half mile south of St. Clair, Michigan.

Launched on Sept. 11, 1870 at Vicksburg (later Marysville), MI, as a barge and quickly converted to a steamer, the *N. Mills* (164'4" x 29'9" x 11'6"), hauled lumber and barges until Sept. 6, 1906, when she was sunk by the steel freighter, *Milwaukee*, with two lives lost. Hardhat divers salvaged many of the *Mills'* components.

RIVER REFUSES TO GIVE UP DEAD

The Body of Wheelsman Barber Hasn't Been Found.

Thorough Search Has Been Made to No Avail.

Survivors of the Wreck Came to This City.

Although a thorough search of the river from the site of the wreck to points below Marine City has been made, the body of Wheelsman James Barber who was drowned in the sinking of the steamer Mills has not yet been found.

Deaths make headlines.
CRIS KOHL COLLECTION

The *N. Mills*. CRIS KOHL COLLECTION

20. *TOKIO*

LORAN:	GPS: 42° 45.240'/082° 28.507'
DEPTH: 15 to 28 feet	LEVEL: Novice-Intermediate

LOCATION: On the chart just south of Recor's Point upstream of Marine City, Michigan.

The large schooner-barge, *Tokio* (222'2" x 38' x 19'), built at West Bay City, MI, in 1889, sank after colliding with the sandsucker, *Homer*, on Oct. 8, 1917, and was abandoned. A hazard to ferry boats (one hit it badly in 1948), the *Tokio* was dynamited in 1963.

21. *JOHN FRANCOMB/DASHING WAVE*

LORAN:	GPS: 42° 42.160'/082° 29.973'
DEPTH: to 18 feet	LEVEL: Novice-Intermediate

Left: The schooner, *John A. Francomb,* at left in photo.
Right: By 1934, the *Francomb* lay visibly abandoned at the McLouth Yards.
Collette Witherspoon did much research in the 1980's on this ship and the *Dashing Wave.*
CRIS KOHL COLLECTION

LOCATION: Off the DNR boat launch ramp south of the old McLouth Yards.

Two abandoned schooners lie just north of Marine City, MI. The *Dashing Wave* (133' x 25' x 10'), built in 1862 at Clayton, NY, was formally abandoned on June 7, 1904. The *John A. Francomb* (180' x 36' x 13'), built at West Bay City, MI, and launched on June 25, 1889, was abandoned just upstream of the *Dashing Wave* in 1934. Many fishing lures are snagged here. Use a boat, as the DNR frowns upon shore diving from the launch ramp.

22. WILLIAM DICKINSON

< DEPTH: 18 to 25 feet   LEVEL: Novice-Intermediate >

LOCATION: This wreck lies along the drop-off on the Michigan side of the river at the southern end of Marine City just off a trailer park.

The tug, *William Dickinson* (78'2" x 19'5" x 10'9"), built at Benton Harbor, Michigan, in 1893, burned to a complete loss on September 16, 1923. Her boiler rising high off the river floor is the most noticeable part of the wreck. Considerable machinery and parts lie scattered around the boiler. Beware of boating traffic.

Above: The tug, *William Dickinson.* ARTIST UNKNOWN. CRIS KOHL COLLECTION. *Left and right:* A diver explores machinery from the tug, *William Dickinson.* PHOTOS BY CRIS KOHL

23. WILLIAM H. WOLF

< DEPTH: 6 to 60 feet   LEVEL: Advanced >

LOCATION: This wreck lies along the drop-off just north of Marshy Creek Park, which is to the south of Sombra, Ontario. You can suit up and wade upstream from that park.

The wooden steamer, *William H. Wolf* (285'5" x 42'5" x 18'5"), began life catastrophically when three people were killed at her launch in 1887 at Milwaukee. But she worked the waters of the Great Lakes successfully for several decades before succumbing to flames on October 20, 1921, with the loss of two lives. Tragedy marred her entry into, and her departure from, the world.

The wreck's superstructure completely burned off, and, once inside the large hull, the diver is protected from the three-knot current. The wreck lies with her broken bow in the shallows and her stern at the bottom of the drop-off. The large

The wooden steamer, *William H. Wolf,* in ice.
CRIS KOHL COLLECTION

217

The *William H. Wolf* after being destroyed by fire in the St. Clair River.
CRIS KOHL COLLECTION

Right: A sense of humor, very evident in the smiling face of diver Greg Schieman, overcomes any difficulties at a depth of 55' at the propeller of the *William H. Wolf.*
PHOTO BY CRIS KOHL

engine, boiler and four-bladed propeller are still in place. The rudder lies flat about 100' off the stern on this combination sand, clay and stone bottom. Beware of boating traffic and entanglement in fishing line.

24. PENOBSCOT

LORAN:	GPS: 42° 40.440'/082° 30.650'
DEPTH: 35 feet	LEVEL: Intermediate

LOCATION: South of Marine City, Michigan.

Launched on March 22, 1880, the schooner, *Penobscot*, was converted to a steam-powered sand dredge (129' x 27'4" x 9'3") in 1908. This ship burned to a total loss at Marine City on Aug. 19, 1925, with no lives lost.

25. UNIDENTIFIED WRECK

LOCATION: Just north of Port Lambton, ON.

The remains of an unidentified wooden ship lie parallel to the river along the drop-off in 12' to 20' of water. China shards have been located here. Use a boat to avoid trespassing on the shoreline private property.

THIS U.S. CHART REPRODUCTION IS NOT FOR USE IN NAVIGATION.

26. HIGHBANKS PARK

DEPTH: To 35 feet	LEVEL: Novice-Intermediate

LOCATION: At the north tip of Walpole Island, where the Snye Channel branches off to the right (southeast) from the St. Clair River. This area can be done from shore or from a boat. Walpole Island is First Nation land. Please respect the rights of private property owners in the area of Highbanks Park, for both scuba entries and exits. This area has been used by

Bottle diving at Highbanks Park. PHOTOS BY CRIS KOHL.

218

The author examines some old bottles and anchors which he found in the St. Clair River. An inflatable boat and outboard motor are ideal for exploring these waters. Two dives yielded five small anchors, each weighing from 10 to 20 pounds. Not bad for a day's fun! PHOTOS BY CRIS KOHL EXCEPT MIDDLE PHOTO, WHICH IS BY KEN SHAW

THE ST. CLAIR PARKWAY SYSTEM

Not to be used for navigation.

picnickers for many years, and the natural split of the Snye and the St. Clair has also made this point a sort of catch-basin for old bottles washed down from upstream. There is a 2-to-3 knot current, with much boating traffic. Beware of fishing lines, snagged and active.

27. SNYE CHANNEL

St. Clair River diving is good from any of the dozen public parks along the Canadian side. The Snye Channel, a branch of the St. Clair River, is also accessible from many spots along the shoreline/roadway, as well as by boat. Its depth reaches 38' and is a good place for learning swiftwater diving. Many old bottles have been found here and continue to be located. Boating traffic is heavy, especially on summer weekends. Use a dive flag. Entanglement in old, snagged fishing line is a possibility, so take along a good, accessible dive knife.

Left: Many parks along the St. Clair River, especially on the Canadian side, offer good entry and exit points for divers. MAP BY CRIS KOHL

28. *BADGER STATE*

LORAN:	GPS: 42° 36.380′/082° 32.910′
DEPTH: 1 to 20 feet	LEVEL: Novice-Intermediate

LOCATION: North Channel opposite Pt. Aux Chenes, southwest of Algonac, MI.

Sister ship to the *Empire State* (which is also a wreck in this book), the wooden steamer,

The *Badger State* as a lumber carrier.
CRIS KOHL COLLECTION

Badger State (213' x 33' x 11'8″), was launched on April 17, 1862, at Buffalo, NY. She was reduced to a lumber carrier in Aug., 1905, after spending three apparently unsuccessful months as a floating casino named the "Poolroom Ship" in the Detroit River. This vessel caught on fire on Dec. 6, 1909, at a dock in Marine City, MI, and was cut loose to drift downstream and burn itself out. No lives were lost. Caution: The river drops off here into the channel to a dangerous depth of 85 feet!

219

29. JOSEPH DUVALL

| DEPTH: 30 feet | LEVEL: Intermediate |

LOCATION: On the bank, s.e. side, Harson's Island, MI, 75' from the Muir House dock.

The small, 131-ton, two-masted schooner, *Joseph Duvall* (103' x 24'3" x 7'6"), built at Manitowoc, WI, in 1874, sank in a collision with a much larger ship, the steel whaleback steamer, *James B. Colgate* (which is also a wreck in this book), on Dec. 5, 1905, with no lives lost. The *Duvall* was dynamited by the Corps of Engineers in the spring of 1906.

30. N. C. WEST

| LORAN: | GPS: 42° 33.265'/082° 37.140' |
| DEPTH: 20 feet | LEVEL: Novice-Intermediate |

LOCATION: At the lower end of the Southeast Bend, St. Clair River.

Built at Fremont, Ohio, and launched in April, 1867, the 145-ton, two-masted, center-board schooner, *N. C. West* (103'6" x 25'5" x 7'4"), was sunk in a collision with the steamer, *Sacramento*, on November 10, 1898. No lives were lost. The wreck was dynamited in the early 1940's as a hazard to navigation.

31. BOTHNIA

| DEPTH: 40 feet | LEVEL: Intermediate |

LOCATION: 600' above the old Star Island House, and 250' from shore.

The Canadian steam barge, *Bothnia* (190' x 38' x 13'8), built in 1895 at Garden Island, Ontario, as the *Jack* (the name was changed in 1896), sank with the loss of one life after the steamer, *Curry*, with a disabled rudder, collided with her on June 26, 1912.

32. HARLOW

| LORAN: | GPS: 42° 34.472'/082° 40.090' |
| DEPTH: 2 to 20 feet | LEVEL: Novice-Intermediate |

LOCATION: Near the western end of the Middle Channel, where it flows into Lake St. Clair's Anchor Bay, behind green marker buoy #13; the wreck is clearly marked on charts.

The wooden steam barge, *Harlow* (154' x 34'4" x 10'7"), was launched as the *Preston* in 1891 at Green Bay, WI, and renamed in 1902. In 1926, when the old ship had outlived its usefulness, it was sunk as a breakwall instead of being scrapped. The hull and prop remain.

33. H. HOUGHTON

| LORAN: | GPS: 42° 37.180'/082° 39.020' |
| DEPTH: 5 to 30 feet | LEVEL: Novice-Intermediate |

LOCATION: Seven miles below Algonac, Michigan, at western end of North Channel.

Launched on Feb. 1, 1889, at West Bay City, MI, the 210-ton, wooden steamer, *H. Houghton* (126' x 27' x 8'2"), burned in the Chenal A Bout Rond on November 20, 1926, with no lives lost from the 11 on board.

34. NELLIE LYON

| LORAN: | GPS: 42° 37.850'/082° 38.151' |
| DEPTH: 20 to 30 feet | LEVEL: Novice-Intermediate |

LOCATION: Western end of the North Channel, southwest of the most westerly fixed bridge on Colony Road. The wreck begins 20' down the drop-off, with the boiler and upright engine most obvious. Launched in 1880 at South Rockwood, MI, as the barge *H. C. Sprague*, renamed *Reliance* in 1906 when converted to a steamer, and given last name in 1910, the *Nellie Lyon* (152' x 29' x 9'7"), burned to a total loss with no lives lost on April 9, 1911.

16. Southeastern Lake Huron

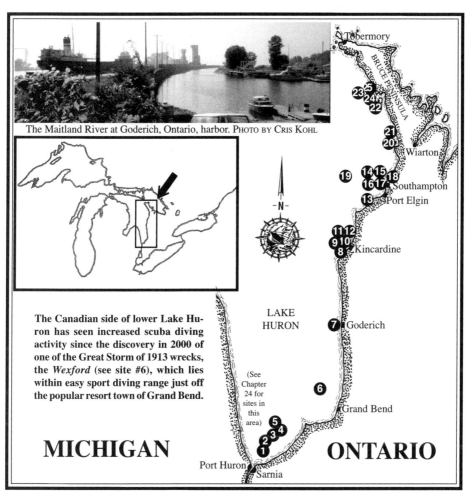

The Maitland River at Goderich, Ontario, harbor. PHOTO BY CRIS KOHL

The Canadian side of lower Lake Huron has seen increased scuba diving activity since the discovery in 2000 of one of the Great Storm of 1913 wrecks, the *Wexford* (see site #6), which lies within easy sport diving range just off the popular resort town of Grand Bend.

(See Chapter 24 for sites in this area)

LAKE HURON

MICHIGAN   ONTARIO

Port Huron / Sarnia

1. *Sweetheart*
2. Mystery "Ghost Fleet" wreck
3. *Aztec/Province*
4. *Sachem*
5. *Yakima*
6. *Wexford*
7. Goderich wrecks
8. Early Kincardine shipwrecks
9. *John S. Miner*
10. *Adelaide Horton*
11. *Singapore*
12. *Ann Maria*
13. *Azov*
14. The "Long Dock"
15. *W. E. Gladstone*
16. *Erie Stewart*
17. *Islet Prince*
18. *General Hunter*
19. Unidentified barge
20. Fishing Islands wrecks
21. *Sarah*
22. *Goudreau*
23. *Africa*
24. *Ripple*
25. *Explorer*

1. SWEETHEART

> LORAN: 30834.0/49671.6   GPS:
> DEPTH: 30 feet   LEVEL: Novice-Intermediate

LOCATION: This wreck lies about three miles north-northeast of Sarnia, Ontario.

The 176-foot-long schooner, *Sweetheart,* was scuttled due to her advanced age. Because of the shallow depth, the wreck is broken and scattered on the sand-and-rock bottom. The keelson, ribbing and planking attract many fish. Beware of disturbing the silt and getting snagged in any fishnets.

Left: The schooner, *Sweetheart.* CRIS KOHL COLLECTION

2. MYSTERY "GHOST FLEET" WRECK

> LORAN: GPS: 43° 06.370'/082° 16.964'
> DEPTH: 40 feet   LEVEL: Intermediate

The remains of an unidentified steamer approximately 175' long, with a steel-sheathed bow, were located in August, 2005, by Bill Simpson of Sarnia, ON, Chris Schmidt of Camlachie, ON, and Fred Felter of MI using a depth sounder. With the propeller being the only machinery remaining on the ship, it is probable that this ship was scuttled, and hence is a member of the "Ghost Fleet of the St. Clair River" (see page 223 for its possible identity!)

3. AZTEC/PROVINCE

> LORAN: 30770.5/49618.3   GPS: 43° 09.830'/082° 18.490'
> DEPTH: 68 feet   LEVEL: Intermediate-Advanced

The remains of the steamer, *Aztec* (180' x 33'3" x 13'9"; built at Marine City, MI, in 1889), and the barge, *Province* (162' x 40' x 10'; built at Fort William, ON, in 1911) lay rotting in Sarnia Bay until the 1936 clean-up, when the dynamited *Aztec* was placed aboard the refloated hull of the *Province* and both were scuttled in lower Lake Huron. The *Aztec* had burned at Marine City on Nov. 9, 1923, and the *Province* had capsized in the St. Clair River on Sept. 28, 1923, with 3 lives lost. Both wrecks were towed to Sarnia and abandoned. These wrecks, now in 68', were found and identified by Jim Stayer and Cris Kohl in 1993.

Left: The wooden steamer, *Aztec,* with a cargo of coal. This ship's huge timbers were loaded onto the *Province* for scuttling. *Right:* The dredge, *Province,* worked along the St. Clair River.
CRIS KOHL COLLECTION

4. SACHEM

> LORAN: 30769.2/49617.6   GPS: 43° 09.90'/082° 18.36'
> DEPTH: 68 feet   LEVEL: Advanced

The wooden steamer, *Sachem* (187' x 33'5" x 14'8"), built at Grand Haven, Michigan, in 1889, burned and sank in the St. Clair River on Oct. 8, 1928. Raised and towed to Sarnia Bay, the ship was scuttled a few weeks later in lower Lake Huron, 13.1 miles southeast of Lexington, Michigan. Located by Bruce and Barbara Campbell of Grand Blanc, Michigan, in May, 1993, the wreck was identified by Jim Stayer and Cris Kohl later that summer. For a scuttled ship, this one has many items of interest on it.

Great Lakes Highlight No. 9

THE GHOST FLEET
OF THE ST. CLAIR RIVER

A hundred years ago, ships sank in the St. Clair River, but these wrecks were nowhere to be found when the first scuba divers searched for them after World War II. The sheer volume of maritime traffic in the dangerous bottleneck called the St. Clair River (connecting Lake Huron with Lake St. Clair and eventually Lake Erie) resulted in over 250 recorded cases of commercial vessel sinkings there. Most of these unfortunate ships were raised and returned to service, but a few remain on the river bottom, and some simply disappeared.

Those ships which sank in the river but disappeared mysteriously from there are part of "The Ghost Fleet of the St. Clair River."

Beginning in the mid-1980's, I researched all of the ships which sank in the St. Clair River. A book about many of them was published in 1987. In the summer of 1993, Jim and Pat Stayer's team and I began finding wrecks in lower Lake Huron, and my mid-1980's research proved to be invaluable for those shipwrecks.

Numerous Great Lakes maritime history books tell us that ships like the *Yakima*, the *Aztec*, the *Province*, and the *Sachem* all sank in the St. Clair River. However, my research indicated that these wrecks had been raised and dumped into Sarnia Bay, this region's "ship's graveyard" in the early 1900's. In the late 1920's and 1930's, municipal clean-ups had these old eyesore shipwrecks raised, towed several miles out into lower Lake Huron, and scuttled. Back then, out of sight was out of mind. There were no worries about the environment.

In 1993, we found the wrecks of the *Yakima*, the *Aztec*, and the *Province*, and that summer, we were able to identify someone else's recent shipwreck discovery as the *Sachem* (see pages 222 and 224 for these wrecks).

These St. Clair River shipwrecks which ended up in Lake Huron received the suitable nickname, "Ghost Fleet of the St. Clair River," from Jim Stayer.

Other ships which sank in the St. Clair River but are not there any more include the sailing ship *Naiad*, the steel steamer *Majestic*, the tug *Constitution*, the schooner *John Kilderhouse*, the 174-foot-long wooden steamer, *Maple Gulf* (formerly the *Pawnee*) -- this one may be the newly discovered "Mystery 'Ghost Fleet' Wreck" on p. 222 -- and others, all awaiting discovery and identification.

Many different newspapers on both sides of the US-Canada border excitedly and extensively publicized our shipwreck discoveries.
CRIS KOHL COLLECTION

Left: The steamer, *Sachem,* burned in the St. Clair River on Oct. 8, 1928, but no history books mention that the ship was raised, towed into Lake Huron, and scuttled. CRIS KOHL COLLECTION. *Right:* Jim Stayer studies a ship's light protector which lies amidst much other wreckage on the *Sachem.*   PHOTO BY CRIS KOHL

5. YAKIMA

LORAN: 30775.1/49612.6	GPS: 43° 10.56′/082° 19.38′
DEPTH: 78 feet	LEVEL: Advanced

The wooden steamer, *Yakima* (279′ x 40′5″ x 20′6″), built at Cleveland in 1887, was the first commercial ship on the Great Lakes to be equipped with electric lights. She stranded and burned in the St. Clair River on June 10, 1905, after which she was towed into Sarnia Bay, abandoned and scuttled in Lake Huron in 1928. Located and identified in 1993 by the team of Jim and Pat Stayer, Tim Juhl, David Fritz and Cris Kohl, this wreck lies 12 miles southeast of Lexington, Michigan, harbor, and 11 miles north of Port Huron, Michigan.

Above: The historic steamer, *Yakima.* CRIS KOHL COLLECTION. *Right:* Jim Stayer videotapes the *Yakima's* huge hull. PHOTO BY CRIS KOHL.

6. WEXFORD

LORAN:	GPS: 43° 24.080′/081° 53.322′
DEPTH: 58 to 78 feet	LEVEL: Advanced

LOCATION: About 7 miles off the Canadian shore northwest of Grand Bend, Ontario.

The steel steamer, *Wexford* (250′ x 40′1″ x 23′7″), was one of eight freighters which disappeared with all hands in lower Lake Huron during the Great Storm of November,

The steamer, *Wexford,* like all the ships lost in the 1913 Storm, had its own set of newspaper headlines. CRIS KOHL COLLECTION

STEAMER WEXFORD LOST ON HURON
WENT DOWN IN SUNDAY'S STORM
BODIES WASHED UP ON THE BEACH

The Bodies Bore Life Preservers Marked "Wexford"---Ship Thought To Have Foundered Between Kettle Point and Bayfield.

Artwork © Robert McGreevy

Above: Michigan artist Robert McGreevy's rendition of the wreck of the *Wexford.* COURTESY OF ROBERT McGREEVY/CTM ASSOCIATES.

Right: A diver glides past the ghostly superstructure of the tragic *Wexford.* PHOTO COURTESY OF OUT OF THE BLUE PRODUCTIONS.

Below: Below deck on the *Wexford,* brass portholes, their glass still intact, remain in place (please keep them that way for other divers to enjoy seeing; Ontario laws protect them, and punishments are severe). A coiled hose and a coffee mug are among the many artifacts found at this site. PHOTOS COURTESY OF OUT OF THE BLUE PRODUCTIONS

1913. This long-sought shipwreck, the subject of several false claims to discovery, was finally found -- accidentally, no less -- by Don Chalmers, a retiree who was out fishing in his sailboat when he passed over this wreck and picked up its presence on his depthsounder in August, 2000. Being a scuba diver, he and two friends were the first to see this ship in 87 years. The *Wexford,* built in Sunderland, England in 1883, was the oldest of the eight ships the storm sank in Lake Huron, and, so far, the only one found sitting upright on the bottom (the others were all flipped upside-down by the storm). The steamers *Hydrus* and *James Carruthers* remain to be located. The *Wexford,* contrary to rumors that she was stripped long ago by divers who could keep a secret, features a chadburn, brass portholes, a brass identification plate on deck, and many fascinating artifacts below deck (penetration diving is only for those with training, experience, attitude and equipment). Respect this tragic site.

Great Lakes Highlight No. 10

THE GREAT STORM OF 1913

The worst storm in recorded Great Lakes history occurred on November 8-10, 1913. This storm was so severe and wide-ranging that ships were lost with all hands in Lakes Michigan, Superior, and Erie, but the hardest hit was Lake Huron. Eight ships went missing in lower Lake Huron, lost with all hands. In all, about 248 sailors lost their lives when their ships sank in this storm. (We say "about 248" because there were no records kept indicating any "free rides" which were often given to friends of the captain's to the ship's destination port, e.g. the *Wexford* was known for sure to have had free riders on board, similar to the schooner *Rouse Simmons* -- the famed "Christmas Tree Ship," see pages 462-464 -- when it disappeared with an undeterminable number of people on board one year earlier while bound from Lake Michigan's north woods to Chicago.)

In a very unusual weather system, three storm fronts collided over the Great Lakes. As a rule, 60-mile-an-hour winds in the Great Lakes do not last for more than four or five hours, but on Sunday, November 9, 1913, they were sustained for a steady 16 hours, with frequent gusts to 79 miles an hour. Waves on the Great Lakes were reported to reach 35 feet in height.

On Lake Huron during the Great Storm, 24 ships were lost or damaged, and

MENOMINEE HERA

SEVEN MEN DROWNED ON BARGE PLYMOUTH

Terrible Gale Which Swept Great Lakes Believed to Have Destroyed Barge Plymouth — Seven Men on Board Probably Drowned—Six of Them Lived in Twin Cities, Including Deputy United States Marshal Christ Keenan—Eager Search Brings no News from Missing Men—Story of Storm told by Survivors on Tug Martin, Which Arrived Last Night from Disaster.

Top row, left to right: The steel steamer, *H. B. Smith,* became one of the first victims of the Great Storm when it sank with all hands in Lake Superior. The barge, *Plymouth,* sank with all hands while at anchor in Lake Michigan.

Left: The steel steamer, *Leafield,* built in England for ocean conditions, struck Angus Island in Lake Superior at the height of the storm, and slid off into deep water, taking its entire crew with it.

Right: Buffalo *Lightship 83* sank in Lake Erie with all hands.

Left and right: A giant "Mystery Ship" was found floating overturned in lower Lake Huron the day after the storm; it took more than a week to identify it.

CRIS KOHL COLLECTION

THE PORT HURON TIMES-HERALD.

BOAT IS PRICE
DIVER IS BAKER
SECRET KNOWN

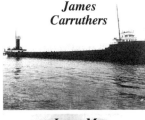

James Carruthers

Hydrus

Argus

These eight ships were lost with all hands in lower Lake Huron during the Great Storm of 1913. Many (but not all) of the bodies washed ashore, mostly on the Canadian side of the lake. The five ships which lie upside-down (attesting to the storm's incredible fury) are the *Price, Regina, Scott, Argus,* and *McGean.* The two still missing: *Carruthers* and *Hydrus.*

CRIS KOHL COLLECTION

Isaac M. Scott

Wexford

Regina

John A. McGean

Charles S. Price

at least 188 sailors' lives were lost; on Lake Superior, 10 ships were lost or damaged with 44 lives lost; on Lake Erie, 17 ships were lost or damaged, with 6 lives lost; and on Lake Michigan, 16 ships were lost or damaged with 10 lives lost. Lake Ontario, the most easterly of the inland seas, was spared the lethal furies of this gale. Ironically, even though its use for saving lives was proven to the world 18 months earlier when *Titanic* sank, wireless (radio) was not carried by any of the ships which sank in the Great Storm. Ships which carried wireless quickly reached harbors of safety after they received the storm warnings.

The *Marine Review* of December, 1913, summed up the nature of this storm: "...Since the lakes have been commercially navigated, no such condition has ever been met with before, and centuries may go by before such a phenomenon may again be experienced...."

Counterclockwise from left: Many Lake Huron sailors' bodies washed a-shore on the Canadian side; five unidentified sailors were given a respectable funeral in Goderich, Ontario, and were buried there in Maitland Cemetery. Historical markers commemorate the Great Storm in both the USA and Canada, but we may never know the exact number of lives lost. CRIS KOHL COLLECTION/PHOTOS BY CRIS KOHL

The Detroit News

DEATH TOTAL ON LAKES MAY BE 273
WILSON READY TO AID REBELS DISASTER GROWS AS NEW REPORTS COME

SAILORS

THE GREAT STORM OF 1913

7. GODERICH WRECKS

DEPTH: 20 feet   LEVEL: Novice-Intermediate

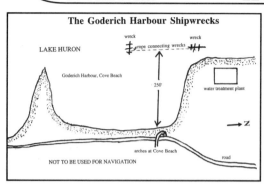

The Goderich Harbour Shipwrecks

LAKE HURON

wreck   wreck
rope connecting wrecks

Goderich Harbour, Cove Beach

250'

water treatment plant

arches at Cove Beach   road

NOT TO BE USED FOR NAVIGATION

LOCATION: These two wrecks lie off the arch over the roadway to Cove Beach, Goderich harbor, Ontario. The wreck to the left (south) is a tugboat from the 1920's that had its machinery removed before it was purposely burned. There is a four-bladed propeller and shaft. The wreck to the right (north) might be two wrecks, but only wood planking and framing remain. Boating traffic is heavy here; use a dive flag. For the best visibility, dive in the spring after a couple days of calm.

8. EARLY KINCARDINE SHIPWRECKS

Broken up in 5'-15' with a sand, gravel and clay bottom just north of the harbor channel are the 374-ton schooner, *A. J. Rich,* storm-stranded with a wheat cargo on Nov. 10, 1864, and, a bit farther out, the sidewheeler, *Bonnie Maggie,* stranded on Oct. 14, 1869.

9. JOHN S. MINER

In under 8' of water lie the broken remains of the 97-ton schooner, *John S. Miner,* grounded on Oct. 15, 1871. Only the bottom timbers remain at the foot of Harbour Street.

10. ADELAIDE HORTON

This 91-ton newly-launched steamer (107' x 18' x 8') struck the pier and broke up on

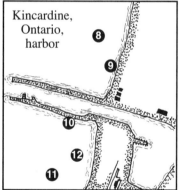

Kincardine, Ontario, harbor

Oct. 19, 1871. She lies in 6' of water. Beware of boaters and fishing lines.

11. SINGAPORE

This schooner (110'9" x 25'4" x 9'9") stranded and broke up on Sept. 15, 1904. Much of this wreck lies under sand, with some timbers visible in 8' of water.

12. ANN MARIA

This schooner (131'2" x 26'3" x 11'3") stranded and broke up on Oct. 7, 1902, with 4 of her 6 sailors lost. The remains lie in 6' of water, much of it buried.

Below: Two stranded schooners at Kincardine, ON: *left,* the *Singapore* (CRIS KOHL COLLECTION); *right,* the *Ann Maria* (ONTARIO ARCHIVES).

13. *Azov*

DEPTH: 6 to 10 feet   LEVEL: Novice

The wreck of the Canadian schooner, *Azov* (108′4″ x 23′7″ x 10′), lies close to shore inside the boundaries of McGregor Point Provincial Park, one concession south of Port Elgin, Ontario. These remains can be seen from the surface on a calm day. Take a boat, as car access to the shore is non-existent. Vis is usually poor, so this is not the most popular dive site. The *Azov,* built in 1866 at Hamilton, Ontario, capsized during a gale on Oct. 25, 1911, about 20 miles east by north of Point aux Barques, Michigan (off the thumb). The hull drifted about 60 miles all the way east across the lake before settling near Port Elgin. The ship's captain, his wife and son, plus the crew,

The *Azov.* ONTARIO ARCHIVES

jury-rigged their yawlboat and sailed to safety in Goderich, Ontario. The wreck was located by the captain's grandson in the 1950's, and an *Azov* anchor, recovered by scuba divers in August, 1956, is on display at the marine museum at Goderich.

14. THE "LONG DOCK"

This now-submerged breakwall (begun in 1871) with wooden cribs begins at Southampton and arches to Chantry Island, with a gap in the middle. Depth: to 25′.

15. *W. E. GLADSTONE*

This small schooner, built at Goderich in 1886, broke up in 15′ along the north wall of the eastern portion of the Long Dock on Nov. 23, 1908. Use a dive flag; boating gets heavy.

16. *ERIE STEWART*

This schooner (117′ x 23′ x 10′), built at Port Dover, Ontario, in 1874, missed the gap on Oct. 7, 1907, rammed the breakwall, and sank. No lives were lost. Her bow lies wedged against the island portion of the Long Dock in the gap. Depth is 18′. Beware of boaters!

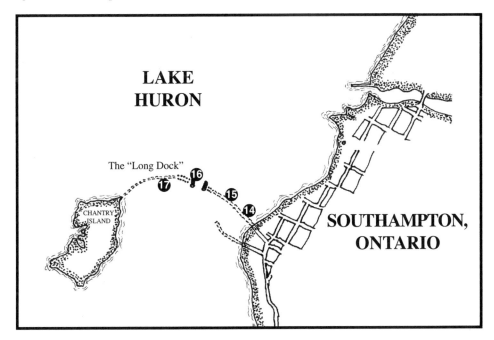

LAKE HURON

The "Long Dock"

CHANTRY ISLAND

SOUTHAMPTON, ONTARIO

The schooner, *Erie Stewart,* in Port Dover harbor, and the steamer, *Islet Prince.* CRIS KOHL COLLECTION

17. ISLET PRINCE

On July 19, 1938, this passenger & freight steamer (118' x 24'6" x 8'), built at Saugatuck, MI, in 1894, burned and sank in 15' at the Long Dock. The few remains are mostly buried.

18. GENERAL HUNTER

LOCATION: This wreck lies buried in sand on shore at Southampton, Ontario.

An ancient vessel, excavated by archaeologists after a portion of it was exposed by weather, is likely the remains of the War of 1812 brig, the *General Hunter,* lost on Lake Huron in 1816. Military buttons from the early 1800's suggest its identity.

19. UNIDENTIFIED DREDGE

DEPTH: 120 feet	LEVEL: Advanced

LOCATION: This huge wreck lies upside-down several miles off Port Elgin, Ontario. Definite identification has not yet been made of this hull.

20. FISHING ISLANDS WRECKS

The Fishing Islands consist of a series of islands and shoals stretching from Chiefs Point about five miles north of Sauble Beach, Ontario, to Pike Bay just south of Stokes Bay and Lyal Island. The largest of the Fishing Islands is Cranberry Island, just off the mainland community of Oliphant. The incredible number of shoals makes this a navigator's nighmare!

The only access is by boat. Since this is an inaccessible area, comparatively little shipwreck search and exploration has been done; the area is ripe for diving.

Some of the known shipwrecks in this area include:

Blanche Shelby: This wooden tug hit a submerged rock on October 15, 1885 and sank almost immediately at the entrance to the channel between Main Station and Burke Island. All hands escaped in the yawl boat.

Phoenix: This 25-ton tug is mostly buried in the sand of the shallow channel between Indian Island and the east shore of Main Station Island. She stranded during a storm and was lost on November 30, 1901. Boiler and machinery were salvaged and only the ship's bottom remains now in about four feet of water. She measured 53'5" x 13'7".

Gold Hunter: Built in 1862 at Milford, Ontario, by John Tait, this schooner struck a shoal off Ghegheto (Round) Island in October, 1890, while attempting to pass the narrow channel to the open lake. She and her cargo of cedar logs went to pieces within days. The vessel's value in 1866 was $8,000, but that had dropped to $2,000 by the time of her loss in 1890. The wreck lies about 600' off the west shore of Ghegheto (Round) Island, near Howdenvale, in 6' to 18' of water. She is on the north side of the reef extending west of the island. The anchors and other items of interest are scattered over a wide area.

21. SARAH

DEPTH: 10 feet	LEVEL: Novice

LOCATION: This wreck lies off the east shore of Burke Island, Ontario.

The two-masted, 65-ton schooner, *Sarah* (73'3" x 19'4" x 6'6"), became trapped in an ice floe and was abandoned on November 28, 1906. The captain, his wife and two crewmen struggled for hours to get their yawl boat through the floe. Originally launched as the *Emma Laura*, she was rebuilt at Port Burwell, Ontario, in 1864 and again at Port Dover in 1871, and in 1881, she was renamed the *Sarah*.

The wreck of the *Sarah* lies broken up in shallow water about 900' off the east shore of Burke Island.

Left: The *Sarah*. CRIS KOHL COLLECTION

22. GOUDREAU

LORAN:	LAT 46° 03' 45" LON 082° 12' 55"
DEPTH: 18 to 28 feet	LEVEL: Novice

LOCATION: This wreck lies 5 miles southwest of Lyal Island, near Stokes Bay, Ontario.

The 2,298-ton steel freighter, *Goudreau* (300' x 40' x 24'8"), built by the Cleveland Ship Building Company and launched as the *Pontiac* on July 3, 1889, set a record in her

Above: The steel steamer, *Goudreau,* stranded and wrecked. CRIS KOHL COLLECTION. *Right and below:* A *Goudreau* winch and cable, and steel sheeting.   PHOTOS BY CRIS KOHL

A *Goudreau* winch and cable. PHOTO BY CRIS KOHL.

first year by hauling a payload of 2,849 tons of ore in a single trip. She sank in a collision with the *Athabasca* in the St. Marys River on July 14, 1891, in 30 feet of water, but was salvaged and returned to service.

Renamed the *Goudreau* in 1916, she stranded with a load of pyrites on a shoal on November 23, 1917, after losing her rudder and trying to make the shelter of Stokes Bay. There were 24 people on board at the time, and fortunately no lives were lost. Much of this wreck's steel was salvaged for the war effort in 1942.

The wreck rests on a rocky shoal, and the visibility is almost always good. The boilers and the engine were salvaged, but two acres of steel hull plates, iron ore cargo, numerous large gears and winches with coiled cable, hatchway frames and steel portholes make this ideal for exploration and photography.

23. AFRICA

DEPTH: 18 to 28 feet	LEVEL: Novice

LOCATION: Near Stokes Bay, Ontario, west of Lyal Island.

The wooden steamer, *Africa* (148' x 26' x 13'), loaded with 1,270 tons of coal, disappeared in a storm on October 7, 1895. The bodies of some of the crew were found along shorelines near Lyal Island. The wreck lies scattered along a wide swath of hazardous shoals just south of the wreck of the *Explorer* southwest of Greenough Point.

The steamer, *Africa*. CRIS KOHL COLLECTION

24. RIPPLE

This tug, built at Chatham, Ontario, in 1884, hit a reef on September 9, 1905 and quickly broke up. The remains of the hull lie upside-down and the rest of the wreck is scattered in less than 10' of water along Ripple Reef off the west side of Lyal Island.

25. EXPLORER

On September 4, 1883, this small, 32.6-ton, two-masted schooner (48' x 16' x 5'6") ran aground in a storm on the rocks at Greenough Bank, northwest of Lyal Island. With her crew of four clinging desperately to the rigging while sailors safe in Greenough Harbor observed them through a telescope, the ship slid into deep water. All four crew perished.

This ship, built in Chatham, Ontario, in 1866, already had a tumultuous history. She disappeared in 1867, taking her two crewmembers with her, but her captain surviving. The ship was found and raised in 1881, with the two crewmembers discovered locked below deck and holes bored into the hull! The ship was returned to service with tragic results only two years later. The detailed story of this ship is told in the chapter called "The Dead Sheriff's Secrets" in the book, *Shipwreck Tales of the Great Lakes* by Cris Kohl.

The late charter boat operator/dive shop owner, Paul LaPointe, searched for and found this wreck in 1975. The *Explorer* lies in 35' of water, broken up, but with much still to see.

The schooner, *Explorer,* resembled this vessel. CRIS KOHL COLLECTION

Right: Newspapers across the Great Lakes published news of the "Captain's Crime" when the *Explorer* was salvaged with its two crewmembers locked inside. CRIS KOHL COLLECTION. But the captain who survived, Sheriff John Waddell, was himself long dead by then. PHOTO BY CRIS KOHL

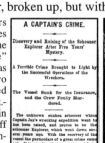

A CAPTAIN'S CRIME.

Discovery and Raising of the Schooner Explorer After Five Years' Mystery.

A Terrible Crime Brought to Light by the Successful Operations of the Wreckers.

The Vessel Sunk for the Insurance, and the Crew Foully Murdered.

The unknown sunken schooner which Captain Jex's wrecking expedition went to has been raised, and proves to be the schooner Explorer, which went down several years ago. With the recovery of the vessel the particulars of a great crime came out. It is not often that mysterious "disasters" can be so fully explained. Late in October, 1807, the Explorer was fitted out at Chatham, Ont., with a stock of goods to trade with the Indians around Georgian Bay

17. Tobermory

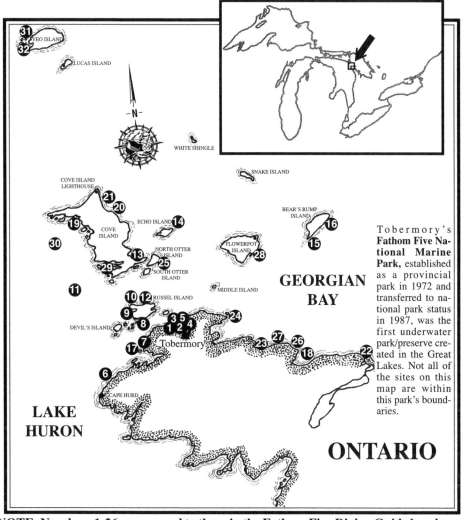

Tobermory's **Fathom Five National Marine Park,** established as a provincial park in 1972 and transferred to national park status in 1987, was the first underwater park/preserve created in the Great Lakes. Not all of the sites on this map are within this park's boundaries.

N<u>OTE</u>: Numbers 1-26 correspond to those in the Fathom Five Diving Guide brochure.

1. *Sweepstakes*	12. *Newaygo*	23. **Dave's Bay**
2. *City of Grand Rapids*	13. *Charles P. Minch*	**(Little Cove)**
3. **Big Tub Lighthouse**	14. *Arabia*	24. **Dunk's Point**
4. **The Anchor**	15. *Marion L. Breck*	25. **North Otter Wall**
5. **The Tugs**	16. *Forest City*	26. *Niagara II*
6. *Cascaden*	17. *Avalon Voyager II*	27. *Lady Dufferin*
7. *China*	18. *Caroline Rose*	28. **Flowerpot I.**
8. *John Walters*	19. **Unidentified**	29. *Points West*
9. *W. L. Wetmore*	20. **Unidentified**	30. **Freighter anchor**
10. *James C. King*	21. **Unidentified**	31. *San Jacinto*
11. *Philo Scoville*	22. **The Caves**	32. *Vita*

Ranked by diving experts as one of the top scuba diving destinations anywhere in the Great Lakes (if not THE top), this mecca offers a variety of superb shipwrecks, excellent underwater visibility, geological formation dives, several scuba dive shops, a large concentration of scuba charter boats, beautiful wilderness scenery, a huge range of accommodations (from rudimentary camping to first class resorts), restaurants (but no fast food chains -- yet!) and interesting land sites for diver and non-diver alike, all in a small area!

I first visited Tobermory in the summer of 1966 after persuading my parents and sister that we absolutely had to satisfy our curiosities about what lay at the end of that long stretch of land called the Bruce Peninsula. I was not disappointed, and I shot 8mm movie film of the quiet harbor and the commercial fishing nets drying on the docks while stretched out on large, cylindrical racks. There were no scuba dive shops in town, and I wasn't a scuba diver yet. In 1972, not long after the discovery of the wonderfully intact schooner, *Arabia,* and the controversy over someone dynamiting the wreck of the *W. L. Wetmore* to salvage the artifacts inside, the first designated underwater park/preserve in the Great Lakes was created there as a provincial park. I took up scuba diving not too long after that. By the time I first went scuba diving at Tobermory, there were dive shops in town and charter boats in the harbor, and the commercial fishing nets drying on the docks had disappeared.

Downtown Tobermory, situated perfectly on the water's edge along protected Little Tub Harbour, was the subject of this 1930's postcard. Note the World War I memorial, now long gone, at the right. CRIS KOHL COLLECTION

With a quarter of a million tourists passing through Tobermory annually nowadays (many of them simply there to catch the ferry to Manitoulin Island, or boaters on a stopover at this maritime crossroads), and 5,500 registered scuba divers visiting each year and doing an average of four dives each, there is much action along the docks and in this town of 600 permanent residents, particularly on summer weekends. Somehow, in spite of all the hubbub, Tobermory retains an appealing, old-fashioned quaintness.

Tobermory's scenic harbor features a reminder of its maritime past, an anchor from the nearby wreck of the schooner, *Charles P. Minch.* PHOTO BY CRIS KOHL

There are 21 known shipwrecks (some unidentified) within five miles of Tobermory, Ontario, inside the boundaries of Fathom Five National Marine Park, plus several more just outside the park. Each visiting scuba diver is required to register at the Diver Registration Center prior to diving (even shore diving) in the park; boaters must also register. There is a registration fee for divers (at press time, about $5.00 for a one day pass, $10.00 for a weekend pass, or $20.00 for an annual pass). You must show a certification card when registering. Use of a dive flag while diving is mandatory. The separate fee for diving the Tobermory area's newest shipwreck, the steel freighter, *Niagara II,* has been removed.

The park's Visitor Centre in the middle of town welcomes all. The scuba diver registration office is about one block away. PHOTO BY CRIS KOHL

1. SWEEPSTAKES

DEPTH: 8 to 20 feet	LEVEL: Novice

LOCATION: This popular shipwreck lies at the head of Big Tub Harbour, Tobermory.

The 218-ton schooner, *Sweepstakes* (119' x 22'8" x 10'1"), built at Burlington, Ontario, in 1867, was driven ashore and seriously damaged at Cove Island in August, 1885, but was pulled off and towed by the tug, *Jessie,* to Big Tub Harbour, where she sank before repairs could be made. Her coal cargo was salvaged.

The *Sweepstake* closely resembled the *Azov*, which was constructed by the same builder. CRIS KOHL COLLECTION

The *Sweepstake's* magnificent windlass attracts diver Joan Forsberg.   PHOTO BY CRIS KOHL

The *Sweepstakes*

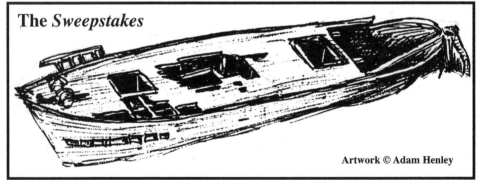

Artwork © Adam Henley

A diver points out the *Sweepstake's* Roman numeral draft markings on the bow.
PHOTO BY CRIS KOHL

The *Sweepstakes* lies about 150' from the head of Big Tub. Because divers' trapped bubbles were damaging the wreck, wooden and wire grates have been installed to prohibit penetration diving. But her external hull and deck exhibit wonderful items, such as a large windlass, an intact starboard railing, the mast holes and Roman numeral bow markings. The *Sweepstakes* is one of the best preserved 1800's Great Lakes schooners to be found, in spite of Nature taking her toll every year. Diver/tourboat hours are limited and staggered during the summer so they don't clash; check the office for times. Please respect the rights of the private landowners around the site.

2. CITY OF GRAND RAPIDS

DEPTH: 5 to 15 feet	LEVEL: Novice

LOCATION: This wreck lies at the head of Big Tub Harbour, Tobermory.

The wooden steamer, *City of Grand Rapids* (123' x 25' x 9'3"), built in 1879 at Grand Haven, Michigan, burned to a total loss on October 29, 1907. This wreck is located about

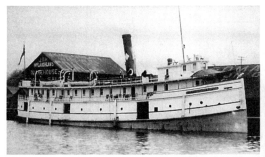

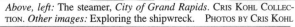

Above, left: The steamer, *City of Grand Rapids*. Cris Kohl Collection. *Other images:* Exploring the shipwreck.   Photos by Cris Kohl

100′ off the starboard bow of the *Sweepstakes,* and is usually explored as part of the same dive. Portions of the engine, boiler and boiler cradle remain.

3. Big Tub Lighthouse

(DEPTH: To 75 feet   LEVEL: Novice-Intermediate)

LOCATION: Lighthouse Point, Big Tub Harbour, Tobermory.
    This shore dive, frequently used for check-out dives by instructors, offers interesting geological features just below the historic (1885) lighthouse. Limited parking is available.

Right: The author, with his second cousin, Christoff Kohl and son, Geoffrey Kohl, after snorkeling at Big Tub Lighthouse.   Photo by Erika Kohl

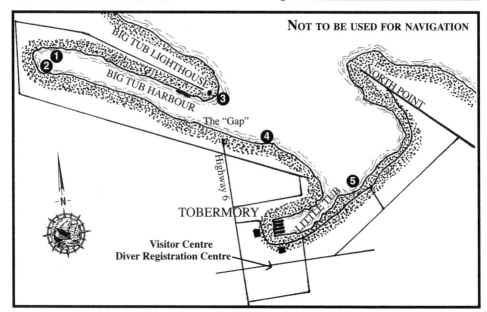

NOT TO BE USED FOR NAVIGATION

BIG TUB LIGHTHOUSE

BIG TUB HARBOUR

NORTH POINT

The "Gap"

Highway 6

LITTLE TUB

-N-

TOBERMORY

Visitor Centre
Diver Registration Centre

4. THE ANCHOR

DEPTH: 70 feet	LEVEL: Intermediate-Advanced

LOCATION: Just off the shoreline almost halfway between Big Tub Harbour and Little Tub Harbour. This shore or boat dive is to a huge, wooden-stocked iron anchor and heavy-linked chain from an unknown vessel. The suit-up and entry area is at the "Gap" just to the

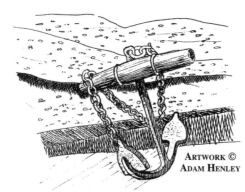

ARTWORK ©
ADAM HENLEY

Left: The solitary anchor and chain. ARTWORK © ADAM HENLEY

Right: Divers at the anchor. PHOTO BY CRIS KOHL

east of the church at the end of Highway 6. Parking is limited. Please respect the rights of adjacent landowners. Be aware of depth, windy wave-producing weather, and boating hazards. Don't miss the anchor! Once you get to the huge underwater boulder, the anchor lies just beyond. Stay at about the 65' level and keep a sharp eye.

5. THE TUGS

DEPTH: To 40 feet	LEVEL: Novice-Intermediate

LOCATION: These four wrecked tugs lie at Little Tub Harbour, Ontario.

The *John & Alex,* a 59' fishing tug built at Port Dover, Ontario, in 1924, burned here on December 6, 1947. A tug reportedly named the *Bob Foote* sank and was abandoned there in 1905. The 68' *Robert K.,* built at Port Dover, Ontario, in 1917, burned on June 23, 1935. The 67' *Alice G.* went aground in gale force winds and sank in November, 1927.

Diver access is from the wooden deck just off the road. For the most part, the first three of these wrecks, all of which burned, are badly broken and scattered in the harbor. The *Alice G.*, however, is nearly intact; her steam engine, boiler, driveshaft and propeller are interesting and photogenic. The stern railing gracefully curving with the lines of the fantail attests to the beauty and workmanship of that era.

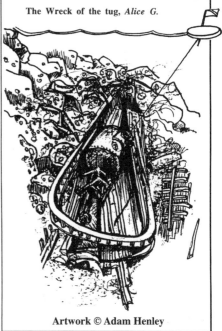

The Wreck of the tug, *Alice G.*

Artwork © Adam Henley

Above: This diver platform offers suit-up/access to the 4 tugs. *Below:* The author's 13-year-old second cousin, Christoff Kohl, explores the stern of the tug, *Alice G.* PHOTOS BY CRIS KOHL

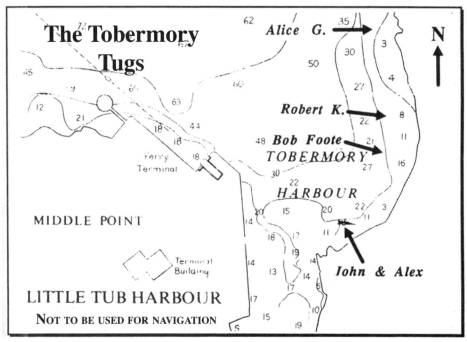

The Tobermory Tugs

N

Alice G.

Robert K.

Bob Foote

TOBERMORY

HARBOUR

John & Alex

MIDDLE POINT

Ferry Terminal

Terminal Building

LITTLE TUB HARBOUR

NOT TO BE USED FOR NAVIGATION

6. CASCADEN

DEPTH: 20 feet	LEVEL: Novice

LOCATION: This wreck lies just northeast of Cape Hurd, Ontario.

The schooner, *Cascaden,* closely resembled this 155-ton sailing ship, the *Maggie Thompson* (114'8" x 26' x 8'), which was built in 1867 and abandoned in 1902. CRIS KOHL COLLECTION

The138-ton wooden schooner, *Cascaden,* built at Southampton, Ontario, in 1866, was wrecked here on October 15, 1871. This site, although still within the park boundaries, is a fair distance southwest of Tobermory, and a boat is required. Wreckage lies scattered over a large, shallow area, and hence this is not a popular dive site. Don't let your boat hit any of the rocky shoals in this region!

A diver closely examines some wooden wreckage from the schooner, *Cascaden.*

PHOTO BY CRIS KOHL

7. CHINA

DEPTH: 10 feet	LEVEL: Novice

LOCATION: This wreck lies southwest of Tobermory, close to shore, but a boat is necessary to reach the site. The wreckage, which can be seen from the surface, lies just on the inside of a small island a short distance southeast of Wreck Point.

The 314-ton schooner, *China* (137' x 23'2" x 11'2"), built at Port Robinson, ON, in 1863, was wrecked on Nov. 20, 1883 (in the same storm which claimed the *John Walters*), at the reef which was later named after her. The wreckage is badly broken up; the largest and most interesting pieces lie close to shore. **Many rocks and ledges form boating hazards.**

No archival photos of the schooner, *China,* have surfaced to date, but the vessel pictured in the upper left was similar in size and appearance. This is the schooner, *Russian* (144' x 26' x 11'), which was built in 1862 and abandoned at Alpena, Michigan, in 1908. CRIS KOHL COLLECTION. A small boat or an inflatable can be used to reach this cove inside China Reef just off Wreck Point (both places named after this shipwreck). This large, shallow wreck attracts many kayakers. Underwater, the broken *China* offers much to see in the way of framing and planking, and visiting divers can truly appreciate 19th-century shipbuilding techniques. PHOTOS BY CRIS KOHL

8. *JOHN WALTERS*

DEPTH: To 15 feet	LEVEL: Novice

LOCATION: This wreck lies off the southwest tip of Russel Island. A boat is necessary to reach the island, and the dive can be done there from shore.

The 176-ton schooner, *John Walters* (108'5" x 23'5" x 8'3"), built at Kingston, Ontario, in 1852 by George Thurston (who also constructed the *Arabia* which lies here at Tobermory), and launched as the *Sarah Bond,* was owned by Henry Patterson of Chatham, Ontario, when she was stranded here on Nov. 20, 1883. The bow lies broken near the shore, while the stern and rudder are in deeper water. The thick keelson and centerboard box are interesting.

No photos of the schooner, *John Walters,* have been located yet, but this ship, the 154-ton schooner, *Alice M. Beers* (109'6" x 24' x 9'), was quite similar. The *Beers,* built at Algonac, Michigan, in 1864, sank after striking a pier at Glen Arbor on Lake Michigan on Sept. 4, 1902. CRIS KOHL COLLECTION. Massive pieces of the *John Walters'* hull and framing, plus the centerboard box, remain on site. PHOTOS BY CRIS KOHL

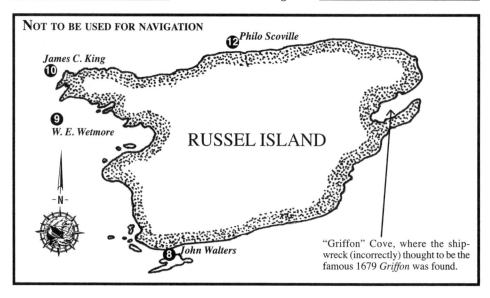

NOT TO BE USED FOR NAVIGATION

Philo Scoville ⑫

James C. King ⑩

⑨ W. E. Wetmore

RUSSEL ISLAND

-N-

⑧ John Walters

"Griffon" Cove, where the shipwreck (incorrectly) thought to be the famous 1679 *Griffon* was found.

9. W. L. WETMORE

LORAN:	LAT 45° 15.200′ LON 081° 42.612′
DEPTH: 28 feet	LEVEL: Novice-Intermediate

LOCATION: This wreck lies just under the northwest tip of Russel Island.

Considered one of the best shipwrecks in the Tobermory area, the wooden steamer, *W.L. Wetmore* (213′7″ x 33′4″ x 12′6″), while towing her usual barges, the *Brunette* and the *James C. King,* was driven ashore on Russel Island in a storm on Nov. 29, 1901. No lives were lost, but only the *Brunette* was salvaged. The *W. L. Wetmore* was launched at Cleveland on May 17, 1871.

Highlights of this site include the massive rudder, the sheared-off propeller, the striking boilers, bow anchor chain, anchor, hawse pipes and much planking with hanging knees and other features. Warning: a west wind will whip up the waves!

Photos of the *Wetmore* on page 244...

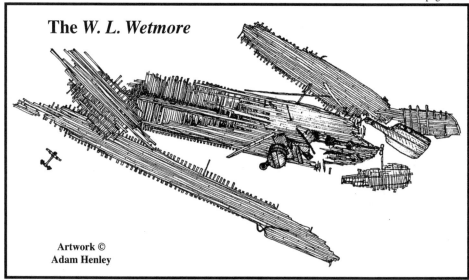

The W. L. Wetmore

Artwork ©
Adam Henley

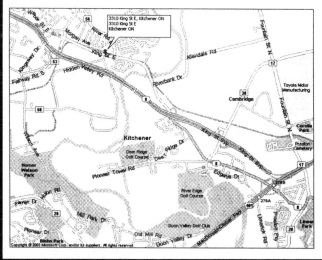

Above, left: The steamer, *W. L. Wetmore. Above, middle:* Many Great Lakes newspapers reported the drama of the storm which ultimately destroyed the *Wetmore* and one of its tows, the *James C. King.* These headlines are from the *Detroit Free Press*, Dec. 3, 1901. BOTH: CRIS KOHL COLLECTION. *Right:* Diver Roy Pickering approaches the sheared-off propeller of the *W. L. Wetmore. Below:* Divers examine the *Wetmore's* chain pile and boilers. PHOTOS BY CRIS KOHL

10. JAMES C. KING

LORAN:	GPS: 45° 16.069'/081° 42.543'
DEPTH: 22 to 93 feet	LEVEL: Intermediate-Advanced

LOCATION: This wreck lies off the northwestern tip of Russel Island.

The schooner-barge, *James C. King* (181'6" x 33' x 13'), built at East Saginaw, Michigan, in 1867, was driven ashore with her towing steamer, the *W. L. Wetmore,* on November 29, 1901. No lives were lost, but, unlike the *Wetmore,* the *James C. King* slid into deep water. The wreck lies on a steep incline, with the rudder lying flat in the shallows close to the broken, split hull. At depth, a capstan and Roman numeral draught markings can be seen.

Above: The schooner-barge, *James C. King,* was wrecked with the *Wetmore* in a 1901 storm. GREAT LAKES MARINE COLLECTION OF THE MILWAUKEE PUBLIC LIBRARY/ WISCONSIN MARINE HISTORICAL SOCIETY. *Left and right:* Diver Roy Pickering explores the *King's* deep bow and its shallow, flat rudder. PHOTOS BY CRIS KOHL

11. NEWAYGO

LORAN:	GPS: 45° 16.238'/081° 45.063'
DEPTH: To 25 feet	LEVEL: Novice

LOCATION: This wreck lies in the Northwest Bank, Devil Island Channel.

The steamer, *Newaygo*. CRIS KOHL COLLECTION

The wooden steamer, *Newaygo* (196' x 37'2" x 13'4"), launched at Marine City, Michigan, on July 18, 1890, stranded in a storm at this site on November 17, 1903, and broke up. No lives were lost. The *Newaygo,* owned by Port Huron businessman Henry McMorran and underway light from Cleveland for French River, Ontario, was towing the schooner-barge, *Checotah*, at the time of loss (the *Checotah* survived this time, but is elsewhere in this book). The highlights of this scattered wreckage are a boiler and the huge, heavily-built bottom of the hull, 160' long. This open site is susceptible to bad weather and west winds.

12. PHILO SCOVILLE

LORAN:	GPS: 45° 16.134'/081° 41.832'
DEPTH: 35 to 95 feet	LEVEL: Intermediate-Advanced

LOCATION: This wreck lies along the north shore of Russel Island.

The 325-ton schooner, *Philo Scoville* (139'5" x 30'4" x 11'3"), constructed at Cleveland in 1863, drifted off course during a storm on October 6, 1889, while enroute light (that is, carrying no cargo) from Collingwood, Ontario, to Escanaba, Michigan. Dragging her anchors, she struck Russel Island, where her captain died when he fell between the ship and some rocks. A Tobermory tug rescued the other four crewmen. Lying on a steep incline, the broken stern lies scattered along the slope in the shallows, while the bowsprit lies in about 93' near the mooring buoy anchor. A ship's anchor about 150' to the east lies at the same depth, with a twin set of anchor chains running uphill along the rocks to about the 30' depth. Part of the stern lies in 35' about 100' west of the main wreckage.

Diver Joe Drummond follows the *Philo Scoville's* twin set of anchor chains down the rocky drop-off.   PHOTO BY CRIS KOHL

13. CHARLES P. MINCH

LORAN:	GPS: 45° 17.670'/081° 42.670'
DEPTH: 20 to 60 feet	LEVEL: Novice-Intermediate

LOCATION: This wreck lies just off the south shore of Tecumseh Cove at Cove Island.

A boat is needed to reach Cove Island; this site can be done as a shore dive from there, or from a boat. The three-masted schooner, *Charles P. Minch* (154'7" x 28'2" x 11'8"), built at Vermilion, Ohio, in 1867, was enroute to Chicago with a lumber cargo on October 26, 1898, when adverse weather forced her into the protected harbor of Tecumseh Cove. When the wind suddenly shifted, the harbor lost its "protected" status, the captain and crew just barely reached the island, and the Minch was destroyed within three hours.

Two mooring buoys usually mark the *Charles P. Minch* sites. The centerboard box,

The *Charles P. Minch*. Cris Kohl Collection

Exploring the *Minch's* hull. Photo by Cris Kohl

sides, bow and bottom of the hull lie on the incline east of the submerged cribs near the head of the cove (a good place to make an entry). The rudder situated west of this mooring buoy is likely from the schooner, *Tecumseh,* wrecked here on Nov. 27, 1882, with a lumber cargo while enroute from Byng Inlet to Windsor. Between the second mooring buoy, about 600' south of the cove, and the shore lie a keel and rudder portion, plus part of the deck. Numerous artifacts, including a .38 revolver, were recovered here years ago.

14. *Arabia*

LORAN: 30202.9/48669.8	GPS: 45° 18.713'/081° 40.444'
DEPTH: 97 to 117 feet	LEVEL: Advanced

LOCATION: This wreck lies to the northeast of Echo Island.

This is the most intact shipwreck in the Tobermory area, as well as one of the deepest. The barque, *Arabia* (131' x 26' x 12'), bound from Chicago to Midland, Ontario, with a corn cargo, began taking on water during heavy seas on October 4, 1884. After hours of pumping, the weary crew took to the yawlboat while the *Arabia* sank. The three-masted ship had been built by George Thurston at Kingston, Ontario, in 1853, and the vessel sailed to Glasgow, Scotland, with a cargo of wheat in 1854. The mostly-intact hull, lying north to south, has two mooring buoys positioned just off the wreck, with a thin line guiding divers from the buoy anchor to the wreck. The bow is impressive with its bowsprit, anchors, catheads,

The
Arabia

Artwork ©
Adam Henley

The Grain-Laden Schooner Arabia
Sinks at the Entrance of
Georgian Bay.

New Iron Lighthouses—The How-
land-Gerlach Collision—A Terrible Struggle.

THE SCHOONER ARABIA SUNK.

WIARTON, Ont., Oct. 5.—The schooner

Above: Newspapers reported the loss of the *Arabia*, with the survival of all four of her crewmembers. CRIS KOHL COLLECTION. Far more scuba divers have not been as lucky. *Right:* Roy Pickering explores the *Arabia's* port rail. PHOTO BY CRIS KOHL

windlass and bilge pump. Deadeyes and pulleys decorate the railings. The afterdeck, separated from the hull, rests against the starboard quarter. the ship's wheel and steering mechanism are located alongside the afterdeck. The three collapsed masts lie alongside the hull. This is a deep, cold, low-visibility (sometimes) site for very experienced divers only. Give this site all the experience and preparation it demands; at least 12 scuba divers have died here over the past 30 years since this shipwreck's 1971 discovery.

15. *MARION L. BRECK*

⟨ **DEPTH: 10 to 100 feet**   **LEVEL: Variable with depth** ⟩

LOCATION: This wreckage lies off the pointy south end of remote Bear's Rump Island.

With much of her canvas lost to the fury of November gales, the schooner, *Marion L. Breck* (127' x 23'6" x 12'), stranded and broke up on October 16, 1900, her crew reaching the safety of Flowerpot Island. This ship, built in 1840 as the *William Penn* at Garden Island, Ontario, lies broken with her cargo of brick fragments scattered over a wide area. A large hull section lies in 75', a section of keel in 50', a capstan and anchor at 25', and the main wreckage at 90'. This is a remote site; use caution.

Underwater images: Joe Drummond makes a steep descent to the *Breck's* hull, finding pieces along the way. PHOTOS BY CRIS KOHL

16. *FOREST CITY*

⟨ **LORAN: 30158.0/48675.1**   **GPS: 45° 18.909'/081° 33.422'**
DEPTH: From 60 to 150 feet   **LEVEL: Advanced to Technical** ⟩

LOCATION: This wreck lies off the northeast side of remote Bear's Rump Island.

Launched at Cleveland on May 7, 1870, as a three-masted schooner, the *Forest City* (213'7" x 33'5" x 21'3") was converted to a steamer two years later. On June 4, 1904, in a dense fog, she struck the island at full steam. Equipment was salvaged before the ship slid into deep water. On shore, a rusty chunk of bow plating marks the ship's impact point. In the water, the broken bow is in 60', while the rest of the ship drops to 150', retaining intactness with depth. Deep coldwater diving is demanding; plan well. Careless and/or inexperienced divers have died here.

The *Forest City*

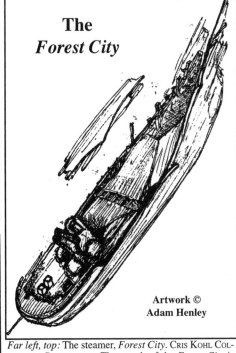

Artwork ©
Adam Henley

Far left, top: The steamer, *Forest City*. CRIS KOHL COLLECTION. *Bottom row:* The wreck of the *Forest City* is marked on shore with a spraypainted triangle. Underwater, a diver studies the *Forest City's* framing bolts at 120′, then drops a bit deeper to the boiler.

PHOTOS BY CRIS KOHL

17. *AVALON VOYAGER II*

DEPTH: To 25 feet   LEVEL: Novice

LOCATION: This totally submerged wreck, which can be seen from the surface, lies just off the west end of Bonnet Island near Hay Bay. A boat (again, an inflatable is ideal) is necessary to reach this site (although the first time I filmed the *Avalon Voyager II* was from a sailboat on which I was living for six weeks, cruising by in the summer of 1981; the *Avalon Voyager II* was still intact and mostly above water, although impaled upon the rocks. A year later, I explored her underwater for my first time). This 325-ton, 135-foot-long wooden propeller, built at Clarenville, Newfoundland in 1946 and launched as the *Twillingate*, with various other name changes (*Thomas V. Hollett* from 1951 to 1967, *Avalon Voyager* from 1967 to 1976, *Avalon Voyager II* from 1976 to 1981) struck rocks off Cape Hurd on October 31, 1980, while enroute from Kincardine to Owen Sound for use there as the floating

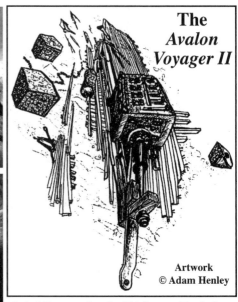

The *Avalon Voyager II*

Artwork
© Adam Henley

Left: A diver examines the thick frames of the *Avalon Voyager II*, while the wreck's toppled bitts offer an interesting view.   PHOTOS BY CRIS KOHL

restaurant she had become. Her anchor failed to hold and she dragged into Hay Bay. Her registration was closed on March 5, 1981. Harsh weather and firebug vandals took their toll on this vessel, but she is still interesting and photogenic.

18. CAROLINE ROSE

LORAN:	GPS: 45° 14.535'/081° 34.572'
DEPTH: 55 feet	LEVEL: Intermediate

LOCATION: This scuttled ship lies in Driftwood Cove, about 4 miles southeast of Tobermory and about half a mile outside the park boundary.

The 250-ton, 132-foot-long schooner, *Caroline Rose,* built in 1940 at Lunenburg, Nova Scotia, was one of the last Grand Banks schooners to be used for fishing (and she is reputed to be one of the three ships pictured on the back of a Canadian $100 bill). Abandoned after being used as a cruise ship and sinking at her dock at Owen Sound, Ontario, the *Caroline Rose* was raised amidst controversy, towed north, and purposely sunk (authorities reportedly would not allow her to be scuttled inside Fathom Five National Marine Park) on August 27, 1990, as a new, intact dive site. Three weeks later, a severe storm moved the wreck 150' closer towards shore, extensively damaging her. She is no longer penetrable but yields an incredible variety of areas to explore and sights to see.

Sights galore on the scuttled schooner, *Caroline Rose,* include a spare propeller (she carried an auxiliary engine) and diver messages written in the silt on her wooden hull.
PHOTOS BY CRIS KOHL

250

19. UNIDENTIFIED

Nothing is known about the backgrounds of these three unidentified shipwrecks (sites #19, 20, and 21) off various parts of Cove Island north of Tobermory.

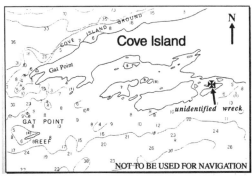

This 62-foot-long section, thought to be a forward hull portion, exists with framing, planking and miscellaneous debris covering a large area. It lies in the shallows (maximum 8' of water) protected by an islet just east of the largest island east of Gat Point.

To reach the unidentified Gat Point wreck, patience, caution, and a boat with very shallow draft are needed, as the area is laced with rocky reefs. What would this schooner say if it could talk? PHOTOS BY CRIS KOHL

20. UNIDENTIFIED

This wreckage, mainly in three chunks of boards lying in 20' to 80', is located beneath a Parks Canada Service sign naming "Cove Island." It's on the east side of Cove Island, just to the southeast of "Cassle's Cove Wreck," site #21.

21. UNIDENTIFIED

Site #21, called "Cassle's Cove Wreck," is a centerboard schooner located below Cove Island lighthouse off Boat Harbour. An 88-foot-long section lies in the sand at 70', while the vessel's sides rest at 60', with the rudder, complete with a decorative, scalloped design carved into the top of its blade, sits on pebbles at 50'.

Right: Cove Island Lighthouse is an excellent place to stop and have lunch between scuba dives.   PHOTO BY CRIS KOHL

22. THE CAVES

DEPTH: 30 feet   **LEVEL: Novice-Intermediate**

LOCATION: These caverns (they are not really "caves" because you never lose sight of light from an opening) are about 10 miles east of Tobermory. Take a boat and forget about hiking in with all your scuba equipment from the parking lot at Cyprus Lake.

Two small, submerged caverns lead from the open bay waters to "The Grotto," a se-

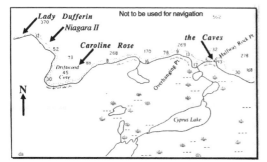

cluded, hushed pool protected by a massive limestone vault, where scuba divers and skinnydippers have been known to encounter each other unexpectedly. Interesting sights, in the shape of underwater rock formations, exist just outside "The Grotto" as well. Dive lights can be used to check out the nooks and crannies of this site, but they are not necessary. The water drops off deeply down the slope beyond these caverns.

Scuba charter boats from Tobermory are lined up at the popular caves divesite. Although technically "caverns," these "cave" dives thrill visitors, and are usually selected as a charterer's second dive. PHOTOS BY CRIS KOHL.

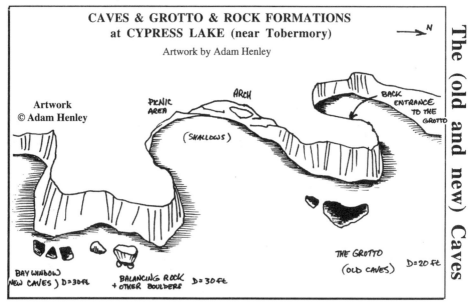

CAVES & GROTTO & ROCK FORMATIONS at CYPRESS LAKE (near Tobermory)

Artwork by Adam Henley

The (old and new) Caves

23. DAVE'S BAY (LITTLE COVE)

DEPTH: To 40 feet   **LEVEL: All levels**

LOCATION: Take Warner Bay Road near the Township Museum east to Little Cove. Besides being a picturesque bay, this site offers interesting geological formations such as glacial erratics, pitting and layered dolomite along the bay's south shore. Used sometimes for diver checkouts, this site offers limited parking at the access point. Please respect the rights of the private property owners here, which is outside the Fathom Five National Marine Park boundaries.

Dave's Bay is located just outside Tobermory.   PHOTO BY CRIS KOHL

24. DUNK'S POINT

DEPTH: To 60 feet   **LEVEL: All levels**

LOCATION: One mile east of Tobermory. A boat (an inflatable is ideal) is necessary. Interesting underwater geological formations, such as glacial pitting, abound. There is an anchor and long chain out here, but the circumstances of their loss is not known. To reach them, begin your swim underwater at Dunk's Point and descend at the gradual dropoff to a

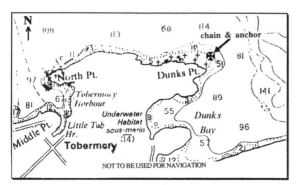

depth of 40'. Follow the contour of the point, swinging north gradually. Ideally, you will eventually encounter a big mound of anchor chain at a depth of about 43'. Follow the chain as it twists and winds and dips over rocks and drops into gulleys on its seemingly endless route to the anchor itself. The anchor, similar to the one at "The Gap," is a wooden stock, iron-fluked one, common on vessels in the late 1800's. Keep a sharp eye; it's easy to miss.

Dan Perry and I found the pile of chain, then followed it, and followed it, and followed it some more, over rocks and through crevices, until we finally reached the Dunk's Point anchor! PHOTOS BY CRIS KOHL

25. NORTH OTTER WALL

This geological dive site has become quite popular in the past decade, featuring steep walls, overhangs (one frequently visited is named "Pablo's Hangover"), a small cave, and examples of geological pitting. With a maximum depth of 40', this site is suitable for all levels of divers.

26. NIAGARA II

LORAN:	GPS: 45° 15.039'/081° 36.179'
DEPTH: From 48 to 98 feet	LEVEL: Intermediate-Advanced

Above: The 54-year-old *Niagara II* in 1984. CRIS KOHL COLLECTION. *Below:* The *Niagara II's* name and final port of call appear on the bridge.   PHOTO BY CRIS KOHL

LOCATION: This wreck lies several miles to the east of Tobermory, close to the wreck of the *Caroline Rose*.

On May 15, 1999, the 700-ton, 180-foot-long former freighter and sand dredge, *Niagara II,* was scuttled for the express purpose of creating another exciting scuba dive site in the Tobermory area. Again, this vessel was sunk just outside the boundaries of Fathom Five National Marine Park because, reportedly, of official opposition to this plan. Several people formed the Tobermory Maritime Association in 1997, found and purchased this ship in 1998, and spent over 1,000 hours cleaning her up before the scuttling.

The *Niagara II,* a steel ship launched in England in 1930, had five different names in the course of her 67-year career, receiving her last name in 1984. In 1990, her engine was removed and she was used as a barge. This is a magnificent site, with enough places to explore on this vessel to occupy a half dozen dives easily. The ship is intact and sits upright, and all doors and hatches have been removed for diver safety. There are railings and passageways galore to guide the diver along. A ship's wheel was added to the wheel-less bridge just prior to the sinking, in effect making this ship complete for the underwater explorer. There was an extra fee charged to dive this wreck, but the cost of scuttling this ship has been recouped, so that fee has been removed.

Divers now steer the *Niagara II* to their favorite destination. PHOTO BY CRIS KOHL

27. LADY DUFFERIN

DEPTH: From 40 to 200+ feet   LEVEL: All levels to Technical

LOCATION: This wreck lies very much broken up in huge, wooden sections about 1.5 miles east of Little Cove and just west of Driftwood Cove.

In October, 1886, the 135-foot-long schooner-barge, *Lady Dufferin,* built at Port Burwell, Ontario, was swept onto the rocks after the towline from the steamer that was towing her parted. The

The *Lady Dufferin* resembled this ship, the schooner *Albany* (140' x 26' x 10'), which was abandoned in 1907 at age 35.   CRIS KOHL COLLECTION

crew escaped with their lives, but the ship was a total loss. To locate this wreck, take a boat to Dufferin Point and look for two small circles painted on the rock wall in a niche. Dive there. The wreck is broken up in slabs on a steep, rocky incline, with a steam engine, probably used

Dan Perry studies wooden slabs from the *Lady Dufferin*. PHOTO BY CRIS KOHL

in lumber salvage, located at about 100'. Technical divers have found more wreckage down the drop-off past 200'. The *Lady Dufferin's* rudder lies at 60' a fair distance away from the main wreck site. Heading east by boat from the beach at Dave's Bay, hug the shoreline, which consists of high limestone cliffs and cedar forests. When you arrive at a small "flowerpot" formation in the limestone cliff about halfway up, dive there to see the rudder. This is about halfway to the *Lady Dufferin* wreckage area from the Dave's Bay parking lot.

28. FLOWERPOT ISLAND

DEPTH: 30 to 150+ feet   LEVEL: Changes with depth

Beautiful Flowerpot Island is a tourist attraction to the north-northeast of Tobermory, with several cruise boats taking sightseers there regularly during summer to explore the island on its several trails and to view the famous "flowerpot" rock formations. Once divers reach the island, they can shore dive in the area just off the "flowerpots," viewing submerged ledges, steep cliffs and underwater rock formations. Take the trail east of the small dock.

Above, left: The famous geological formations called"flowerpots," for which Tobermory is famous, have long been photographed, as seen in this early 1900's postcard. CRIS KOHL COLLECTION. *Above, right:* The layered limestone formations continue underwater at Flowerpot Island.   PHOTO BY CRIS KOHL

255

29. POINTS WEST

DEPTH: 50 feet   **LEVEL: Intermediate**

LOCATION: Just east of Harbour Island, off the southwest side of Cove Island.

The *Points West*, a 32-foot-long wooden vessel, served the Tobermory area as a guide boat, later in her career even working as a scuba dive boat. Built in 1956 as the *Flowerpot,* she was scuttled in October, 1984, 300' east of Harbour Island. She sits intact on the sand in an area of usually poor visibility.

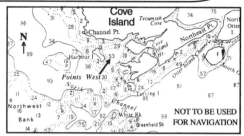

30. FREIGHTER ANCHOR

An unknown vessel lost a huge, modern anchor about one mile south of Gat Point on Cove Island. It lies in open water at a depth of 75', reportedly at **GPS: 45° 17.885'/081° 46.449'.**

31. SAN JACINTO

LORAN: 30242.7/48619.1   **GPS: 45° 24.273'/081° 47.722'**
DEPTH: 80 feet   **LEVEL: Advanced**

The San Jacinto

Artwork
© Adam Henley

LOCATION: This wreck lies off the northwest side of Yeo Island.

The 265-ton schooner, *San Jacinto,* launched in 1856 at Buffalo, New York, foundered in heavy weather off Yeo Island a fair distance north of Tobermory on June 20, 1881, with no lives lost. Located by charterboat operator Paul LaPointe in 1990, the *San Jacinto's* hull is split open, but she is quite intact; bilge pump, windlass, rigging, tools and many other items are found at the site.

Divers hooked this wooden, two-sheave block onto this metal bilge pump at the *San Jacinto* site.   PHOTO BY CRIS KOHL

32. VITA

The opulent steam yacht, *Vita* (86'4" x 18'4" x 6'8"), built at Trenton, MI, in 1888, was wrecked on November 5, 1910, under unknown circumstances. Her broken remains lie in 2' to 18' of water between the daymark on Yeo Island and the rocks of Manitoba Ledge.

18. Eastern Bruce Peninsula

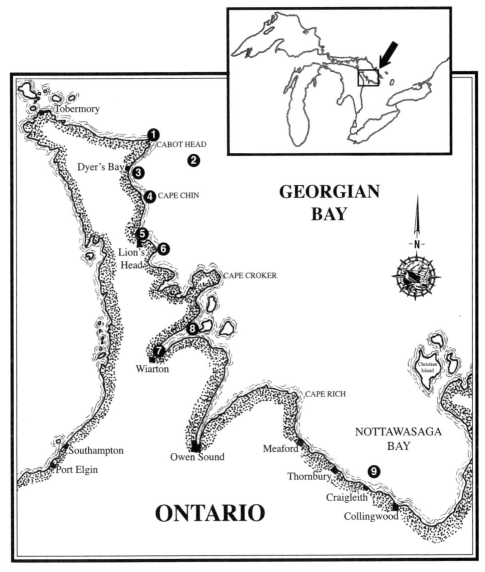

Tobermory

1 CABOT HEAD

2

Dyer's Bay
3

4 CAPE CHIN

5
6

Lion's
Head

CAPE CROKER

GEORGIAN
BAY

-N-

8

7

Wiarton

Christian
Island

CAPE RICH

NOTTAWASAGA
BAY

Southampton
Port Elgin

Owen Sound

Meaford

Thornbury

Craigleith

Collingwood

9

ONTARIO

1. *Gargantua*
2. *Thomas R. Scott*
3. Dyer's Bay
4. Cape Chin wreck
5. Lion's Head wrecks

6. *Old Concord*
7. Wiarton wrecks
8. Underwater forest
9. *Mary Ward*

1. GARGANTUA

> **DEPTH: To 10 feet**   **LEVEL: Novice**

LOCATION: The northwest corner of Wingfield Basin, a small, protected bay at Cabot Head. Shore access is possible; ask permission of the lighthouse grounds keeper for access to Wingfield Basin. It's a bit of a swim; using a boat is better.

The large, wooden tug, *Gargantua* (130' x 32'1" x 15'4"), was built at McLouth Shipyard, Marine City, Michigan, as the *Seafarer* in 1919. On December 6, 1952, after her machinery had been removed, she was under tow in Georgian Bay when she took shelter from heavy

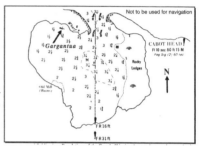

The *Gargantua.* CRIS KOHL COLLECTION

seas in Wingfield Basin, where she sat until she sank. This mostly-above-water eyesore wreck was never popular with local cottage owners. In 1971, a mysterious fire destroyed her superstructure. Most of this wreck remains high and dry; snorkel/dive around her hull.

2. THOMAS R. SCOTT

> **DEPTH: 393 feet**   **LEVEL: Technical**

LOCATION: This wreck lies off Dyer's Bay.

In July, 1994, the submersible from the Canadian Navy diving ship, HMCS *Cormorant,* doing a geological study, picked up a sonar image ahead of it that resembled a schooner. The searchers almost ran right into the shipwreck, since the visibility in that area is perpetually bad: about 6'. But they clearly read the name, *Thomas R. Scott,* on the port side. The wreck sits upright and is very intact.

The wooden steamer, *Thomas R. Scott* (129' x 28' x 7'6"), built at Grand Haven, Michigan, in 1887, became waterlogged and sank on September 2, 1914 (by coincidence, the real-life Thomas R. Scott, a lumber, shipping and ranching businessman after whom this

The *Thomas R. Scott (left).* CRIS KOHL COLLECTION

vessel was named, died four days later at his ranch in Arizona.) Contact the Canadian Navy or their geologists for the coordinates to this deep shipwreck.

3. DYER'S BAY

> **DEPTH: To 90 feet**   **LEVEL: Variable**

There was a waterfront resort, consisting of several old, wooden buildings, which was used by scuba divers in the 1980's and 1990's, but has since been sold. Off this resort, which sits to the south of the dock, lies a large, wooden-stocked anchor, imported to this site by scuba instructors, with 12' of immense chain on it in 42' of water. About one mile south via boat from the town of Dyer's Bay is the impressive rock formation, both above and under water, called "The Devil's Face." Canyon-like passageways, cliffs and caverns abound.

Right: A diver explores "The Devil's Face." PHOTO BY CRIS KOHL

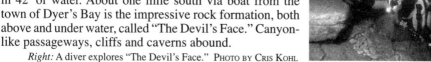

4. CAPE CHIN WRECK

⟨ **DEPTH: 20 and 70 feet**   **LEVEL: Novice/Advanced** ⟩

Approach by boat, since this part of the Bruce Peninsula is lined with privately-owned cottages. Three chunks of unidentified schooner wreckage lie near Cape Chin just off the brown cottage with the gazebo near shore, south of three telephone poles. Just off the boulders used as a retaining wall, sitting on the sand, lie two of the pieces, 60' and 35' in length, in 20' of water. They can usually be seen from the surface. In 1992, we found an additional 35-foot piece in 70' just off the shallow portions. All the sections consist of a heavy, thick keelson, with

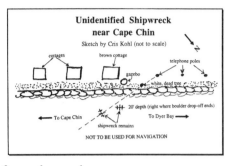

many ribs emanating; it appears that they came from a large schooner.

5. LION'S HEAD WRECKS

⟨ **DEPTH: To 15 feet**   **LEVEL: Novice** ⟩

Sailing vessels in the lumber industry at the beginnng of the 20th century found

themselves being abandoned to age in the many Georgian Bay harbors. Two of these unidentified wrecks lie in Lion's Head harbor. The more accessible of the two lies with the remains of its bow right against the shore of a small, rounded peninsula of land to the southeast of the public beach. These skeletal remains, probably of a sailing vessel, are about 140' long. A bit farther east and about 200' off shore in 15' of water are the remains of a tugboat. Beware of boating traffic here, especially in the summertime.

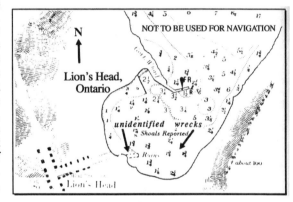

6. OLD CONCORD

⟨ **DEPTH: 60 feet**   **LEVEL: Intermediate** ⟩

LOCATION: This wreck lies off Gun Point, near Lion's Head, Ontario.

Located by Norm Black and Don Knowles in 1974, the 318-gross-ton schooner-barge, *Old Concord* (166' x 27'8" x 11'2"), launched in June, 1855, at Newport (present-day Marine City), Michigan, stranded and sank in July, 1888. The ship's wheel, steering gear, rudder, huge hull slabs and other items are on site.

7. WIARTON WRECKS

⟨ **DEPTH: 12 to 15 feet**   **LEVEL: Novice** ⟩

The identified remains of three wooden ships lie just off the shore of Colpoy's Bay north of the town of Wiarton, and can be done as shore dives or by boat. The flattened lower hull of the passenger ship, *City of Chatham* (136'3" x 28'5" x 9'), built in Toronto in 1888, lies just north of the Wiarton fish hatchery. The ship had been partially stripped in 1921 and removed to Wiarton for a rebuilding which never happened. Farther north along the shore, just south of the pier at the community of Colpoy's Bay, lie the remains of the *Lothair,* a Scottish-built barge (and the closer wreck to shore, with its stern post reaching close to the

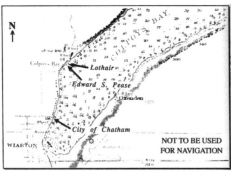

Above: The active passenger and freight steamer, *City of Chatham.*
CRIS KOHL COLLECTION

NOT TO BE USED FOR NAVIGATION

The *City of Chatham* Shipwreck

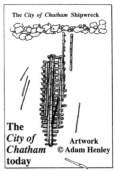

The *City of Chatham* today

Artwork © Adam Henley

surface) and the *Edward S. Pease,* a lumber barge with sails. They lie end-to-end, flat and broken up, purposely sunk in the early 1900's in front of Whicher's Mill to form a mill pond as protection for the log rafts. The mill company had paid $200 each for them.

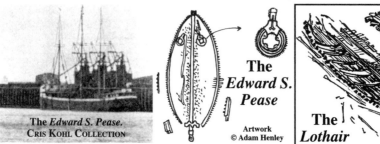

The *Edward S. Pease.*
CRIS KOHL COLLECTION

The *Edward S. Pease*

Artwork © Adam Henley

Artwork © Adam Henley

The *Lothair*

8. UNDERWATER FOREST

DEPTH: To 34 feet   LEVEL: Novice

Diver and past mayor of Wiarton, Ontario, Alan Given, located this underwater forest in 1977 on the northwest side of Gundersen Shoal in Colpoy's Bay, but thought little of it until 1993, when he sawed off some samples underwater and sent them to botanists. They were excited. They were 4,500 to 7,600 years old. Underwater forests, which give us a date at which water levels rose from the retreat of the last Ice Age, can also be found adjacent to nearby Cyprus Lake and a bit south of it in 40' to 60', Johnson Harbour on the west side of the Bruce Peninsula, and just off Cape Croker, as well as off Chicago in Lake Michigan.

9. *MARY WARD*

DEPTH: To 15 feet   LEVEL: Novice

Lying between Craigleith, Ontario, and the Mary Ward Ledges in Georgian Bay are the engine, propeller and much broken wreckage from the wooden steamer, *Mary Ward* (139' x 25'6" x 11'6"), built in Montreal as the *North* in 1864, and stranded and sunk on November 24, 1872, with the loss of 8 crewmembers who tried to reach shore in a lifeboat. A boat is necessary to reach this hard-to-find site.

Left: Drawing of the steamer, *Mary Ward.*
PUBLIC ARCHIVES OF CANADA

Right: A geographic feature was named after this wreck: the Mary Ward Ledges.

Not to be used for navigation.

19. Penetanguishene

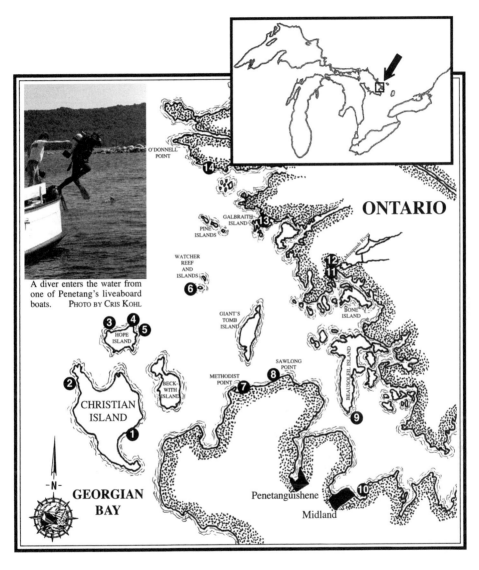

A diver enters the water from one of Penetang's liveaboard boats. PHOTO BY CRIS KOHL

ONTARIO

O'DONNELL POINT

GALBRAITH ISLAND

PINE ISLANDS

WATCHER REEF AND ISLANDS

Musquash River

BONE ISLAND

GIANT'S TOMB ISLAND

HOPE ISLAND

BECK-WITH ISLAND

BEAUSOLEIL ISLAND

SAWLONG POINT

METHODIST POINT

CHRISTIAN ISLAND

-N-

GEORGIAN BAY

Penetanguishene

Midland

1. *Saucy Jim*
2. *Mapledawn*
3. *Michigan*
4. *Lottie Wolf*
5. *Marquette*
6. *Thomas Cranage*
7. *Reliever*
8. *Luckport*
9. *Wawinet*
10. *Midland City*
11. *Chippewa*
12. *Ontario*
13. *Galbraith Island tug*
14. *W. J. Martin*

1. SAUCY JIM

> **DEPTH: 5 feet**   **LEVEL: Novice**

LOCATION: This wreck lies off the sandy beach just east of the government dock at Christian Island. Built at Meaford, Ontario, in 1887, the small steam tug, *Saucy Jim*, burned to a total loss on November 18, 1910. Her boiler rises above the water's surface to act as a location marker for those wishing to snorkel/dive her broken, scattered remains.

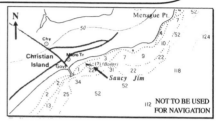

2. MAPLEDAWN

> **LORAN: 29655.3/48931.5**   **LAT 44° 51' 52" LON 080° 14' 50"**
> **DEPTH: 10 to 30 feet**   **LEVEL: Novice-Intermediate**

LOCATION: This wreck lies off the northwest side of Christian Island.

The steel freighter, *Mapledawn* (349'1" x 40'2" x 21'3"), actually started life as the *Manola* (which is also in this book) when she was launched at Cleveland in 1890. As the *Manola*, her bow half sank in Lake Ontario. Later, a new bow half was constructed for the *Manola's* orphaned stern half, the resulting whole ship being named the *Mapledawn.* Although lives were lost when her original bow half sank in Lake Ontario, none was lost when the *Mapledawn,* loaded with barley,

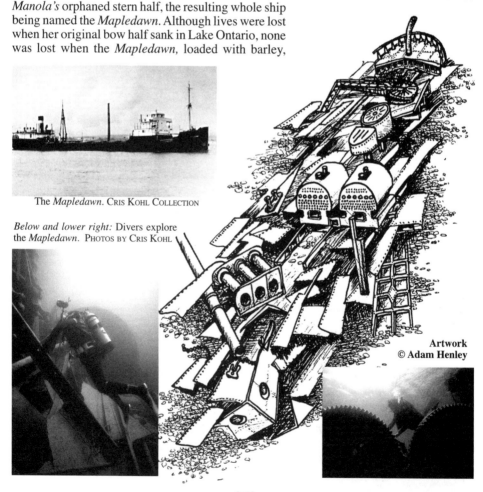

The *Mapledawn.* CRIS KOHL COLLECTION

Below and lower right: Divers explore the *Mapledawn.* PHOTOS BY CRIS KOHL

Artwork © Adam Henley

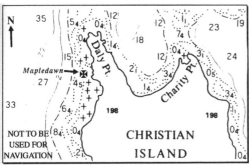

Divers in the 1950's could easily find the *Mapledawn*. Today the wreck is completely submerged. PHOTOGRAPHER UNKNOWN. CRIS KOHL COLLECTION

stranded in a blinding snowstorm on November 30, 1924. Some machinery was salvaged at that time, but more of this wreck was recovered for its metal during the time of need in World War II. The considerable remaining wreckage includes the winch, chains, engine, gigantic boilers and the propeller at the deepest part in 30' of water about 50' off the stern.

3. MICHIGAN

> **LORAN: 29637.73/48912.73   LAT 44° 54' 58" LON 080° 12' 15"**
> **DEPTH: To 15 feet   LEVEL: Novice**

LOCATION: This wreck lies off the northwest corner of Hope Island, Georgian Bay.

The steel barge, *Michigan* (296'5" x 41'3" x 15'6"), launched at West Bay City, Michigan, on October 30, 1890, as a railroad carferry, was lightering the grain cargo from the stranded steamer, *Riverton,* at this site on November 24, 1943, when the gales of November blew the *Michigan* onto the rocks as well. Suddenly the salvage ship needed salvaging! Ironically, the *Riverton* was eventually recovered and returned to service, but the *Michigan* became a total loss. Giant gears, machinery and much metalwork offer intriguing sights here.

The steel barge, *Michigan,* sank in 1943. CRIS KOHL COLLECTION. The *Michigan* shipwreck covers a large area, with divers exploring the site as thoroughly as possible.   PHOTOS BY CRIS KOHL

BARGE "MICHIGAN" BREAKS UP ON LOTTIE WOLFE SHOAL AND WILL BE A TOTAL LOSS

The lighter "Michigan" from Owen Sound is lying with a broken back on the Lottie Wolfe Shoal, in the lee of the S. S. Riverton, aground on the same shoal since November 14. The Michigan had gone to lighten the stricken Riverton, and met the same fate herself in a wicked gale on the night of November 23, which swept her on to the rocks near midnight.

The Michigan, owned by John Harrison and Sons of Owen Sound in preparation to sending out a tow-line to the lighter Michigan

4. LOTTIE WOLF

LORAN: 29501.9/48914.3	GPS:
DEPTH: 18 feet	LEVEL: Novice

LOCATION: This wreck lies about 450' from the lighthouse dock, off the northeast corner of Hope Island, southern Georgian Bay.

The three-masted, 126' schooner, *Lottie Wolf*, launched at Green Bay, Wisconsin, in 1866, sailed for Midland, Ontario, from Chicago with a cargo of corn when she struck a rock during severe weather on October 16, 1891. Purposely run aground to avoid sinking in deep water, the vessel broke up after the crew abandoned ship. The remains lie scattered on a sandy bottom, with the sides of the hull off the south and west of the main wreckage area.

Artist's conception of the *Lottie Wolf*.
ARTIST UNKNOWN. CRIS KOHL COLLECTION

5. MARQUETTE

LORAN: 29620.0/48917.0	GPS:
DEPTH: 29 to 45 feet	LEVEL: Novice-Intermediate

LOCATION: The wreck of the *Marquette* lies off the northeast corner of Hope Island.

The schooner, *Marquette,* closely resembled this ship, the *Emerald*.
CRIS KOHL COLLECTION

NOT TO BE
USED FOR
NAVIGATION

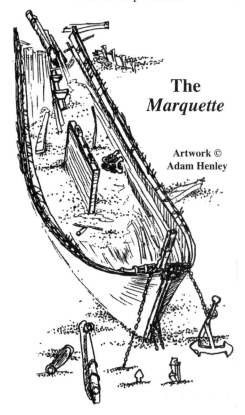

The
Marquette

Artwork ©
Adam Henley

The 139'3" bark, *Marquette,* built at Newport (today's Marine City), Michigan, in 1856, foundered with a cargo of corn and no lives lost on November 28, 1867. Known as "The Hope Island Wreck" for about 10 years after divers located it in 1975, her identity

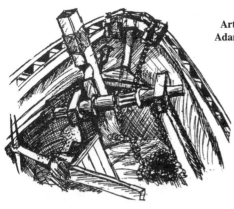

Artwork ©
Adam Henley

Left: Detail of the *Marquette's* bow. ART BY ADAM HENLEY. *Right:* Exploring the windlass and chain at the *Marquette's* bow. PHOTO BY CRIS KOHL

was established in the mid-1980's. Although pilfered of many of its artifacts shortly after its discovery by divers who probably were unaware that they were hurting sport scuba diving in the Great Lakes, this wreck has quite a few interesting items left at the site: two wooden-stocked anchors (with chains still connecting them to the windlass), a samson post, a capstan lying on its side in the sand beside the hull, double framing on its hull, a centerboard box, a centerboard winch, the main mast step, hatch coaming, planksheers, transom wing, and a portion of the rudder.

6. *THOMAS CRANAGE*

LORAN: 29593.6/48906.0	LAT 44° 56' 39" LON 080° 05' 27"
DEPTH: To 25 feet	LEVEL: Novice

LOCATION: This wreck lies off "The Watchers" Islands, southern Georgian Bay. The *Thomas Cranage* (305' x 43' x 20'7"), was, for a short time after her launch on July

The steamer, *Thomas Cranage*, and news of its stranding.   CRIS KOHL COLLECTION

CRANAGE HITS REEF; MAY GO TO PIECES

Bay City Steamer, Grain Laden, is Reported Out Six Feet For-ward Near Tiffin, Ont.

Special to The Free Press.
Bay City, Mich., September 25.—The steamer Thomas Cranage, owned by the Cranage Steamship company, of this city, carrying grain from Duluth to Tiffin, Ont., ran on a reef outside Tiffin harbor, Georgian Bay, this morning, and is believed to be in danger of going to pieces. Her bow is six feet out.

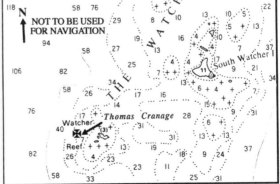

NOT TO BE USED FOR NAVIGATION

Thomas Cranage

29, 1893, at West Bay City, Michigan, the Great Lakes' largest wooden steamer. On September 25, 1911, while on a voyage from Duluth, Minnesota, to Tiffin, Ontario, with a cargo of wheat, the *Thomas Cranage* struck Watcher Reef. Salvage efforts proved futile, and the ship broke to pieces in the early fall.

The broken remains of this vessel include the impressive triple expansion engine, the steel-reinforced rudder and much planking. The propeller and boilers were likely salvaged, as they are absent. This open site is susceptible to adverse westerly weather.

The *Thomas Cranage's* triple expansion engine and extensive wooden hull make unique photographic subjects.   PHOTOS BY CRIS KOHL

7. RELIEVER

Scattered along the bay bottom in about 12' of water about 100' off Way's Point, Ontario (near Methodist Point), lie the hull and other remains of the wooden steamer, *Reliever* (216' x 36' x 18'), launched at West Bay City, Michigan, on April 1, 1888, as the *Germanic*. The

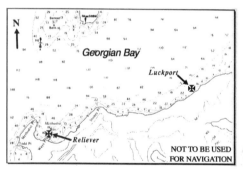

The *Reliever*. CRIS KOHL COLLECTION

ship caught on fire while loading lumber on November 3, 1909. The flaming vessel, cut adrift to save the dock, grounded at Way's Point and burned to a total loss.

8. LUCKPORT

The 126' wooden steamer, *Luckport,* built as the *St. Magnus* at Hamilton, Ontario, in 1880, burned to the waterline west of Sawlog Point in December, 1934. Only the charred hull remains about 200' off shore. The privately-owned land here precludes shore access.

Left: The *Luckport* (middle vessel). CRIS KOHL COLLECTION

9. WAWINET

LORAN: 29501.9/48970.7	LAT 44° 49' 30" LON 079° 05' 54"
DEPTH: 25 feet	LEVEL: Novice-Intermediate

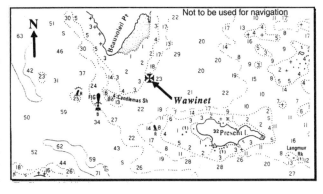

The 87' private yacht, *Wawinet,* built in 1904 and purchased by Bertrand Corbeau of Penetanguishene in 1938, became one of Georgian Bay's most tragic marine accidents. On September 21, 1942, returning from Honey Harbour to Penetanguishene with Corbeau and colleagues from the Midland Foundry & Machine Company, the vessel heeled over while making a sudden turn. Her lower windows were, unfortunately, open, and the ship filled and sank within two minutes, with 25 of the 42 people on board, including Corbeau, losing their lives. The survivors swam to nearby Beausoleil Island where they were soon rescued.

The *Wawinet,* upright and intact, faces bow southeast. The weakened hull of the wreck should be entered only with the greatest of care, training and preparation. Silt stirs up easily.

10. MIDLAND CITY

This site can be reached by shore or boat. Lying in 3' to 12' of water, only the bottom of

the hull remains of the *Midland City* in Tiffin Basin, just east of the easternmost dock. This composite (built of both wood and steel or iron) passenger and freight steamer spent an incredible 84 years working on the Great Lakes! Built as the *Maud* at Kingston in 1871 by George Thurston, the *Midland City* (149'2" x 33'2" x 6'4") was dismantled and deliberately burned on May 7, 1955 near the Wye River. Beware of busy boating traffic here.

The passenger steamer, *Midland City.* CRIS KOHL COLLECTION

11. CHIPPEWA

The 94' wooden steamer, *Chippewa,* built in 1874 at Muskoka Mills, Ontario, at the mouth of the Musquash River, was abandoned near her birthplace in 1906, 3/4 mile up the Musquash River from the extreme southern end of Longuissa Point. She lies in 6' to 20'.

12. ONTARIO

About 1.5 miles up the Musquash River from the extreme southern end of Longuissa Point, the abandoned wooden barge, *Ontario* (131' x 24'), lies in 6' to 12' off the north bank. This ship, built at Welland, Ontario, in 1867, worked mainly in the lumber trade before old age forced her abandonment in the early 1900's. The Musquash River poses certain navigation problems, mainly deadheads and rocks near its mouth, and getting past the first set of rapids (keep to starboard.) Beware of any current and some boating traffic while diving or snorkeling.

13. GALBRAITH ISLAND
WRECK

This unidentified, wooden tug lies in 2' to 10' of water in a quiet cove at the northeast corner of Galbraith Island. A 53-foot-long keel section and some framing remain. Considering the seclusion of this wreck nestled in a quiet cove, this site is good for snorkeling or novice shipwreck diving.

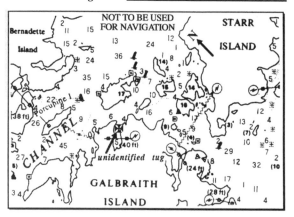

14. *W. J. MARTIN*

The small, 75' wooden steamer, *W. J. Martin,* burned to a complete loss in November, 1905, only two months after she was launched at Midland, Ontario. She lies at Middle Rock, between Ward Island and Fairlie Island, in 5' to 20' of water. Her boiler is the highlight.

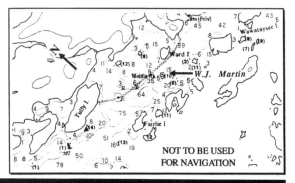

20. Parry Sound

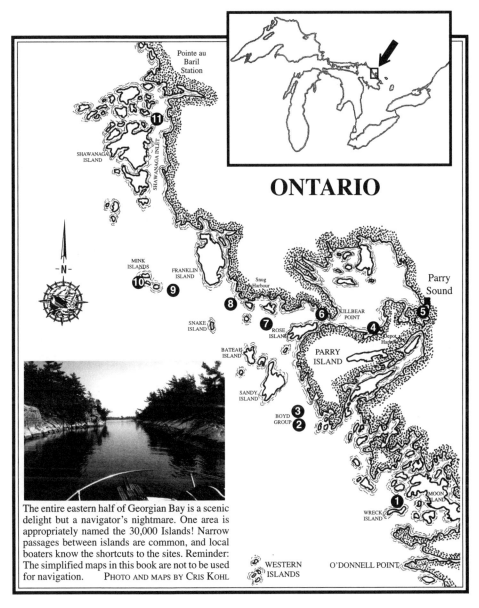

ONTARIO

Parry Sound

The entire eastern half of Georgian Bay is a scenic delight but a navigator's nightmare. One area is appropriately named the 30,000 Islands! Narrow passages between islands are common, and local boaters know the shortcuts to the sites. Reminder: The simplified maps in this book are not to be used for navigation.   PHOTO AND MAPS BY CRIS KOHL

1. *Waubuno*
2. *Emma*
3. **Blackmore Island wreck**
4. **Depot Harbour**
5. *Ella Ross*
6. **Harold Point**

7. *Atlantic*
8. *Jane McLeod*
9. *Midland*
10. *Seattle*
11. *Metamora*

1. *WAUBUNO*

LORAN:	LAT 45° 07' 15" LON 080° 09' 58"
DEPTH: To 15 feet	LEVEL: Novice

LOCATION: This wreck lies in an inlet on the southern tip of Bradden Island, just north of Wreck Island, halfway between the Musquash River and Parry Sound.

The wooden, sidewheel steamer, *Waubuno* (135' x 18'3" x 7'), worked on Georgian Bay for 14 years before becoming a mystery vessel. On November 22, 1879, the *Waubuno* left Collingwood, Ontario, with passengers and freight bound for Parry Sound. Later, a logging crew on shore heard the heavily-laden vessel's distress whistles in a blinding snowstorm. Then she simply disappeared with all 30 people on board. The following spring, this washed-up hull was located, but no bodies were ever found. The ship had been built in 1865 at Port Robinson, Ontario. The hull provides a habitat for pike, perch and bass. The engine, boiler and other machinery are all absent. Keep off the adjoining private property.

Left: The tragic sidewheeler, *Waubuno*. CRIS KOHL COLLECTION. *Above and below:* Examining the *Waubuno's* hull. Often schools of bait fish use this wooden hull as a home. The wreck of the *Waubuno* is marked on charts, but the fact that Bradden Island is privately owned is not; please respect the rights of the cottagers and keep off the island.   PHOTOS BY CRIS KOHL

2. *EMMA*

DEPTH: 4 to 20 feet	LEVEL: Novice

LOCATION: This wreck lies in a small cove formed by three islands in the Boyd Group of the 30,000 Islands, just to the northeast of Bald Island.

Launched at Collingwood, Ontario, on May 1, 1894, the 75-ton steam yacht, *Emma* (89'3" x 18' x 6'6"), on her way from Parry Sound to Owen Sound, Ontario, to take advantage of busy summer tourism, caught on fire and burned to a

Right: The steam yacht, *Emma*. PUBLIC ARCHIVES OF CANADA

270

Left: The Canadian steam yacht, *Emma,* plied Parry Sound waters at the turn of the last century before burning in 1912. This detail from an early 1900's colorized postcard shows women and children in Victorian garb, probably out picnicking, waving to people on the passing steamer, *Emma.* CRIS KOHL COLLECTION. *Above and below:* Bolts, boards and nails are all that remain of the *Emma* in a secluded little cove. PHOTOS BY CRIS KOHL

total loss on the Fourth of July, 1912. No lives were lost. Only the broken, bottom portion of the hull remains; her engine and boiler were salvaged shortly after her loss.

3. BLACKMORE ISLAND WRECK

DEPTH: 10 to 20 feet   **LEVEL: Novice**

LOCATION: This wreck lies off the northwest side of Blackmore Island, between that island and tiny Bayview Island, and just to the south of Schade Island. It is believed that this solidly-built, unidentified vessel, which is about 85′ in length and 20′ in beam, was used as a scow in this area's lumber trade.

4. DEPOT HARBOUR

DEPTH: To 30 feet   **LEVEL: Novice-Intermediate**

Depot Harbour is the community just to the west of Parry Sound, Ontario. It sits about halfway between Parry Sound and Killbear Provincial Park. Access is by boat.

The old, submerged cribs at this formerly thriving community offer excellent exploration possibilities. The intricate pattern of logs attests to the construction skills of a much earlier generation. Don't get lost or tangled up inside any

271

of the passageway structures between cribs. "Cribs" were wooden-framed, rock-filled, submerged bases used to support an above-water dock superstructure. Beware: A portion of these cribs is caving in. Do not penetrate!

25-30 feet!

To shore

Depot Harbour

Artwork ©
Adam Henley

5. ELLA ROSS

DEPTH: 20 feet	LEVEL: Novice

LOCATION: This wreck lies in Parry Sound harbor off the Coast Guard Station.

The iron steamer, *Ella Ross* (99'2" x 27'8" x 6'4"), launched as the *Gypsy* at Montreal in 1873, burned to a complete loss at her dock in Parry Sound on June 5, 1912. The superstructure burned off, and the hull lies mostly buried in the bottom of the harbor, but inside the hull are the boiler, engine and other mechanical components.

The *Ella Ross*. CRIS KOHL COLLECTION

6. HAROLD POINT IN KILLBEAR PARK

DEPTH: 40 to 90 feet	LEVEL: Variable

Harold Point is an impressive rock formation in Killbear Provincial Park, and you can drive your vehicle into the park. However, it is a bit of a walk from the nearest parking lot to Harold Point. This natural, rocky setting provides views of underwater boulders and fish.

Harold Point in Killbear Provincial Park attracts cliff jumpers as well as scuba divers (look out below!) This rocky peninsula also serves well as a sunset vantage point.
PHOTO BY CRIS KOHL

7. ATLANTIC

> **LORAN: 29661.88/48743.12   LAT 45° 20′ 02″ LON 080° 15′ 39″**
> **DEPTH: 6 to 50 feet   LEVEL: Novice-Intermediate**

LOCATION: This wreck lies several miles west of Parry Sound, along the northwestern edge of Spruce Rocks, to the north of Spruce Island.

Flames fanned by the fierce gales of November 10th, 1903, destroyed, for the second and last time, the combination passenger and package freight steamer, *Atlantic* (147′ x 30′ x 11′). No lives were lost, although in her first incineration on May 18, 1882, when she was

Left: The wooden steamer, *Atlantic,* was built on the solid hull of the tragic *Manitoulin.*
CRIS KOHL COLLECTION

Right: The *Atlantic's* bow was often heavy with excursionists.
ONTARIO ARCHIVES

named the *Manitoulin*, about 30 people perished. Her relatively new hull at that time was raised and the vessel was rebuilt and renamed. She had been constructed originally at Owen Sound, Ontario, in 1880.

The Atlantic

Easily located are the propeller and the huge rudder which lie in less than 10′ of water. The superstructure totally burned off or caved in on the hull, and, lying there with the stern in the shallows and the bow in the deeper water, the seascape of tangled debris, which includes chain, capstan, gears, boiler, engine and other machinery, proves irresistible to divers. A modern snowmobile sits at the bottom. Boating hazards are many, as this wreck lies in the shoal-strewn, island-dotted "30,000 Islands." A strong west wind can prove dangerous at this open site.

Right: These divers are standing on the rocky shoal which snagged the burning *Atlantic* in 1903. Boating can be challenging here! PHOTO BY CRIS KOHL

Artwork © Adam Henley

Exploring the *Atlantic's* propeller, smokestack, and engine. PHOTOS BY CRIS KOHL

8. JANE MCLEOD

DEPTH: 20 to 25 feet   **LEVEL: Novice**

LOCATION: This wreck lies off the south part of McLeod Island, in the 30,000 Islands. The 117' schooner, *Jane McLeod*, built at St. Catharines, Ontario, in 1868, stranded on November 4, 1890, when her anchor chain parted. Her captain and crew camped on the

Below: The island right where the *Jane McLeod* wrecked. PHOTO BY CRIS KOHL

inhospitable, rocky island for five days before they were rescued. Autumn winds battered their schooner to pieces. Lying about 100' from the island, the stern is slightly deeper than the bow. Scattered portions of this vessel cover a wide area. This area is susceptible to sudden, adverse westerly wind conditions.

Wooden frames and anchor chain remain of the *Jane McLeod*. PHOTOS BY CRIS KOHL

Artwork © Adam Henley

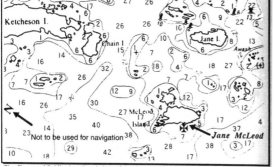

Not to be used for navigation

9. MIDLAND

LORAN: 29708.4/48718.5   **GPS:**
DEPTH: 50 feet   **LEVEL: Intermediate**

This wreck lies on the east side of the Mink Islands, southeast of the site of the *Seattle*. Built at Midland, Ontario, in 1896 as the *D. L. White,* this 56-ton wooden tug (62' x 13' x 6'8"), foundered in 1923. Her name had been changed to *Midland* in 1908. Sitting on a clay bottom, the site features the steeple compound engine, bilge pump, and the rudder and propeller a bit off the wreck. This site's remoteness makes it potentially dangerous.

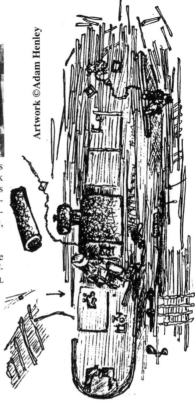

Artwork ©Adam Henley

Above: The *Midland,* as the *D. L. White,* took sportsmen to remote areas in the early 1900's. INSTITUTE FOR GREAT LAKES RESEARCH, BOWLING GREEN, OHIO.

Left: A diver examines the steam engine on the *Midland.* PHOTO BY CRIS KOHL

The Midland
Artwork by Adam Henley

10. SEATTLE

LOCATION: This wreck lies in 15'-25' of water just west of Green Island, in the Mink Islands. LORAN 29735.6/48706.8.

The wooden steamer, *Seattle* (160'7" x 36'5" x 9'9"), built in Oscoda, Michigan, in 1892, stranded here after engine failure in heavy seas on November 11, 1903. No lives were lost. The boiler and other wreckage can be seen from the surface. Sights include the propeller, engine and steering quadrant.

The steamer, *Seattle.* CRIS KOHL COLLECTION

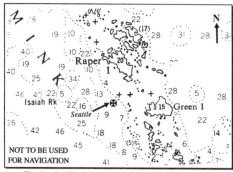

Top Right: The *Seattle's* propulsion system, including its propeller *(below).* PHOTOS BY CRIS KOHL

11. *METAMORA*

Above: The steamer, *Metamora.*
PUBLIC ARCHIVES OF CANADA.
Below: The *Metamora* after the fire.
CRIS KOHL COLLECTION

Located at the east end of Nadeau Island in the Shawanaga Inlet, the wooden tug, *Metamora* (115' x 39'3" x 10'8"), built at Cleveland in 1864, burned to a total loss on September 29, 1907. This novice site has a maximum depth of 15'. The stern section is the most alluring, since it contains the rudder, steam engine and propeller. The boiler, which protrudes above the water, serves as the base for a navigational daymark. This site also offers crayfish galore!

Below: The *Metamora's* boiler has been the island for a navigational daymark for many years. On charts, it is shown as both a shipwreck and a daymark.

Right: The *Metamora's* massive propeller sits upright a short distance below the surface.

PHOTOS BY CRIS KOHL

21. Northern Georgian Bay

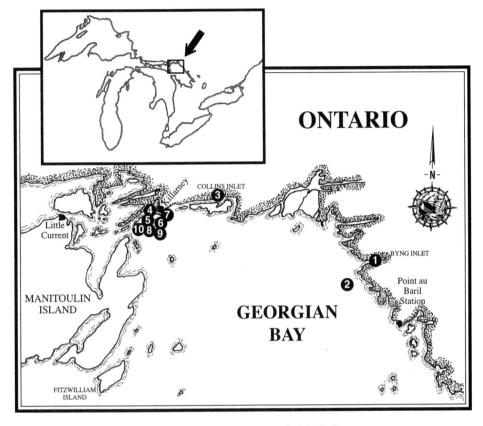

ONTARIO

COLLINS INLET

Killarney

Little Current

BYNG INLET

Point au Baril Station

MANITOULIN ISLAND

GEORGIAN BAY

FITZWILLIAM ISLAND

1. *Northern Belle*
2. *James Reid*
3. Collins Inlet
4. Killarney Channel
5. *Wilma Ann*

6. *M. J. Low*
7. *Dove* and *Branch II*
8. "Parking Lot"
9. "Silica Wall"
10. "Boat Rock Wall"

---

1. NORTHERN BELLE

DEPTH: 10 feet	LEVEL: Novice

The *Northern Belle*. CRIS KOHL COLLECTION

LOCATION: This wreck rests along the south shore of Byng Inlet, west of Old Mill Island. It can usually be located visually from the surface.

The wooden steamer, *Northern Belle* (129' x 22'6" x 9'5"), launched as the *Gladys* on May 21, 1875, at Marine City, Michigan, burned to a total loss in the narrows at Byng Inlet on November 6, 1898. For over 20 years, she had served the tiny lumbering communities between Sault Ste. Marie and Collingwood. Beware of the current and occasional boating traffic at this site.

277

2. JAMES REID

DEPTH: 70 feet	LEVEL: Advanced

LOCATION: This wreck lies off Byng Inlet. Draw a line from the Bell buoy at the western edge of Magnetewan Ledges to the red "AM2" buoy at Morden Rock. The wreck lies halfway between these two points and just a bit east of that line.

The large, iron-hulled tugboat, *James Reid* (117' x 23' x 12'7"), built in 1875 at Wilmington, Delaware, as the *Protector,* was purchased by famous Great Lakes shipwreck salvager, Tom Reid, in 1893 and was later renamed after his father. The ship

The powerful tug, *James Reid*. CRIS KOHL COLLECTION

foundered in August, 1917. Located in the late 1970's, this wreck sits upright and offers much to see.

3. COLLINS INLET

DEPTH: To 30 feet	LEVEL: Novice-Intermediate

LOCATION: This site lies six miles east of Killarney, Ontario.

The town of Collins Inlet, created in the 1880's, soon boasted a sawmill, boarding house, private residences, a store and a school. The community, however, came to a grinding halt when the mill burned down in 1917 and lumber operations were moved to Midland. Every building save one is a ruin. Access is by car or boat. By car, go west on Highway 637 from highway 69 for 21 miles. Turn onto the old unsurfaced Pike Road down to the present-day fish camp at Collins Inlet. Boaters can launch at Killarney. Ruins of docks and pilings where the lumber-laden schooners and steamers once tied up, plus turn-of-the-century cast-offs or losses, can easily be seen. Beware of sunken logs, trees and branches.

4. KILLARNEY CHANNEL

This novice-intermediate dive to 30' will take the diver to parts of burned and abandoned vessels, as well as garbage and losses from over the years. Boating season traffic is heavy!

5. WILMA ANN

In 65' to 80' adjacent to the Kokanongwi Shingle, southwest of Killarney, the fishing tug, *Wilma Ann,* built in 1932, was scuttled in 1983 as a dive site. She sits upright in mud, intact, including open holds, the wheelhouse and the after structure.

6. M. J. LOW

In 65' northeast of Killarney, this intact wooden fishing vessel was scuttled in 1951.

7. DOVE AND BRANCH II

These two wooden cabin cruisers lie in 23' past Killarney east light at Red Rock Point.

8. "PARKING LOT"

Three cars, two half-tons, and a large truck cab lie near site #7 in 15' to 30' of water.

9. "SILICA WALL"

Off the Indusmin Silica Mine near Killarney, this advanced wall dive drops to 120'. The wall offers views of rocks covered with white silica, a hard, glassy mineral.

10. "BOAT ROCK WALL"

This steep wall dive to 110' for advanced divers is near Badgeley Island off Killarney.

22. Manitoulin Island

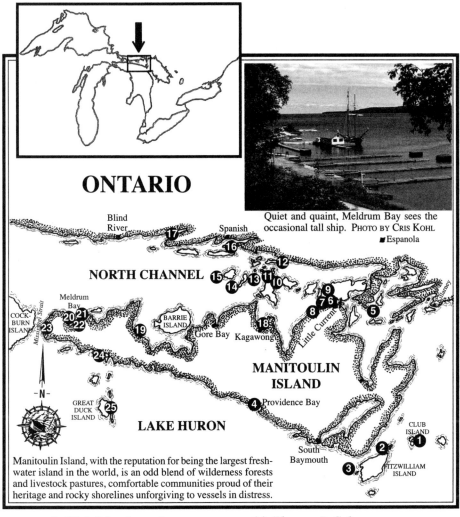

ONTARIO

Quiet and quaint, Meldrum Bay sees the occasional tall ship. PHOTO BY CRIS KOHL

Manitoulin Island, with the reputation for being the largest freshwater island in the world, is an odd blend of wilderness forests and livestock pastures, comfortable communities proud of their heritage and rocky shorelines unforgiving to vessels in distress.

1. Club Island wreck
2. *Michigan*
3. *City of Cleveland*
4. *Clarence E.*
5. *India*
6. *Alexandria*
7. *Hiawatha*
8. *B. B. Buckhout*
9. *Edward Buckley*
10. *Jacqueline*
11. *North Wind*
12. *Iroquois*
13. *Emma E. Thompson*
14. *Thomas J. Cahoon*
15. *Chamberlain* and *Webb*
16. *Wanipitee*
17. *Winona*
18. *Everett*
19. *Michipicoten*
20. *Winslow*
21. *Alberta M.*
22. *Laura H. Lee*
23. *Burlington*
24. *Joyland*
25. *Bielman* and *Chattanooga*

1. CLUB ISLAND WRECK

DEPTH: 15 feet   **LEVEL: Novice**

LOCATION: This unidentified wreck lies in Club Island Harbour, which is about 20 miles north of Tobermory and six miles east of Rattlesnake Harbour on Fitzwilliam Island. This popular (we shared the harbor with 14 other boats the one night we spent there) overnight spot for boaters cruising between the North Channel and Tobermory is on the island's east side. This 57' metal-sheathed shipwreck lies 150' from shore opposite the fishing shanties.

2. *MICHIGAN*

PHOTO BY CRIS KOHL

Rattlesnake Harbour, Ontario

✠ *Michigan* shipwreck

DEPTH: To 15 feet   **LEVEL: Novice**

LOCATION: This wreck lies in the well-sheltered Rattlesnake Harbour on the northern portion of Fitzwilliam Island, about 20 miles north of Tobermory. The 180' schooner-barge, *Michigan,* in operation until the 1930's, lies along the shoreline near the abandoned fishing shanties. A steel rod marks the bow. The wreck of the *Wauseda II* lies at the very eastern end

Right: The author relaxes on a dock ruin at Rattlesnake Harbour, his sailboat at anchor in the distant left background.
PHOTO SET-UP BY CRIS KOHL

of the inlet. Reportedly a small wreck lies along the south shore of the bay, and another one just to the east of the *Michigan.* Submerged logs and tree branches clutter the clay bottom of this bay, so explore with caution. And yes, there are rattlesnakes on the island.

3. *CITY OF CLEVELAND*

LORAN: 30256.2/48587.4   **GPS: 45° 28.222'/081° 50.723'**
DEPTH: 10 to 30 feet   **LEVEL: Novice**

LOCATION: North of Perseverance Island, off the outlying shoal of Little Perseverance Island, 9 miles from South Baymouth, Manitoulin Island, and 18 miles north of Tobermory.

The twin-decked, four-masted, wooden steamer, *City of Cleveland* (255'7" x 39'5" x 18'4"), launched at Cleveland on June 17, 1882, ran aground in a blinding snowstorm and southwest gales on September 15, 1901, with her 2,300 tons of iron ore and no lives lost. The crew rowed to Fitzwilliam Island, from where they were rescued. This immense vessel, with her bow in the shallows, is one of the most impressive shallow-water shipwrecks you will ever see. The tall steam engine, seemingly on stilts, the massive boilers, the rudder and a huge propeller are very interesting and photogenic.

The huge steamer, *City of Cleveland,* was wrecked dramatically in 1889 *(left),* but was salvaged and returned to service. Twelve years later, she stranded again, but became a total loss. CRIS KOHL COLLECTION. *Right:* Tim Philp studies some machinery from the *City of Cleveland's* engine. PHOTOS BY CRIS KOHL

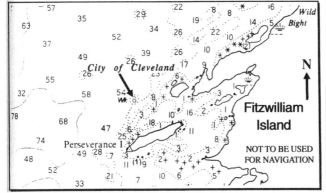

4. CLARENCE E.

The tug, *Clarence E.,* which sank in 1936, lies in 25' of water off the northwest tip of the wharf at Providence Bay, southern Manitoulin Island. This can be a shore or boat dive.

5. INDIA

LORAN:	LAT 45° 58' 15" LON 081° 45' 55"
DEPTH: 20 to 30 feet	LEVEL: Novice

LOCATION: This wreck, correctly marked on the chart of this area, lies off the northeast side of West Mary Island, 8 miles east of Little Current, Ontario.

The wooden steamer, *India* (216'9" x 36'4" x 15'), built at Garden Island near Kingston, Ontario, in 1899, burned to a total loss on September 4, 1928. The vessel's keel, mast, boiler and propeller are the highlights of a visit to this popular site. Schools of sunfish and bass swim between the machinery, while lazy ling lie between the beams.

Left: The *India,* ablaze. CRIS KOHL COLLECTION. *Right:* Exploring the *India's* remains. PHOTO BY CRIS KOHL

6. ALEXANDRIA

The small, wooden steamer, *Alexandria* (91' x 25'), launched at Chatham, Ontario, in 1902, burned at Little Current in 1927. Her remains, mainly a boiler and wood debris, rest on the rock bottom in 24' of water at the east end of the government dock at Little Current. Beware of heavy boating traffic in the summer months.

7. HIAWATHA

The 93-foot-long, 163-ton steamer, *Hiawatha,* built at Dresden, Ontario, in 1874, spent most of her life plying the waters of the St. Clair River before being moved and abandoned up here in 1930. Much wood, a propeller and some pulleys and bracing form the main part of this site in 5' to 30' of water. A small barge lies beside her. She is at the northeast edge of Low Island, which is, in fact, connected to Manitoulin Island. Divers can drive right up to the wreck site and suit up there. This wreck is also marked on the local nagivation chart.

Left: The small passenger steamer, *Hiawatha,* was often pictured on postcards of the St. Clair River. CRIS KOHL COLLECTION. *Middle:* The *Hiawatha* was abandoned at Manitoulin Island in the 1930's.   PHOTO BY CRIS KOHL

8. B. B. BUCKHOUT

The schooner-barge, *B. B. Buckhout* (158'2" x 28'8" x 10'), built at East Saginaw, Michigan, in 1873, transferred to Canadian ownership in 1912 and seemingly disappeared into history at that point. The long-unidentified lumber-laden shipwreck just west of Narrow Island was identified as the *B. B. Buckhout* by researcher Richard Hammond of Little Current. She lies in 40' just south of green buoy "J63" on the east side of the limestone shoal. One story tells of the *Buckhout,* while being towed by the tug, *Maitland,* stranding on that reef in November, 1912 and sinking before she could be salvaged. This wreck, with its vast amount of lumber (some divers have wondered if this isn't really TWO wrecks), is broken up and shows signs of having caught on fire as well.

Left: The lumber-laden *B. B. Buckhout.* CRIS KOHL COLLECTION.

Right: Diver Sean Moore swims along the *Buckhout's* charred timbers. PHOTO BY CRIS KOHL

9. EDWARD BUCKLEY

Southwest off Mink Island, a few miles to the northwest of Little Current, in about 110' of low-visibility water, lie the remains of the wooden steamer, *Edward Buckley* (154'3" x 31' x 10'6"), burned to a complete loss on September 1, 1929. The *Buckley,* built at Manitowoc, Wisconsin, in 1891, was located and identified in 1993 by researcher/diver Richard Hammond of Little Current. The anchor chain begins in 70' of water and follows the slope down to the shipwreck. The ship's engine, propeller and hull await the experienced.

The *Edward Buckley.* CRIS KOHL COLLECTION

282

10. *JACQUELINE*

The *Jacqueline* is a double-ender railroad car ferry which was abandoned on the west side of the only bay on the north tip of Clapperton Island. She lies in the shallows (5' to 12' of water), with parts in 40', between the 1st and 2nd stone beaches, before the drop-off.

11. *NORTH WIND*

LORAN: 30343.3/48293.4	GPS: 46° 03.45'/082° 12.56'
DEPTH: 80 to 110+ feet	LEVEL: Advanced

LOCATION: This wreck lies just east of Robertson Rock, off the north side of Clapperton

The *North Wind*. CRIS KOHL COLLECTION

A diver examines a section of piping on the *North Wind*. PHOTO BY DAVID OSTIFICHUK

Island. A plastic jug, which often disappears, sometimes marks the site.

The steel freighter, *North Wind* (299'5" x 40'8" x 21'6"), launched at Cleveland on July 31, 1888, stranded on Robertson Rock on July 1, 1926, and slid into deep water two hours later. No lives were lost.

Aquatic visitors usually land on the bow, with its twin anchors and anchor winch. Portholes can be seen between 80' and 100', and a four-bladed propeller rests on the deck at 110'. Wonderful sights await those trained divers who penetrate carefully.

12. *IROQUOIS*

The remains of the wooden steamer, *Iroquois* (112' x 20' x 8'7"), lie in 25' to 30' of water at East Rock in McBean Channel. Built at Wiarton, Ontario, in 1902, the ship burned to a total loss on Oct. 24, 1908. The green channel marker is about 650' away from this hull.

The *Iroquois*, and *(right)*, news of its loss. CRIS KOHL COLLECTION

BOAT BURNS AMID ROCKS

Little Steamer Iroquois, With 17 Passengers and Crew of 8, Making McBean Channel, Georgian Bay, Hits West Rock in Haze of Smoke.

WRECKED STEAMER BURSTS INTO FLAME

H. A. J. Kotcher, of Detroit, Assists Terror-Stricken Women and Babies When Rafting Tug Comes to Rescue—Lifeboats Were Useless.

Missing her way in the smoke pall that hung over McBean channel, Georgian Bay, Saturday, the little Canadian steamer Iroquois, with 17

13. *EMMA E. THOMPSON*

LORAN: 44927.9/57943.0	GPS:
DEPTH: 30 feet	LEVEL: Novice

LOCATION: This wreck lies off the northeast side of Innes Island.

The wooden steamer, *Emma E. Thompson* (125'9" x 27'6" x 12'8"), built at Saginaw, MI, in 1875, sought shelter from

The *Emma E. Thompson*. CRIS KOHL COLLECTION

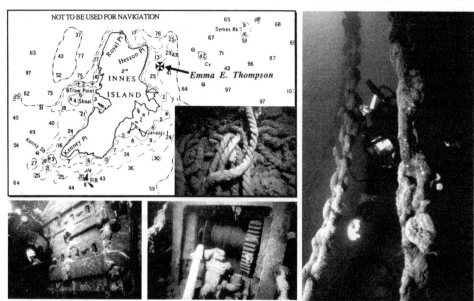

Above: The wreck of the *Emma E. Thompson* offers a huge boiler and door, a windlass, 1914 rope, and much more! *Right:* Three anchor chains arch dramatically off the *Emma E. Thompson's* bow.   PHOTOS BY CRIS KOHL

a storm behind Innes Island, but caught on fire and sank on May 28, 1914. No lives were lost. The wreck sits upright and intact, and is sometimes marked with a plastic jug. This is a fascinating wreck to explore: rudder, engine, boiler, rope, tools, chains, pumps, and three sets of anchor chains cascading in graceful arcs down the bow. One chain leads to a half-buried anchor. Richard Hammond of Little Current, ON, found this wreck in 1992.

14. THOMAS J. CAHOON

Off the southwest side of Innes Island, at Kenny Point and inside Kenny Shoal, in a maximum of 20′ of water, lie the remains of the 166′ schooner-barge, *Thomas J. Cahoon,* launched in 1881 at Saginaw, Michigan, and, lumber-laden, stranded here in a storm on October 11, 1913. She can usually be seen from the surface. LORAN: 30398.1/48286.1

Lack of conservation has disintegrated a *Cahoon* windlass, recovered during World War II, displayed at Gore Bay.   PHOTO BY CRIS KOHL

15. PORTER CHAMBERLAIN AND H. J. WEBB

These wrecks lie west of Darch Island, off Egg Island at Wallace Rock, north of Gore Bay (LORAN: 30437.9/48267.4), in 7′ to 30′ of water. The wooden steamer, *Porter Chamberlain* (134′ x 26′ x 10′3″) was towing the schooner, *H. J. Webb* (167′ x 28′4″ x 11′5″), both ships loaded with lumber, when the *Chamberlain* caught on fire and ran aground. Her cohort also ended up stranding and burning. No lives were lost in that incident on November 11, 1901. The *Chamberlain's* boiler can be seen from the surface, and there is little evidence of burning on these wrecks. There are large areas of frames, but not much intact hull. There is a centerboard trunk, prop blade, and many other items at this big site.

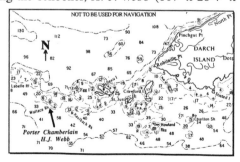

Left: The wooden steamer, *Porter Chamberlain,* was towing the schooner, *H. J. Webb (right),* both lumber-laden, when they burned at Darch Island in 1901. CRIS KOHL COLLECTION

16. WANIPITEE

The *Wanipitee,* a general purpose, mail/passenger/freight tug, sank in 20' to 30' next to Ethel Rock in the middle of boat-busy Little Detroit Passage near Spanish, Ontario.

17. WINONA

The passenger/freight steamer, *Winona* (110' x 21'), built in 1902 at Port Stanley, burned and sank in 10' on the south shore of the entrance to Spragge Harbour on November 13, 1931.

The *Winona.* CRIS KOHL COLLECTION

18. EVERETT

The 56-foot, wooden fishing tug, *Everett,* was abandoned in about 1940 along the east side of the bay at Kagawong Harbour. Ship's ribs can be found in 10'. A boiler sits on shore.

19. MICHIPICOTEN

Built in 1883 in Wyandotte, MI, as the *E.K. Roberts,* the wooden steamer, *Michipicoten,* caught fire and burned on Oct. 10, 1927, off Cook's Dock. The burned-out hull sits in 25'.

The steamer, *Michipicoten,* a year before she burned. CRIS KOHL COLLECTION

20. WINSLOW

Located in 20' about 200' offshore in the harbor opposite the Net Shed Museum in Meldrum Bay, the tug, *Winslow* (120' x 19'), built in 1865, burned on August 21, 1911.

The *Winslow.* CRIS KOHL COLLECTION

21. ALBERTA M.

The 38.09-gross-ton, 69-foot-long steamer, *Alberta M.,* built in Goderich, ON, in 1907, was operated as a fishing tug until the spring of 1946, when it ran aground on the east side of Welsh Island and fell into disrepair. The wreck lies in 2' to 15' of water. **GPS: 45° 54.92'/083° 05.26'**

Left: The small steamer, *Alberta M.,* worked in the commercial fishing industry. CRIS KOHL COLLECTION. *Right:* The main wreckage of the *Alberta M.* lies shallow. PHOTO BY CRIS KOHL

285

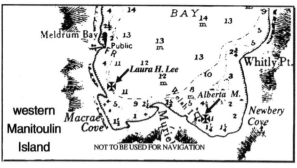

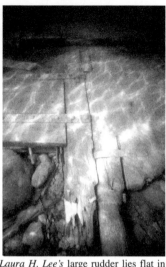

22. *LAURA H. LEE*

Originally a tea boat converted to a lumber hooker, this small tug sank in November, 1929, when a sudden gale knocked over a kerosene lamp which set the boat ablaze. The wreckage lies scattered in 5' to 20' of water.

LAT 45° 55.40'   LON 083° 06.76'

The *Laura H. Lee's* large rudder lies flat in about five feet of water. PHOTO BY CRIS KOHL

23. *BURLINGTON*

DEPTH: 23 feet	LEVEL: Novice

LOCATION: In a bay on the north side of the Mississagi Straits Lighthouse. There are telephone poles in the camping area at the water's edge; where the wires enter the water on their way over to Cockburn Island is where the *Burlington* lies. Telephone pole number 721 is the closest one to the water. You can get a campsite right at the entry point!

The steambarge, *Burlington.* CRIS KOHL COLLECTION

The wooden steamer, *Burlington* (137' x 25'3" x 12'), launched in 1857 at Buffalo, New York, caught on fire while at anchor at the Mississagi Straits Lighthouse on August 24, 1895, and burned to a complete loss. She had been on her way from Detroit to Manitoulin Island to load up with lumber. The tug, *James Storey,* took her crew of 12 to Meldrum Bay, from where they found transportation home.

The electrical cable that was extended to Cockburn Island in the late 1980's runs right over the wreck of the *Burlington!* Where were the heritage politicians when this was planned? The *Burlington's* salvageable items (prop, anchors, windlass, capstan, boiler, engine) were recovered shortly after the fire, but visiting divers can

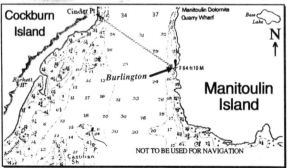

The shoreline is rocky here at the Mississagi Straits Lighthouse at the extreme western end of Manitoulin Island, but it has ledges for suiting up to dive the *Burlington* site. PHOTO BY CRIS KOHL

Many interesting items remain at the *Burlington* site: wooden hull, chain, engine components, etc. PHOTOS BY CRIS KOHL

still appreciate the rudder with chain, a pump, the engine mount and huge sections of framing and planking at this scattered site.

24. *JOYLAND* (THE "HONEYMOON WRECK")

DEPTH: To 16 feet   **LEVEL: Novice**

LOCATION: This wreck lies just off the southeast shore of Burnt Island Harbour, in the southwest corner of Manitoulin Island.

Built in 1884 at Detroit as the wooden steamer, *William A. Haskell* (250'5" x 37' x 14'3"), this vessel carried package freight around the Great Lakes. Her name was changed to *Joyland* in 1916 when sold to Canadian interests, who converted her to a sandsucker in 1924. The *Joyland* ran aground here in 1926 and was abandoned. Someone set her on fire in 1930, destroying all of her superstructure.

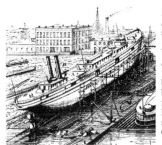

Left: The *William A. Haskell* under construction in Detroit in 1884. Art by Seth Arca Whipple (1855-1901) *Right:* The *Joyland* in 1930, just before she burned. The ship had been abandoned here for four years already. Notice the sand scoops over the stern. CRIS KOHL COLLECTION

There is a virtually overgrown road/trail starting at the main road and running right to the water's edge. Search for it carefully on the right before you reach the commercial fishing community of Burnt Island.

Lying 100' offshore and perpendicular to it, with the bow facing the land, the *Joyland* is very shallow, but offers MANY worthwhile shipwreck sights, such as a four-bladed propeller, boiler (the second boiler was recovered in 1934 and sits on shore, acting as a guide to this site), massive hull, spikes, bolts, sandsucker scoops, prop shaft and more. This site has, for years, been nicknamed the "Honeymoon Wreck" because my friend who told me about it came here on her honeymoon; she, a new diver, explored the *Joyland* with her

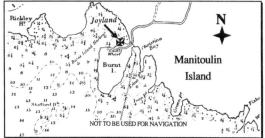

N

Manitoulin Island

NOT TO BE USED FOR NAVIGATION

The *Joyland* is a casual shore dive. PHOTO BY CRIS KOHL

287

The huge *Joyland* boiler, gears, propeller, and other machinery half-buried in the Lake Huron sands at Burnt Island offer underwater exploration galore for diver Sean Moore.

PHOTOS BY CRIS KOHL

husband. Actually, there *is* a certain romance to this place....

25. *C. F. Bielman* and *Chattanooga*

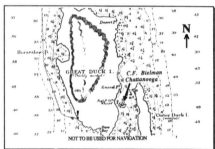

The old steamer, *C. F. Bielman* (291' x 41' x 19'8"), and the schooner-barge, *Chattanooga* (308' x 45' x 24'), both built in West Bay City, Michigan, in the late 1800's but by competitors, were derelicts by the 1930's. Both became breakwalls/docks at the fishing wharf on the southeast side of Great Duck Island, 13 miles south of Manitoulin Island. The reluctant *C. F. Bielman* swamped her towing tug, the *Monarch* (also in this book) in the St. Clair River on July 6, 1934, with the loss of four lives, when she was on her way to the island. The *Chattanooga's* hull is filled with stone, and both vessels lie at a maximum depth of 20'. The *Bielman's* rudder and propeller are in place, but her engine and boiler were removed. Part of her hull lies on the beach.

Both the long, sleek *C.F. Bielman (left)* and the huge barge *Chattanooga (right)* ended up sunk as breakwalls in the 1930's for the commercial fishery at Lake Huron's Great Duck Island.

CRIS KOHL COLLECTION

If you make it up to the north shore of Manitoulin Island, you're in the North Channel -- the best boat cruising waters in all of the Great Lakes! Stay a while and explore the many islands and hidden coves in between diving.

The author enjoys the multi-island view from this perch on Croker Island in the beautiful North Channel of Lake Huron, looking down at his sailboat, and several others, anchored in numerous bays and coves.

PHOTO SET-UP BY CRIS KOHL

23. DeTour

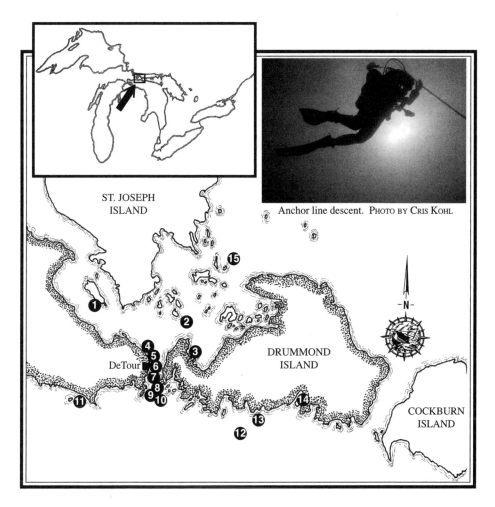

ST. JOSEPH ISLAND

Anchor line descent. PHOTO BY CRIS KOHL

DeTour

DRUMMOND ISLAND

COCKBURN ISLAND

-N-

1. *Rome*
2. *J. C. Ford*
3. Pigeon Cove schooner
4. Kelly's dock
5. *Two Myrtles/Alice C.*
6. *Superior*
7. *John W. Cullen*
8. *Sainte Marie*

9. *General*
10. Frying Pan Island dock
11. Saddlebag Island wreck
12. *John B. Merrill*
13. *Agnes W.*
14. *Troy*
15. *E. J. LaWay, Jr.*

1. ROME

LORAN: 30946.31/48073.02   GPS: 46° 05.212'/084° 00.763'
DEPTH: 15 feet   LEVEL: Novice

LOCATION: This wreck lies at the entrance to the harbor on the west side of Lime Island, Michigan.

The steamer, *Rome*. CRIS KOHL COLLECTION

The wooden steamer, *Rome* (265' x 36'10" x 16'3"), built at Cleveland in 1879 and launched as the *Chicago* (she was renamed *Rome* in 1901), burned to a total loss on November 17, 1909, off Lime Island in the St. Marys River. This older style vessel, with the midship, external arched braces, was carrying a cargo of cement and hay when she burned. No lives were lost. The burned-out hull was put to use when it was filled with limestone blocks and sunk as a breakwall. Although her stern is considerably broken, the bow remains quite intact. With the many protruding planks and spikes at this site, beware of getting snagged on any of them. A general garbage dump site lies adjacent, but low visibility plagues this area.

2. J. C. FORD

LORAN: 30984.87/48116.97   GPS: 46° 02.663'/083° 50.172'
DEPTH: 5 to 15 feet   LEVEL: Novice

LOCATION: This wreck lies just east of Little Trout Island.

The 432-ton wooden steamer, *J.C. Ford* (172' x 31'8" x 13'), burned to a complete loss with no lives lost on November 26, 1924. This vessel had been built 35 years earlier in 1889 at Grand Haven, Michigan, as a package freighter, but had been converted to a crane-equipped bulk carrier just the year before her demise.

This site, with its large debris field, usually has surprisingly good visibility, and the wreck can be seen from the surface. The large propeller remains connected to the shaft and engine, with the hull in several large sections surrounded by tools and other

The steamer, *J. C. Ford,* in her final year. CRIS KOHL COLLECTION

hardware. Burbots, bass, crayfish and freshwater sponges are often seen here.

3. PIGEON COVE SCHOONER

LORAN: 30888.20/48130.46   GPS: 46° 01.453'/083° 48.422'
DEPTH: 4 to 15 feet   LEVEL: Novice

LOCATION: This wreck lies in the eastern bay of Pigeon Cove, just south of Nick's Marina and a bit north of a sandbar.

This unidentified vessel, definitely a schooner, lies shallow enough to be a hazard to local boaters, who sometimes mark the wreck with a plastic jug so they can steer clear of it. The hull is fairly intact and rises about ten feet off the bottom. The wreck, with damage at both ends, lies east-to-west. This ship was equipped with a steam cargo winch; a donkey boiler is present. Local anglers have left equipment here, including fishing line. Be careful!

4. KELLY'S DOCK

LORAN: 30922.91/48126.55   GPS: 46° 00.36'/083° 54.252'
DEPTH: 4 to 18 feet   LEVEL: Novice

LOCATION: This site lies north of DeTour village and about 300' off shore.

The entire shoreline is private property, so a boat is necessary to reach this site. Because the submerged dock comes close to the surface, a plastic jug is often used to indicate its presence to boaters. Several cribs can be found here, some filled with rocks and others hollow and penetrable (for the trained and experienced only). Beware of ships of all sizes.

5. *TWO MYRTLES/ALICE C.?*

LORAN: 30922.54/48131.61   GPS: 45° 59.842'/083° 53.941'
DEPTH: 10 to 15 feet   LEVEL: Novice

LOCATION: This wreckage lies about 250' to 300' north of the east-west DeTour Harbor breakwall.

The 80' steamer, *Two Myrtles,* built at Manitowoc, Wisconsin, in 1889, was abandoned here in the 1930's. The remains of at least one other abandoned vessel, possibly the *Alice C.*, lie intermingled with the disturbed *Two Myrtles* (a 1970's construction crane raised the *Two Myrtles* from the water, at which point she broke into pieces and fell back in!) This scattered site can be shore-accessed from the marina or the breakwall.

6. *SUPERIOR*

LORAN: GPS: 45° 59.632'/083° 53.918'
DEPTH: 10 to 15 feet   LEVEL: Novice-Intermediate

LOCATION: This wreck lies near the entrance to the harbor at DeTour Village.

Launched as the sloop, *Mentor,* in 1881 at Manitowoc, Wisconsin, the wooden scow-steamer (she was converted to a bulk freighter in 1887 and to a self-unloading sandsucker in 1916 when her name was changed), *Superior* (142'3" x 30'5" x 9'2"), was moored for the night at DeTour when she caught fire and burned to a total loss on June 11, 1929. Visibility seldom exceeds 3' at this site, which consists mostly of large timbers, but it is accessible from shore.

The *Superior.*
CRIS KOHL COLLECTION

7. *JOHN W. CULLEN*

LORAN: 30922.89/48133.32   GPS: 45° 59.302'/083° 53.641'
DEPTH: 5 to 40 feet   LEVEL: Novice

LOCATION: This wreck lies between DeTour Village and Frying Pan Island, and about 300' east of the boiler from the *Sainte Marie.*

The wooden steamer, *John W. Cullen* (141' x 29' x 10'8"), launched at Milwaukee in 1883 as the *George C. Markham,* received her name change in 1920. She was abandoned in 1933. Mainly large timbers comprise this site; beware of the spikes protruding from the wreckage and avoid getting any of your equipment caught on them.

The *John W. Cullen.* CRIS KOHL COLLECTION

291

8. SAINTE MARIE

LORAN: 30922.25/48136.69	GPS: 45° 59.303'/083° 53.639'
DEPTH: 0 to 40 feet	LEVEL: Novice

LOCATION: This wreck lies between DeTour Village and Frying Pan Island.

Launched as a railroad carferry in 1893 at Wyandotte, Michigan, the *Sainte Marie* (288' x 53' x 19'5"), carried 18 cars each trip across the Straits of Mackinac, which she did almost daily for 19 years. She became a barge in 1912 and was abandoned in 1927 at DeTour. This vessel can be done as a shore dive, as divers can wade a fair distance in the shallows to the wreck site. The boiler and large timbers form most of the visuals at this site. Avoid the spikes!

The carferry, *Sainte Marie:* Attracting summer crowds and overpowering winter ice. CRIS KOHL COLLECTION

9. GENERAL

LORAN: 30923.52/48137.01	GPS: 45° 59.202'/083° 53.829'
DEPTH: 15 to 20 feet	LEVEL: Novice

LOCATION: This wreck lies off the northwest end of Frying Pan Island.

The tug, *General* (97'5" x 24' x 10'), launched at West Bay City, Michigan, in 1900, spent the years between 1910 and 1919 at the bottom of the St. Marys River in 40' of water off Lime Island. A collision with the huge steel ship, *Athabasca,* on November 30, 1910, took three lives and sank the 132-ton tug. After she was raised and returned to service, the *General* spent another 11 years working the northern waters, until she burned and sank at DeTour on April 7, 1930, and remained in place. Boaters can anchor near the large boulders at the site. Although the tug's large equipment, such as her boiler and engine, were removed after she sank, her hull offers much to see. Visibility in this area is generally good.

10. FRYING PAN ISLAND DOCK

These submerged docks, once the holding spot for vessels which were salvaged by the Durocher Company, are similar to Kelly's Dock, only deeper (they begin in 4', but have ledges at the 45' and 90' levels.). Discards from the salvage company's raised ships also ended up on the bottom here. The island is privately owned; stay on your boat. Debris fields lie along the island's north, east and south sides. Beware of large freighters passing nearby.

11. SADDLEBAG ISLAND WRECK

LORAN: 30973.3/48137.2	GPS: 45° 57.081'/084° 01.498'
DEPTH: 10 to 25 feet	LEVEL: Novice

LOCATION: This wreck lies off the southeastern end of Saddlebag Island.

It's a long swim from a park on shore; use a boat to take you to this small, unidentified freighter. Reportedly it sank with a cargo of farm equipment, most of which was salvaged. What little remains is the highlight of the dive, since not much of the ship is left.

12. JOHN B. MERRILL

> LORAN: 30880.28/48191.97   GPS: 45° 54.981'/083° 43.912'
> DEPTH: 30 to 80 feet   LEVEL: Intermediate-Advanced

LOCATION: This shipwreck lies on the west side of Holdridge Shoal.

Considered the best shipwreck dive in the DeTour area, the three-masted schooner,

John B. Merrill (189' x 34' x 13'3"), foundered in a storm on October 14, 1893, with a cargo of coal and no lives lost. This ship, built at Milwaukee, Wisconsin, in 1873, was lost in the same storm which destroyed the *Dean Richmond* (which is also in this book) and several other vessels.

Located in 1992 by John Steele and Sam Mareci, the *John B. Merrill* shows evidence of having

The *John B. Merrill*. ARTIST UNKNOWN. CRIS KOHL COLLECTION

broken up on the rocks in the shallows, then slid into deeper water. Her anchor lies in 30', with chain cascading down to 65' where the forward keelson is located. The hull's starboard side lies with the outside facing up in about 70'; the port side lies with the inside facing up in 75'. Decking has been turned upside down near the bow area in 80'. Because the ship is broken up like this, there are no actual penetration opportunities. Beware of loose overhangs near the bow. The debris field is fairly extensive. Enjoy exploring it!

13. AGNES W.

> LORAN: 30869.88/48191.39   GPS: 45° 55.453'/083° 42.501'
> DEPTH: 2 to 12 feet   LEVEL: Novice

LOCATION: This wreck lies off Traverse Point.

Built at Milwaukee, Wisconsin, in 1887, and launched as the *Roswell P. Flower,* the huge, wooden bulk freight steamer, *Agnes W.* (264' x 38' x 17'6"), was renamed in honor of a new owner's wife in 1915. The vessel stranded on Drummond Island on July 12, 1918, and was pounded to pieces by the powerful storm. Machinery was recovered, but the bottom part of the hull lies in place, and the debris field is extensive. The wreck can be seen from the surface.

The large steamer, *Agnes W.*
CRIS KOHL COLLECTION

14. *TROY*

LOCATION: This wreck lies just off the eastern shoreline of Scammon Cove in about

8' to 12' of water, near the community of Johnswood on Drummond Island. The remains of this large, broken wreck can be seen from the surface.

The schooner-barge, *Troy,* (191'3" x 30' x 10'), built at Marine City, Michigan, in 1872, and used mainly in the lumber trade, was abandoned in this cove in 1921, almost half a century after she was launched. The remains of at least one other abandoned vessel, possibly the steamer, *Silver Spray,* lie north of the *Troy.*

The schooner-barge, *Troy.* CRIS KOHL COLLECTION

15. *E. J. LAWAY, JR.*

LOCATION: This wreck lies off the Seine Islands in the North Channel, in about 53' of water, north of Drummond Island, about 500' inside the USA side of the border.

Built in 1914 at Cheboygan, Michigan, the small, 70-ton, wooden steamer, *E. J. LaWay, Jr.* (73'1" x 20'7" x 6'), foundered in a storm on April 19, 1929, with no lives lost. The wreck lies very close to the international border, about 500' inside the USA.

24. Sanilac Shores

LAKE
HURON

Sanilac Shores, designated in 1988, is one of Michigan's 11 underwater preserves. This designation serves only to let scuba divers know that there is a particularly high concentration of located shipwrecks within these preserve boundaries. Some shipwreck sites shown here lie outside the preserve boundaries. All shipwrecks and their artifacts in Michigan's Great Lakes waters are protected by state and federal laws.

White Rock
Forestville
Richmondville
Forester
Port Sanilac
Lexington

KETTLE POINT

(See Chapter 16 for sites in this area)

MICHIGAN

ONTARIO

-N-

PORT HURON

SARNIA

1. *Col. A. B. Williams*
2. *Checotah*
3. *New York*
4. *Charles A. Street*
5. *F. B. Gardner*
6. *City of Milwaukee*
7. *North Star*
8. *Mary Alice B.*
9. *Canisteo*
10. *Regina*
11. *Sport*
12. *Eliza H. Strong*
13. *John Breden*
14. *Queen City*
15. *City of Genoa*
16. *Charles S. Price*
17. *Clayton Belle*
18. *Amaranth*

1. COL. A. B. WILLIAMS

LORAN: 30779.1/49407.2	GPS: 43° 36.234'/082° 30.804'
DEPTH: 73 to 84 feet	LEVEL: Advanced

LOCATION: This wreck lies 12.4 miles north-northeast of Port Sanilac.

Artwork © Pat Stayer

The schooner, *Col. A.B. Williams* (sometimes listed as the *A.B. Williams;* 110' x 24' x 9'9") foundered with her coal cargo in an 1864 storm. The wreck sits upright and quite intact, with her masts and cabin missing, but this is the norm for Great Lakes shipwrecks. Her stern has collapsed, but the bow and midship area gives quite a profile, offering hatches, a huge windlass, two winches, a bilge pump and a stove. This wreck was discovered in 1957 by Garth Meyer. The bow anchors and wheel were removed in the 1960's; one anchor sits in front of the Sanilac Historical Museum in Port Sanilac.

2. CHECOTAH

LORAN: 30761.3/49413.5	GPS: 43° 36.103'/082° 28.169'
DEPTH: 95 to 117 feet	LEVEL: Advanced

LOCATION: This wreck lies 12.3 miles north-northeast of Port Sanilac, Michigan.

The schooner-barge, *Checotah* (198'7" x 34'1" x 12'4"), built at Toledo, Ohio, in 1870, as the *George B. Russell,* foundered in a violent storm on October 30, 1906, with the crew safely taking to the yawl boat. Earlier, the ship had spent seven years (1882-1889) on the bottom of the St. Marys River after sinking, with the loss of three lives, in a collision with the steamer, *Northerner.* In 1890, the restored ship was renamed *Checotah.* Discovered in the early summer of 1988 by Gary Biniecki, Tim Juhl and Jim and Pat Stayer (known collectively at that

The schooner-barge, *Checotah.* CRIS KOHL COLLECTION

time as the Great Lakes Shipwrecks Exploration Group), the wreck sits upright, but with some damage to the stern deck and the starboard gunwhale. At the bow are the winch, windlass, capstan, port anchor and a donkey steam boiler, while the stern displays the rudder, steering gear and ship's wheel. Visibility is sometimes low in this part of Lake Huron.

CHECOTAH
1870 - Oct. 30, 1906
Discovered June 28, 1988

Artwork © Pat Stayer

3. NEW YORK

LORAN: 30761.0/49411.9	GPS: 43° 36.230'/082° 28.267'
DEPTH: 95 to 118 feet	LEVEL: Advanced

NEW YORK
1856 - Oct. 13, 1876
Found Aug. 12, 1988

Artwork © Pat Stayer

LOCATION: This wreck lies 12.3 miles north-northeast of Port Sanilac, Michigan.

The wooden steambarge, *New York* (184'8" x 29'4" x 11'8"), foundered with the loss of one life on October 14, 1876, while she was towing three barges, also laden with lumber, from Cove Island. The *New York* had been built in 1856 at Buffalo, New York. This wreck was located in August, 1988, while the group that had found the nearby *Checotah* a month earlier (Gary Biniecki, Tim Juhl and Jim and Pat Stayer) were heading to that site. The two wrecks lie only a few hundred feet apart. The *New York* sits upright, bow pointing south, with her twin oscillating steam engines, boiler and upright starboard bracing arch the site's highlights. Also of interest to divers are the smokestack hole, gauges and other machinery.

4. CHARLES A. STREET

LORAN: 30818.2/49413.1	GPS: 43° 35.50'/082° 27.50'
DEPTH: 5 to 15 feet	LEVEL: Novice

The steamer, *Charles A. Street.* CRIS KOHL COLL.

LOCATION: This wreck lies about 11.5 miles north of Port Sanilac, Michigan.

The wooden steamer, *Charles A. Street* (165'3" x 31'4" x 12'), caught on fire and was steered towards shore, where she stranded and burned to a complete loss. No lives were lost. The *Charles A. Street,* built at Grand Haven, Michigan, in 1888, usually carried coal or lumber. The top of the engine rises close to the surface, and the hull is broken and scattered.

5. F. B. Gardner

> **LORAN: 30802.4/49446.8**   **GPS: 43° 31.63'/082° 31.77'**
> **DEPTH: 55 feet**   **LEVEL: Intermediate**

LOCATION: This wreck lies 6.5 miles north of Port Sanilac, Michigan.

The wooden schooner-barge, *F.B. Gardner* (177'2" x 31'3" x 10'), built in 1855 at

Sheboygan, Wisconsin, plied and worked on Great Lakes waters for nearly five decades. On September 15, 1904, in tow of the steamer, *D. Leuty,* the *F. B. Gardner* suddenly caught on fire and burned to a total loss. Her sunken remains, a hazard to navigation, were dynamited. This wreck was located by Mike Kohut, using information from Chet Reddeman, in 1973. A huge windlass, complete with chain, is the main attraction amidst all the hanging knees and other ship's parts and equipment scattered at this site.

The schooner-barge, *F. B. Gardner.* INSTITUTE FOR GREAT LAKES RESEARCH, BOWLING GREEN, OH

6. City of Milwaukee

> **LORAN:**   **GPS:**
> **DEPTH: 168 feet**   **LEVEL: Technical**

LOCATION: This wreck lies about 12 miles northeast of Port Sanilac, Michigan.

The schooner, *City of Milwaukee* (139' x 30' x 11'), is one of the few Great Lakes

The fascinating, gargoyle-like figurehead of the *City of Milwaukee*.
PHOTO BY DAVID TROTTER/UNDERSEA RESEARCH ASSOCIATES

vessels to have been built with a distinctive, elegant figurehead -- this one in the shape of a ferocious, open-mouthed dragon. Built in Cleveland in 1861, the *City of Milwaukee* sank in a storm on November 5, 1875, with no loss of life. The wreck was located by Dave Trotter (Undersea Research Associates) and his team on July 7, 1990. The vessel's stern has virtually disintegrated (probably crushed in the sinking), while her bow, with windlass and both anchors, is quite intact. At midship, masts, spars and booms crisscross the hull. Highlighted by the distinctive figurehead, this wreck is one of the prime examples of the preserving powers of our freshwater Great Lakes.

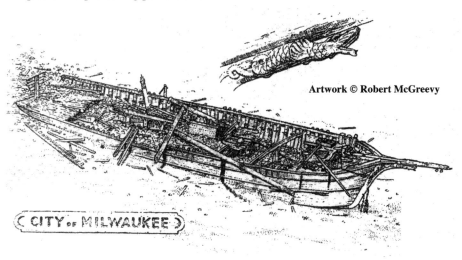

Artwork © Robert McGreevy

7. NORTH STAR

LORAN: 30787.3/49508.1	GPS: 42° 23.959'/082° 26.518'
DEPTH: 85 to 99 feet	LEVEL: Advanced

The *North Star.* CRIS KOHL COLLECTION

LOCATION: This wreck lies 5.3 miles east-southeast of Port Sanilac, Michigan.

The steel package freighter, *North Star* (299'5" x 40'8" x 21'6"), launched at Cleveland on February 12, 1889, sank in early morning fog after the steamer, *Northern Queen,* collided with her starboard side on November 25, 1908. No lives were lost, but the ship and her cargo of wheat and shingles were a total loss.

Located in the 1960's by John Steele, the Great Lakes' first modern wreck hunter, the *North Star* lies upright, broken into two main pieces due to the

North Star
Sank November 25, 1908

Artwork © Pat Stayer

Joan Forsberg explores the *North Star.* PHOTO BY CRIS KOHL

collision. The pilot house remains intact on the bow, while the enormous engine and boiler grace the stern. The cargo holds are also explorable in this very large shipwreck area.

The *Mary Alice B.* (then the *Quintus), far right,* and her sister tugs at Duluth in 1931. Cris Kohl Collection

8. *MARY ALICE B.*

LORAN: 30790.8/49521.0	GPS: 43° 22.309'/082° 26.301'
DEPTH: 82 to 98 feet	LEVEL: Advanced

LOCATION: This wreck lies 8.4 miles northeast of Lexington, Michigan.

The tug, *Mary Alice B.* (62'1" x 17' x 6'3"), launched as the *Quintus* at Duluth, Minnesota, in 1931 and renamed the *Bonanka* in 1962 and *Lomax* in 1972, received her final name in

The *Mary Alice B.*
Photo courtesy of Bill Hoey

Pat Stayer takes the helm of the *Mary Alice B.* Photo by Cris Kohl

Pat examines the tug's name still visible on the bow. Photo by Cris Kohl

Artwork © Pat Stayer

MARY ALICE B.
Built 1931-Sank Sept. 5, 1975
Discovered July 8, 1992

her final year afloat (1975). On September 5th of that year, she became waterlogged and sank with no lives lost. About ten years later, Wayne Brusate began searching for her, but found the *Regina* and *Sport* instead (both are in this chapter). Jim and Pat Stayer's team located the *Mary Alice B.* on July 8, 1992. She sits upright and is very intact, complete with the ship's wheel, pilot house, horns, searchlight, stacked dishes in the galley, and engine compartment.

9. CANISTEO

LORAN:	GPS: 43° 14.142'/082° 18.292'
DEPTH: 98 feet	LEVEL: Advanced

LOCATION: This wreck lies about 15 miles east-northeast of Lexington, Michigan.

The wooden steamer, *Canisteo* (191' x 34'3" x 12'2"), launched in 1886 at Mount Clemens, Michigan, was burned and scuttled on Oct. 25, 1920. The wreckage includes a large, four-bladed propeller, hull planking and framing, and small items like tools and a milk can.

Above, large photo: Pat Stayer explores the propeller of the wooden steamer, *Canisteo* (lower left; CRIS KOHL COLLECTION), which was scuttled off Lexington, Michigan, in 1920. Located by the Stayers' team in 1997, these wreck remains were identified when Cris Kohl found archival material describing the scuttling and Pat located an engine cover with the ship's name on it (*upper right*). A milk can (*lower right*) was found on the wreck. CRIS KOHL PHOTOS. The detailed story of the *Canisteo* was given its own chapter called "The Challenge of Shipwreck Identification" in the book, *Shipwreck Tales of the Great Lakes,* by Cris Kohl.

10. REGINA

LORAN: 30801.7/49534.9	GPS: 43° 20.456'/082° 26.888'
DEPTH: 60 to 83 feet	LEVEL: Advanced

LOCATION: This wreck lies about 6.5 miles northeast of Lexington, Michigan.

The steel freighter, *Regina* (249'7" x 42'6" x 20'5"), constructed in Scotland in 1907, capsized and sank with all hands during the Great Storm of November 10-13, 1913, which claimed seven other steel ships and their entire crews in lower Lake Huron (they were the *Charles S. Price, Wexford, Argus, Isaac M. Scott, John McGean,* all in this book, and the

Left: The steamer, *Regina*. CRIS KOHL COLLECTION. *Right:* A diver studies the brass letters which make up the *Regina's* name on her overturned bow. PHOTO BY CRIS KOHL

REGINA
Built 1907 - Sank Nov. 9, 1913
Discovered by Garry Biniecki
July 1, 1986

Artwork© **Pat Stayer**

Left: A diver explores the large propeller at the top of the upside-down wreck of the *Regina*. *Right:* The *Regina's* bell on exhibit at a Michigan dive show. *Below:* The modern freighter *Cuyahoga* shows that the wreck of the *Regina*, marked with a plastic jug *(circled)*, lies in the busy shipping lane. PHOTOS BY CRIS KOHL

yet-to-be-located *James Carruthers* and *Hydrus*). The *Regina* was discovered on July 1, 1986, by Gary Biniecki, Wayne Brusate and John Severance, reportedly while they were searching for the tug, *Mary Alice B*. The *Regina,* at anchor when she met her end, lies upside-down, bow facing north, with much of her general cargo spilled onto the lake bottom. Her propeller and rudder are impressive. Penetration is possible only for those with proper training, experience, preparedness and attitude, but there is so much to see on the outside of the wreck that this site has become one of the prime destinations of divers in Lake Huron.

11. SPORT

LORAN: 30824.9/49569.2	GPS: 43° 15.995′/082° 27.925′
DEPTH: 35 to 50 feet	LEVEL: Novice-Intermediate

LOCATION: This wreck lies 3.0 miles east of Lexington, Michigan.

The tug, *Sport* (56'7" x 14'7" x 9'), constructed at Wyandotte, Michigan in 1873 and one of the first composite (both steel and wood) vessels built, sank with no lives lost in a

Above: The tug, *Sport,* at dockside. CRIS KOHL COLLECTION.

Above: The *Sport* marker on board the U.S. Coast Guard cutter, *Bramble,* just prior to being lowered to the shipwreck site in 1992. PHOTO BY CRIS KOHL

Below: Joan Forsberg approaches the *Sport's* propeller. PHOTO BY CRIS KOHL

Artwork © Pat Stayer

SPORT
1873 - 1920

Right: Joan examines the *Sport's* wheel. PHOTO BY CRIS KOHL

storm on December 13, 1920. Found by diver Wayne Brusate in June, 1987, in his quest to locate the *Mary Alice B.*, the historic *Sport* lies on her keel with a starboard list, intact save for her missing cabin. Inside the hull and in plain view, since much of the decking is missing, are the engine and boiler. An anchor and winch sit on the bow, while the stern offers the propeller (broken off and lying flat), steering chain and ship's wheel. On August 4, 1992, the *Sport* became the recipient of the State of Michigan's first underwater historical marker, which stands mounted on a post next to the shipwreck. A $1,000.00 reward remains in place for information leading to the discovery of the diver who stole the *Sport's* bell.

12. ELIZA H. STRONG

LORAN: 30847.0/49570.4	GPS: 43° 15.77'/082° 30.66'
DEPTH: 24 to 28 feet	LEVEL: Novice

The *Eliza H. Strong*.
CRIS KOHL COLLECTION

LOCATION: This wreck lies 0.9 mile from Lexington, Michigan, harbor.

The wooden steamer, *Eliza H. Strong* (205' x 36'7" x 11'), built at Marine City, Michigan, in 1874, had a tumultuous history of sinkings and recoveries before succumbing once and for all on October 26, 1904, when she burned and sank with no loss of life. Her machinery was salvaged and the hull, a hazard to navigation, was dynamited. As can be imagined, this site is broken and widely scattered, with considerable decking, her keel and the propeller.

13. JOHN BREDEN

LORAN: 30823.4/49595.7	GPS: 43° 12.638'/082° 26.248'
DEPTH: 51 feet	LEVEL: Intermediate

LOCATION: This wreck lies 5.4 miles southeast of Lexington, Michigan, harbor.

The three-masted schooner, *John Breden* (130' x 25'2" x 11'), built at Port Dalhousie, Ontario, in 1862, was, in her later years, reduced to a towbarge. On July 21, 1899, loaded with twice her rated carrying capacity of coal and towed by the tug, *Winslow* (which is also in this book), the *John Breden's* seams opened and she foundered with the loss of three lives. Located by Gary Biniecki and Nathan Butler on October 14, 1994, the wreck lies broken into huge pieces with an extensive debris field that contains the wooden-stocked anchors, the windlass and the ship's wheel, along with many other items.

14. QUEEN CITY

LORAN: 30831.2/49622.3	GPS: 43° 09.125'/082° 25.712'
DEPTH: 50 feet	LEVEL: Intermediate

The *Queen City* by Eric Heyl. CRIS KOHL COLLECTION

LOCATION: This wreck lies 9.3 miles southeast of Lexington, Michigan, harbor.

The sidewheel steamer, *Queen City* (292' x 30'7" x 12'7"), constructed at Buffalo, New York, in 1848, was, with the decline in passenger business after the railroads were built, converted into a lumber barge in 1862. On August 17, 1863, the *Queen City* struck rocks, broke up and sank, the crew safely abandoning ship. In late 1991, David Losinski and Paul Schmitt located this broken up wreck, with its round arches and brackets for paddlewheels.

15. CITY OF GENOA

LORAN: 30805.2/49625.0	GPS: 43° 08.78'/082° 22.31'
DEPTH: 55 to 65 feet	LEVEL: Advanced

LOCATION: This wreck lies 11.4 miles southeast of Lexington, Michigan, harbor.

The wooden steamer, *City of Genoa* (301' x 42'5" x 20'1"), built at West Bay City, Michigan, in 1892, sank in a collision in the St. Clair River on August 26, 1911. She was raised and towed into Sarnia Bay, where she sat for several years before having her large equipment removed

The *City of Genoa*. CRIS KOHL COLLECTION

and being set ablaze by vandals. In 1915, she was scuttled in Lake Huron several miles north of the river. Located by Detroit-area diver, Bud Uren, in 1983, the *City of Geno*a (once referred to as the "Wheelbarrow Wreck" because of the wheelbarrow which sat in her hull), bow pointing north, is an enormous hull with a boiler cradle, propeller shaft and valves. When I last saw her, only the wheel of that wheelbarrow was left.

Frank Troxell on the *City of Genoa*. PHOTO BY CRIS KOHL

Sanilac Shores

16. CHARLES S. PRICE

LORAN: 30799.6/49622.5	GPS: 43° 09.174'/082° 21.771'
DEPTH: 47 to 72 feet	LEVEL: Intermediate-Advanced

LOCATION: This wreck lies 11.4 miles southeast of Lexington, Michigan.

The large, steel freighter, *Charles S. Price* (504' x 54' x 30'), built at Lorain, Ohio, in 1910, was one of the victims of the Great Storm of November 8-11, 1913. When the blizzard

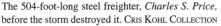

The 504-foot-long steel freighter, *Charles S. Price,* before the storm destroyed it. CRIS KOHL COLLECTION

After the Great Storm of November 8-11, 1913, an upside-down hull of a steel freighter was seen floating in lower Lake Huron. CRIS KOHL COLLECTION

abated, an enormous, overturned hull was left floating offshore. Identification was not immediately possible, since several steel freighters went missing in this storm. After eight days, a hardhat diver identified the "Mystery Ship" as the *Charles S. Price.* Two days later, she sank. There were no survivors to tell what had happened. *Price* bodies washed ashore, including one wearing a *Regina* lifebelt, hinting at a collision between the two ships. But

Aquatic Adventures of MI!

**5 Star PADI IDC Facility offering
Recreational to Technical training
Sales, service, mixed gases and travel!**

**Aquatic Adventures
of MI, LLC
2100 Grand River Annex
Suite 100
Brighton, MI 48114
Ph: 866-600-DIVE**

www.aquaticadventuresofmi.com

Left: A diver examines stern lettering placed upon the rudder of the *Charles S. Price. Below:* Failed salvage attempts broke most of the hull. *Right:* That same dramatic, over-turned hull and its upside-down bow can be explored to-day.   Photos by Cris Kohl

that was not so. More than likely, human scavengers on shore returned the lifejacket to the wrong corpse when they noticed that the law was nearby.

This wreck lies upside-down and the steel hull is collapsing badly. She is in noticeably worse shape now than she was 20 years ago when I first visited her. Penetration dives are not recommended.

17. CITY OF PORT HURON

LORAN:	GPS: 43° 13.404'/082° 29.058'
DEPTH: 43 feet	LEVEL: Novice-Intermediate

The wooden steamer, *City of Port Huron* (169' x 30'5" x 10'2"), built at Port Huron, Michigan, in 1867, sprang a leak and sank off Lexington, Michigan, on September 4, 1876, with a cargo of iron ore. No lives were lost, and much of the machinery was recovered shortly after it sank. This wreck was located by David Losinski and Paul Schmitt in 2001.

18. CLAYTON BELLE

LORAN:	LAT 43° 07' 42" LON 082° 26' 06"
DEPTH: 36 feet	LEVEL: Novice-Intermediate

The 139-foot, 300-ton schooner, *Clayton Belle,* collided with the *Thomas Parsons* and sank in a matter of minutes with four lives lost on April 10, 1882. The surviving sailors had jumped onto the *Parsons* and attempted to launch a lifeboat to rescue their companions, but the *Parsons'* crew would not help. The *Clayton Belle*, built in 1854 at Clayton, NY, was heavily loaded with pig iron, which was recovered a short time after the sinking.

19. AMARANTH

LORAN:	GPS: 43° 02.390'/082° 26.567'
DEPTH: 5 to 13 feet	LEVEL: Novice

The two-masted, 330-ton schooner, *Amaranth* (134'6" x 25' x 10'6"), built at Milan, Ohio, in 1864, was used as a towbarge at the end of her career. On September 7, 1901, a foggy, stormy day, the ship was driven ashore in the shallows above Port Huron while in tow of the steamer, *John H. Pauly*, and became a total loss, soon pounded to pieces. Her crew was saved by the *Pauly*. This wreck lies mostly buried in the lake bottom.

Right: The loss of the *Amaranth*. Cris Kohl Collection

308

25. Michigan's Thumb

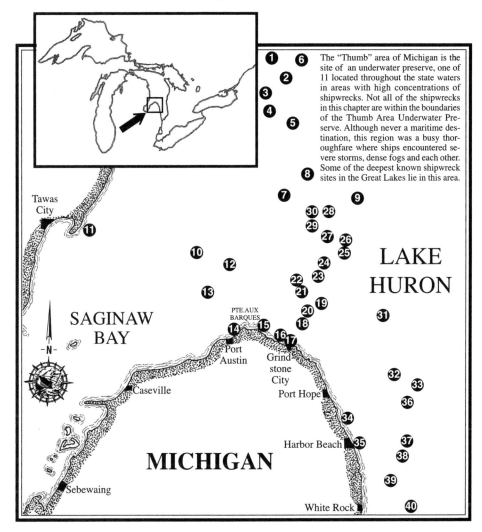

The "Thumb" area of Michigan is the site of an underwater preserve, one of 11 located throughout the state waters in areas with high concentrations of shipwrecks. Not all of the shipwrecks in this chapter are within the boundaries of the Thumb Area Underwater Preserve. Although never a maritime destination, this region was a busy thoroughfare where ships encountered severe storms, dense fogs and each other. Some of the deepest known shipwreck sites in the Great Lakes lie in this area.

LAKE HURON

Tawas City

SAGINAW BAY

-N-

PTE.AUX BARQUES

Port Austin

Grind stone City

Caseville

Port Hope

MICHIGAN

Harbor Beach

Sebewaing

White Rock

1. *W. C. Franz*
2. *Edward U. Demmer*
3. *1930's biplane*
4. *S. H. Kimball*
5. *A. Everett*
6. *H. P. Bridge*
7. *Curran* and *McPhail*
8. *Frank H. Goodyear*
9. *Minnedosa*
10. *Metropole*
11. *Goshawk*
12. *City of Detroit*
13. *Troy*

14. **Anchor: P. A. Reef**
15. *Berlin*
16. *Jacob Bertschy*
17. **Anchor: Kinch Rd.**
18. *Philadelphia*
19. *Albany*
20. *Iron Chief*
21. **Dump barge/scow**
22. *Anna Dobbins*
23. *E. P. Dorr*
24. *Governor Smith*
25. *Emma L. Nielsen*
26. *Fred Lee*

27. *Detroit*
28. *Daniel J. Morrell* **bow**
29. *Daniel J. Morrell* **stern**
30. *Argus*
31. *Hunter Savidge*
32. **Mystery schooner**
33. *John McGean*
34. *Marquis*
35. *Chickamauga*
36. *Dunderberg*
37. *Waverly*
38. *Glenorchy*
39. *Goliath*
40. *Arctic*

1. W. C. FRANZ

> **LORAN: 30768.7/48893.3**   **GPS: 44° 38.862'/082° 54.379'**
> **DEPTH: 200 to 230 feet**   **LEVEL: Technical**

Launched as the *Uranus* at Wyandotte, Michigan on April 20, 1901, and, after being sold to Canadian interests in 1913, renamed the *W. C. Franz* (346' x 48' x 24'11"), this 3,429-ton steel ship sank with four lives lost after a collision in thick fog with the steamer, *Edward E. Loomis*, on Nov. 21, 1934. Dave Trotter and his team found this wreck in 2000.

Left to right: The steel steamer, *W. C. Franz,* easily passed through pack ice. CRIS KOHL COLLECTION. An electronic image, and the *Franz's* bell. SIDESCAN AND PHOTO COURTESY OF DAVID TROTTER/UNDERSEA RESEARCH ASSOCIATES

2. EDWARD U. DEMMER

> **DEPTH: 210 feet**   **LEVEL: Technical**

The 4,651-ton steel steamer, *Edward U. Demmer* (423'9" x 51'9" x 28'), sank with her 7,000 tons of coal cargo in a collision with the steamer, *Saturn,* on May 20, 1923, in dense fog. No lives were lost, the crew being rescued by two passing steamers. Launched as the *Admiral* in 1899 at Wyandotte, MI, it was renamed *Demmer* in 1920. It rests upside-down.

The
Edward U. Demmer
Artwork © Robert McGreevy

The steamer, *Edward U. Demmer.* CRIS KOHL COLLECTION. The underwater *Demmer.* COURTESY OF ROBERT MCGREEVY

3. 1930's BIPLANE

> **DEPTH: 210 feet**   **LEVEL: Technical**

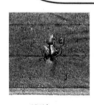

In 2006, Dave Trotter and his team, while wreck hunting, found a Douglas 0-38 biplane, one of only 156 built between 1931 and 1934 for training. The pilot was not with his plane.

Left: This little speck on sidescan sonar paper does, upon close examination, resemble an airplane. *Right:* This is the skeleton of this 128 mph 1930's biplane. SIDESCAN AND PHOTO COURTESY OF DAVID TROTTER/UNDERSEA RESEARCH ASSOCIATES

4. S. H. KIMBALL

> **DEPTH: 210 feet**   **LEVEL: Technical**

The 319-ton schooner-barge, *S. H. Kimball* (138'5" x 26'5" x 12'6"), built at Vermilion, Ohio, in 1864, sank on May 8, 1895, with her cargo of soft coal and no lives lost after colliding with the steamer which was towing her, the *George Stone*. The two had become separated, and met head-on in thick fog. The steamer rescued the *Kimball's* crew.

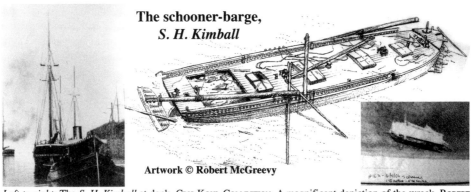

The schooner-barge, *S. H. Kimball*

Artwork © Robert McGreevy

Left to right: The *S. H. Kimball* at dock. CRIS KOHL COLLECTION. A magnificent depiction of the wreck. ROBERT MCGREEVY. The *Kimball* sidescan image. SIDESCAN COURTESY OF DAVID TROTTER/UNDERSEA RESEARCH ASSOCIATES

5. *A. EVERETT*

DEPTH: 210 feet	LEVEL: Technical

The 1,088-ton wooden steamer, *A. Everett* (211′5″ x 34′8″ x 17′2″), launched June 24, 1880, at Cleveland, Ohio, was cut by ice and sunk on April 30, 1895, the crew being rescued by the passing steamer, *Eber Ward* (which, years later, was also sunk by ice and is also in this book!). The *Everett* was enroute from Chicago to Buffalo with 48,000 bushels of corn.

The *A. Everett.* CRIS KOHL COLLECTION

The *A. Everett*

Artwork © Robert McGreevy

6. *H. P. BRIDGE*

DEPTH: 215 feet	LEVEL: Technical

This wreck was reportedly located by Dick Race in the 1970's while he was searching for a modern barge, then found in 2004 by Dave Trotter and his team. The three-masted, 426-ton bark, *H. P. Bridge* (164′4″ x 30′2″ x 12′6″), built in 1864 at Detroit, sank on May 11, 1869, after colliding in dense fog with the steamer, *Colorado.* No lives were lost. All three masts are upright on this intact wreck, and the bow sports a unique eagle figurehead.

Left: A sidescan sonar image of the *H. P. Bridge* reveals much about what type of ship it was and its present condition. SIDESCAN COURTESY OF DAVID TROTTER/UNDERSEA RESEARCH ASSOCIATES

The *Curran* and the *McPhail*

See next page....

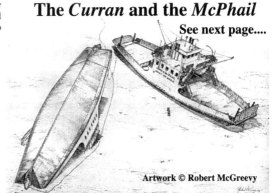

Artwork © Robert McGreevy

7. JAMES W. CURRAN AND JOHN A. MCPHAIL

> LORAN: 30761.1/49047.4   GPS:
> DEPTH: 176 feet   LEVEL: Technical

On May 9, 1964, two auto ferries which had run between the two Sault Ste. Marie's were being towed by a tugboat to Kingston, ON, when they sank. The *James W. Curran* (103′ x 34′ x 8′2″), built at Collingwood, ON in 1947, and the *John A. McPhail* (104′6″ x 36′1″ x 8′6″), built at Collingwood, ON, in 1955, foundered in a severe squall. No lives were lost. These ships were found by Stan Stock in the 1980's. See art on previous page.

8. FRANK H. GOODYEAR

> DEPTH: 160 feet   LEVEL: Technical

Launched at Lorain, Ohio, in 1902, the 4,815-ton steel freighter, *Frank H. Goodyear* (416′ x 50′ x 28′), sank with great loss of life (18 of the 23 people on board) on May 23, 1910, after colliding with the steamer, *James B. Woods*. Dave Trotter and his team found this wreck in 2000. The owner's luxury railroad car is still mounted in midship on deck!

The *Frank H. Goodyear:* ship, railroad car, and tragedy. CRIS KOHL COLLECTION

9. MINNEDOSA

> DEPTH: 160 feet   LEVEL: Technical

The four-masted schooner, *Minnedosa* (243′ x 35′6″ x 16′9″), was the largest sailing ship ever built on the Canadian side of the Great Lakes. Launched on April 26, 1890, at Kingston, ON, she sank with all hands in the severe storm of Oct. 20, 1905 while under tow. This wreck was located in 1991 after a long search by Dave Trotter and his team.

Left: The huge sailing ship, *Minnedosa,* proved to be too big to sail on the inland seas. CRIS KOHL COLLECTION. Right: A bottle, jugs, and a fathometer sit near a *Minnedosa* cabin. PHOTO COURTESY OF DAVID TROTTER/ UNDERSEA RESEARCH ASSOCI-

10. METROPOLE

> DEPTH: 210 feet   LEVEL: Technical

The 190-ton wooden steamer, *Metropole* (118′ x 22′7″ x 7′), launched as the *Sakie Shepherd* on June 23, 1883, at Huron, Ohio, at Cleveland in 1887, had its name changed in

1901. On Aug. 3, 1903, a leak developed and the ship sank, with the crew rowing ashore in the lifeboat. This wreck is intact!

Left : The little steamer, *Metropole.* CRIS KOHL COLLECTION. *Right:* The *Metropole's* crew painted their initials inside the hull, still visible today. PHOTO COURTESY OF DAVID TROTTER/UNDERSEA RESEARCH ASSOCIATES

11. GOSHAWK

LORAN: 31049.3/49055.5	GPS: 44° 14.95'/083° 24.96'
DEPTH: 40 to 50 feet	LEVEL: Intermediate

LOCATION: This wreck lies 3 miles northeast of Tawas Point, Michigan.

The schooner-barge, *Goshawk* (180' x 32'4" x 11'5"), built at Cleveland in 1866, foundered with a cargo of salt on June 16, 1920, after having served on the Great Lakes,

Below: The lumber-laden *Goshawk* under tow. CRIS KOHL COLLECTION. *Right:* Bill Atkins, of the 1992 survey team, approaches the *Goshawk's* wheel. PHOTO BY CRIS KOHL

mostly in the lumber trade, for over half a century! No lives were lost in the sinking, the crew having taken to the lifeboats. Located in 1990 by A&T Recovery of Chicago, IL, the *Goshawk* was the subject of an intense survey in August, 1992, by the Underwater Archaeological Society of Chicago, the author and others. At the wreck site, only the rudder post is taller than the average rise of 5'. The many artifacts include a windlass, capstan, bilge pump, donkey boiler, ship's wheel and four anchors! Much timber criss-crosses this busy site.

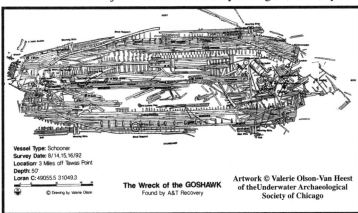

Vessel Type: Schooner
Survey Date: 8/14,15,16/92
Location: 3 Miles off Tawas Point
Depth: 50'
Loran C: 49055.5 31049.3
© Drawing by Valerie Olson
The Wreck of the GOSHAWK
Found by A&T Recovery
Artwork © Valerie Olson-Van Heest of the Underwater Archaeological Society of Chicago

12. CITY OF DETROIT

LORAN: 30889.5/49101.2	GPS: 44° 12.472'/083° 00.841'
DEPTH: 176 feet	LEVEL: Technical

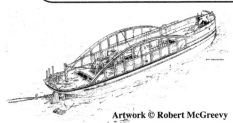

Artwork © Robert McGreevy

LOCATION: This wreck lies due north of Port Austin, Michigan.

The wooden bulk freight steamer, *City of Detroit* (167' x 27'7" x 12'1"), built at Marine City, Michigan, in 1866, foundered in a storm on Dec. 4, 1873, with all 20 hands and a cargo of barrelled flour and wheat. The wreck lies upright and intact in deep water.

13. TROY

LORAN: 30909.0/49131.6	GPS: 44° 08.655'/083° 01.939'
DEPTH: 97 feet	LEVEL: Advanced

LOCATION: This wreck lies about 7 miles north of Pointe aux Barques, Michigan.

The wooden steamer, *Troy* (182' x 27' x 11'), foundered in heavy seas with the loss of

The
Troy

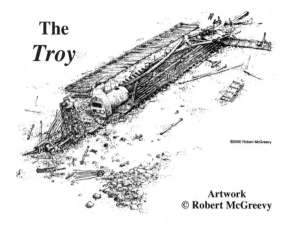

©2000 Robert McGreevy

Artwork
© Robert McGreevy

23 lives on October 18, 1859. Discovered in 1999, the scattered wreck site includes the engine, boiler, propeller, four anchors and much wooden decking and planking.

14. ANCHOR: PORT AUSTIN REEF

This wooden-stocked anchor lying in 15' of water with approximately 200' of chain attached to it was lost at this location (**LORAN: 30904.4/49172.2**) from an unidentified vessel in unknown circumstances. This is a novice dive.

15. *BERLIN*

LORAN: 30869.2/49170.7	GPS:
DEPTH: 10 feet	LEVEL: Novice

LOCATION: This wreck lies about one mile northwest of Grindstone City, Michigan. Four lives were lost when the schooner, *Berlin* (111'6" x 24' x 11'), built in 1854 at Milan, Ohio, stranded here in violent weather on November 8, 1877. Waves washed the captain, cook and a deckhand overboard, while the captain's son perished from exposure while lashed to the rigging. Two others survived. The lumber/limestone cargo lies scattered.

16. *JACOB BERTSCHY*

LORAN: 30862.8/49181.4	GPS: 44° 03.419'/082° 53.133'
DEPTH: 10 feet	LEVEL: Novice

LOCATION: This wreck lies 900' southeast of Grindstone City pier, 1/4 mile off shore.

The 433-gross-ton, wooden bulk freight steamer, *Jacob Bertschy* (139'8" x 27'4" x 9'3"), built at Sheboygan, WI, in 1867, stranded on Sept. 3, 1879, with a cargo of shingles and wheat. She broke up shortly afterwards; no lives were lost. The wreckage lies scattered.

Left: The wooden steamer, *Jacob Bertschy*. INSTITUTE FOR GREAT LAKES RESEARCH, BOWLING GREEN, OHIO

17. ANCHOR: KINCH ROAD

This wooden-stocked anchor lying in 20' of water with approximately 300' of chain attached to it was lost at this location (**LORAN: 30834.8/49184.7 GPS: 43° 03.388'/082° 49.331'**) from an unidentified vessel in unknown circumstances. This is a novice dive.

18. *PHILADELPHIA*

LORAN: 30786.44/49183.96	GPS: 44° 04.120'/082° 42.992'
DEPTH: 105 to 125 feet	LEVEL: Advanced

LOCATION: This wreck lies about 5.5 miles northeast of Pointe aux Barques, Michigan. The iron-hulled propeller, *Philadelphia* (236' x 34'3" x 14'), built at Buffalo, New York, in 1868, collided with the steamer, *Albany* (see site #19) on November 7, 1893, with

Two steamers, similar in size and appearance, sank after colliding with one another on November 7, 1893. *Left,* the *Philadelphia,* and *right,* the *Albany.* BOTH GREAT LAKES HISTORICAL SOCIETY

the loss of 16 lives and a cargo of coal and general merchandise.

Shipwreck hunter John Steele located the *Philadelphia* in the spring of 1973. The wreck's noteworthy sights include the engine, two boilers, rudder, propeller, stern capstan, and, on the port deck, a load of cast iron stoves, some of which have spilled onto the lake floor or into the cargo holds. The bow damage from the collision is evident, and the port bow anchor on the lake floor leans against the hull. This wreck, and others in this underwater preserve, is usually buoyed in the springtime.

19. ALBANY

LORAN: 30773.1/49166.8	GPS: 44° 06.351'/082° 42.016'
DEPTH: 132 to 149 feet	LEVEL: Technical

LOCATION: This wreck lies about 2.5 miles to the northeast of the *Philadelphia*.

Launched at Wyandotte, Michigan, in 1885, the steel bulk freight steamer, *Albany* (267' x 38'5" x 13'8"), sank first in the collision with the *Philadelphia* (site #18) on November 7, 1893, and lies in slightly deeper water. She went down with eight crewmembers and her grain cargo. The wreck sits upright and intact.

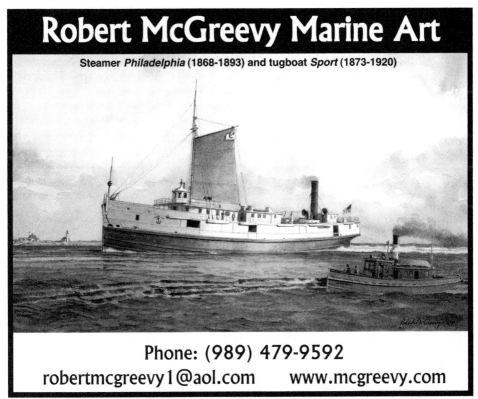

20. IRON CHIEF

LORAN: 30779.0/49172.0	GPS: 44° 05.632'/082° 42.588'
DEPTH: 135 feet	LEVEL: Technical

The steamer, *Iron Chief.*
CRIS KOHL COLLECTION

The author and the *Iron Chief's* anchor at Harbor Beach.
PHOTO BY JOAN FORSBERG

LOCATION: This wreck lies about four miles northeast of Grindstone City, Michigan.

Launched as a schooner at Wyandotte, Michigan, on July 12, 1881, the *Iron Chief* (212'4" x 35' x 17'6"), converted to a bulk freight steamer, sprang a leak after breaking a stern pipe and foundered in heavy seas with her coal cargo on October 3, 1904. The crew was rescued by the steamer, *Andrew Carnegie.* Machinery is the site's highlight.

21. DUMP BARGE/SCOW

LORAN: 30836.6/49150.8	GPS: 44° 07.401'/082° 51.276'
DEPTH: 77 feet	LEVEL: Advanced

LOCATION: This unidentified wreck lies about six miles north-northeast of Grindstone City, Michigan, near the wreck of the *Anna Dobbins* (see site #22 in this chapter).

22. ANNA DOBBINS

LORAN:	GPS: 44° 08.111'/082° 51.277'
DEPTH: 90 feet	LEVEL: Advanced

LOCATION: This wreck lies about six miles north-northeast of Grindstone City.

The wooden tug, *Anna Dobbins* (101'8" x 18' x 10'), foundered on September 24, 1886, after a stern bearing gave way, breaking the stern pipe. No lives were lost. The upright wreck sits intact. The vessel had been built at Buffalo, New York, in 1862.

23. E. P. DORR

LORAN: 30780.0/49145.5	GPS: 44° 08.790'/082° 43.960'
DEPTH: 175 feet	LEVEL: Technical

LOCATION: This wreck lies about seven miles north-northeast of Grindstone City.

The huge, 300-ton, wooden tug, *E.P. Dorr* (161' x 25'), collided with the steamer, *Oliver Cromwell,* in June, 1856. The tug, built at Buffalo, New York, was only one year old at the time of loss. This is a deep site which requires special technical training and experience.

24. GOVERNOR SMITH

LORAN: 30763.3/49141.3	GPS: 44° 09.333'/082° 42.001'
DEPTH: 178 to 197 feet	LEVEL: Technical

LOCATION: This wreck lies about eight miles north-northeast of Grindstone City, Michigan.

The wooden freighter, *Governor Smith* (240' x 42' x 23'4"), built in 1889 at Wyandotte, Michigan), sank in a collision in thick fog with the larger steel steamer, *Uranus,* on August 19, 1906. The *Uranus* rescued the *Smith's* crew, but

Left: The *Governor Smith.* CRIS KOHL COLLECTION

the cargo of grain and package freight was lost. This deep, intact wreck is for only the specially trained.

25. *EMMA L. NIELSEN*

LORAN: 30763.9/49129.9	GPS: 44° 10.878'/082° 42.611'
DEPTH: 190 feet	LEVEL: Technical

LOCATION: This wreck lies about nine miles north-northeast of Grindstone City.

The three-masted schooner, *Emma L. Nielsen* (98'2" x 20'6" x 6'2"), launched at Manitowoc, Wisconsin, in 1883, sank in a collision in fog with the 346' steel steamer, *Wyandotte*, on June 26, 1911, with no lives lost. This deep, but beautifully intact, shipwreck was found by Dave Trotter in April, 1980.

The
Emma L. Nielsen

The *Emma L. Nielsen*.
CRIS KOHL COLLECTION

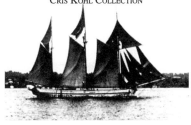

Artwork
© Robert McGreevy

26. *FRED LEE*

LORAN: 30780.83/49115.23	GPS: 44° 12.422'/082° 45.556'
DEPTH: 200 feet	LEVEL: Technical

LOCATION: The *Fred Lee* lies about ten miles north-northeast of Grindstone City.

Built at Port Huron, Michigan, in 1896, the tug, *Fred Lee* (70' x 16' x 9'), also known as the *Frederick A. Lee,* foundered with the entire crew of five on Friday the 13th of November, 1936. Dave Trotter and his team located this wreck in 1996. The hull is intact, with an anchor on the bow, chain out of a hawsepipe, a winch with braided steel cable and a steel ship's wheel.

The tug, *Frederick A. Lee.*
CRIS KOHL COLLECTION

27. DETROIT

LORAN: 30776.4/49105.4   GPS: 44° 13.611'/082° 45.436'
DEPTH: 180 feet   LEVEL: Technical

This wreck, 10 miles NNE of Grindstone City, was found by Dave Trotter's team on June 5, 1994. Built at Newport (Marine City), MI, in 1846, the sidewheel steamer, *Detroit* (157' x 23'3" x 10'), sank in a collision in fog with the bark, *Nucleus,* on May 25, 1854, with no lives lost. The site's highlight, her bell, with "New York 1844" on it, was stolen recently.

28 & 29. DANIEL J. MORRELL (BOW & STERN) -- SEE PAGE 319.

30. ARGUS

LORAN: 30790.6/49068.2   GPS:
DEPTH: 220 feet   LEVEL: Technical

LOCATION: This wreck lies just to the northwest of the middle of a line drawn from the bow to the stern of the *Daniel J. Morrell.*

A victim of the Great Storm of November 9-11, 1913, the steel freighter, *Argus* (416' x 50' x 28'), disappeared with all 24 crew and her cargo of soft coal. The 10-year-old ship had been launched at Lorain, Ohio. Located in 1972, this wreck, like all the other victims of that storm in lower Lake Huron, except the *Wexford,* lies upside down.

The *Argus.*
CRIS KOHL COLLECTION

31. HUNTER SAVIDGE

LORAN: 30742.3/49175.8   GPS: 44° 06.52'/082° 35.058'
DEPTH: 150 feet   LEVEL: Technical

The schooner, *Hunter Savidge.*
CRIS KOHL COLLECTION

LOCATION: This wreck lies about 10 miles east-northeast of Grindstone City, Michigan.

Found by Dave Trotter's team on Aug. 13, 1988, the two-masted, 152-ton schooner, *Hunter Savidge* (117' x 26'6" x 8'2"), capsized on Aug. 20, 1899, after being hit by a sudden white squall. Five lives were lost. The vessel had been built at Grand Haven, Michigan, in 1879. The wreck hit the bottom hard bow-first and is fairly broken up; the masts all snapped and tumbled forward, but she is a prime example of a well-equipped Great Lakes schooner.

32. MYSTERY SCHOONER

LORAN: 30746.4/49239.2   GPS: 43° 57.851'/082° 35.018'
DEPTH: 145 feet   LEVEL: Technical

LOCATION: This wreck lies about 8 miles north-northeast of Harbor Beach, Michigan.

This unidentified schooner is called, by some divers, the "Challenge," but since no schooner of that name went down in this lake, that designation appears to have been given as a nickname referring to the daunting task of identifying her. The wreck has small ornamentation beneath her bowsprit, akin to a figurehead, indicative of an early design.

33. JOHN A. MCGEAN

LORAN: 30723.8/49245.9   GPS: 43° 57.198'/082° 31.718'
DEPTH: 198 feet   LEVEL: Technical

LOCATION: This wreck lies about 8 miles northeast of Harbor Beach, Michigan.
Built at Lorain, Ohio, in 1908, the large steel freighter, *John McGean* (432' x 52' x 28'),

Great Lakes Highlight No. 11

THE *DANIEL J. MORRELL*:
THE SHIP WHICH BROKE IN HALF

BOW HALF:

LORAN: 30761.4/49068.4	GPS: 44° 18.320'/082° 45.161'
DEPTH: 205 feet	LEVEL: Technical

STERN HALF:

LORAN: 30803.7/49086.3	GPS: 44° 15.478'/082° 50.088'
DEPTH: 218 feet	LEVEL: Technical

LOCATION: This wreck lies about 12 miles north of Grindstone City, Michigan.

The 60-year-old steel freighter, *Daniel J. Morrell* (586'5" x 58'2" x 27'9"), is another of the tragic yet legendary modern losses on the Great Lakes. She broke in half in a furious storm on Nov. 29, 1966, and from her crew of 29 men, there was but one survivor, Dennis Hale, who spent 36 hours on a liferaft before the Coast Guard finally found him. The wreck's bow half begins at 100', with the top of the mast; the pilot house is at 142', and from there, it's another 70' of massive shipwreck before one reaches the lake bottom. This site is definitely for trained, experienced, cautious deep divers only. After the *Morrell* broke in two, the stern half steamed off into the night for an incredible five miles before sinking! It lies slightly deeper than the bow, but is not quite as interesting.

Clockwise, from upper left: The *Daniel J. Morrell* in the 1960's; Dennis Hale later identified himself as the sailor standing at the very bow. REV. PETER VAN DER LINDEN COLLECTION. An early photo of the *Daniel J. Morrell*. CRIS KOHL COLLECTION. Dennis Hale, 30 years after surviving the sinking, gazed reflectively at the yard in West Bay City, Michigan, where the *Morrell* had been launched in 1906. PHOTO BY CRIS KOHL. The *Morrell's* halves, as they look today. Artwork © Robert McGreevy. *Center:* The top of the *Morrell's* mast, the letter "C" for the Cambria Steamship Company, and Joan Forsberg emerging from the pilot house. PHOTOS BY CRIS KOHL

went missing with all hands (23) in the Great Storm of November 9-11, 1913, one of eight ships in lower Lake Huron to do so. The *McGean* was located by Dave Trotter and his team in 1986. She lies upside-down, and it's a deep dive to see lots of steel hull. Five of the six Lake Huron Storm of 1913 wrecks located to date lie upside-down, so the odds are that the other two, the *Hydrus* and the *James Carruthers,* will also be upside-down when found.

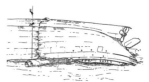

Artwork © Robert McGreevy

Left: The steel freighter, *John McGean.* CRIS KOHL COLLECTION

34. MARQUIS

LORAN: 30795.0/49266.4	GPS:
DEPTH: 15 feet	LEVEL: Novice

LOCATION: This wreck lies about three miles south of Port Hope, Michigan.

The three-masted schooner-barge, *Marquis* (148' x 29'), was caught in a blizzard on November 12, 1892, and stranded. The entire crew survived, thanks in part to the local lifesaving team. Because it is so shallow, the wreck is badly broken up and scattered.

35. CHICKAMAUGA

LORAN: 30787.9/49294.0	GPS: 43° 50.952'/082° 37.425'
DEPTH: 32 feet	LEVEL: Novice

LOCATION: This wreck lies about half a mile east of Harbor Beach, Michigan.

The schooner-barge, *Chickamauga* (322' x 45' x 21'5"), loaded with iron ore and towed by the steamer, *Centurion,* encountered immense seas on September 12, 1919, and stranded one mile north of Harbor Beach. Her crew was removed before the hull was twisted into an unsalvageable condition. She had been built at West Bay City, Michigan, in 1898. The wreck was moved to its present location the

The *Chickamauga.* CRIS KOHL COLLECTION

following year to clear the harbor entrance. The wreck lies broken and scattered over a wide area. This is too far offshore to be a shore dive; a boat is required.

36. DUNDERBERG

LORAN: 30740.7/49257.3	GPS: 43° 55.640'/082° 33.390'
DEPTH: 143 to 157 feet	LEVEL: Technical

LOCATION: This wreck lies about five miles northeast of Harbor Beach, Michigan.

Located by Kent Bellrichard in 1971, the three-masted schooner, *Dunderberg* (186' x 33' x 13'), built at Detroit in 1867, worked in the grain trade. She was loaded with 40,000 bushels of corn and five passengers on August 13, 1868, in her second season afloat, when the steamer, *Empire State,* collided with her. One life, a female passenger, was lost.

The wreck is upright, intact and pristine. The bow displays a large windlass, both anchors and catheads. The thick railings are crowded with deadeyes and belaying pins. The open hatches invite exploration. Fair-sized sections of two masts remain in place and upright. Much running rigging lies on deck and off the wreck on the hard clay bottom. But the highlight of this site is the figurehead: a carved alligator, jaw dropped, tongue protruding,

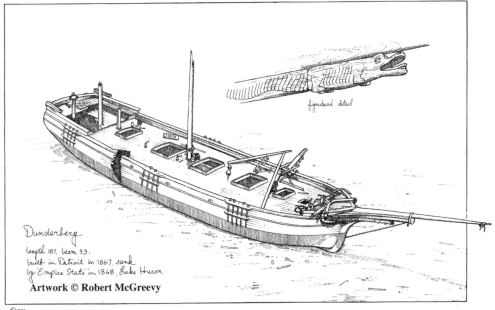

Dunderberg
length 187, beam 33.
built in Detroit in 1867, sank
by 'Empire State' in 1868, Lake Huron.

figurehead detail

Artwork © Robert McGreevy

©1982

The schooner, *Dunderberg,* proudly exhibits her unique and finely-crafted alligator figurehead and other ornate carvings just below the bowsprit. PHOTOS BY CRIS KOHL

each eye still glinting with a dab of red paint, plus grapes, birds and curled vines, clustered leaves and arched branches carved into the trim boards curving back from the bowsprit.

The *Dunderberg,* with its superb craftsmanship, is deemed one of the finest, best-preserved and most intact shipwrecks in the Great Lakes.

37. WAVERLY

LORAN:	GPS:
DEPTH: 121 feet	LEVEL: Advanced

LOCATION: This wreck lies just north of the *Glenorchy* (site #38), about eight miles east of Harbor Beach, Michigan.

The wooden steamer, *Waverly* (191'2" x 33'7" x 13'4"), built at Buffalo, New York, and launched on May 28, 1874, sank in a collision with the steamer, *Turret Court,* on July 22, 1903. No lives were lost, but the ship, with her coal cargo, was a complete

The *Waverly.* CRIS KOHL COLLECTION

loss. This wreck, first located by John Steele, is quite broken up.

Left and *right:* A *Waverly* nameboard washed ashore at Port Franks, Ontario, and it has been used for 100+ years on this former resort/post office/hotel building called the "Waverly." PHOTOS TAKEN AND SUBMITTED BY D. M. GIBBS

38. GLENORCHY

LORAN: 30750.4/49314.2	GPS: 43° 48.580'/082° 31.792'
DEPTH: 100 to 120 feet	LEVEL: Advanced

LOCATION: This wreck lies about ten miles east-southeast of Harbor Beach, Michigan.

Built in 1902 at West Bay City, Michigan, and launched as the *A. E. Stewart,* the steel freighter, *Glenorchy* (356' x 50' x 28'), collided in dense fog with the steamer, *Leonard B. Miller,* and sank with no lives lost. The wreck sits upright and has penetration opportunities for properly trained and equipped divers.

The *Glenorchy.*
CRIS KOHL COLLECTION

39. GOLIATH

LORAN: 30761.8/49326.5	GPS: 43° 47.007'/082° 32.720'
DEPTH: 104 feet	LEVEL: Advanced

LOCATION: This wreck lies about ten miles southeast of Harbor Beach, Michigan.

The package and bulk freight steamer, *Goliath* (131' x 25' x 9'), also referred to as *Goliah,* exploded on Lake Huron on September 13, 1848, taking 18 souls with her. The ship

The *Goliath*

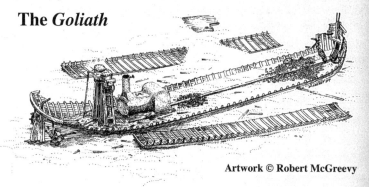

Artwork © Robert McGreevy

Goliath's engine.
PHOTO BY CRIS KOHL

had caught on fire, and sparks reached her cargo of bricks, general freight and 200 kegs of blasting powder. Discovered by Dave Trotter's team in 1984, the *Goliath's* main features are her tall, upright engine, boiler, stove, and unique, early propellers.

40. ARCTIC

LORAN: 30748.4/49371.4	GPS: 43° 41.460'/082° 28.710'
DEPTH: 136 feet	LEVEL: Technical

Located by Dave Trotter's team in 1987, the steamer, *Arctic* (193'7" x 28'1" x 10'8"), sprang a leak and foundered on Sept. 5, 1893, with no lives lost. The engine is distinctive.

26. Thunder Bay

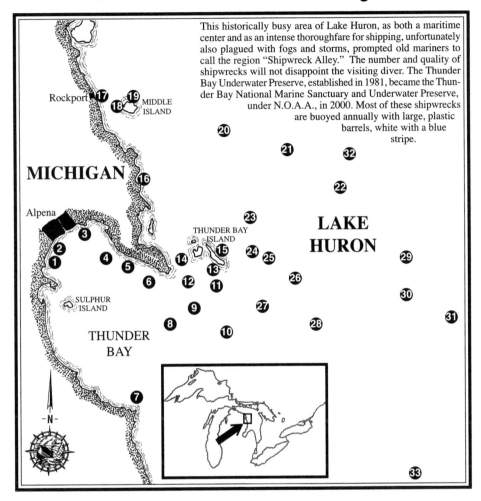

This historically busy area of Lake Huron, as both a maritime center and as an intense thoroughfare for shipping, unfortunately also plagued with fogs and storms, prompted old mariners to call the region "Shipwreck Alley." The number and quality of shipwrecks will not disappoint the visiting diver. The Thunder Bay Underwater Preserve, established in 1981, became the Thunder Bay National Marine Sanctuary and Underwater Preserve, under N.O.A.A., in 2000. Most of these shipwrecks are buoyed annually with large, plastic barrels, white with a blue stripe.

1. *Shamrock*	12. **North Point wrecks**	23. *D. M. Wilson*
2. *Harvey Bissell* (?)	13. *Monohansett*	24. *O. E. Parks*
3. *William P. Rend*	14. *New Orleans* (1)	25. *Lucinda Van Valkenburg*
4. *Oscar T. Flint*	15. **Limestone walls**	26. *W. P. Thew*
5. *Scanlon's barge*	16. *Maid of the Mist*	27. *E. B. Allen*
6. *Barge No. 1*	17. **Rockport cribbing**	28. *Pewabic*
7. *Nellie Gardner* (?)	18. *Portsmouth*	29. *Isaac M. Scott*
8. *Montana*	19. **Limestone formations**	30. *Viator*
9. **Salvage barge**	20. *New Orleans* (2)	31. *Monrovia*
10. *Grecian*	21. *Nordmeer*	32. *Kyle Spangler*
11. *James Davidson*	22. *D. R. Hanna*	33. *W. H. Gilbert*

1. SHAMROCK

LORAN: 30908.2/48651.4	GPS: 45° 02.98'/083° 25.85'
DEPTH: 12 feet	LEVEL: Novice

LOCATION: This wreck lies south of the Alpena city marina, 2/3 mile off shore.

The wooden passenger and freight steamer, *Shamrock* (146' x 30' x 11'), built in 1875 at St. Clair, Michigan, as the schooner-barge, *John W. Hannaford,* foundered on June 26, 1905, off the mouth of the Thunder Bay River which flows through Alpena. The entire crew escaped unharmed. The vessel had just been converted to a steamer the year before her demise. This wreckage, for years thought to be that of the steamer, *P. H. Birckhead,* which was lost later that same year, 1905, contains boiler parts, propeller, shaft and hull portions.

2. HARVEY BISSELL (?)

LORAN: 30904.5/48649.7	GPS: 45° 03.27'/083° 25.38'
DEPTH: 14 feet	LEVEL: Novice

LOCATION: This unidentified 148-foot-long wooden wreck lies 600' east of the marina and breakwall. The highlights of this site include the huge keelson and stern post.

Indications suggest that this wreck is the 496-ton schooner-barge, *Harvey Bissell* (162'4" x 33'6" x 12'4"), launched as a bark on May 28, 1866, at Toledo, Ohio, and stranded while in tow of the steamer, *David W. Rust,* on Nov. 24, 1905. No lives were lost.

The *Harvey Bissell.* CRIS KOHL COLLECTION

3. WILLIAM P. REND

LORAN: 30981.0/48649.5	GPS: 45° 03.69'/083° 23.49'
DEPTH: 15 to 22 feet	LEVEL: Novice

LOCATION: This wreck lies almost a mile east of the Huron Portland Cement Plant.

The William P. Rend. CRIS KOHL COLLECTION

The barge, *William P. Rend* (287'6" x 40' x 21'6"), a former steamer named the *George G. Hadley* launched in 1888 at West Bay City, Michigan, stranded on September 22, 1917, with no loss of life. She had been reduced to a barge just the year before her demise. As the *George G. Hadley,* this vessel collided with and sank the whaleback steamer, *Thomas Wilson* (which is also in this book) outside Duluth, Minnesota, harbor on Lake Superior in 1902. There is a partial cargo of limestone on board the wreck of the *William P. Rend,* with the rudder post, valves and boiler.

4. OSCAR T. FLINT

LORAN: 30879.8/48671.9	GPS: 45° 01.48'/083° 20.69'
DEPTH: 28 to 36 feet	LEVEL: Novice

LOCATION: A mile off shore and four miles southeast of Thunder Bay River.

The wooden steamer, *Oscar T. Flint* (218' x 37' x 15'7"), burned to a total loss during the night while at anchor on November 25, 1909, with no lives lost, the captain barely escaping from the forward part of the ship where the fire started. This vessel was built in 1889 at St. Clair, Michigan. Much of the hull remains intact, plus two wooden-stocked

MARINE IS MENACE TO NAVIGATION

Hull of Burned Steamer Flint, Sinks at Alpena, Mich.

Alpena, Mich., Nov. 26.—The hull of the steamer Oscar T. Flint, which burned yesterday, sank last night in five fathoms of water. With twenty feet of water over her decks, she lies directly in the course of vessels, and is a menace to navigation.

The *Oscar T. Flint* and news of its loss. CRIS KOHL COLLECTION. *Right:* Exploring the *Flint's* remains. PHOTOS BY CRIS KOHL

anchors, a windlass and much more remain at this interesting site.

5. SCANLON'S BARGE

LORAN: 30870.2/48669.1	GPS: 45° 02.02'/083° 19.40'
DEPTH: 5 to 15 feet	LEVEL: Novice

LOCATION: This wreck lies off the middle south shore of North Point.

This gravel dredging barge is broken into three pieces, and scattered among them are a crane boom, steam winches, boiler, two-cylinder steam engine and anchor.

6. *BARGE NO. 1*

LORAN: 30865.0/48680.8	GPS: 45° 00.84'/083° 18.08'
DEPTH: 45 feet	LEVEL: Intermediate

LOCATION: This wreck lies about one mile off the tip of North Point.

The enormous wooden vessel named simply *Barge No. 1* (309'9" x 44'2" x 12'), was built at West Bay City, Michigan, in 1895 and launched as a railroad carferry before being converted to a bulk freight barge at Chicago in 1912. The ship stranded on the rocks of North Point in a storm on November 8, 1918, and wind and waves moved her into deeper water. The sidewalls of the hull are intact, as is the steering quadrant at the stern.

Barge No. 1's wooden hull at the bow. PHOTOS BY CRIS KOHL

Barge No. 1's steering quadrant at the stern. PHOTOS BY CRIS KOHL

7. *NELLIE GARDNER* (?)

LORAN: 30893.7/48737.9	GPS: 44° 53.55'/083° 19.50'
DEPTH: 15 to 20 feet	LEVEL: Novice

LOCATION: Just north of South Point, between Scarecrow and Bird Islands.

The 178-foot-long, 567-gross-ton schooner-barge, *Nellie Gardner,* built in 1873 at

Marine City, Michigan, stranded with a cargo of coal after breaking her towline in a storm on October 14, 1883. The crew reached shore in their yawl boat.

This wreck, once called the *Molly H.* or the *Molly T. Horner* by early divers, sits broken up and scattered on a mixed sand and stone bottom, with the ribs and sidewalls comprising most of this site.

It is also possible that this wreck is that of the *William Stephens*, a 117' schooner built in 1855 at Cleveland and stranded and broken up in a storm here on Nov. 15, 1863.

8. *MONTANA*

LORAN: 30855.9/48699.9	GPS: 44° 59.04'/083° 15.90'
DEPTH: 33 to 74 feet	LEVEL: Intermediate-Advanced

LOCATION: This wreck lies southwest of Thunder Bay Island.

The wooden steamer, *Montana* (236'3" x 36' x 14'), launched on June 18, 1872 at Port Huron, Michigan, burned to a total loss on September 7, 1914. No lives were lost.

This shipwreck is one of the most popular scuba dive sites in the Alpena area. The hull is intact and upright, with nautical items such as windlass, anchor chain, capstan, boiler, rudder and huge, four-bladed propeller. The highlight is the towering steam engine.

Above: The steamer, *Montana.* CRIS KOHL COLLECTION. *Others:* Divers explore the *Montana's* tall engine and propeller. PHOTOS BY CRIS KOHL

9. CARBIDE SALVAGE BARGE

LORAN: 30839.5/48707.5	GPS: 44° 58.557'/083° 13.151'
DEPTH: 90 feet	LEVEL: Advanced

LOCATION: This wreck lies off North Point to the northwest of the *Grecian*.
This 68-foot-long salvage barge with a wheelhouse was used in the *Grecian* salvage.

10. *GRECIAN*

LORAN: 30832.7/48713.3	GPS: 44° 58.500'/083° 11.783'
DEPTH: 70 to 105 feet	LEVEL: Advanced

LOCATION: About 10.5 miles east of Alpena harbor.
The steel freighter, *Grecian* (296'2" x 40'4" x 21'1"), built at Cleveland in 1891, hit a rock and sank near DeTour, Michigan, on June 7, 1906. Refloated, she was being towed to Detroit for major repair work when the temporary patch gave way on June 15, 1906. The

Grecian sank for the second time in eight days, only this time, it was permanent, as further salvage attempts failed.

This popular site, buoyed in season like most of the other shipwrecks in this designated area, offers much to see at the deck level of 70′: tools, railing, bitts and machinery. The propeller rests in 105′. Penetration is possible into the holds for experienced, trained divers. The bow portion of the *Grecian* has collapsed, giving the false impression that the wreck is broken in two, so the intact stern is the more popular part to explore.

Above: The steel steamer, *Grecian.* CRIS KOHL COLLLECTION. *Right:* Diver Roy Pickering approaches the emergency steering at the stern of the *Grecian,* and later takes a close look at a pair of on-deck bitts.   PHOTOS BY CRIS KOHL

11. JAMES DAVIDSON

LORAN:	GPS: 45° 01.871′/083° 11.764′
DEPTH: 70 feet	LEVEL: Intermediate-Advanced

LOCATION: This wreck lies two miles northeast of Thunder Bay Island.

The wooden steamer, *James Davidson* (231′ x 37′ x 19′), built at West Bay City, MI, in 1874, stranded on a reef half a mile off Thunder Bay Island Light on October 4, 1883, with a cargo of coal. It broke up and sank over the next few days. Ribs and planking remain.

12. NORTH POINT WRECKS

LORAN: 30846.3/48688.4	GPS: 45° 00.46′/083° 14.99′
DEPTH: 15 feet	LEVEL: Novice

LOCATION: This site lies to the east off the tip of North Point.

Three shipwrecks lie broken and scattered, with some interesting large pieces, such as a windlass and a large steel anchor, as well as other ship's parts.

These wrecks are likely the 212′ wooden steamer, *B. W. Blanchard* (launched on July 19, 1870, at Cleveland, and stranded and broke up here on Nov. 29, 1904), the schooner-barge, *John T. Johnson* (which was in tow of the *Blanchard* on Nov. 29, 1904, and was also lost), and the 193′ steamer, *Galena,* stranded here with all hands lost on Sept. 25, 1872.

13. *MONOHANSETT*

> **LORAN: 30822.6/48681.4** **GPS: 45° 01.89'/083° 11.90'**
> **DEPTH: 14 to 20 feet** **LEVEL: Novice**

LOCATION: This wreck lies about 600' off the old dock at Thunder Bay Island.

The wooden steamer, *Monohansett* (164'8" x 31'9" x 9'4"), launched as the *Ira H. Owen* on June 26, 1872 at Gibraltar, Michigan, and renamed in 1882, burned to a total loss on November 23, 1907; 12 on board, no lives were lost. The site's highlights include an enormous boiler, a large propeller and considerable wooden hull (bottom portion only).

Left: The steamer, *Monohansett*. CRIS KOHL COLLECTION. *Right:* Diver Roy Pickering did a 70-minute dive exploring the *Monohansett's* main wreckage and debris field, over and over and over again. PHOTO BY CRIS KOHL

14. *NEW ORLEANS* (1)

> **LORAN: 30836.2/48673.1** **GPS: 45° 82.469'/083° 14.240'**
> **DEPTH: 15 feet** **LEVEL: Novice**

LOCATION: This wreck lies between North Point and Sugar Island.

The 610-ton wooden, passenger and freight sidewheel steamer, *New Orleans,* ran aground in a dense fog on June 11, 1849, and became a total loss. All of the ship's crew and passengers, however, survived and used a small boat to reach Thunder Bay Island, where the hospitable lighthouse keeper took care of them until they could be transported to the mainland. The *New Orleans,* the oldest shipwreck in the area, was built in Detroit in 1844.

This wreck lies broken and scattered over a wide area.

15. LIMESTONE WALLS

> **DEPTH: 20 to 70 feet** **LEVEL: Dependent upon depth**

Off the southeast shore of Thunder Bay Island, a limestone wall drops to a depth of about 70', with a variety of shipwreck artifacts scattered around the bottom of the wall.

16. *MAID OF THE MIST*

> **LORAN:** **GPS: 45° 06.917'/083° 19.021'**
> **DEPTH: 6 feet** **LEVEL: Novice**

LOCATION: This wreck lies two miles northeast of Thunder Bay Island.

The small, 110-ton, two-masted schooner, *Maid of the Mist*, built at St. Clair, MI, in 1863, was loading cedar posts on South Nine Mile Point when a storm arose. The ship was scuttled in order to save it, but it was destroyed. It lies nearly flattened to the bottom.

17. ROCKPORT CRIBBING

Cribbing, the base of old docks, supports much fish life at Rockport, north of Alpena.

Great Lakes Highlight No. 12

THE *PEWABIC*:
LAKE HURON'S DEATH SHIP

LORAN: 30795.6/48723.3   **GPS: 44° 57.920'   083° 06.158'**
DEPTH: 148 to 168 feet   **LEVEL: Technical**

In one of the worst maritime accidents on the Great Lakes, the wooden passenger and freight steamer, *Pewabic* (200'3" x 31'1" x 12'5"), sank in a collision with her sister ship, the *Meteor,* on August 9, 1865, resulting in approximately 90 lives from the *Pewabic* being lost. The *Pewabic,* launched in September, 1863, at Cleveland, carried a valuable cargo of copper ingots, and several hardhat divers died during

The only known photograph of the tragic steamer, *Pewabic*. REV. PETER VAN DER LINDEN COLLECTION

salvage attempts in subsequent years. For the record, these copper ingots were embossed on three sections: the first had the initials of one of the four particular copper mines it came from ["PW" stood for the Pewabic (Mining Company); "F", for the Franklin (Mining Company); "H", for the Hancock (Mining Company); and "Q", for the Quincy (Mining Company)]; the second section read "LST" for Lake Superior Transit; the third read "MC" for "Mining Company."

The wreck is deep and generally intact, although the upper works were removed long ago by a succession of salvagers. A *Pewabic* anchor sits outside the local museum in Alpena. This very real shipwreck has reached the status of "legend."

Clockwise from immediate left: The *Pewabic's* valuable, embossed, copper cargo ingots ignited many treasure expeditions. PHOTO BY CRIS KOHL. People died in this diving bell. Tons of ingots were recovered. Tough Margaret Goodman went *Pewabic* treasure hunting. CRIS KOHL COLLECTION. This dark wreck today displays its engine and small artifacts. PHOTOS BY JIM & PAT STAYER. Modern divers recovered silverware. PHOTO BY CRIS KOHL

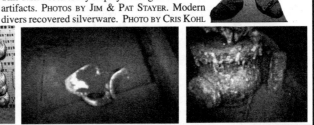

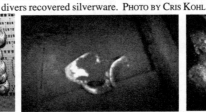

18. PORTSMOUTH

> **LORAN: 30847.6/48588.2** **GPS: 45° 11.87′/083° 20.03′**
> **DEPTH: 15 feet** **LEVEL: Novice**

Portsmouth. CRIS KOHL COLLECTION

LOCATION: This wreck lies off the west side of Middle Island.

The wooden package freighter, *Portsmouth* (176′ x 29′ x 11′), built at Buffalo, New York, in 1853, tried to ride out a storm while at anchor on November 10, 1867, but the anchors dragged and the ship stranded on Middle Island, where she caught fire and burned before breaking up. Her cargo was pig iron. The scattered wreckage is home to many fish.

19. LIMESTONE FORMATIONS

> **DEPTH: 20 to 70 feet** **LEVEL: Dependent upon depth**

A limestone wall and interesting formations, including room-like spaces created by springs, can be found off Middle Island.

20. NEW ORLEANS (2)

> **LORAN: 30808.0/48613.7** **GPS: 45° 10.06′/083° 12.85′**
> **DEPTH: 115 to 147 feet** **LEVEL: Advanced-Technical**

LOCATION: This wreck lies about 4 miles east-southeast of Middle Island, and about 10 miles north of the Thunder Bay Island Lighthouse.

The wooden steamer, *New Orleans* (231′8″ x 38′ x 13′6″), built at Marine City, Michigan, in 1885, sank with a cargo of coal after a collision with the much larger steel freighter, *William R. Linn*, on June 30, 1906. No lives were lost. The middle part of this generally intact steamer is broken up and split at the coal bunker. The bow lies in the shallower part, with the stern deepest.

Left: The *New Orleans.* CRIS KOHL COLLECTION. *Right:* The forward-most mast and rail on the *New Orleans.* PHOTO BY CRIS KOHL

21. NORDMEER -- SEE PAGES 332-333

22. *D. R. Hanna*

> **LORAN: 30771.47/48666.73**   **GPS: 45° 05.0316'/083° 05.2035'**
> **DEPTH: 97 to 138 feet**   **LEVEL: Advanced-Technical**

The *D. R. Hanna.*
CRIS KOHL COLLECTION

LOCATION: This site is about 6.5 miles northeast of Thunder Bay Island Lighthouse.

The steel freighter, *D. R. Hanna* (532' x 56' x 31'), launched in 1906 at Lorain, Ohio, sank with a wheat cargo in a dense fog after a collision with the steamer, *Quincy A. Shaw,* on May 16, 1919. All 32 on board survived. A hardhat diver located the wreck five months after she sank, but because she lies upside-down at that depth, salvage was not attempted. The wreck is penetrable, but only well-trained divers should attempt this.

23. *D. M. Wilson*

> **LORAN:**   **GPS:**
> **DEPTH: 45 feet**   **LEVEL: Intermediate**

LOCATION: This wreck lies two miles north-northeast of Thunder Bay Island.

Launched on May 24, 1873, at St. Clair, Michigan, the wooden steamer, *D. M. Wilson* (179'1" x 32'7" x 12'2"), sprang a leak on Oct. 27, 1894, and sank. Her crew was rescued by the *Sylvanus J. Macy.* The decking is gone, but the hull and many artifacts are present.

24. *O. E. Parks*

> **LORAN: 30809.5/48674.3**   **GPS:**
> **DEPTH: 45 feet**   **LEVEL: Intermediate**

LOCATION: This wreck lies west of Thunder Bay Island.

Built at Saugatuck, Michigan, in 1891, the 392-ton, wooden steamer, *O. E. Parks* (134'4" x 27'7" x 11'), grounded with a cargo of pulpwood on a reef four miles west of Thunder Bay Island during a storm on May 3, 1929, and was totally destroyed. No lives were lost. This is one of the many wrecks found by Stan Stock in this area.

Left: The wooden steamer, *O. E. Parks.* CRIS KOHL COLLECTION

25. *Lucinda Van Valkenburg*

> **LORAN: 30807.50/48672.85**   **GPS: 45° 03.3907'/083° 10.2208'**
> **DEPTH: 65 to 72 feet**   **LEVEL: Advanced**

LOCATION: This wreck is located two miles northeast of Thunder Bay Island.

The schooner, *Lucinda Van Valkenburg* (137'8" x 26'3" x 12'8"), built at Tonawanda, NY, in 1862, was run down by the steamer, *Lehigh,* in the fog on June 1, 1887, with no lives lost. This wreck, found by Stan Stock in 1981, is partially intact. The decks are collapsed, but the centerboard and trunk remain upright. The coal cargo was partially salvaged.

26. *W. P. Thew*

> **LORAN: 30802.7/48769.6**   **GPS: 45° 02.6097'/083° 09.0399'**
> **DEPTH: 76 to 86 feet**   **LEVEL: Advanced**

LOCATION: This wreck lies 1.8 miles east of the Thunder Bay Island Lighthouse.

The small, wooden steamer, *W. P. Thew* (132'5" x 24'2" x 8'3"), named after William

Great Lakes Highlight No. 13

SALTWATER VISITORS

Ocean-going vessels have been visiting the Great Lakes at least since the year 1857 -- when the British *Madeira Pet* made its famous trip to Chicago. Some of the pre-Seaway ocean ships which became permanent denizens of the underwater Great Lakes include the German World War I U-boat, the *UC-97*; the Australian convict ship, the *Success*; and the regular Dutch visitor to Milwaukee, the *Prins Willem V*.

Many ocean ships regularly entered the inland seas prior to the construction of the St. Lawrence Seaway in the late 1950's, but that engineering feat opened the floodgates to world trade. Yet only three ocean ships fell victim to the Great Lakes as shipwreck victims since then: the *Monrovia* in 1959, the *Francisco Morazan* in 1960, and the *Nordmeer* in 1966.

Surprisingly, three ocean ships lie sunk off Alpena's Thunder Bay:

NORDMEER

LORAN: 30790.7/48634.7	GPS: 45° 08.07'/083° 09.35'
DEPTH: To 40 feet	LEVEL: Novice

LOCATION: This better-known wreck lies 7 miles northeast of Thunder Bay Island.

The steel ocean-going freighter, *Nordmeer* (470'8" x 60'9" x 28'2"), which means "North Sea" in German, stranded during a clear, calm night on Thunder Bay Island Shoals with a cargo of steel coils on November 19, 1966. Somebody wasn't paying attention. The crew of 43 was removed in two shifts several days apart once it became apparent that the Great Lakes' gales of November were going to claim this ship, which had been built at Flensburg, Germany, in 1954. Only a very small portion of this once mighty ship remains above water, and the engine room and other below deck areas are now collapsed and impenetrable. But the fascination of exploring this site lies in the fact that around every corner there appears a new scene of immense wreckage to explore. This was a big ship, and it covers a lot of bottomlands. Fortunately, it's shallow. A wooden storm-sunk salvage barge lies on the *Nordmeer's* port side.

The German *Nordmeer*.
CRIS KOHL COLLECTION

Left: In 1986, 20 years after her stranding, much of the *Nordmeer's* superstructure remained above water. *Right:* Diver Roy Pickering explored the *Nordmeer's* intact engine room. PHOTOS BY CRIS KOHL

Left: By the early 2000's, only a small portion of the *Nordmeer's* hull remained above water. *Right:* Diver Joan Forsberg swims between broken sheets of steel hull at the *Nordmeer* site.
PHOTOS BY CRIS KOHL

VIATOR

LORAN: 30766.4/48715.6	GPS: 44° 59.488'/083° 02.256'
DEPTH: 175 feet	LEVEL: Technical

Built at Bodo, Norway in 1904, the 231'-long, 619-ton steel freighter, *Viator,* sank in the fog after a collision with the freighter, *Ormidale,* on October 31, 1935. No lives were lost, but her cargo of sardines went to the bottom (she also carried pickled herring and cod liver oil). Kent Bellrichard found the wreck in late 1975.

MONROVIA

LORAN: 30723.83/48729.52	GPS: 44° 59.0014'/082° 55.4029'
DEPTH: 90 to 150 feet	LEVEL: Advanced-Technical

LOCATION: This wreck lies about 13 miles southeast of Thunder Bay Island.

The steel, 6,674-ton, ocean-going freighter, *Monrovia* (447'7" x 56'2" x 26'3"), built in Scotland in 1943, owned in Liverpool, England, sailing under Liberian registry and bound for Chicago with a Greek crew and a cargo of steel from Belgium (talk about a festival of nations!), sank in U.S. waters after a collision in thick fog with the Canadian freighter, *Royalton,* on June 25, 1959. It was the *Monrovia's* first (and last!) trip to the Great Lakes. As water gushed into her gashed port side, the 29 crew were rescued by the freighter, *Norman W. Foy* (thanks to its radar); most of the steel cargo was subsequently salvaged using dynamite. The *Royalton's* captain testified that the *Monrovia* "struck us on the bow," but he forgot to mention *Monrovia* "struck" with her port side (kind of like getting punched in the fist by somebody's face). The inquiry found both captains responsible. This wreck, long popular among experienced divers, sits upright mostly intact, with her superstructure, hull and cargo holds. Considerable

The Liberian *Monrovia.*
CRIS KOHL COLLECTION

machinery remains on deck. Penetration is possible, but tricky, and has proven fatal here.

Joan Forsberg explores the wreck of the *Monrovia.*
Left: The deck debris.
Right: Inside a cabin.
PHOTOS BY CRIS KOHL

Left: The *W. P. Thew.* CRIS KOHL COLLECTION. *Above and right:* Diver Roy Pickering interacts with the *Thew's* wreckage and fish life. PHOTOS BY CRIS KOHL

Plymouth Thew by his son, Richard, who had the ship built at Lorain, Ohio, in 1884, sank after a collision (again in thick fog) with the steamer, *William Livingston*, on June 22, 1909. The *W.P. Thew* carried no cargo and lost no lives. The wreck's boilers and engine remain upright, with considerable hull still in place and an anchor with chain near the bow.

27. E. B. ALLEN

LORAN: 30811.6/48693.1	GPS: 45° 00.88'/083° 09.81'
DEPTH: 92 to 106 feet	LEVEL: Advanced

LOCATION: This wreck lies 2.5 miles southeast of Thunder Bay Island.

The 111'-long schooner, *E. B. Allen*, sank on Nov. 18, 1871, after colliding with the bark, *Newsboy*, in thick fog common to this area. No lives were lost. The 275-ton *Allen* was built in 1864 at Ogdensburg, NY, and was sailing from Chicago to Buffalo with a grain cargo at the time of loss. This shipwreck has her windlass, anchor chains and rudder in place.

28. PEWABIC -- SEE PAGE 329.

29. ISAAC M. SCOTT

LORAN: 30758.3/48686.8	GPS: 45° 02.98'/083° 02.20'
DEPTH: 180 feet	LEVEL: Technical

The steel freighter, *Isaac M. Scott* (504" x 54' x 30'), built at Lorain, Ohio, in 1909 and another of the victims lost with all hands (28) in the Great Storm of November 9-11, 1913, lies upside-down about 11 miles east of Thunder Bay Island Lighthouse. This wreck was located by Kent Bellrichard's team in September, 1975, while searching for the *Viator* (which is site #30 on this page).

The *Isaac M. Scott.*
CRIS KOHL COLLECTION

30. VIATOR -- SEE PAGE 333.

31. MONROVIA -- SEE PAGE 333.

32. KYLE SPANGLER

The schooner, *Kyle Spangler* (130'7" x 26'1" x 11'1"), built at Black River (now Lorain), OH, in 1856, sank after colliding with the schooner, *Racine*, on November 7, 1860. Found by Stan Stock on July 30, 2003, the cabin is intact, and the masts are upright with crowsnests.

33. W. H. GILBERT   LORAN: 30765.8/48795.0

Built at West Bay City, Michigan, in 1892, the steel steamer, *W. H. Gilbert* (328' x 42'5" x 20'5"), carrying a cargo of coal, sank after a collision with the *Caldera* on May 22, 1914; no lives were lost. She lies in 225' of water 17.7 miles off Thunder Bay Island.

27. Northwestern Lake Huron

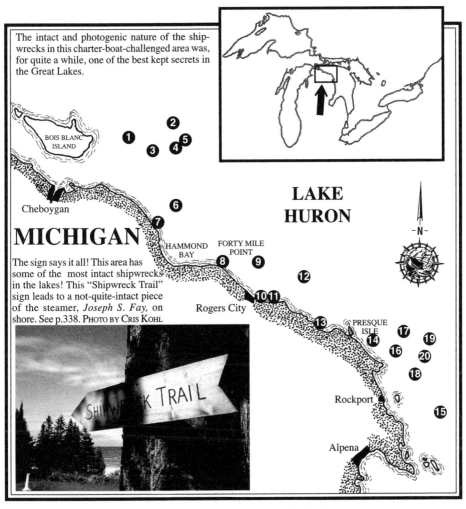

The intact and photogenic nature of the shipwrecks in this charter-boat-challenged area was, for quite a while, one of the best kept secrets in the Great Lakes.

BOIS BLANC ISLAND

Cheboygan

MICHIGAN

HAMMOND BAY

FORTY MILE POINT

The sign says it all! This area has some of the most intact shipwrecks in the lakes! This "Shipwreck Trail" sign leads to a not-quite-intact piece of the steamer, *Joseph S. Fay*, on shore. See p.338. Photo by Cris Kohl

Rogers City

LAKE HURON

-N-

PRESQUE ISLE

Rockport

Alpena

1. *Newell A. Eddy*
2. *Nightingale*
3. *Robert Burns*
4. *James R. Bentley*
5. *Persian* (?)
6. *Henry J. Johnson*
7. *John Jewett* (?)
8. *Joseph S. Fay*
9. *F. T. Barney*
10. *Duncan City*
11. *W. G. Mason*
12. *Northwestern*
13. *American Union*
14. *Malabar*
15. *Defiance*
16. *John J. Audubon*
17. *Cornelia B. Windiate*
18. *Typo*
19. *Norman*
20. *Florida*

1. NEWELL A. EDDY

LORAN: 31067.0/48194.8	GPS: 45° 46.880'/084° 13.825'
DEPTH: 145 to 168 feet	LEVEL: Technical

LOCATION: This wreck lies to the east of Bois Blanc Island.

The three-masted schooner-barge, *Newell A. Eddy* (242' x 40' x 16'), built at West Bay City, Michigan, in 1890, foundered in a storm with a cargo of grain and all nine hands near Spectacle Reef on April 20, 1893, while in tow of the steamer, *Charles A. Eddy,* bound from Chicago for Buffalo. Widely reported as "The Great Gale," this was the worst spring storm in recorded Great Lakes history, with at least 15 vessels wrecked or stranded. Three days later, the passing steamer, *G.W. Morley,* passed the *Eddy's* quarter deck and cabin. The relatively new *Newell A. Eddy* was valued at the time of loss at an immense $105,000, and carried insurance for $95,000. The *Newell A. Eddy* was accidentally located on July 25, 1992 by the University of Michigan scientific research vessel, *Laurentian,* while demonstrating sidescan sonar to students. The wreck's masts are still standing and rise to within 80' of the surface (sometimes a line and buoy are tied to one of these masts). While the stern section is broken or absent, the bow is upright and virtually intact, with capstans, bow nameplates, an eagle figurehead and bow machinery in place.

2. NIGHTINGALE

LORAN: 31037.6/48211.3	GPS:
DEPTH: 45 to 70 feet	LEVEL: Intermediate-Advanced

LOCATION: This wreck lies off Spectacle Reef.

The 138', 272-ton, two-masted schooner, *Nightingale,* built at Conneaut, Ohio, in 1856, stranded and sank on September 18, 1869, with no lives lost. She was carrying a cargo of iron ore at the time. This shipping loss was cited for justifying the construction of the Spectacle Reef Lighthouse, and much of this wreckage was removed in 1872 when the lighthouse was being built. What remains of this shipwreck was reportedly found by John Steele.

3. ROBERT BURNS

LORAN: 31151.56/48207.67	GPS: 45° 42.08'/084° 26.35'
DEPTH: 65 feet	LEVEL: Advanced

LOCATION: This wreck lies east-northeast of Cheboygan, Michigan.

Built at Port Huron, Michigan, in 1848, the 307-gross-ton, two-masted brig, *Robert Burns,* (121'2" x 25'7" x 10'4") foundered with all ten hands and a cargo of grain on November 17, 1869. She was raised and quickly lost again. The claim that she was the last full-rigged brig on the inland seas is doubtful. The wreck is broken up, but some equipment remains.

4. JAMES R. BENTLEY

LORAN: 31057.7/48251.1	GPS: 45° 41.317'/084° 09.315'
DEPTH: 165 feet	LEVEL: Technical

LOCATION: This wreck lies east of Bois Blanc Island and north of Hammond Bay.

Discovered by John Steele in 1984, the three-masted schooner, *James R. Bentley* (178'5" x 34' x 13'4"), built at Fairport, Ohio, in 1867, foundered in a storm on Nov. 12, 1878, no lives lost. The mizzenmast is upright; the other masts have toppled. The stunningly unique dragon figurehead remains on display in a Wisconsin museum; Michigan law enforcers decid-

The dramatic dragon figurehead: safe in a museum. PHOTO BY CRIS KOHL ed to make an example of the diver who recovered that figurehead from Michigan waters and donated it to a Wisconsin museum. In a unique but costly legal turnaround based on the interpretation of the law's wording, this diver was granted ownership of this shipwreck by the court!

5. PERSIAN (?)

LORAN: 31055.0/48246.0	GPS: 45° 41.949'/084° 09.161'
DEPTH: 159 to 172 feet	LEVEL: Technical

LOCATION: This wreck lies north of Hammond Bay.

All ten men on board the wheat-laden, 128' schooner, *Persian*, lost their lives when the ship sank after a collision with the schooner, *E. B. Allen* (which is also in this book) on September 16, 1868. The *Persian* was built in 1855 at Oswego, New York. Some recent identification doubts have been cast. The wreck sits upright and is very intact.

6. HENRY J. JOHNSON

LORAN: 31050.0/48285.3	GPS: 45° 38.043'/084° 06.260'
DEPTH: 160 feet	LEVEL: Technical

LOCATION: This wreck lies north of Hammond Bay.

The wooden steamer, *Henry J. Johnson* (260' x 40'2" x 19'6"), built at Cleveland in 1888, collided in dense fog with the steamer, *Fred Pabst,* on July 24, 1902. The *Henry J. Johnson* was downbound from Escanaba, Michigan, with a cargo of iron ore. No lives were lost. The wreck sits upright and intact in deep water.

The *Henry J. Johnson.* CRIS KOHL COLLECTION

7. JOHN JEWETT (?)

LOCATION: This wreck lies in 10′ to 12′ of water 3/4 miles south of the Hammond Bay Refuge Harbor entrance road, 500′ off **LAT 45° 34.85′ LON 084° 09.01′** on shore.

This unidentified vessel may be the schooner, *John Jewett*, (92′ x 21′ x 8′), built in 1866 at Vermilion, Ohio, and stranded with no lives lost on October 18, 1898.

8. JOSEPH S. FAY

LORAN: 31007.3/48381.6	GPS:
DEPTH: 15 feet	LEVEL: Novice

LOCATION: Off Forty Mile Point Lighthouse, six miles north of Rogers City.

Launched at Cleveland in 1871, the wooden bulk freight steamer, *Joseph S. Fay* (215′6″ x 33′6″ x 14′8″), foundered in the infamous October 20, 1905

The wooden steamer, *Joseph S. Fay.*
PHOTO BY CRIS KOHL

The steamer, *Joseph S. Fay.*
CRIS KOHL COLLECTION

storm which also sank the *Tasmania*, the *Siberia* and the *Sarah E. Sheldon* (which are all in this book). The *Joseph S. Fay* was transporting a cargo of iron ore towards Ashtabula, Ohio, when she began to leak and was beached to avoid sinking in deep water. But instead of being recoverable later, the ship was destroyed by the pounding waves. These shipwreck remains lie about 800′ off shore. It's a long swim with occasional current. Use a boat. The broken up wreck, which is visible from the surface, is home to a wide variety of freshwater fish: perch, suckers, burbots....

9. F. T. BARNEY

LORAN: 30984.45/48391.22	GPS: 45° 29.1389′/083° 50.5631′
DEPTH: 160 feet	LEVEL: Technical

LOCATION: This wreck lies north of Rogers City, Michigan.

The two-masted, coal-carrying schooner, *F. T. Barney* (130′6″ x 25′ x 11′), sank in a collision with the schooner, *Tracy J. Bronson,* on Oct. 23, 1868. Built in Vermilion, Ohio, in 1856, this vessel, identified by Stan Stock in 1989, displays a mast with a crowsnest!

The *F. T. Barney* features many items of interest to visiting divers, among them, the ship's wheel, of course, and a lantern on the lake floor off the starboard side, both examined here by Nathan Kroll.   PHOTOS BY CRIS KOHL

Great Lakes Highlight No. 14

THE *CORNELIA B. WINDIATE'S* STRANGE DISAPPEARANCE

LORAN: 30824.6/48525.3	GPS: 45° 19.566'/083° 19.622'
DEPTH: 165 to 185 feet	LEVEL: Technical

This schooner closely resembled the *Cornelia B. Windiate*.   PATRICK LABADIE COLLECTION

LOCATION: In northwestern Lake Huron, off Presque Isle, Michigan.

Found when Paul Ehorn was at the helm of colleague John Steele's boat the same morning in May, 1986, that they had found the *Norman* nearby, the three-masted schooner, *Cornelia B. Windiate* (138'6" x 26'2" x 11'6"), built at Manitowoc, Wisconsin, in 1874, disappeared with all hands after leaving Milwaukee for Buffalo with a cargo of wheat on November 28, 1875. She sits upright and immaculately intact in 185' of water, making this a technical dive.

What was strange about the *Windiate's* disappearance was how total it was. No bodies were recovered, and not so much as even a single board was found anywhere, so even a rough guess as to where the ship sank would have been just a wild guess. Some old sailors argued that the *Windiate* went down somewhere off

Diver Jim Stayer videotapes his descent along the *Windiate's* upright forward mast before reaching the deck and heading for the stern. PHOTOS BY CRIS KOHL

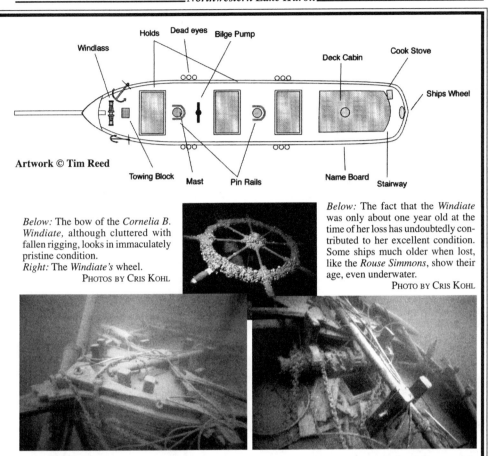

Holds Dead eyes Bilge Pump

Windlass

Deck Cabin Cook Stove

Ships Wheel

Artwork © Tim Reed

Towing Block Mast Pin Rails Name Board Stairway

Below: The bow of the *Cornelia B. Windiate,* although cluttered with fallen rigging, looks in immaculately pristine condition.
Right: The *Windiate's* wheel.
PHOTOS BY CRIS KOHL

Below: The fact that the *Windiate* was only about one year old at the time of her loss has undoubtedly contributed to her excellent condition. Some ships much older when lost, like the *Rouse Simmons*, show their age, even underwater.
PHOTO BY CRIS KOHL

the Fox Islands in Lake Michigan, because no one in the towns of St. Ignace and Mackinaw City had seen her pass through the Straits of Mackinac. But it wouldn't have been the first time that a ship made it through that narrow channel undetected....

Joyce Hayward of Ohio successfully led a team of divers through a difficult survey of this deep shipwreck in 2003.

For detailed information about the history and the discovery of the *Cornelia B. Windiate*, read the chapter entitled "...Unless Some Diver Discovers Her" in the book, *Shipwreck Tales of the Great Lakes,* by Cris Kohl.

These images further show the intact nature of the *Cornelia B. Windiate* shipwreck. *Left:* The ship's transom, with the yawl boat lying off one side. *Right:* A rarity: an intact stern cabin.   PHOTOS BY JOHN VEBER

10. DUNCAN CITY

Built in 1883 at Manitowoc, Wisconsin, the tug, *Duncan City* (77'5" x 19'8" x 9'2"), abandoned since 1926, lies in 15' two miles west of Adams Pt. **LORAN: 30968.2/48436.5**

11. W. G. MASON LORAN: 30963.1/48439.2 GPS: 45° 24.62'/083° 19.61'

Built in 1898 at Port Huron, MI, the tug, *W. G. Mason* (84' x 20'5" x 10'5"), was scuttled in 17'-22' of water in Swan Bay near Calcite, MI, in 1923. Prop and rudder are highlights.

12. NORTHWESTERN

LORAN:	GPS: 45° 26.940'/083° 41.671'
DEPTH: 129 to 135 feet	LEVEL: Advanced-Technical

Once thought to be the schooner, *Perseverance*, this shipwreck is more likely the 217-ton schooner *Northwestern* (114'9" x 23'2" x 8'3"), built in the 1840's and sunk in a collision with the wooden steamer, *Monticello*, on September 30, 1850. The schooner, bound from Oswego to Chicago with a cargo of salt, sank quickly, but the steamer rescued the crew.

Left: The *Northwestern* resembled this vessel, the *Robert Howlett*. CRIS KOHL COLLECTION

Left: This older bow design helps determine when the ship was built. *Right:* The *Northwestern* was blessed with numerous crocks and jugs, all of which were stolen by a diver in 2005.
PHOTOS BY CRIS KOHL

13. AMERICAN UNION

The huge, 543-ton schooner (185' x 25' x 13'), built at Cleveland in 1862, stranded in a storm on May 6, 1894, at Thompsons Harbor. It lies in 12' to 14'. **LORAN: 30915.4/48483.2**

14. MALABAR

The *Malabar*, a yacht reputedly once owned by President Coolidge, burned in the 1980's and lies in 129', rising 6' off the bottom. **GPS: 45° 18.849'/083° 24.381'**

15. DEFIANCE

LORAN:	GPS: 45° 14.060'/083° 16.710'
DEPTH: 186 feet	LEVEL: Technical

The two-masted schooner, *Defiance* (115'8" x 26'2" x 10'3"), built at Perrysburg, Ohio, in 1848, sank with a cargo of wheat after a collision with the brig, *John J. Audubon* (see site #16), on October 20, 1854. No lives were lost. This wreck was located by divers in 1996.

16. JOHN J. AUDUBON

LORAN:	GPS: 45° 17.348'/083° 20.381'
DEPTH: 178 feet	LEVEL: Technical

LOCATION: This technical dive site lies in deep (178′) water north of Presque Ile.

Built in 1854 at Cleveland, the 370-ton, two-masted brig, *John J. Audubon,* sank later that same year. On the night of October 20, 1854, the schooner, *Defiance,* struck her amidship, and both vessels sank. Found by Stan Stock, the *Audubon* sits upright and is intact.

The magnificent wreck of the *John J. Audubon.* PHOTO BY JOHN VEBER

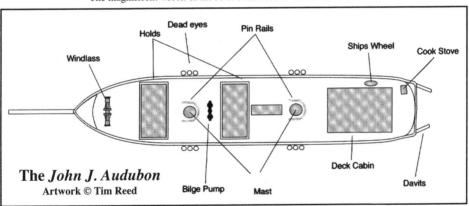

Windlass
Holds
Dead eyes
Pin Rails
Ships Wheel
Cook Stove

The *John J. Audubon*
Artwork © Tim Reed

Bilge Pump   Mast

Deck Cabin

Davits

Left: The *John J. Audubon* bow was steered by means of a tiller instead of a ship's wheel. *Right:* The ship's artistic lines can be readily seen at the transom. DIGITAL IMAGES BY DAN LINDSAY OF SEA-VIEW DIVING (SEE PAGE 156 FOR THE AD)

17. *CORNELIA B. WINDIATE* -- SEE PAGES **340-341.**

18. TYPO

> **LORAN: 30825.7/48543.4**   **GPS: 45° 17.497′/083° 18.964′**
> **DEPTH: 180 feet**   **LEVEL: Technical**

The three-masted schooner, *Typo* (137′8″ x 26′2″ x 11′3″), built at Milwaukee in 1873, sank six miles east-southeast of Presque Isle Light after a collision with the steamer, *W. P. Ketcham,* on October 14, 1899. Four lives were lost. The wreck lies masts up and stern broken in 170′ of water, making this a technical dive site. **LORAN: 30825.7/48543.4**

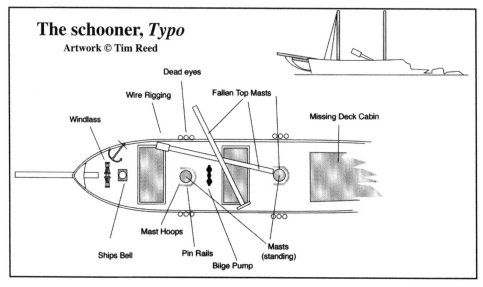

The schooner, *Typo*
Artwork © Tim Reed

Dead eyes
Wire Rigging
Fallen Top Masts
Windlass
Missing Deck Cabin
Mast Hoops
Ships Bell
Pin Rails
Masts (standing)
Bilge Pump

19. NORMAN

> **LORAN: 30809.2/48537.3**   **GPS: 45° 18.668′/083° 16.735′**
> **DEPTH: 210 feet**   **LEVEL: Technical**

The *Norman.* CRIS KOHL COLLECTION

Found by John Steele and Paul Ehorn the same morning in May, 1986, that they found the *Cornelia B. Windiate* nearby, the steel steamer, *Norman* (296′5″ x 40′4″ x 24′), traveling light, sank within three minutes after a collision in thick fog with the Canadian steamer, *Jack,* on May 30, 1895, with the loss of three lives. The little steamer, *M. Sicken,* rescued the rest of the crew, and the *Jack* was kept afloat only by her lumber cargo! The *Norman* was launched at Cleveland on August 30, 1890, and sits intact on a 45-degree list in 210′ of water.

20. FLORIDA

> **LORAN: 30813.0/48544.1**   **GPS: 45° 17.781′/083° 17.002′**
> **DEPTH: 195 feet**   **LEVEL: Technical**

The wooden steamer, *Florida* (270′3″ x 40′2″ x 15′4″), built at Buffalo in 1889, sank with a cargo of grain and general merchandise in 12 minutes after she was struck in a dense fog by the steamer, *George W. Roby,* on May 20, 1897. No lives were lost. This wreck, located in 1994, is upright and amazingly intact.

28. Sites near Lake Huron

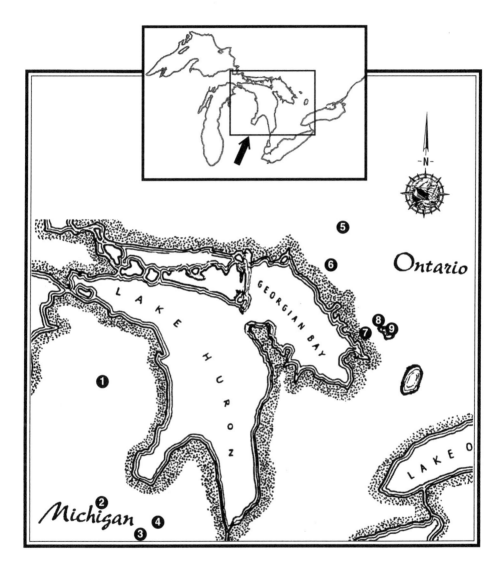

1. Higgins Lake
2. Brockway Lake
3. Orchard Lake
4. Stony Lake
5. *John Fraser*
6. Kawigamog Lake
7. Bala Falls/Moon River
8. *Nipissing*
9. *Waome*

1. HIGGINS LAKE

LOCATION: Ten miles south of Grayling, MI, just east of the I 75/US 27 intersection.

This enormous lake, comprising almost 10,000 acres of surface space, reaches depths up to 135' in the lake's northwest corner, but most of the many scuba divers that enjoy this lake stay considerably shallower. This lake features a couple of "sunken islands" where vast numbers of fish congregate. Two state parks with boat launching ramps, as well as one independent launching facility, line the lake. There are several picnic/public access areas from where divers can do shore dives to explore the lake.The lake's visibility is exceptional, upwards of 50' on occasion. Sunken logs, boats and ice fishing shelters lie on the bottom.

The main dive areas of Higgins Lake are:

1. Michigan Central Park in the northwest corner of the lake. Features include two fish habitats in 20' of water, a dive platform with a plexiglass bubble, and a cabin cruiser in 45' of water.

2. North State Park at the northern tip of the lake. A shore dive can be done from the first road east of the park entrance. A dive tower is located in 30' of water straight out from the road. A large fish habitat can be found in 25' of water just east of the tower in front of the conservation school.

3. A "sunken island" in the middle of the northwest portion of the lake. This is a boat dive to a depth of about 30'. The "island" is comprised of a large rock pile which includes expansion joints from the nearby expressway (a great fish habitat).

4. Shore dives from East Street (features several weed beds) and West Street (weed beds plus sunken pine trees).

5. Point Detroit in the middle of the lake is a boat dive to weed beds which feature abrupt drop-offs on both sides. Lots of fish.

6. Flag Point is a boat dive (no shore access) featuring huge weed beds and an abrupt drop-off to 80'. Weeds are anywhere from 5' to 20' down, and include lots of fish.

7. Another "sunken island" at the south end of the lake is a boat dive. The island is from ankle deep on the west side to about 10' down on the east side, with abrupt drop-offs on both sides.

8. West shore drop-off, in the southernmost part of the lake, for both shore and boat dives, features several fish habitats along this drop-off.

2. BROCKWAY LAKE

LOCATION: Take US 131 to the Jefferson Road (Morley) exit, go east about 10 miles to 100th Avenue, and turn left (north). At the first road, which is Three Mile Road, turn right. Signs indicate the way to public access. A boat is not necessary.

Brockway Lake is a 14-acre body of water with a maximum depth of 30'. It is wonderful for either scuba diving or snorkeling. The "marl" was excavated from the sides of the lake, so there are walls up to 25' tall at the water's edge. Considerable aquatic life, such as bass, northern pike, perch, bluegills and sunfish, can be found around the many sunken logs. A shallow underwater island rises in the middle of the lake.

3. ORCHARD LAKE

LOCATION: A few miles southwest of Pontiac, Michigan. The main entry point is on the west side of Orchard Lake Road approximately 100 yards north of Pontiac Lake Road. Signs indicate the way to public access. A boat is not necessary.

Orchard Lake is popular for ice diving, when the lake is free from crowds of boaters found there in the summer. Depths to about 25'. Considerable aquatic life can be found in this lake.

4. STONY LAKE

LOCATION: A few miles north of Pontiac, Michigan. Take M-24 north of Pontiac, go through the towns of Lake Orion and Oxford, and Stony Lake is one mile north of Oxford on the west side of the road. The Stony Lake Beach Club on the east side of the lake is a good meeting point. It charges a fee, but it also has toilets and a changing room on site. Numerous sunken attractions, like small boats, plus a wide variety of fish life, make this an interesting lake to explore.

5. JOHN FRASER

LOCATION: This wreck lies at a depth of 50′ just east of Goose Island in the center of Lake Nipissing in the northern Georgian Bay area of Ontario.

The oak-hulled steamer, *John Fraser,* built in 1888 at Sturgeon Falls on Lake Nipissing, was making its final run of the year across the lake on November 7, 1893. Seven crewmembers and 17 lumberjacks were aboard. In the middle of the lake, fire broke out near the boiler. Some people sought refuge in a scow which the *John Fraser* was towing, while others took to a lifeboat which overturned, drowning its occupants. Tragically, there were only 7 survivors from the 24 people on board. In 1972, the burned out hull was located, along with the steam engine, boiler and piping, by members of the North Bay Scuba Club. Often buoyed at the beginning of the year, this site suffers from poor visibility, and divers must use caution not to become entangled in the twisted pipes and rails.

6. KAWIGAMOG LAKE (LOST CHANNEL) -- SEE ALSO P. 348-349

LOCATION: This lake lies east of Highway 69 and just off road 522 down Lost Channel Road, halfway between Parry Sound and Sudbury, Ontario.

This is a shore dive for novice to intermediate divers, with a maximum depth of 16′. At the edge of this lake lie the remains of the steamer, *Douglas L.,* and two barges. Hundreds of people lived and worked in this thriving community called the Lost Channel in the early 1900's, but they, their descendants and most signs of their habitation are now gone. The *Douglas L.* was a small steamer, about 70′ in length, which carried goods and settlers to the more remote parts of Kawigamog Lake until approximately 1930 when the vessel was abandoned at this site. The barges were simple carriers towed behind a steamer. You can drive right up to this site, although the road is primitive. The low visibility in tea-colored water could be a problem for the inexperienced, but exploring the hull and boiler of the *Douglas L.,* with the many diver-friendly bass, is interesting.

See pages 348 and 349 for archival and other photographs, a map, and artwork of this ship-and-barges site.

7. BALA FALLS/MOON RIVER

A site for every level of diver experience is at Bala Falls on the Moon River, at the western side of Lake Muskoka, Ontario. With a depth from 22′ to 100′, and several levels of underwater cliffs, one can go deep or stay shallow. Many pieces of pottery and china have been located here. This site is adjacent to the Foodland grocery store in Bala. There is, of course, a current; stay within your level of experience. In Moon River below the waterfalls, the constant, cleansing current creates good visibility, as well as a variety of large game fish finding the base of the falls an ideal feeding spot.

8. NIPISSING

LOCATION: The wreck of the steamer, *Nipissing,* lies off Blueberry Island in the northern part of Lake Joseph, Ontario. Access is from a gravel road connected to Highway 69 just past Hamer Bay. A boat is needed to reach this novice site in 10′ to 23′ of water. The broken up steamer, *Nipissing,* which can be seen from the surface, abounds with fish life and is excellent for underwater photography. The rock and sand bottom prevents silting, so good visibility is almost always guaranteed. Beware of occasional boating traffic.

The LOST CHANNEL AREA
on Lake Kawigamog

("Kawigamog" in Ojibwa means "where the waters turn back")

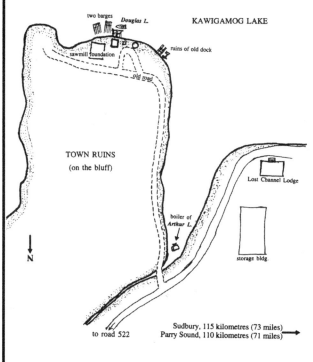

two barges   Douglas L.   KAWIGAMOG LAKE

sawmill foundation   ruins of old dock

old road

TOWN RUINS
(on the bluff)

Lost Channel Lodge

boiler of
Arthur L.

storage bldg.

N

to road 522

Sudbury, 115 kilometres (73 miles)
Parry Sound, 110 kilometres (71 miles)

Sketch by Cris Kohl (not to scale)

Above left: The sideroad to the Lost Channel is clearly marked along road 522. This is a seldom-visited area for scuba diving. *Above right:* Sean Moore tries hard to stay dry as he checks out the divesite of the *Douglas L.* and the two barges.

PHOTOS BY CRIS KOHL

Below left: The small steamer, *Arthur*, was less than 50′ in length, but it became vital for transporting people and goods along this water system.

CRIS KOHL COLLECTION

Below right: Only the boiler remains of the steamship *Arthur*; it lies in the shallows near the Lost Channel Lodge.

PHOTO BY CRIS KOHL

The *Douglas L.* and Barges

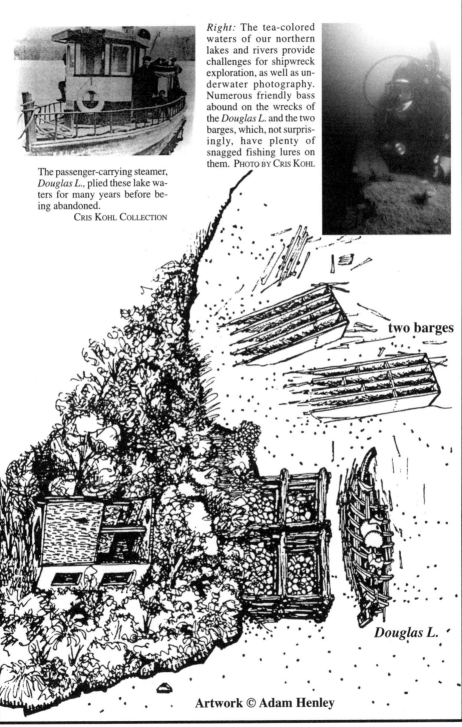

Right: The tea-colored waters of our northern lakes and rivers provide challenges for shipwreck exploration, as well as underwater photography. Numerous friendly bass abound on the wrecks of the *Douglas L.* and the two barges, which, not surprisingly, have plenty of snagged fishing lures on them. PHOTO BY CRIS KOHL

The passenger-carrying steamer, *Douglas L.,* plied these lake waters for many years before being abandoned.
CRIS KOHL COLLECTION

two barges

Douglas L.

Artwork © Adam Henley

9. WAOME

LOCATION: This shipwreck lies off the west side of Keewaydin Island in the northern part of Lake Muskoka near Milford Bay, Ontario.

The steamer, *Waome* (78' x 14'), launched as the *Mink* at Gravenhurst, Ontario, in 1912, received her name change on May 28, 1929. *Waome* (pronounced "Way-OH-mee") is an Ojibwa word meaning "water lily." On October 6, 1934, on her final run of the season (hasn't that so often been the case?), and carrying the

The steamship, *Waome,* sank on October 6, 1934, with the loss of three lives, and is a popular dive site today.
CRIS KOHL COLLECTION

captain, 5 crew, and a passenger (an old-fashioned minister who preferred to travel by ship rather than on the new bus line), the *Waome* headed towards Beaumaris. A sudden, powerful gust knocked the ship onto her port side and water gushed into her holds. Within a minute, the ship sank, taking with her a crewmember and the minister. The elderly captain died of a heart attack as he swam for his life on the surface, but the other four reached the island.

This very popular wreck sits upright and intact in 50' to 74' of dark, tea-colored water. Penetration diving is possible, but should be done only by trained, experienced divers.

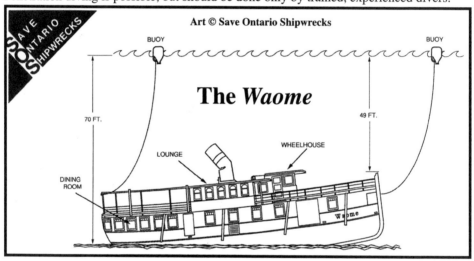

There is a popular wall dive on Lake Muskoka opposite the wreck of the *Waome*, specifically off the northwest side of Keewaydin Island. A boat is needed to reach this advanced site. The rock wall drops to about 80', while the rubble extends to approximately 115'. This wall dive displays nature in a powerful way. Don't drop anything at this site! Depth and low visibility can be problems. Keep an eye on your depth gauge and bottom time.

29. Straits of Mackinac

The Round Island Lighthouse, Straits of Mackinac. PHOTO BY CRIS KOHL

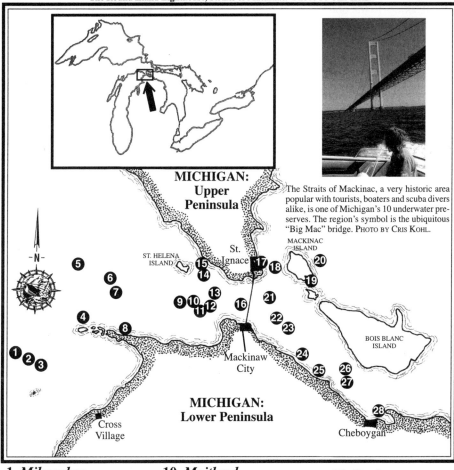

MICHIGAN: Upper Peninsula

The Straits of Mackinac, a very historic area popular with tourists, boaters and scuba divers alike, is one of Michigan's 10 underwater preserves. The region's symbol is the ubiquitous "Big Mac" bridge. PHOTO BY CRIS KOHL.

MACKINAC ISLAND

ST. HELENA ISLAND

St. Ignace

BOIS BLANC ISLAND

Mackinaw City

MICHIGAN: Lower Peninsula

Cross Village

Cheboygan

1. *Milwaukee*
2. *J. H. Tiffany*
3. *Cayuga*
4. *Canisteo*
5. *Richard Winslow*
6. *Uganda*
7. *Colonel Ellsworth*
8. *Anglo Saxon* and *J. A. Smith*
9. *Fred McBrier*

10. *Maitland*
11. *Northwest*
12. *Sandusky*
13. *Eber Ward*
14. Chuck's barge
15. *C. H. Johnson*
16. *Minneapolis*
17. St. Ignace harbor
18. Clam bucket barge
19. M. I. harbor wreck

20. Rock maze
21. *William Young*
22. *M. Stalker*
23. *Cedarville*
24. *Wm. H. Barnum*
25. *Albemarle*
26. *J. H. Outhwaite*
27. *St. Andrew*
28. *Leviathan*

1. MILWAUKEE

> **LORAN: 31407.2/48077.8   GPS: 45° 43.5740′/085° 14.8660′**
> **DEPTH: 97 feet   LEVEL: Advanced**

LOCATION: This pre-Civil War wreck lies 5.2 miles southwest of Grays Reef Light.

Built in 1853 at Cleveland, the 185′ wooden, wheat-laden steamer, *Milwaukee,* bound from Milwaukee to Buffalo, sank in a collision with the schooner, *J. H. Tiffany,* which also sank and lies nearby (see Site #2), on Nov. 29, 1859. No lives were lost from the *Milwaukee.*

This shipwreck sits upright but is not intact; only the starboard quarter portion of the hull still stands upright. The remainder of the wreck has collapsed outward, or, in the case of the decking, to the bottom of the hull. Salvage in the 1870's removed much equipment, but the propeller, windlass and fallen wheel are still there. The *J. H. Tiffany* is very close, with the *Cayuga* (Site #3) 2.8 miles from the *Milwaukee.*

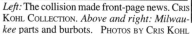

Left: The collision made front-page news. CRIS KOHL COLLECTION. *Above and right: Milwaukee* parts and burbots. PHOTOS BY CRIS KOHL

2. J. H. TIFFANY

> **LORAN: 31402.0/48081.7   GPS: 45° 43.352′/085° 12.678′**
> **DEPTH:103 feet   LEVEL: Advanced**

LOCATION: This pre-Civil War wreck lies 4.8 miles southwest of Grays Reef Light.

The 137′ schooner, *J. H. Tiffany,* built in 1856 at Cleveland, sank with the loss of five lives and a cargo of railroad iron after her collision with the steamer, *Milwaukee* (see Site #1) on November 29, 1859. Time and the 1870's salvage of her valuable cargo broke up and flattened the wreck of the *J. H. Tiffany.* The remains are basic and minimal.

Both collision shipwrecks (Sites #1 and #2) were located in modern times (1985) by scuba divers from Muskegon, Michigan, namely Brian Scott, Craig Scott, Dave Scott, George Manning and Bill Salsbury, and John Makuch from Detroit.

3. CAYUGA

> **LORAN: 31390.4/48089.8   GPS: 45° 43.2505′/085° 11.3958′**
> **DEPTH: 75 to 102 feet   LEVEL: Advanced**

LOCATION: This wreck lies 3.6 miles southwest of Grays Reef Light.

The steel freighter, *Cayuga,* (290′ x 40′8″ x 13′6″), launched on April 2, 1889 at Cleveland, sank in a collision with the steamer, *Joseph L. Hurd* on May 10,1895. One life was lost from the *Hurd,* which did not sink. Lengthy, costly salvage failed to raise the *Cayuga,* and instead cost one hardhat diver his life (Great Lakes lore has that diver still trapped beneath the small

The steel steamer, *Cayuga.* CRIS KOHL COLLECTION

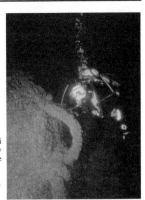

The *Cayuga*
and the sunken
salvage barge

Artwork © Chuck & Jeri Feltner (Drawing by Chuck Feltner & Dave Donovan)

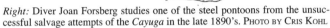

Right: Diver Joan Forsberg studies one of the steel pontoons from the unsuccessful salvage attempts of the *Cayuga* in the late 1890's. PHOTO BY CRIS KOHL

salvage barge next to the wreck). John Steele and Gene Turner of Illinois located the *Cayuga* in the spring of 1969. The wreck today is upright and quite intact, lying on an angle to portside, with salvage pontoons still strapped onto her sides and vast opportunities for trained and experienced divers to penetrate below deck.

4. CANISTEO

LORAN: 31341.9/48070.8	**GPS: 45° 47.32'/085° 04.75'**
DEPTH: 15 feet	**LEVEL: Novice**

LOCATION: This wreck lies 0.6 mile east of Waugoshance Light.

The 196' wooden steamer, *Canisteo,* not to be confused with the other wooden steamer, *Canisteo,* which lies in Lake Huron, was launched in 1862 at Buffalo and sank in a collision with the schooner, *George Murray,* on Oct. 14, 1880, with a cargo of corn and lard, but no lives lost. This wreck, located from the air in 1988 by Chuck and Jeri Feltner and Mike Kohut, was moved by the ice and wind over the years about half a mile east of the place where she originally sank. The machinery was salvaged, so only broken wood remains.

5. RICHARD WINSLOW

LORAN: 31356.4/48026.4	**GPS: 45° 50.45'/085° 09.48'**
DEPTH: 32 feet	**LEVEL: Novice**

LOCATION: This wreck lies 1.4 miles west of White Shoals Light.

The 216' schooner, *Richard Winslow*, built in 1871 at Detroit, foundered with an iron ore cargo and no lives lost on September 5, 1898. The wreck was dynamited to remove her as a hazard to navigation, so the wreckage lies scattered over a wide area.

6. UGANDA

> **LORAN: 31321.7/48047.2** **GPS: 45° 50.30'/085° 03.49'**
> **DEPTH: 185 to 207 feet** **LEVEL: Technical**

LOCATION: This wreck lies 4.3 miles due east of White Shoals Light.

Launched at West Bay City, Michigan, in 1892, the wooden steamer, *Uganda* (291' x 41' x 19'8"), was cut by ice on April 19, 1913, while carrying a cargo of corn from Milwaukee to Buffalo. No lives were lost in this sinking. Located by Chuck and Jeri Feltner and Stan Stock in 1983, the *Uganda's* depth and the strong current make her a difficult dive. She sits upright and intact, with her midship cabin the only one still in place. Engine, boiler, anchors and much more mechanical equipment remain at this site.

The *Uganda*.
CRIS KOHL COLLECTION

7. COLONEL ELLSWORTH

> **LORAN: 31317.2/48067.7** **GPS: 45° 48.6999'/085° 00.9900'**
> **DEPTH: 70 to 84 feet** **LEVEL: Advanced**

LOCATION: This wreck lies 6.2 miles east-southeast of White Shoals Light.

The schooner, *Colonel Ellsworth* (137'8" x 26' x 11'8"), built in 1861 at Euclid, Ohio, sank in a collision with the schooner, *Emily B. Maxwell,* on September 2, 1896. She carried no cargo and lost no lives. The *Maxwell* stayed afloat and in service for another 13 years before sinking in Lake Erie. The *Colonel Ellsworth,* located by Dick Race of Chicago in 1968, is upright, intact and penetrable, with much to see (windlass, mast, etc.) in spite of some salvage (e.g. her anchors) done shortly after she sank.

8. ANGLO SAXON AND J. A. SMITH

> **LORAN: 31309.63/48102.82.0** **GPS: 45° 45.24'/084° 57.25'**
> **DEPTH: 12 feet** **LEVEL: Novice**

LOCATION: These wrecks lie 12.3 miles east of Old Mackinac Point.

Two towed ships, the 134' schooner, *Anglo Saxon*, built in 1864 at Port Dalhousie, ON, and the 138' scow schooner, *J. A. Smith* (138'3" x 26'4" x 9'4"), built at Algonac, MI, in 1871, stranded on Sept. 8, 1887, and were total losses. Their broken remains lie intermingled.

9. FRED MCBRIER

> **LORAN: 31287.8/48085.3** **GPS: 45° 48.339'/084° 55.320'**
> **DEPTH: 96 to 104 feet** **LEVEL: Advanced**

LOCATION: This wreck lies 9.3 miles west of Old Mackinac Point.

Launched at West Bay City, Michigan, in 1881, the comparatively small wooden steamer, *Fred McBrier* (161' x 31' x 12'), laden with iron ore, sank in a collision with the steamer, *Progress,* on Oct.

Left: The *Fred McBrier* appeared on an early 1900's postcard, even though it sank in 1890! CRIS KOHL COLLECTION. *Right:* Engine machinery on the *McBrier.* PHOTO BY CRIS KOHL

3, 1890, with no lives lost. Located in 1967 by Jim Ryerse from nearby St. Ignace, the wreck displays considerable machinery, such as her engine, boiler, and windlass, but lies in an area plagued with frequently silty water, reducing visibility considerably.

10. *MAITLAND*

LORAN: 31273.1/48092.7	GPS: 45° 48.250'/084° 52.547'
DEPTH: 84 feet	LEVEL: Advanced

LOCATION: This wreck lies 7.1 miles west of Old Mackinac Point.

The bark, *Maitland* (133'7" x 25'9" x 11'6"), built at Goderich, ON, along the Maitland River, in 1861, sank with a corn cargo after colliding with both the steamer, *Golden Harvest*, and her tow, the schooner, *Mears*, on June 11, 1871. No lives were lost. The *Maitland* sits upright, intact and penetrable, with much equipment (e.g. windlass, bilge pump) on deck.

Left: The schooner, *Margaret Dall*, closely resembled the *Maitland*. The *Dall* was storm-wrecked on South Manitou Island on Nov. 16, 1906, with no lives lost. CRIS KOHL COLLECTION. *Right:* The *Maitland* sports an enormous windlass, examined here by Joan Forsberg. PHOTO BY CRIS KOHL

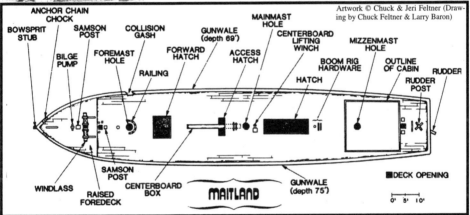

Artwork © Chuck & Jeri Feltner (Drawing by Chuck Feltner & Larry Baron)

MAITLAND

11. NORTHWEST

> **LORAN: 31270.2/48102.2**   **GPS: 45° 47.440'/084° 51.520'**
> **DEPTH: 73 feet**   **LEVEL: Advanced**

LOCATION: This wreck lies 6.2 miles west of Old Mackinac Point.

Ice punctured the hull (a common malady among ships in the Straits) of the 233' schooner, *Northwest,* on April 6, 1898, and she sank with her cargo of corn but no lives lost. Built in 1873 at Bangor, Michigan, the *Northwest* was located in 1978 by Chuck and Jeri

Feltner. This wreck, although broken up and in disarray, is very interesting and, as long as you can maintain bow and stern bearings, easy to navigate. The rudder lies flat off the stern.

Left: The schooner, *Northwest.* CRIS KOHL COLLECTION. *Right:* Joan Forsberg and *Northwest* machinery. PHOTO BY CRIS KOHL.

12. SANDUSKY

> **LORAN: 31262.0/48100.9**   **GPS: 45° 47.9733'/084° 50.2651'**
> **DEPTH: 70 to 84 feet**   **LEVEL: Advanced**

LOCATION: This wreck lies 5.2 miles west of Old Mackinac Point.

The brig, *Sandusky* (110' x 25'1"), built in 1848 at her namesake, Sandusky, Ohio, foundered with all seven hands and a grain cargo in a storm on September 20, 1856. The wreck, located by Chuck and Jeri Feltner's team on May 2, 1981, sits upright and intact,

An unidentified *Sandusky* lookalike. AUTHOR'S COLLECTION

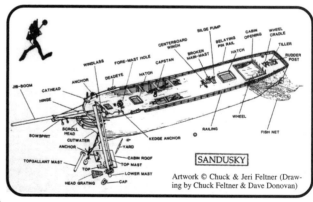

Artwork © Chuck & Jeri Feltner (Drawing by Chuck Feltner & Dave Donovan)

Below: The *Sandusky's* upright bowsprit, chains still in place, and scrolled figurehead; Joan Forsberg and the starboard anchor. PHOTOS BY CRIS KOHL

with magnificent sights such as the scroll figurehead (even though this one, compliments of several Detroit area divers from the Ford Seahorses Scuba Dive Club, is a precise replica of the original, which was damaged in a bungled theft attempt in 1988 and is now in a museum), completely intact bowsprit with chains, bow anchors, and windlass. The *Sandusky,* excellently preserved, is the oldest located and most visited shipwreck in the Straits of Mackinac.

13. *EBER WARD*

LORAN: 31253.7/48096.9	GPS: 45° 48.7503'/084° 49.1213'
DEPTH: 111 to 142 feet	LEVEL: Advanced-Technical

LOCATION: This wreck lies 4.6 miles west-northwest from Old Mackinac Point.

Built in 1888 at West Bay City, Michigan, the wooden steamer, *Eber Ward* (213'2" x 37' x 22'2"), lost five lives and her cargo of corn on April 20, 1909, after she sank when ice holed her hull. Found by Chuck and Jeri Feltner in 1980, this double-decked wreck sits facing south, upright, intact and penetrable (by trained and experienced divers only, please).

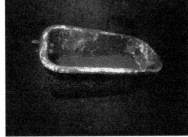

Left: The steamer, *Eber Ward,* and her Capt. LeMay appeared in print after the ship's loss. CRIS KOHL COLLECTION. *Right:* Shipwreck sights include an *Eber Ward* bathtub.   PHOTO BY CRIS KOHL

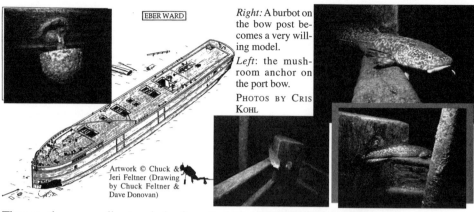

EBER WARD

Right: A burbot on the bow post becomes a very willing model.

Left: the mushroom anchor on the port bow.

PHOTOS BY CRIS KOHL

Artwork © Chuck & Jeri Feltner (Drawing by Chuck Feltner & Dave Donovan)

Three anchors, as well as two holes from the ice, grace her bow area. Her machinery includes a large steam engine, a scotch boiler and a four-bladed propeller. Quite a few shipwreck items lie on the lake bottom just off the wreck, particularly at the stern.

14. CHUCK'S BARGE

LORAN: 31255.8/48074.3	GPS:
DEPTH: 33 to 43 feet	LEVEL: Novice-Intermediate

LOCATION: This wreck lies about one mile east-southeast of St. Helena Island.

This upside-down barge, about 60' long, was located by Chuck and Jeri Feltner in 1982. It is a dump scow used to dispose of dredge material, as the bottom consists of two hinged doors covering large openings. It is believed to have been lost in the 1940's.

15. *C. H. Johnson*

> **LORAN: 31247.0/48061.7** **GPS: 45° 52.20'/084° 50.08'**
> **DEPTH: 13 feet** **LEVEL: Novice**

LOCATION: This wreck lies on the north shore of Gros Cap, Upper Peninsula, 9 miles northwest of Old Mackinac Point.

Constructed in 1870 at Marine City, Michigan, the 137' schooner, *C. H. Johnson,* stranded with a small cargo of large stone blocks while attempting to ride out a storm on September 23, 1895. No lives were lost when the ship sank. Lying at such a shallow depth, the wreck is broken up, but the keelson and many of the ribs are still in place. The cargo of about 20 large (8' x 4' x 2') stone blocks remain. This dive site can be done by boat or from shore.

16. *Minneapolis*

> **LORAN: 31226.2/48111.2** **GPS: 45° 48.502'/084° 43.898'**
> **DEPTH: 124 feet** **LEVEL: Very Advanced**

LOCATION: This wreck lies 1.5 miles north-northwest from Old Mackinac Point.

Carrying a cargo of wheat from Chicago to Buffalo as early in the shipping season as possible, the wooden steamer, *Minneapolis* (226'3" x 34' x 11'2"), was (you guessed it!) holed by ice and sunk with no lives lost on April

Left: The steamer, *Minneapolis.* CRIS KOHL COLLECTION. *Right:* The engine deep on the dark *Minneapolis.*   PHOTO BY CRIS KOHL.

4, 1894. Other ships which jumped the gun and sank in the Straits due to ice include the *Eber Ward, Uganda, Northwest* and (the day before the *Minneapolis* sank) the *William H. Barnum*. All are described in this chapter.

Mackinac divers Fred Leete and Dick Charboneau located this wreck in 1963. The *Minneapolis* sits upright, largely intact, with her bow broken off. The most interesting items are the steam engine, boiler, four-bladed propeller, and her upright smoke stack which rises to a depth of 75'. The usually poor visibility and strong currents make this a site for very experienced divers only. It is 500' southwest of the Mackinac Bridge's main south tower.

17. ST. IGNACE HARBOR

St. Ignace, Michigan, is one of the oldest cities in the United State, and, for most of its history, it relied heavily upon water transportation for people and goods. As a result, its harbor is strewn with an immense variety of artifacts, such as discarded or lost tools, machinery, anchors, pottery, household items, or pieces of wreckage from ships. There are two popular places for divers to enter the harbor: at the northernmost point of the bay at the end of Hazelton Street, and near the south end of the harbor off State Street, right from the city park. Stay out of the busy ferry lanes and display a dive flag. Depths: to 25 feet.

18. CLAM BUCKET BARGE

LORAN:	GPS: 45° 51.273'/084° 41.061'
DEPTH: 115 feet	LEVEL: Advanced

LOCATION: This unidentified shipwreck lies between St. Ignace and Mackinac Island. The clam bucket barge, nicknamed after its metal scoop, was located in Sept., 2000.

19. MACKINAC ISLAND HARBOR WRECK

LORAN: 31180.1/48110.1	GPS:
DEPTH: 52 feet	LEVEL: Intermediate

LOCATION: This wreck lies 150' inside the east breakwall, Mackinac Island harbor.

Lying upside-down, this unidentified wooden wreck, about 100' long and 22' wide, is mounted with a centerboard in her hull. So much of this wreck lies buried in the muddy bottom that penetration is impossible. Beware of heavy boating traffic.

20. ROCK MAZE

LORAN: 31155.3/48080.0	GPS: 45° 51.817'/084° 36.391'
DEPTH: To 35 feet	LEVEL: Novice

LOCATION: This site lies about 900' east of Mackinac Island's Arch Rock.

Caverns, walls and rock pillars with interesting patterns rise 30' from the bottom.

21. WILLIAM YOUNG

LORAN:	GPS: 45° 48.772'/084° 41.939'
DEPTH: 100-118 feet	LEVEL: Advanced

LOCATION: This wreck lies 1 mile east of the Mackinac Bridge. The schooner-barge, *William Young* (138'6" x 26'2" x 11'6"), built in 1863 at Madison Dock, Ohio, sank on Oct. 5, 1891, while in tow of the steamer, *Nashua*. No lives were lost from the coal-laden *Young*. This wreck was accidentally found while Tom Farnquist of the Great Lakes Shipwreck Historical Society was sidescanning for the body of a Mackinac Bridge suicide victim in August, 2002. The registration numbers carved into a main beam identified this very intact vessel (see drawing).

The *William Young* had dimensions very similar to those of the *Hattie Hutt* (pictured). CRIS KOHL COLLECTION

The William Young

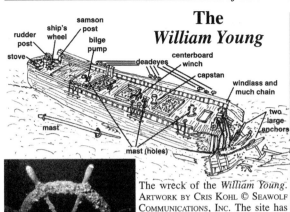

The wreck of the *William Young.* ARTWORK BY CRIS KOHL © SEAWOLF COMMUNICATIONS, INC. The site has many interesing items, such as the wheel *(left),* bilge pump (studied by hoodless, gloveless Mark Kistner -- they grow them tough up there!) and windlass with massive anchor chain *(right).*   PHOTOS BY CRIS KOHL

22. M. STALKER

LORAN: 31213.6/48125.9	GPS: 45° 47.633'/084° 41.040'
DEPTH: 85 feet	LEVEL: Advanced

LOCATION: This wreck lies 2.3 miles east of Old Mackinac Point.

The schooner, *M. (Martin) Stalker* (135'2" x 25' x 10'6"), built in 1863 at Milan, Ohio, sank on Nov. 5, 1886, in a collision with the barge, *Muskoka,* which was one of three vessels in tow of the Canadian steamer, *Isaac May.* The *M. Stalker,* loaded with iron ore and riding out a storm at anchor, sank with no lives lost.

This shipwreck was located in July, 1967, by Dick Campbell, Fred Leete, Dick Race and John Steele. With her bow pointing north-northwest, the *M. Stalker* sits upright and intact, except for the stern, which is broken up. Items of interest include her windlass, bilge pump, wire rigging, centerboard and winch, and mast portions. Beware of current and visibility-

Painting of the *M. Stalker.* ARTIST UNKNOWN. CRIS KOHL COLLECTION

reducing silt, as well as the Mackinac Island ferry boats, in whose path this wreck lies.

23. CEDARVILLE -- SEE PAGE 363.

24. WILLIAM H. BARNUM

> **LORAN: 31205.5/48153.3** **GPS: 45° 44.7147'/084° 37.8359'**
> **DEPTH: 58 to 75 feet** **LEVEL: Intermediate-Advanced**

LOCATION: This wreck lies 5.6 miles east-southeast of Old Mackinac Point.

Built in 1873 at Detroit, Michigan, the wooden steamer, *William H. Barnum* (218'6" x 34'8" x 21'4"), foundered with a cargo of corn half a mile off shore on April 3, 1894, with no lives lost after ice opened the seams of her hull.

Located in 1963 by a team lead by Norm McCready of Indianapolis, the *William T. Barnum,* one of the most popular dive sites in the Straits, is upright and largely intact. Fascinating visuals include the boiler, steam engine, windlass and other machinery. The stern was destroyed when she was dynamited for the removal of her rudder. There are numerous opportunities for wreck penetration, particularly at the bow, for those trained and experienced in that type of diving.

Left: The steamer, *William H. Barnum,* at Buffalo, from a contemporary postcard. CRIS KOHL COLLECTION

Left: The large boiler is only one of the many machinery items at the *Barnum* site.

Right: Diver Joan Forsberg prepares to enter the *Barnum's* hull.

PHOTOS BY CRIS KOHL

25. ALBEMARLE

> **LORAN: 31188.7/48183.1** **GPS: 45° 42.9446'/084° 33.7824'**
> **DEPTH: 12 feet** **LEVEL: Novice**

LOCATION: This wreck lies 9.4 miles east-southeast from Old Mackinac Point.

The 154' schooner, *Albemarle,* built in 1867 at Buffalo, New York, stranded with an iron ore cargo on November 6, 1867, and broke up. No lives were lost. The wreck lies scattered. Primarily ribs, a centerboard box, and hull planking make up this site.

Above: The three-masted schooner, *Albemarle,* closely resembled the *Delos DeWolf.* CRIS KOHL COLLECTION. *Right:* Pat Stayer videotapes the decking and keel at the *Albemarle* site. PHOTOS BY CRIS KOHL

Great Lakes Highlight No. 15

COLLISION IN THE STRAITS:
THE *CEDARVILLE*

LORAN: 31210.7/48130.6   **GPS: 45° 47.230'/084° 40.253'**
DEPTH: 40 to 106 feet   **LEVEL: Intermediate-Advanced**

LOCATION: This wreck lies 2.8 miles east of Old Mackinac Point.

Launched as the *A. F. Harvey* on April 9, 1927, at River Rouge, Michigan, the steel freighter, *Cedarville* (588'3" x 60'2" x 30'8"), received her name change in 1957. She sank with the tragic loss of ten lives on May 7, 1965, after a collision in dense fog with the Norwegian freighter, *Topdalsfjord*. All but one of the bodies were recovered.

One of the best known and most frequently visited shipwrecks in the Straits, the immense *Cedarville* lies on her starboard side and remains quite intact, but don't rush inside this wreck. The daring rescue of a desperate diver lost inside the engine room in July, 2000, where an extra tank of air with a regulator had to be passed to him through a porthole before trained cave divers went in and got him out, made it clear that penetration diving is only for the trained, experienced, and totally prepared. Don't even think about doing this large wreck in a single dive; buoy markers are placed at the bow and at the stern. Take your pick.

Left: The freighter, *Cedarville*. CRIS KOHL COLLECTION. *Right:* Diver Sharon Troxell peers out of the heavily tilted pilot house. PHOTO BY CRIS KOHL

Artwork © Robert McGreevy

26. J. H. OUTHWAITE

> LORAN: 31187.3/48184.3   GPS: 45° 42.28'/084° 33.18'
> DEPTH: 30 feet   LEVEL: Novice

LOCATION: This wreck lies 9.7 miles southeast of Old Mackinac Point.

Built in 1886 at Cleveland, the 224' wooden steamer, *J.H. Outhwaite,* with a cargo of iron ore, stranded and burned to a complete loss with no lives lost on November 28, 1905, a victim of one of the worst storms in recorded Great Lakes history. Forty ships and almost the same number of lives were lost in this late autumn blizzard. The anchors, engine and boiler were salvaged. What remains today is mostly the hull, much of which is unfortunately covered in a sand bank. The wreck lies north to south, with her smokestack and other pieces of wreckage off the midship port side.

Left: J.H. Outhwaite. CRIS KOHL COLLECTION

27. ST. ANDREW

> LORAN: 31180.2/48195.1   GPS: 45° 42.0488'/084° 31.7725'
> DEPTH: 62 feet   LEVEL: Intermediate-Advanced

LOCATION: This wreck lies 11.4 miles southeast of Old Mackinac Point.

The 135' schooner, *St. Andrew,* built in 1857 at Milan, Ohio, sank at night with a cargo of corn in a collision with the schooner, *Peshtigo,* on June 26, 1878. No lives were lost from

A *St. Andrew* lookalike ship. CRIS KOHL COLLECTION. *Right:* Exploring the *St. Andrew.* PHOTOS BY CRIS KOHL

the *St. Andrew,* but the *Peshtigo* also sank, taking two of her crew to the bottom. The *Peshtigo* remains to be found.

The *St. Andrew* sits upright and, for the most part, intact, with the stern broken up but the bow virtually untouched. Her interesting windlass is of an old-fashioned design, and her centerboard box remains intact. There is usually good visibility here with no current.

28. LEVIATHAN

> LORAN: 31156.5/48228.0   GPS: 45° 39.65'/084° 25.95'
> DEPTH: 12 feet   LEVEL: Novice

LOCATION: This wreck lies at the mouth of Duncan Bay, 1.5 miles east-northeast of the mouth of the Cheboygan River.

Built at Buffalo in 1857, the wooden steamer, *Leviathan* (125'2" x 26' x 10'6"), worked as a wrecking tug her entire career, saving ships from destruction. She, however, could not save herself when she caught fire at the Cheboygan, Michigan, dock on November 12, 1891, and burned to a complete loss. She was raised, stripped of any useful gear, and scuttled nearby, out of the way. This broken wreck sits upright, consisting only of large timbers. The site, at least, is weather-protected, and the visibility is usually good.

30. Northeastern Lake Michigan

The "Naubinway Wreck," also called the "Millecoquins River Shipwreck," embedded in the northern Lake Michigan shoreline, was found by a young boy when nature uncovered a portion of it in 1990. A major excavation and professional survey followed in Sept., 1991. This unidentified wreck appears to be that of a small schooner which apparently stranded here some time in the 1840's and became a total loss. Marine architect Ted McCutcheon calculated that this 63-ton vessel measured 62' x 17'5" x 6'5". A large penny coin dated 1833 was found in the foremast step; it was customary to place a coin under the mast of a new ship for good luck. After the survey work, the wreck was re-covered completely with sand to help preserve it.

"Naubinway Wreck"

See Ch. 29

Cross Village

LAKE MICHIGAN

Petoskey

See Ch. 31

Charlevoix

-N-

Traverse City

MICHIGAN

A movement is underway to created an additional Michigan Underwater Preserve encompassing the Grand Traverse Bay area.

Ancient rock carvings, whose images depict a mastodon hunt, were reportedly found recently by divers in Traverse Bay.

1. *Carl D. Bradley*
2. *Niko*
3. *Lucy Clark*
4. **Petoskey Diver Memorial**
5. *Elizabeth*
6. *Keuka*
7. *Gloria*
8. *Alide J. Rogers*
9. *Metropolis*
10. *Lauren Castle*
11. *Tramp*
12. **unidentified barge**
13. **"Elmwood Wreck"**
14. *Nyord*

1. CARL D. BRADLEY -- SEE PAGE 367

2. NIKO

LORAN: 31451.0/48006.8	GPS:
DEPTH: 35 feet	LEVEL: Novice

LOCATION: This wreck lies between Garden Island and Hog Island.

The wooden steamer, *Niko* (189' x 35' x 13'), built at Trenton, Michigan, in 1889, sprang a leak and sank on November 2, 1924, with no lives lost. This wreck lies broken up over a wide area.

The *Niko*.
CRIS KOHL COLLECTION

3. LUCY J. CLARK

LORAN:	GPS: 45° 39.954'/085° 01.103'
DEPTH: to 63 feet	LEVEL: Intermediate-Advanced

LOCATION: This wreck lies between Cross Village, MI, and Waugoshance Point.

The two-masted, 293-ton schooner, *Lucy J. Clark* (137' x 26'), built in 1863, stranded near Cross Village on Nov. 2, 1883. On Nov. 11, after a tug had pulled her free, the ship sank with the loss of three lives. The hull has collapsed outwards, but much remains of interest.

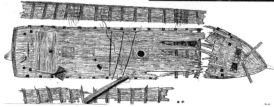

Above, left: Media attention was given to the August, 2006, discovery and identification of the *Lucy J. Clark* by George and Kim Bommarito, and Matt Paulus. *Above, right:* The first photographs of the sunken *Lucy J. Clark*. PHOTOS BY MATT PAULUS, SUBMITTED BY GEORGE BOMMARITO. *Left:* The *Clark's* layout; art by George Bommarito.

4. PETOSKEY DIVER MEMORIAL

LORAN:	GPS: 45° 22.881'/084° 57.315'
DEPTH: About 30 feet	LEVEL: Novice

LOCATION: This site sits about 1,000' off shore east of the Petoskey municipal marina.

This unusual site consists of several plaques honoring scuba divers who have contributed to the sport (e.g. Dr. William Kenner, who was the driving force behind the legislation to protect Michigan shipwrecks). The centerpiece is a marble crucifix, intended for a church but arriving from Italy slightly damaged. Divers were allowed to place it underwater as a memorial. Park your car at a waterfront park along Lake St. Beware of boating traffic.

If going by boat, please anchor at the buoy, or at least 100' due east, to avoid damage.

5. ELIZABETH

LOCATION: This small wreck lies in Round Lake at Charlevoix, MI, in the middle of a shipping lane, with much vessel traffic to and from Lake Michigan. Avoid on weekends. This intermediate site in about 30' of water lies at **GPS: 45° 18.950'/085° 15.090'**

Great Lakes Highlight No. 16

THE TRAGIC LOSS OF THE
CARL D. BRADLEY

LOCATION: This wreck lies almost six miles west-northwest of Boulder Reef Light.

LORAN: 32427.2/49190.4	GPS: 43° 29.84'/086° 29.93'
DEPTH: 300 to 365 feet	LEVEL: Technical

Launched on April 9, 1927, at Lorain, Ohio, the steel freighter, *Carl D. Bradley* (623'2" x 65'2" x 30'2"), is one of a handful of modern, but very tragic, shipwrecks in the Great Lakes. The ship broke in two in a violent storm on November 18, 1958, with the loss of 33 of her 35 crew, most of whom came from Rogers City, Michigan. This is the second-largest shipwreck in the lakes, the *Edmund Fitzgerald* being longer (729' in length -- see pages 568-569).

The wreck lies deep in an area of predominantly low visibility, with the pilot house being the shallowest point at 300'. Cameras on remote-operated vehicles (ROV's) have taken underwater images of this wreck, but the first diver to reach the *Carl D. Bradley* was Detroit-area technical diver, Mirek Standowicz, on July 6, 2001, using trimix gases.

Right: Mirek Standowicz. PHOTO BY CRIS KOHL

Above: The *Carl D. Bradley*, the largest ship on the lakes when launched in 1927, became the largest ship ever lost in the inland seas when it sank with nearly all hands in 1958. CRIS KOHL COLLECTION. *Below:* Artist Robert McGreevy captured the details of the upright, sunken *Bradley*.

Boat Carrying 35 Sinks; Two Saved

Vessel Breaks Up in Lake Michigan

Only First Mate Elmer Fleming *(standing, at right)* and deckhand Frank Mays survived the 1958 *Bradley* sinking. Fleming died in 1969. CRIS KOHL COLLECTION

Below: At his Florida retirement home, Frank Mays recreates the tuck position which helped save his life on the raft in 1958. He proudly displays his *Bradley* china collection. PHOTOS BY CRIS KOHL

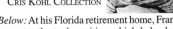
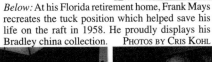

Artwork © Robert McGreevy

6. KEUKA

LORAN: 31495.5/48304.4	**GPS: 45° 18.334'/085° 14.289'**
DEPTH: 35 to 50 feet	**LEVEL: Novice-Intermediate**

LOCATION: This wreck lies in Lake Charlevoix, half a mile from shore and about 2.5 miles from the point where this lake meets Lake Michigan.

Launched at Mount Clemens, Michigan, on June 19, 1889, as the *A. Stewart,* the lumber

The schooner-barge, *Keuka.* CRIS KOHL COLLECTION

schooner-barge, *Keuka* (172' x 32'4" x 12'), given her last name in 1925, reportedly spent her final years afloat as an offshore speakeasy in the Charlevoix area. Scuttled in the early 1930's because she had become an eyesore, the *Keuka* sits upright and her bow cabins can be penetrated by trained and experienced divers. Penetration to the cargo holds is possible from a forward hatch only, as all the other hatches were covered with a hardwood dance floor. Summer offers the poorest visibility due to algae growth; spring and autumn are the best diving time, although ice diving at this site is also popular.

7. GLORIA

LOCATION: This wooden recreational sailboat, possibly built in the early 1900's, lies straight out from the Northport, Michigan, marina entrance.

8. ALIDE J. ROGERS

LOCATION: This wreck lies 4.5 miles north of the tip of the Old Mission Point.

The 340-ton, two-masted schooner, *Alide J. Rogers* (130' x 26' x 12'), built in 1862 at Madison Dock, Ohio, sank on Oct. 8, 1898, becoming a total loss with her cargo of pig iron. The wreck lies in 50' of water at **GPS: 45° 03.153'/085° 28.821'**

9. METROPOLIS

LOCATION: This wrecks lies 3.0 miles southeast of Old Mission Point.

Built in 1857 at Cleveland, Ohio, the two-masted 246-ton schooner, *Metropolis* (126'5" x 28'3" x 11'6"), sank on Nov. 27, 1886, and became a total loss. The keelson rests in less than 10' of water; other hull parts lie in 90+ feet. **GPS: 44° 58.192'/085° 27.938'**

10. LAUREN CASTLE

The steel tug, *Lauren Castle* (97'9" x 21'5" x 10'8"), built in 1906 at Chester, PA, sank in 392' 7 miles north of Traverse City in West Bay on Nov. 5, 1980, with one life lost.

11. TRAMP

Built in 1926 at Rogers City, MI, the 25-ton fish tug, *Tramp* (54'8" x 16' x 4'4"), sank during the 1970's in 45' of water on the southeast side of Marion Island.

12. UNIDENTIFIED BARGE

This barge lies in 80' near Traverse City, MI, at **GPS: 44° 47.064'/085° 37.824'**

13. "ELMWOOD WRECK"

Lying in 20' close to shore, this unidentified fish tug was reputedly dragged from 80' in a net by the Michigan DNR to its present location: **GPS: 44° 47.261'/085° 38.115'**

14. NYORD

A double-ended sailboat, sunk in the 1970's, lies in 55': **GPS: 44° 46.402'/085° 36.006'**

31. Manitou Passage

Manitou Passage is part of Michigan's underwater preserve system created by legislation supported and largely drafted by sport scuba divers in 1980. This region offers two kinds of scuba diving: fascinating shipwrecks and historic dock ruins. Both attract large numbers of freshwater fish and both are buoyed annually.

LAKE MICHIGAN

NORTH MANITOU ISLAND

SOUTH MANITOU ISLAND

Leland

GOOD HARBOR BAY

PYRAMID POINT

Glen Haven   Glen Arbor

SLEEPING BEAR NATIONAL LAKESHORE

MICHIGAN

Empire

Sleeping Bear National Lakeshore is the dramatic setting for many shipwrecks.
PHOTO BY CRIS KOHL

1. Aral dock
2. Empire dock
3. *James McBride* and *General Taylor*
4. *J. S. Crouse*
5. Glen Haven dock
6. Port Oneida dock
7. *Flying Cloud*
8. *Rising Sun*
9. *Walter L. Frost*
10. *Francisco Morazan*
11. *Three Brothers*
12. *P. J. Ralph*
13. *Congress*
14. Burton's wharf
15. *Moore/Vought?*
16. *William T. Graves*
17. *Alva Bradley*
18. Unidentified wreck
19. Crescent dock
20. *Stormer dock*
21. Pickard's wharf
22. *Supply*
23. *Montauk*

1. ARAL DOCK

LORAN: 31899.9/48488.8	GPS: 44° 45.49'/086° 03.34'
DEPTH: To 15 feet	LEVEL: Novice

LOCATION: At the end of County Road 610 (Esch Road).

Aral, once a bustling lumber town with a large mill, saw considerable shipping traffic stop at its dock until the timber was depleted and business moved farther north in the early 1900's. This site, just off a popular swimming beach with ample parking, boasts underwater pilings that run offshore for about 600', and sights include anchor chain and a propeller. The National Park Service forbids removal of any items from these waters.

2. EMPIRE DOCK

LORAN: 31895.5/48482.0	GPS: 44° 46.24'/086° 04.01'
DEPTH: To 20 feet	LEVEL: Novice

LOCATION: At the municipal park at the western end of the village of Empire.

Also a popular swimming beach with much convenient parking, this site, submerged pilings of a dock which catered to lumber trade ships, lies just off the concrete structures visible on shore. As with every site in this area, shifting sands alternately cover and uncover submerged items. North of this dock, in 12', lie tree stumps believed to be 3,000 years old.

3. *JAMES McBRIDE* AND *GENERAL TAYLOR*

LORAN: 31864.9/48408.7	GPS: 44° 53.69'/086° 04.55'
DEPTH: 5 to 15 feet	LEVEL: Novice

LOCATION: Off Sleeping Bear Point. Use a boat; it's a long shore walk to this site.

The oldest known shipwreck site in this area, the brig, *James McBride* (121' x 25'), launched on April 1, 1848 at Irving, New York, was perhaps best known in its time as the first vessel to deliver a cargo to Chicago from saltwater (it was salt from the British West Indies in 1848). A powerful autumn gale forced the *James McBride* ashore on October 19, 1857. No lives were lost, but the ship was pounded to pieces. Today, these large pieces prove to be quite interesting (when they are not covered by the constantly shifting sands). The sternpost rises to within 5' of the surface.

Another ship became a total wreck here. The accident-prone wooden steamer, *General Taylor* (173' x 26' x 11'), launched at Buffalo, NY, on Aug. 24, 1848, was caught in a storm, driven ashore, and wrecked, along with her cargo of general merchandise and flour, on Oct. 3, 1862. No lives were lost. A large piece of the hull was washed ashore in the 1950's.

This wreck, lying stern to shore, plus the remains of others, can be seen from the top of the dunes at Sleeping Bear Point.

4. *J. S. CROUSE*

LORAN: 31840.7/48401.7	GPS: 44° 55.28'/086° 01.30'
DEPTH: 10 to 20 feet	LEVEL: Novice

LOCATION: This wreck lies at Glen Haven dock off County Road 209.

The small wooden steamer, *J. S. Crouse* (89'7" x 16'8" x 7'5"), built at Saugatuck, Michigan, in 1898, burned with a cargo of potatoes and lumber and sank on November 15, 1919, with no casualties. This type of freight vessel, popularly called a "rabbit boat," had its pilot house at the stern (unusual for a

The *J. S. Crouse*. CRIS KOHL COLLECTION

Great Lakes ship), and was often seen with its midship area loaded tall with cargo, e.g. lumber or coal.

With roadside parking available, this site is popular as a shore dive. Charred timbers indicate parts of this shipwreck.

5. GLEN HAVEN DOCK

LORAN: 31840.7/48401.7	GPS: 44° 55.31'/086° 01.31'
DEPTH: 12 to 25 feet	LEVEL: Novice

LOCATION: Off County Road 209, east of the U.S. Life Saving Service Station in Leelanau County, and just offshore from the old fruit storage building.

Sites at this submerged lumber dock, marked by several groups of pilings, include a horse-drawn cart which ran on rails and the remains of two broken and scattered shipwrecks.

6. PORT ONEIDA DOCK

LORAN: 31807.4/48397.1	GPS: 44° 57.09'/085° 56.44'
DEPTH: 7 to 20 feet	LEVEL: Novice

LOCATION: North of Glen Arbor at the end of Kilderhouse Road.

The usual shifting sands cover and uncover items from this dock's past, as well as the remains of a small schooner which stranded here and lie in about 14' of water.

7. *FLYING CLOUD*

LORAN:	GPS: 44° 56.19'/085° 57.39'
DEPTH: 4 to 14 feet	LEVEL: Novice

LOCATION: Off the southwest side of Pyramid Point.

Built in 1852 at French Creek, New York, the two-masted schooner, *Flying Cloud* (124' x 25'6"), stranded with a cargo of oats on October 29, 1892, after her anchors lost their grip while she tried to ride out the powerful gale which also sank the schooner *Ostrich* and the steel steamer, *W.H. Gilcher*. No lives were lost from the *Flying Cloud*. Three sections of wooden wreckage lie in the sand and rocks, one in about 5' and the others in about 14'.

8. *RISING SUN*

LORAN: 31799.5/48386.8	GPS: 44° 58.23'/085° 55.97'
DEPTH: 7 to 12 feet	LEVEL: Novice

LOCATION: About 300' north of Pyramid Point.

Launched as the *Minnie M.* in 1884 at Detroit, the wooden steamer, *Rising Sun* (133'3"

x 26' x 10'8"), received her new name in 1915, just in time for her loss on October 29, 1917. She stranded with a cargo of cedar posts; no lives were lost. The steam engine and prop shaft, plus wooden framing, remain at the site; sometimes the boiler is uncovered.

The little, wooden steamer, *Rising Sun,* was a beautiful ship while afloat *(left)*, and a dramatic shipwreck when lost *(above)*.   BOTH CRIS KOHL COLLECTION

9.   WALTER L. FROST

LORAN: 31859.0/48339.4	GPS: 44° 59.749'/086° 08.549'
DEPTH: 10 to 14 feet	LEVEL: Novice

LOCATION: This wreck lies about 600' due south of the very visible wreck of the steel freighter, *Francisco Morazan*.

The wooden steamer, *Walter L. Frost* (235'7" x 36'9" x 12'9"), built in 1883 at Detroit and carrying corn and general merchandise from Chicago to Ogdensburg, NY, stranded during a thick fog on Nov. 4, 1903, and was abandoned 10 days later. After much salvaging over the years, and some unintentional crushing from the *Morazan* in 1960, only the hull's bottom remains. A buoy usually marks her stern.

The wooden steamer, *Walter L. Frost*. Thick fog put her right onto the island. BOTH CRIS KOHL COLLECTION

10.   FRANCISCO MORAZAN

LORAN: 31858.5/48339.3	GPS: 44° 59.07'/086° 08.09'
DEPTH: To 20 feet	LEVEL: Novice

LOCATION: This large wreck, partially above water, lies about 900' off the island.

The most visited shipwreck in the Manitous, the ocean-going steel freighter, *Francisco Morazan* (246'9" x 36'10" x 16'8"), stranded in bad weather on November 29, 1960. No lives were lost and the cargo of lard and hides was salvaged, but the entire ship, launched as the *Arcadia* in Hamburg, Germany, in 1922, remains here. Visiting boaters usually tie off the wreck. The bow is sand-filled, but the machinery in the stern is of interest. Caution: seagull droppings make exploring the rusting, steel superstructure slippery and dangerous.

The *Francisco Morazan*. CRIS KOHL COLLECTION

11. THREE BROTHERS

LORAN: 31839.2/48339.3	GPS: 45° 00.651'/086° 05.500'
DEPTH: 5 to 45 feet	LEVEL: Novice-Intermediate

LOCATION: This wreck lies a few feet from shore off Sandy Point, S. Manitou Island.

The wooden steamer, *Three Brothers* (162' x 31'4" x 11'8"), launched in 1888 at Milwaukee as the *May Durr,* leaking and beached on South Manitou Island on September 27, 1911, was broken by autumn weather with no lives lost. The wreck was covered deeply with sand until early 1996. The sudden appearance of a

The heavily loaded *Three Brothers*. CRIS KOHL COLLECTION

nearly perfectly intact shipwreck prompted a whirling dervish of scuba activity. The bow is broken, but the stern is intact, although filled with much sand, the weight of which is threatening to destroy its intact nature. Take part in the free diver registration program at the ranger station before diving and obtain an update on the wreck's condition.

12. *P. J. RALPH*

LORAN: 31839.5/48333.5	GPS: 45° 01.11'/086° 06.01'
DEPTH: 10 to 45 feet	LEVEL: Novice-Intermediate

LOCATION: This wreck lies at the south end of South Manitou Island harbor.

The seams opened in heavy weather on the wooden steamer, *P. J. Ralph* (211'4" x 37' x 14'), on September 8, 1924, and she was beached just off this island. Salvage never came for this ship. Built at Marine City, Michigan, in 1889, the *P. J. Ralph's* pulpwood cargo was all that was salvaged. A large part of the hull and all of the steam engine remain at this site.

The steamer, *P. J. Ralph.* CRIS KOHL COLLECTION

13. *CONGRESS*

LORAN: 31834.3/48330.4	GPS: 45° 01.49'/086° 05.45'
DEPTH: 165 feet	LEVEL: Technical

LOCATION: This very deep wreck lies in South Manitou Island harbor.

The large wooden steamer, *Congress* (267'4" x 35'5" x 14'2"), launched at Cleveland in 1867 as the *Nebraska*, was waiting out a storm safely tied to the dock in the shelter of South Manitou Island on October 4, 1904, when she caught on fire. The storm suddenly became the lesser of two evils, but the *Congress* burned to a total loss, fortunately with no lives lost. This very deep shipwreck, seemingly out of place in a region where no shipwreck or dock site is deeper than 45', sits in an area of extreme silt and usually very bad visibility (from 3' to 8'). This wreck site has been buoyed only in recent years.

WAS DESTROYED
BY FIRE

Steamer Congress Burned at
South Manitou Island.

CARGO OF PINE LUMBER

A Total Loss—Life Savers to the
Rescue—Steamer Formerly
an Excursion Boat.

Special Telegram to The Blade.
Glen Haven, Oct. 5.—The steamer Congress, while lying in shelter from the storm at South Manitou Island last night, was destroyed by fire and her cargo of pine lumber will also be a total loss.
The Congress came into shelter in the

Right: The loss of the steamer, *Congress,* was reported by many Great Lakes newspapers, including this one, the *Toledo* (Ohio) *Blade,* on October 5, 1904. CRIS KOHL COLLECTION

Above: The steamer, *Congress,* underway. *Right:*
The *Congress* on fire. BOTH CRIS KOHL COLLECTION

14. Burton's wharf

> **LORAN:** 31833.4/48334.1   **GPS:** 45° 01.31'/086° 05.01'
> **DEPTH:** 5 to 65 feet   **LEVEL:** Novice to Advanced

LOCATION: In the center of the crescent which forms South Manitou Island harbor.

At the end of an old roadway that runs through the Bay Campground, you will find the remnants of the old, busy Burton's wharf, the main dock on this island. Because of the high volume of shipping traffic in the old days, and due to the fast-sloping shoreline here, this dock runs as deep as 45'. A bit beyond, in 65', sits a jeep. If only it could talk...

15. *H. D. Moore/Annie Vought?*

> **LORAN:**   **GPS:** 45° 02.02'/086° 04.44'
> **DEPTH:** 10 to 12 feet   **LEVEL:** Novice

LOCATION: This wreck lies about 300' off shore on the north side of Gull Point.

The identity of this broken up schooner is in question. It is either the *H. D. Moore* (103'3" x 23'5" x 7'7"), built at Saugatuck, MI, in 1874 and stranded on Sept. 10, 1907, while seeking shelter, no lives lost, or the 199' *Annie Vought*, built at Fairport, OH, in 1867, and stranded on November 21, 1892, again with no lives lost. Only the hull's bottom remains.

It this shipwreck the schooner, *H. D. Moore* (pictured left, Cris Kohl Collection) or the schooner *Annie Vought?*

16. *Alva Bradley*

> **LORAN:** 31798.5/48339.2   **GPS:** 45° 02.27'/085° 59.26'
> **DEPTH:** 20 to 27 feet   **LEVEL:** Novice

LOCATION: This wreck lies on the shoal at the south end of North Manitou Island.

The three-masted schooner, *Alva Bradley* (192'2" x 32' x 20'2"), built in 1870 at Cleveland, foundered during a gale with a cargo of steel billets on October 13, 1894, with no lives lost. The site, located by Dave Trotter in 1990, displays the ship's wheel, blocks, chains, deadeyes, belaying pins, keelson, many tools, some machinery and much of the cargo of steel billets.

The *Alva Bradley*.
Cris Kohl Collection

17. *William T. Graves*

> **LORAN:** 31802.8/48330.7
> **GPS:** 45° 02.95'/086° 00.45'
> **DEPTH:** 10' to 20'   **LEVEL:** Novice

LOCATION: North Manitou Shoal, far off shore.

The huge, three-masted barkentine, *William T. Graves* (207' x 35'5" x 14'2"), launched at Cleveland in 1867, stranded on North Manitou Island during a blinding snowstorm on October 31, 1885. The ship had been heading to Buffalo from Chicago with a corn cargo. A large piece of the stern section lies flat on the sandy bottom. This shallow site is a fair distance off shore; a boat is necessary to reach it.

18. UNIDENTIFIED WRECK (EX-*J. B. NEWLAND*)

LORAN: 31803.3/48338.1   **GPS: 45° 02.29'/086° 00.01'**
DEPTH: 4 to 10 feet   **LEVEL: Novice**

LOCATION: This wreck lies off the southern end of North Manitou Island.

The broken up deck and hull of a wooden sailing vessel, with the rudder about 100' to the southwest, comprise this site. Although this is approximately where the schooner, *J. B. Newland,* stranded on September 8, 1910, and for years, divers have been calling this shipwreck the *J. B. Newland,* that vessel was recovered and returned to service under Canadian registry for several more years before finally being scuttled in Lake Ontario in 1929. The identity of these shipwreck pieces remain a mystery.

19. CRESCENT DOCK

LORAN: 31802.2/48288.4   **GPS: 45° 06.58'/086° 03.34'**
DEPTH: 5 to 25 feet   **LEVEL: Novice**

LOCATION: On the west side of North Manitou Island, off the big barn.

Many boulders lie interspersed at this site, which is marked by the tops of pilings.

20. STORMER DOCK

LORAN: 31784.4/48316.2   **GPS: 45° 05.02'/085° 48.60'**
DEPTH: 5 to 20 feet   **LEVEL: Novice**

LOCATION: Across from the old cemetery on North Manitou Island.

Pilings and some small machinery can be viewed on the gravel bottom.

21. PICKARD'S WHARF

LORAN: 31773.7/48296.5   **GPS: 45° 07.16'/085° 58.29'**
DEPTH: 5 to 25 feet   **LEVEL: Novice**

LOCATION: This site lies on the east side of North Manitou Island, about 600 north of the National Park Service dock. Items from bygone eras can be viewed on the sand bottom.

22. SUPPLY

LORAN: 31769.8/48285.0   **GPS: 44° 58.22'/085° 58.48'**
DEPTH: 8 to 10 feet   **LEVEL: Novice**

LOCATION: This wreck lies about 200' from shore off Vessel Point.

The brig, *Supply* (132' x 29'3" x 10'5"), built in 1855 at Buffalo, New York, stranded here with a cargo of 300,000 bricks in Nov., 1869. Piles of bricks still lie amidst the wreckage.

23. MONTAUK

LORAN: 31759.6/48270.6   **GPS: 45° 09.54'/085° 59.51'**
DEPTH: 35 feet   **LEVEL: Novice**

LOCATION: This wreck lies about 1000' off shore and is usually not buoyed.

The two-masted schooner, *Montauk* (137'5" x 25'9" x 12'6"), built at Oswego, NY, in 1863, stranded in a gale on November 23, 1882. The wreck lies in two sections on rocks.

32. Eastern Lake Michigan

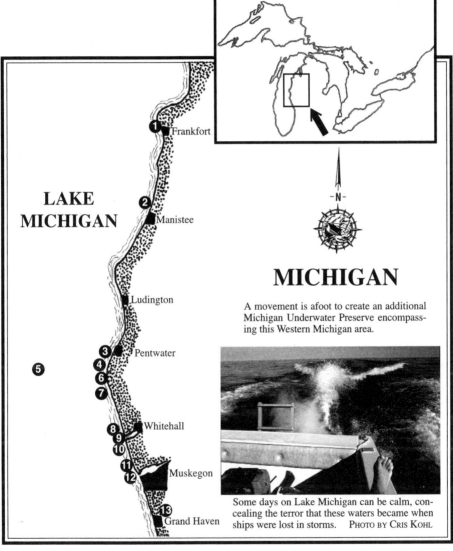

LAKE MICHIGAN

Frankfort

Manistee

Ludington

Pentwater

Whitehall

Muskegon

Grand Haven

-N-

MICHIGAN

A movement is afoot to create an additional Michigan Underwater Preserve encompassing this Western Michigan area.

Some days on Lake Michigan can be calm, concealing the terror that these waters became when ships were lost in storms.   PHOTO BY CRIS KOHL

1. *Ida*
2. *T. S. Christie*
3. *Anna C. Minch*
4. *Novadoc*
5. *Willliam B. Davock*
6. *Daisy Day*
7. *Brightie*

8. *State of Michigan*
9. *Interlaken*
10. *Salvor*
11. *Helen*
12. *Henry Cort*
13. *Manistee*

1. IDA

LOCATION: About 200' off shore from the Congregational Church Assembly beach access (ask permission if you plan to dive from there) two miles north of Frankfort, MI.

The three-masted schooner, *Ida* (120'4" x 27' x 8'3"), built at Milwaukee in 1867, was abandoned by her crew in a raging storm when she began to founder on Sept. 29, 1908. She drifted to shore and broke up with a lumber cargo. Much wood and anchor chain remain.

2. T. S. CHRISTIE

LORAN:	GPS: 44° 17.65'/087° 21.25'
DEPTH: 40 feet	LEVEL: Novice-Intermediate

LOCATION: About four miles north of Manistee, Michigan.

The wooden steamer, *T. S. Christie* (160' x 30'3" x 12'), built at West Bay City, Michigan, and launched on April 25, 1885, was stranded in a snow storm on November 8, 1933, with a cargo of cordwood. The crew reached shore safely in a lifeboat.

The wreck of the steamer, *T. S. Christie* *(background)*. CRIS KOHL COLLECTION

3. ANNA C. MINCH -- SEE PAGE 379.

4. NOVADOC -- SEE PAGE 379.

5. WILLIAM B. DAVOCK -- SEE PAGE 379.

6. DAISY DAY

LOCATION: In shallow water about 50' off Little Point Sable, Michigan.

Built at Manistee, Michigan, in 1880, the 146-ton wooden steam barge, *Daisy Day* (103'4" x 21' x 8'), stranded and was a total loss on October 11, 1891. No lives were lost.

7. BRIGHTIE

LORAN: 32427.4/49190.4	GPS: 43° 29.75'/086° 29.99'
DEPTH: 70 feet	LEVEL: Advanced

LOCATION: This wreck lies about 8 miles north of Whitehall, Michigan.

The schooner-barge, *Brightie* (182' x 33'2" x 13'), launched at Cleveland in 1868, foundered with a cargo of pulpwood on August 23, 1928. No lives were lost. The *Brightie*, located by Gene Turner, sits 1.5 miles off shore, intact and penetrable.

Left: The *Brightie.* CRIS KOHL COLLECTION

8. STATE OF MICHIGAN

LORAN: 32453.7/49263.5	GPS: 43° 23.21'/086° 27.91'
DEPTH: 75 feet	LEVEL: Advanced

LOCATION: This wreck lies about two miles northwest of Whitehall, Michigan.

A connecting rod from her steam engine accidentally piercing her hull, the wooden steamer, *State of Michigan* (165' x 29' x 10'), sank with no lives lost on October 18, 1901. The vessel was launched as the *Depere* in 1873 at Manitowoc, WI. She sits on a sandy bottom, upright and intact except for her stern, which hit the lake bottom first and hard.

See photo of the *State of Michigan* on page 380...

Great Lakes Highlight No. 17

THE 1940 ARMISTICE DAY STORM

One of the worst storms in Great Lakes history reached its peak on Armistice Day (November 11), 1940, sinking three steel freighters on Lake Michigan, two of them with all hands. Once the 125-mile-per-hour winds subsided, the world learned that 70 lives had been lost and several more ships were stranded and damaged. The three which are total losses are:

ANNA C. MINCH

LORAN: 32326.8/49030.4	GPS: 43° 45.799′/086° 27.748′
DEPTH: 36 to 45 feet	LEVEL: Intermediate

LOCATION: This wreck lies about 1.5 miles south of Pentwater, Michigan.

The steel freighter, *Anna C. Minch* (380′ x 50′ x 28′), built at Cleveland in 1903, foundered with everyone on board (24 people) and a cargo of coal in the notoriously severe Armistice Day Storm of November 11, 1940. This is a huge site of steel wreckage.

Left: The *Anna C. Minch.* CRIS KOHL COLLECTION

NOVADOC

LORAN: 32366.2/49064.4	GPS: 43° 41.819′/086° 30.970′
DEPTH: 12 to 15 feet	LEVEL: Novice

LOCATION: About halfway between Ludington and Whitehall, off Juniper Beach near the town of Pentwater, Michigan.

The steel freighter, *Novadoc* (252′8″ x 43′3″ x 17′8″), stranded and broke in half with the loss of two lives and her coal cargo in the Armistice Day Storm of 1940. A few men on board the small fish tug, *Three Brothers,* overcame great difficulties posed by the violent, towering seas and, with a superb display of seamanship, maneuvered close enough to the shipwreck to rescue the remaining

After the storm, the wrecked *Novadoc.*
CRIS KOHL COLLECTION

17 crewmembers. The *Novadoc* had been built at Wallsend-on-Tyne, England in 1928. Today, this steel shipwreck lies broken up in shallow water.

WILLIAM B. DAVOCK

LORAN: 32402.4/49066.0	GPS: 43° 40.445′/086° 36.380′
DEPTH: 215 to 240 feet	LEVEL: Technical

LOCATION: This wreck lies 2.9 miles off Little Sable Light.

The third steel freighter lost in the Armistice Day Storm of November 11, 1940, the *William B. Davock* (420′ x 52′ x 23′), catastrophically foundered with all 32 hands and her coal cargo. This ship, built in 1907 at St. Clair, Michigan, and located in deep water in 1982, may have collided with the *Anna C. Minch,* which also sank with all hands, but evidence is lacking.

Left: The *William P. Davock.* CRIS KOHL COLLECTION

Left: The *State of Michigan.* CRIS KOHL COLLECTION.

Right: The barge, *Interlaken*, at Sturgeon Bay, WI, with the abandoned hull of the *Vermillion* in the foreground. CRIS KOHL COLLECTION

9. INTERLAKEN

LOCATION: Just off the harbor at White Lake, Michigan.

The barge, *Interlaken* (170' x 34'2" x 11'), built at Algonac, MI, in 1893, stranded and sank on Oct. 1, 1934, with no lives were lost. It was reportedly found from the air in 2004.

10. SALVOR

LORAN: 32467.1/49355.9	GPS: 43° 15.49'/086° 22.19'
DEPTH: 25 to 30 feet	LEVEL: Novice

LOCATION: This wreck lies almost three miles north of the Muskegon Lighthouse.

The pseudo-whaleback steamer, *Turret Chief* (253' x 44' x 22'), built in England in 1896, was reduced to a barge in 1927 and renamed *Salvor*. She foundered in a storm on Sept. 26, 1930, with 5 lives lost. The wreck sits upright, partially buried in sand.

Left: The *Salvor.* CRIS KOHL COLLECTION

11. HELEN

LOCATION: Off Muskegon's Pere Marqette northside beach.

The scow schooner, *Helen* (90' x 23' x 7'), built at Milwaukee in 1881, stranded and capsized with the loss of all six hands, including her eccentric captain and his wife, on Nov. 18, 1886. Shifting sands cover and uncover this wreck in a few feet of water.

Right: The *Helen* entering Manitowoc (WI) harbor. CRIS KOHL COLLECTION

12. HENRY CORT

LOCATION: This wreck lies alongside the north Muskegon, Michigan, breakwall.

The whaleback steamer, *Henry Cort* (320' x 42' x 25'), built at Superior, WI, in 1892 as the *Pillsbury,* stranded here on Nov. 30, 1934, with one life lost. She lies broken and scattered in 48' to 55' of water.

EXTRA THE MUSKEGON CHRONICLE EXTRA

ALL ABOARD SAFE AS FREIGHTER CORT WRECKS

COAST GUARD MEMBER LOST OVERBOARD

WASHED FROM ... RESCUE TRY ... IS MARKED ... MEN BROUGHT ASHORE
BOAT GOING TO ... BY HEROISM ... BY COAST GUARDSMEN
SINKING CORT ... AFTER BREAK OF DAY

The wrecked whaleback steamer, *Henry Cort*, received considerable newspaper coverage. CRIS KOHL COLLECTION

For an entire chapter about the whaleback, *Henry Cort*, and its several sinkings, see *Shipwreck Tales of the Great Lakes* by Cris Kohl.

13. MANISTEE

LORAN: 32472.9/49487.1	GPS: 43° 04.75'/086° 12.17'
DEPTH: 25 feet	LEVEL: Novice

LOCATION: In Spring Lake (which flows into Lake Michigan), at Ferrysburg, near Grand Haven, Michigan.

The steamer, *Manistee* (202' x 32' x 21'9"), launched at Benton Harbor, Michigan, on April 22, 1882, as the *Lora*, renamed *Alice Stafford* in 1897, and *Manistee* in 1905, burned at Johnston Brothers' dock on June 28, 1914. No lives were lost.

Left: The *Manistee.* CRIS KOHL COLLECTION

33. Southeastern Lake Michigan

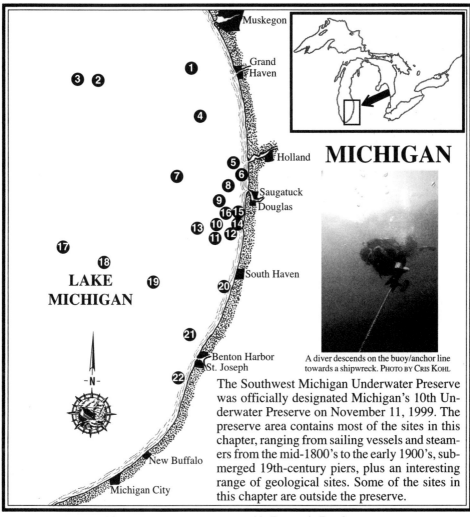

A diver descends on the buoy/anchor line towards a shipwreck. PHOTO BY CRIS KOHL

The Southwest Michigan Underwater Preserve was officially designated Michigan's 10th Underwater Preserve on November 11, 1999. The preserve area contains most of the sites in this chapter, ranging from sailing vessels and steamers from the mid-1800's to the early 1900's, submerged 19th-century piers, plus an interesting range of geological sites. Some of the sites in this chapter are outside the preserve.

1. *Ironsides*
2. Commercial barge
3. *Michigan*
4. Potter's barge
5. 27-foot sailboat
6. Crane and barge
7. North shore tug
8. *Francie*
9. Hatch cover
10. South Haven clay bank
11. *Verano*
12. Donny's Reef
13. *Rockaway*
14. Pier Cove
15. Glenn Pier
16. John Butler II clay banks
17. *H. C. Akeley*
18. *Hennepin*
19. *Ann Arbor No. 5*
20. *City of Green Bay*
21. *Havana*
22. Grand Mere Rocks

1. IRONSIDES

LORAN: 32525.20/49494.50	GPS: 43° 02.903'/086° 19.138'
DEPTH: 109 to 122 feet	LEVEL: Advanced

LOCATION: This wreck lies about four miles west of Grand Haven, Michigan.

The wooden, twin-propellered steamer, *Ironsides* (218'8" x 31'7" x 12'9"), built in 1864 at Cleveland, foundered in heavy seas on September 15, 1873, with a cargo of grain, pork, flour and passengers; 21 of the 50 people on board perished.

This shipwreck's stern, with its twin propellers and rudder, sits at the shallower end, in 109' of water, while the broken up bow rests in 122'. The twin hogging arches sag towards the center of the hull in midship, and rise above the boilers, piping and engine. This wreck is just outside the Southwest Michigan Underwater Preserve. However, the removal of anything from this site is a violation of state and/or federal laws.

The steamer, *Ironsides,* from *American Steam Vessels,* 1895. Drawing by Samuel Ward Stanton.   CRIS KOHL COLLECTION

2. COMMERCIAL BARGE

LORAN:	GPS: 42° 46.800'/086° 24.020'
DEPTH: 250 feet	LEVEL: Technical

LOCATION: This wreck lies about 7.5 miles west of Grand Haven, Mi.

This unidentified barge, discovered in 2004, lies in very deep water a fair distance off shore, so more caution than usual should be used by any technical divers venturing to this site. Lacking any equipment suggests that this "clean" barge was scuttled.

3. MICHIGAN

LORAN:	GPS:
DEPTH: 270 feet	LEVEL: Technical

The *Michigan*. CRIS KOHL COLLECTION

LOCATION: About 8.5 miles west of Grand Haven, MI.

The iron, bulk freight steamer, *Michigan* (203'9" x 35' x 11'7"), built in 1881 at Wyandotte, MI, became trapped in Lake Michigan ice on Feb. 9, 1885. Some crewmembers hiked over the ice to shore (12 hours!) for supplies several times. The *Michigan's* hull finally gave out after 42 days, sinking on March 19, 1885, with no lives lost; the entire crew was taken off by a tugboat. This upright wreck was found in the summer of 2005 by the Michigan Shipwreck Research Associates.

Left: Sidescan image of the *Michigan. Below, left:* Her anchors stowed on deck, Todd White photo. *Below:* The *Michigan's* double wheel, Todd White photo.
COURTESY OF VALERIE VAN HEEST/MICHIGAN SHIPWRECK RESEARCH ASSOCIATES

4. "POTTER'S BARGE"

LORAN:	GPS: 42° 53.660'/086° 22.212'
DEPTH: 200 feet	LEVEL: Technical

LOCATION: In deep water halfway between Grand Haven and Holland, Michigan. This unidentified work barge will appeal to technical divers only, due to its depth.

5. 27-FOOT SAILBOAT

LORAN: 32604.5/49681.9	GPS: 42° 45.73'/086° 14.84'
DEPTH: 22 feet	LEVEL: Novice

LOCATION: This small, modern wreck lies off Holland, Michigan.

This 27-foot sailboat is usually marked with a small, plastic buoy, and is a popular site among local divers.

6. CRANE AND BARGE

LORAN: 32616.3/49713.1	GPS: 42° 42.71'/086° 13.92'
DEPTH: 45 to 55 feet	LEVEL: Intermediate

LOCATION: This site is about one mile off shore between Holland and Saugatuck.

This unidentified barge and crane were apparently lost in a storm while under tow. The wooden barge sits somewhat settled in the sand bottom, while the crane (**LORAN: 32616.4/ 49713.2 GPS: 42° 42.75'/086° 13.85'**) lies nearby.

7. NORTH SHORE TUG

LORAN: 32666.87/49732.95	GPS: 42° 40.165'/086° 19.441'
DEPTH: 150 feet	LEVEL: Technical

LOCATION: This wreck lies about 8 miles off Saugatuck, Michigan.

This old tugboat was towed out of Saugatuck harbor and scuttled. It lies in deep water pointing east. Penetration is possible at this site for trained and experienced divers. Beware of snagged fishing lines and loose railing and other items at the site which could cause entanglement. The wheel house sits upside-down about 30' to the southwest of the hull.

8. *FRANCIE*

LORAN: 32644.7/49724.1	GPS: 42° 41.350'/086° 16.932'
DEPTH: 92 to 102 feet	LEVEL: Advanced

LOCATION: This wreck lies about two miles west of Saugatuck harbor.

The sailing vessel, *Francie,* was a Chesapeake Bay oyster dredge working in the commercial fishing industry before being converted to a passenger/pleasure boat. The vessel sank at her dock in the 1980's, when local divers reportedly raised the hulk and scuttled her.

9. HATCH COVER

LORAN:	GPS: 42° 38.920'/086° 14.517'
DEPTH: 50 feet	LEVEL: Intermediate

This lone piece of wreckage (a search for its ship/wreck has been made in close proximity to the hatch, but with no luck) is home to a fair number of fish.

10. SOUTH HAVEN CLAY BANK

LORAN: 32706.1/49840.4	GPS: 42° 30.454'/086° 15.737'
DEPTH: 50 to 60 feet	LEVEL: Intermediate

Small grottos, trenches and projections rising to 15' in height are part of this multi-acre ancient beach zone, formed thousands of years ago as the last Ice Age glaciers melted.

11. VERANO

LORAN: 32707.72/49843.95	**GPS:** 42° 30.21'/086° 15.96'
DEPTH: 50 feet	**LEVEL:** Inermediate

LOCATION: This wreck lies near the Clay Banks about 7 miles north of South Haven.
The pleasure yacht, *Verano* (88'3" x 16' x 8'), constructed at Morris Heights, New York, at the height of the "Roaring '20's" (1925), foundered with all three people on board on August 28, 1946. Located in September, 1994, by scuba divers Tom Tanczos and Robert Trowbridge, the *Verano's* site highlights include the ship's wheel, windlass, compass, pottery, twin engines, propeller and the ignition key still in place. The bow and the stern sections lie 185' apart.

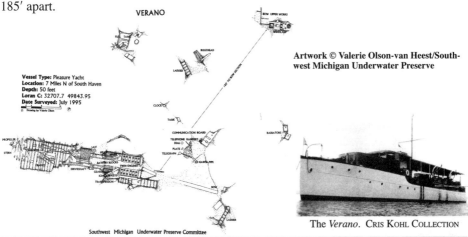

Artwork © Valerie Olson-van Heest/Southwest Michigan Underwater Preserve

The *Verano*. CRIS KOHL COLLECTION

12. DONNY'S REEF

> **LORAN: 32745.51/49890.85**   **GPS: 42° 25.484'/086° 16.999'**
> **DEPTH: 25 to 40 feet**   **LEVEL: Novice-Intermediate**

LOCATION: This site lies several miles north of South Haven and 1/2 mile off shore.
Concrete stuctures and other manmade items were dumped among the natural glacial
formations here, and as a result, the reef hosts a variety of fish life.

13. *ROCKAWAY*

> **LORAN: 32747.0/49878.1**   **GPS: 42° 25.63'/086° 17.65'**
> **DEPTH: 70 feet**   **LEVEL: Advanced**

LOCATION: This wreck lies 2 miles off shore and 2.5 miles northwest of South Haven.
Launched in October, 1866, at Oswego, New York, the schooner scow, *Rockaway* (106'
x 24' x 7'), foundered in a late season storm on November 18, 1891, with a load of lumber.
No lives were lost.

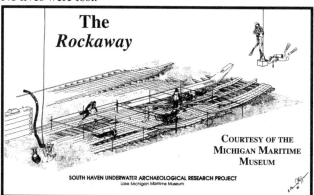

The Rockaway

COURTESY OF THE
MICHIGAN MARITIME
MUSEUM

SOUTH HAVEN UNDERWATER ARCHAEOLOGICAL RESEARCH PROJECT
Lake Michigan Maritime Museum

This wreck, located
accidentally by a fisherman
in Sept., 1983, was almost
completely excavated by
marine archaeologists in
1984; most of her artifacts,
such as the ship's wheel, were
recovered and conserved for
museum exhibition. The
wreck itself, in three main
sections, still exhibits her upright centerboard box, anchor
chain and a windlass about
35' forward of the bow.

14. PIER COVE

> **LORAN: 32667.1/49793.5**   **GPS: 42° 35.16'/086° 14.29'**
> **DEPTH: 5 to 20 feet**   **LEVEL: Novice**

LOCATION: This pier lies about about 14 miles north of South Haven, Michigan.
The mid-1800's community of Pier Cove was one of the busiest ports on Lake Michigan,
with steamers transporting lumber, fruit and passengers. But commercial routes changed
over the years, and, by 1917, the piers were no longer used because commercial activity had
ceased. Today, they make an interesting shore dive, revealing numerous small artifacts from
the boom years.
Take US 31 to Hwy 89, go west to 70th Street, go south to the historic marker for Pier
Cove. Park in the public parking area and head north on the beach, keeping an eye out for a
piling visible from shore. That's the dive site; go from there.

15. GLENN PIER

> **LORAN: 32697.5/49833.5**   **GPS: 42° 31.22'/086° 15.20'**
> **DEPTH: 5 to 20 feet**   **LEVEL: Novice**

LOCATION: This pier lies about 10 miles north of South Haven, Michigan.
This once-busy community pier was about 650' long in its heyday when local farmers
could get their produce, mostly fruit, to the large Chicago market within one day. The lumber
trade and, later, the resort industry, also accounted for considerable maritime traffic to this

pier. Today, pilings poking their heads out of the water are the only above-water reminders of those old days. The site includes underwater views of old tools, bottles and machinery.

To reach this shore dive site, take 96 to exit 30, go south to the community of Glenn, go west on 114th to a two-track road which will take you to the shoreline. Do not dive here in heavy seas, as entries and exits become dangerous, and the visibility will be reduced to very low levels.

Parking is a problem on summer weekends because this site is popular with swimmers.

16. John Butler II Clay Banks

LORAN:	GPS: 42° 34.964'/086° 15.358'
DEPTH: 50 to 55 feet	LEVEL: Intermediate

LOCATION: This site lies off Pier Cove, Michigan.

Originally mistaken for shipwreck debris in 1998 during a sidescan sonar survey, these irregular, underwater peaks and valleys offer an interesting close-up view of the remnants of glacial movement.

17. *H. C. Akeley*

LORAN:	GPS: 42° 39.520'/086° 31.640'
DEPTH: 240 to 260 feet	LEVEL: Technical

LOCATION: This wreck lies about 13.5 miles west of Saugatuck, Michigan.

Launched on April 26, 1881, at Grand Haven, MI, the wooden steamer, *H. C. Akeley* (230'3" x 35'2" x 20'2"), enroute with corn from Chicago to Buffalo, foundered in a storm on Nov. 13, 1883, with 6 of the 18 lives lost. This wreck, at first thought to be the fabled *Chicora*, was found in 2001 by the Michigan Shipwreck Research Associates.

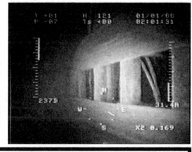

Above: The sinking of the *H. C. Akeley*. Artist Unknown. Cris Kohl Collection. *Left:* Sidescan sonar image of the *Akeley*. *Right:* a ROV (remote-operated vehicle) image of the wreck. Courtesy of Valerie van Heest/Michigan Shipwreck Research Associates

The wreck of the *H. C. Akeley*. ART BY VALERIE VAN HEEST. COURTESY OF MICHIGAN SHIPWRECK RESEARCH ASSOCIATES

18. *HENNEPIN*

LORAN:	GPS:
DEPTH: 230 feet	LEVEL: Technical

LOCATION: This historic wreck lies about 13 miles west of South Haven, Michigan.

Launched in 1888 at Milwaukee as the *George H. Dyer*, and renamed the *Hennepin* (214' x 35'8" x 17'3") in 1898, she sank in a storm on August 18, 1927, with no lives lost. This ship, significant for becoming the Great Lakes' first self-unloader in 1902, was found in 2006 by the Michigan Shipwreck Research Associates. The *Hennepin* is very intact! The wheel is exposed (the housing was blown off when the ship sank), the bow capstan cover is embossed with the original ship's name, and the A-frame self-unloading mechanism rises to a depth of 170'.

The first self-unloader, the *Hennepin*. CRIS KOHL COLLECTION

388

Left to right: The wheel on the *Hennepin,* photographed by Bob Underhill; sidescan sonar image of how the *Hennepin* first appeared; the self-unloading frame rises high above the *Hennepin's* deck, in this Todd White photo. COURTESY OF VALERIE VAN HEEST/MICHIGAN SHIPWRECK RESEARCH ASSOCIATES

The Hennepin

This detailed artwork depicts the many interesting items on the wreck of the historic *Hennepin.* DRAWING BY ROBERT DOORNBOS WITH VALERIE VAN HEEST. SIGNED AND NUMBERED 16" X 20" PRINTS ARE AVAILABLE AT WWW.VALERIEVANHEEST.COM/SHIPWRECKART.HTM

19. *ANN ARBOR NO. 5*

LORAN:	GPS: 42° 22.765'/086° 27.430'
DEPTH: 120 to 160 feet	LEVEL: Technical

LOCATION: This unusual wreck lies eight miles WSW of South Haven, Michigan.

This 2,884-ton, steel railroad car ferry (360' x 56'3" x 18'9"), built in 1910 at Toledo, Ohio, was, in later years, cut down (literally--the upper works were removed) to a powered barge, and supposedly "scrapped" in 1970. It was, however, taken out into the lake that year and scuttled. It sank oddly: it juts out of the bottom at a dramatic 45-degree angle, bow embedded in 160', propellers suspended freely at 120', and railroad car tracks still on deck. This wreck was found in 2005 by the Michigan Shipwreck Research Associates.

Left to right: The *Ann Arbor No. 5*. CRIS KOHL COLLECTION. This is the image of the *Ann Arbor No. 5* as it appeared on the sidescan sonar monitor when the wreck was found. A diver explores the area around *Ann Arbor No. 5's* propeller, in a photo by Todd White. COURTESY OF VALERIE VAN HEEST/MICHIGAN SHIPWRECK RESEARCH ASSOCIATES

20. CITY OF GREEN BAY

LORAN: 32773.4/49926.6	GPS: 42° 22.01'/086° 17.97'
DEPTH: 6 to 15 feet	LEVEL: Novice

LOCATION: This wreck lies close to shore off South Haven, Michigan.

The three-masted schooner, *City of Green Bay* (128'5" x 24'5" x 12'5"), was prone to wanderlust and collisions. On October 3, 1887, she stranded two miles south of South Haven in a fierce storm (which also claimed the nearby schooner, *Havana,* both ships coincidentally loaded with iron ore for St. Joseph, Michigan). The U.S. Life Saving Service crew's out-of-character bungled rescue efforts (only one crewmember from the seven was recovered alive), caused head-rolling controversy.

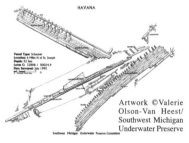

Artwork © Valerie Olson-Van Heest/ Southwest Michigan Underwater Preserve

This wreck has washed so close to shore over the years that it is now a shore dive. The keelson, centerboard box and frames remain.

21. HAVANA

LORAN: 32888.1/50024.9	GPS: 42° 11.690'/086° 25.631'
DEPTH: 52 feet	LEVEL: Intermediate

LOCATION: This wreck lies about one mile off shore and six miles north of St. Joseph.

The two-masted schooner, *Havana* (135' x 25' x 10')*,* built at Oswego, New York, in 1871, foundered with her iron ore cargo during the same storm that claimed the nearby *City of Green Bay* (see site #20) on October 3, 1887, with the loss of three of the seven lives on board. Their ship sinking fast, the men had all clambered into the rigging, but when the main-mast toppled over, three of them drowned. The bold crew of the tug, *Hannah Sullivan,* rescued the remaining four, heroically triumphing over the heavy seas and howling winds.

Artwork ©Valerie Olson-Van Heest/ Southwest Michigan Underwater Preserve

Located by Gene Turner, the wreck of the *Havana,* although broken up, features the keelson, hull framing, centerboard box and hanging knees.

22. GRAND MERE ROCKS

LORAN: 33013.58/50135.37	GPS: 42° 00.328'/086° 33.753'
DEPTH: 15 to 23 feet	LEVEL: Novice

LOCATION: This site lies about 3/4 of a mile off shore from St. Joseph, Michigan.

This unique geological formation runs parallel to the shoreline for a length of about one mile. As usual, fly a dive flag. Boating traffic is heavier here than elsewhere in the area.

34. Sites off Indiana

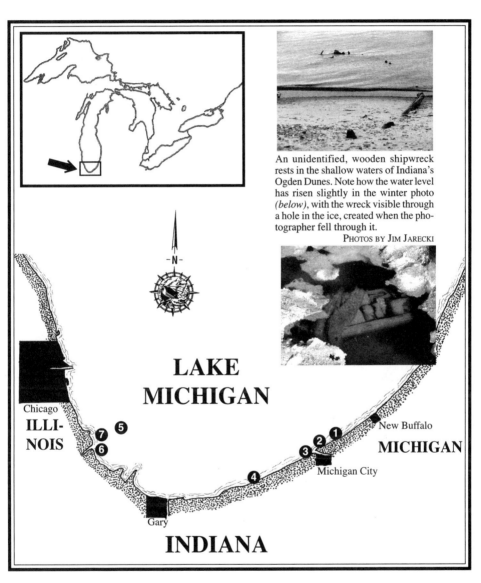

An unidentified, wooden shipwreck rests in the shallow waters of Indiana's Ogden Dunes. Note how the water level has risen slightly in the winter photo *(below)*, with the wreck visible through a hole in the ice, created when the photographer fell through it.

PHOTOS BY JIM JARECKI

LAKE
MICHIGAN

Chicago
ILLI-
NOIS

New Buffalo

MICHIGAN

Michigan City

Gary

INDIANA

1. *Frank W. Wheeler*
2. *Eureka*
3. *Muskegon*
4. *J. D. Marshall*

5. *Barge No. 2*
6. *George F. Williams*
7. *Material Service*

1. FRANK W. WHEELER

> **LORAN: 33228.7/50278.9**   **GPS: 41° 44.64'/086° 51.98'**
> **DEPTH: 30 to 40 feet**   **LEVEL: Novice**

LOCATION: About 1,200' off shore, 2.5 miles east of Michigan City, Indiana.

The wooden steamer, *Frank W. Wheeler* (265'5" x 40'5" x 19'4"), built at West Bay City, Michigan, in 1887, stranded about a quarter of a mile off shore with a cargo of 2,100 tons of coal from Buffalo to Chicago during a blizzard on December 3, 1893, and became a total loss. The local lifesaving crew rescued all 16 sailors on the *F. W. Wheeler* in two trips. When asked how he ran ashore at Michigan City when he was heading for Chicago, Captain George Trotter stated, "I can only account for it by the fact that my compass was out of order, and led me to this side of the lake. Early the previous evening, I shut down the speed and did not know how many miles I had gone. Consequently I lost reckoning...."

The *Frank W. Wheeler.* Bad navigation put the ship here.   CRIS KOHL COLLECTION

Broken into three main sections, this wreck is covered/uncovered by shifting sands and offers newly-exposed portions each spring. A huge winch sits on a large portion of decking.

2. EUREKA

> **LORAN: 33237.4/50281.2**   **GPS: 41° 44.28'/086° 53.06'**
> **DEPTH: 30 feet**   **LEVEL: Novice**

LOCATION: This wreck lies just to the north-northeast of Michigan City, Indiana.

The 240' sidewheeler, *Eureka,* built at Newport (now Marine City), Michigan, in 1864, stranded and was a total loss on October 12, 1873. The wreck lies broken up and scattered.

3. MUSKEGON

> **LORAN: 33266.0/50293.5**   **GPS: 41° 42.71'/086° 56.15'**
> **DEPTH: 25 feet**   **LEVEL: Novice**

LOCATION: About 1/2 mile off shore, two miles west of Michigan City, Indiana, harbor.

Launched as the attractive passenger steamer, *Peerless,* in 1872 at Cleveland, and running mostly between Chicago and Duluth, in 1907, this now-aging, wooden vessel was renamed *Muskegon* (211' x 39'9" x 12'5") and converted first to a bulk freighter and later to a sandsucker. It was a sad swan song to a long career. The ship burned to a total loss at Michigan City on October 6, 1910. No lives were lost. The burned out hulk was towed beyond the harbor and abandoned.

Left: The *Muskegon* as the passenger ship, *Peerless.*
Above: The charred remains of the *Muskegon.*
BOTH REV. PETER VAN DER LINDEN COLLECTION

4. J. D. MARSHALL

LORAN: 33329.3/50309.3	GPS: 41° 40.04′/087° 04.20′
DEPTH: 32 feet	LEVEL: Novice

The steamer, *J. D. Marshall*.
CRIS KOHL COLLECTION

LOCATION: This wreck lies about one-third mile north of the water tower near the western boundary of the Indiana Dunes National Park, halfway between Gary and Michigan City.

The wooden steamer, *J. D. Marshall* (154′5″ x 33′5″ x 12′), built in 1891 at South Haven, Michigan, capsized with the loss of four lives on June 10, 1911, and floated close to shore several days later. Ironically, the company which lost the *Muskegon* (see site #3) used the insurance money which they received from that loss to buy the *J. D. Marshall*. Tools and machinery lie on the lake bottom near the wreck, the huge propeller and boiler being the main components here.

5. BARGE NO. 2

LORAN: 33407.62/50205.75	GPS: 41° 44.82′/087° 26.99′
DEPTH: 42 feet	LEVEL: Intermediate

LOCATION: This wreck lies about three miles off the Calumet breakwall.

Barge No. 2 (324′6″ x 44′ x 11′) was part of the Lake Michigan (Railroad) Car Ferry Transportation Company fleet which included identical *Barge No. 3* and *Barge No. 4*, both of which sank in Lake Erie (and are in this book), and *Barge No. 1*, converted to a freight barge after the car ferry business failed, and which sank off Alpena, Michigan (and is also in this book).

Built at West Bay City, Michigan, in 1895, *Barge No. 2* struggled in a Lake Michigan storm on Sept-

Barge No. 2, with railroad cars. CRIS KOHL

ember 29, 1906. She was carrying 30 railroad cars, about half filled with lumber and the rest with iron ore. Her seams opened and she capsized with her heavy cargo just inside the breakwall at Chicago, with the loss of three lives. In the spring of 1907, the U.S. Army Corps of Engineers towed the hulk out into the lake and sank her at her present location. Then realizing that she lay in the shipping lane and was a danger to navigation, they dynamited her in August, 1907. The wreck lies in many pieces, scattered over a wide area.

6. GEORGE F. WILLIAMS

LORAN: 33446.7/50230.6	GPS: 41° 41.82'/087° 30.67'
DEPTH: 15 feet	LEVEL: Novice

LOCATION: This wreck lies about one mile west of the Hammond Water Intake plant. Launched on July 24, 1889, at West Bay City, Michigan, the wooden steamer, *George*

F. Williams (280' x 41'4" x 20'3"),was abandoned in 1913 and reportedly towed to her final resting place about 400' off shore and sunk on April 21, 1915. It took until 1988 for divers to locate this wreck; she was found by Tim Early. Besides her long, flattened hull, the site exhibits her scotch boiler and propeller. The Underwater Archaeological Society of Chicago did an extensive survey of this site in 2001. Beware of boating traffic, particularly annoying little "water fleas."

The *George F. Williams*.
GREAT LAKES HISTORICAL SOCIETY

7. MATERIAL SERVICE

> **LORAN: 33426.3/50201.4**　　**GPS: 41° 44.50'/087° 30.50'**
> **DEPTH: 22 to 38 feet**　　**LEVEL: Novice-Intermediate**

LOCATION: This wreck lies about 2000' northeast of Calumet Harbor Light, Illinois.

The barge, *Material Service* (239'7" x 40'1" x 13'9"), built in 1929 at Sturgeon Bay, Wisconsin, foundered with terrible loss of life (15 died from the 22 who were on board) with a cargo of sand and gravel on July 29, 1936.

The wreck is marked by buoy "WR10." Anchor next to the wreck, since it is illegal to tie a boat to a government buoy. Visibility is usually low (about 7'), but can improve considerably after several calm days in early spring. The ship's large holds are open and invite exploration by trained and experienced penetration divers. Warning: the silt stirs up easily and reduces visibility to zero! The stern shows scattered steel and pipes (signs of dynamiting), and the propellers are still in place, although half buried in the lake bottom.

Left: The steel barge, *Material Service*, passing under a Chicago bridge. CRIS KOHL COLLECTION. *Right:* Sidescan sonar image of the *Material Service* shipwreck. COURTESY OF DOUG GOSSAGE, GOOSE'S SCUBA. *Immediately below:* Sturgeon Bay, Wisconsin, where the barge had been built, expressed its anguish in its headline. *Below:* Diver Joan Forsberg examines one of the twin propellers, and later explores inside the shipwreck. PHOTOS BY CRIS KOHL.

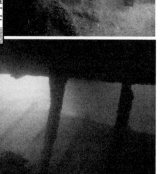

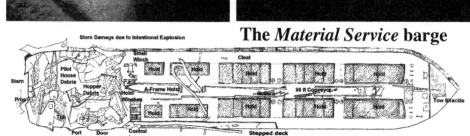

The *Material Service* barge

Artwork © Underwater Archaeological Society of Chicago.

35. Chicago

Zion

Waukegan

Wilmette

Evanston

ILLINOIS

CHICAGO

LAKE MICHIGAN

Hammond   Gary

INDIANA

On average, 60 or 70 "tall ships" arrived at, or departed from, Chicago's busy harbor every single day during sailing seasons in the mid-1800's. Many became shipwrecks just off shore. Today, the Windy City is occasionally visited by large vessels such as this reproduction of the famous HMS *Bounty*.   PHOTO BY CRIS KOHL

The captain-at-the-helm statue at Navy Pier, flanked by Cris Kohl and son, Geoff, is one of the very few reminders in Chicago that this city owes its existence to Great Lakes ships and sailors.
PHOTO BY JOAN FORSBERG

1. Underwater forest
2. *Louisville*
3. *David Dows*
4. "Mystery Wreck"
5. *Luther Loomis*
6. *Desmond*
7. *Tacoma*
8. *Silver Spray*
9. *Illinois* and "Holly barge"
10. *Dispatch Boat #1*
11. 12th Street Wreck
12. *Rainbow*
13. Four-Mile Crib
14. Caissons

15. East Tug
16. South Tug/"Tym barge"
17. North Tug
18. *Iowa*
19. "Mike's Wreck"
20. *Flora M. Hill*
21. North Ave. schooner
22. Box barge
23. *Rotarian*
24. "Val's Wreck"
25. *David A. Wells*
26. *Wings of the Wind*
27. *Lucille*

28. *The Straits of Mackinac*
29. *Wells Burt*
30. *Carrier*
31. *George Morley*
32. *Searcher*
33. *UC-97*
34. *St. Mary*
35. *Lady Elgin*
36. *Seabird*
37. Grain barge
38. Zion Schooners
39. Zion Subchaser
40. *Thomas Hume* (?)

1. UNDERWATER FOREST

> **DEPTH: 80 feet**　　　　　**LEVEL: Advanced**

LOCATION: Just to the northeast of the wreck of the *Louisville*.

Tree stumps estimated to be between 7,000 and 8,000 years of age rise one to two feet off the lake bottom; similar sites exist off Tobermory and in Georgian Bay off Wiarton, Ontario (reference p. 149 of *Dive Ontario Two!*, 1994, by Cris Kohl, for a photo of one.)

2. LOUISVILLE

> **LORAN: 33366.0/50205.6**　　　**GPS: 41° 46.16'/087° 20.39'**
> **DEPTH: 60 feet**　　　　　　　**LEVEL: Intermediate-Advanced**

LOCATION: 7 miles off shore; 3 miles east-southeast of the *David Dows* (site #2).

The wooden steamer, *Louisville* (137'5" x 25'6" x 11'2"), launched at Buffalo, New York, in 1853, sank following a fire on board on September 29, 1857. One life was lost, that of the *Louisville's* fireman, who drowned when his lifeboat capsized in the turbulence created by the still-revolving propeller as his ship was sinking. The *Louisville,* one of the first propeller-driven vessels on the Great Lakes, lies just north of the Indiana-Illinois state line.

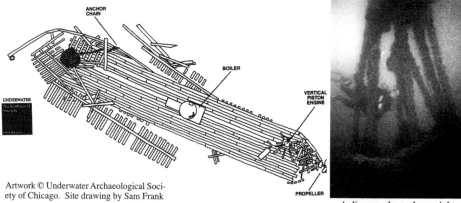

Artwork © Underwater Archaeological Society of Chicago. Site drawing by Sam Frank

A diver explores the upright, eight-legged steam engine of the historic ship, *Louisville*.
PHOTO BY JIM JARECKI

The site includes the upright engine, boiler, part of the smokestack, propeller, anchor chain and much piping and wooden hull and decking. Local charters boats and/or the Underwater Archaeological Society of Chicago buoy this site annually.

3. DAVID DOWS -- SEE PAGES 400-401

4. "MYSTERY WRECK"

> **LORAN:**　　　　　　　　　**GPS: 41° 47.555'/087° 23.929'**
> **DEPTH: 50 feet**　　　　　　**LEVEL: Novice-Intermediate**

LOCATION: Just north-northwest of the wreck of the *Louisiana*, seven miles off shore.

The long hull, ribs and planking of this unidentified wooden vessel have been flattened by time and nature. The stern appears surprisingly square.

5. LUTHER LOOMIS

The small, 29-ton tugboat, *Luther Loomis,* built in 1889, caught on fire in the Calumet River in 1913 and was towed out into Lake Michigan and allowed to sink there.

Great Lakes Highlight No. 18

DAVID DOWS: THE SAILING GIANT

LORAN: 33383.6/50201.7   **GPS: 41° 45.95'/087° 23.58'**
DEPTH: 40 to 45 feet   **LEVEL: Intermediate**

LOCATION: This wreck lies north of Indiana Shoals, five miles off the nearest shore.

Launched amidst great fanfare at Toledo, Ohio, on April 21, 1881, the 1,347-net-ton schooner, *David Dows* (265'4" x 37'6" x 18'), it was hoped, would revive the use of sailing ships over steamships for commercial purposes on the Great Lakes. She was, after all, the largest schooner in the world. The solid logs which comprised the masts, from bow to stern, reached a height, respectively, of 93', 97', 97', 93', and 88'. Add to that the topmasts, at 65' in height each, and which were attached as extensions to the tops of the masts, and the *David Dows'* mainmast towered an incredible 162' above the ship's deck! The mighty vessel was designed to carry an impressive 140,000 bushels of grain, and she had two, not just one, centerboards. The ship was designed to be handled by a relatively small crew of only 12 sailors, about twice the number that Great Lakes schooners typically carried.

The large schooner, *David Dows,* appears manageable in this Louden Wilson artwork. CRIS KOHL COLLECTION

But the largest (and the only five-masted) schooner on the inland seas proved too difficult to maneuver in the confined waters of the Great Lakes, even with her competent crew and a steam donkey engine to raise and lower her gigantic, heavy sails. After two collisions, the second one involving the loss of four lives, this maritime white elephant was demoted to a towbarge. As such, the *David Dows,* carrying a cargo of coal, foundered in a storm while at anchor on November 30, 1889, with no lives lost.

The five-masted schooner, *David Dows,* largest sailing vessel built on the Great Lakes. CRIS KOHL COLLECTION

The storm appears to have broken the ship in two. The stern portion, located in 1964, remains considerably intact, with its centerboad box, rudder, and rudder post. The bow portion has not been located. At that shallow a depth, the mightiest of the Great Lakes sailing ships ever constructed was soon, for the most part, flattened by time and nature. Despite that, many items of interest remain at this relatively shallow site. Coal, likely from her last cargo, lies scattered near the centerboard box. The double-planked hull construction is quite visible as the diver swims around the stern hull segment. The starboard side has broken away and lies flat on the lake floor. At this depth, the visiting diver has time to explore all around the actual hull itself, just off the main wreck site.

The *David Dows* is a prime case where "bigger" was not necessarily "better."

The huge schooner, *David Dows,* was wrecked in lower Lake Michigan in 1889. She was the largest sailing ship ever constructed on the Great Lakes, but her career record was disappointing. Considering this ship's reputation, her broken remains in shallow water often fail to dazzle scuba diving visitors.

PHOTOS BY JOE OLIVER

6. DESMOND

Built in 1892 at Port Huron, Michigan, the wooden steamer, *Desmond,* capsized off the South Chicago breakwall on Dec. 8, 1917, with the loss of seven lives. This shallow site, known to divers many years ago, has failed to be relocated in recent years.

The 160-foot-long steamer, *Desmond.* CRIS KOHL COLLECTION

7. TACOMA

LORAN: 33417.7/50178.9	GPS: 41° 46.22'/087° 31.37'
DEPTH: 27 to 35 feet	LEVEL: Novice-Intermediate

LOCATION: This wreck lies near Chicago's Clark Point Shoal, 2.5 miles north-northwest of the Calumet Harbor Light.

The wooden, steam-powered tug, *Tacoma* (73'4" x 18' x 9'), foundered with no lives lost on November 4, 1929. Built in 1894 at Benton Harbor, Michigan, the little tug had simply grown too old to handle Lake Michigan. The wreck sits on a sand bottom with the propeller and steam engine the highlights of this site, which is buoyed annually by local dive shops, charter boats and/or the Underwater Archaeological Society of Chicago.

The *Tacoma's* steam engine. PHOTO BY JIM JARECKI

The tug, *Tacoma.* CRIS KOHL COLLECTION

Tacoma's rudder and propeller. PHOTO BY JIM JARECKI

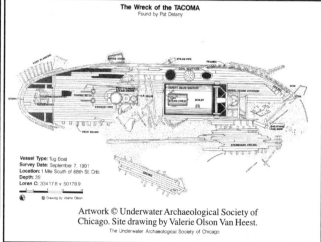

The Wreck of the TACOMA
Found by Pat Delany

Vessel Type: Tug Boat
Survey Date: September 7, 1991
Location: 1 Mile South of 68th St. Crib
Depth: 35
Loran C: 33417.8 x 50178.9

Artwork © Underwater Archaeological Society of Chicago. Site drawing by Valerie Olson Van Heest.
The Underwater Archaeological Society of Chicago

8. SILVER SPRAY

The passenger steamer, *Silver Spray* (115' x 21'10" x 8'3"), launched as *Bloomer Girl* in 1894 at Ludington, Michigan, caught on fire on July 15, 1914, after stranding on Morgan Shoal with 200 passengers; no lives were lost. The ship broke up, with the hull and superstructure washing ashore and used for bonfires. Today, only the boiler remains, and can be seen from Lakeshore Drive near 49th St.

3919 Oakton~ Skokie, Illinois 60076
(847) 674-0222 Fax (847) 674-0275
www.scubasystems.org

IN-STORE 86°POOL
PADI 5-Star Facility

SCUBA & SNORKELING CENTER

Excellent customer service since 1975

- ➢ Equipment Sales
- ➢ Rentals & Repairs
- ➢ Prescription Masks
- ➢ Nitrox, Tri-Mix, & Argon Fills
- ➢ Group & Private Classes
- ➢ Tec Deep Classes
- ➢ Children's Classes and Parties
- ➢ Dive Travel
- ➢ Great Lakes Wreck Diving

9. *ILLINOIS* DREDGE AND "HOLLY BARGE"

> **LORAN: 33403.1/50128.4** **GPS: 41° 49.99'/087° 34.26'**
> **DEPTH: 24 to 33 feet** **LEVEL: Novice**

LOCATION: About two miles east of 33rd Street, Chicago.

The hydraulic sand dredge, *Illinois,* reputedly the largest on the Great Lakes at the time, sank in a storm on Dec. 9, 1907. Much of Chicago's shoreline sand was carried by this dredge. Notable features of this site include a large pump, boom supports and an auger.

On May 6, 2000, a 120' long barge which had been used by the Holly Towing Company (hence the name, "Holly barge") was scuttled next to the *Illinois* to give this shallow area some added pizzazz. Penetration into the barge's holds is possible for trained, experienced divers.

This site is buoyed annually by local dive shops, charter boats and/or the Underwater Archaeological Society of Chicago.

Above: The "Holly barge" sinking on May 6, 2000. PHOTO BY CRIS KOHL

Left: The "Holly barge" is used for dive training.
Above: Joan Forsberg points towards the *Illinois* wreck from the "Holly barge."
Below: The helicoidal auger at the bow of the *Illinois.*
PHOTOS BY CRIS KOHL

The *Illinois* dredge

PIPE TO TRANSPORT SAND SLURRY
PORT BOOM SUPPORT
MACHINERY PLATFORM
AUGER DRIVE SHAFT
UNDERWATER Archeological Society
CENTRIFUGAL PUMP (12" Diameter)
CABLE REEL
MACHINERY PLATFORM
STARBOARD BOOM SUPPORT
THREE BLADED HELICOIDAL AUGER

Artwork © Underwater Archaeological Society of Chicago. Site drawing by Sam Frank

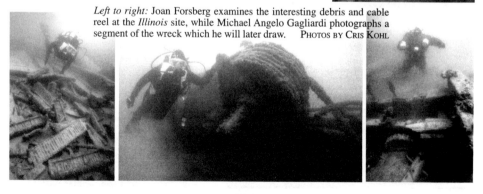

Left to right: Joan Forsberg examines the interesting debris and cable reel at the *Illinois* site, while Michael Angelo Gagliardi photographs a segment of the wreck which he will later draw. PHOTOS BY CRIS KOHL

10. DISPATCH BOAT #1

LOCATION: This small wreck lies about three miles east of Burnham Harbor.
This wooden tug burned and sank off Chicago on April 3, 1935, with no lives lost. This gas screw vessel was built in 1928.

11. 12TH STREET WRECK

LOCATION: On the north edge of 12th Street Beach, Chicago, behind the planetarium.
An unidentified shipwreck, a schooner estimated to be 150′ in total length (some of it is buried under the concrete walkway) is embedded in the sand, stones, and rocks on the edge of this beach.

Underwater Archaeological Society of Chicago members do a winter survey of the 12th St. Wreck in the shadows of the nation's tallest buildings. PHOTOS BY CRIS KOHL

12. RAINBOW

LORAN: 33397.5/50098.5	GPS: 41° 52.10′/087° 36.46′
DEPTH: 20 feet	LEVEL: Novice

LOCATION: About a mile south-southeast of the Chicago harbor entrance.
The 3-masted schooner, *Rainbow* (125′ x 27′ x 10′), built in 1855 at Buffalo, New York, sank with her lumber cargo on May 18, 1894. She lies broken up and scattered.

13. FOUR-MILE CRIB

LORAN: 33379.9/50106.3	GPS: 41° 52.400′/087° 32.700′
DEPTH: 30 feet	LEVEL: Novice-Intermediate

LOCATION: This site lies four miles straight out of Chicago harbor.
For a change from shipwrecks, dive around the base of this historic site. Keep your eyes open for old tools and machinery discarded by crib workers years ago.

14. CAISSONS

LORAN: 33365.71/50092.0	GPS: 41° 53.69′/087° 32.01′
DEPTH: 45 to 50 feet	LEVEL: Intermediate

LOCATION: This unusual site lies about a mile east beyond the Four-Mile Crib.
The infamous Chicago Fire of 1871 killed about 300 people and destroyed much of the city. The survivors were determined to rebuild their homes and businesses as fast as possible. But what would they do with all the rubble? The simple solution in those pre-environmental-concerns times was to load it onto dredges and dump it into the lake. The caissons is the location where this 1871 fire rubble was reputedly dumped. It covers a large area underwater, and many interesting items, such as watches and jugs, have been found over the years by divers. It is unclear as to why this site is called the "caissons," since a caisson is, among other things unrelated to water, a watertight chamber used in construction work under water (which this site is not), or a float for raising a sunken vessel (which this site is also not). Another name for the "bends" is "caissons disease," so don't dive this site too long!

15. EAST TUG

LORAN: 33365.8/50099.0	GPS: 41° 53.30'/087° 31.25'
DEPTH: 45 feet	LEVEL: Intermediate

This unidentified tug sits about a mile east of the Four-Mile Crib.

16. SOUTH TUG AND "TYM BARGE"

LORAN: 33360.9/50087.6	GPS: 41° 54.345'/087° 31.680'
DEPTH: 42 feet	LEVEL: Intermediate

LOCATION: This two-sites-in-one is about 900' southwest of the North tug.

This unidentified steam-powered tug, approximately 60' long, features its engine, boiler and propeller, along with scattered pottery pieces. Next to it is the "Tym barge," which was a relatively small (30' in length by 15' in beam) wooden, barrel/submarine-shaped experimental fuel-oil tank barge. Michael Tym of Chicago constructed this prototype for the Navy in 1942. No additional barges were manufactured, and this one was left to deteriorate in the harbor; divers moved it into the lake in 1999. Both wrecks can be visited on a single dive. This site is usually buoyed by the local charter boats and/or dive shops and/or the UASC.

17. NORTH TUG

LORAN: 33359.8/50084.0	GPS: 41° 54.50'/087° 31.82'
DEPTH: 45 feet	LEVEL: Intermediate

LOCATION: This wreck lies just north of the South tug and Tym barge.

This unidentified tug, about 70' long, displays its engine, boiler and propeller.

Great Lakes Highlight No. 19

THE *EASTLAND*:
THE WORST MARITIME DISASTER

The *Eastland*. CRIS KOHL COLLECTION

The worst maritime disaster in Great Lakes history, besides being the most horrendous, is also the most absurd and senseless.

Early on the morning of Saturday, July 24, 1915, the passenger excursion steamer named the *Eastland*, tied to a shoreline dock in the shallow Chicago River in the heart of the largest city on the Great Lakes, capsized onto her port side. More than 800 of the 2,400+ people on board perished within 50 feet of shore, the majority of them women and children.

The Western Electric Company, expecting 7,000 people consisting of their employees, their families and their friends, had chartered five steamers for this massive round-trip, day-long, company picnic excursion across Lake Michigan to Michigan City, Indiana. The *Eastland*, largest and fastest of the five steamers, filled up first. Before the ship left port, the tragedy struck.

More than 800 people died, including 22 entire families (mother, father, and children). Recovery of bodies seemed like a never-ending horror, particularly since most of the dead were young mothers and little children. Several Chicago undertakers worked nonstop for days at a time.

Numerous reasons were given for the disaster: suspected overcrowding, with no organized control of passenger numbers; most of the passengers gathering

Below: The Jenks Shipbuilding Company had launched the 265-foot-long, steel-hulled *Eastland* at Port Huron, Michigan, on May 6, 1903. Twelve years later, hundreds of Chicagoans, entombed inside that steel hull, met unimaginable, horrifying deaths. Recovering the hundreds of bodies required a dozen hardhat divers and 14 heartbreaking days. CRIS KOHL COLLECTION

For more detailed information about the *Eastland* disaster, see Chapter 14, "Great Lakes Death Ship: The *Eastland*" in the book, *Titanic, The Great Lakes Connections* by Cris Kohl.

Most of the *Eastland* victims died inside the capsized ship, but many drowned in the Chicago River. Makeshift morgues were set up in nearby buildings like the Second Regiment Armory, which today is the home of Harpo Studios where Oprah Winfrey's talk show is taped.　CRIS KOHL COLLECTION

on the river, or port, side of the vessel; an incompetent engineer below deck changing the water ballast frequently between the port and starboard tanks; the sleek, narrow ship's design as a cargo freighter making the vessel tilt and sway due to her high center of gravity; additional lifeboats, liferafts and lifejackets, added as a result of recent safety legislation passed in response to *Titanic's* loss in 1912, adding tons of weight to the top part of an already topheavy ship (as it was, the disaster occurred so swiftly that there was no time to launch even a single lifeboat or for any passenger to don a lifejacket!); and recent structural changes, like pouring 30+ tons of concrete between the deck and the main floor for repairs, adversely affecting the ship's stability.

Angry citizens of Chicago filed hundreds of lawsuits and litigation lingered for decades. Lawyers tried (unsuccessfully) to argue that the accident occurred "upon the high seas," which would have merited federal jurisdiction. In 1935, the courts finally determined that the company which owned the *Eastland* was liable only to the extent of the salvage value of the vessel, which turned out to be minimal.

The *Eastland* itself was righted within three weeks, but no one wanted the grim vessel any more. Finally, the ship was sold by the insurance company to the Naval Reserves for $42,000.00 on Nov. 21, 1917; $36,000.00 of that money was paid to the salvage company which raised the ship. For nearly three decades afterwards, sailors felt uneasy about being on a vessel, renamed the USS *Wilmette*, in which more than 800 people had died. Decommissioned on Nov. 28, 1945, the *Wilmette*/ex-*Eastland* was offered for sale, but no buyers could be found. On Nov. 2, 1948, the scrapping of the most hated ship in Chicago began in a wrecking yard on the South Branch of the Chicago River.

It made front page news in Chicago.

Libby Hruby was one of the lucky ones; she was only ten years old when she survived the *Eastland* disaster. *Above,* she attended the *Eastland* commemorative service at the disaster site in 2002. The memory of the tragedy stayed clear in her mind all her life. Sadly, she died in 2004 at age 99. PHOTO BY CRIS KOHL

18. IOWA

LORAN: 33373.7/50087.1	GPS: 41° 53.76'/087° 33.76'
DEPTH: 35 to 40 feet	LEVEL: Novice-Intermediate

LOCATION: This wreck lies about 4 miles east of Navy Pier, between two cribs.

The steamer, *Iowa*. CRIS KOHL COLLECTION

Launched as the *Menominee* in 1872 at Manitowoc, Wisconsin, this wooden steamer was constructed to replace the steamer, *Navarino,* which had been destroyed in the big Chicago fire of October 9, 1871. In fact, the steam engine from the *Navarino*, only a year old at the time of the burning, was placed into the *Menominee*. On the verge of being abandoned due to age, the ship was completely rebuilt in 1896 and renamed *Iowa* (202'5" x 36'4" x 12'). As such, this vessel experienced a string of at least six strandings and collisions which earned her the reputation of being a jinxed ship. Finally, the *Iowa,* with a cargo of general merchandise on her 13th trip of the year, was crushed by the ice off Chicago harbor and sank on February 4, 1915. The crew and the single passenger simply stepped onto the ice and walked to shore. The hull was partially removed, some cargo and machinery (engine and boilers) were salvaged and the rest was dynamited as a navigation hazard.

Re-located in the late 1950's and in 1976, the *Iowa* lies scattered over a broad area. The remains of an old truck lie there, amidst kitchen items such as plates. Enough machinery remains at this site (even after the salvage and dynamiting) to make it interesting.

19. "MIKE'S WRECK"

LORAN: 33376.5/50087.4	GPS: 41° 53.73'/087° 34.16'
DEPTH: 40 feet	LEVEL: Intermediate

This unidentified schooner, about 140' long, named after a charter boat captain who reportedly passed away while attempting to rescue a diver in trouble, is moderately intact.

20. FLORA M. HILL

LORAN: 33375.4/50077.0	GPS: 41° 54.34'/087° 35.08'
DEPTH: 37 feet	LEVEL: Novice-Intermediate

LOCATION: About 1.2 miles north-northeast of the Chicago Harbor Light.

Constructed in 1874 at Philadelphia, Pennsylvania, as the lighthouse tender, *Dahlia* and given her final name on May 12, 1910, the iron-hulled steamer, *Flora M. Hill* (130'9" x 25' x 10'5"), on a run from Kenosha to Chicago, was crushed by ice and sank about 600' southeast of the Two-Mile Crib on March 11, 1912. The 32 crew and passengers, one of them the female cook, walked on the dangerous ice to the safety of the crib and were later picked up by a tugboat. Ironically, the *Flora M. Hill* had been taken to Ferrysburg, Michigan, in 1909-1910 to install heavy plating which would give her year-round working capability

Left: The steamer, *Flora M. Hill.* CRIS KOHL COLLECTION

Right: Exploring the *Hill's* iron hull. PHOTO BY JIM JARECKI

410

by enabling her to go through the ice. The wreck was later dynamited as a navigation hazard.

With her stern aimed at the Two Mile Crib and her bow pointing southwest, the *Flora M. Hill* features iron hull plates, a boiler, propeller and rudder as its highlights. Remnants of her cargo of brass beds and automobile running lamps are still evident.

Sidescan sonar image of the steamer, *Flora M. Hill*.
COURTESY OF DOUG GOSSAGE, GOOSE'S SCUBA

21. NORTH AVENUE SCHOONER

LORAN: 33375.9/50070.4	GPS: 41° 54.73'/087° 35.85'
DEPTH: 30 feet	LEVEL: Novice

LOCATION: This wreck lies about 1.5 miles out in the lake east of North Avenue. This unidentified schooner has a fairly substantial debris field scattered to its south.

22. BOX BARGE

LORAN: 33339.0/50104.7	GPS: 41° 54.079'087° 26.267'
DEPTH: 60 feet	LEVEL: Advanced

LOCATION: This small, metal box-shaped wreck lies about 7.7 miles east of Chicago. This wreck, upright with an open hold, has a deck equipped with tow blocks and cleats.

23. *ROTARIAN*

LORAN: 33317.0/50072.0	GPS: 41° 57.016'/087° 26.066'
DEPTH: 80 to 84 feet	LEVEL: Advanced

LOCATION: About 8.2 miles east-northeast of the Chicago harbor entrance.

Launched as the *A. Wehrle, Jr.* on July 17, 1889, at Sandusky, Ohio, this wooden steamer received the name *Rotarian* (146'8" x 41'9" x 9') in 1919. In 1928, the ship was dropped from documentation as "abandoned," but she was docked at Clark Street, Chicago, and used successively as a dance hall, as the home for the Cook County Democrats and as a restaurant. She sank at her slip on Oct. 10, 1930 "of old age" and was scuttled in Lake Michigan on September 28, 1931.

The remains of the *Rotarian* lie a considerable distance offshore, but there is much to see: boiler, hull and much wood debris scattered from this scuttled wreck. Photos next page.

Left: Early in the *Rotarian's* career when the ship was still in Ohio and named the *A. Wehrle, Jr.* CRIS KOHL COLLECTION. *Above:* Prohibition beer bottles amidst the *Rotarian's* wreckage. *Right and below right:* Joyce Hayward photographs the *Rotarian*, the ship with the colorful history. *Below left:* The boiler.
PHOTOS BY CRIS KOHL

24. "VAL'S WRECK"

LORAN:	GPS: 41° 55.504'/087° 27.065'
DEPTH: 63 feet	LEVEL: Intermediate-Advanced

LOCATION: This wreck lies about 7.5 miles east of Chicago, Illinois.

That UASC romantic devil, Keith Pearson, gave the location coordinates of this unidentified shipwreck to former girlfriend Val Olson on her birthday, so it has been called "Val's Wreck" ever since. Stripped and broken up, with the bow buried under sand, this appears to be a large (100'+) tug with only a 4'-diameter propeller left of its machinery, so it was probably scuttled; 1920's art deco debris lies on and around the wreck, perhaps dumped later.

25. DAVID A. WELLS

DEPTH: 43 feet	LEVEL: Novice-Intermediate

Lost in the severe *Alpena* Storm of Oct. 16, 1880, the 3-masted schooner, *David A. Wells* (134' x 26' x 12'), built in 1866 at Port Huron, Michigan, sank with all (8) hands and an iron ore cargo. She lies mostly embedded, with frame ends sticking out of the lake bottom.

26. WINGS OF THE WIND

LORAN: 33357.5/50064.1   **GPS:** 41° 55.86′/087° 33.50′
DEPTH: 40 to 45 feet   **LEVEL:** Intermediate

LOCATION: This wreck lies about 3.5 miles north-northeast of the Chicago harbor entrance.

The two-masted schooner, W*ings of the Wind* (142′ x 26′ x 10′), built in 1855 at Buffalo, NY, sank with her coal cargo after a collision with the large bark, *H. P. Baldwin,* on May 12, 1866. The brand new *H. P. Baldwin,* basically undamaged, rescued the *Wings of the Wind's* crew. The coal cargo salvage later in 1866 destroyed the schooner's stern.

Located in 1987 by professional divers who revealed its location to sport divers, this shipwreck was reportedly soon stripped of most of

Top, right: The *Wings of the Wind* sports a large windlass. PHOTO BY CRIS KOHL. *Right:* Sidescan sonar image of the *Wings of the Wind.* COURTESY OF DOUG GOSSAGE, GOOSE'S SCUBA

Great Lakes Highlight No. 20

CONSTRUCTIVE SHIPWRECK:
THE *REUTAN*

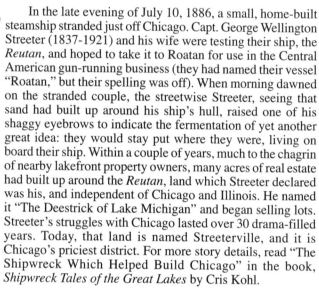

CAPT. GEORGE
WELLINGTON
STREETER.

In the late evening of July 10, 1886, a small, home-built steamship stranded just off Chicago. Capt. George Wellington Streeter (1837-1921) and his wife were testing their ship, the *Reutan*, and hoped to take it to Roatan for use in the Central American gun-running business (they had named their vessel "Roatan," but their spelling was off). When morning dawned on the stranded couple, the streetwise Streeter, seeing that sand had built up around his ship's hull, raised one of his shaggy eyebrows to indicate the fermentation of yet another great idea: they would stay put where they were, living on board their ship. Within a couple of years, much to the chagrin of nearby lakefront property owners, many acres of real estate had built up around the *Reutan*, land which Streeter declared was his, and independent of Chicago and Illinois. He named it "The Deestrick of Lake Michigan" and began selling lots. Streeter's struggles with Chicago lasted over 30 drama-filled years. Today, that land is named Streeterville, and it is Chicago's priciest district. For more story details, read "The Shipwreck Which Helped Build Chicago" in the book, *Shipwreck Tales of the Great Lakes* by Cris Kohl.

Counterclockwise from upper left: 'Cap' Streeter could actually look formal and elegant. Ma & Cap Streeter kept the land authorities at bay for many years while living on 186 acres of land created after their steamer, the *Reutan*, stranded in Chicago's shallows. Often Cap's conflicts landed him in jail temporarily. The land his shipwreck created is today named Streeterville, and all the tall skyscrapers in this late 1920's postcard are sitting there. Even a Chicago tour ship today is named "Cap Streeter." Streeter died in 1921 at the age of 83, still fighting for "his" land.   Cris Kohl Collection; modern photos by Cris Kohl

CAP. STREETER
DIES DEFYING
GOLD COAST
'Ma' and His Dog With
Old Fighter on Boat
When End Came.

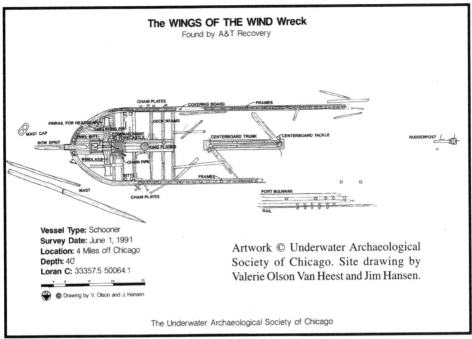

The WINGS OF THE WIND Wreck
Found by A&T Recovery

Vessel Type: Schooner
Survey Date: June 1, 1991
Location: 4 Miles off Chicago
Depth: 40'
Loran C: 33357.5 50064.1

Artwork © Underwater Archaeological Society of Chicago. Site drawing by Valerie Olson Van Heest and Jim Hansen.

© Drawing by V. Olson and J. Hansen

The Underwater Archaeological Society of Chicago

its small artifacts. Only the forward half of this schooner remains intact, with her bowsprit, chains, windlass and centerboard trunk photogenically in place. A fallen mast lies off her port bow. A mooring buoy is attached annually to this site charter boat operators and/or by the Underwater Archaeological Society of Chicago.

27. LUCILLE

LORAN: 33355.1/50033.9	GPS: 41° 57.87'/087° 36.23'
DEPTH: 30 feet	LEVEL: Novice

LOCATION: This wreck lies 1/4 mile off the Wilson Avenue crib.

The 159-gross-ton steamer, *Lucille* (100' x 23'), referred to as a "wood swill boat," was built by the Miller Brothers at Chicago for Shufeldt Distillery in 1884. The ship was sunk by ice on February 2, 1893, after ferrying 30 tunnel workers and supplies (sand, cement, brick, coal, and foodstuffs) to the crib. Located by Harry Zych, this shipwreck site features a bow stem, keelson, framing, planking, and chain.

28. THE STRAITS OF MACKINAC

LORAN: GPS: 42° 02.726'/087° 30.894'
DEPTH: 38 to 78 feet   LEVEL: Novice to Technical

LOCATION: This wreck lies several miles northeast of Chicago's Navy Pier.

Sunk on April 10, 2003, the old ferry, *The Straits of Mackinac*, is the largest of the scuttled ships used to create a Great Lakes dive site, and the most frequently visited site in Lake Michigan. Launched at River Rouge, MI, on May 28, 1929, the *The Straits of Mackinac* (196'1" x 48'1" x 14'7") carried tourists and their autos across the Straits of Mackinac for nearly 30 years. After hauling supplies to Mackinac Island until 1968, the ship was retired.

Above: The Straits of Mackinac appeared on many postcards from the 1930's to the 1960's. CRIS KOHL COLLECTION. On April 10, 2003, a powerful tugboat pushed the ship out of the Calumet River to the northeast past Chicago. Patrick Hammer, the chief organizer and investor, prayed for a successful sinking. Hank Fiene, who was the liaison between the Neptune's Nimrods Dive Club of Green Bay and Chicago interests in obtaining this vessel, stood by in his inflatable. As the ship sank, water spouts spurted from the pressure below. PHOTOS BY CRIS KOHL
Below: The Straits of Mackinac sank in exactly 100 minutes after her seacocks were opened. Today, all levels of scuba divers, from novice (deck level diving) to technical (penetration diving), can explore the largest ship sunk in the Great Lakes for the purpose of creating a dive site. UASC's Keith Pearson jumped at a chance to buy one of the ship's original portholes and bolted it to the vessel on deck prior to the sinking. Don't miss it! PHOTOS BY CRIS KOHL

29. WELLS BURT

LORAN: 33325.5/49977.6   GPS: 42° 02.739'/087° 37.092'
DEPTH: 38-45 feet   LEVEL: Intermediate

LOCATION: This wreck lies about three miles east of Evanston, Illinois.

DEADLY GALES

The Large Schooner Wells Burt Sunk at Grosse Point, Near Chicago.

The Captain and Ten of the Crew of the Ill-fated Vessel Drowned.

Woeful Wrecks Washed Ashore by the Terrible Storm of Last Sunday.

Additional Particulars of the Gale That Swept the Lakes with Fearful Fury.

CRIS KOHL COLLECTION

The majestic *Wells Burt*.
ARTIST UNKNOWN. CRIS KOHL COLLECTION

The huge, three-masted schooner, *Wells Burt* (201' x 33'5" x 14'2"), launched on July 12, 1873 at Detroit, Michigan, foundered in a storm on May 20, 1883, with the loss of all 11 people on board and her cargo of coal. Hardhat divers soon recovered the two anchors and her masts, while the rest of the ship was already settling into the soft lake bottom.

Located in 1988 by professional divers from A & T Recovery of Chicago, the wreck of the *Wells Burt* was found to be in excellent condition in spite of its shallow site. Facing northwest with a slight port list, she sits embedded in about 8' of clay, but her hold is open and accessible through the hatches. A capstan and a windlass remain on deck. The wreck was surveyed and photographed extensively by the Underwater Archaeological Society of Chicago. Maintaining the integrity of the shipwreck succeeded for a while, but in late 1990 or early 1991, a diver stole 10 of the large deadeyes from the site; there is a reward of $2,000.00 offered for information leading to the arrest and conviction of the thief. Contact the Illinois Historic Preservation Agency or the State Police if you know the whereabouts of these irreplacable items. This site is buoyed annually.

The schooner, *Wells Burt*

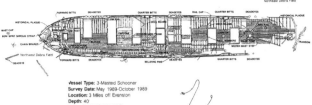

Vessel Type: 3-Masted Schooner
Survey Date: May 1989-October 1989
Location: 3 Miles off Evanston
Depth: 40'
Loran C: 33325.4 49977.7

Artwork © Underwater Archaeological Society of Chicago. Site drawing by Valerie Olson

Below: Close-up of a *Wells Burt* deadeye. ART BY MICHAEL ANGELO GAGLIARDI

Clockwise, from upper right: The buoy marker is anchored off the *Wells Burt* to protect the shipwreck; a line runs to the bow. Joan Forsberg approaches a fallen bilge pump. Joyce Hayward examines three, huge deadeyes chained to the wreck, and later, the bow capstan.   PHOTOS BY CRIS KOHL

Great Lakes Highlight No. 21

THE *UC-97*:

THE GREAT LAKES' SUNKEN U-BOAT

LORAN:	LAT 42° 10' LON 087° 20'
DEPTH: About 250 feet	LEVEL: Technical

LOCATION: This wreck lies about 19 miles off Wilmette, Illinois.

A German U-boat, spotted by a sailor from a Great Lakes freighter in the middle of Lake Michigan on August 16, 1919, scared the daylights out of him. But the ship was only a harmless war prize, brought to the United States and towed to Chicago after Germany's defeat in World War I (1914-1918). The German mine-laying submarine, *UC-97* (185' x 18' x 12'), launched at Hamburg, Germany, on March 17, 1918 and technically renamed the *"USS Ex-UC97"* when the US Navy took over her command, was towed around Great Lakes ports to stimulate the sale of post-war Victory Bonds by giving buyers a close-up view of an enemy submarine.

The Treaty of Versailles, which ended World War I, called for the destruction of all German weapons of war within three years of confiscation. Accordingly, on June 7, 1921, the USS *Hawk* towed the German sub out into the middle of Lake Michigan and the Navy training ship, the USS *Wilmette* (formerly the disastrous passenger steamer, *Eastland,* which had capsized at dock in Chicago on July 24, 1915, taking over 800 people to a watery grave) used her as target practice. Eighteen rounds of 4-inch shells put the submarine on the bottom.

The approximate location, given above, is from the log of the USS *Hawk.* Reportedly the Navy located the submarine in 1977, with verification given by the Combined Great Lakes Naval Association from their vessel, *Neptune,* and in 1992, A & T Recovery, a commercial salvage company, also located the shipwreck. In spite of its bombardment, the *UC-97* appears to be upright and quite intact, with a slight starboard list, according to remote-operated video shown recently to the public. Her number, *UC-97,* is clearly visible.

Plans to raise the *UC-97* from this great depth and place it on public exhibit have apparently fallen through, as funding has not been forthcoming.

Left: On board the confiscated German *UC-97*, memorial services were held on May 8, 1919, marking the 4th anniversary of the loss of the *Lusitania.* The submarine was later sunk in Lake Michigan after her Victory Bonds tour. US NAVY PHOTO. *Right: UC-97's* anti-netting teeth dominate this photo.   CRIS KOHL COLLECTION

Great Lakes Highlight No. 22

CHICAGO'S SUNKEN AIRPLANES

When the USA became embroiled in WWII in December, 1941, a plan which had been suggested years earlier was quickly activated: turning Lake Michigan into a training ground for Naval aircraft carrier pilots. Between 1942 and 1945, 17,820 pilots received training here, including future President George H. W. Bush. The two ships used for training were former Great Lakes excursion ships:

Seeandbee/Wolverine

Greater Buffalo/Sable

Above: The 6,381-ton sidewheel passenger steamer, SS *Seeandbee* (484'5" x 58' x 24'), launched at Wyandotte, Michigan, on Nov. 9, 1912, was the largest sidewheel steamer in the world at the time. *Below:* After a speedy 59-day conversion into an aircraft carrier with a flight deck 558'6" long, the ship was renamed USS *Wolverine* and commissioned on Aug. 12, 1942. The Navy had paid $756,500.00 for it. After the war, a Milwaukee company paid $46,789.00 for it and scrapped the ship in late 1947. CRIS KOHL COLLECTION

Above: The 7,739-ton sidewheel passenger steamer, SS *Greater Buffalo* (518'7" x 58' x 21'3"), launched at Lorain, Ohio, on Oct. 27, 1923, became the largest sidewheel steamer in the world at the time. *Below:* Converted into an aircraft carrier with a deck 535' long, the ship was renamed USS *Sable* and commissioned on May 8, 1943. The Navy likely paid more for this newer ship than it had for the *Seeandbee*. After the war, a Canadian company paid $126,176.00 for it and scrapped the ship in late 1948. CRIS KOHL COLLECTION

Left: Of the tens of thousands of training flights on Lake Michigan during the war, several were unsuccessful. Estimates vary: between 100 and 300 planes ended up on the lake bottom. CRIS KOHL COLLECTION. *Right:* A raised WWII aircraft graces Chicago's Midway airport. PHOTO BY CRIS KOHL

421

30. CARRIER

LOCATION: About 1,500 feet off shore from Main Street, Evanston, IL, in 30'.

The old schooner, *Carrier* (123' x 26' x 8'6"), built in 1865 at Marine City, Michigan, and used as the Chicago Yacht Club clubhouse in her final ten years, sank while under tow to Waukegan, Illinois, on Sept. 30, 1923. She lies broken up and scattered.

The *Carrier, left,* as a Chicago yacht club-house, and *right,* on Sept. 30, 1923, towed away by *Subchaser 412,* donated to be the new clubhouse of the Naval Scouts of Wau-kegan. CRIS KOHL COLLECTION

31. GEORGE W. MORLEY

LORAN: 33338.8/49970.2	GPS: 42° 02.67'/087° 40.14'
DEPTH: 20 feet	LEVEL: Novice

BIG SHIP IS BURNED

Propeller George W. Morley Destroyed on Evanston Shore.

ESCAPE OF THE CREW

Boat Takes Fire En Route from Milwaukee to Chicago.

Spectacular Blaze Witnessed by Thousands on the Beach of the Northern Suburb.

With a fierce fire raging in her hold, the freight steamer George W. Morley was beached o nthe Evanston shore early last night, where she burned to the water's edge. The fire was discovered when the boat was seven miles off shore, running under full

LOCATION: This wreck lies about 300' off Greenwood Avenue, Evanston, Illinois.

Launched in April, 1888, at West Bay City, Michigan, the wooden steamer, *George W. Morley* (192'9" x 34' x 21'), caught fire and stranded on December 5, 1897, with no lives lost. The ship was travelling light between Milwaukee and Chicago. Her engine was salvaged in October, 1898. The bottom part of the hull lies broken, with other pieces scattered.

The wooden steamer, *George W. Morley,* and news of its fiery demise. CRIS KOHL COLLECTION

32. SEARCHER

LOCATION: About 17 miles off Chicago's Northerly Island, in 160 feet of water.

This 60-ton, 65' steel fishtug sank with 3 lives lost (the Coast Guard airlifted 3 others) on Dec. 27, 1985. Three commercial divers, including Keith Pearson, recovered the bodies.

33. UC-97 -- SEE PAGE 420

34. ST. MARY

LORAN: 33259.3/49882.5	GPS: 42° 11.482'/087° 35.927'
DEPTH: 110 feet	LEVEL: Advanced

LOCATION: This wreck lies 8 miles northeast of Wilmette, Illinois, harbor.

The two-masted schooner, *St. Mary* (114' x 25'), received very little press coverage at the time of her tragic loss because she sank on the exact date that the *Lady Elgin* went down (see site #35), and the latter totally eclipsed the former in the media. Built in 1848 at Perrysburg, Ohio, the *St. Mary* sank with the loss of all 7 hands on September 8, 1860. This west-facing, collapsed-but-intact shipwreck, located by A & T

The *St. Mary* resembled the *J. U. Porter* (114'3" x 25' x 7'). CRIS KOHL COLLECTION

Windlass
The St. Mary

Recovery in 1989, offers exquisite views of a large wooden stock anchor with its stem through a hawsepipe, a folding bow anchor, a windlass and anchor chain, a rudder with draft marks and the ship's wheel in place. Identification is not 100% yet. Regardless, it's a unique site!

Left: The bow of the *St. Mary,* with the windlass predominant. PHOTO COLLAGE BY MICHAEL ANGELO GAGLIARDI

Below: The same subject converted to art. ART BY MICHAEL ANGELO GAGLIARDI

Left: One of the anchors on the wreck of the schooner, *St. Mary,* lies mostly buried in the lake bottom, with only a massive fluke exposed. PHOTO BY CRIS KOHL

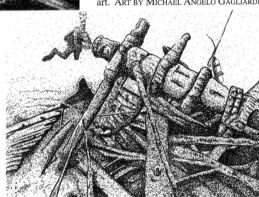

Great Lakes Highlight No. 23

THE *LADY ELGIN*: PRE-CIVIL WAR SHIPWRECK

LOCATION: This wreck lies broken and widely scattered in about 55 feet of water 4.3 miles due east of the harbor at Fort Sheridan, IL. It is an intermediate level dive.

The elegant sidewheel passenger steamer, *Lady Elgin* (251' x 31'8" x 11'1"), built at Buffalo, New York, in 1851, sank after a collision off Winnetka, Illinois, with the small, lumber-laden schooner, *Augusta,* on the stormy night of September 8, 1860. The damaged *Augusta* limped into Chicago, but the mortally stricken *Lady Elgin,* with a gaping hole in her port side, ran desperately for shore in heavy weather but broke into pieces and sank within

The *Lady Elgin* sinking. CRIS KOHL COLLECTION

30 minutes. She was bound from Chicago to Milwaukee with a large passenger list which included several civic officials, and enormous loss of life ensued, with estimates ranging from 282 to 373 people perishing, most of Irish descent from Milwaukee. Some history analysts have argued that the loss of the *Lady Elgin* transferred political control of Milwaukee from the Irish to the Germans.

The *Lady Elgin* had had her share of misfortunes, among them striking a rock off Manitowoc on August 30, 1854, and sinking right when she reached dock, with no lives lost, and catching on fire from sparks blown from another steamer on October. 17, 1857, damaging only the deck and one stateroom before the flames were extinguished.

This shipwreck, located by Harry Zych in 1989 (and he had reportedly been searching for her and the *Seabird* --see site #36-- since 1973), is badly broken up and scattered, with the bow and the boiler lying about a mile apart, connected by a vast debris field. Essentially the wreckage is divided into four main fields. A years-long court case over this shipwreck's ownership ensued, with Harry Zych fighting the state of Illinois. The court gave ownership to Harry Zych, or perhaps more correctly, to his non-profit organization, the Lady Elgin Foundation. It is illegal for anyone else to visit the site, and there is a reason for that. During the court proceedings, unknown (as yet) scuba divers stole a number of articles from the bow section, items which will, in all likelihood, never be seen again. Harry's plans are to find a permanent display for the salvaged artifacts, possibly to include a traveling exhibit. Despite court rulings giving ownership of the *Lady Elgin* to Harry Zych, dive boats regularly visit this site. Prior to the court's decision, the various *Lady Elgin* wreck debris sites were catalogued in a study done by the Underwater Archaeological Society of Chicago. To date, Harry Zych has spent years unsuccessfully searching in several states for a museum which will exhibit the artifacts from this controversial shipwreck.

Headlines across the land related the tragedy of the *Lady Elgin* sinking. CRIS KOHL COLLECTION

VOLUME XIV.

APPALLING LAKE DISASTER.

Collision and Fearful Loss of Life.

LOSS OF THE STEAMER

LADY ELGIN

NEARLY 300 LIVES LOST.

98 Persons Saved.

Military and Fire Companies of Milwaukee Among the Lost.

RECEPTION OF THE NEWS HERE.

Particulars of the Disaster.

35. *LADY ELGIN* -- SEE PAGE 424.

36. *SEABIRD*

LORAN: 33264.1/49759.9	GPS: 42° 18.892′/087° 49.262′
DEPTH: 30 feet	LEVEL: Novice-Intermediate

LOCATION: About 1/2 mile northeast of the Great Lakes Naval Training Center Harbor.

Another one of the dozen worst Great Lakes maritime disasters, the sidewheel passenger and freight steamer, *Seabird* (190′8″ x 27′5″ --excludes paddlewheels-- x 10′9″), was built at Newport (today's Marine City), Michigan, in 1859. She also carried double 26′ diameter paddlewheels. On April 9, 1868, running between Milwaukee and Chicago on her third run of the season, she caught on fire off Waukegan, Illinois. An unwitting porter had carelessly thrown hot ashes from the heater stove over the side -- lamentably the windward side! A thousand sparks flew like moths back on board ship

Drawing of the *Seabird*.
ARTIST UNKNOWN. CRIS KOHL COLLECTION

onto the lower deck, right into the cargo of newly varnished buckets and straw. Approximately 72 lives (the estimates ran from 50 to 100) were lost. Only three people survived this horrible catastrophe: C.A. Chamberlain, Edwin Hanneberry and James H. Leonard. The blazing ship burned to the waterline before drifting close to shore and sinking.

The *Seabird* was located by Harry Zych in 1989, the same year he found the *Lady Elgin* (see site #35), and he immediately initiated court proceedings for ownership of both shipwrecks. At last count, the State of Illinois owns the *Seabird*. The highlights of this site include the large boiler and a rarity: a large, intact paddlewheel. Because the paddlewheel is deteriorating, please use the utmost caution when you are near it and make sure you practice

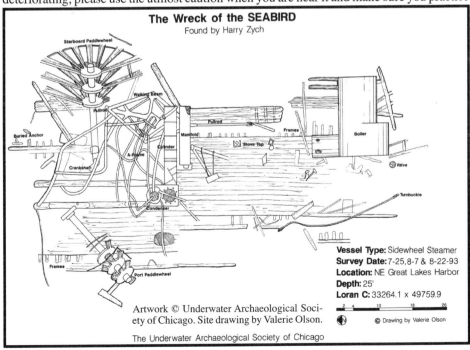

The Wreck of the SEABIRD
Found by Harry Zych

Starboard Paddlewheel
Walking Beam
Pullrod
Pullrod
Buried Anchor
Manifold
Frames
Boiler
Stove Top
Cylinder
A-Frame
Crankshaft
Valve
Condenser
Turnbuckle
Frames
Port Paddlewheel

Vessel Type: Sidewheel Steamer
Survey Date: 7-25,8-7 & 8-22-93
Location: NE Great Lakes Harbor
Depth: 25′
Loran C: 33264.1 x 49759.9

Artwork © Underwater Archaeological Society of Chicago. Site drawing by Valerie Olson.

© Drawing by Valerie Olson

The Underwater Archaeological Society of Chicago

Seabird sights: a paddlewheel, a kettle on timbers, and Joan Forsberg with ship's tools. PHOTOS BY CRIS KOHL

buoyancy skills. Don't wreck the wreck with carelessness or clumsiness. Many small artifacts have been laid out to make it easier for divers to see and appreciate them. Please do not remove anything from this site. It is illegal and unethical. The wreck of the *Seabird* is buoyed annually by local charter boats operators, dive shops, or the UASC.

37. GRAIN BARGE

LORAN:	GPS: 42° 22.43'/087° 42.20'
DEPTH: 112 feet	LEVEL: Advanced

LOCATION: This wreck lies about 4 miles off Waukegan, Illinois.

An unnamed, steel-hulled grain barge (150' x 45') suddenly foundered with a full cargo of grain in the late summer of 2002 while being towed by the tug, *Herbert C. Jackson*.

38. ZION SCHOONERS

LORAN: 33202.1/49672.0	GPS: 42° 27.158'/087° 47.786'
DEPTH: 20 feet	LEVEL: Novice

LOCATION: These wrecks lie just off the Zion (Illinois) Power Plant.

These two unidentified schooners, each about 100' long, were probably aging vessels abandoned at this site. They are broken up and lying in such a way that at least part of one appears to be lying on top of the other. A donkey boiler, often used on schooners and barges to provide steam-powered assistance with the loading and uploading of cargo, rests on one wreck. Construction debris, likely from the power plant on shore, is strewn about the site.

39. ZION MINESWEEPER

LORAN: 33199.0/49668.0	GPS: 42° 27.535'/087° 47.814'
DEPTH: 12 feet	LEVEL: Novice

LOCATION: This wreck lies 400' off shore from Illinois Beach State Park, about 1 mile north of the Zion Power Plant.

Long referred to as the "Zion Mystery Ship" and the "old minesweeper," this 110'-long wooden vessel is actually a decommissioned Navy subchaser. Intense research done by members of the Underwater Archaeological Society of Chicago, spearheaded by Tony Kiefer, has concluded that this shipwreck is likely that of the *SC 419* (although the *SC 418* and *SC 416* are also contenders), part of the Navy's 440-strong "Splinter Fleet" of subchasers built during World War I. Many were sold to France, while some, after the war, were converted to civilian use. This one was scuttled for the creation of a breakwall in front of a private residence, likely in the mid-1930's. If it is the *SC 419*, she was built at Milwaukee by the Great Lakes Boat Building Corporation. Research is ongoing.

The wreck lies on its port side, exposing its copper-clad, steel-reinforced wooden hull. The engine and the propeller are missing, but the propeller shaft remains intact. Several steel tanks, used either for extra fuel or water storage, are on board.

40. *THOMAS HUME* (?)

⟨ **DEPTH: 150 feet** **LEVEL: Technical** ⟩

LOCATION: This wreck lies about 24 miles northeast of Chicago, Illinois.

The schooner, *Thomas Hume* (131'6" x 26'3" x 8'4"; official #95135; 209.79 gross tons; 199.31 net tons; built as the *H. C. Albrecht* in Manitowoc, Wisconsin, in 1870), owned by the Hackley & Hume Lumber Company of Muskegon, Michigan, departed Chicago for Muskegon across Lake Michigan with another Hackley & Hume ship named the *Rouse Simmons* on May 21, 1891, to pick up lumber cargoes. The seas worsened, the *Simmons* turned back to Chicago, and the *Thomas Hume*, pressing on, went missing without a trace with all 7 hands, creating one of the lake's greatest mysteries. (The *Rouse Simmons* also went missing with all hands 21 years later; see pages 462-464). A sunken schooner located off Michigan City, Indiana, in 1905 and claimed to be the *Thomas Hume* turned out to be 175' long, much longer than the *Hume*.

A shipwreck located in deep water in 2003 by A & T Recovery could be the wreck of the *Thomas Hume*. The dimensions appear to be correct. The port bow anchor rests in place, while much anchor chain has spilled off the starboard bow side and is mounded on the lake bottom with the starboard anchor. The stern, which appears to have hit the lake bottom first, is damaged, and masts lie fallen across the wreck. The deck appears to be in very good condition. Solid identification, like a nameboard, or registration and/or tonnage numbers carved in a hatch beam, is still sought.

Shipwreck hunting off Chicago is tricky because of small, pointy clay mounds which rise several feet off the lake bottom. This one is examined by UASC diver Scott Reimer.   PHOTO BY CRIS KOHL

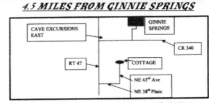

Shipwreck Conservation: Changing Attitudes

Since the year 1679, the Great Lakes have seen more than 15,000 different commercial ships ply their waters. These were sailing vessels until the year 1816, when the first steamer on the Great Lakes was launched in the Kingston, Ontario, area at the eastern end of Lake Ontario. As the invention of steam-powered watercraft perfected itself, the predominance of sail toppled in 1874 when, for the first time, steamships outnumbered sailing craft on the inland seas. The mass production of steel ships began in the 1890's, with 600-footers becoming the norm by 1906. The last wooden-hulled steamer slid down the launchramp in the Great Lakes in 1902, and by the 1930's, most wooden ships had been abandoned or scuttled in ships' graveyards which dotted the region. In 1958, the largest ship on the freshwater seas, the *Edmund Fitzgerald,* was built, only to become, in 1975, the lakes' largest and last major shipwreck tragedy. In 1972, the first of the "thousand-footers," of which there are now a dozen laboring with massive bulk cargoes on the upper Great Lakes, was launched.

When ships sank, people did everything possible to recover them, or to salvage the cargo and as many parts of the ship as possible. On the Great Lakes, professional hardhat divers performed salvage jobs by the early 1850's and reached the height of their profession during the five-decade span, from 1870 to 1920, when most of the shipwrecks occurred, a dark era for the shipping industry, but 50 golden years for a number of famous commercial salvagers headquartered around the Great Lakes. Salvage regulations were written into the shipping acts of both Canada and the United States, and "wreckers" were members of a

Since shipwrecks are historic and nonrenewable, most divers realize that removing artifacts is irresponsible. PHOTO BY CRIS KOHL

dangerous but noble and elite profession. Even in the 1930's, recovery was the norm, with shipwreck conservation little more than a twinkle in an archaeologist's eye.

By the time World War II ended in 1945, the world, including the Great Lakes, was a very different place. Electronic devices provided greater safety for ships, with shipwreck frequency being reduced from a few a week in 1900 to a handful a year by 1950.

There was also a new invention capturing the imaginations of adventurers in 1950, something called a self-contained underwater breathing apparatus, or s.c.u.b.a. for short. Gradually this new breed of modern-day explorer using this scuba invention went in quest of shipwrecks, not only to explore but also to salvage, not on a commercial scale but for personal "tokens of accomplishment" which proclaimed their elite membership status. In the 1950's and '60's, thousands of ships' parts, from the smallest deadeyes to the largest anchors, were removed from Great Lakes waters by people feeling empowered by their new ability to breathe underwater without the constraint of massively heavy equipment, and free from hoses and lines connecting them to the surface. What was shrugged off in the late 1800's as being merely a Jules Verne type of science fiction dream had become a reality by the mid-1900's.

Underwater archaeology training begins with sessions on dry land. Save Ontario Shipwrecks helps train divers.　PHOTO BY CRIS KOHL

By 1970, the results were noticeable. Parallel to the California experience, where spearfishermen and women had switched from free-breathing to scuba equipment, making the taking of fish as easy as shooting them in a barrel, Great Lakes divers noticed something amiss in their waters as well. Off California, the once-plentiful supply of fish to spear had become heavily depleted. In the Great Lakes, new scuba divers would visit a shipwreck once, then never again, because there was nothing left to see but a bare hull. In California, divers placed a moratorium on spearing fish so that the reefs could replenish themselves, but in the Great Lakes, it was heartbreaking to see

Members of shipwreck conservation groups like S.O.S. try out marine archaeology in pool sessions. PHOTO BY CRIS KOHL

Shipwreck surveys produce important information. Joyce Hayward measures Lake Erie's *Conemaugh*. PHOTO BY CRIS KOHL

what had become of many nonrenewable shipwrecks. A scuba diver who was dynamiting the wreck of the *W. L. Wetmore* at Tobermory in the early 1970's prompted the creation of the Great Lakes' first underwater park or preserve, Fathom Five Provincial Park, in 1972. In 1976, Ontario produced its Heritage Act, and in 1981, Michigan passed its Great Lakes Bottomlands Act, both serving to protect our submerged cultural resources. Also in Ontario

The Underwater Archaeological Society of Chicago offers activities which include *(above)* doing winter survey work, when the water is low, of a shipwreck embedded in Chicago's shoreline; having a professional artist give lessons in drawing shipwrecks; Tony Kiefer, Don Doherty, and others taking measurements of *The Straits of Mackinac* before it was scuttled as a shipwreck site off Chicago; Scott Reimer checking survey equipment while heading out into Lake Michigan to do survey work; *(below)* Tom Pakenas measuring parts of "Val's Wreck;" Tony Kiefer detailing the dimensions of the propeller from the same wreck. PHOTOS BY CRIS KOHL

Shipwreck survey groups have fun while producing educational materials. *Left:* In 1992, members of UASC, SOS, and others, worked together to survey the wreck of Lake Huron's *Goshawk*.

PHOTO SET-UP BY CRIS KOHL

Right: Survey reports and plastic shipwreck slates, available to the public, are often produced. © UASC.   CRIS KOHL COLLECTION

in 1981, scuba divers who were genuinely concerned about the pillaging of our underwater history formed marine conservation groups called Preserve Our Wrecks (P. O. W.) in the Kingston area and Save Ontario Shipwrecks (S. O. S.) with chapters all across the province (and even one in Ohio today). These groups also took the initiative to create settings where scuba divers could learn about ship construction, shipwreck research, and marine archaeology techniques, even working hand-in-hand with professional marine archaeologists in surveying shipwreck sites. In the late 1980's, the Underwater Archaeological Society of Chicago (U. A. S. C.) was formed after divers splintered off from the Chicago Maritime Society. Since then, more groups, such as the Great Lakes Shipwreck Preservation Society in Minnesota, and others in New York, Michigan, Wisconsin, and Ohio, continue to educate people about our maritime history and to save our Great Lakes wrecks, undoubtedly the world's best preserved shipwrecks, from those few who still feel that "wrecking" is a noble calling but are increasingly viewed as self-centered looters.

Trying to sink legal teeth into shipwreck looters has been a problem, despite some highly publicized cases such as the theft of one of the enormous anchors from the *Tasmania*, a shipwreck in Canadian waters off Lake Erie's Point Pelee by two boatloads of Ohio divers in 1987. A small army of investigators, including Save Ontario Shipwrecks (particularly the Windsor chapter), a Toledo journalist and several government agencies, flew into action, with the results being the return of the anchor to the *Tasmania* site and the prosecution of those responsible for its theft. It took the perpetrators years and heavy legal fees just to get their boats back. But their big mistake had been in clandestinely transporting heritage material across an international border, an action which prompted the U.S. Customs Service to join the investigation. What can be done about divers who remove things from shipwrecks, but don't leave the country? A few minor cases of theft from shipwrecks have recently been taken to court with successful results, e.g. the divers who removed blocks from the Lake Huron wreck of the *New York*. However, the anticipated high-profile case which would set a lasting precedent among scuba divers remained elusive, in spite of the fact that shipwreck looting was still going on. There remains a $1,000 reward for the conviction of the party responsible for the theft of the tugboat *Sport's* bell, and P.O.W. has offered a similar reward over the theft of a metal plate from the historic dredge, *Munson*, off Kingston.

There is one unfortunate case of trying to make a high-profile example of a diver. Well-known Illinois shipwreck locator, Paul Ehorn, had, many years ago, removed the truly unique dragon-shaped figurehead from the site of the schooner, *James R. Bentley,* in Michigan waters, taken the time and spent the money to conserve that unusual and "at risk" wooden artifact, then donated it to the Manitowoc Maritime Museum, which put it on display under glass in an elaborate housing. In 1998, the Michigan Department of Natural Resources had Paul Ehorn charged with the theft of that artifact. In a daring challenge to the wording of the laws, hinging mainly upon the word "embedded," Paul Ehorn was not only exonerated of the crime, but ended up receiving ownership of the *James R. Bentley!* In 2001, he legally removed one of the *Bentley's* huge anchors as a DNR boat watched him wave his court-issued ownership papers. Selling that anchor would recoup some of his legal expenses, which reportedly reached close to six figures; this legal action also cost taxpayers a lot.

Authorities, divers, and other "stakeholders," could, and should, work better together. We hope that education, in the long run, will ultimately protect our Great Lakes shipwrecks.

36. Milwaukee

MILWAUKEE

LAKE MICHIGAN

WISCONSIN

Racine

-N-

Kenosha

Zion

ILLINOIS

Waukegan

Milwaukee has a rich maritime history which is little known to most people. Harbor, maritime traffic, lighthouses, shipbuilding, shipwrecks -- all of these nautical elements were solid realities in creating Milwaukee's important role on the Great Lakes. *Below,* a circa 1906 postcard depicts a commercial vessel passing a Milwaukee lift bridge. CRIS KOHL COLLECTION

1. WISCONSIN

LORAN: 33147.41/49634.04	GPS: 42° 31.961'/087° 42.524'
DEPTH: 90 to 130 feet	LEVEL: Advanced

LOCATION: This wreck lies 6.5 miles east-southeast of Kenosha, Wisconsin.

Nine lives were lost from the 68 on board when the iron steamer, *Wisconsin* (209' x 40' x 20'9"), foundered in a storm on October 29, 1929. Built at Wyandotte, Michigan, in 1881, the ship was carrying a cargo of iron castings, automobile parts and oil at the time of loss.

Dick Race of Chicago located the *Wisconsin* in 1961. The port anchor chain winds around the bow and trails off to where her anchor lies firmly embedded in the sandy lake bottom. The superstructure is broken and/or missing. The smokestack lies lengthwise on the deck, its red paint still showing. The windlass sits below the capstan on deck. Three vintage 1920's automobiles grace the rear cargo hold. Beware of strong currents and darkness.

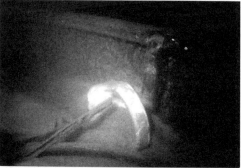

The *Wisconsin*. CRIS KOHL COLLECTION

Numerous sinks lie along the deck of the *Wisconsin*, evidence of her 100 staterooms.　PHOTO BY JON ZEAMAN

The wreck of the Wisconsin, as viewed by an underwater artist. ART BY AND © MICHAEL ANGELO GAGLIARDI

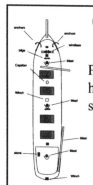

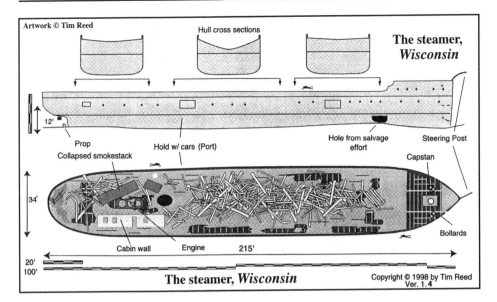

Artwork © Tim Reed

Hull cross sections

The steamer,
Wisconsin

12'

Prop
Collapsed smokestack

Hold w/ cars (Port)

Hole from salvage
effort

Steering Post

Capstan

34'

Cabin wall   Engine   215'

Bollards

20'
100'

The steamer, *Wisconsin*

Copyright © 1998 by Tim Reed
Ver. 1.4

2. ROSINCO

> **LORAN: 33089.6/49586.8**   **GPS: 42° 37.515'/087° 37.650'**
> **DEPTH: 195 feet**   **LEVEL: Technical**

LOCATION: This wreck lies about 10 miles off Kenosha, Wisconsin.

The steel-hulled diesel-powered luxury yacht, *Rosinco* (88' x 15' x 7'8"), struck some floating timber in the middle of the night and surprisingly sank within 10 minutes on April 18, 1928, while enroute from Milwaukee to Chicago. The seven men on board took to the motorized tender and another boat in tow. Built as the *Georgiana III* at Wilmington, Delaware, in 1916, the *Rosinco* (renamed in 1925 from the name *Whitemarsh* given her in 1919) is upright, intact and in excellent condition, with penetration possible for trained/experienced

Early scuba divers found a variety of interesting items on the wreck of the *Rosinco*: *left*, a silver plate and silverware; *above:* detail of the *"Rosinco"* name and pennant engraved in the silver plate; *right*, the ship's wheel.
PHOTOS BY CRIS KOHL

divers in her main cabin and outer rooms along the main deck. Commercial fishermen found this wreck in 1961 when they snagged it in their nets. The State of Wisconsin recently had this wreck placed on the National Register of Historic Sites.

3. EVRA FULLER

LOCATION: In 35' of water about 400'-500' east of the Racine Harbor entrance.

The 217-net-ton schooner, *Evra Fuller* (132'9" x 26'3" x 9'9"), constructed as the *Lena Johnson* at Fort Howard, Wisconsin, in 1873, stranded on Racine Reef with a load of lumber on October 8, 1893, and broke up, but the majority of the vessel washed in close to shore. The wreck, broken and scattered, lies in muddy water busy with boating traffic. Caution!

4. KATE KELLY

> **LORAN: 33053.5/49467.7**   **GPT: 42° 46.676'/087° 43.410'**
> **DEPTH: 45 to 55 feet**   **LEVEL: Intermediate**

The *Kate Kelly's* windlass.
ART BY AND © MICHAEL ANGELO GAGLIARDI

LOCATION: This wreck lies almost two miles east of the Wind Point Lighthouse.

Built in 1867 at Tonawanda, NY, the twin-masted schooner, *Kate Kelly* (126' x 26' x 10'), stranded in a severe gale on May 13, 1895. With the crew of 7 in the rigging, the storm broke the doomed vessel free from her perch, spiriting her towards shore. Unfortunately, the entire crew was lost, along with 6,000 hemlock railroad ties she carried. The wreck, found by Dan Johnson in July, 1983, lies quite intact, with a windlass in place and pulleys and deadeyes in the sand.

5. LUMBERMAN

LORAN: 33026.4/49400.0	**GPS: 42° 52.172'/087° 45.420'**
DEPTH: 53 to 70 feet	**LEVEL: Advanced**

LOCATION: This wreck lies about 10 miles north of Wind Point, Wisconsin.

The three-masted, twin-centerboarded schooner, *Lumberman* (126'5" x 23'5" x 7'1"), built at Blendon's Landing (Grand Haven), Michigan, in the spring and summer of 1862, capsized on April 7, 1893, on her first trip of the season. This low-draft ship, traveling light (i.e. with no cargo) was easy prey for a strong western squall. As she sank, the vessel righted herself, and the five crew clung to her above-water masts until the steamer, *Menominee*, rescued them. The wreck's masts were later removed by a salvage company.

The *Lumberman,* located on July 16, 1983, by Dan Johnson, Eric Smith and Patricia

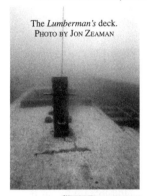

The *Lumberman's* deck.
PHOTO BY JON ZEAMAN

THE LUMBERMAN

GALDEL DRAWING NO SCALE 4-28-01
DRAWN FROM VIDEO BY BRAD FRIEND

3 MAST SCHOONER (WOOD) SIX MILES off OAK CREEK WISCONSON

The wreck of the *Lumberman.*
ART BY AND © MICHAEL
ANGELO GAGLIARDI

Please turn to p. 585 to see our Lockwood Pioneer Diving Museum ad

Insko (who reportedly initially had plans to raise the ship in her entirety), sits upright and intact, with her empty cargo holds open to divers who want to swim from one end of the wreck to the other without impediment. Many items that were on her in 1983 (such as nameboards on her sides and moonshine bottles in the cabin) have now been lost, but this wreck still has enough artifacts to make her wonderful to explore. The *Lumberman* was the subject of survey and shore-up work in the summer of 2001.

6. GRACE A. CHANNON

LORAN: 32963.2/49388.1	GPS: 42° 55.76'/087° 36.12'
DEPTH: 185 to 198 feet	LEVEL: Technical

LOCATION: This wreck lies 6.8 miles southeast of Oak Creek, Wisconsin.

The schooner, *Grace Channon* (169' x 29'), built in 1873 at East Saginaw, Michigan, sank after a collision with the steam barge, *Favorite,* broke a large hole in her port side on

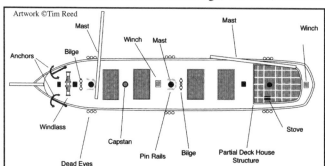

August 2, 1877. The seven-year-old son of a co-owner, sleeping below deck, died in this sinking, while the *Favorite* rescued the others. This wreck, located in April, 1985, by Kent Bellrichard and his team, sits upright, intact and in remarkably good shape, with an intact cabin. Rigging lies on the deck.

7. NO. 6 DREDGE (OLD 906)

LORAN: 32996.0/49329.1	GPS: 42° 57.92'/087° 47.24'
DEPTH: 50 to 75 feet	LEVEL: Intermediate-Advanced

LOCATION: This wreck lies four miles southeast of Milwaukee, Wisconsin.

No. 6 Dredge (this is the same one formerly referred to as *Dredge 906*) (110' x 40' x 11'5") was a 685-gross-ton, steel-hulled, box-type, nonself-propelled, uninspected, unregistered "vessel" which took the lives of 9 men when it foundered while under tow in a storm on May 23, 1956. *No. 6 Dredge* was built in 1912.

This wreck, one of Milwaukee's most popular scuba dive sites, lies upside-down, resting on two retracted spuds (steel arms sunk into the lake bottom to hold the dredge in place during work).Truly interesting sights include the massive crane, boiler and dredging machinery. Be totally in charge of your buoyancy so as not to stir up the considerable silt at this site; cave diving techniques are handy here. Penetrate the wreck only if you are trained and experienced.

No. 6 (906) Dredge.
CRIS KOHL COLLECTION

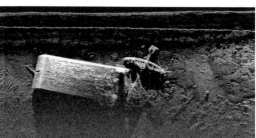

An electronic sidescan view of *No. 6 (906) Dredge.*
SIDESCAN IMAGE COURTESY OF JERRY GUYER

No. 6 Dredge's bitts hang upside-down just above the lake floor; a diver examines the boiler. PHOTOS BY JON ZEAMAN

8. CHICAGO PARK BOAT

LORAN:	GPS: 42° 50.45' /087° 48.30'
DEPTH: 40 feet	LEVEL: Novice-Intermediate

This ex-Coast Guard, aluminum patrol boat was reportedly last used by a Chicago park company and sank in April, 1982. Intact and upright, it sits considerably buried in the sand.

9. *NORLOND*

LORAN: 32999.9/49320.5	GPS: 42° 58.434'/087° 48.671'
DEPTH: 65 feet	LEVEL: Advanced

LOCATION: Three miles southeast of Milwaukee.

The wooden steamer, *Norlond* (152'5" x 25' x 9'4"), built as the *Eugene C. Hart* in 1890 at Manitowoc, WI, foundered in heavy weather on Nov. 13, 1922, with no lives lost. The wreck lies broken and scattered, with her boiler just to the west of the main wreckage.

Below: The steamer, *Norlond.* CRIS KOHL COLLECTION. *Center:* Sidescan sonar image of the wreck of the *Norlond.* COURTESY OF JERRY GUYER. *Right:* A portion of the propulsion components at the *Norlond* site.   PHOTO BY JON ZEAMAN

10. "SANDY'S WRECK"

This unidentified wooden hull was located by Jerry Guyer on Nov. 9, 2004. It sits in 35' of water, with dimensions of 112' by 25'. Location: **GPS: 43° 01.00'/087° 51.50'**

11. *VOLUNTEER*

LORAN: 33008.5/49304.5	GPS: 42° 58.88'/087° 51.72'
DEPTH: 15 feet	LEVEL: Novice

LOCATION: This wreck lies just outside the breakwall south of Milwaukee. Beware of boating traffic!

The *Volunteer*. Cris Kohl Collection

The wooden steamer, *Volunteer* (270'8" x 41'6" x 20'4"), built in 1888 at Trenton, Michigan, was deemed too costly to rebuild when she aged, so she was dismantled, burned and abandoned at this location in 1914. Wreckage includes wooden planking and piping.

Right: The wreck of the *Volunteer*. Art by and © Michael Angelo Gagliardi

12. SEBASTOPOL

LORAN: 33009.1/49301.3	GPS: 42° 59.03'/087° 52.14'
DEPTH: 10 to 12 feet	LEVEL: Novice

LOCATION: Inside the outer breakwall off Milwaukee's South Shore Beach, straight out from Oklahoma Avenue.

Built at Cleveland in 1855, the wooden sidewheel steamer, *Sebastopol* (230' x 26' x 14'), didn't last her first season on the Great Lakes. With confusing shore lights misleading the ship's navigation during heavy weather, the *Sebastopol* stranded on September 18, 1855. Four crewmembers died during the safe evacuation of the 60 passengers, and the ship broke up. Ship's framing and planking remain, with occasional bits of cargo or baggage in between.

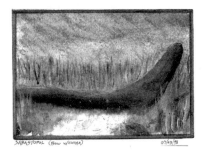

The *Sebastopol* shipwreck frames, two different views: *left,* an artist's rendition, ART BY AND © MICHAEL ANGELO GAGLIARDI, and *right,* a photographer's view. PHOTO BY JON ZEAMAN

SABASTOPOL (BOW W/CHINA)   07/23/98

13. "JERRY'S WRECK"

LORAN: 33000.4/49280.9	GPS: 43° 00.87'/087° 52.53'
DEPTH: 41 feet	LEVEL: Intermediate

LOCATION: This wreck lies less than a mile north of Milwaukee harbor.
This unidentified wooden shipwreck, apparently a steam-powered sandsucker about 112' long, lies broken and scattered.

14. SUMATRA

LORAN: 32997.4/49272.4	GPS: 43° 01.42'/087° 53.01'
DEPTH: 35 feet	LEVEL: Novice

The 204' schooner-barge, *Sumatra,* built in 1874 at Black River, Ohio, foundered in a gale on September 30, 1896, with the loss of four lives and her cargo of railroad iron.

15. HIRAM R. BOND

LORAN:	GPS: 43° 02.12' /087° 52.30'
DEPTH: 40 feet	LEVEL: Novice-Intermediate

The wooden, unrigged scow, *Hiram R. Bond* (65' x 14'), built in 1888 at Milwaukee, sank carrying sand on May 29, 1905, after being rammed in the fog by the steel carferry, *Pere Marquette No. 20.* No lives were lost. Jerry Guyer found this wreck on May 10, 2003.

16. EDWARD E. GILLEN

LORAN: 32981.5/49284.0	GPS: 43° 01.44'/087° 49.18'
DEPTH: 62 to 74 feet	LEVEL: Advanced

LOCATION: This wreck lies 2.5 miles east of Hoan Bridge, Milwaukee, Wisconsin.
The old, wooden tugboat, *Edward E. Gillen* (56'5" x 15'3" x 7'9"), began her long life as the *Erastus C. Knight* at Buffalo, New York, in 1908. Just before noon on June 3, 1981,

Above: The tug, *Edward E. Gillen.* CRIS KOHL COLLECTION.
Right: A folding bunk inside the wreck. PHOTO BY JON ZEAMAN

the *Edward E. Gillen* rolled over and sank after a wire parted suddenly while helping the Coast Guard test the towing winch on one of their vessels. No lives were lost.

The *Edward E. Gillen* sits upright, intact and penetrable by the trained and experienced.

17. PRINS WILLEM V

LORAN: 32979.6/49286.9	GPS: 43° 01.35'/087° 48.59'
DEPTH: 48 to 90 feet	LEVEL: Advanced

LOCATION: This wreck lies three miles east of Milwaukee, Wisconsin.

Another "saltie" (ocean-going freighter) that never made it out of the Great Lakes (just like the *Nordmeer, Monrovia* and *Francisco Morazan,* which are all in this book), the steel freighter, *Prins Willem V* (250'5" x 42'1" x 14'7"), built in the Netherlands in 1948, sank in a freak collision with the tug, *Sinclair's* tow on October 14, 1954. No lives were lost, and the *Prins Willem V* sank with the loss of her cargo of automotive parts, animal hides and jukeboxes.

The *Prins Willem V.* CRIS KOHL COLLECTION. The sidescan outline of the "Willy." COURTESY OF JERRY GUYER

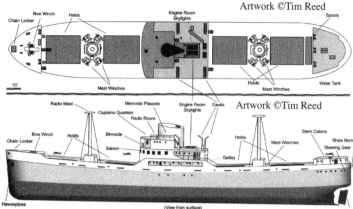

Artwork ©Tim Reed

Artwork ©Tim Reed

Various scenes of the wreck of the *Prins Willem V*: photos reflect the fact that this shipwreck lies practically on its side, but superstructure railing is in ample evidence, and a swim through the pilot house is the highlight of any dive here; the ship's name is still visible on her stern (3 PHOTOS AT LEFT BY PETE TOMASINO); the galley offers much to see (e.g. stove in background), and steel steps lead ever deeper inside the shipwreck (2 PHOTOS, BELOW AND RIGHT, BY JON ZEAMAN)

The *"Willy"* is the most popular dive site in the Milwaukee area, and perhaps in all of Lake Michigan. Memorable explorations can be made by remaining outside the hull; the *Prins Willem V* is a huge, multi-leveled shipwreck which has been unforgiving towards scuba divers who overestimate their abilities or foresake their precautions. Once again, penetration diving is only for the trained, experienced and prepared.

18. *MILWAUKEE FIRE BOAT 23*

GPS: 43° 00.94'/087° 48.18'
DEPTH: 75 feet   LEVEL: Intermediate

The famous firm of Rieboldt, Wolter & Co. built the 2nd and 3rd of Milwaukee's fire tugs: the *MFD* (Milwaukee Fire Dept.) *17*, launched as the *James Foley* (99' x 24'4" x 10'2"), in 1893, and the nearly identical *MFD 23*, launched as the *August F. Janssen*, in 1896. Decades later, these old tugs were scuttled off Milwaukee, the *MFD 23* stripped of nearly everything and ironically set ablaze on July 27, 1923, and the *MFD 17* was simply sunk, engine and all, on May 12, 1930. Jerry Guyer located the remains of the historic *MFD 23* on Jan. 10, 2005--see sidescan at right.

19. "WILLY BARGE I"

> GPS: 43° 00.68'/087° 48.28'
> DEPTH: 70 feet   LEVEL: Intermediate

"Willy Barge I"

LOCATION: This wreck lies close to the famous wreck of the *Prins Willem V*, hence its nickname.

This unidentified wooden hull, approximately 80 feet long and with a 29-foot beam, was located by wreck hunter Jerry Guyer on September 10, 2005. This ship was likely scuttled.

20. "WILLY BARGE II"

> GPS: 43° 00.36'/087° 47.47'
> DEPTH: 75 feet   LEVEL: Intermediate

LOCATION: This wreck lies close to the famous wreck of the *Prins Willem V*, hence its nickname.

This unidentified wooden hull, approximately 125 feet in length and 35 feet in beam, was found by Jerry Guyer on November 15, 2005. This ship was likely scuttled.

21. "WILLY BARGE III"

> GPS: 43° 00.81'/087° 47.19'
> DEPTH: 80 feet   LEVEL: Intermediate

"Willy Barge III"

LOCATION: This wreck lies close to the famous wreck of the *Prins Willem V*, hence its nickname.

This unidentified wooden hull, approximately 125 feet in length and 35 feet in beam, was found by Jerry Guyer on November 30, 2005. This ship was likely scuttled.

22. *TRANSFER*

> GPS: 43° 01.09'/087° 45.85'
> DEPTH: 110 feet   LEVEL: Advanced

LOCATION: This wreck lies east of the *Prins Willem V*.

The large schooner-barge, *Transfer* (200' x 34'), sank in 1910. This wreck was located by Jerry Guyer of Milwaukee on April 6, 2005.

23. "DEAN'S WRECK"

> GPS: 43° 02.58'/087° 46.60'
> DEPTH: 122 feet   LEVEL: Advanced

Transfer

LOCATION: This wreck lies a couple of miles to the north-northeast of the well-known wreck of the *Prins Willem V.*

This unidentified shipwreck, lying at a depth of 122 feet of water, was first located by commercial fishermen in the mid-1980's, and again recently in 2004.

The sidescans in the right column: "Willy Barge I," "Willy Barge III," and *Transfer,* are COURTESY OF JERRY GUYER

24. UNIDENTIFIED WRECK

LORAN:	GPS: 43° 02.67′ /087° 46.56′
DEPTH: 122 feet	LEVEL: Advanced

LOCATION: This shipwreck lies very close to the one nicknamed "Dean's Wreck."

This unidentified shipwreck lying in 122 feet of water was unintentionally found while running sidescans from different directions on "Dean's Wreck."

25. BOILERS

LORAN:	GPS: 43° 02.70′ /087° 48.20′
DEPTH: 80 feet	LEVEL: Intermediate-Advanced

LOCATION: These items lie north of the *Prins Willem V* wreck.

This set of boilers, measuring about 15 feet by 12 feet, but missing the rest of the shipwreck, was first located in the mid-1980s.

26. CAISSON

LORAN: 32955.4/49273.4	GPS: 43° 03.24′/087° 45.58′
DEPTH: 150 feet	LEVEL: Technical

At first thought to be a section of a scuttled railroad bridge, this very large, upright, round cylinder, about 75′ in diameter and standing 60′ tall, with masonry on its interior walls, still awaits identification. Kent Bellrichard and his team found this in Dec., 1975.

27. *ST. ALBANS*

LORAN: 32951.8/49269.1	GPS: 43° 03.79′/087° 45.65′
DEPTH: 160 to 178 feet	LEVEL: Technical

LOCATION: This wreck lies about seven miles off Milwaukee, Wisconsin.

The wooden steamer, *St. Albans* (135′6″ x 25′8″ x 11′), launched at Cleveland on July 18, 1868, was sunk by ice northeast of Milwaukee on January 30, 1881, with no

Left: The *St. Albans* at Cleveland. CRIS KOHL COLLECTION. *Below:* A burbot and netting adorn the *St. Albans'* deck. PHOTO BY JON ZEAMAN

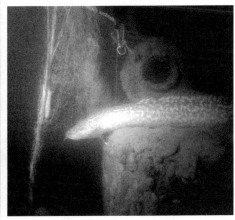

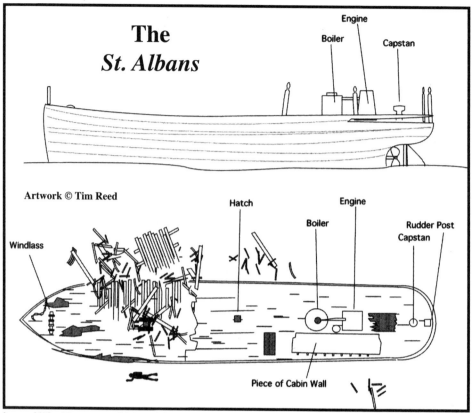

The St. Albans

Engine

Boiler

Capstan

Artwork © Tim Reed

Hatch

Engine

Boiler

Rudder Post

Capstan

Windlass

Piece of Cabin Wall

loss of life. Her crew of 21 and 6 passengers (2 men and 4 women) took to the four lifeboats and, with great difficulty, reached shore, but the cargo of flour (1,000 barrels and 1,800 sacks) and four head of livestock was lost.

This wreck was located by Kent Bellrichard, Richard Zaleski and their team on the day in late December, 1975, when they found the *EMBA* and the caisson/railroad bridge as well. The ship's double wheel was removed by divers in January, 1976, but there remains a lot for the visiting diver still to see of this mostly intact, upright steamer in deep water.

28. EMBA

LORAN: 32949.6/49271.6	GPS: 43° 03.72′/087° 45.05′
DEPTH: 170 feet	LEVEL: Technical

The *EMBA* (which stands for "Excelsior Marine Benevolent Association"), ex-*A.C. Tuxbury*. CRIS KOHL COLLECTION

LOCATION: This wreck lies off Milwaukee's North Point.

Built in 1890 at West Bay City, Michigan, the three- (later two) -masted schooner, *EMBA* (ex-*A.C. Tuxbury*) (128′5″ x 24′5″ x 12′5″), was converted to a twin-masted schooner-barge, a towed ship often carrying lumber or coal. This vessel was scuttled in 1932. This site was one of three located in a single day of scanning by Kent Bellrichard, Richard Zaleski and their group in late December, 1975 (the other two were the

446

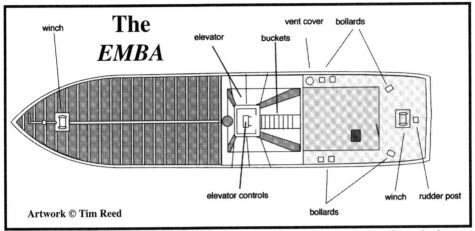

The EMBA

winch — elevator — vent cover — bollards — buckets — elevator controls — bollards — winch — rudder post

Artwork © Tim Reed

St. Albans and the caisson/railroad bridge). Because the wreck lies broken from the impact with the lake bottom, there are few penetration possibilities here.

29. SCUTTLED SCHOONER

LORAN:	GPS: 43° 03.80′ /087° 43.40′
DEPTH: 210 feet	LEVEL: Technical

LOCATION: This wreck lies to the north-northeast of the *St. Albans* wreck.

This large schooner has an approximate length of 150′ and a beam of 30′, and it sits upright, but empty (suggesting that it was scuttled). There are also signs of fire damage.

30. *APPOMATTOX*

LORAN: 32969.4/49231.1	GPS: 43° 05.35′/087° 52.24′
DEPTH: 15 to 23 feet	LEVEL: Novice

LOCATION: This wreck lies just south of the first north pier off Atwater Beach, Whitefish Bay, Wisconsin, about 450′ off shore.

The large wooden steamer, *Appomattox* (319′8″ x 42′ x 23′), launched on July 25, 1896 at West Bay City, Michigan, stranded on November 2, 1905, with a coal cargo. Broken and scattered, the wreck lies on a sand and gravel bottom, with the boiler just to the east.

The wooden steamer, *Appomattox*.
CRIS KOHL COLLECTION

31. *JOSEPHINE*

LORAN:	GPS: 43° 05.39′ /087° 52.43′
DEPTH: 10 feet	LEVEL: Novice

LOCATION: About 70′ off shore north of Atwater Beach, 3 piers down the beach.

The wooden steam barge, *Josephine* (99′ x 25′ x 6′), built at Milwaukee in 1874, sank with a sand cargo after hitting a rock on April 15, 1888. She is broken and scattered in sand.

32. MILWAUKEE

LORAN: 32943.2/49208.7   GPS: 43° 08.178'/087° 49.925'
DEPTH: 90 to 125 feet   LEVEL: Advanced

LOCATION: This wreck lies 3.5 miles northeast of North Point, Milwaukee

The steel railroad car steamer, *Milwaukee* (338' x 56' x 19'5"), tragically foundered in an autumn storm on October 22, 1929, while bound from Milwaukee for Muskegon,

Left: The carferry, *Milwaukee. Right:* This postcard view shows the ship from its stern angle, giving an idea of how wide open the railroad car doors were. BOTH CRIS KOHL COLLECTION

Michigan, with a load of railroad cars. All 52 people who were on board perished. Launched on December 6, 1902, at Cleveland with the long name *Manistique-Marquette & Northern No. 1,* she was given a more managable name, *Milwaukee,* in 1908.

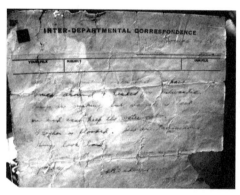

Left: The tragic note which a crewmember was able to write and encase before the *Milwaukee* sank with all hands. NATIONAL ARCHIVES, GREAT LAKES BRANCH, CHICAGO, PHOTO BY CRIS KOHL. *Below:* Sidescan sonar image of the *Milwaukee.* COURTESY OF JERRY GUYER

This is a challenging dive, as the visibility is frequently low (15' or less) and the maze of wires and twisted cables invite entanglement. Some of the railroad cars can be explored, since this part of the wreck is relatively open. One car contains a cargo of bathtubs and toilet

Views of the *Milwaukee* shipwreck: The ship's name painted (and still readable) above a door, and a porthole still in place. PHOTOS BY JON ZEAMAN

seats, while another holds three automobiles. The wreck is split in some places, with thick silt filling the crevices. Do not disturb the silt, as it will destroy your visibility and possibly your orientation. Very experienced divers with proper training, conditions and equipment can enter the shipwreck.

For more detailed information about the loss of the *Milwaukee*, see *The 100 Best Great Lakes Shipwrecks, Volume II*, by Cris Kohl. That book contains the complete text of the desperate message which was sent out by a doomed crewmember and picked up on shore days later.

33. ISLAND CITY

LORAN: 32908.5/49138.1	GPS: 43° 14.30'/087° 50.71'
DEPTH: 135 to 140 feet	LEVEL: Technical

LOCATION: This wreck lies southeast of Port Washington, Wisconsin.

Captain William R. Wood, who drifted ashore unconscious at the bottom of the 9' yawl boat and was found by a farmer, was this shipwreck's sole survivor (the other two crewmen drowned). The small, 52-net-ton, two-masted, lumber-laden schooner, *Island City* (81' x 17' x 6'), built in 1859 at St. Clair, Michigan, sank on April 8, 1894, while enroute from Ludington, Michigan, to Milwaukee. The 26-year-old captain had every dollar he owned invested in his little schooner. Sailors who knew him at Milwaukee collected donations so he could purchase some necessities and pay for passage back home across the lake.

This little shipwreck is badly broken up with commercial fishing nets snagged on her pieces. It is surprising that the site is in such bad shape, considering how deep it lies (depth usually ensures greater intactness and preservation). Apparently she sank so fast that her deck was blown off the hull from the great pressure of the air trying to escape from below.

34. TENNIE AND LAURA

LORAN:	GPS: 43° 15.63' /087° 43.64'
DEPTH: 319 feet	LEVEL: Technical

LOCATION: This wreck lies 12 miles northeast of Milwaukee.

Tragedy led to the finding of this shipwreck. It was while searching for the lost fish tug, *Linda E.*, which sank in 1998 with the loss of several lives after being struck by a steel, government boat, that this shipwreck was unintentionally located. At first referred to as "the mystery schooner," research and ROV (Remote-Operated Video) findings suggested that the wreck was that of the small, 56-ton scow-schooner, *Tennie and Laura* (73' x 19' x 5'6"). This two-masted workhorse vessel, built at Manitowoc, Wisconsin, in 1876, capsized and sank on August 8, 1903, with a cargo of lumber and the loss of the mate, half of her two-man crew. The captain survived when he was rescued by a passing steamer.

37. Wisconsin's East Coast

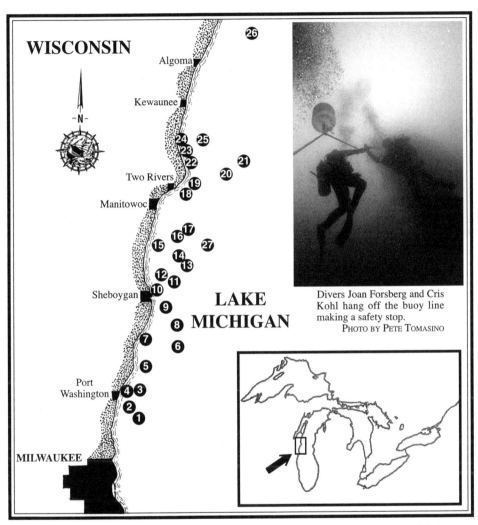

WISCONSIN

-N-

Algoma

Kewaunee

Two Rivers

Manitowoc

Sheboygan

LAKE
MICHIGAN

Port
Washington

MILWAUKEE

Divers Joan Forsberg and Cris
Kohl hang off the buoy line
making a safety stop.
PHOTO BY PETE TOMASINO

1. *Northerner*	10. *Phoenix*	19. *S. C. Baldwin*
2. *Mahoning*	11. *Helvetia*	20. *Vernon*
3. Cat sailboat	12. *Selah Chamberlain*	21. *Rouse Simmons*
4. *Toledo*	13. *Silver Lake*	22. *Pathfinder*
5. *Niagara*	14. *Walter B. Allen*	23. *Continental*
6. *Byron*	15. *McMullen & Pitz dredge*	24. *Francis Hinton*
7. *Atlanta*	16. *Floretta*	25. *America*
8. *Advance*	17. *Home*	26. *Daniel Lyons*
9. *Hetty Taylor*	18. *Henry Gust*	27. *Gallinipper*

1. NORTHERNER

LORAN: 32874.7/49091.8	GPS: 43° 18.89'/087° 49.45'
DEPTH: 122 to 138 feet	LEVEL: Technical

LOCATION: This wreck lies southeast of Port Washington, Wisconsin.

The twin-masted, 77-gross-ton "pocket schooner," *Northerner* (78' x 18' x 7'), constructed in 1859 at Wells Island, Michigan, foundered in severe weather on November 29, 1868, with a cargo of cord wood below deck. No lives were lost. This almost totally intact, upright site includes the railing, windlass, masthead, a mainmast which rises 75' above her deck, centerboard winch, bowsprit, anchor chain and, the most unique feature of this site, her figurehead, still with signs of white paint on it and which closely resembles the figurehead on the *Sandusky* in the Straits of Mackinac.

The *Northerner's* figurehead.
PHOTO BY JON ZEAMAN

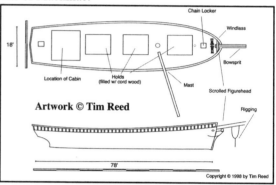

Artwork © Tim Reed

2. MAHONING

LORAN:	GPS: 43° 20.47'/087° 51.21'
DEPTH: 53 feet	LEVEL: Intermediate

LOCATION: This wreck is located just southeast of Port Washington, Wisconsin.

Divers Brad Ingersoll and Jim Bach located the wreck of the *Mahoning* in the summer of 2005. Another diver immediately claimed to have found it years earlier, but hadn't shared that knowledge. It's the sharing that counts. Built at Black River (Lorain), Ohio, in 1848, the brig, *Mahoning* (119' x 25'5" x 9'8"), capsized on Nov. 13, 1864, while being towed to port in a leaky condition. Two lives were lost. This collapsed wreck rises 3' off the bottom.

3. CAT SAILBOAT

LORAN:	GPS: 43° 23.83'/087° 49.36'
DEPTH: 70 feet	LEVEL: Intermediate

LOCATION: Straight out from the harbor at Port Washington, Wisconsin.

A modern sailboat with a catamaran-shaped hull, about 35 feet in length with a narrow 10-foot beam, sank under unknown circumstances. Found by Jerry Guyer on Aug. 1, 2005.

4. TOLEDO

LORAN:	GPS:
DEPTH: 20 feet	LEVEL: Novice

LOCATION: This wreck lies about 300' off the northern Port Washington breakwall out from the water pumping station.

Launched at Buffalo in 1854, the 179' wooden passenger and freight steamer, *Toledo*, was carrying a total of about 50 passengers and crew, plus a cargo of general merchandise, when she encountered extremely harsh weather on October 24, 1856 (this was only about one month after the tragic loss of the *Niagara*; see site #5). Initially attempting to ride out the storm at anchor, Captain John Densham sensed disaster unless he beached his ship. He gave the orders to raise the anchors, and, in doing so, one of the chains fouled and an enormous wave crashed a heavy anchor against the ship's hull, splitting her bow. The mortally wounded *Toledo* was swept towards land by the wind and waves, but soon went to the bottom, taking with her all but three members of the hardy crew who managed to reach shore alive. The victims were buried alongside those from the *Niagara* in the Port Washington Union Cemetery; a *Toledo* anchor recovered in 1900 is on display at this cemetery. Salvagers recovered the *Toledo's* boiler and engine in 1857.

The wreck lies broken and scattered on the sand bottom, much of it (e.g. smokestack) being alternately covered and uncovered at the whim of nature.

5. *NIAGARA*

LORAN: 32800.0/48988.5	GPS: 43° 29.31'/087° 46.49'
DEPTH: 55 feet	LEVEL: Intermediate

LOCATION: This wreck lies about seven miles northeast of Port Washington and about two miles off Harrington Beach in the town of Belgium, Wisconsin.

The wooden sidewheel passenger and freight steamer, *Niagara* (245' x 33'6" x 14'), one of the numerous (about 25 in all) fast and opulent "palace steamers" which carried thousands of immigrants from the East to the Midwest in the years 1844 to 1857 just before the construction of railroad connections, caught on fire in the

The *Niagara*. ARTIST UNKNOWN.
CRIS KOHL COLLECTION

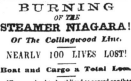

BURNING
OF THE
STEAMER NIAGARA!
Of The Collingwood Line.
NEARLY 100 LIVES LOST!
Boat and Cargo a Total Loss.

We are pained to be obliged to record another dreadful lake disaster, in the loss by fire of the steamer *Niagara*, of the Collingwood Line, last night, off Port Washington, about 20 miles north of this city.

We are indebted to Mr. Wm. Snow, of the firm of Snow & Williams, of this city, who came up on the *Traveler* last night, for the following particu-

Above: News of the many lives lost in this disaster spread quickly. *Milwaukee Sentinel*, Sept. 26, 1856.
CRIS KOHL COLLECTION

middle of the afternoon on September 23, 1856 off Port Washington. Captain Miller immediately ordered the ship steered towards shore, about five miles away, but within five minutes, the steam engine quit, and the blazing ship drifted helplessly. The flames, the smoke and the language barrier combined to create panic among the primarily Scandinavian passengers. In the ensuing chaos, about 60 people perished from the approximately 180 on board. The *Niagara* is one of the worst (in terms of loss of life) disasters to happen on the Great Lakes. Many of the deceased lie in Port Washington Union Cemetery.

The *Niagara* site displays vast piping, an upright paddlewheel, and the flat anchor for the marker buoy provided by the State of Wisconsin. Diver Joan Forsberg explores this interesting shipwreck. PHOTOS BY CRIS KOHL

Built at Buffalo, New York, in 1845, the *Niagara* spent most of her life transporting people between the eastern and western ends of Lake Erie. She was, however, traveling between Collingwood, Ontario, and Chicago, Ilinois, when the disaster occurred.

The wreck and cargo lie broken up and scattered, with the bow facing shore. Much of the keel, ribs and machinery remains, with the hull broken in two with the sides fallen outward. The walking beam and engine rise 15' off the bottom. One paddlewheel is nearly intact, the other, quite damaged. The three huge (8' x 18') and impressive boilers lie 278' to the north-northeast of the main wreckage. This site is buoyed annually by the State Historical Society of Wisconsin.

6. BYRON

LORAN: 32736.4/48929.0	GPS: 43° 36.29'/087° 41.29'
DEPTH: 135 feet	LEVEL: Technical

LOCATION: This wreck lies off Sheboygan, Wisconsin.

The small schooner, *Byron,* only about 40' long, sank after a collision with the larger schooner, *Canton,* on May 8, 1867. This wreck is difficult to locate because it rises only 3' off the lake floor. Do not drag an anchor into any shipwreck to locate it, particularly this fragile little beauty. Anchors cause damage. Using a knowledgeable dive charter to visit this site is preferred. This wreck lies intact, with centerboard, fallen mast, attached tiller and a capstan just off the wreck.

7. ATLANTA

LORAN: 32969.4/49231.1	GPS: 43° 34.23'/087° 46.89'
DEPTH: 90 feet	LEVEL: Advanced

LOCATION: This wreck lies just offshore from the town of Cedar Grove, Wisconsin.

The wooden passenger and freight steamer, *Atlanta* (200' x 32'2" x 13'6"), launched at Cleveland on April 25, 1891, burned to a total loss on March 18, 1906, with one life lost (a fireman from the *Atlanta's* crew fell into the lake and drowned while attempting to enter a lifeboat). The fire spread quickly, assisted by the large cargo of wooden furniture and pianos. The tug, *Tessler,* under the command of Captain G.H. Smith, came to the rescue and removed most of the passengers and crew, later returning to the burning wreck and towing it to shore.

The *Atlanta.* CRIS KOHL COLLECTION

This shipwreck lies about 450' off shore, and rises 3' to 5' off the bottom, with the bow pointing north. This vast site sits in a busy boating area; stay close to your dive flag.

8. ADVANCE

LORAN: 32741.2/48919.3	GPS: 43°36.71'/087° 49.91'
DEPTH: 83 feet	LEVEL: Advanced

LOCATION: This wreck lies about 9 miles southeast of Sheboygan, 2.5 miles off shore.

The two-masted schooner, *Advance* (117' x 25' x 9'), built in 1853 at Milwaukee and heading to Chicago with a cargo of tan bark, foundered in a storm on September 8, 1885, with all five men on board, including Captain M. Paulson and his son, George.

The wreck, reportedly located by Robert Van Der Puy and Ray Larson in 1978, but not publicized by them until 1982, is surprisingly, for this depth, broken up, with most of it sitting on sand in a large pile, with pieces scattered nearby.

9. HETTY TAYLOR

LORAN: 32700.9/48885.5	GPS: 43° 40.89'/087° 39.30'
DEPTH: 97 to 107 feet	LEVEL: Advanced

LOCATION: This wreck lies southeast off Sheboygan, Wisconsin.

The 85-gross-ton, two-masted schooner, *Hetty Taylor* (84' + bowsprit x 22'6" x 8'), built in 1874 at Milwaukee, capsized on August 26, 1880, in a storm because her lumber cargo on deck made her topheavy. The crew reached shore in a lifeboat. A salvage crew steamed out immediately in the tug, *Messenger,* in an attempt to tow in the overturned ship before she sank, but upon arriving at the site, they found only the top 8' of a mast above water. She was already on the bottom. Today she makes an excellent dive site.

The *Hetty Taylor,* buoyed annually by the State Historical Society of Wisconsin, lies upright and considerably intact, with her photogenic bow (bowsprit and chains in place, windlass and anchor chain on deck) and portside in excellent condition. The pilothouse, in good shape, sits off the broken starboard side, and the rudder lies in the damaged stern.

Left: Steve Radovan takes a close look at the *Hetty Taylor's* windlass. *Right:* The *Hetty Taylor's* cabin lies off the starboard side of the wreck near the stern.   PHOTOS BY CRIS KOHL

10. PHOENIX

LORAN:	GPS:
DEPTH: 8 feet	LEVEL: Novice

LOCATION: This wreck lies just north of the Sheboygan city boat ramp.

The wooden passenger and freight sidewheel steamer, *Phoenix* (144' x 26' x 11'), built in 1845 at Cleveland, was fated to become another of the worst tragedies in Great Lakes history. In the middle of the night on November 21, 1847, the ship, loaded with package freight and almost 250 people (mostly Dutch immigrant families), caught on fire from an overheated boiler and burned to a total loss, with about 180 to 200 men, women and children being lost. The ship carried only two lifeboats which saved a total of 43 lives, including the captain's. The tug, *Delaware,* rescued three sailors who clung to the *Phoenix's* steering chains at the stern, and also towed in the burnt out hulk to Sheboygan, where burnt bodies (plus coins and machinery) were recovered and the hull was allowed to sink. Relocated in modern times in 1982 by Jim Brotz, Jim Jetzer and Bill Wangemann, the *Phoenix's* hull lies mostly buried in a soft bottom.

The tragic *Phoenix.*
CRIS KOHL COLLECTION

11. HELVETIA

LORAN: 32650.7/48824.2	GPS: 43° 47.31'/087° 36.49'
DEPTH: 165 feet	LEVEL: Technical

LOCATION: About 10 miles northeast of Sheboygan.

This old ship's bare hull was purposely burned on Lake Michigan on September 10, 1921. She had outlived her usefulness after almost half a century of hauling bulk cargoes such as lumber around the Great Lakes. Built at Tonawanda, New York, in 1873, the large schooner, *Helvetia* (204'5" x 35'6" x 13'8"), was located in 1975. Beware of commercial fishing nets snagged onto this deep hull.

The schooner, *Helvetia.*
CRIS KOHL COLLECTION

12. SELAH CHAMBERLAIN

LORAN: 32670.7/48828.0	GPS: 43° 46.12'/087° 34.47'
DEPTH: 75 to 88 feet	LEVEL: Advanced

LOCATION: This wreck lies two miles north of Sheboygan Point, Wisconsin.

The wooden steam barge, *Selah Chamberlain* (212' x 34' x 14'), built at Cleveland in 1873, sank in a collision in dense fog and heavy seas with the steamer, *John Pridgeon, Jr.,* on Wednesday, October 13, 1886, with the loss of 5 lives when the 16 crew rushed for the lifeboat. The *Chamberlain* was bound light from Milwaukee to Escanaba, Michigan. The *Pridgeon,* having turned around in an unsuccessful attempt to locate the sinking ship in the fog, continued to Chicago and reported the matter.

This, one of Wisconsin's most popular dive sites, was found by early shipwreck hunter

John Steele in the 1960's. The wreck of the *Selah Chamberlain,* sitting upright on a sand bottom, displays her engine and boiler, the site's highlights. Other items include the propeller and tools lying around the deck. Shifting sands cover and uncover portions of the wreck steadily, so each new visit will yield new things to see.

Joan Forsberg takes a detailed look at the many intricacies of the *Selah Chamberlain's* large steam engine. PHOTOS BY CRIS KOHL

13. SILVER LAKE

LORAN: 32637.5/48819.5	GPS: 43° 48.39′/087° 34.65′
DEPTH: 209 feet	LEVEL: Technical

LOCATION: This wreck lies about 8.5 miles northeast of Sheboygan, Wisconsin.

A 337′ steel Pere Marquette Railroad carferry ran down and sank the small, two-masted scow schooner, *Silver Lake* (95′ x 20′ x 7′6″), on May 28, 1900, in a heavy fog. The lumber-laden *Silver Lake* was struck midship port side, cutting her almost in two. The cook, Henry Eastman, 45 and single, lost his life. The ship, valued at $1,500, carried no insurance. Located by John Steele and his team (Bill Cohrs, Steve Radovan, Jim Brotz and Wally Bissonnette) on May 22, 1977, this wreck sits upright and mostly intact, with the foremast rising to 138′.

14. WALTER B. ALLEN

LORAN: 32637.3/48748.0	GPS: 43° 49.822′/087° 36.521′
DEPTH: 158 to 170 feet	LEVEL: Technical

LOCATION: This wreck lies about 9 miles northeast of Sheboygan, Wisconsin.

The twin-masted, 137′ schooner, *Walter B. Allen,* built at Ogdensburg, NY, in 1866, foundered in a fierce storm on April 16, 1880, with no lives lost. Located by Kent Bellrichard in May, 1975, this upright wreck has both masts still standing 70′ above the deck, rising to a depth of 90′. Her bowsprit, a windlass and the salvage steam engine remain in place behind the first hold. An upright lifeboat lies off the starboard quarter. Catheads, each with a chain and a built-in-pulley, adorn the bow, and five deadeyes still grace the starboard side.

Left: Reaching the top of a *Walter B. Allen* mast at a depth of 90 feet places the diver at about the halfway point to the bottom. *Right:* The steam engine on deck failed to pump the water out of the *Allen*.   PHOTOS BY CRIS KOHL

15. McMULLEN & PITZ DREDGE

LORAN: 32632.6/48746.5	GPS: 43° 53.52′/087° 40.31′
DEPTH: 85 feet	LEVEL: Advanced

LOCATION: This wreck lies about halfway between Sheboygan and Manitowoc.

Located by Steve Radovan in November, 1984, this work dredge sank in a storm off Cleveland, Wisconsin, on November 18, 1919, with no lives lost. Features include a full-length crane boom, a boiler and huge cleats. Penetration is possible for the trained and experienced.

Right: Steve Radovan, the dredge's discoverer, explores the many pulleys, cables and other machinery.   PHOTOS BY CRIS KOHL

457

16. *Floretta*

LORAN: 32576.4/48732.4	GPS: 43° 57.02'/087° 32.13'
DEPTH: 181 feet	LEVEL: Technical

LOCATION: This wreck lies about 11 miles southeast of Manitowoc, Wisconsin.

The schooner, *Floretta* (134' x 26' x 11'), constructed at Detroit in 1868, foundered with her iron ore cargo on September 18, 1885. No lives were lost. The wreck is mostly intact, with three anchors at the bow, but the visibility is usually poor and commercial fishing nets are snagged on the wreck, posing serious danger to the diver.

17. *Home*

LORAN: 32585.5/48732.4	GPS: 43° 56.83'/087° 33.28'
DEPTH: 165 feet	LEVEL: Technical

LOCATION: This wreck lies about 10 miles southeast of Manitowoc, Wisconsin.

The small, two-masted schooner, *Home* (84' x 23'), built in Lower Sandusky, Ohio, in 1843, sank after a collision with another ship on October 23, 1858. Located by Steve Radovan in April, 1981, this site is infrequently visited due to her depth, usually poor visibility and the potentially dangerous commercial fish nets draped over most of the wreck.

18. *Henry Gust*

LORAN: 32501.1/48619.9	GPS:
DEPTH: 80 feet	LEVEL: Advanced

The *Henry Gust*. CRIS KOHL COLLECTION

LOCATION: This wreck lies about three miles east of Two Rivers, Wisconsin.

The steam-powered fishing tug, *Henry Gust,* was built in 1893 at Milwaukee. After 1929, this aging ship was shortened by ten feet (from 72' to 62') to bypass mandatory inspection requirements for vessels over 65' in length. But the vessel was already on her last legs, and in 1935, she was stripped of her reusable brass and copper items, towed into Lake Michigan and scuttled. Her boiler, propeller and other machinery remain in place.

19. *S. C. Baldwin*

LORAN: 32487.1/48598.0	GPS: 44° 10.944'/087° 29.007'
DEPTH: 76 feet	LEVEL: Advanced

LOCATION: North of Two Rivers, about 2.3 miles southeast of Rawley Point.

One life was lost when the wooden steamer-converted-to-a-bulk-freight-barge-in-1903, *S. C. Baldwin,* (160' x 30' x 11'), with a stone cargo and under tow of the tug, *Torrent,* capsized and sank on August 27, 1908. The *S. C. Baldwin* was built in 1871 at Detroit and named after a Spring Lake, MI, business man (who died 5 months after this ship sank!)

The wreck of the *S. C. Baldwin* sits upright and is surprisingly intact, rising 7' off the bottom. Avoid getting snagged on the considerable wire rigging.

The steamer, *S. C. Baldwin*. CRIS KOHL COLLECTION

20. VERNON

LORAN: 32462.2/49599.2	GPS: 44° 12.106'/087° 24.749'
DEPTH: 175 to 205 feet	LEVEL: Technical

LOCATION: This wreck lies about 6 miles east of Rawley Point Lighthouse.

Built in 1886 at Chicago, the wooden steamer, *Vernon* (158'7" x 25'5" x 18'8"), foundered in a gale on October 29, 1887, with 41 lives lost from the 42 on board (16 passengers and 26 crew); a sole survivor, one of the passengers, clung to a raft for two days before being rescued. Milwaukee shipwreck hunter Kent Bellrichard located this wreck on July 12, 1969.

The *Vernon* is upright and quite intact. The carved bow is a diver attraction, as is the copper sheathed tip of the bow itself. Penetration is possible for experienced, properly trained divers, particularly into the deck level cabins. Buoys are often placed at both bow and stern.

The *Vernon* has a highly ornamental bow.
ARTWORK © MICHAEL ANGELO GAGLIARDI

Above, left: The steamer, *Vernon*. *Above:* When Axel Stone turned out to be the sole survivor from the wreck of the *Vernon*, he appeared on stage in Chicago and elsewhere. BOTH CRIS KOHL COLLECTION

21. ROUSE SIMMONS -- SEE PAGES 462-464.

22. PATHFINDER

LORAN: 32473.5/48552.3	GPS: 44° 14.69'/087° 30.68'
DEPTH: 10 feet	LEVEL: Novice

LOCATION: This wreck lies about 2.5 miles north of Two Rivers Point, Wisconsin.

The three-masted schooner, *Pathfinder* (188' x 31'), built in Detroit in 1869, attempted to ride out heavy seas with her anchors set, but they failed to hold and she stranded with her cargo of 1,053 tons of iron ore on November 19, 1886. No lives were lost. This notorious storm sank or stranded at least 29 other Great Lakes vessels, a few of which were recovered. Among those total losses was, at Marquette, Michigan, the schooner, *Florida* (which is also in this book). The *Pathfinder's* anchors and other items were salvaged, but the wreck lies scattered where she broke up.

23. CONTINENTAL

LORAN: 32476.8/48561.2	GPS: 44° 13.83'/087° 30.52'
DEPTH: 25 feet	LEVEL: Novice

LOCATION: One mile north of Rawley Point. The wooden steamer, *Continental* (244'7" x 36'4" x 19'2"), stranded in a severe snow storm on December 13, 1904, enroute to Manitowoc to pick up a cargo. None of the 20 lives was lost. The ship, built at Cleveland in 1882, broke up over the winter.

Today, wooden ribs (framing) and decking emerge from the sandy bottom of the lake. Her upright engine rises very close to the surface (boaters: beware!)

Left: The *Continental.* CRIS KOHL COLLECTION

24. FRANCIS HINTON

LORAN: 32548.9/48614.3	GPS: 44° 06.67'/087° 37.88'
DEPTH: 20 feet	LEVEL: Novice

The *Francis Hinton,* carried a cargo of lumber on her deck (and below) on the day she sank. CRIS KOHL COLLECTION

FRANCIS HINTON IS DRIVEN ASHORE

Steam Barge Crew Escape, But Lose All Their Belongings.

Manitowoc, Wis., Nov. 16.—The steam barge Francis Hinton en route from Manistique, Mich., to Chicago, with lumber, went ashore today two miles

The day she sank. CRIS KOHL COLLECTION

LOCATION: This wreck lies about 4.5 miles north of Two Rivers, Wisconsin.

Built at Manitowoc, Wisconsin, in 1889, the wooden steamer, *Francis Hinton* (152'2" x 30'9" x 10'8"), bound for Chicago from Manistique, Michigan, with a heavy cargo of lumber (Norway pine), ultimately stranded and broke in two on November 16, 1909. Captain John Campbell (who was 86 years old) had anchored his leaking ship offshore, but ordered the line cut so his vessel, which he knew was doomed, would sink in shallow water. Once it drifted west and stranded, he and his crew reached shore safely in their lifeboat.

This shipwreck lies somewhat broken and scattered, but not flattened as badly as other wrecks in such shallow water. The propeller is in place and the boiler rises to within 10' of the surface. This site is buoyed annually by the State Historical Society of Wisconsin.

The *Francis Hinton* breaking up. CRIS KOHL COLLECTION

25. AMERICA

LORAN: 32423.1/48498.5	**GPS: 44° 21.01'/087° 26.84'**
DEPTH: 112 to 130 feet	**LEVEL: Advanced**

LOCATION: This wreck lies about 9 miles north of Two Rivers Light, Wisconsin.

Heading to Escanaba, Michigan, from Chicago, empty in order to pick up an iron ore cargo destined for Michigan City, Indiana, the three-masted schooner, *America* (137' x 26' x 11'), built at Port Huron, Michigan, in 1873, collided at full speed the night of September 28, 1880, with the braided steel towline between an unlighted tug and her equally unlighted towbarge. The impact put a large hole in the schooner's bow and she went down within minutes, but with her stern floating for several days afterwards. The strain of salvage tugs towing her in caused her to sink totally. Her crew had escaped to shore in their yawlboat.

The wreck, located on Sept. 3, 1977, by John Steele, Jim Brotz, Kent Bellrichard, Rich Zaleski and Jim Jetzer, faces east, upright and relatively intact, with her open deck and cargo holds inviting exploration. Beware of snagged lines at this popular fishing spot. The wheel was recovered several years ago and is now in the Manitowoc Maritime Museum.

26. DANIEL LYONS

LORAN: 32283.5/48329.1	**GPS: 44° 40.22'/087° 17.71'**
DEPTH: 95 feet	**LEVEL: Advanced**

LOCATION: Several miles northeast of Algoma, Wisconsin, and 3 miles off shore.

Built at Oswego, NY, in 1873, the three-masted, 318-ton, grain-laden schooner, *Daniel Lyons,* sank after the schooner, *Kate Gillett,* sliced halfway through the *Lyons'* starboard side on October 18, 1878. No lives were lost. This wreck is quite broken up.

27. GALLINIPPER

LORAN:	**GPS: 43° 54.82'/087° 29.07'**
DEPTH: 230 feet	**LEVEL: Technical**

LOCATION: This shipwreck lies 10.4 miles due east of Cleveland, Wisconsin.

The schooner, *Gallinipper* (95' x 22' x 7'), built in Milwaukee in 1846 on the hull of the schooner, *Nancy Dousman* (which was built at Black River, OH, in 1833, sunk in the Straits of Mackinac in 1834, raised about 10 years later, then used again as a hull), foundered in a storm on July 7, 1851. This wreck, which has detractors claiming it is not the *Gallinipper* and from which divers illegally removed the wheel recently, was located by the legendary Great Lakes shipwreck hunter, John Steele, in the 1970's.

Great Lakes Highlight No. 24

Above: The *Rouse Simmons*, set inside the frame of a circa 1912 Christmas card. BOTH CRIS KOHL COLLECTION

THE *ROUSE SIMMONS*,
THE CHRISTMAS TREE SHIP

> **LORAN: 32437.7/48550.7**   **GPS: 44° 16.646'/087° 24.856'**
> **DEPTH: 155 to 168 feet**   **LEVEL: Technical**

LOCATION: This wreck lies east-northeast of Two Rivers Point, Wisconsin.

The three-masted schooner, *Rouse Simmons* (123'5" x 27'6" x 8'4"), launched at Milwaukee in August, 1868, is the famous "Christmas Tree Ship," so-named because Chicago's Capt. Herman Schuenemann packed northern Michigan evergreen trees into her holds and onto her deck for the last trip of the year to take advantage of the profitable Chicago Christmas market. The *Simmons* was carrying just such a cargo when she foundered in a fierce blizzard off Kewaunee, WI, on Nov. 23, 1912. All 16 (estimated number) people on board perished. Capt. Schuenemann's brave widow and daughters kept up the Christmas Tree tradition for another 20 years. This wreck, upright and intact, was located by Kent Bellrichard in October, 1971. Skeletal evergreen trees remain in her hold.

Below: The "Christmas Tree Ship," the *Rouse Simmons,* loaded with evergreen trees. CRIS KOHL COLLECTION

SHIP LEFT BY RATS
LOST IN LAKE WITH
ALL HANDS ABOARD

Schooner Rouse Simmons,
With Christmas Trees,
Believed Wrecked

MAN WHO QUIT BOAT TALKS

Seaman Says Superstition and
Heavy Cargo Drove Him
From His Berth.

Left: Superstition attended the tragic loss of the *Simmons.* CRIS KOHL COLLECTION. *Below:* Capt. Schuenemann's body was never found, but his name and an evergreen tree grace his widow's headstone.   PHOTO BY CRIS KOHL

The schooner, *Rouse Simmons*, is an exciting, deep dive. Upright in 165', the *Simmons* exhibits *(clockwise from right)* her bow, windlass and chain, broken decking on both starboard and port sides revealing skeletal branches of 1912 Christmas trees, and an interesting stern, examined by diver Steve Radovan.　PHOTOS BY CRIS KOHL

Improved visibility in the Great Lakes in recent years has made underwater photography an easy delight. These *Rouse Simmons* photos were taken by the author in 2004.

The late 1800's-early 1900's tradition of bringing Christmas trees to the (virtually treeless) prairie port of Chicago by ship was rekindled in the year 2000 by the old USCG icebreaker, *Mackinaw*. The original "Captain Santa," Capt. Herman Schuenemann, had often given away trees to needy families in Chicago; the *Mackinaw* has brought 1,000+ trees to Navy Pier each December and given them to families in need. The new *Mackinaw*, which replaced the old one in 2006, continues this tradition. PHOTOS BY CRIS KOHL

Legacies of the *Christmas Tree Ship*

"The story of the *Rouse Simmons*... is the Great Lakes' unique entry in the catalogue of all things Christmas."

-- Cris Kohl, *Wreck Diving Magazine*, Issue 4 (2004)

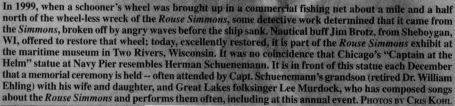

In 1999, when a schooner's wheel was brought up in a commercial fishing net about a mile and a half north of the wheel-less wreck of the *Rouse Simmons*, some detective work determined that it came from the *Simmons*, broken off by angry waves before the ship sank. Nautical buff Jim Brotz, from Sheboygan, WI, offered to restore that wheel; today, excellently restored, it is part of the *Rouse Simmons* exhibit at the maritime museum in Two Rivers, Wisconsin. It was no coincidence that Chicago's "Captain at the Helm" statue at Navy Pier resembles Herman Schuenemann. It is in front of this statue each December that a memorial ceremony is held -- often attended by Capt. Schuenemann's grandson (retired Dr. William Ehling) with his wife and daughter, and Great Lakes folksinger Lee Murdock, who has composed songs about the *Rouse Simmons* and performs them often, including at this annual event. PHOTOS BY CRIS KOHL

Jim Brotz

The Ehlings with Lee Murdock

38. Door County & Green Bay

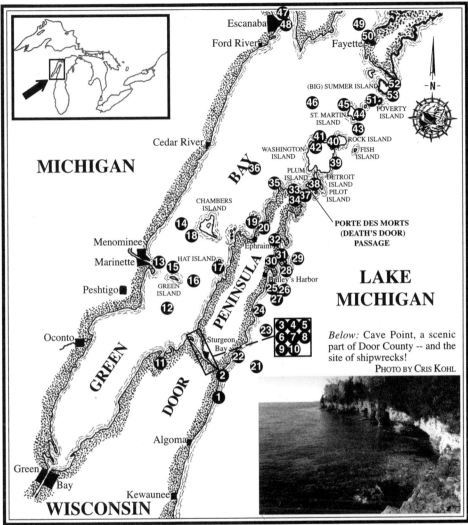

Below: Cave Point, a scenic part of Door County -- and the site of shipwrecks!
PHOTO BY CRIS KOHL

1. *Ottawa*
2. *Coast Grd. brkwall*
3. *Adriatic*
4. *Joys*
5. *Fountain City*
6. *Dan Hayes*
7. *Vermilion*
8. *Joseph L. Hurd*
9. *Bullhead Pt. wrecks*
10. *J. S. Williams*
11. *Little Sturgeon Bay*
12. *W. L. Brown*
13. *Sidney O. Neff*
14. *May Queen*
15. *Wisconsin*
16. *Erie L. Hackley*
17. *Carrington*
18. *Jennibell*
19. *Meridian*
20. *Sister Bay wreck*
21. *Lakeland*
22. *City of Glasgow*
23. *Ocean Wave*
24. *Jacksonport wrecks*
25. *Australasia*
26. *Emeline*
27. *Christina Nilsson*
28. *Michael J. Bartelme*
29. *Frank O'Connor*
30. *Moonlight Bay*
31. *Boaz*
32. *Cherubusco*
33. *Table Bluff*
34. *Wisconsin Bay*
35. *Fleetwing*
36. *R. J. Hackett*
37. *Resumption*
38. *Pilot Island wrecks*
39. *Winfield Scott*
40. *Iris*
41. *Pride*
42. *Louisiana*
43. *Roen barge & tug*
44. *Eagle*
45. *St. Martin I. wall*
46. *E. R. Williams*
47. *Nahant*
48. *John Weber*
49. *Big Bay de Noc*
50. *Fayette*
51. *Erastus Corning*
52. *C. C. Hand*
53. *Misc. Summer Island wrecks*

1. OTTAWA

> **LORAN: 32395.6/46144.5**   **GPS: 46° 52.84'/090° 46.25'**
> **DEPTH: 20 feet**   **LEVEL: Novice**

LOCATION: This wreck lies about 6 miles north of Algoma, Wisconsin.

The two-masted schooner, *Ottawa* (113' x 25' x 7'6"), built at Grand Haven, Michigan, in 1874, stranded on her first trip of the season less than a mile off shore in heavy fog and building seas while bound from Manistique, Michigan for Chicago with a lumber cargo on Thursday, April 13, 1911. The crew of five lost their lives when they attempted to reach shore in a yawl boat.They should have remained with their ship, which stayed so intact that the decks had to be dynamited later so salvagers could remove the cargo.

The wrecked *Ottawa*.
CRIS KOHL COLLECTION

Hull framing and some planking remain of this shipwreck, flattened by time and nature in the shallows where she hit the rocks.

2. COAST GUARD BREAKWALL

> **DEPTH: To 35 feet**   **LEVEL: Novice**

LOCATION: The northern breakwall close to the navigation light at the eastern entrance of the Sturgeon Bay Canal.

Many fish tend to congregate here, including burbots, carp, alewives and, in the autumn when there are also many fishermen in this area, salmon. The bottom is sand and the visibility is generally good.

3. ADRIATIC

> **DEPTH: 10 to 20 feet**   **LEVEL: Novice**

The *Adriatic*. CRIS KOHL COLLECTION

LOCATION: This wreck lies south of the yacht club and north of the docks northwest of the old railroad bridge on the east side of the bay, on the southeasterly end of the old Leatham Smith Co. dock.

Built at West Bay City, Michigan, in 1889, the three-masted schooner, *Adriatic* (202' x 34'7" x 16'6"), worked as a stone barge all of her life. She was laid up at the dock in 1927 and sank in 1930 where she lies today. This wreck consists basically of her ribs. Beware of boating traffic, low visibility and snagged fishing line.

4. JOYS

> **DEPTH: 10 to 20 feet**   **LEVEL: Novice**

LOCATION: This wreck lies next to the remains of the *Adriatic* (see site #3).

Built for the lumber trade at Milwaukee in 1884, the wooden steamer, *Joys* (131' x 28'2" x 9'9"), burned to a total loss at Sturgeon Bay on Christmas Day, 1898. The wreck lies flat and broken. Be cautious of boating traffic and fishing lines.

The *Joys*. CRIS KOHL COLLECTION

5. FOUNTAIN CITY

DEPTH: 10 to 30 feet   LEVEL: Novice

The *Fountain City,* after the fire.
CRIS KOHL COLLECTION

LOCATION: This wreck lies off Sunset Park on the north side of Sturgeon Bay.

Built at Cleveland in 1857, the wooden steamer, *Fountain City* (209'11" x 30'3" x 13'6"), caught on fire at the coal dock in Sturgeon Bay on May 5, 1896, was cut loose to save the dock, stranded and had her fire extinguished, but she was still declared a total loss. Wreckage, mainly ribs and planks, is spread over a large area in a busy boating portion of the bay known for generally low visibility (5' to 8')

6. DAN HAYES

DEPTH: 6 to 8 feet   LEVEL: Novice

LOCATION: About 400' off the abandoned Graef & Nebel quarry jetty, Sturgeon Bay.

The scow-schooner, *Dan Hayes* (112' x 24'2" x 7'), built at Fairport, Ohio, in 1868, was demoted to a stone-hauling barge by 1900 and abandoned in 1905. Flattened timbers remain.

7. VERMILLION

DEPTH: 9 to 13 feet   LEVEL: Novice

LOCATION: This wreck lies about 50' off shore in the northern part of Sturgeon Bay, off one of the old stone quarry pits along county highway "B," near the *J. Hurd* (site #8).

This abandoned wreck, formerly thought to be the wooden steamer, *Mueller*, was recently identified by Door County maritime historian Jon Paul Van Harpen as the *Vermillion*. (The *Mueller's* stern end is displayed at the waterfront park opposite the old stone quarry, but the rest of the ship was removed.) The *Vermillion* (252' x 42' x 20'4"), built in 1887 at Trenton, Michigan, as the *J. C. Gilchrist*, was sunk as a breakwater at the Leathem & Smith quarry in 1922. Usually visible from shore, this stone-filled, abandoned ship rises about 5' at the bow.

8. JOSEPH L. HURD

DEPTH: to 30 feet   LEVEL: Novice

LOCATION: This wreck lies near the *Vermilion* (site #7), about 100' off the stone quarry, and just to the north of the new cement fishing dock.

The wooden steamer, *Joseph L. Hurd* (128'5" x 24'5" x 12'5"), launched on September 1, 1869 at Detroit, stranded with a cargo of crushed stone 9 miles northwest of the Sturgeon

Left: The *Joseph L. Hurd,* prior to abandonment in 1913 (CRIS KOHL COLLECTION) and, *right,* what is left of the same ship today underwater. PHOTO BY CRIS KOHL

Bay Ship Canal on September 23, 1913, but was released and towed to the old Leatham Smith quarry dock at the northwest end of Sturgeon Bay, where the ship was scuttled. The *Joseph L. Hurd* is perhaps most (in)famous for her collision with the steamer, *Cayuga,* (which is also in this book) near the Straits of Mackinac in 1895.

The bow half of the wreck is fairly intact, but the stern has broken off. Visibility is usually good, but boating traffic is steady. Use a dive flag.

9. BULLHEAD POINT WRECKS

> **DEPTH: 10 to 15 feet**   **LEVEL: Novice**

LOCATION: Three abandoned wooden ships rest at the foot of the old Sawyer Quarry dock at Bullhead Point, Sturgeon Bay, in a busy boating and fishing area:

❶ The wooden steamer, *Empire State* (212' x 33' x 18'6"), constructed at Buffalo, New York, in 1862, spent her first 44 years carrying passengers before being reduced to a barge; she was abandoned at Bullhead Point in 1929 after suffering a fire on board.

❷ The wooden barge, *Ida Corning* (168' x 31'3" x 10'9"), launched in 1881 at East Saginaw, Michigan, and named after a lumberman's one-year-old daughter, was abandoned in 1928.

❸ The three-masted schooner, *Oak Leaf* (final measurements 160' x 31'2" x 10'7"), built at Cleveland in 1866 and converted to a barge in 1917, was abandoned in 1928.

All three ships worked together in the stone trade in the final years of their careers, and all three burned on June 21, 1931, but their hulls offer excellent exploration opportunities.

❶ The *Empire State*. CRIS KOHL COLLECTION

❷ The *Ida Corning*. CRIS KOHL COLLECTION

❸ The *Oak Leaf*. CRIS KOHL COLLECTION

Ida Corning

Empire State

Oak Leaf

The three abandoned wrecks at Bullhead Point

Archival photos above: CRIS KOHL COLLECTION. An aerial view of Bullhead Pt. shows Sturgeon Bay (background) and the three abandoned wrecks. *Left:* Joan Forsberg examines one of the wooden hulls. *Right:* Three ship eras and styles can be viewed here: the freighter *Edward Ryerson* (background), a small pleasure boat, and an abandoned heritage ship. PHOTOS BY CRIS KOHL

10. *J. S. WILLIAMS*

> **DEPTH: 15 to 20 feet**   **LEVEL: Novice**

LOCATION: These vessel remains lie about one mile south of the large quarries on County Highway "B," off a small access road to the water. In the water, to the south, a sand and concrete finger runs into the bay. The remains of three unidentified ships lie scattered together here. Go farther. There is a second finger, off which you will find the *J. S. Williams*.

Launched as the three-masted schooner, *Phoenix,* in 1868 at Henderson, Minnesota and renamed the *J. S. Williams* (121' x 26') in 1896, this vessel toiled mainly in the lumber and stone trades before being abandoned in the spring of 1902. Flattened wooden framing and planking are all that remain of this once-beautiful sailing ship.

11. LITTLE STURGEON BAY

DEPTH: To 20 feet	LEVEL: Novice

LOCATION: Off Claflin Memorial Park at the end of Lime Kiln Road near the west entrance to Little Sturgeon Bay.

Fish life and the broken remains of a small, wooden ship are found at this site.

12. *W. L. BROWN*

LORAN: 32261.6/48096.8	GPS: 44° 57.96'/087° 33.05'
DEPTH: 80 feet	LEVEL: Advanced

LOCATION: This wreck lies near the middle of Green Bay off Peshtigo, Wisconsin.

Launched at Oshkosh, Wisconsin, in 1872 as the *Neptune,* and, in 1880, renamed the *W. L. Brown* (140' x 28' x 13'), this wooden steamer sprang a leak and foundered about one mile off Peshtigo Reef in Green Bay on October 21, 1886. The vessel was carrying an iron ore cargo from Escanaba, Michigan, to De Pere, Wisconsin, and no lives were lost. The boiler, anchors, chain and engine were salvaged, but today's divers will see both masts still standing, bilge pumps and other artifacts on deck, rudder and propeller tips at the stern, and intact wooden railings on this upright wreck. This is usually a low-visibility (4' to 8') site in orange water, so penetration diving is not recommended here.

The *W. L. Brown.* CRIS KOHL COLLECTION

13. *SIDNEY O. NEFF*

LORAN: 32233.2/48015.2	GPS: 45° 05.55'/087° 34.69'
DEPTH: 15 feet	LEVEL: Novice

LOCATION: About one-quarter mile south of the Marinette lighthouse.

Launched as a schooner-barge at Manitowoc, Wisconsin, in 1890, the *Sidney O. Neff* (149'6" x 30'2" x 10'4"), was converted to a bulk freight steamer in 1897 and worked mainly in the lumber trade until she was scuttled in June, 1940, due to age. The wreck lies broken and scattered over a large area. Highlights include the windlass and other machinery.

The *Sidney O. Neff* in the Chicago River. CRIS KOHL COLLECTION

14. *MAY QUEEN*

LORAN:	GPS:
DEPTH: 80 feet	LEVEL: Advanced

LOCATION: About one-quarter mile south of the Marinette lighthouse.

The little, two-masted, 12-ton coasting schooner, *May Queen* (38'3" x 12'2" x 4'6"), built at Menominee, Michigan, in 1875, sank in Green Bay with a cargo of fish after developing a leak on December 4, 1882, with all four crewmembers surviving. Commercial fishermen had long been snagging their nets on this wreck, and finally, in 2002, one of them lowered an underwater camera to view the obstruction. Divers were informed and made their first dive to this site in 2004. This small shipwreck is slightly damaged, possibly from the snagged fishnets, but many artifacts and sailors' personal effects remain on site.

15. WISCONSIN

LORAN: 32213.4/48040.2	GPS: 45° 04.74'/087° 29.50'
DEPTH: 85 feet	LEVEL: Advanced

LOCATION: This wreck lies just to the north of Green Island.

The wooden steamer, *Wisconsin* (187' x 30'5" x 12'2" after 1918), launched at Detroit in 1882 as the *F. & P. M. No. 1* (*Flint and Pere Marquette Railroad No. 1*), received her new name in 1906. When she grew old, she was converted to a schooner-barge in 1918. Finally, she was abandoned at Marinette in 1935. The government paid to have her removed, and a local entrepreneur set up a spectacular show with many people ferried to Green Island to watch this ship burn to the waterline and sink.

Steel frames around the hull give a rib cage effect to this upright shipwreck. Her bilge pumps and other machinery lie inside her hull, while the anchor chain sits at the bow and her rudder is in place. Take a dive light, as it is usually dark with only 5' to 10' of visibility.

Left: The *Wisconsin* in early years. GREAT LAKES MARINE COLLECTION OF THE MILWAUKEE PUBLIC LIBRARY/WISCONSIN MARINE HISTORICAL SOCIETY

16. ERIE L. HACKLEY

LORAN: 32209.5/48058.2	GPS: 45° 03.71'/087° 27.37'
DEPTH: 99 to 112 feet	LEVEL: Advanced

LOCATION: This wreck lies to the northeast of Green Island, Green Bay.

The small, wooden steamer, *Erie L. Hackley* (79' x 17'4" x 5'2"), foundered in a storm on October 3, 1903, with 11 lives lost (8 passengers and 3 crew, including the captain) from the 19 on board. The ship had been launched on August 11, 1882, at Muskegon, Michigan. Located by Frank Hoffman in 1980, the *Erie L. Hackley* sits upright and is mostly intact. In place are her engine, boiler, the cargo of red bricks, some decking and her hull. Take along a light, as it is dark at this poor visibility site.

The *Erie L. Hackley.*
CRIS KOHL COLLECTION

17. CARRINGTON

LORAN: 32167.4/48067.4	GPS: 45° 05.58'/087° 19.32'
DEPTH: 35 to 55 feet	LEVEL: Intermediate

LOCATION: This wreck lies about 3/4 of a mile south-southwest of Hat Island.

The two-masted, 215' schooner, *Carrington,* heading for Chicago with a cargo of pig iron and shingles, stranded on Oct. 30, 1870, on Hat Island Reef due to confusion about lights. The crew was safely removed, but a storm arose and destroyed the *Carrington.* The wreck lies broken in two, with much framing and decking. Beware of the adjacent boulder.

Left: The *Carrington* closely resembled this ship, the *Cataract.* CRIS KOHL COLLECTION

18. JENNIBELL

LORAN: 32176.1/48013.3	GPS: 45° 09.04'/087° 25.11'
DEPTH: 105 feet	LEVEL: Advanced

LOCATION: This wreck lies about 1.5 miles southwest of Chambers Island.

Laden with lumber products, the two-masted, 94' schooner, *Jennibell* (sometimes spelled *Jenny Bell*), capsized in a squall on Sept. 17, 1881, but stayed afloat. She sank only after becoming waterlogged while under tow in a salvage attempt. Frank Hoffman located this wreck in 1961. His colleagues tried to raise her (as he did later with the *Alvin Clark* in 1969) but they succeeded only in breaking her in two. The *Jennibell* sits upright with deadeyes, windlass, chain, centerboard winch and cordwood cargo in place. Visibility is often poor (5' to 10').

Right: This schooner, the *Trade Wind,* was similar in appearance to the *Jennibell.* CRIS KOHL COLLECTION

19. MERIDIAN

LORAN: 32084.1/48030.2	GPS: 45° 12.92′/087°08.59′
DEPTH: 28 to 45 feet	LEVEL: Intermediate

LOCATION: This wreck lies just south of the Sister Islands.

The twin-masted schooner, *Meridian* (120'3" x 23'), built in 1848 at Black River, Ohio, stranded and broke up on Oct. 23, 1873. The wreck is broken and scattered over a wide area on a sand and clay bottom. Much framing and considerable decking comprise this site.

Left: The *Meridian* suffered from a paucity of photographs of itself, but the schooner, *Fearless,* came close to being a lookalike. CRIS KOHL COLLECTION. *Right:* Joan Forsberg explores the *Meridian's* bow. PHOTO BY CRIS KOHL

20. SISTER BAY WRECK

DEPTH: 10 to 20 feet	LEVEL: Novice

LOCATION: Southwest of the boat launch at the end of Country Lane, at the base of Sister Bay. An unidentified wooden vessel, about 50' long, lies in these shallow waters, with wreckage lying on shore marking the site. Use a dive flag; traffic can get busy here.

21. LAKELAND

LORAN: 32219.3/48274.5	GPS: 44° 47.57′/087° 11.49′
DEPTH: 190 to 210 feet	LEVEL: Technical

LOCATION: This wreck lies about 6 miles off the Sturgeon Bay Ship Canal.

Launched as the *Cambria* in 1887 at Cleveland, the iron-hulled ship was renamed *Lakeland* (280' x 40' x 20') in 1910. She was one of the first three steamers on the Great Lakes to have a triple expansion engine. Converted from a bulk freighter to a combination passenger and package freight steamer in 1910, she sprang a leak and foundered on December 3, 1924. None of the 30 lives on board was lost, but the thirty 1924 automobiles all went

Contemporary newspaper ad for sailing on the *Lakeland.* CRIS KOHL COLLECTION

The sinking *Lakeland.* CRIS KOHL COLLECTION

Underwater images of the deep wreck of the steamer, *Lakeland,* show the hull to be intact, but some of the decking appears bent and twisted or otherwise damaged. A fairly intact 1924 automobile is visible in a hatch opening.
PHOTOS BY KIM BRUNGRABER

to the bottom. One auto, a Rollins, was raised in 1979, with considerable damage done to the vehicle. The *Lakeland* lies upright, intact -- and deep!

22. *CITY OF GLASGOW*

> **DEPTH: 8 to 10 feet**   **LEVEL: Novice**

LOCATION: About 400' off the community of Lily Bay, 3 miles north of the canal.

The wooden steamer, later a barge, *City of Glasgow* (297' x 41' x 24'2"),was built at West Bay City, Michigan, in 1891. It was after she burned off Green Bay on December 3, 1907, that her hull was converted to a barge. She stranded during a strong southern gale at her final resting place, where she broke in two, on October 6, 1917. Her anchors and chain were salvaged. Her broken hull lies in two large sections some distance apart.

City of Glasgow.
CRIS KOHL COLLECTION

One end of the *City of Glasgow* today.
AERIAL PHOTO BY CRIS KOHL

Great Lakes Highlight No. 25

THE RAISING OF THE *ALVIN CLARK*

In July, 1969, Frank Hoffman and his team of divers successfully raised, from 100′ of Green Bay (Lake Michigan) water, a completely intact wooden schooner which they nicknamed the Mystery Ship until research identified it as the *Alvin Clark* . This 106-foot-long vessel, built at Trenton, Michigan in 1846, had foundered in a gale off Chambers Island on June 29, 1864, with the loss of three lives. After being raised and cleaned up, the *Alvin Clark* operated as a museum for several years. But then the vessel began to deteriorate quickly, massive conservation being prohibitively expensive for this huge, wooden artifact, and Hoffman being unable to locate any sources of funding. The *Alvin Clark's* maintenance turned into a costly problem, and even Hoffman's desperate attempt to destroy the ship, just to rid himself of it, failed. The vessel which had stayed perfectly preserved for 105 years on the lake bottom crumbled within 25 years on the surface. The broken remains were trucked to the local garbage dump.

The *Alvin Clark*, raised from Green Bay in 1969 but unable to be conserved properly, began hogging and warping fewer than 20 years later. This historic vessel's tragic fate only a few years after these photos were taken provided a hard-learned lesson for would-be salvagers. For more details of this story, read chapter two of *Shipwreck Tales of the Great Lakes* by Cris Kohl.   PHOTOS BY CRIS KOHL

23. OCEAN WAVE

LORAN:	**GPS: 44° 52.994'/087° 09.128'**
DEPTH: 105 feet	**LEVEL: Advanced**

LOCATION: In Whitefish Bay, Wisconsin, two miles off Cave Point.

Constructed on Harsens Island in the St. Clair River in 1860, the small, 74-ton scow-schooner, *Ocean Wave* (73' x 20 x 7'), sank at night with a cargo of building stone on September 23, 1869, after striking some floating object. The crew rowed safely to shore. Located by commercial fishermen in 2003 when they brought up a small mast which had snagged their nets, the *Ocean Wave* wreck site (its identification determined by Jon Paul Van Harpen) features many interesting items, including an intact windlass with anchor chain, an anchor at the bow's base, a portion of decking with the stern cabin still attached, a long bowsprit which remains upright, and a unique, open-beaked eagle figurehead just beneath the bowsprit.

This scow schooner, with its box-like appearance, closely resembled the *Ocean Wave*.   CRIS KOHL COLLECTION

The *Ocean Wave*, in 105' of water, offers many interesting items for divers such as Joan Forsberg to explore *(clockwise from left)*: the windlass, the figurehead, the separated cabin and decking, and the upright bowsprit.
PHOTOS BY CRIS KOHL

24. JACKSONPORT WRECKS

DEPTH: To 12 feet	LEVEL: Novice

LOCATION: Off the municipal waterfront park in Jacksonport, Wisconsin.

Framing and planking from two schooners lie interspersed: the 21-year-old *Perry Hannah* (125' x 26' x 10'5") was wrecked here in the Great Storm of Oct. 16-17, 1880, and on Sept. 8, 1885, the 17-year-old *Cecilia* (118'2" x 25'7" x 8'4") also storm-wrecked there.

25. AUSTRALASIA

DEPTH: 20 feet	LEVEL: Novice

LOCATION: In shallow waters of Whitefish Bay, Wisconsin.

The large, wooden steamer, *Australasia* (282' x 39' x 21'2"), built in 1884 at West Bay City, Michigan, burned to a total loss on Oct. 17, 1896, with no lives lost. Much of the ship was salvaged. Located in August, 2005, by two men on personal watercraft, only parts of the bow and the stern remain uncovered by sand.

The steamer, *Australasia*. CRIS KOHL COLLECTION

26. EMELINE

LORAN:	GPS: 45° 03.555'/087° 06.969'
DEPTH: to 20 feet	LEVEL: Novice

The 170-ton schooner, *Emeline* (115' x 22' x 7'), built at Vicksburg (later Marysville), Michigan in 1862, capsized, was towed to Baileys Harbor, and sank on Aug. 8, 1896. Today, mainly lower hull framing and planking, and the centerboard trunk, remain visible.

27. CHRISTINA NILSSON

DEPTH: to 15 feet	LEVEL: Novice

The schooner, *Christina Nilsson* (139' x 26'2" x 11'3"), built in 1871 at Manitowoc, WI, was storm-wrecked in Bailey's Harbor near the old lighthouse on Oct. 24, 1884, with no lives lost. Mostly framing remains.

The remains of the schooner, *Christina Nilsson*. AERIAL PHOTO BY CRIS KOHL

28. MICHAEL J. BARTELME

DEPTH: 18 feet	LEVEL: Novice

LOCATION: This wreck lies at the south end of Cana Island.

Launched on April 20, 1895 at West Bay City, Michigan, as the *John J. McWilliams* (and renamed *Central West* in 1916 and given her last name in the final year of her life) the huge, steel steamer, *Michael J. Bartelme* (352' x 44'8" x 22'8"), named after a dock

The stranded *Michael J. Bartelme*. CRIS KOHL COLLECTION. Salvage cables remain on shore. PHOTO BY CRIS KOHL

superintendent who lived from 1881 to 1970, stranded in a storm on Cana Island on October 4, 1928, and was declared a total loss. The wreck was mostly scrapped by 1934. The site today consists of steel, rigging, valves, cables and pumps, plus machinery, all of which makes for good underwater photography in an area of generally good visibility. Take a boat, as the lighthouse property is accessible only to lighthouse tourists (it's a long walk anyway!)

29. *FRANK O'CONNOR*

LORAN: 32078.7/48115.9	GPS: 45° 06.87'/087° 00.73'
DEPTH: 50 to 70 feet	LEVEL: Intermediate-Advanced

LOCATION: This wreck lies about two miles off Cana Island.

The steel-strapped, wooden steamer, *Frank O'Connor* (301' x 42'5" x 22'8"), launched on September 17, 1892, at West Bay City, Michigan, as the *City of Naples* (she was renamed

The huge, wooden steamer, *Frank O'Connor*.
CRIS KOHL COLLECTION

Only one of the four daily Chicago newspapers reported the loss of the *Frank O'Connor*. CRIS KOHL COLLECTION

COAL SHIP BURNS ON LAKE

Steamer Takes Fire Off Wisconsin Peninsula; Crew Flees in Boats.

[By The Associated Press.]

Sturgeon Bay, Wis., Oct. 3.—The steamer Frank O'Connor of the O'Connor Transportation company, North Tonawanda, N. Y., bound down on its way from Buffalo to Milwaukee with 3,000 tons of hard coal, was completely destroyed by fire last evening while five miles off Taylor island, in the vicinity of Bailey's Harbor.

Capt. William J. Hayes ordered the crew to the boats and the men reached Sturgeon Bay late Thursday night.

Contrary to information in several history books and websites, Mr. Frank O'Connor did not die in WWI; here he is at his home in Tonawanda, NY, enjoying a beer in the late 1960's! He lived from 1901 until 1974. PHOTO COURTESY OF KEVIN J. O'CONNOR AND MARY DOINO.

At the *Frank O'Connor's* stern, divers will find the fallen steering quadrant/rudder, and the upright, four-bladed propeller. PHOTO BY CRIS KOHL

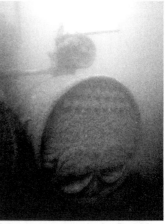

For most visitors to the wreck of the *Frank O'Connor*, the top of the steam engine is the first thing they see. Schools of shiny baitfish flit often past the wreck; schools of large whitefish are seen less frequently. The enormous boiler helped power this vessel.   PHOTOS BY CRIS KOHL

in 1916), burned with a cargo of coal on October 2, 1919. Her crew safely abandoned the blazing ship after her seacocks were ordered opened to hasten her sinking.

Located by divers Sam Mareci and Tom Beaudwin in 1990, the *Frank O'Connor* sits upright with most of her artifacts and much machinery in place, including her 20'-tall triple expansion steam engine, two large scotch boilers, a steam windlass, a capstan, much bow chain, a rudder and steering quadrant lying flat and a large four-bladed propeller. An anchor illegally removed by Chicago divers in 1991 outraged local divers to the point where an out-of-court settlement was reached: the anchor today resides at the Cana Island Lighthouse overlooking the site where the ship met its end. This site, likely the most popular in Door County, is buoyed annually at both bow and stern by the State Historical Society of Wisconsin.

30. MOONLIGHT BAY

DEPTH: 25 feet	LEVEL: Novice

LOCATION: On the north side of Moonlight Bay, south off Highway "Q."

Interesting rock formations, old net stakes and fish make up the highlights of a dive near the boat ramp.

31. *BOAZ*

LORAN: 32082.4/48093.8	GPS: 45° 08.31'/087° 03.10'
DEPTH: 15 feet	LEVEL: Novice

LOCATION: In North Bay in a small cove southwest of Marshall's Point.

Launched at Sheboygan, Wisconsin, in 1869, the three-masted, oak-hulled schooner, *Boaz* (118'9" x 22' x 7'), sailing from Pierpont, Michigan, towards Racine, Wisconsin with a load of lumber, sought shelter from a strong gale in this bay on November 9, 1900. She anchored safely and her crew, having little faith in the 31-year-old wooden vessel, abandoned ship, boarding a steamer which had also taken shelter there. Her cargo was removed and the *Boaz* sank shortly afterwards. Her centerboard and trunk, plus two pump shafts and much of the hull, form the highlights of this site.

The *Boaz*. CRIS KOHL COLLECTION

478

32. CHERUBUSCO

LORAN: 32084.5/48090.2	GPS: 45° 08.46'/087° 03.72'
DEPTH: 8 to 10 feet	LEVEL: Novice

LOCATION: This wreck lies in the middle of North Bay, Door Peninsula, Wisconsin. This old vessel, built in Milwaukee in 1848, was a bark-rigged scow named the *Cherubusco* (144' x 27' x 9'4"). After a career in the lumber business, she was beached in a waterlogged condition considerably north of her destination while enroute from Chicago to Manitowoc with a lumber cargo in November, 1872, and was abandoned in place.

Most of the *Cherubusco's* lower hull lies intact, with the bow, centerboard and trunk, and sternpost in place. The port side is in good condition, but the starboard side lies buried in the sand.

33. TABLE BLUFF

DEPTH: 10 to 110 feet	LEVEL: Novice to Advanced

LOCATION: Along the northern wall of Table Bluff.

Geologic formations (steep walls, boulders, outcroppings) form the highlights of any underwater exploration here. This is a boat dive, unless you happen to be staying at the lodge which adjoins the cliff. Caution: the ferry to Washington Island passes close by.

34. WISCONSIN BAY

DEPTH: 25 to 55 feet	LEVEL: Novice to Intermediate

LOCATION: Off Shastal's dock, at the end of Timberline Road, just northwest of the boat launch. The dock itself is private property, so a boat is required to dive here. This bay

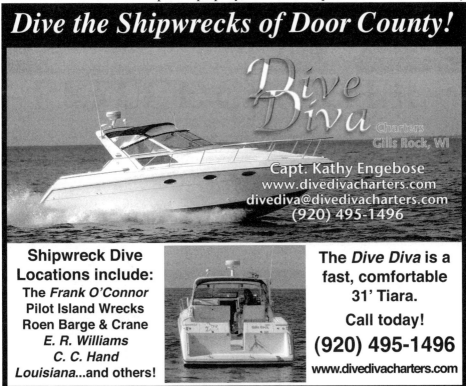

offers quite a lot: schools of fish, submerged dock cribbing in 25', a 34' commercial gill net fishing boat in 55' of water about 200' in front of Shastal's dock, and a 40' fishing tug in 55' of water about 400' 70 degrees off Shastal's dock.

35. *FLEETWING*

> LORAN: 32041.11/48006.22   GPS: 45° 17.25'/087° 02.99'
> DEPTH: 10 to 30 feet   LEVEL: Novice

LOCATION: This wreck lies in the southwest part of Garrett Bay, Door County.
The three-masted schooner, *Fleetwing* (136' x 29' x 12'), built in 1867 at Manitowoc,

The *Fleetwing*. CRIS KOHL COLLECTION

The *Fleetwing* today.
PHOTO BY CRIS KOHL

Wisconsin, was enroute with a cargo of lumber from Menominee, Michigan, to Chicago, when, on the night of September 26, 1888, heading into a northwest gale, Captain Andrew McGraw mistook another bluff for Table Bluff, and sailed at full speed into Garrett Bay instead of the open waters into Lake Michigan through Death's Door Passage. In the darkness, he hit a dead end, grinding his vessel's wooden hull upon the rocky beach with such force that a mast sheared off. Fortunately, the crew all reached land safely, but their ship soon broke in two. This site, buoyed annually by the State Historical Society of Wisconsin, consists of several sections of hull, scattered over an area 500' long. Four sections, from the hull and decking, lie broken 200' to 300' east-northeast of the boat landing at Garrett Bay Road, while the fifth section lies about 500' north-northeast of the boat launch.

36. *R. J. HACKETT*

> LORAN: 32057.7/47938.8   GPS: 45° 21.510'/087° 11.092'
> DEPTH: 10 to 20 feet   LEVEL: Novice

LOCATION: On the east side of Whaleback Shoal, about 7 miles from the mainland.
The wooden *R. J. Hackett* (211'2" x 32'5" x 19'2") was the first of a new kind of Great

The *R. J. Hackett*. CRIS KOHL COLLECTION

The broken engine of the *R. J. Hackett*.   PHOTO BY CRIS KOHL

Lakes ship: the bulk freight steamer, with continuous cargo holds, 24-foot hatch centers, the engine as far aft as possible and the pilothouse right on the bow. Launched at Cleveland in 1869, she became the first steamer to deliver iron ore to that city on August 14, 1871. On November 12, 1905, she caught on fire and was purposely stranded on Whaleback Shoal, but she became a total loss. The crew escaped in two yawlboats.

Much decking and machinery lies scattered on the white sand and pebbles bottom, with highlights being the engine, boilers, and propeller. Be careful here; this is a remote site.

480

37. RESUMPTION

```
DEPTH: 5 to 15 feet          LEVEL:  Novice
```

LOCATION: This wreck lies off the southeast side of Plum Island in Death's Door.

The schooner, *Resumption* (143'4" x 29' x 10'3"), built at Milwaukee in 1879, stranded here on Nov. 7, 1914 and became a total loss. Only portions of the hull's bottom remain.

The wreck of the *Resumption*. CRIS KOHL COLLECTION

38. PILOT ISLAND WRECKS

```
LORAN: 32006.5/48032.3      GPS: 45° 37.64'/086° 55.31'
DEPTH: 20 to 50 feet         LEVEL:  Novice-Intermediate
```

LOCATION: These wrecks lie off the northwest side of Pilot Island, Death's Door. The broken remains of three wooden ships rest at this site:

1. The scow-schooner, *Forest* (115'6" x 23', after 1880 rebuild), built in 1857 at Newport (later Marine City), Michigan, stranded here in a gale on October 28, 1891. All 5 crew rowed to the safety of the lighthouse.

2. The schooner, *J. E. Gilmore* (137'7" x 25'4"), constructed at Three Mile Bay, NY, in 1867, was blown onto the reef on October 17, 1891. No lives were lost.

3. The schooner, *A. P. Nichols* (145'2" x 30'2" x 11'9"), launched at Madison Dock, Ohio, in 1861, was driven onto the island in the gale of Oct. 28, 1891. No lives were lost.

This group site consists of a large debris field near a cement dock. The sand and gravel bottom turns silty the deeper it gets. This jumble of wreckage from three ships is worth the effort to

This photo, taken on October 29 or 30, 1891, shows the *A. P. Nichols* on the right and a broadside view of the *J. E. Gilmore,* left. The sunken *Forest* lies between them. These are the Pilot Island wrecks.   CRIS KOHL COLLECTION

get out there. A boat capable of handling unexpectedly bad weather, usually from the northwest, is needed. Currents can sometimes be moderate.

Pilot Island and portions of its three shipwrecked schooners. PHOTOS BY CRIS KOHL

Great Lakes Highlight No. 26

THE *GRIFFON*:

FIRST WRECK ON THE UPPER LAKES

One of our smallest ships became the greatest mystery in the Great Lakes! Explorer Robert Cavalier, Sieur de la Salle, built and launched a 45-foot-long sailing vessel along the Niagara River near Lake Erie in the year 1679. Named the

The *Griffon*. CRIS KOHL COLLECTION

Griffon, it was the first ship ever to sail the upper (that is, upstream of Niagara Falls) Great Lakes.

The ship and its large crew sailed across Lakes Erie, Huron, and Michigan, and loaded valuable furs at or near Washington Island at the mouth of Green Bay, before beginning the return leg of this maiden voyage with only a handful of crewmembers, the others canoeing on to explore new lands.

But the little ship, with its crew, furs, and cannons, disappeared. In the past 300+ years, more than 16 sites

A statue of explorer La Salle stands near downtown Chicago. PHOTO BY CRIS KOHL

have laid claim to being the fabled *Griffon*, and all have been either unproved or outrightly disproved. The cannons or a recognizable figurehead, say -- smoking guns in this game of identification -- have remained elusive.

The last place where La Salle, the owner, saw the *Griffon* was off Washington Island (and hence the choice of Door County for

The route of the *Griffon*. MAP BY CRIS KOHL

this page's inclusion), but the wreck of the *Griffon* could lie anywhere between there and the place where it was built, the most likely locations being northern Lake Michigan and northern Lake Huron -- and that covers an overwhelmingly huge area!

When it is finally found, whether by design or by accident, the *Griffon*, this longlost holy grail of the Great Lakes, will cause major stirs.

For details of the *Griffon's* story and the many discovery claims made over the years, read the 68-page flagship first chapter of *Shipwreck Tales of the Great Lakes* by Cris Kohl.

Numerous *Griffon* historical markers dot the Great Lakes, this one at the mouth of the St. Clair River. PHOTO BY CRIS KOHL

39. WINFIELD SCOTT

LORAN: 31968.5/48000.2	GPS: 45° 21.75'/086° 51.39'
DEPTH: 10 feet	LEVEL: Novice

LOCATION: Off Hog Island, about 2000' to the east of Washington Island.
The two-masted, 213-ton schooner, *Winfield Scott,* sometimes called the *General W. Scott,* built in Cleveland in 1852, capsized while enroute from Menominee, Michigan, to Chicago with a lumber cargo on August 30, 1871. Her crew clung to her overturned hull for 13 hours until rescued by a passing steamer. This wreck, sitting on shifting sands, lies broken and scattered, with the main section displaying its bilge, keelson and centerboard trunk.

40. IRIS

DEPTH: To 5 feet	LEVEL: Novice

LOCATION: Near shore in Jackson Harbor, Washington Island, WI. The small schooner, *Iris* (74' x 19'2" x 6'6"), built in Port Huron, MI, in 1866, was abandoned here in 1913.

41. PRIDE

LORAN: 31975.1/47963.5	GPS: 45° 29.77'/086° 38.76'
DEPTH: 40 to 60 feet	LEVEL: Intermediate

LOCATION: North end of Washington Island, in Washington Harbor, broken and scattered in 40' to 60' of water. This site, like the nearby *Louisiana,* offers superb visibility. The small, two-masted schooner, *Pride* (87' x 20'), built at Sandusky, OH, in 1849, stranded in a storm on November 29, 1901. No lives were lost.

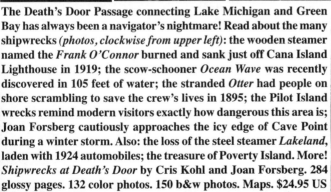 

42. *Louisiana*

LORAN: 31975.7/47964.7	**GPS: 45° 23.98'/086° 55.36'**
DEPTH: 1 to 25 feet	**LEVEL: Novice**

LOCATION: At the north end of Washington Island on the southeast side of the harbor.
Launched on May 12, 1887, at Marine City, Michigan, the wooden steamer, *Louisiana* (267' x 39' x 20'), was driven ashore during the Great Storm of 1913 on November 10th. She caught on fire and was a total loss; no lives were lost.

A boat is needed to reach this site; the property adjacent to the wreck is private. This site, buoyed annually by the State Historical Society of Wisconsin, features most of this ship's hull and some decking sitting on a rock and sand bottom. Most of the machinery was salvaged in 1920, but much of interest remains here.

MARINE

THE LOUISIANA A WRECK

Beached in Gale, Breaks in Two and Burns.

The Steamer Louisiana, owned by J. R. Davock & Co., of Cleveland, is a

Clockwise from above left: The wooden steamer, *Louisiana*. CRIS KOHL COLLECTION. When the Great Storm of 1913 began, the Louisiana sought shelter in Washington Harbor. AERIAL PHOTO BY CRIS KOHL. However, the *Louisiana* became the Great Storm's first of many victims. CRIS KOHL COLLECTION. Joan Forsberg explores what remains underwater of this huge steamer.
PHOTOS BY CRIS KOHL

43. ROEN BARGE (AND TUG)

LORAN: 31885.0/47967.7	**LAT 45° 28.70' LON 086° 40.20'**
DEPTH: 75 to 110 feet	**LEVEL: Advanced**

LOCATION: 2.8 miles south of the old Poverty Island Lighthouse.
The tug and steam barge owned by modern-day salvager John Roen sank in a storm in

October, 1969. The upside-down steambarge is penetrable by the trained and experienced. Tools lie scattered at this site. The tug lies a fair distance away and would be a separate dive.

The Roen barge.
PHOTOS BY KIM BRUNGRABER

44. *Eagle*

DEPTH: 12 feet	**LEVEL: Novice**

LOCATION: Off St. Martin Island, just out from the old lighthouse dock.
A 32' diveboat, the *Eagle,* stranded and broke up here in the 1960's.

45. St. Martin Island Wall

DEPTH: 45 to 125 feet　　　　LEVEL: Intermediate-Advanced

LOCATION: Off the northeast side of St. Martin Island.

This wall dive features unique, white, limestone formations, but there is no hint that they exist above water -- these are visible underwater only. Be careful with depth and time.

46. E. R. Williams

LORAN:	GPS: 45° 31.970'/086° 44.910'
DEPTH: 95 to 105 feet	LEVEL: Advanced

LOCATION: Off St. Martin's Island, Michigan.

The three-masted schooner, *E. R. Williams* (137'2" x 26' x 11'6"), sank with her iron ore cargo during a violent storm on September 22, 1895, while in tow of the steamer, *Santa Maria*. The crew (6 men, 1 woman, 1 dog) launched their yawl boat with great difficulty and reached Big Summer Island, where a passing steamer picked them up. This site, found in the mid-1990's, features many items of interest, including a stove 40' off the stern.

Clockwise from above left: Initially it was reported that the schooner, *E. R. Williams,* was lost in a storm with all hands. Fortunately, the entire crew survived. The *Williams* resembled the *Penokee,* seen here under full sail. Cris Kohl Collection. Some of the wondrous sights on this shipwreck include both wooden-stocked anchors still in place at the bow, and the upright bowsprit with chains remaining attached.　　　Photos by Cris Kohl

47. NAHANT

DEPTH: 5 to 25 feet   LEVEL: Novice-Intermediate

The *Nahant*. CRIS KOHL COLLECTION

This is a shore dive in Escanaba Harbor, between the green can buoy and the municipal dock.

The wooden steamer, *Nahant* (213'3" x 35' x 16'2"), built at Detroit in 1873, burned at Escanaba to a total loss with two lives lost on Nov. 29, 1897. The bow is flattened, and the boiler rests to the east of the hull. This wreck is usually buoyed. Beyond the wreck, it drops off to 80'! The *Nahant's* bell and rudder are at a nearby museum.

48. JOHN WEBER

DEPTH: 45 to 60 feet   LEVEL: Intermediate

This is a shore dive in Escanaba Harbor, between the green can buoy and the municipal dock. Launched at Black River (Lorain), Ohio, in 1856, the two-masted schooner, *John Weber* (93' x 25'6" x 10'), sprang a leak and was scuttled in Escanaba on Oct. 6, 1875, becoming a total loss. This wreck is fairly intact, but beware of fishing line and low visibility.

49. BIG BAY DE NOC BUGGY

DEPTH: 20 feet   LEVEL: Novice

A horse and buggy reportedly went through the ice a long time ago next to the present-day green can buoy. Although dilapidated, the buggy remains recognizable.

50. FAYETTE

DEPTH: To 20 feet   LEVEL: Novice

LOCATION: Snail Shell Harbor at the historic town of Fayette, Michigan, offers interesting shore dives to see an old fishing boat, pilings from the old smelter, and many artifacts. Reportedly the friendly park personnel allow divers to drive in and drop off gear.

51. ERASTUS CORNING

DEPTH: 30 to 65 feet   LEVEL: Intermediate

LOCATION: Off the west side of Poverty Island. The enormous, three-masted, 832-ton schooner, *Erastus Corning* (204'3" x 35'3" x 14'5"), built in Tonawanda, NY, in 1867, stranded and became a total loss on May 21, 1889, while in tow of a steamer.

52. C. C. HAND

DEPTH: To 22 feet   LEVEL: Novice   GPS: 45° 34.75'/086° 37.80'

LOCATION: Off the east side of Summer Island. Built in 1890 at Cleveland, Ohio, the wooden steamer, *C. C. Hand* (265'7" x 41'5" x 22'3"), burned to a total loss off Big Summer Island on Oct. 7, 1913, with no lives lost. This very photogenic wreck lies in clear water!

53. MISCELLANEOUS SUMMER ISLAND SHIPWRECKS

From a plane, one can see the outlines of five shipwrecks along the east side of Big Summer Island. Most were filled with rocks and scuttled, and three of them are so close together that they touch, including the large schooner, *Mattie C. Bell* (181' x 35'4" x 11'5"), which wrecked 200' off shore naturally in a blizzard on Nov. 27, 1895, with no lives lost.

39. Sites near Lake Michigan

1. Heart Lake
2. Hardy Dam Pond
3. Murray Lake
4. Gull Lake
5. Lake Cora
6. Paw Paw Lake
7. Diamond Lake
8. Stone Lake
9. France Park
10. Haigh Quarry
11. Pearl Lake
12. Lake Geneva
13. Racine Quarry
14. Lannon Quarry
15. Devils Lake
16. Green Lake
17. Red Granite Quarry
18. Gilbert Lake
19. Wazee Lake

1. HEART LAKE

LOCATION: One mile north of the town of Waters, Michigan, which is west of exit #270 on I-75 between Gaylord and Grayling, Michigan. Access on the lake's south side.

Heart Lake, small at only 62.5 acres but with a maximum depth of about 123', is known for incredible visibility, a mostly sand bottom, and large numbers of bass (both largemouth and smallmouth). Sunken logs which were on their way to the sawmill at the water's edge years ago are another of the visual treats here. Look out for boaters and water skiers.

2. HARDY DAM POND

LOCATION: In Newaygo State Park, Newaygo County, 7 miles west of exit #125 on Highway 131, and 40 miles northeast of Muskegon, Michigan.

The huge, 4,000-acre Hardy Dam Pond, created in 1932 by the damming of the Muskegon River, reaches a maximum depth of 110'. Many fish and sunken logjams, as well as a steel bridge in 60', attract scuba divers. Beware of entanglement on monofilament line.

3. MURRAY LAKE

LOCATION: About 12 miles east-northeast of Grand Rapids, 7 miles north of Lowell.

Murray Lake, covering 320 acres in a horseshoe shape, reaches a depth of about 72' and offers considerable aquatic life to see, such as perch, bluegills, bass and sunfish. This lake is also popular for night diving and ice diving. Lalley Avenue at the south end of Murray Lake will take you to Causeway Drive, which leads to public access.

4. GULL LAKE

LOCATION: Straddling Kalamazoo County and Barry County, 10 miles northwest of Battle Creek, Michigan, and 12 miles northeast of Kalamazoo, Michigan.

The 2,030-acre Gull Lake, often used for diving charity events, is known for its excellent visibility and has a maximum depth of about 110', with considerable aquatic life plus old, unwanted farm equipment and automobiles which were placed on the ice in early spring and allowed to sink as the ice melted, located in 10' to 40'. Streets circle this lake, allowing access to its waters. There are also two parks where divers can suit up, enter and exit the lake: Ross Township Park near the town of Yorkville at the southwest corner of Gull Lake, and Prairieville Township Park at the north end. Beware of much boating traffic in summer.

5. LAKE CORA

LOCATION: Five miles west of Paw Paw, Michigan; public access is via 46th Street and West Street on this circular lake's west side. Lake Cora, covering 197 acres with a maximum depth of 59', is used for diver checkouts, as well as recreational exploration.

6. PAW PAW LAKE

LOCATION: This 900-acre lake in Berrien County, near Lake Michigan 10 miles northeast of Benton Harbor, Michigan, is not to be confused with the 126-acre lake of the same name only a few miles to the east in Kalamazoo County near Kalamazoo, Michigan.

The large Paw Paw Lake, just north of Watervliet, Michigan, has a maximum depth of 90'. The best public access for scuba diving is at the northeastern end of the lake off North Watervliet Road. This old resort lake, busy on weekends, is good for bottle diving.

7. DIAMOND LAKE

LOCATION: Southeast of Cassopolis, Michigan, east-northeast of Niles, Michigan.

The 1,020-acre Diamond Lake has historic Diamond Isle, popular with Chicago people in the 1890's as a vacation destination complete with a large hotel, in the middle of it. A twin-decked 65' excursion steamer, the *South Bend,* from that era, lies broken in several large pieces, including her boiler, at a depth of about 40' off the northeast side of the island. Located in the 1970's by Zoltan and Diane Tiser, the pieces of this wreck were moved closer together by them and other divers for easier diver exploration in April, 1989. The wreck site is usually buoyed. Diamond Lake reaches maximum depths of 42' off Diamond

Isle's west side, 50' off its north side, and 64' off its east side. Public access is from the southwest end of the lake. A boat is necessary to reach the wreck of the *South Bend*.

8. STONE LAKE

LOCATION: At Middlebury, Indiana, just east of Elkhart, Indiana.

Stone Lake, maximum depth: 26', contains much which has been placed specifically for scuba divers to explore: small boats, a car, a swing set and many other fun items.

9. FRANCE PARK

LOCATION: 4 miles east of Logansport, Indiana, about 60 miles south of South Bend.

This stone quarry, maximum depth: 35', offers good visibility (10' to 25') in early spring and fall when swimmers are absent, and views of rare paddlefish and freshwater jellyfish.

10. HAIGH QUARRY

LOCATION: About 35 miles south-southwest of Chicago, in Kankakee, Illinois.

This 12-acre, spring-fed quarry teems with catfish, perch, bluegill, sunfish, crappie, bass and rare paddlefish, as well as mining equipment left behind when the quarry flooded. Visibility is usually excellent, with east access to the water. Land features include change houses, bbq grills and picnic tables in a park-like setting. There are five scuba training platforms in the shallows, as well as five in the deep area.

At Haigh Quarry, a 33' cabin cruiser, fully explorable, is one of the many underwater sights. PHOTO BY JIM JARECKI

11. PEARL LAKE

LOCATION: Off Highway 251, South Beloit, Illinois, just south of Wisconsin.

This small lake, with a maximum depth of 85', has had numerous items, such as small boats and several vehicles, placed in it for diver exploration. There are also training platforms.

12. LAKE GENEVA

LOCATION: In the center of the triangle formed by Chicago-Madison-Milwaukee.

Lake Geneva, popular with scuba divers, is very large: 5,262 acres, with a maximum depth of 144'. No night-diving or shore-diving are allowed, but boats and motors can be rented. Divers must register with the Water Safety Patrol in Lake Geneva or Fontana. The lake offers gamefish, old tools, bottles and shipwrecks (all the manmade items are protected by the State of Wisconsin; please do not remove them). The shipwrecks include the excursion steamers, *Lady of the Lake* (93' x 22'), which sank in 1893 and lies in 35' of water in Buttons Bay at the southeast end of Lake Geneva, and the 115' *Lucius Newberry*, which sank in 1891, the wreckage of which was located in 1981 in 65' of water 300' off Geneva Bay Estates in the northeast part of the lake. The lake also has cribs and an old hotel dump.

13. RACINE QUARRY

LOCATION: Just outside the northwest corner of Racine, Wisconsin.

This spring-fed quarry, with an average depth of 45' to 60', but with a deep, sulphur-layered hole in 85', offers a couple of cars and a former city dump in the far corner.

14. LANNON QUARRY

LOCATION: Just outside Menomonee Falls, WI, just west of Milwaukee.

This 8-acre limestone quarry in a park system has a maximum depth of 50. Quarry machinery, fish and snagged monofilament line (take a knife!) are found here.

15. DEVILS LAKE

LOCATION: Off Highway 123, northwest of Madison, and southeast of Baraboo, WI.

Devils Lake State Park is perhaps the most popular inland dive site in Wisconsin, open year round and offering camping and picnicking. Rock formations and gamefish are common in this 45' maximum depth lake. This spring-fed lake has a silty bottom.

16. GREEN LAKE

LOCATION: About 40 miles southwest of Appleton, WI, off highway 23.

Four boat launches provide access to Green Lake; shore diving is restricted.

17. RED GRANITE QUARRY

LOCATION: About 30 miles west of Oshkosh, in the town of Red Granite, WI.

Although most divers stay in 30' to 90', this deep quarry descends to 238'! The water is cold, clear, and full of game fish but little vegetation. Open water dive classes are held here.

18. GILBERT LAKE

LOCATION: In Waushara County off County Road K near 22nd Street.

Lush aquatic vegetation coats the bottom (in a max. of 60') of this clear-water lake.

19. WAZEE LAKE

LOCATION: This lake is located 60 miles southeast of Eau Claire, Wisconsin, near the town of Black River Falls. From I-94, take exit 116, which is Route 54, and follow Route 54 east 10 miles until you see the signs for Wazee Lake.

Wazee Lake was once the Jackson County Iron Mine quarry, which operated from 1961 until April, 1983, when domestic steel markets crashed. The company closed the mine and took with them several high-capacity pumps which had kept the mines dry. At an estimated rate of 800 gallons of water per minute, the lake quickly formed. Wazee Lake is today the deepest inland lake in Wisconsin, reaching a max. depth of 355'. Circular roads wind around the pit (underwater), and mining artifacts, like chains and pipes, abound. Fish cribs and training platforms exist. Aquatic life includes trout, bluegills, catfish , and bass. Summer visibility averages 35'. Open year round. There is a vehicle fee and a diving fee.

40. Whitefish Point

Whitefish Point is one of Michigan's eleven Underwater Preserves; most, but not all, of the shipwrecks in this chapter lie within that Preserve's boundaries (the exceptions are the *Aurania, A. A. Parker,* and the *Cyprus*.) *Below:* Cris Kohl and Joan Forsberg explore Whitefish Point's shoreline. PHOTO BY DARRYL ERTEL

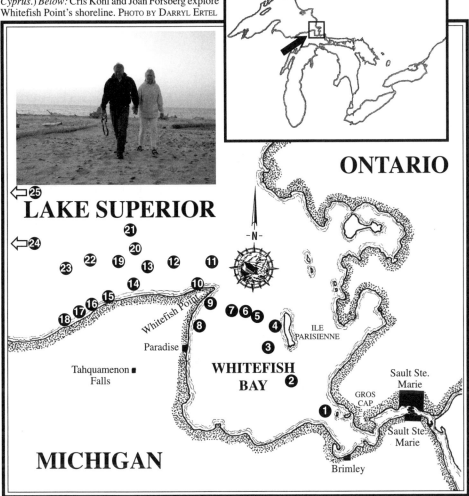

ONTARIO

LAKE SUPERIOR

-N-

Whitefish Point

Paradise

ILE PARISIENNE

Tahquamenon Falls

WHITEFISH BAY

Sault Ste. Marie

GROS CAP

Sault Ste. Marie

MICHIGAN

Brimley

1. *Sagamore*	10. *Ora Endress*	19. *Niagara*
2. *Samuel Mather*	11. *John B. Cowle*	20. *John Mitchell*
3. *Panther*	12. *Myron*	21. *John M. Osborne*
4. *Aurania*	13. *Miztec*	22. *Eureka*
5. *Comet*	14. *M. M. Drake*	23. *Indiana*
6. *Superior City*	15. *Saturn*	24. *A. A. Parker*
7. *Zillah*	16. *Alex. Nimick*	25. *Cyprus*
8. *Sadie Thompson*	17. *Neshoto*	
9. *Vienna*	18. *Allegheny*	

1. SAGAMORE

LORAN: 31072.9/47771.8	**GPS: 46° 31.089'/084° 37.927'**
DEPTH: 42 to 63 feet	**LEVEL: Intermediate-Advanced**

LOCATION: This wreck lies at the entrance to the St. Marys River, Whitefish Bay.

The uniquely-designed whaleback steamer-barge, *Sagamore* (308' x 38' x 24'), launched at Superior, Wisconsin, on July 23, 1892, sank nine years and six days later, on July 29, 1901, after a collision with the steamer, *Northern Queen*. Three of the eight lives on board the *Sagamore* were lost that foggy day. The wreck sits upright and mostly intact. The wide open hatches provide easy access for a swim throughout the wreck, and the collision damage

The "pigboat," *Sagamore*.
CRIS KOHL COLLECTION

Examining the *Sagamore's* triple fairleads.
PHOTO BY CRIS KOHL

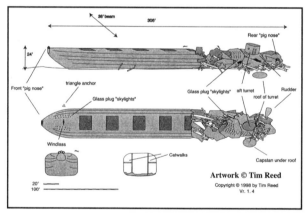

is clear near the stern. The triple bow fairleads are impressive, as is the sheer size of this wreck. This excellent site lies in the shipping lane directly out of the Sault locks, with immense freighters pouring out of there almost non-stop. Call the U.S. Coast Guard at the Soo (Sault Ste. Marie, MI) at 906-635-3273 or VHF 16 to let them know you will be anchored at this site. Maybe they can get the freighters to go around your boat, but don't count on it.

2. SAMUEL MATHER

LORAN: 31086.7/47734.8	GPS: 46° 34.275'/084° 42.345'
DEPTH: 150 to 172 feet	LEVEL: Technical

LOCATION: This wreck lies 16 miles southeast of Whitefish Point, Michigan.

Launched at Cleveland on April 9, 1887, the wooden steamer, *Samuel Mather* (246' x 40' x 19'3"), was sunk in a collision with the new steel steamer, *Brazil*, on November 22, 1891, while downbound with a cargo of wheat. No lives were lost.

The *Samuel Mather,* located by Tom Farnquist and his team in May, 1978, is one of the best preserved and most intact shipwrecks off Whitefish Point. The wreck sits upright and penetrable. The stern mast towers high off the deck, and the rudder, four-bladed propeller, trumpet-shaped dorades (air vents), the engine and much rigging are of interest. Use caution: this is a remote deep dive. *Below*: The *Samuel Mather.* ART BY AND © KEN MARSCHALL, COURTESY OF TOM FARNQUIST/GREAT LAKES SHIPWRECK HISTORICAL SOCIETY

The steamer, *Samuel Mather.* CRIS KOHL COLLECTION

The *Samuel Mather*   SIDESCAN © AND COURTESY OF TOM FARNQUIST/ GREAT LAKES SHIPWRECK HISTORICAL SOCIETY

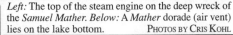

Left: The top of the steam engine on the deep wreck of the *Samuel Mather. Below:* A *Mather* dorade (air vent) lies on the lake bottom.   PHOTOS BY CRIS KOHL

3. PANTHER

> **LORAN: 31105.8/47685.9**   **GPS: 46° 38.300'/084° 48.369'**
> **DEPTH: 88 to 110 feet**   **LEVEL: Advanced**

LOCATION: Off Parisienne Island, about 10 miles southeast of Whitefish Point.

The *Panther.* CRIS KOHL COLLECTION

The wooden steamer, *Panther* (247'6" x 35'8" x 22'2"), built at West Bay City, Michigan, in 1890, sank with a wheat cargo on June 26, 1916, in a collision with the steamer, *James J. Hill.* No lives were lost. Upright and reasonably intact, the *Panther's* decks have collapsed, but interesting items may be viewed on deck: tools, dishes and portholes. The more intact stern offers the engine, smokestack, boiler, winch, stove and much of the cargo.

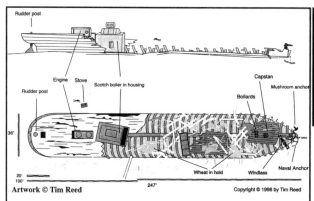

Artwork © Tim Reed

Toppled bitts are only a small part of the interesting collection of shipwreck parts at the *Panther's* stern. Other items include the rudder post, engine, steering quadrant and a stove.   PHOTO BY CRIS KOHL

4. AURANIA

> **LORAN:**   **GPS:**
> **DEPTH: 440 feet**   **LEVEL: Technical**

LOCATION: Off Parisienne Island, about 8.5 miles east-southeast of Whitefish Point.

The *Aurania.* CRIS KOHL COLLECTION

Launched as a steel tow barge at Chicago on August 31, 1895, and converted in 1899 when an engine was added, the steamer, *Aurania* (352' x 44'2" x 21'9"), carrying a coal cargo, was trapped in late ice which penetrated her hull, and she sank off Parisienne Island on April 29, 1909. The 20 crew walked several miles across the ice to a nearby steamer. This deep wreck, reportedly located in 1972, has been visited by technical divers.

5. COMET

> **LORAN: 31111.4/47638.1**   **GPS: 46° 43.007'/084° 52.012'**
> **DEPTH: 205 to 230 feet**   **LEVEL: Technical**

LOCATION: This deep wreck lies 4.6 miles southeast of Whitefish Point, Michigan.

The wooden, twin-arched steamer, *Comet* (182' x 29'2" x 11'2"), built in Cleveland in 1857, sank in a collision with the Canadian sidewheel steamer, *Manitoba*, on August 26, 1875, with the loss of 10 of the 20 lives on board and the cargo of pig iron ingots and copper and silver ore.

Located in the summer of 1980 by the Great Lakes Shipwreck Historical Society, this site lies in the main shipping channel. The bow is detached and partially buried, while the exposed engine has the ship's name ornately painted on it. The large debris field is interesting.

Left: The *Comet.* ONTARIO ARCHIVES.

Right: Sidescan sonar image of the wreck of the *Comet.* SIDESCAN © AND COURTESY OF TOM FARNQUIST/GREAT LAKES SHIPWRECK HISTORICAL SOCIETY

6. SUPERIOR CITY

LORAN: 31112.0/47633.5	GPS: 46° 43.51'/084° 52.37'
DEPTH: 210 to 270 feet	LEVEL: Technical

LOCATION: This wreck lies 4.0 miles southeast of Whitefish Point, Michigan.

Launched at Lorain, Ohio, on April 13, 1898, the steel steamer, *Superior City* (429' x 50' x 24'7"), sank in a collision with the 580' steamer, *Willis L. King,* on August 20, 1920, with the loss of 29 of her 33 crew (the four survivors were blown clear of the ship when her boilers exploded) and her iron ore cargo. Located by John Steele in 1972, this deep wreck shows explosion damage in her stern area. Use extreme caution at this site.

Left: The *Superior City.* CRIS KOHL COLLECTION. *Below:* SIDESCAN © AND COURTESY OF TOM FARNQUIST/GREAT LAKES SHIPWRECK HISTORICAL SOCIETY

7. ZILLAH

LORAN: 31123.6/47624.3	GPS: 46° 43.705'/084° 54.965'
DEPTH: 230 to 250 feet	LEVEL: Technical

LOCATION: This wreck lies 2.8 miles south-southeast of Whitefish Point, Michigan.

Launched as the *Edward Smith* at West Bay City, Michigan, on March 31, 1890, and renamed the *Zillah* (201'7" x 37' x 13') in

The *Zillah*. CRIS KOHL COLLECTION

1901, this wooden steamer foundered on August 29, 1926, with no lives lost. Carrying a cargo of limestone at the time of her loss, the *Zillah* sits upright and mostly intact in very deep water. Use every precaution here.

STEAMSHIP ZILLAH SUNK IN WHITE FISH BAY; CREW IS SAVED

Bottom of Old Wooden Vessel, Storm Laden, Seemed to Drop Out

Whitefish Point, Mich., Aug. 30 (AP)—The steamer Zillah, a 200-foot freighter, with a cargo of stone, sprang a leak off here yesterday and went down. The crew

CRIS KOHL COLLECTION

The deep wreck of the *Zillah* is intact and can be penetrated, at increased peril at that depth. *Left:* An open doorway with white paint still visible on the walls. *Right:* The engine throttles. VIDEO FREEZE-FRAMES BY DARRYL ERTEL

8. SADIE THOMPSON

LORAN: 31150.1/47619.8	GPS: 46° 42.537'/084° 59.878'
DEPTH: 85 to 116 feet	LEVEL: Advanced

LOCATION: This wreck lies 4.1 miles west-southwest of Whitefish Point, Michigan.

The old barge, *Sadie Thompson,* built in the 1890's, broke from her moorings in a storm in the early 1950's while involved in the construction of the breakwall and pier at Whitefish Point Harbor of Refuge while under contract to the U.S. Army Corps of Engineers.

Located by the Great Lakes Shipwreck Historical Society (Tom Farnquist's group) and contracted wreckhunter Dave Trotter in August, 1992, the *Sadie Thompson* rests almost upside-down and displays her steam crane, huge gears, spindle and a large bell, among many other items. Penetration is possible for trained, experienced and prepared divers. This relatively protected site lies in the lee of Whitefish Point.

Ohio diver Steve Whitman explores under the nearly-overturned barge, *Sadie Thompson,* to view her massive gears, winches and bitts.
PHOTO BY CRIS KOHL

9. *VIENNA*

LORAN: 31135.8/47610.2	GPS: 46° 44.415'/084° 57.912'
DEPTH: 118 to 148 feet	LEVEL: Advanced-Technical

LOCATION: This wreck lies 1.6 miles west-southwest of Whitefish Point, Michigan.

The wooden steamer, *Vienna* (191'4" x 33'8" x 14'1"), launched at Cleveland on June 19, 1873, carried a cargo of iron ore when she collided with the steamer, *Nipigon,* on September 17, 1892. No lives were lost. Following the collision, the *Nipigon* was towing the *Vienna* towards shore when the latter ship sank.

Scuba divers Kent Bellrichard and Tom Farnquist located the *Vienna* in 1974. She sits upright, rising 30' off the lake bottom. From her artistic, curved stern railing to the collision damage at her bow, the *Vienna* offers much to see, including a lifeboat near midship and tools strewn about the deck. Penetration is possible for the trained and experienced. This site is buoyed annually, as are most of the wrecks in the Whitefish Point Underwater Preserve.

The *Vienna*. CRIS KOHL COLLECTION

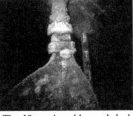

The *Vienna's* rudder and deck tools. PHOTOS BY CRIS KOHL

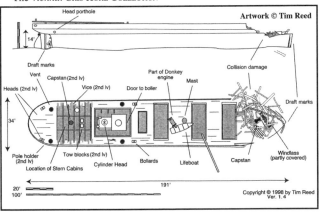

Joyce Hayward prepares to photograph a winch. PHOTO BY CRIS KOHL

The wreck of the *Vienna*. ART BY AND © KEN MARSCHALL, COURTESY OF TOM FARNQUIST/GREAT LAKES SHIPWRECK HISTORICAL SOCIETY

10. ORA ENDRESS

> **LORAN: 31133.8/47592.8**   **GPS:**
> **DEPTH: 13 to 15 feet**   **LEVEL: Novice**

LOCATION: This wreck lies about one mile west of Whitefish Point, Michigan.

The *Ora Endress*. CRIS KOHL COLLECTION

The 56-net-ton fishing tug, *Ora Endress* (58' x 15' x 6'), built at Manitowoc, Wisconsin, in 1910, capsized on September 13, 1914, with the Whitefish Point lighthouse keeper and two other men rescuing all 11 crewmembers. The wreck, uncovered when sands shifted in early 1997, lies with her hull intact (but the cabin is missing) with much machinery in and around the hull. Sands continue to shift around this wreck.

11. JOHN B. COWLE

> **LORAN: 31125.1/47579.4**   **GPS: 46° 48.315'/084° 57.870'**
> **DEPTH: 180 to 220 feet**   **LEVEL: Technical**

LOCATION: This wreck lies 2.3 miles north-northwest of Whitefish Point, Michigan.

The steel steamer, *John B. Cowle* (420' x 50'2" x 24'), loaded with iron ore, sank on July 12, 1909, in a tragic collision in thick fog with the steel steamer, *Isaac M. Scott* (which did not sink in this episode, but rather four years later in Lake Huron; that wreck is also in this book), with 14 of the 24 on the *Cowle* perishing. The *John B. Cowle*, launched in September, 1902, at Port Huron, Michigan, was located by Kent Bellrichard and his team in the summer of 1972 (he also found the *Isaac M. Scott*). This wreck, angled on a slope, offers an intact pilothouse at the shallowest point.

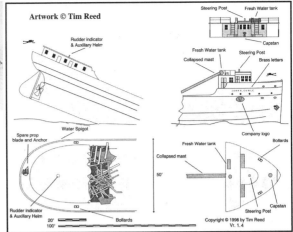

Artwork © Tim Reed

Above: The steel steamer, *John B. Cowle.* CRIS KOHL COLLECTION. *Right:* Detailed wreck site drawings for the *John B. Cowle.* ART BY, COURTESY OF, AND © TIM REED

Copyright © 1998 by Tim Reed
Vr. 1.4

12. *MYRON*

LORAN: 31142.9/47566.5	GPS: 46° 48.463′/085° 01.646′
DEPTH: 42 to 52 feet	LEVEL: Intermediate

LOCATION: This shipwreck lies 4.2 miles NW of Whitefish Point.

The wooden steamer, *Myron* (186′ x 32′6″ x 13′), launched as the *Mark Hopkins* in 1888 at Grand Haven, MI, was renamed in 1902 and foundered in a severe storm on Nov. 22, 1919, with the loss of 17 of the 18 lives on board (only the captain survived). The wreck lies broken in basically two clusters: the bow with its anchor chain tapestry, and the stern, with its propeller and engine (with the boiler lying nearby).

The *Myron* and her tows, depicted in an early 1900's postcard which was colorized. CRIS KOHL COLLECTION

The full story of the *Myron* is told in the chapter, "The Captain's Jinx," in *Shipwreck Tales of the Great Lakes* by Cris Kohl.

Right: Myron victims were chopped out of the ice and buried on a hillside overlooking the lake. PHOTO BY CRIS KOHL

Above: At first, all hands were feared lost when the *Myron* sank; her captain was not rescued until the next day. CRIS KOHL COLLECTION. *Left:* Diver Gary Elliott examines the *Myron's* bow. *Center:* The *Myron's* bow, from a distance. *Right:* Joan Forsberg takes a close look at the *Myron's* boiler. PHOTOS BY CRIS KOHL

13. *MIZTEC*

LORAN: 31156.9/47561.2	GPS: 46° 48.073'/085° 04.500'
DEPTH: 45 to 50 feet	LEVEL: Intermediate

LOCATION: This wreck lies 5.5 miles west-northwest of Whitefish Point, Michigan.

The *Miztec (at right)* with the steamer, *Aztec.* CRIS KOHL COLLECTION

The schooner-barge, *Miztec* (194'1" x 34'6" x 14'), built at Marine City, Michigan, in 1890, carried heavy bulk cargoes, usually towed by the steamer *Myron* (see site #12). She survived the storm which sank the *Myron* in 1919. However, as if responding to some powerful summons to be with her old partner, the *Miztec* foundered in a severe gale on May 15, 1921, not far from where the *Myron* sank. The entire *Miztec* crew perished. Today, the wreck lies broken, but with much hardware and many tools still to explore and examine.

14. *M. M. DRAKE*

LORAN: 31167.5/47569.3	GPS: 46° 46.75'/085° 05.87'
DEPTH: 42 to 50 feet	LEVEL: Intermediate

LOCATION: 6.0 miles west of Whitefish Point.

The wooden steamer, *M. M. Drake* (201' x 34'5" x 14'6"), built at Buffalo, New York, in 1882, attempted to remove the crew of the sinking barge, the 213' *Michigan,* which she was towing, when an enormous wave crashed the wooden vessels together on Oct. 2, 1901. Both ships sank, with the loss of the *Michigan's* cook. The *Michigan* remains to be located.

Above: 18 months after the *Myron* sank, the *Miztec* was lost at the same place. CRIS KOHL COLLECTION. *Left:* The donkey steam engine lies on the bow. *Right:* Steve Whitman explores the *Miztec*. PHOTOS BY CRIS KOHL

The *Drake,* although broken and scattered, offers a photogenic boiler, a propeller shaft (but the prop is gone), wooden hull and a variety of tools.

Left: The *M. M. Drake* CRIS KOHL COLLECTION. *Right:* The *Drake's* steering post and rudder at the Whitefish Point museum. PHOTO BY CRIS KOHL

15. SATURN

LORAN:	GPS:
DEPTH: 32 feet	LEVEL: Novice

LOCATION: About 8 miles west of Whitefish Point.

The 233-ton schooner barge, *Saturn,* built at New Jerusalem, Ohio, in 1872, sank later that same year which claimed all seven hands when the vessel stranded on Nov. 27, 1872.

The *Saturn*, along with the *Jupiter* (also lost with all hands), both towed by the tug, *John A. Dix*, carried iron ore from Marquette to Wyandotte, MI. This wreck was found by Darryl Ertel, Dave Heyboar, and Sarah Wilde in August, 2006.

Left: The *Saturn's* bow stem, with Roman numeral draft markings, lies on a portion of sandy lake bottom. *Right:* Much of the hull's framing and planking remain intact and embedded in the bottom of the lake. PHOTOS BY DARRYL ERTEL

16. *ALEX. NIMICK*

LORAN: 31203.3/47555.2	GPS:
DEPTH: 15 to 22 feet	LEVEL: Novice

LOCATION: This wreck lies 11.2 miles west of Whitefish Point, Michigan.

Launched on January 25, 1890, at West Bay City, Michigan, the wooden steamer, *Alex. Nimick* (298'4" x 40' x 21'), stranded in a strong gale on September 20, 1907, with the loss of six lives. Pounded to pieces, the wreck lies scattered in shallow water.

Left: The steamer, *Alex. Nimick.* CRIS KOHL COLLECTION

17. *NESHOTO*

LORAN: 31181.2/47527.4	GPS:
DEPTH: 15 feet	LEVEL: Novice

LOCATION: About 2.5 miles east of Crisp Point, Michigan.

The wooden steamer, *Neshoto* (284'2" x 42'5" x 22'), built at Cleveland, Ohio, in 1889, carried iron ore when she stranded due to dense forest fire smoke on Sept. 27, 1908. The 16 crew were rescued by the Crisp Point Life Saving Station just before the gales increased, turning the *Neshoto* broadside to the waves and pounding her to pieces.

Left: The steamer, *Neshoto.* CRIS KOHL COLLECTION

18. *ALLEGHENY*

LOCATION: Off Crisp Point, Michigan, about 13 miles west of Whitefish Point.

Erie, Pennsylvania, saw the launch of the 689-ton, three-masted schooner, *Allegheny*

(187' x 33' x 13'1"), on Sept. 13, 1873. Forty years later, this ship, reduced to a towbarge, was carrying lumber,

Left: The *Allegheny,* in an early 1900's hand-colored postcard. CRIS KOHL COLLECTION. *Right:* A fallen capstan on the *Allegheny.* PHOTO BY DARRYL ERTEL

Left: A diver examines the huge timbers and a hawse pipe with chain on the wreck of the *Allegheny*. *Right:* The sides of the hull have collapsed outwards, exposing the hanging knees. PHOTOS BY DARRYL ERTEL

when it broke away from its steamer, *M. T. Greene*, in a storm on June 6, 1913, and stranded. The Vermilion Point Life Saving crew rescued 6 of the 7 on the *Allegheny*. This wreck, in 28′ of water, was found in August, 2006, by Darryl Ertel, Dave Heyboar, and Sarah Wilde.

19. NIAGARA

LORAN: 31168.3/47543.9	GPS: 46° 49.173′/085° 07.488′
DEPTH: 96 to 108 feet	LEVEL: Advanced

LOCATION: 7.8 miles WNW of Whitefish Point.

Built at Tonawanda, New York, in 1873, the schooner-barge, *Niagara* (204′6″ x 34′ x 14′), with a cargo of iron ore, foundered on September 7, 1887, with her entire crew (9 lives) in a severe gale after breaking her tow line from the steamer, *Australasia*. Today, that iron ore cargo forms the highest point of this broken shipwreck. The sides of the hull lie alongside the cargo, with numerous bits of equipment lying scattered.

A *Niagara* anchor adorns the Superior College campus in nearby Sault Ste. Marie, MI. PHOTO BY CRIS KOHL

20. JOHN MITCHELL

LORAN: 31153.6/47545.6	GPS: 46° 49.930′/085° 04.839′
DEPTH: 120 to 150 feet	LEVEL: Advanced-Technical

LOCATION: This wreck lies 6.6 miles northwest of Whitefish Point, Michigan.

The steel steamer, *John Mitchell* (420′ x 52′ x 23′), constructed at St. Clair, Michigan, in 1907, sank within five minutes of colliding with the 354′ steel steamer, *William H. Mack*, on July 9, 1911. Three lives were lost from the 34 on board. This wreck, located in 1972 by John Steele and his crew (Bill Cohrs, Kent Bellrichard and Tom Farnquist), lies upside-down, the bow buried in the sand and the propeller and rudder in about 120′. Inside, porcelain toilets hang from above, while the engine room and crew quarters are penetrable for trained, experienced and prepared divers.

The *John Mitchell*.
CRIS KOHL COLLECTION

21. JOHN M. OSBORNE

LORAN: 31149.5/47528.2	GPS: 46° 51.990′/085° 05.169′
DEPTH: 150 to 170 feet	LEVEL: Technical

LOCATION: This wreck lies 8.3 miles northwest of Whitefish Point, Michigan.

The wooden steamer, *John M. Osborne* (178′1″ x 32′1″ x 14′), sank in dense fog after being struck by the 305′ steel steamer, *Alberta,* on July 27, 1884, with the loss of four lives

Above: The *John M. Osborne.* ARTIST UNKNOWN. CRIS KOHL COLLECTION. *Right:* The *Osborne* wreck. ART BY AND © KEN MARSCHALL, COURTESY OF TOM FARNQUIST/GREAT LAKES SHIPWRECK HISTORICAL SOCIETY. *Below:* Tim Reed's *Osborne* art. *Lower right:* The bow and anchor. PHOTO BY CRIS KOHL

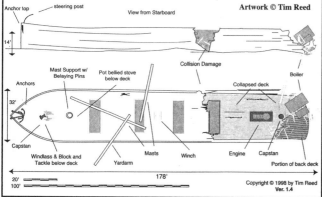

(three from the *Osborne* and one from the *Alberta*). The *John M. Osborne,* upright and quite intact, was located in 1984 by the Great Lakes Shipwreck Historical Society and the Odyssey Foundation of Lansing, Michigan. Both bow anchors are in place, as are a capstan and winches, and the cargo holds are open for penetration. The stern offers the boiler and engine.

22. EUREKA

LORAN: 31181.2/47524.4	GPS: 46° 50.15'/085° 10.76'
DEPTH: 48 to 54 feet	LEVEL: Intermediate

LOCATION: This wreck lies 10.3 miles west-northwest of Whitefish Point, Michigan.
This 138' schooner-barge foundered with all six lives on board and a cargo of iron ore on October 20, 1886. Her rudder box stands upright in the midst of broken planking.

23. INDIANA

LORAN: 31215.1/47520.3	GPS: 46° 48.66'/085° 17.16'
DEPTH: 103 to 118 feet	LEVEL: Advanced

LOCATION: This wreck lies 14.1 miles west-northwest of Whitefish Point, Michigan.
Launched at Vermilion, Ohio, in 1848, the early propeller-driven steamer, *Indiana* (146'6" x 23' x 10'10"), laden with iron ore, foundered on June 6, 1858, with no lives lost.

THE *INDIANA* WRECK SITE

Drawing by David S. Robinson, Smithsonian Institution

Located in 1972 by John Steele and his team mates, Bill Cohrs and Kent Bellrichard, this historic shipwreck was extensively salvaged by museums, including Washington's Smithsonian, which raised the engine and boiler. Much remains here, e.g. prop shaft, stem and sternposts with Roman numeral markings, and iron ore scattered on deck.

24. A. A. PARKER

LOCATION: This wreck lies in about 220' of water off the harbor town of Grand Marais, Michigan, about 52 miles to the west of Whitefish Point.
The wooden steamer, *A. A. Parker* (246'9" x 38'2" x 20'9"), launched as the *Kasota* at Cleveland in 1884 (name changed in 1892), foundered with a cargo of iron ore after springing a leak in a northwest gale on September 19, 1903. All on board were rescued by the U.S. Life Saving crew. This long-sought wreck was located, upright and intact, on June 28, 2001, by Tom Farnquist and his team.

The steamer, *A. A. Parker.*
CRIS KOHL COLLECTION

25. CYPRUS

LOCATION: About 8 miles north of Deer Park, MI, west-northwest of Whitefish Point.
The brand new, steel steamer, *Cyprus* (420' x 52' x 28'), built at Lorain, Ohio, in 1907, sank on October 11, 1907, only a few weeks after being launched, with the loss of 22 of the 23 lives on board. Only the wheelsman, Charles Pitz of Toledo, survived (he remained a sailor and died in 1961). Tom Farnquist and the Great Lakes Shipwreck Historical Society located this wreck in late August, 2007. The *Cyprus* lies on its starboard side in 420' to 460' of water.

The new steamer, *Cyprus.* CRIS KOHL COLLECTION

41. Munising

Munising, Michigan, is the hub of activity for the Alger Underwater Preserve, one of the state's eleven special areas recognized as encompassing a high concentration of shipwrecks.

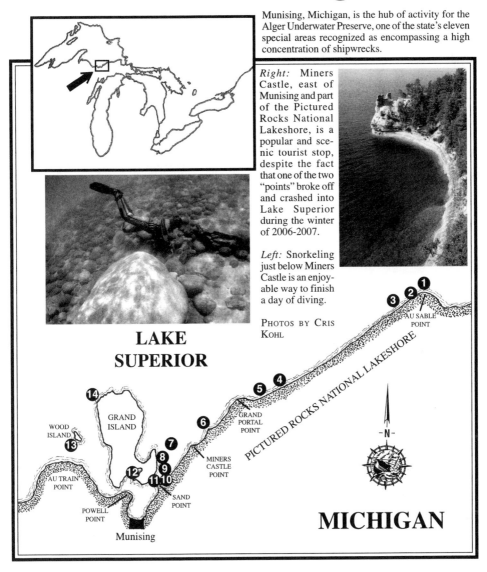

Right: Miners Castle, east of Munising and part of the Pictured Rocks National Lakeshore, is a popular and scenic tourist stop, despite the fact that one of the two "points" broke off and crashed into Lake Superior during the winter of 2006-2007.

Left: Snorkeling just below Miners Castle is an enjoyable way to finish a day of diving.

PHOTOS BY CRIS KOHL

LAKE SUPERIOR

AU SABLE POINT

PICTURED ROCKS NATIONAL LAKESHORE

GRAND PORTAL POINT

GRAND ISLAND

WOOD ISLAND

MINERS CASTLE POINT

AU TRAIN POINT

SAND POINT

POWELL POINT

Munising

-N-

MICHIGAN

1. *Gale Staples*	8. *Herman H. Hettler*
2. **Au Sable shore wrecks**	9. *Manhattan*
3. *Kiowa*	10. **Sand Point wrecks**
4. *Superior*	11. **Smith Moore**
5. *Wabash*	12. *Bermuda*
6. *George*	13. *Chenango*
7. *Steven M. Selvick*	14. *F. Morrell*

1. GALE STAPLES

LORAN:	GPS: 46° 40.80'/086° 09.10'
DEPTH: 20 feet	LEVEL: Novice

LOCATION: This wreck lies about 3/4 mile to the northwest of the Au Sable lighthouse.

The wooden bulk freight steamer, *Gale Staples* (277'2" x 42' x 24'7"), launched as the *William B. Morley* at Marine City, Michigan, in 1888, stranded off Au Sable light on October 1, 1918, with no lives lost. She is broken up in a widely scattered debris field which includes both boilers, visible from the surface, about 250' apart, with most of the wreckage around the more westerly boiler: propeller, folding anchor, iron-sheathed wooden rudder, capstan, tools and much miscellaneous machinery and fittings.

The *Gale Staples*.
CRIS KOHL COLLECTION

2. AU SABLE SHORE WRECKS

LORAN:	GPS: 46° 40.15'/086° 10.08'
DEPTH: To 6 feet	LEVEL: Landlubber to Novice

The remains of the *Sitka* and the *Mary Jarecki* lie along shore. PHOTO BY CRIS KOHL

LOCATION: These two wrecks lie 0.5 and 1.25 miles west of the Au Sable Lighthouse.

Two wooden shipwrecks lie badly broken up along the shoreline and out a bit into very shallow water. The remains of the steamer, *Sitka* (272'5" x 40'5" x 19'4"), built at West Bay City, Michigan, in 1887, and stranded and broken up here on October 4, 1904, with no lives lost, rest closer to the lighthouse. The steamer, *Mary Jarecki* (179'6" x 32'7" x 13'2"), built at Toledo, Ohio, in 1871, stranded with an iron ore cargo on July 4, 1883, and broke to pieces with no lives lost. Chunks of her hull lie 200' east of the Hurricane River; the above co-ordinates are for her broken boiler in 6' of water.

3. KIOWA

LORAN: 31499.78/47425.19	GPS: 46° 38.71'/086° 13.21'
DEPTH: 25 to 35 feet	LEVEL: Novice

LOCATION: This wreck lies 3.8 miles southwest of the Au Sable Lighthouse.

The *Kiowa*. CRIS KOHL COLLECTION

The wrecked *Kiowa*. CRIS KOHL COLLECTION

508

The steel freighter, *Kiowa* (251' x 43'6" x 22'2"), resembled a "salty" (an ocean-going ship) with her midship bridge and masts, cranes and booms. In fact, she was built for World War I in Europe, but she slid down the Detroit launch-ramp too late (May 18, 1920). On November 30, 1929, she stranded in a severe gale with 5 lives lost. Partially salvaged

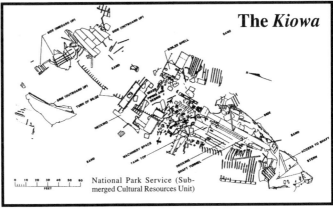

The *Kiowa*

National Park Service (Submerged Cultural Resources Unit)

for World War II, much remains here: pieces of steel hull, pumps, generators, piping and valves.

4. SUPERIOR

LORAN: 31577.1/47429.1	GPS: 46° 33.45'/086° 24.91'
DEPTH: 6 to 33 feet	LEVEL: Novice

LOCATION: This wreck lies 7.3 miles northeast of Miners Castle Point.

The sidewheel passenger steamer, *Superior* (191' x 27'8" plus 22' for the paddlewheels x 11'2"), became the most tragic, in terms of lives lost, shipwreck in Lake Superior when she stranded in heavy seas and broke up on October 30, 1856, with the loss of 35 lives from the 50 on board. Captain Hiram Jones, who had lost three ships earlier (the *Ben Franklin* in 1850, the *Albany* in 1853 and the *E. K. Collins* in 1854) reportedly made no effort to save himself this time. The *Superior* was built at Perrysburg, Ohio, in 1845. The wreck lies broken and scattered around the base of Spray Falls, with her boilers visible from the surface.

This dramatic drawing depicts the loss of the steamer, *Superior,* on Lake Superior.
ARTWORK BY EDWARD PUSICK, COURTESY OF FREDERICK STONEHOUSE

5. WABASH

LOCATION: This wreck lies 6.0 miles northeast of Miners Castle Point.

The schooner-barge, *Wabash* (140' x 26' x 12'), built at Toledo, Ohio, in 1873, stranded and broke up with a cargo of coal and no lives lost in a storm on Nov. 16, 1883. Keelson and frames lie in 8' of water (**GPS: 46° 32.86'/086° 26.80'**), sometimes hidden by shifting sands, while hull pieces and coal cargo lie in 16' to 48' (**GPS: 46° 33.65'/086° 26.30'**)

6. GEORGE

LORAN: 31604.48/47430.63	GPS: 46° 30.96'/086° 31.25'
DEPTH: 15 feet	LEVEL: Novice

LOCATION: About 150' off shore, 1.9 miles northeast of Miners Castle Point.

Launched as the *George Murray* at Manitowoc, Wisconsin, in 1873, the large, three-masted schooner, *George* (202'8" x 34' x 13'8"), stranded in a severe gale and broke up with a coal cargo and no lives lost on October 24, 1893. Much equipment was later salvaged. The ship's bare frames remain.

The *George*. ARTIST UNKNOWN. CRIS KOHL COLLECTION

7. STEVEN M. SELVICK

LORAN: 31629.3/47427.0	GPS: 46° 29.53'/086° 35.87'
DEPTH: 45 to 65 feet	LEVEL: All levels

The tug, *Lorain,* later the *Steven M. Selvick*. GREAT LAKES MARINE COLLECTION OF THE MILWAUKEE PUBLIC LIBRARY/WISCONSIN MARINE HISTORICAL SOCIETY

LOCATION: Between Grand Island and Miners Castle Point, 6 miles north-northeast of Munising.

The tug, *Steven M. Selvick* (68'7" x 17' x 11'), launched in 1915 at Cleveland as the *Lorain,* was purposely scuttled to create a new scuba dive site on June 1, 1996. This tug aided in the construction of the Mackinac Bridge in 1957, and Mr. Steven M. Selvick was married on board this vessel on June 19, 1982. Her exterior is impressive and, with caution, the inside of the pilot house, engine room, galley, messroom and crew quarters can be explored. Take a light.

The *Selvick's* deck railing and dorade. PHOTO BY PETE TOMASINO

Joan Forsberg at the *Selvick's* propeller. PHOTO BY CRIS KOHL

Above: Inside the *Steven M. Selvick's* pilothouse. PHOTO BY PETE TOMASINO. *Left and right:* There is much to explore on this interesting tugboat, whether one remains above the wreck's deck, or goes inside. Shipwreck penetration does require special training. PHOTOS BY CRIS KOHL

The old lighthouse on Grand Island off Munising, Michigan, was recently restored. PHOTO BY CRIS KOHL

8. HERMAN H. HETTLER

> **LORAN: 31632.18/47431.39**   **GPS: 46° 29.03'/086° 35.98'**
> **DEPTH: 20 to 36 feet**   **LEVEL: Novice**

Herman H. Hettler. CRIS KOHL COLLECTION. *Below:* An anchor from the *Hettler,* recently returned to the site. PHOTO BY PETE TOMASINO

A diver studies the *Hettler's* hull. PHOTO BY CRIS KOHL

LOCATION: This wreck lies two miles north of Sand Point.

Built in 1890 at West Bay City, Michigan, as the *Walter Vail,* the wooden steamer, *Herman H. Hettler* (210' x 34'7" x 13'2"), renamed in 1913, was driven ashore at Grand Island in a blizzard on November 23, 1926, and broke in two with no lives lost. Today, the wooden hull and decking, broken into large pieces, sit on the rocky lake bottom. The huge boiler is also on site, along with much piping and a bathtub. An anchor raised in 1961 by local divers was returned to the site in 1996.

9. MANHATTAN

> **LORAN: 31638.20/47438.13**   **GPS: 46° 28.02'/086° 36.56'**
> **DEPTH: 20 to 40 feet**   **LEVEL: Novice**

LOCATION: 0.8 mile north of Sand Point.

Burned after stranding off the south end of Grand Island with a cargo of wheat on October 26, 1903, with no lives lost, the wooden steamer, *Manhattan* (252'3" x 38' x 19'3"), built in 1887 at Wyandotte, Michigan, today offers aquatic visitors views of hull timbers, some machinery and her rudder. Much of this wreck was salvaged shortly after her loss, but she remains interesting.

Views of the *Manhattan* shipwreck: *left,* a portion of the propulsion system; *center,* chains, cables and hull timbers which, *right,* are fairly extensive. PHOTOS LEFT AND CENTER BY PETE TOMASINO, RIGHT BY CRIS KOHL

10. SAND POINT WRECKS

LOCATION: These wreck remains lie in the shallows just north and east of Sand Point. Remnants of at least three shipwrecks lie in these shifting sands:

1. The schooner, *Mary M. Scott* (138'6" x 26'6" x 11'8"), built at Conneaut, Ohio, in 1857, stranded and broke up with a cargo of iron ore on November 2, 1870, with no lives lost. What is likely the *Mary M. Scott's* centerboard trunk, keelson, frames and mound of iron ore in the middle of her hull lie in 15' of water at **GPS: 46° 27.54'/086° 36.37'.**

2. The schooner-barge, *Elma* (165'2" x 30' x 11'), launched in 1873 at Marine City, MI, stranded in immense seas at Miners Castle on Sept. 29, 1895, with one life lost. Her hull, it is believed, drifted down to Sand Point and broke up. An anchor and chain in 43' of water off Miners Castle, believed to be from the *Elma,* lie at **GPS: 46° 29.55'/086° 33.74'.**

3. The lumber-laden steam barge, *Michael Groh* (120'4" x 23'8" x 8'6"), built at Cleveland in 1867, stranded in a storm on Nov. 22, 1895 at Miners Castle, drifted down to Sand Point, broke up and lies in two sections in 10' to 12' of water at **GPS: 46° 27.74'/086° 35.59'** and at **GPS: 46° 27.73'/086° 35.86'.** She was extensively salvaged.

11. SMITH MOORE

LORAN: 31642.2/47442.1	GPS: 46° 27.33'/086° 37.06'
DEPTH: 91 to 105 feet	LEVEL: Advanced

LOCATION: 2.9 miles northeast of Munising, between Grand Island and Sand Point.

Launched on July 29, 1880 at Cleveland, the wooden steamer, *Smith Moore* (223'4" x 35' x 18'2"), carrying iron ore, sank after a collision with the *James Pickands* (which is also in this book) on July 13, 1889, with no lives lost. The wreck sits upright, with her engine, boiler and deck hardware increasingly threatened and covered by shifting sands from Sand Point.

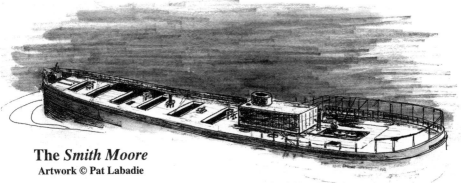

The *Smith Moore*
Artwork © Pat Labadie

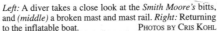

Left: A diver takes a close look at the *Smith Moore's* bitts, and *(middle)* a broken mast and mast rail. *Right:* Returning to the inflatable boat. PHOTOS BY CRIS KOHL

12. BERMUDA

> **LORAN: 31647.8/47431.2**   **GPS: 46° 27.89'/086° 38.81'**
> **DEPTH: 12 to 30 feet**   **LEVEL: Novice**

LOCATION: This wreck lies in protected Murray Bay at southern Grand Island.

The two-masted schooner, *Bermuda* (136' x 26' x 11'9"), launched in April, 1860, at Oswego, New York, foundered in a storm in Munising Bay on October 15, 1870, with the loss of three lives and her iron ore cargo. In October, 1883, she was raised and towed into Murray Bay, where her chains slipped and she again sank. Much of her iron ore cargo was salvaged. This well-preserved, intact shipwreck is one of the most visited sites in all the Great Lakes. Explorable above, beside and below deck, this wreck features a bow samson post, three hatches, railing and rudder post.

The *Bermuda* (two views)
Artwork © Pat Labadie

Below: Diver Joan Forsberg examines one of the *Bermuda's* several hatches and, later, a wooden barrel on the stern deck *(middle)*. It is possible to swim from one end of this wreck to the other inside, below deck. *Right:* A diver at the stern studies the steering post. PHOTOS BY CRIS KOHL

13. CHENANGO

> **LORAN: 31665.2/47391.1**   **GPS: 46° 30.10'/086° 44.76'**
> **DEPTH: 15 feet**   **LEVEL: Novice-Intermediate**

This iron ore-laden schooner-barge stranded on November 20, 1875; no lives were lost. The bottom of the hull and the rudder lie in 15' about 1,000' southwest of Wood Island.

14. F. MORRELL

> **LORAN:**   **GPS: 46° 32.85'/086° 42.88'**
> **DEPTH: 15 feet**   **LEVEL: Novice-Intermediate**

This 144', 369-ton schooner stranded with iron ore on Nov. 7, 1874, off the northwest edge of Grand Island. No lives were lost. Sights include capstans, chains and iron ore.

42. Marquette

The Marquette Underwater Preserve, one of eleven such designations created by the State of Michigan, was established in 1990 to promote conservation of the area's submerged historical resources.

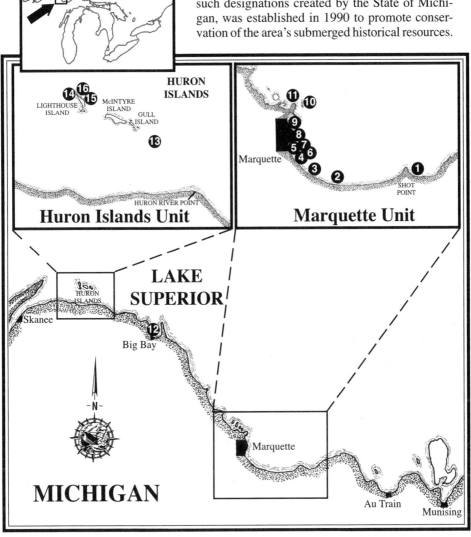

Huron Islands Unit

HURON ISLANDS

LIGHTHOUSE ISLAND
McINTYRE ISLAND
GULL ISLAND

Marquette Unit

Marquette

SHOT POINT

HURON RIVER POINT

LAKE SUPERIOR

HURON ISLANDS

Skanee

Big Bay

-N-

MICHIGAN

Marquette

Au Train

Munising

1. *George Sherman*
2. *Queen City*
3. *Charles J. Kershaw*
4. *DeSoto*
5. *Florida*
6. **F-106B parts**
7. *Superior* **and** *Marion L.*
8. *D. Leuty*
9. *J. H. Sheadle* **parts & "Iron Man"**
10. **"Gold Mine" pinnacle**
11. **Black Rocks**
12. **Big Bay lumber dock**
13. *Southwest*
14. *Huron Island*
15. *Arctic*
16. *George Nestor*

1. GEORGE SHERMAN

LORAN:	GPS: 46° 29.89'/087° 09.63'
DEPTH: 10 to 12 feet	LEVEL: Novice

LOCATION: About 12 miles east-southeast of Marquette, just east of Shot Point.

The 323-ton schooner, *George Sherman* (139'8" x 26'2" x 11'6"), built at Cleveland in 1862, stranded at Shot Point with a coal cargo in a blinding snowstorm which destroyed or stranded many other vessels in the Great Lakes on October 23, 1887. No lives were lost, but the ship quickly broke up. Basically three portions of the wooden hull remain amidst a scattered debris field to be explored in shallow water.

2. QUEEN CITY

LORAN:	GPS: 46° 29.42'/087° 18.64'
DEPTH: 10 to 13 feet	LEVEL: Novice

LOCATION: 150' off Chocolay Beach, about 5 miles southeast of Marquette.

The 368-ton, two-masted schooner, *Queen City* (137' x 25'7" x 11'3"), constructed at Vermilion, Ohio, in 1855, lost her anchors while trying to ride out a gale and stranded on November 18, 1864 with a cargo of firebricks. The crew was saved, but the vessel broke up. The remains, when not covered by sand, include the port side of the hull, plus the neatly-stacked bricks in the cargo hold just aft of the high-profile centerboard trunk.

3. CHARLES J. KERSHAW

LORAN:	GPS: 46° 30.56'/087° 21.81'
DEPTH: 25 feet	LEVEL: Novice

LOCATION: This wreck lies about two miles south-southeast of Marquette.

The wooden steamer, *Charles J. Kershaw* (223' x 37'3" x 19'9"), built at Bangor, Michigan, in 1874, was towing the schooner-barges, *Henry A. Kent* and *Moonlight,* on Sept.

The *Charles J. Kershaw.*
CRIS KOHL COLLECTION

29, 1895, when the steamer lost power and all three were stranded by the high seas. Members of Marquette's U.S. Life Saving Service made daring rescues of the *Kershaw's* crew, while the schooners' crews simply jumped onto land. The *Detroit Free Press* of Oct. 10, 1895, reported that "The recent gale removed the last trace of the *Kershaw,* which broke its spinal column on Chocolay reef...." The two

This widely-reproduced photograph dramatically shows the stranded schooner-barges, *Henry A. Kent* and *Moonlight,* while salvage ships work on the *Kershaw.* CRIS KOHL COLLECTION

schooners were recovered and returned to service eight months later. This wreck lies broken and scattered, with the huge boiler being the site's highlight.

4. DESOTO

LORAN:	GPS: 46° 32.07'/087° 23.55'
DEPTH: 8 to 10 feet	LEVEL: Novice

LOCATION: About 1000' north of the Shiras Generating Plant, inside an old dock.

Launched on April 10, 1856 at Cleveland, the bark, *DeSoto* (160'10" x 33'8" x 11'7"), stranded and broke up on Dec. 4, 1869. Some framing and planking make up this site.

5. *FLORIDA*

LORAN:	GPS: 46° 32.10′/087° 23.55′
DEPTH: 90 feet	LEVEL: Advanced

LOCATION: South of Whetstone Brook and just north of the *DeSoto* wreck site.

The two-masted schooner, *Florida* (139′ x 26′ x 11′), built at Oswego, New York, in 1868, was dashed against the Marquette docks during a blizzard on November 17, 1886, with the loss of one life. Partly buried in the sand are framing and planking just outside the cribs of an old dock.

Left: The stranded schooner, *Florida*. CRIS KOHL COLLECTION

6. F-106B PARTS

LORAN:	GPS: 46° 31.71′/087° 23.75′
DEPTH: 20 to 22 feet	LEVEL: Novice

LOCATION: Near the Shiras Generating Plant, Marquette, Michigan.

This F-106B fighter plane from the nearby K.I. Sawyer Air force Base lost power and crashed after the pilot bailed out safely on June 12, 1974. The engine and most of the fuselage were recovered, but pieces of this aircraft remain lodged in the shifting sands.

7. *SUPERIOR* AND *MARION L.*

LORAN:	GPS: 46° 32.50′/087° 23.35′
DEPTH: 18 to 22 feet	LEVEL: Novice

LOCATION: Inside the Lower Harbor at Marquette, Michigan.

These two abandoned fish tugs lie in an area of heavy boating traffic; caution must be used here, including the use of a dive flag. The *Marion L.* lies along the south side of Thill's dock, while the *Superior* rests across the slip on the north side of the Association dock.

8. *D. LEUTY*

LORAN:	GPS: 46° 32.76′/087° 22.44′
DEPTH: 5 to 40 feet	LEVEL: Novice-Intermediate

LOCATION: This wreck lies about 800′ off Lighthouse Point near downtown Marquette.

The wooden steamer, *D. Leuty* (179′ x 33′6″ x 12′6″), stranded in a snowstorm while trying to enter Marquette harbor on October 31, 1911, with a cargo of logs. No lives were lost, but the ship broke up. Her engine, boiler and machinery were salvaged. Three large sections of wooden hull remain at this site, which is one of the area locations usually buoyed. The huge rudder lies in 40′, with tools, fasteners and piping scattered in more shallow water. Unfortunately, this is not a shore dive, as the nearest public access is about 1/4 mile from the wreck. That's a long swim; use a boat instead.

D. Leuty. CRIS KOHL COLLECTION

9. *J. H. SHEADLE* PARTS AND "IRON MAN"

The steamer, *J. H. Sheadle,* left behind her rudder and a propeller blade when she backed into the rocky reef on Nov. 20, 1920. These items lie in 15′ of water at **GPS: 46° 34.08′/ 087° 23.17′**. The *Sheadle* was repaired and remained in service until scrapped in 1980. The "Iron Man" is the human-shaped water intake for the long-defunct charcoal plant.

10. "GOLD MINE" PINNACLE

This finger of granite rises from the sandy lake bottom at 150' to about 12' from the surface, and features steep walls and overhangs. Divers named it "Gold Mine" because of snagged fishing equipment they found on it. The controllable depth makes diving experience level variable. The pinnacle, marked on charts, is just east of the Presque Isle Point Rocks.

11. BLACK ROCKS

This site, at the northernmost tip of Presque Isle Park north of Marquette and featuring unusual geological formations, is accessible from shore with depths from 10' to 50'.

12. BIG BAY LUMBER DOCK

This all-weather site, about 800' north of the Big Bay Harbor of Refuge, offers interesting artifacts among the old timber cribs, ballast stones and an old railroad car from the old dock.

13. *SOUTHWEST*

LORAN: 31851.9/46890.0	GPS: 46° 56.42'/087° 56.11'
DEPTH: 88 to 110 feet	LEVEL: Advanced

LOCATION: This wreck lies one mile southeast of Gull Island in the Huron Islands.

The schooner, *Southwest* (137'2" x 26'1" x 11'), built at Ogdensburg, New York, in 1866, stranded and eventually sank in deep water on September 19, 1898, while upbound light. No lives were lost. The forest fire smoke which the captain blamed for the disaster also caused the loss of the steamer, *Colorado*, (which is also in this book) off the Keweenaw at about the same time. Discovered by divers in 1978, the remains of the *Southwest* are broken up, but there is much to see that is of interest. This wreck, usually buoyed, can be reached by boat from either the Big Bay Harbor of Refuge or the marina at Skanee.

14. *HURON ISLAND*

LOCATION: This wreck lies just north of the rocks on the north side of the channel between Lighthouse Island and the small island immediately next to it. The 40' wooden launch, *Huron Island,* lying on her side and collapsed in about 15' of very clear water, was used as the lighthouse launch until it sank in 1922. Sand partially covers the engine.

15. *ARCTIC*

LORAN:	GPS: 46° 57.74'/087° 59.85'
DEPTH: 5 to 100 feet	LEVEL: Variable (Advanced)

LOCATION: Off the middle of the eastern side of Lighthouse Island in the Hurons.

The sidewheel steamer, *Arctic* (236'6" x 30' x 12'), launched at Newport (later Marine City), Michigan, in late April, 1851, stranded in thick fog on May 29, 1860. No lives were lost. The main wreckage field contains many artifacts, such as broken china and wooden timbers, with the ship's bow located in the shallow channel between Lighthouse Island and the small island at the south end. Part of her engine and hull lie in 20' on the west side.

16. *GEORGE NESTOR*

LORAN:	GPS: 46° 57.99'/088° 00.20'
DEPTH: 20 to 100 feet	LEVEL: Advanced

LOCATION: 1/4 mile north of the *Arctic,* near the northern tip of Lighthouse Island.

The schooner-barge, *George Nestor* (207' x 35' x 14'), built at Baraga, Michigan, in 1887, stranded in a storm on April 30, 1909, with 6 lives lost. The wreck is very scattered.

The *George Nestor.* CRIS KOHL COLLECTION

43. Keweenaw

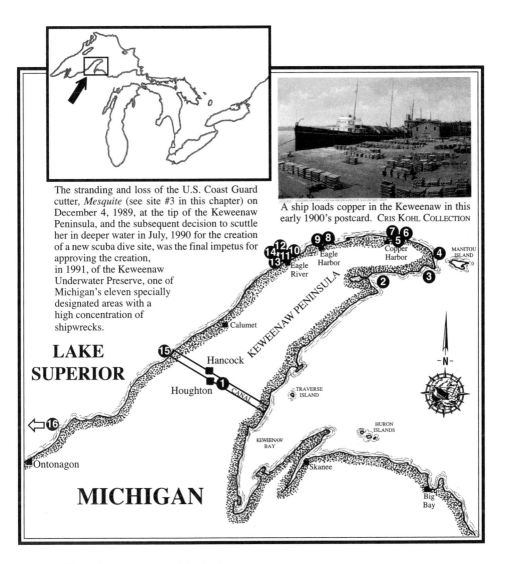

The stranding and loss of the U.S. Coast Guard cutter, *Mesquite* (see site #3 in this chapter) on December 4, 1989, at the tip of the Keweenaw Peninsula, and the subsequent decision to scuttle her in deeper water in July, 1990 for the creation of a new scuba dive site, was the final impetus for approving the creation, in 1991, of the Keweenaw Underwater Preserve, one of Michigan's eleven specially designated areas with a high concentration of shipwrecks.

A ship loads copper in the Keweenaw in this early 1900's postcard. CRIS KOHL COLLECTION

1. **The Canal wrecks (9 sites)**
2. *Langham*
3. *Mesquite*
4. *Scotia*
5. *Wasaga*
6. *City of Superior*
7. *John Jacob Astor*
8. *John L. Gross*
9. *Traveller*
10. *City of St. Joseph* and *Transport*
11. *Tioga*
12. *James Pickands*
13. *Colorado* and *Fern*
14. *William C. Moreland*
15. *Maplehurst*
16. *Panama*

1. THE CANAL WRECKS (9)

The Portage Ship Canal, also called the Keweenaw Waterway, encompasses a lake, a pond, two rivers and some manmade canal work to provide convenient marine access across the base of the long Keweenaw Peninsula. This lengthy waterway contains both natural and abandoned shipwrecks. Here are nine of them, from east to west:

1. The wooden steamer, *Alfred P. Wright* (286' x 41'5" x 22'3"), built at Cleveland in 1888, burned with a wheat cargo on Nov. 16, 1915, at the canal's lower entry. She lies in 10' to 15' of water. **LORAN: 31954.2/46749.5 GPS: 46° 57.96'/088° 26.41'**

2. Also lying at the lower entry, the wooden passenger steamer, *International* (80'8" x 26'4" x 7'4"), burned on Nov. 2, 1913, with no one aboard. Built at Buffalo, NY, in 1889, she lies in 3' to 10' of water. **LORAN: 31948.3/46743.0 GPS: 46° 58.97'/088° 25.84'**

The *Alfred P. Wright*.
CRIS KOHL COLLECTION

3. The wooden steamer, *Charles H. Bradley* (201' x 37' x 13'6"), built at West Bay City, Michigan, in 1890, grounded then burned in lower Portage Lake on October 9, 1931, with no lives lost. She lies in 2' to 5' of water. **GPS: 47° 02.14'/088° 29.02'**

The steamer, *Charles H. Bradley*, underway *(left)*, and ablaze in the canal *(right)*.
CRIS KOHL COLLECTION

4. The wooden steamer, *Samoa* (205'5" x 34'5" x 17'7"), built at Detroit as the *Thomas W. Palmer* in 1880, burned to a total loss on Sept. 21, 1909, in the Torch Lake part of the ship canal at the old Osceola Mills. This wreck was located in 2000 by Randy Beebe.

BURNS TO THE WATER'S EDGE

The Steamer Samoa Is Complete Loss on Torch Lake.

Milwaukee, Wis., Sept. 21.—An Evening Wisconsin special from Calumet, Mich., says:
    The steamer Samoa, owned by H. W. Baker of Detroit. was burned to the

The *Duluth Evening Herald* on Sept. 21, 1909, spread the news about the loss of the steamer, *Samoa*. BOTH, CRIS KOHL COLLECTION

5. The wooden steam yacht, *Sea Fox* (101'6" x 16' x 6'8"), launched as the *Azalea* at Detroit in 1895, was abandoned in about 1930. She lies in 5' to 15' of water across from the Michigan Tech water plant. Site sights: engine, boiler, rudder, sink, bathtub and head.

6. The schooner-barge, *Mediator* (127'3" x 27'5" x 10'), built at Cape Vincent, NY, in 1862, stranded in a storm on Sept. 18, 1898. Towed to Houghton, the damaged ship was abandoned. She lies in 20'. **LORAN: 31942.4/46640.1 GPS: 47° 07.30'/088° 33.00'**

7. The small, wooden steam yacht, *Morgan* (64'6" x 12'4" x 6'1"), built in 1891 at Rome, NY, was abandoned in about 1928. She lies in 4' to 15' of water about 100' east of the Houghton Super 8 Motel (let's hope they never change names!) just off the south shore.

8. The iron passenger steamer, *Uarda* (95'3" x 12'5" x 8'3"), built at Buffalo, NY, in 1881, burned on June 4, 1912, with no lives lost. She lies in 15' to 20' of water near the wreck of the *Sailor Boy* (see next site). **GPS: 47° 07.42'/088° 35.30'**

9. The wooden excursion steamer, *Sailor Boy* (91' x 24' x 6'5"), launched on January 6, 1891 at West Bay City, Michigan, burned on May 12, 1923 and drifted to 300' east of Osceola Point, where she lies in 10' to 20' of water about 30' off shore.

2. LANGHAM

> **LORAN: 31758.1/46675.8**   **GPS: 47° 22.37'/087° 55.53'**
> **DEPTH: 90 to 106 feet**   **LEVEL: Advanced**

LOCATION: In Bete Grise Bay, 2.0 miles east of the entrance to Lac La Belle.
Launched as the *Tom Adams* at West Bay City, Michigan, in 1888, the wooden steamer,

Langham (281'1" x 41'4" x 20'), burned to a total loss with a coal cargo but with no lives lost on October 23, 1910. Features include the ship's two boilers, engine and much machinery still in place. The *Langham* is the identical sister ship to the *Robert L. Fryer* (which is also in this book).

The *Langham*. CRIS KOHL COLLECTION

A burbot explores the upright remains of the steamer, *Langham*.   PHOTOS BY PETE TOMASINO

MARINE
LANGHAM IS TOTAL LOSS

Vessel Is Sunk in 120 Feet
of Water Off Kewee-
naw Point.

Crew of Eighteen Made Way
to Shore in Ship's
Yawls.

Details of the burning of the steamer Langham, off Keweenaw point in Lake Superior, Sunday afternoon, which were not received yesterday, have been learned here. The Langham was burned and sank in 120 feet of water six miles from shore of Bete de Gris.

3. MESQUITE

> **LORAN: 31714.6/46712.8**   **GPS: 47° 22.38'/087° 55.55'**
> **DEPTH: 82 to 112 feet**   **LEVEL: Advanced**

LOCATION: This wreck lies in Keystone Bay, southwest of Keweenaw Point.

The U.S. Coast Guard cutter/buoy tender, *Mesquite* (180' x 37' x 14'), built at Duluth, Minnesota, in 1942, stranded on Keweenaw's notorious rocks on December 4, 1989, and became a total loss, with no lives lost. The wreck was moved into deeper water on July 14, 1990, as

The *Mesquite*.
INSTITUTE FOR GREAT LAKES RESEARCH, BOWLING GREEN, OHIO

Descending to the *Mesquite*. PHOTO BY CRIS KOHL. Sights on the wreck: a crane, portholes, and a stainless steel galley below deck.   PHOTOS BY PETE TOMASINO

a dive site. Almost everything, excluding most Coast Guard insignia, was left on board! There is much to see on deck and along the hull. Penetration diving should be done only by trained and experienced divers. As with all Great Lakes shipwrecks, please leave all (repeat: ALL) items in place on the *Mesquite*.

4. SCOTIA

LORAN: 31697.8/46710.5	GPS: 47° 25.86'/087° 42.28'
DEPTH: 15 to 25 feet	LEVEL: Novice

LOCATION: About 150' off the old rocket launch platform at High Rock Point.

Lost in a blinding blizzard on October 24, 1884, the iron package freighter, *Scotia* (231' x 35'6" x 25'), ran hard aground on Keweenaw's tip and broke up. A passing steamer saved the crew. Built at Buffalo, New York, in 1873, the *Scotia's* engine and boiler were salvaged shortly after her loss. More recently, one of her propellers was placed on exhibit at nearby Fort Wilkins State Park. Today, the wreck lies broken and scattered. A rough terrain roadway runs 7 miles from US 41 to the shore, but boat access would be easier.

5. WASAGA

LORAN:	GPS: 47° 28.22'/087° 52.93'
DEPTH: 25 to 36 feet	LEVEL: Novice

The *Wasaga*.
CRIS KOHL COLLECTION

LOCATION: In the harbor at Copper Harbor, Michigan.

While taking shelter from a storm at Copper Harbor on November 6, 1910, the wooden steamer, *Wasaga* (238'2" x 35'6" x 14'8"), launched as the *Wissahickon* on July 1, 1876 at Buffalo, New York, caught on fire and burned to a total loss with no lives lost. She sank with a cargo of farm implements bound for Canada. Salvage efforts recovered the engine, boiler and much machinery and cargo. Although this wreck (the keel and some cargo) lies just off Harbor Haus Restaurant in Copper Harbor, it is best accessed by boat.

6. CITY OF SUPERIOR

LORAN:	GPS: 47° 28.40'/087° 51.72'
DEPTH: 15 to 35 feet	LEVEL: Novice

LOCATION: This wreck, accessible from shore, lies off the Copper Harbor lighthouse.

Launched on July 18, 1857, at Cleveland, the wooden steamer, *City of Superior* (187'8" x 29'3" x 11'1"), was lost in her first year. She struck a reef off Copper Harbor on November 10, 1857, and became a total loss, including her cargo of barrelled copper, but with no lives lost. Much of this ship and her cargo were salvaged at that time, so today, only small pieces of her hull remain to be explored.

7. JOHN JACOB ASTOR

LORAN: 31725.4/46643.3	GPS: 47° 28.34'/087° 51.88'
DEPTH: 10 to 35 feet	LEVEL: Novice

LOCATION: This shore-dive wreck lies directly off the old Fort Wilkins dock.

The 112-gross-ton, two-masted, wooden brig, *John Jacob Astor* (77'8" x 21'8" x 7'7"), is the oldest known shipwreck site in Lake Superior. Constructed at Black River, Ohio, and shipped in pieces to Sault Ste. Marie where she was launched in August, 1834, the first U.S. commercial vessel on the big lake. The *Astor* stranded and broke up in strong winds on September 21, 1844. Her machinery and rigging were recovered, but the broken and scattered remains are interesting. Artifacts from this wreck are on exhibit at Fort Wilkins State Park and the Copper Harbor Lighthouse Museum.

8. *JOHN L. GROSS*

```
LORAN: 31789.2/46575.5        GPS: 47° 27.58'/088° 09.30'
DEPTH: 20 to 30 feet          LEVEL: Novice
```

LOCATION: This wreck lies just inside the entrance to Eagle Harbor, on the west side.

The two masted schooner, *John L. Gross* (131'5" x 25'7" x 10'1"), built in 1857 at Vermilion, Ohio, stranded in a storm on October 30, 1873, and was pounded to pieces with a coal cargo but no lives lost. Originally thought to be the sidewheeler, *Gazelle* (which grounded here on Sept. 8, 1860, but was mostly removed), the *John L. Gross* site features ribs, keel, much coal and some of the hull still standing.

9. *TRAVELLER*

```
LORAN: 31788.7/46577.0        GPS: 47° 27.53'/088° 09.09'
DEPTH: 15 to 30 feet          LEVEL: Novice
```

LOCATION: This wreck lies just inside the entrance to Eagle Harbor, on the east side.

Built in 1852 at Newport (now Marine City), Michigan, the sidewheel steamer, *Traveller* (199'1" x 29' x 10'1"), burned to a complete loss on August 17, 1865. This flattened wreckage, off the old Eagle Harbor Life Saving Station, sits on a shifting sand bottom, broken but nonetheless an interesting and enjoyable shore dive. This site is often buoyed.

10. *CITY OF ST. JOSEPH* AND *TRANSPORT*

```
LORAN: 31777.6/46581.4        GPS: 47° 28.20'/088° 06.75'
LORAN: 31777.5/46582.2        GPS: 47° 28.10'/088° 06.58'
DEPTH: 25 to 35 feet          LEVEL: Novice
```

LOCATION: About 1/4 mile off Little Grand Marais harbor, east of Eagle Harbor.

Near the terrible beginning of World War II, two barges were lost off the Keweenaw on September 21, 1942. The steel barge, *City of St. Joseph* (254' x 34' x 16'6"), built as the passenger steamer, *City of Chicago,* in 1890 at West Bay City, Michigan, renamed in 1915, was converted to a barge in 1938. The iron barge, *Transport* (254'1" x 45'9" x 14'), launched as a steamer on January 24, 1880 at Wyandotte, Michigan, and working mainly as a railroad car ferry on the Detroit River, was reduced to a barge in 1933. Both pulpwood-laden barges were towed by the tug, *John Roen,* which survived. However, one life, the *City of St. Joseph's* captain's wife, was lost when the barges stranded.

The wrecks lie about 300' apart, with the *Transport* closer to shore. Much machinery remains at the *City of St. Joseph* site, which is usually marked with a buoy.

The *City of St. Joseph (left)* and the *Transport (right)*. CRIS KOHL COLLECTION

11. *TIOGA* (LORAN: 31817.3/46556.3

GPS: 47° 26.31'/088° 16.21')

LOCATION: This wreck lies three miles east of Eagle River, Michigan.

The iron package steamer, *Tioga* (285'5" x 38'9" x 25'7"), built at Buffalo, NY, in 1884, stranded with a wheat cargo on Nov. 26, 1919, and broke up with no lives lost. This popular wreck lies in 28' to 35' of water, with her boilers, machinery and hull pieces scattered.

The *Tioga*. CRIS KOHL COLLECTION

12. *JAMES PICKANDS* (LORAN: 31825.1/46553.2 GPS: 47° 25.46'/088° 18.02')

Located today on Sawtooth Reef in 10' to 30' of water, the wooden steamer, *James Pickands* (232'6" x 40' x 19'2"), built at Cleveland in 1886, stranded and broke up with her iron ore cargo on Sept. 22, 1894. No lives were lost. Her boilers and rudder are the highlights. This popular wreck lies scattered with the *Colorado* and the *Fern* (see site #13).

13. *COLORADO/FERN* (LORAN: 31824.5/

46553.4 GPS: 47° 25.72'/088° 17.95')

The wooden steamer, *Colorado* (254'6" x 35' x 13'), built in 1867 at Buffalo, NY, stranded in smoky conditions on Sept. 19, 1898, with a flour cargo and no lives lost. The 65' tug, *Fern,* lost with all 5 hands in a storm while salvaging the *Colorado* on June 29, 1901, lies nearby. Both these wrecks lie scattered with the *James Pickands* in 10' to 30' of water.

The *Colorado*. CRIS KOHL COLLECTION

14. *WILLIAM C. MORELAND* (LORAN: 31832.9/

46551.0 GPS: 47° 25.07'/088° 19.61') LOCATION: In 25' to 40', on Eagle River Shoals off Eagle River, Michigan. This new steel steamer (580' x 58' x 32'), left only her unsalvaged bow half after stranding and breaking in two on Oct. 18, 1910. Flattened by nature, this wreck, found by Jerry Eliason, Kraig Smith, and Larry Rice in 1982, offers interesting machinery.

Salvaging the *Moreland*. CRIS KOHL COLLECTION

15. *MAPLEHURST*

(GPS: 47° 13.90'/088° 38.05')

In 15' to 20' of water 225' west of the North Entry, this steel steamer (235'1" x 36'8" x 15'4"), grounded in a storm and broke up with 11 lives lost on Dec. 1, 1922.

The *Maplehurst,* before and after its tragic demise. CRIS KOHL COLLECTION

16. *PANAMA* (LORAN: 32200.8/46518.9

GPS: 46° 50.17'/089° 32.89')

LOCATION: In 5' to 20' of water off Mineral Point, 14 miles west of Ontanagon, MI.

Launched as the *John Craig* at Trenton, MI, on May 19, 1888, the wooden steamer, *Panama* (290' x 41' x 25'), coal-laden, stranded and broke up in heavy seas on Nov. 21, 1906.

The *Panama*. CRIS KOHL COLLECTION

44. Apostle Islands

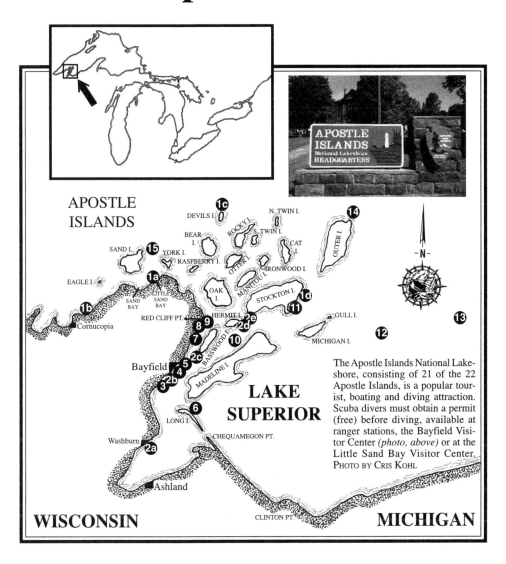

APOSTLE
ISLANDS

DEVILS I.

N. TWIN I.

BEAR I.

ROCKY I.

S. TWIN I.

CAT I.

OUTER I.

SAND I.

YORK I.

RASPBERRY I.

OTTER I.

IRONWOOD I.

EAGLE I.

OAK I.

MANITOU I.

STOCKTON I.

-N-

LITTLE SAND BAY

SAND BAY

RED CLIFF PT.

HERMIT I.

GULL I.

Cornucopia

MICHIGAN I.

Bayfield

BASSWOOD I.

MADELINE I.

LAKE
SUPERIOR

The Apostle Islands National Lakeshore, consisting of 21 of the 22 Apostle Islands, is a popular tourist, boating and diving attraction. Scuba divers must obtain a permit (free) before diving, available at ranger stations, the Bayfield Visitor Center *(photo, above)* or at the Little Sand Bay Visitor Center. PHOTO BY CRIS KOHL

LONG I.

Washburn

CHEQUAMEGON PT.

Ashland

WISCONSIN

CLINTON PT.

MICHIGAN

APOSTLE ISLANDS
National Lakeshore
HEADQUARTERS

1. "Caves" (4 sites)
2. Dock ruins (5 sites)
3. *Charlotte* and barge
4. *Fin McCool*
5. Pickup truck
6. *Lucerne*
7. *Fedora*
8. *H. D. Coffinberry*

9. *Ottawa*
10. *T. H. Camp*
11. *Noquebay*
12. *Marquette*
13. *Moonlight*
14. *Pretoria*
15. *Sevona*

1. "CAVES"

That which scuba divers call the "caves" here are nothing at all like cave-diving in Florida, for example. These are caverns, overhangs, short tunnels and other interesting geological formations that are about the closest thing to real caves in the Great Lakes. In the Apostle Islands, there are four recommended "cave" areas, all requiring boat access:

1a. **Little Sand Bay** (north and west of), with depths to 30′, usually with 50′+ of visibility.

1b. **Squaw Bay**, northeast of the town of Cornucopia, with depths to 35′.

1c. **Devils Island** (north end), depths to 30′, stratified sandstone extending 60′ back.

1d. **Stockton Island** (east end of), with depths to 35′.

2. DOCK RUINS

Dock ruins usually consist of submerged cribs (timber boxes with rocks in them) which formed the solid foundations for docks, and pilings, short, thick telephone poles to which vessels were often docked with ropes. Not only are the interesting tools and other equipment from a long-gone era viewable here (please remember that it is illegal to remove any of these non-renewable submerged cultural resources), but the fish life around these old docks is often prolific. There are five recommended historic docks to explore underwater:

2a. **Washburn** (at the south end, off the point in Vandeventer Bay), with depths to 40′.

2b. **Bayfield** (south of; the dock is often marked with a green buoy), with depths to 80′.

2c. **Basswood Island** (south end, LORAN 32406.7/46176.0), depths to 35′.

2d. **Hermit Island** (southeast end, LORAN 32381.4/46171.0), depths to 30′.

2e. **Stockton Island** (southwest end; LORAN 32367.7/46170.8), depths to 35′.

3. *CHARLOTTE* AND BARGE

LOCATION: This wreck lies near the marine railroad in Pikes Bay south of Port Superior.

The 28-net-ton tug, *Charlotte* (62′ x 17′6″ x 6′6″), built in Erie, Pennsylvania, in 1912, worked mainly in Lake Superior towing and commercial fishing before being abandoned due to age and condition in 1943. She lies in 3′ to 6′ of water, with parts of her frames and stem protruding from the water.

An unknown barge or scow, believed to have been abandoned in the 1930's and subsequently gutted by fire, lies in shallow water near the *Charlotte*.

4. *FIN MCCOOL*

LORAN: 32423.3/46171.4	GPS:
DEPTH: 10 to 20 feet	LEVEL: Novice

LOCATION: This wreck lies just down the hill from the Seagull Bay Motel, at the south end of the Apostle Islands Yacht Club Harbor, in Bayfield harbor.

The oak barge, *Fin McCool* (135′ x 34′ x 7′7″), built at nearby Ashland, Wisconsin, in 1926, worked in the local lumber trade until it sank in Bayfield harbor in 1964 and was abandoned. It lies in what is today a private marina. In years of low levels in the Great Lakes, parts of this wreck will appear above water. Often this wreck, which features most of its original deck equipment, such as steam winches and cable drums, is buoyed by local divers. It is also a popular ice diving location.

5. PICKUP TRUCK

Off the Bayfield harbor breakwall, in 65′ of water, rest the remains of a 1932 Ford pickup truck in relatively good condition (the chrome still shines and a door still opens). Parking for this shore dive is available inside the marina near Bayfield's city park. Huge, flat concrete slabs on the lake side of the breakwall mark the entry point. At a depth of 6′, a yellow polypropylene line is secured to a wooden part of the breakwall. The truck, lying on its side, lies at the end of this line about 150′ off shore.

6. LUCERNE

LORAN: 32434.6/46234.9	GPS: 46° 43.389'/090° 46.035'
DEPTH: 15 to 24 feet	LEVEL: Novice

LOCATION: This wreck lies off the northeast side of Long Island, Wisconsin.

The three-masted schooner, *Lucerne* (195' x 34' x 14'), built in 1873 at Tonawanda, New York, sank with a large cargo of iron ore while attempting to ride out a severe snowstorm on November 19, 1886. Her anchor slipped and her centerboard hit the lake bottom, snapping the keel. Later, a nearby lighthouse keeper spied the ship's masts standing out of the water. Upon closer examination, he saw that three of the crew had lashed themselves to the rigging to keep from being swept overboard. Their lifeless bodies were coated with several inches of ice. All ten men on board the *Lucerne* perished.

Below. left: The schooner, *Lucerne*. ARTIST UNKNOWN. CRIS KOHL COLLECTION. *Below, right: Lucerne* artifacts in the Canal Park museum in Duluth.PHOTO BY CRIS KOHL. *Right:* The *Lucerne* was but one of several victims of that storm. CRIS KOHL COLLECTION

This site, which features the centerboard and trunk, an amazingly intact bow with a capstan, windlass, samson post and chain, intact starboard railing and a large ore cargo field, is buoyed annually by the State Historical Society of Wisconsin.

7. FEDORA

LORAN: 32403.3/46153.5	GPS: 46° 51.588'/090° 46.709'
DEPTH: 0 to 10 feet	LEVEL: Novice

LOCATION: Just south of Red Cliff Point.

The composite (iron frame, ribs and keel with oak planking) bulk freight steamer, *Fedora* (282'2" x 41'5" x 20'1"), built at West Bay City, Michigan, in 1889, burned to a complete loss on September 20, 1901 with no lives lost. A kerosene lamp had started the fire in

The *Fedora* then. CRIS KOHL COLLECTION

the engine room. Her machinery was salvaged, but some boiler plates and the immense hull, with its engine beds, remain in place.

The *Fedora* now. PHOTO BY CRIS KOHL

8. H. D. COFFINBERRY

LORAN: 32395.8/46144.4	GPS: 46° 52.978'/090° 45.814'
DEPTH: 3 to 6 feet	LEVEL: Novice

LOCATION: This wreck lies along the shore in Red Cliff Bay, Wisconsin.

The wooden bulk freight steamer, *H.D. Coffinberry* (191'4" x 33'5" x 13'4"), launched at East Saginaw, Michigan, in 1874, was abandoned at Ashland in 1912 after a long career hauling coal, grain, iron ore and lumber. Her hull was towed to its present site in 1917 and stripped of its machinery. Only the lower part of the wooden hull remains to be seen today.

Left: The *H. D. Coffinberry*. CRIS KOHL COLLECTION. *Right:* The remains of the *Coffinberry* today. PHOTO BY CRIS KOHL

9. OTTAWA

LORAN: 32395.8/46144.4	GPS: 46° 52.978'/090° 45.814'
DEPTH: 12 to 20 feet	LEVEL: Novice

LOCATION: This wreck lies next to the *H. D. Coffinberry* in Red Cliff Bay, Wisconsin.

Launched as the *Boscobel* at Chicago in 1881 and renamed in 1903 when it changed to Canadian ownership, the large, wooden tug, *Ottawa* (151' x 28'4" x 13'7"), burned to a complete loss with no lives lost on November 29, 1909. The fire had begun in the coal bunker. She was one of the most powerful tugboats in the world when she was built, and worked at salvaging many lost ships, including the *Sevona,* for famous Great Lakes wreckers Jim and Tom Reid of Sarnia, Ontario. Her machinery was recovered, but the large, wooden hull remains in place.

The tug, *Ottawa,* working on the wreck of the *Sevona.* CRIS KOHL COLLECTION

10. T. H. CAMP

LORAN:	GPS:
DEPTH: 178 feet	LEVEL: Technical

LOCATION: This wreck lies off the west side of Madeline Island, Wisconsin.

The wooden fishing tug, *T. H. Camp* (65'4" x 15' x 6'), built at Cape Vincent, NY, in

Left: The *T. H. Camp's* intact pilot house frames the ship's wheel in its windows. *Right:* The whistles remain attached to the smokestack. PHOTOS BY KEN MERRYMAN

1876, sank in a storm after striking a reef. No lives were lost (the crew was rescued by a sailboat), but the cargo of lumber supplies went to the bottom. This tug, worth $4,000 when lost, was located in 1991 by Ken Merryman, Andrew Merryman, and Ray Julian.

11. NOQUEBAY

> **LORAN: 32351.3/46184.6**   **GPS: 46° 55.568'/090° 32.717'**
> **DEPTH: 10 to 15 feet**   **LEVEL: Novice**

LOCATION: This wreck lies 300' off Stockton Island in Julian Bay.

The huge schooner-barge, *Noquebay* (205'2" x 34'7" x 12'5"), built at Trenton, Michigan, in 1872, caught fire on October 8, 1905, with a lumber cargo while in tow of the steamer, *Lizzie Madden*. The *Noquebay* was beached, where she burned to a total loss. No lives were lost. Her lumber cargo and anchors were salvaged. Shifting sands continually change this site, which includes the ship's wheel and steering gear, and many interesting scattered parts.

Left: The *Noquebay* underway, loaded with lumber. CRIS KOHL COLLECTION.
Right: Roman numeral depth draft markings on the *Noquebay*.
PHOTO BY CRIS KOHL

12. MARQUETTE

> **LORAN:**   **GPS:**
> **DEPTH: 210 feet**   **LEVEL: Technical**

LOCATION: This wreck lies about five miles east of Michigan Island, Wisconsin.

Launched at Cleveland on April 21, 1881, the wooden steamer, *Marquette* (235' x 35'7" x 18'5"), sank with its iron ore cargo after springing a leak and trying to reach the nearest land on Oct. 15, 1903. No lives were lost. This wreck was found in 2005 by Jerry Eliason, Kraig Smith, Randy Beebe, and Ken Merryman. The stern appears to have hit first.

Left: The wooden steamer, *Marquette.*
Right: It was considered odd that this ship sank in such calm conditions. BOTH, CRIS KOHL COLLECTION. *Below:* Divers examine the *Marquette's* bell, lying flat on the bottom, and her four-bladed propeller.
PHOTOS BY KEN MERRYMAN

SANK IN QUIET WATER

Strange Foundering of the Steamship Marquette.

Ashland, Wis., Oct. 16.—The phenomenon was witnessed, during the early hours of yesterday morning, of a vessel sinking in Lake Superior with the weather conditions the finest they have been for months, with no sea and but little wind. The steamer Marquette sprung aleak be-

529

13. *MOONLIGHT*

> **LORAN:**   **GPS:**
> **DEPTH: 240 feet**   **LEVEL: Technical**

LOCATION: This wreck lies about eight miles east of Michigan Island, Wisconsin.

Launched as a schooner at Milwaukee on March 13, 1874, the *Moonlight* (205'9" x 33'6" x 14'2") was used as an iron-ore-carrying barge being towed by the steamer, *Volunteer,* when it foundered with no lives lost. This shipwreck was located in August, 2004, by Jerry Eliason, Kraig Smith, Randy Beebe, and Ken Merryman.

Above left: The *Moonlight* was once a graceful sailing ship, but was reduced to a tow-barge later in life. CRIS KOHL COLLECTION. *Left and right:* A diver approaches a bow anchor on the *Moonlight,* and a toppled capstan. PHOTOS BY KEN MERRYMAN

14. *PRETORIA*

> **LORAN: 32288.0/46141.1**   **GPS: 47° 05.36'/090° 23.66'**
> **DEPTH: 55 feet**   **LEVEL: Intermediate**

LOCATION: This wreck lies one mile off the northeast shore of Outer Island.

The three-masted schooner-barge, *Pretoria* (338'4" x 44' x 23'), launched at West Bay City, Michigan, on July 28, 1900, foundered with the loss of five of the ten lives on board and her iron ore cargo in the fierce gale of Sept. 2, 1905. The *Pretoria* was one of the largest sailing vessels ever to ply Great Lakes waters. Her two huge anchors were recovered in the summer of 1961 for exhibit at the Madeline Island Historical museum. The wreck is broken and scattered, with no penetration possibilities, but the site yields views of the iron-reinforced keelson, bitts, hanging knees, cargo, much planking and a hatch cover.

The immense *Pretoria.*
CRIS KOHL COLLECTION

15. *SEVONA*

> **LORAN: 32388.1/46032.9**   **GPS: 47° 00.410'/090° 54.520'**
> **DEPTH: 16 to 20 feet**   **LEVEL: Novice**

LOCATION: This wreck lies on Sand Island Reef, northeast of Sand Island.

The tragic loss of the steel steamer, *Sevona* (372'5" x 41' x 24'6"), resulted in 7 of the 24 people on board losing their lives when the ship stranded during a severe storm on Sept. 2, 1905. Launched as the *Emily P. Weed* in 1890 at West Bay City, Michigan, the *Sevona* to-

day lies scattered (from nature and salvage attempts), with steel and iron ore cargo covering a wide area.

The *Sevona,* underway *(left),* and a total, tragic wreck *(right)* in the Apostle Islands.
BOTH, CRIS KOHL COLLECTION

45. Minnesota's Superior Shore

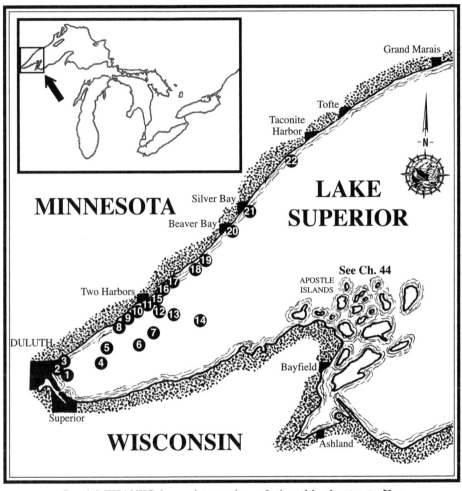

MINNESOTA

LAKE SUPERIOR

WISCONSIN

Grand Marais

Tofte

Taconite Harbor

Silver Bay

Beaver Bay

Two Harbors

DULUTH

Superior

See Ch. 44

APOSTLE ISLANDS

Bayfield

Ashland

Special THANKS for assistance in updating this chapter to Ken Merryman of Superior Trips Scuba Charters, www.superiortrips.com

1. *Thomas Wilson*
2. **Duluth breakwall**
3. *Amethyst*
4. *May Flower*
5. *A. C. Adams*
6. *Onoko*
7. *Benjamin Noble*

8. **Stony Point**
9. *Niagara*
10. **Knife River ruins**
11. *Samuel P. Ely*
12. *Harriet B.*
13. *Robert Wallace*
14. *Thomas Friant*

15. **Agate Bay merchant dock**
16. **Flood Bay wayside**
17. *Lafayette*
18. **Gooseberry Falls State Park**
19. *Madeira*
20. *Just For Fun*
21. *Hesper*
22. *Amboy* and *George Spencer*

1. THOMAS WILSON

BOW--DEPTH: 54 to 70 feet	GPS: 46° 46.955'/092° 04.163'
STERN--DEPTH: 54 to 70 feet	GPS: 46° 47.010'/092° 04.155'
LORAN: 32605.3/45820.1	LEVEL: Advanced

LOCATION: This wreck lies about 7/8 mile off the Duluth harbor entrance.

Above: The whaleback steamer, *Thomas Wilson.* CRIS KOHL COLLECTION. *Below:* The wreck of the whaleback, *Thomas Wilson,* lies in usually murky water just outside Duluth harbor.   PHOTOS BY KEN MERRYMAN

The whaleback steamer, *Thomas Wilson* (308' x 38' x 24'), launched on April 30, 1892, at West Superior, Wisconsin, was the 19th vessel built of this particular and uniquely-Great-Lakes design. The *Thomas Wilson* sank within 3 minutes with 9 lives lost after a collision with the wooden steamer, *George G. Hadley,* on June 7, 1902. The *Hadley,* which also sank, was later recovered and returned to service as the *William P. Rend,* only to sink at Alpena, Michigan, in 1917 (her story is also in this book).

The *Thomas Wilson,* dynamited shortly after her sinking as a hazard to navigation, lies with her bow and stern somewhat intact,

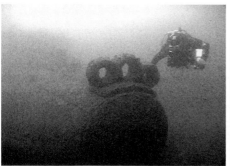

but her midship area destroyed. Visibility is often bad, reduced even more after a storm, but increased if the wind has been out of the northwest for a couple of days. Penetration diving is possible with almost zero visibility to be expected because of the silt. Cave-diving techniques and precautions are mandatory. Two anchors from the *Thomas Wilson,* raised in 1973 and 1978, are exhibited at the Canal Park Museum.

Of the 44 whalebacks ever constructed, the first 6 were built at Duluth, Minnesota, the next 34 at West Superior, Wisconsin, then one at Everett, Washington, two in Brooklyn, New York, and one in England. Several "near-whalebacks" were constructed by various shipyards in both the U.S.A. and England.See pages 534-535 for the story of whalebacks.

2. DULUTH BREAKWALL

LOCATION: About 600' off the Fitger Inn Complex on Lake Superior.

With depths from 5' to 45', this novice dive offers views of the old, submerged docks, cribs, tools, chains and other artifacts from the 1800's. Please do not remove these items.

3. AMETHYST

DEPTH: 7 to 10 feet	LEVEL: Novice

LOCATION: About 375' off shore off Park Point, Duluth, Minnesota.

The shipwreck found in the Duluth shallows under the ice is likely that of the *Amethyst*. PHOTOS BY KEN MERRYMAN

Ice skaters on Feb. 15, 2007, enjoying a brisk but sunny day, were surprised to look through the clear ice -- at a shipwreck in shallow water! The main contender is the tug, *Amethyst* (45'3" x 11'4" x 5'4"), built at Buffalo in 1868, and burned here on Oct. 25, 1888.

4. *MAY FLOWER*

LORAN:	GPS: 46° 48.193'/092° 00.665'
DEPTH: 90 feet	LEVEL: Advanced

LOCATION: This wreck lies about 4 miles out of Duluth 500' off the shipping lane.

Built at Sturgeon Bay, Wisconsin, in 1888, the 230-ton scow-schooner, *May Flower* (147' x 27' x 7'), worked in the inland seas for only three years before capsizing and sinking in a storm on June 2, 1891, with a cargo of sandstone. Only the captain drowned. This wreck was found in 1990 by brothers Gerry and Peter Buchanan, and Ken Engelbrecht.

Please turn to p. 536 for photos of the *May Flower*....

Great Lakes Highlight No. 27

WHALEBACKS:
A UNIQUE GREAT LAKES DESIGN

Whalebacks were the brainchild of a man named Alexander McDougall (1845-1923) from Duluth, MN. In the late 1880's, he designed, patented, and constructed a rounded, steel ship which resembled a pig-nosed, semi-submarine, or a long, curved, steel whale, with the idea that heavy seas would just roll off the streamlined contours of

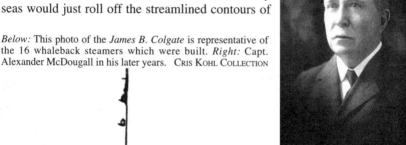

Below: This photo of the *James B. Colgate* is representative of the 16 whaleback steamers which were built. *Right:* Capt. Alexander McDougall in his later years. CRIS KOHL COLLECTION

his unique creation. Forty-four whalebacks were built between 1888 and 1898 before modern technology advanced to the point where the whalebacks' design proved impractical, the ships were too small, and, as a result, they became uneconomical for hauling bulk freights.

Eight whalebacks lie wrecked in the Great Lakes, three still awaiting discovery; the others were either scrapped or lie in saltwater seas. The eight Great Lakes whaleback shipwrecks, listed chronologically, are: barge *104*, foundered in Lake Erie outside Cleveland on November 11, 1898; barge *115* stranded on Pic Island in northern Lake Superior on December 18, 1899 becoming not only a total loss, but also historically the last shipwreck of the 1800's in the

Left: The *Christopher Columbus* was a unique ship, being the only passenger excursion whaleback ever constructed. Built for Chicago's 1893 Columbia Exposition, the *Columbus* carried more passengers than any other Great Lakes vessel in her long career, which ended when the ship was scrapped in 1936. The metal was ultimately sold to Japan, which used it for its munitions build-up prior to World War Two. *Below:* Famous East Coast maritime artist Samuel Ward Stanton spent some time exhibiting his work at Chicago's Columbia Exposition of 1893, during which he sketched many Great Lakes ships, including the *Christopher Columbus*. Stanton published this in his 1895 book, *American Steam Vessels*.

CRIS KOHL COLLECTION

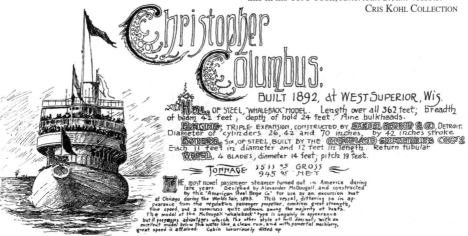

Great Lakes (see page 564); the barge *Sagamore* sank after a collision with another ship in eastern Lake Superior on July 29, 1901, with the loss of three lives (see page 492); the steamer, *Thomas Wilson*, sank outside Duluth harbor on June 7, 1902, following a collision with another steamer in which nine lives were lost (see page 532); barge *129* was wrecked on Lake Superior in a collision with its own towing steamer, the *Maunaloa*, on October 13, 1902; the steamer, *James B. Colgate*, sank in Lake Erie in the Black Friday Storm of October 20, 1916, with only the captain surviving (see page 168); the steamer, *Clifton*, launched as the *Samuel Mather*, foundered with all hands in a Lake Huron storm on September 22, 1924; the steamer, *Henry Cort*, was destroyed in a storm which smashed it against the breakwater at Muskegon, Michigan, on November 30, 1934, with one life lost (see page 380). The *104*, the *129*, and the *Clifton* remain to be found.

Left: The *Meteor* is the only one of the 44 whalebacks ever constructed which remains intact above water, as a museum in Superior, Wisconsin, examined by diver Don Edwards.

Right: Joan Forsberg is dwarfed by the *Meteor's* bow.

PHOTOS BY CRIS KOHL

The wreck of the *May Flower* (read her story on page 533) offers divers many exciting views of a bow anchor, windlass, steering post and numerous other items not pictured here.
PHOTOS BY KEN MERRYMAN

5. *A. C. ADAMS*

LORAN: GPS: 46° 49.180'/091° 59.300'
DEPTH: 118 feet   LEVEL: Advanced

LOCATION: Off the Lester River outside Duluth.
Built at Buffalo in 1881, the 41-ton tug, *A. C. Adams* (62' x 16' x 9'), worked in Duluth from 1894 until being "abandoned" (scuttled) in 1923. This wreck was found by Ken Merryman in Oct., 1990, while helping officials search for barrels of contaminants discarded in the 1950's.

Right: The rudder of the *A. C. Adams*. PHOTO BY KEN MERRYMAN

6. *ONOKO*

DEPTH: 220 feet   LEVEL: Technical

The *Onoko*.
CRIS KOHL COLLECTION

LOCATION: This deep shipwreck lies about 13.5 miles east of Duluth and 6.5 miles south of Knife Island.
The *Onoko* (287'3" x 38'8" x 20'7"), launched at Cleveland on Feb. 16, 1882, as the first iron-hulled steam freighter on the Great Lakes, sprang a leak and sank on Sept. 14, 1915, with a wheat cargo and no lives lost. Found by Jerry Eliason, Jerrod Eliason, and Kraig Smith in June, 1988, the *Onoko* lies upside down.

7. *BENJAMIN NOBLE*

DEPTH: 360 feet   LEVEL: Technical

LOCATION: This wreck lies off Knife Island, Minnesota.
The steel steamer, *Benjamin Noble* (239'2" x 42'2" x 18'8"), launched on April 28,

1909, at Wyandotte, Michigan, foundered on April 27, 1914, with a heavy cargo of steel rails, tragically taking all 20 lives which were on board with it to the bottom of Lake Superior.

Located on November 1, 2004, by Jerry Eliason, Kraig Smith, Randy Beebe, and Ken Merryman, this wreck rests upright but deeply buried in a rare soft part of Lake Superior's bottom. Only 3' of the fantail rises above the lake floor. The rail cargo is visible through open hatches.

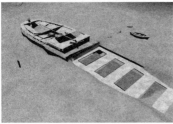

Above, left: The *Benjamin Noble* had a short, tragic career. CRIS KOHL COLLECTION. *Left:* How the wreck sits on the bottom. ART BY KEN MERRYMAN. *Right:* The superstructure, including the stern cabin, imploded during the sinking. PHOTO BY KEN MERRYMAN

8. STONY POINT

LOCATION: Take Stony Point Rd. for 3/4 mile off U.S. 61, 11 miles n. of Lester River.

This novice shore-dive site, popular among those divers interested in geology, runs from 10' to 40' deep along very old lava ledges, with interesting lava crevices and boulders along the northeast side in 15' of water. You will also see agates embedded in the lava.

9. NIAGARA

LORAN:	GPS: 46° 56.680'/091° 46.360'
DEPTH: 65 to 95 feet	LEVEL: Advanced

LOCATION: This wreck lies 500' due south of the middle of Knife Island.

The tug, *Niagara*. CRIS KOHL COLLECTION

Launched in 1872 at Detroit, the tug, *Niagara* (130' x 24'7" x 8'7"), stranded along Knife Island during a heavy northeast gale on June 4, 1904, and broke in two. No lives were lost, as the 13 people on board were removed by a tug dispatched to the scene. The engine, boiler and other machinery were salvaged soon afterwards.

The wreckage of the wooden hull consists of the bow section lying in four slabs on a rocky slope, with the stern still missing.

STRIKES ON ROCKS

Tug Niagara From Sault Strands on Knife Island.

Crew and Two Women Passengers Rescued By Tug Edna G

The sea tug Niagara, one of the largest boats of her class on the lakes, and owned by the Perry Towing company, of Sault Ste. Marie, went on the rocks at Knife Island at 7 p. m., Saturday, and was dashed to pieces. Practically total loss, except the boilers and engine, which it is hoped may be saved. No lives were lost. There was a crew of eleven men on board, with two wo-

Above, left: The *Niagara* stranded and broke up on June 4, 1904, and the loss was reported two days later in the *Duluth Evening Herald*. CRIS KOHL COLLECTION. *Above,* divers explore the *Niagara's* starboard side and, *below,* the bow. PHOTOS BY KEN MERRYMAN

The tug, *Niagara*

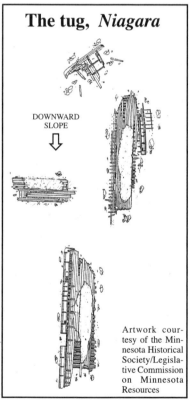

DOWNWARD SLOPE ⇩

Artwork courtesy of the Minnesota Historical Society/Legislative Commission on Minnesota Resources

10. KNIFE RIVER RUINS

LOCATION: Just off the mainland to the northwest of the *Niagara* site and Knife I.

This old pulpwood dock at the mouth of the Knife River, owned by the Alger Smith logging railroad which ceased operations in about 1919, offers a shore dive in about 5' to 25' of water. Avoid any northern rivers in the spring or early summer, as the run-offs produce strong currents and poor visibility. Divers can park at the end of the river's mouth road.

11. SAMUEL P. ELY

LORAN: GPS: 47° 00.700′/091° 40.685′
DEPTH: 30 feet   LEVEL: Novice-Intermediate

LOCATION: Along the inner west breakwall halfway between shore and the light.
The schooner-barge, *Samuel P. Ely* (200′ x 31′6″ x 13′8″), built as a three-masted

schooner at Detroit in 1869, stranded and sank along the breakwall with no cargo or lives lost on October 30, 1896.

A boat is required to reach this site, which is one of the most popular shipwreck dives along this north shore. The wreck, sitting on sand, is easily penetrated because of the missing hatch covers. The bow and stern ends are broken, but wooden railings, the deck, a bilge pump and a winch greet visiting divers. The site is often marked with a buoy, or paint along the breakwall. Recently, conservation work has been done here by the Great Lakes Shipwreck Preservation Society.

Samuel P. Ely. ARTIST UNKNOWN. CRIS KOHL COLLECTION

An underwater exploration of the *Samuel P. Ely* is fun, easy and relaxing. PHOTOS BY KEN MERRYMAN

12. HARRIET B.

DEPTH: 650 feet   LEVEL: Technical

LOCATION: This shipwreck is located three miles out of Two Harbors, Minnesota.

The *Harriet B.* was found in 2006 when Jerry Eliason, Kraig Smith, Randy Beebe, and Ken Merryman were testing some sidescan sonar equipment. The wreck, although broken near the bow, is fairly intact. The *Harriet B.* (282′6″ x 53′ x 19′4″), launched as a composite hull railroad car ferry in 1895 at Toledo,

The *Harriet B.* CRIS KOHL COLLECTION

Ohio, and named the *Shenango No. 2*, was converted to an unpowered barge in 1921. It sank with no loss of life after a collision with the steamer, *Quincy A. Shaw,* on May 3, 1922, in thick fog while under tow.

The *Harriet B.'s* pilot house washed ashore after the sinking.
0CRIS KOHL COLLECTION

Great Lakes Highlight No. 28

THE STORMS OF 1905

The year 1905 was notorious on the Great Lakes for a series of devastating storms.

Three storms proved especially disastrous. The first, on September 2nd, struck the southwest corner of Lake Superior at the Apostle Islands the hardest, sinking the huge barge, *Pretoria* (with the loss of five of her ten men), and the steel freighter, *Sevona* (with the loss of seven from the 24 on board).

The second storm that year occurred on October 20th, with Lakes Huron and Erie being the hardest hit. The immense barge, *Minnedosa* was lost with all hands

Left: Newspapers across the Great Lakes reported the disastrous effects of the October 20th storm.

Right: A commemorative photo collage of the November 28th storm was printed. CRIS KOHL COLLECTION

Right: The bad news of stranded ships along Lake Superior's unforgiving shoreline went on for days after the November 28th storm.

off Michigan's thumb, while simultaneously, ships in Lake Erie were sinking: the *Tasmania* with all hands, and also the steamers *Siberia* and *Sarah E. Sheldon*.

Lake Superior received the worst of the final big storm that year, on November 28th. The large, steel barge, *Madeira*, became a total wreck near Split Rock, Minnesota, with the loss of her First Mate. Nearby, the wooden steamer, *George Spencer*, and her schooner-barge, *Amboy*, became total losses, and the steamer, *Lafayette*, was driven ashore and broken in two. Many other vessels stranded along Superior's shoreline; most were eventually recovered, repaired, and returned to service. The most tragic disaster, however, took place right at the Duluth harbor entrance breakwall. The steel steamer, *Mataafa*, stranded while trying to enter port during the storm. Nine lives were lost because no one could reach the men on the broken vessel; that ship was later repaired and returned to service. All of the vessels named on this page, excluding the *Mataafa* (which was scrapped in 1964 after a long life), are shipwreck sites described in this book.

13. ROBERT WALLACE

DEPTH: 240 feet   LEVEL: Technical

LOCATION: This wreck lies approximately 8 miles south of Knife River, Minnesota. The wooden steamer, *Robert Wallace* (209' x 36' x 19'6"), built in Cleveland in 1880,

sank with her iron ore cargo in a storm on Nov. 17, 1902. The *Ashland*, the barge she was towing, bucked so wildly that it tore out the *Wallace's* stern post, causing steam pipes to burst and the ship to flood. Ironically, the ship which sank the *Wallace* rescued her crew.

Located and identified by Jay Hanson and Ron Smith in October, 2006, the *Robert Wallace* has her name still legible on her stern. Ironically again, the stern is the most intact part of this shipwreck, being in near-perfect condition up to the rail. The engine

The *Robert Wallace*. CRIS KOHL COLLECTION

and boiler are also very viewable there

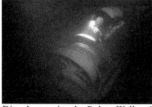

Diver's examine the *Robert Wallace's* windlass, and the surprisingly intact stern section. PHOTOS BY KEN MERRYMAN

14. THOMAS FRIANT

DEPTH: 305 feet   LEVEL: Technical

LOCATION: This shipwreck lies about 12 miles southeast of Knife River, Minnesota. The wooden steamer, *Thomas Friant* (96' x 18'3" x 7'8"),

built at Grand Haven, Michigan, in 1884, sprang a leak after ice cut into her hull and sank on January 6, 1924. No lives were lost, as the captain, mate and six fishermen who were on board took to the lifeboat, rowing ashore by midnight. This wreck, located by Jerry Eliason, Kraig Smith, Randy Beebe, and Ken Merryman in May, 2004, is in near-perfect condition, with her smoke stack upright, the binnacle with its brass compass on deck, her wheel in place, and her name still legible.

Bell, wheel, binnacle: amazing sights on the *Friant*. PHOTOS BY KEN MERRYMAN

15. AGATE BAY MERCHANT DOCK AND FISHING TUGS

LOCATION: Northwest of the public boat launch at Agate Bay.

The old dock lies in about 10' of water, with the remains of 3 abandoned fishing tugs in about 25' of water approximately 70' off shore. This shore dive is suitable for novice divers.

16. FLOOD BAY WAYSIDE

LOCATION: About one mile northeast of Two Harbors, immediately off shore from the parking area in 2' to 20' of water lies an assortment of artifacts from the old mining days (chains, railroad spikes, nails, axles, gears and rails). Please leave these items in place.

17. LAFAYETTE

LORAN:	GPS: 47° 05.693'/091° 32.960'
DEPTH: 6 to 30 feet	LEVEL: Novice

LOCATION: A boat is required to reach this site four miles northeast of Two Harbors.

The large, steel steamer, *Lafayette* (454' x 50' x 28'5"), along with several other ships, succumbed to one of the worst storms in Great Lakes history. On November 28, 1905, the light *Lafayette,* buffetted by strong gales and lashing waves, collided with her equally empty barge consort, the *Manila,* before stranding and breaking in two on the inhospitable rocky shoreline near Encampment Island. One life was lost. The *Manila* was later recovered, and the *Lafayette's* stern half was refloated and taken

The wrecked *Lafayette* bow.
CRIS KOHL COLLECTION

to Duluth, with the bow half deemed a total loss and left in place. Scrap iron salvage during the two World Wars left little of the *Lafayette's* bow other than some steel plates, railing and pipes to the south and east of Lafayette Bluff. The large steamer had been launched at Lorain, Ohio, on May 31, 1900.

18. GOOSEBERRY FALLS STATE PARK

LOCATION: Off U.S. 61 at Gooseberry Falls State Park.

The *Belle P. Cross*. CRIS KOHL COLLECTION

This novice shore dive to 30' will be of interest to geology and shipwreck buffs alike, as there are massive lava formations, as well as portions of the wooden steamer, *Belle P. Cross* (146' x 26' x 12'), built at Trenton, Michigan, in 1870, and stranded at the mouth of the Gooseberry River in a blinding snowstorm on April 29, 1903. The ship broke up with her lumber cargo and no lives lost, and the pulverized remains lie scattered over a wide area.

19. MADEIRA

LORAN:	GPS: 47° 12.360'/091° 21.480'
DEPTH: 25 to 110 feet	LEVEL: Intermediate-Advanced

The *Madeira*. CRIS KOHL COLLECTION

LOCATION: This wreck lies at the base of Golden Cliff, NE of Split Rock Point.

The three-masted, schooner-rigged, steel barge, *Madeira* (436' x 50'2" x 24'2"), built at Chicago in 1900, was wrecked in the same storm that destroyed the nearby *Lafayette* (site #17). On November 28, 1905, this huge barge stranded and broke up with the loss of the First Mate.

There is a small parking area behind a locked gate along U.S. 61 for divers only; a vehicle permit is required, and you must inquire at the Split Rock park office for access. From that parking lot, a short trail runs down to the water's edge, where divers can suit up and swim a few hundred feet over to the wreck site. The *Madeira,* usually buoyed at the base of the cliff, lies basically in 3 large sections of steel. The bow is upside-down in 40' to 50' of water, while the stern, with its steam winch and open hatches, rests on its starboard side in 65'. A small, roofless pilot house sits at 75'. In spite of being torn apart as with a giant can opener, this shipwreck offers interesting scuba diving.

Exploring the *Madeira's* angled steel pieces. PHOTOS BY CRIS KOHL

Artwork: Minnesota Historical Society/Legislative Commission on Minnesota Resources

20. JUST FOR FUN

DEPTH: 30 feet   LEVEL: Novice   GPS: 47° 15.55'/091° 17.15'

LOCATION: At Beaver Bay, Minnesota, near the harbor's retaining wall.
This modern-era, ferrocement sailboat hull is an easy dive. Beware of boating traffic.

21. HESPER

DEPTH: 35 to 55 feet   LEVEL: Intermediate   GPS: 47° 16.25'/091° 16.30'

LOCATION: This wreck lies along the west breakwall of Silver Bay harbor, Minnesota.
Built at Cleveland in 1890, the wooden bulk freight steamer, *Hesper* (250'3" x 41'6" x 20'2"), stranded during a severe gale on May 3, 1905, and slid into deeper water in two main pieces in the harbor at Silver Bay. No lives were lost. The large machinery was salvaged that year. Located in August, 1961 by divers Don Franklin and Curtis Anderson,

the *Hesper* was further salvaged of smaller pieces, including the

The *Hesper.* CRIS KOHL COLLECTION

nameplate, bell and compass binnacle. A boat is needed to reach this site, and the wreck lies near the midway point along the breakwall from shore. The site features the large, wooden hull, with the sides collapsed, and the rudder.

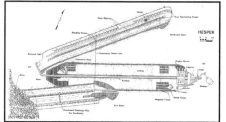

Artwork © Great Lakes Shipwrecks Preservation Society.

22. AMBOY AND GEORGE SPENCER

DEPTH: 3 to 18 feet   LEVEL: Novice   GPS: 47° 28.675'/090° 59.900'

LOCATION: 1 mile southwest of Sugar Loaf Cove, in 3' to 20' of water 50' from shore.
The wooden steamer, *George Spencer* (230'5" x 37'2" x 18'8"), built at Cleveland in 1884, and her tow, the schooner-barge, *Amboy* (209'3" x 34'2" x 14'4"), also from Cleveland in 1874, stranded in the storm of Nov. 28, 1905. A keelson part of the *Amboy* lies on shore.

46. Isle Royale

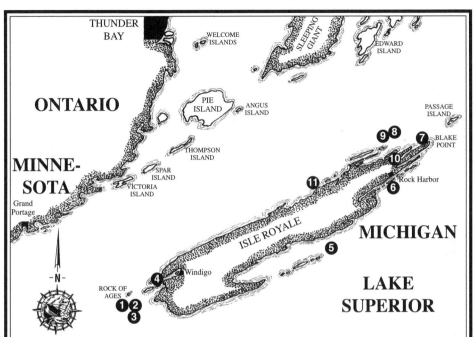

Isle Royale, the largest island in the largest Great Lake, with its wilderness remoteness and tempting inaccessibility, is the Mecca of Great Lakes diving, beckoning scuba divers from afar with its handful of legendary shipwrecks. It offers some of the most challenging shipwreck diving and post-diving conditions in the world. Converted to National Park status in 1940, Michigan's Isle Royale lies only a few miles off Minnesota and Ontario. All the shipwreck sites except the *Kamloops* and the Five Finger Bay tug have surface buoys provided by the Park Service. The main rules at present are:

1. Boats from Canada must clear customs.
2. Scuba divers must register at a ranger station before diving and obtain a free permit.
3. A standard dive flag must be used.
4. Disturbance or removal of anything underwater is prohibited.
5. Compressor use is restricted to certain locations and hours. (There are no airfill stations on the island, so you have to bring your own.)
6. There is a daily use fee for anyone visiting the island. Campers need a camping permit.
7. The shipwreck *America* is closed to diving during certain hours (presently noon to 2:00 PM) to allow visitors on the passenger ferry to view the wreck.

Plan this trip of a lifetime carefully. Contact Isle Royale National Park at (906) 482-0986.

Special THANKS for assistance in updating this chapter to Ken Merryman of Superior Trips Scuba Charters, www.superiortrips.com

1. *Cumberland*	**5.** *Glenlyon*	**9.** *Chester A. Congdon*
2. *Henry Chisholm*	**6.** *Algoma*	**10.** **Five Finger Bay Tug**
3. *George M. Cox*	**7.** *Monarch*	**11.** *Kamloops*
4. *America*	**8.** *Emperor*	

1. CUMBERLAND

> **LORAN: 31927.24/46066.70**   **GPS: 47° 51.465'/089° 19.650'**
> **DEPTH: 20 to 90 feet**   **LEVEL: Advanced**

LOCATION: This wreck lies intermingled with the remains of the *Henry Chisholm* (see site #2 below) near Rock of Ages Reef and Light, off the western end of Isle Royale.

The wooden sidewheel steamer, *Cumberland* (204'5" x 26' x 10'7"), launched on August 9, 1871, at Port Robinson, Ontario, stranded on the Rock of Ages Reef on July 23, 1877, and finally broke and sank several weeks later during storms after salvage attempts failed. No lives were lost in the stranding.

The wreck site is a jumble of timber slabs and machinery, such as engine boilers, rudder, paddlewheel and propeller.

The paddlewheel steamer, *Cumberland,* was wrecked at Isle Royale in 1877.   CRIS KOHL COLLECTION

The wooden steamer, *Henry Chisholm,* joined the wreck of the *Cumberland* in 1898.
GREAT LAKES HISTORICAL SOCIETY

2. HENRY CHISHOLM

> **LORAN: 31927.24/46066.70**   **GPS: 47° 51.459'/089° 19.679'**
> **DEPTH: 20 to 90, and 140 feet   LEVEL: Advanced-Technical**

LOCATION: This wreck lies intermingled with the remains of the *Cumberland* (see site #1 above) near Rock of Ages Reef and Light, off the western end of Isle Royale.

This wooden steamer (256'5" x 39'3" x 20'3"), launched on Aug. 28, 1880, at Cleveland, stranded and sank at Rock of Ages Reef on Oct. 21, 1898, with no lives lost. Her engine lies on the reef's other side in 145' at **LORAN: 31936.1/46068.0   GPS: 47° 51.450'/089° 19.796'**.

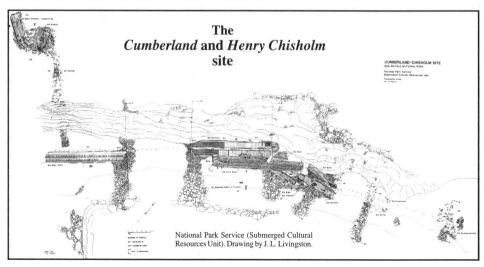

The
Cumberland* and *Henry Chisholm
site

CUMBERLAND/CHISHOLM SITE
ISLE ROYALE NATIONAL PARK
National Park Service
Submerged Cultural Resources Unit

National Park Service (Submerged Cultural Resources Unit). Drawing by J. L. Livingston.

546

3. GEORGE M. COX

> **LORAN: 31934.9/46069.8**   **GPS: 47° 51.462'/089° 19.385'**
> **DEPTH: 12 to 97 feet**   **LEVEL: Intermediate-Advanced**

LOCATION: This wreck lies along Rock Island Reef, near the Rock of Ages Light.

The wooden steamer, *George M. Cox* (259' x 40'5" x 26'6"), launched as the *Puritan* on May 1, 1901, at Toledo, Ohio, and renamed by wealthy new owner George M. Cox in honor of himself in early 1933, ran hard aground on her first trip of the season with 121 people on board on May 27, 1933. Fortunately, all were safely removed. Salvage efforts failed and the ship broke up, but much of her machinery and equipment had been recovered.

The *George M. Cox,* the second-most visited shipwreck at Isle Royale (after the popular *America* nearby), lies within a mile of the *Cumberland/Henry Chisholm* site. The highlights of this shipwreck site are the four (!) large boilers (she was a fast ship!), the rudder lying flat, and the vast amount of broken steel. Much scattered steel debris, mainly from the bow, lies in the shallows, but the bulk of the shipwreck (and the most interesting part, which happens to be the stern half) rests between 50' and 97'.

Above: The *George M. Cox* failed to complete her maiden voyage under her new name, opting instead to pose for one of the more dramatic series of Great Lakes shipwreck photos. CRIS KOHL COLLECTION

bow

Artwork: National Park Service (Submerged Cultural Resources Unit). Drawing by J. Livingston and L. Nordby.

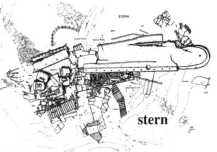

stern

Below: Diver Don Edwards examines the several boilers at the site. PHOTO BY CRIS KOHL

Some salvage occurred over several months before the *Cox* finally broke up and sank. CRIS KOHL COLLECTION

4. AMERICA

LORAN: 31909.2/46082.2	GPS: 47° 53.628'/089° 13.345'
DEPTH: 4 to 85 feet	LEVEL: Intermediate-Advanced

LOCATION: This wreck lies just outside Washington Harbor at western Isle Royale. The steel-hulled passenger and freight steamer, *America* (182'6" x 31' x 11'), launched on April 2, 1898, at Wyandotte, MI, struck a rocky reef in the darkness of night and became an unsalvageable total loss on June 7, 1928. Fortunately, there were no lives lost, as all 47 passengers and crew took to the lifeboats. Unfortunately, a dog tied to the stern went down with the ship. Today, the wreck

The active *America*.
CRIS KOHL COLLECTION

The passive *America*. CRIS KOHL COLLECTION

of the *America* is the most visited dive site at Isle Royale. She sits on a 45-degree angle on the incline with a 30-degree list to port. Her bow in the shallows offers tantalizingly photogenic visuals with a windlass, pump and bitts. Narrow passageways into the wreck offer access to the galley, the dining salon, various staterooms with several below-deck corridors, and the engine room. Don't get snagged on any of the debris below deck. The pride of the *America's* crew remains evident where, years ago, they painted the American flag, still visible today, onto the side of the engine. At the stern, the deepest part of the wreck, the propeller and taffrail are of interest.

The *America* in profile

Artwork: National Park Service (Submerged Cultural Resources Unit). Drawings by (left) H. Thom McGrath, and (right) Jerry Livingston.

S. S. AMERICA SINKS; ALL HANDS SAVED

DULUTH, June 7.—The steamer America, a great lakes passenger boat, sank near Isle Royale at 4.30 a.m., Booth Fisheries, owners, were informed today.
The crew of 30 and from 15 to 20 passengers, were saved, the vessel which operated between Duluth, Isle Royale, Fort William and Port Arthur, was leaving Washington Harbor, on Isle Royale, when she struck a reef which split the hull.

CRIS KOHL COLLECTION   *America* site map. Drawing by Jerry Livingston.

Left: Diver Karen Della-Mattia ventures below deck in the *America*. PHOTO BY JOE LARK. *Below:* Don Edwards explores the bow. PHOTO BY CRIS KOHL *Right:* Karen at the propeller. PHOTO BY JOE LARK

5. GLENLYON

LORAN: 31808.65/46188.57	GPS: 47° 57.178'/088° 44.824'
DEPTH: 10 to 100 feet	LEVEL: Novice to Advanced

LOCATION: On Isle Royale's south side, at Glenlyon Shoal north of Menagerie Island. The steel freighter, *Glenlyon* (328' x 42'5" x 20'5"), launched as the *William H. Gratwick* at West Bay City, Michigan, in 1893, headed for Siskiwit Bay seeking shelter from a storm, but instead stranded on a reef on November 1, 1924, with a cargo of wheat. No lives were lost in this mishap. Broken wreckage, such as the triple expansion engine, rudder, capstan and spare propeller blades, lies widely scattered in 10' to 50' of water, with parts of the separated stern cabin sitting in 100'.

The *Glenlyon*. CRIS KOHL COLLECTION

National Park Service (Submerged Cultural Resources Unit). Drawing by J. Livingston and L. Nordby

The freighter, *Glenlyon*

Diver Karen Della-Mattia explores the *Glenlyon's* components. PHOTOS BY JOE LARK

6. ALGOMA

LORAN: 31748.36/46187.83	GPS: 48° 06.431'/088° 32.335'
DEPTH: 15 to 100 feet	LEVEL: Intermediate-Advanced

LOCATION: On the south side of Mott Island, southwest of Rock Harbor, Isle Royale. Built in Glasgow, Scotland in 1883, the steel passenger steamer, *Algoma* (262'8" x 38'2" x 23'3"), stranded on Nov. 7, 1885, with the loss of 45 lives from the 59 on board. Those lost were on the bow when the ship broke in half and that part of the wreck was swept into deep water. It has not yet been located. Engine, boiler and other machinery were salvaged in 1886. Today's divers explore the stern half, broken and scattered in three gullies.

Left: Archival views of the *Algoma* wreck. CRIS KOHL COLLECTION

National Park Service (Submerged Cultural Resources Unit) Drawing by Larry Nordby.

7. MONARCH

LORAN: 31702.4/46171.3	GPS: 48° 11.334'/088° 25.957'
DEPTH: 10 to 150 feet	LEVEL: All levels possible here

LOCATION: This wreck lies on the north side of Blake Point, eastern Isle Royale.

The wooden passenger and freight steamer, *Monarch* (240' x 35' x 14'8"), launched at Sarnia, Ontario, in 1890, grounded hard onto the inhospitable and uninhabited shoreline called the Palisades during a blinding snowstorm on December 6, 1906. One man reached shore with a rope, which he tied to a tree so the other 60 people could escape the sinking ship hand over hand along that line. One life was lost when a young crewman slipped from the rope.

Massive pieces of hull and decking, as well as some scattered machinery (the engine and boiler were salvaged), comprise this site, which is extensive in shallow water (to 70'), but less so in deeper water.

Above: The regal *Monarch* proudly underway. *Below:* The *Monarch* dethroned at the Palisades, Dec., 1906.   CRIS KOHL COLLECTION

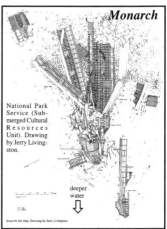

Monarch

National Park Service (Submerged Cultural Resources Unit). Drawing by Jerry Livingston.

deeper water

8. EMPEROR

Bow--DEPTH: 25-175 feet	GPS: 48° 12.003'/088° 29.525'
Stern--DEPTH: 110-175 feet	GPS: 48° 12.018'/088° 29.606'
LORAN: 31711.8/46150.6	LEVEL: Intermediate-Technical

LOCATION: This wreck lies off the Canoe Rocks, eastern Isle Royale.

Launched on December 17, 1910, at Collingwood, Ontario, the huge, steel, bulk freight steamer, *Emperor* (525' x 56'1" x 27'), carrying a cargo of iron ore, struck the rocks and sank on June 4, 1947, with the loss of 12 of the 33 people on board. At the time of her launching, she was the largest ship ever built in Canada.

Above: Emperor. CRIS KOHL COLLECTION

Below: Crew's quarters underwater.   PHOTO BY JOYCE HAYWARD

The hull, although split, forms a long line of massive, cracked steel running down a rocky slope, with her propeller and rudder sitting at the deep end. This wreck is so enormous that you cannot see it all in one dive (or even a few!). Fortunately, the shallow bow and the deep stern are buoyed separately. At the bow, the large anchor and open holds are impressive, while the stern offers the ship's galley, crew's quarters (with bunkbeds), skylights and large dorades, or air vents. Penetration is only for specially trained and experienced divers.

Don Edwards studies the *Emperor's* engine.   PHOTO BY JOE LARK

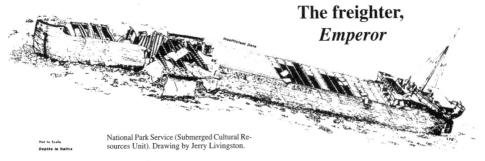

The freighter, *Emperor*

National Park Service (Submerged Cultural Resources Unit). Drawing by Jerry Livingston.

Not to Scale
Depths in Italics

9. CHESTER A. CONGDON

Bow--DEPTH: 60-120 feet	**GPS: 48° 11.559'/088° 30.815'**
Stern--DEPTH: 20-220 feet	**GPS: 48° 11.620'/088° 30.881'**
LORAN: 31717.5/46147.8	**LEVEL: Intermediate-Technical**

LOCATION: Off Congdon Shoal near the Canoe Rocks, northeastern Isle Royale.

The steel freighter, *Chester A. Congdon* (532' x 56'2" x 26'5"), launched as the *Salt Lake City* at Chicago on August 29, 1907, and renamed in 1912, stranded in thick fog on the rocks with her huge cargo of wheat and broke in two over the reef on November 6, 1918. No lives were lost in this simple but costly accident.

The *Congdon* site is in two parts, with the bow and its intact (but empty) pilot house

Chester A. Congdon

National Park Service (Submerged Cultural Resources Unit). Drawing by Jerry Livingston.

Above: The wrecked *Chester A. Congdon.* CRIS KOHL COLLECTION. *Below:* The *Congdon's* pilot house. PHOTO BY JOE LARK

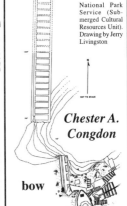

stern

National Park Service (Submerged Cultural Resources Unit). Drawing by Jerry Livingston

Chester A. Congdon

bow

resting in 60' to 120' of water, with the forward mast being less deep. The stern section on the other side of the reef, not usually buoyed as the Park does not encourage diving this deep, sits on a steep angle in 20' to 220' of water; the engine room and stern cabins are here.

10. FIVE FINGER BAY FISH TUG

LOCATION: Three-quarters of the way to the end of the southwesterly-most arm of Five Finger Bay, in 10' to 17' of water. **GPS: 48° 09.325'/088° 31.303'.** An unidentified 40' fish tug sits upright, with intact cabins and engine, plus a few tools. Found in the 1970's, this is a good dive when the lake is too rough, but visibility rarely exceeds 15'.

Right: The Five Finger Bay fish tug. PHOTO BY KEN MERRYMAN

11. KAMLOOPS

Bow--DEPTH: 240-270 feet	GPS: 48° 05.121'/088° 46.031'
Stern--DEPTH: 180-270 feet	GPS: 48° 05.118'/088° 46.000'
LORAN: 31786.1/46124.5	LEVEL: Technical

The *Kamloops*. CRIS KOHL COLLECTION

LOCATION: About 300' off Twelve O'Clock Point, north shore of Isle Royale.

The *Kamloops* story is one of the more tragic Isle Royale shipwreck tales. Built in England in 1924, this steel freighter (250' x 42'9" x 24'3") foundered in a severe early winter storm on December 6, 1927, alongside rocky Isle Royale. Not all of the crew of 20 men and 2 women perished immediately; some reached the island by lifeboat and froze or starved to death slowly. One woman left a heart-wrenching note in a bottle to her parents. The bodies were found the following spring.

The *Kamloops* was located in 1977, with divers Ken Merryman, Randy Saulter, and Ken Engelbrecht being the first to explore and identify her. She lies on her starboard side, bow deeper than stern, and very intact, with the perfectly preserved ship's wheel chain-and-padlocked in place so it won't get lost. The Park does not encourage diving this deep site, so there is no surface buoy here.

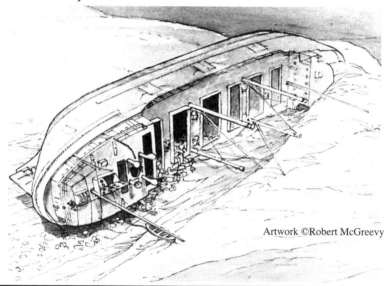

Artwork ©Robert McGreevy

47. North Shore Superior

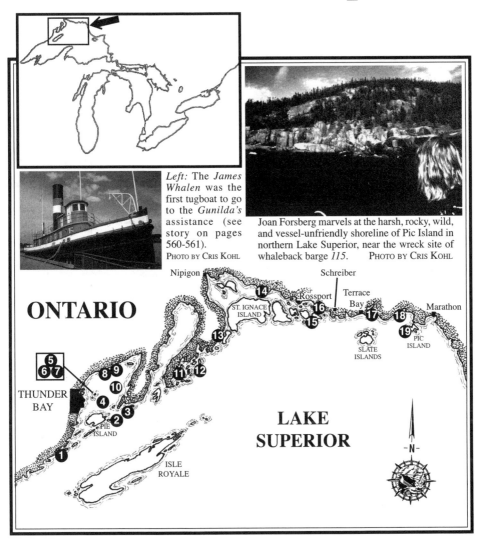

Left: The *James Whalen* was the first tugboat to go to the *Gunilda's* assistance (see story on pages 560-561). PHOTO BY CRIS KOHL

Joan Forsberg marvels at the harsh, rocky, wild, and vessel-unfriendly shoreline of Pic Island in northern Lake Superior, near the wreck site of whaleback barge *115*. PHOTO BY CRIS KOHL

1. *Howard*
2. *Monkshaven*
3. *Theano*
4. *Gray Oak*
5. *Green River*
6. *Robert L. Fryer*
7. *Puckasaw*
8. "Wally Sank Six Boats"
9. *Gordon Gauthier*
10. Thunder Bay ships' graveyard
11. *W. J. Emerson*
12. *St. Andrew*
13. *Neebing*
14. *Mary E. McLachlan*
15. *Ontario*
16. *Gunilda*
17. *Rappahannock*
18. *Judge Hart*
19. Whaleback Barge *115*

1. HOWARD

LORAN:	GPS: 48° 04.871'/089° 21.794'
DEPTH: 40 to 120 feet	LEVEL: Intermediate-Advanced

LOCATION: Off the south end of Victoria Island, south-southwest of Thunder Bay.

One of the oldest vessels active on Lake Superior, the 195-ton wooden tug, *Howard* (114'5" x 22'2" x 10'), launched at Wilmington, Delaware, in 1864 as the gunrunner *Admiral D.D. Porter,* received her last name in 1889. On June 13, 1921, she stranded on Victoria Island, caught fire and burned to a total loss with no lives lost.

The main wreckage of the *Howard,* including her 300 horsepower steeple compound

The tug, *Howard.*
REV. PETER VAN DER LINDEN COLLECTION

Right: Don Edwards and the *Howard's* propeller. *Below:* Don examining the *Howard's* firebox door.   PHOTOS BY JOE LARK

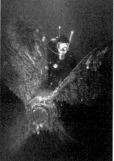

engine, lies between 40' and 60', with her propeller at 50'. The fact that a barge lies in 90' to 100' lends truth to the rumor of two wrecks at this site, one almost atop the other. Divers can suit up on Victoria Island at the navigation light and walk out into the lake along the shallow reef. The wreck lies on the right side of the reef facing the mainland.

2. MONKSHAVEN

DEPTH: 3 to 70 feet	LEVEL: Intermediate-Advanced

LOCATION: Off the s. side of Angus Island.

The steel steamer, *Monkshaven* (249' x 36'1" x 17'5"), a canaler-type freighter built in England in 1882, stranded for the 2nd time in as many years in the Thunder Bay area on October 10, 1906, when she broke free from her moorings and impaled herself on the rocks of Angus Island. Fall weather completed her destruction. Steel was salvaged during World War II. Found by Ken Engelbrecht, Randy Saulter, and Ken Merryman in 1978, there is much of interest at this broken and scattered site.

The demise of the *Monkshaven.*
CRIS KOHL COLLECTION

3. THEANO

LOCATION: This wreck reportedly lies in 320' of water off tiny Trowbridge Island, four miles east of Thunder Cape, Ontario.

Sometimes when ships sank, the shoal or the point of land which caused their demise was named after them (e.g. in northern Lake Huron alone, Jennie Graham Shoal was named after the schooner which sank there in 1880, Carter Rock received its name after the schooner, *J. S. Carter,* crashed into it and sank in 1890, and also in 1890, when the schooner, *Jane McLeod,* sank in Georgian Bay's 30,000 islands, two islands, Jane Island and McLeod Island, were named after it! The reverse was the case for the steel freighter, *Theano,* which was named after Lake Superior's Theano Point (north of Sault Ste. Marie) to commemorate the

The steel steamer, *Theano*. Note the midship cabins. Cris Kohl Collection. The *Theano's* name and port of call (Newcastle, England) are legible on the transom; the ship's wheel is in excellent condition. Photos by Ken Merryman

father of the *Theano's* Norwegian ship master, who drowned off that point.

Built at Slikkerveer (Rotterdam), Netherlands in 1890, the *Theano* (241'8" x 36' x 17'1") was transferred to British ownership in 1900 before coming to the Great Lakes in 1901. The ship was driven onto Trowbridge Island in a snow storm on Nov. 17, 1906. Once safely abandoned by her crew of 20, the ship's boiler exploded, and the hull slid into the deep water around the island with its cargo of steel rails. This wreck, in excellent condition, was found in 2005 by Jerry Eliason, Ken Merryman, Kraig Smith, and Randy Beebe.

4. GRAY OAK

LORAN: 31800.7/45915.7	GPS:
DEPTH: 108 feet	LEVEL: Advanced

LOCATION: This wreck lies about two miles southeast of the Welcome Islands.

The flat-bottomed, blunt-nosed scow-schooner, *Gray Oak* (133'7" x 31'7" x 9'), launched at Bayfield, Wisconsin, on June 20, 1885, was scuttled in about 1911. The hull and glass in the windows are intact. White letters on the hull clearly spell out the name *GRAY OAK*, with additional lettering obliterated.

Right: The *Gray Oak's* wheel. Photo by Joe Lark

5. ROBERT L. FRYER

LORAN: 31801.7/45902.4	GPS:
DEPTH: To 35 feet	LEVEL: Novice-Intermediate

LOCATION: This wreck lies at "B" Island, in the Welcome Islands, Thunder Bay.

The wooden steamer, *Robert L. Fryer* (290' x 41'6" x 20'), built in 1888 at West Bay City, Michigan, became

The *Robert L. Fryer.*
CRIS KOHL COLLECTION

a display of spectacular entertainment when it was towed to the Welcome Islands and set on fire on July 29, 1930. Part of the island burned as well. It is easy to locate this wreck, since a piece of the hull breaks the surface. Highlights include the boiler, propeller and rudder. A small unidentified wreck lies next to the *Fryer,* while portions of three other scuttled wrecks lie nearby.

Newspaper ad for the *Robert L. Fryer's* burning. CRIS KOHL COLLECTION

6. GREEN RIVER

DEPTH: 50 to 80 feet	LEVEL: Advanced

LOCATION: This wreck lies 450' north of the *Robert L. Fryer* wreck (site #5).

The wooden steamer, *Green River* (275' x 40' x 22'), launched on October 1, 1887, at West Bay City, Michigan, as the *Gogebic,* was reduced to a barge and renamed *Green River* in 1921. She was dismantled and scuttled at the Welcome Islands on November 5, 1932. The deck (at 50') and rudder are intact, and penetration is possible; training and a dive light are necessary.

The wooden steamer, *Green River.*
RALPH ROBERTS COLLECTION

7. PUCKASAW

LORAN: 31801.4/45901.3	GPS:
DEPTH: 55 to 80 feet	LEVEL: Advanced

Lying very close to the *Green River* (site #6), the tug, *Puckasaw,* (96' x 26' x 12'4"), built at Sturgeon Bay, WI, in 1910, as the *John Hunsader* (renamed in 1921), was scuttled in 1934. Several old boilers weighed down this intact, upright hull when she was scuttled.

Left: The tug, *Puckasaw,* is a penetrable shipwreck. CRIS KOHL COLLECTION

8. "WALLY SANK SIX BOATS"

In the early 1990's, Wally Peterson of Thunder Bay arranged for the sinking of six boats, including a decrepit, old 32' Chris Craft named *Sho-Nuff,* as a dive training site. They sit in 20' to 47' of water off the conservation area at Silver Harbour. A short trail runs from the parking lot to the water; in between are picnic tables, outhouses and tables. All the boats are roped together underwater, with the first boat being about 50' offshore. Fly a dive flag!

9. GORDON GAUTHIER

The 26-ton wooden tug, *Gordon Gauthier* (52'7" x 13'9" x 6'4"), built at Wallaceburg, Ontario, in 1884, burned at a quarry dock at Port Arthur harbor on Oct. 8, 1911. Today, she sits in 15' of water at Mary Island, off Silver Harbour, ON. The propeller was removed in 1974 by divers who would have received $25 for its scrap metal value; instead, they sold it to an appreciative diver for the same amount. Today, it is displayed in a dive shop in Thunder Bay, ON.

The *Gauthier* propeller. PHOTO BY CRIS KOHL

10. THUNDER BAY SHIPS' GRAVEYARD

DEPTH: 190 to 250 feet   LEVEL: Technical

In the 1920's and '30's, various levels of government in both Canada and the U.S.A. allocated funds for harbor clean-ups to eliminate the eyesores created by the half-submerged hulks of ships abandoned due to age and condition. The most famous of these ships' graveyards lie off Kingston, Ontario; Sarnia, Ontario; Sturgeon Bay, Wisconsin; and Thunder Bay, Ontario. The latter place recently added vastly to its numbers when Ryan LeBlanc, to prove his historical research, sidescanned Thunder Bay with colleagues Gerry Buchanan, Ken Engelbrecht and Dan Kuss in July, 2001, and located 26 to 30 scuttled ships in deep water just to the west of the known ships' graveyard in the Welcome Islands.

Among the many scuttled vessels in this deep site are:

The steamer, *Corunna*. CRIS KOHL COLLECTION

The steamer, *Corunna* (241' x 34'1" x 21'), built at Leith, Scotland, in 1891, with its "saltie" characteristic of a midship pilot-house, was dismantled and scuttled in 1938. The *Corunna* and the *Niagara* are the only two metal-hulled ships known to be in this graveyard.

The iron steamer, *Niagara* (159' x 21' 1" x 10'4"), launched at Glasgow, Scotland, in 1856 as the *Druid,* was used early in her career by the Nova Scotia government as a lighthouse supply ship for lonely Sable Island in the North Atlantic. Converted from a paddle-wheeler to a propeller-driven vessel in 1894, she was sold in 1900 by the Canadian government to a private company in Quebec for $2,150; she was already an old ship then. Renamed *Niagara* in 1901, she operated as an excursion steamer on Lake Ontario until 1911, when she was sold for freight use at

The steamer, *Niagara.* CRIS KOHL COLLECTION

Port Arthur, Ontario. She was scuttled on October 1, 1936.

The wooden tugboat, *Mary Ann,* is believed to be the first vessel registered in the new country called Canada after the Confederation of four British colonies on July 1, 1867.

The tug, *Mary Ann.* CRIS KOHL COLLECTION

557

11. W. J. Emerson

LOCATION: Off distant Bennett Island, at the old Number 10 Light, in 30' of water. This 19-ton, 70' tug, built in 1910, sank on Oct. 9, 1933. The wreck lies broken.

12. St. Andrew

LOCATION: This wreck lies off the rocks at the south end of tiny Bachand Island.

The wooden steamer, *St. Andrew* (192'6" x 41' x 12'4"), built at St. Catharines, Ontario, in 1885, as the *W. B. Hall,* changed her name after her 1897 rebuild. She stranded at Bachand Island and slipped into deeper water (40' to 60'). No lives were lost. Her machinery was salvaged and she lies broken, with her many parts forming a sizeable debris field.

The *St. Andrew.* CRIS KOHL COLLECTION

13. Neebing

LORAN:	GPS: 48° 39.80'/088° 07.80'
DEPTH: 60 to 100 feet	LEVEL: Advanced

Five lives were lost when the gravel carrier, *Neebing* (193' x 40'5" x 12'3"), built in 1892 at Toledo, Ohio, as the *John B. Ketcham II,* foundered on Sept. 24, 1937, off the north tip of Moss Island in the Nipigon Straits. The ship and crane are intact. *Right:* The *Neebing.* CRIS KOHL COLLECTION

14. Mary E. McLachlan

LORAN: 31454.5/46053.0	GPS: 48° 54.66'/087° 48.06'
DEPTH: 16 to 33 feet	LEVEL: Novice-Intermediate

LOCATION: This wreck lies about one mile off the mainland in Mountain Bay.

The huge four-masted schooner, *Mary E. McLachlan* (251' x 41' x 16'2"), launched on March 2, 1893, at West Bay City, Michigan, foundered on Nov. 7, 1921, with no loss of life. Located on May 16, 1981, by Ryan LeBlanc, this wreck is loaded with interesting items, but the visibility here is often reduced because of the outflow from two nearby rivers.

Above: The *Mary E. McLachlan* after being cut down to two masts. CRIS KOHL COLLECTION. *Right:* The *McLachlan's* bell was raised years ago and donated to a local historical society. PHOTO BY CRIS KOHL

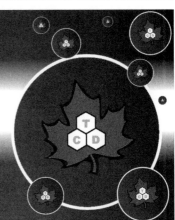

Great Lakes Highlight No. 29

THE LUXURY YACHT *GUNILDA*

DEPTH: 257 feet   **LEVEL: Technical**

LOCATION: This wreck lies just north of McGarvey Shoal near Rossport, Ontario.

The 385-gross-ton, palatial steel steam yacht, *Gunilda* (195'--with her bowsprit-- x 24'7" x 14'2"), built at Leith, Scotland, in 1897, was owned by multimillionaire William Harkness of Cleveland. He was entertaining his family and a number of friends on a cruise off Lake Superior's north shore when the *Gunilda* scraped hard aground on McGarvey Shoal, a rocky pinnacle near the town of Rossport, Ontario. Nonplussed, Harkness arranged for the tug, *James Whalen*, to release his yacht. When told that a second tug would be required to keep the *Gunilda* upright, Harkness balked. So, on August 11, 1911, the *Whalen* pulled, and the *Gunilda* capsized and sank in deep water. Harkness and his party returned home by train and he bought himself another boat.

Proclaimed "the most beautiful shipwreck in the world" by the 1980 Cousteau expedition, the *Gunilda* sits upright, intact, deadly (two divers have died here, one in 1970, the other in 1989), controversial (years ago, a diver claimed to have acquired the salvage rights to this wreck and that he planned to raise it), and carefully watched by the local residents.

The fabulous luxury yacht, *Gunilda*. NATIONAL ARCHIVES OF CANADA

If you were a multimillionaire and this were your luxury yacht, would you be too cheap to hire a <u>second</u> tugboat to help get it off the rocks?   Cris Kohl Collection

Right: One of the *Gunilda's* masts was grappled to the surface years ago and stands outside the Rossport Inn, where the passengers and crew were taken after their ship sank in 1911. Ryan LeBlanc stands next to it on Aug. 8, 1989, its brass marker commemorating Charles King Hague, who, on Aug. 8, 1970, became the first diver to die on the deep *Gunilda*. Ryan was one of the first divers in the world to utilize trimix (see p. 49)--which the team he was on blended specifically in the early 1980's to explore the *Gunilda*. Photo by Cris Kohl

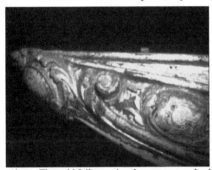

Above: The gold foil covering the ornate wooden bow scrollwork still glitters and shines, but a *Gunilda* deck-mounted searchlight has stayed dark. *Below:* Possibly the most impressive of the many unique sights on the *Gunilda* is her binnacle (which houses the ship's compass) and the vessel's wheel.
Images by Dan Lindsay of Sea-View Diving (see page 156 for the ad)

Left: The *Gunilda's* entire superstructure remains amazingly intact. *Right:* The bow anchors remain chocked in their standard position.

Photos by
Darryl Ertel

15. *ONTARIO*

> **LORAN: 31426.7/46178.0**   **GPS: 48° 45.20'/087° 31.99'**
> **DEPTH: 10 to 40 feet**   **LEVEL: Novice-Intermediate**

LOCATION: Around the most eastern peninsula on Battle Island, 7 miles south of Rossport, Ontario.

Built at Chatham, Ontario, in 1874, the wooden steamer, *Ontario* (181' x 35' x 12'2"), smashed onto the rocks in the shallows off Battle Island on August 10, 1899, with a cargo of coal. No lives were lost. Located by Ryan LeBlanc in 1977, this wreck lies broken and scattered on a rock and sand bottom. One boiler sits on shore (great landmark!), while the other lies nearby in 10' of water.

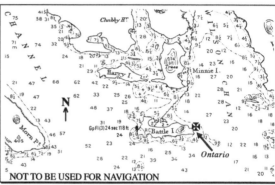

Above: The wooden steamer, *Ontario*. CRIS KOHL COLLECTION. *Below, left:* Joyce Hayward and Ryan LeBlanc explore the *Ontario's* shorebound boiler. *Below, right:* Ryan examines the *Ontario's* planking. PHOTOS BY CRIS KOHL

NOT TO BE USED FOR NAVIGATION

16. *GUNILDA* -- SEE PAGES 560-561.

17. *RAPPAHANNOCK*

> **DEPTH: 35 to 85 feet**   **LEVEL: Advanced**

LOCATION: This wreck lies in Jackfish Bay, near Schreiber, Ontario.

The *Rappahannock*. CRIS KOHL COLLECTION

The wooden steamer, *Rappahannock* (308'1" x 42'5" x 21'2"), launched on June 6, 1895, at West Bay City, Michigan, was beached in a 70-mile-per-hour gale in Jackfish Bay on July 25, 1911. No lives were lost as the ship sank along the steep underwater incline.

Located by Ryan LeBlanc in 1979, the *Rappahannock* is in excellent shape, with an intact hull, capstan, and a unique covered walkway held up by carved wooden supports. Below, there is a carpenter's bench, a

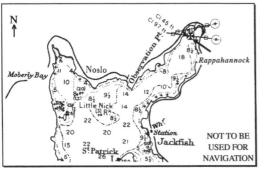

Right: Ryan Le-Blanc glides past the ship's wheel lying flat on the deck. PHOTO BY CRIS KOHL

Right, below: Diver Joe Lark explores the *Rappahannock's* intact stern cabin. PHOTO BY JOYCE HAYWARD

stove with utensils, and much machinery, including the engine. To reach this usually-buoyed site, launch an inflatable boat (anything bigger won't fit) at Jackfish Lake, head towards Lake Superior, and go through an extremely narrow channel under the Jackfish Bay railway culvert into Jackfish Bay.

18. *JUDGE HART*

LORAN:	LAT 48° 47' 34" LON 086° 38' 23"
DEPTH: 180 to 210 feet	LEVEL: Technical

LOCATION: This wreck lies at Fitz-simmons Rocks and Barclay Island, close to Simon's Reef in Ashburton Bay, west of Neys Provincial Park, off Superior's north shore, Ontario.

Built in England in 1923, the steel steamer, *Judge Hart* (252'2" x 43'2" x 17'8"), carried grain

The steel freighter, *Judge Hart.*
CRIS KOHL COLLECTION

Breathtaking in its beauty, the *Judge Hart's* pilot house remains amazingly intact. PHOTO BY DARRYL ERTEL

The magnificently intact nature of the *Judge Hart* can be seen from the condition of its binnacle *(left)* and its deck rails and ladders *(right)*. PHOTOS BY DARRYL ERTEL

for most of her Great Lakes career, which ended on Nov. 27, 1942, when she stranded with a grain cargo and sank. No lives were lost.

The *Judge Hart,* located on June 16, 1990, by divers Jerry Eliason and Kraig Smith, sits upright and incredibly intact, including all equipment, like the wheel, in the pilot house.

19. WHALEBACK BARGE *115*

DEPTH: 40 to 80 feet   LEVEL: Intermediate-Advanced

LOCATION: This wreck lies off the middle west side of Pic Island, Lake Superior.

Whaleback barge *115*. CRIS KOHL COLLECTION

The whaleback barge *115* (256' x 36'1" x 18'9"), built at Superior, Wisconsin, in 1891, stranded with her iron ore cargo on Pic Island on Dec. 18, 1899, becoming the last Great Lakes shipwreck of the 1800's. After a dramatic fight for survival lasting several days, the eight crewmembers reached safety on the mainland.

Located by Ryan LeBlanc in 1980, barge *115* sits broken on the rocky bottom, with only her bow and deckhouse intact. A windlass lies among the large sheets of steel.

Right: Wreckage from barge *115* can be found 50' up the cliff on Pic Island. PHOTO BY CRIS KOHL

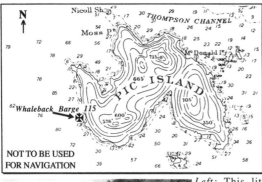

N ↑

NOT TO BE USED FOR NAVIGATION

Left: This little nook on Pic Island's rocky shoreline near the wreck offers a safe harbor. PHOTO BY CRIS KOHL

Right: Examining machinery from barge *115.* PHOTO BY JOE LARK

564

48. Eastern Lake Superior

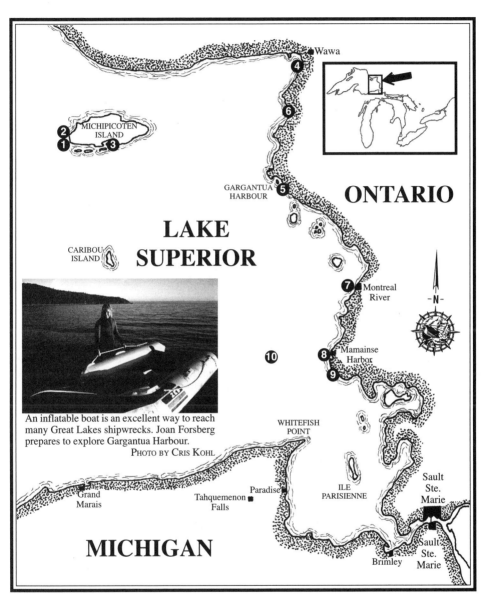

An inflatable boat is an excellent way to reach many Great Lakes shipwrecks. Joan Forsberg prepares to explore Gargantua Harbour.
PHOTO BY CRIS KOHL

1. *Chicago*
2. *Strathmore*
3. *Hiram R. Dixon*
4. *Acadia*
5. *Columbus,* **dredge and cribs**

6. *Golspie*
7. **Montreal River harbor**
8. *William O. Brown*
9. *Batchawana*
10. *Edmund Fitzgerald*

1. CHICAGO

LORAN:	GPS: 47° 43.84'/085° 57.91'
DEPTH: 10 to 70 feet	LEVEL: Intermediate-Advanced

LOCATION: This wreck lies in Schafer Bay at the western end of Michipicoten Island.

The healthy *Chicago*.
CRIS KOHL COLLECTION

The steel package freighter, *Chicago* (324'2" x 44' x 14'), launched on Sept. 28, 1901, at Buffalo, New York, with a cargo of zinc ingots and steel fence posts, stranded at this remote location 35 miles off the mainland on October 23, 1929, with no lives lost from the 31 crew. The wreck lies on her port

The wrecked *Chicago*.
GREAT LAKES HISTORICAL SOCIETY

side on a slope with visual treats that include the stern deck capstan, the zinc ingots cargo, two chains running down a stern hawsepipe, a chain locker, her propeller and hub, and a stream anchor. The broken bow in the shallows displays a windlass and other interesting nautical items.

2. STRATHMORE

LORAN:	GPS: 47° 44.64'/085° 57.36'
DEPTH: 5 to 35 feet	LEVEL: Novice-Intermediate

LOCATION: This wreck lies a bit north of the *Chicago* (site #1) in Schafer Bay.

The *Strathmore*.
CRIS KOHL COLLECTION

Launched in 1871 at Detroit as the *Gordon Campbell* and given her last name in 1906, the wooden freight steamer, *Strathmore* (207' x 33' x 21'), ran onto the rocks at Michipicoten Island while downbound with a grain cargo on Nov. 14, 1906, caught on fire and sank, with no harm to her crew. An underwater photographer's delight resting on a rock and sand bottom, this wreck displays big eccentric rods and a propulsion system with the propeller. At Quebec Harbour on southern Michipicoten Island, a set of *Strathmore* bitts sit on a dock (so now they're "bollards"), and her rudder reclines on a lawn.

3. HIRAM R. DIXON

LOCATION: In 10' - 15' at the east end of Quebec Harbour, on the south side of Michipicoten I. The wooden steamer, *Hiram R. Dixon* (147'2" x 20'6" x 9'), built at Mystic, Conn., in 1883, burned to a total loss on August 18, 1903. Her hull was damaged during the salvage of her machinery. Cribs and the remains of another small wreck lie nearby.

The *Hiram W. Dixon*.
CRIS KOHL COLLECTION

4. ACADIA

LOCATION: This wreck lies in 10' to 30', at the mouth of the Michipicoten River.

The *Acadia*. ONTARIO ARCHIVES

The steamer, *Acadia* (177' x 26' x 12'3"), built of early composite hull construction and launched at Hamilton, Ontario, on May 1, 1867, exactly two months to the day before Canada became a country, stranded with a grain cargo on November 5, 1896, while seeking shelter. No lives were lost, but the ship was pounded to pieces, which today lie scattered over a wide area between boulders and include hull pieces, steam fittings and tools.

5. *COLUMBUS*, DREDGE AND CRIB

LOCATION: These submerged cultural resources lie in Gargantua Harbour, Ontario.

A rough, adventurous dirt road runs 9 long miles from the main highway to a parking lot, from which it is only a couple more miles of hiking with your scuba gear to reach pretty Gargantua Harbour. It's rough, but it's worth it. The harbor is lined with scenic submerged cribs and an abandoned dredge, while the wreck of the large wooden tug, *Columbus* (136'2" x 25'2" x 11'8"), launched as the *John Owen* in 1874 at Detroit and burned to a total loss with no lives lost on Sept. 10, 1909, lies in 0' to 27' of water near the harbor's center. The wreck features the towering engine, propeller, boiler, a capstan, and much interesting debris.

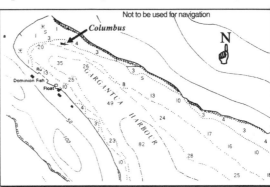

Not to be used for navigation
Columbus

Reaching the wreck of the tug, *Columbus (above, left,* INSTITUTE FOR GREAT LAKES RESEARCH, BOWLING GREEN STATE UNIVERSITY, OHIO), in Gargantua Harbour will be a trip you will never forget (for the black flies or the mosquitoes alone!) The engine rises above the water. The abandoned fishing village has a couple of buildings left standing. A dredge,submerged along the shoreline, features an impressive winch at its deeper stern end. PHOTOS BY CRIS KOHL

Columbus' propeller and stern area *(left)*, its angled fore & aft compound engine *(below)*, and her toppled boiler approached by diver Joan Forsberg *(right)*, are highlights.   PHOTOS BY CRIS KOHL

Great Lakes Highlight No. 30

THE LEGEND AND THE MYSTIQUE OF THE *EDMUND FITZGERALD*

LORAN:	LAT 46° 59′ 9″ LON 085° 06′ 6″
DEPTH: 529 feet	LEVEL: Legally off limits

Lying just inside Canadian waters is the most famous Great Lakes shipwreck of them all, thanks in large part to Gordon Lightfoot's haunting, popular ballad about her. Several years ago, I offered the editor of a high-circulation scuba diving magazine in Germany an article about diving on Great Lakes shipwrecks, and he responded, "Only if it is about the *Edmund Fitzgerald*."

The steel freighter, *Edmund Fitzgerald* (729′3″ x 75′ x 39′), built in 1958 at River Rouge, MI, foundered in an extremely violent storm with all 29 lives lost on Nov. 10, 1975. Broken in half, this controversial wreck lying in 529′ of cold, dark, Lake Superior water has been visited by submersibles many times, but only once, in September, 1995, by a pair of trimix divers, Terrence Tysall and Mike Zee, who reportedly spent eight minutes on the wreck and then three hours coming back up. They have no desire to do it again. The wreck victims' families have asked that no further visitations take place to the largest shipwreck in the Great Lakes. In 2006, the Ontario government declared the wreck of the *Edmund Fitzgerald* (and the *Hamilton* and the *Scourge* in Lake Ontario) to be off limits to further visits. But the inexplicable mystique of the *Edmund Fitzgerald* persists.

The *Edmund Fitzgerald* bucked the fabled gales of November while crossing Lake Superior; one storm proved particularly bad. ARTWORK © PETER RINDLISBACHER, USED WITH PERMISSION. FOR INFORMATION ABOUT MR. RINDLISBACHER'S ART, CONTACT THE CANADIAN SOCIETY OF MARINE ARTISTS, OR GO TO WWW.ULTRAMARINE.CA

This is the Mariner's Church in downtown Detroit, appearing a bit out of place in the shadow of the towering Renaissance Center. It was here that the minister, upon hearing of the loss of the freighter, *Edmund Fitzgerald,* with its 29 crewmembers, walked to the belfry and rang the church's bells 29 times, once for each man on the *Edmund Fitzgerald.* A journalist for one of Detroit's two daily newspapers, upon hearing about the ringing, wrote an article about it which received wide distribution. Annual commemorative services, always well attended, have been held ever since. A ship's bell is rung 29 times (the author had the honor of ringing it at the 1987 memorial service), accompanying a reading of the names of each crewmember. PHOTOS BY CRIS KOHL

Rev. Ingalls is the man who famously rang the church bells 29 times when he heard the tragic news about the *Fitzgerald's* loss. He presided over annual *Fitzgerald* commemorative services until his death in 2006.
PHOTO BY CRIS KOHL

Canadian folksinger, Gordon Lightfoot, flanked by Joan Forsberg and Cris Kohl, spent much time on the Great Lakes in his sailboat. When he read about the *Fitzgerald's* loss in 1975, particularly the part about the tolling of the bells 29 times in Detroit, he was inspired to write a song about it. It was a huge hit in 1976. PHOTO SET-UP BY CRIS KOHL

Capt. Donald Erickson made it safely into Whitefish Bay in his ship, the *William Clay Ford,* but turned around and went back out into the storm to search for any *Fitzgerald* survivors when he heard the news of that ship's disappearance.   PHOTO BY CRIS KOHL

The largest ship on the Great Lakes in 1958 became the largest shipwreck in our freshwater seas in 1975. The *Edmund Fitzgerald* wreck site lies 900′ inside the Canadian border. The Great Lakes Shipwreck Museum at Whitefish Point, close to the wreck site, displays much of her history.   CRIS KOHL COLLECTION

This *Edmund Fitzgerald* life ring is on display in the Mooretown Museum, Ontario.
PHOTO BY CRIS KOHL

6. GOLSPIE

LOCATION: This wreck lies at the mouth of Old Woman River in Old Woman Bay.

The wooden steamer, *Golspie* (183'6" x 34' x 22'), launched as the *Osceola* in 1882 at West Bay City, MI, stranded in a blizzard on Dec. 4, 1906 and broke up. Her boiler remains.

The *Golspie*, when the ship was still named the *Osceola*.   CRIS KOHL COLLECTION

7. MONTREAL RIVER HARBOR

LOCATION: A boat is necessary to reach the mouth of the harbor, where two unidentified tugs lie in 24' to 35' of water. Keep someone on board to watch for boating traffic.

8. WILLIAM O. BROWN

LOCATION: In 30' of water at Mamainse Point lie the remains of the 400-ton, two-masted schooner, *William O. Brown*, lost in a ruthless west-southwest snow-battering gale which also sank 3 other ships on Nov. 28, 1872. The *Brown* stranded and broke up with the loss of 6 of her 9 crew and her wheat cargo. Pieces of this ship lie scattered over a wide area.

9. BATCHAWANA

LOCATION: In 4' to 35' on the north side of Rousseau Island off Coppermine Point.

The steamer, *Batchawana*. CRIS KOHL COLLECTION

Launched as the *Robert A. Packer* in 1881 at Bay City, MI, burned in 1902, and rebuilt and renamed in 1906, the wooden steamer, *Batchawana* (209' x 33'8" x 16'1"), burned to a final total loss on June 26, 1907, with no lives lost. Divers with stamina have done this as a shore dive from the mainland, but a small boat is much preferred. Spikes and bolts lie in the shallows, with slabs of hull and pieces of machinery scattered in the slightly deeper water.

CANADIAN BOAT BURNS

Steamer Batchawanna, Loaded With Ore, is a Total Loss.

Crew Launched Small Boats and Easily Saved Themselves.

Sault Ste. Marie, June 27.—The Canadian steamer Batchawanna, loaded with iron ore consigned to the Algoma Steel company at Sault Ste. Marie, burned last night off Copper Point, on the north shore

News of the *Batchawana's* demise.
CRIS KOHL COLLECTION

Diver Frank Troxell takes a good look at the *Batchawana's* damaged, four-bladed propeller.
PHOTO BY CRIS KOHL

10. EDMUND FITZGERALD -- SEE PAGES 568-569

49. St. Marys River

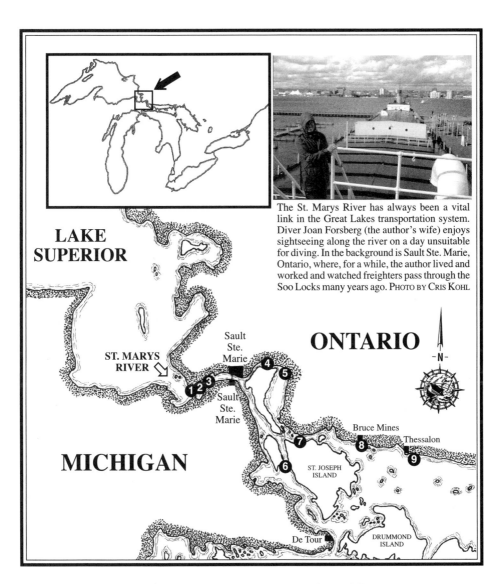

The St. Marys River has always been a vital link in the Great Lakes transportation system. Diver Joan Forsberg (the author's wife) enjoys sightseeing along the river on a day unsuitable for diving. In the background is Sault Ste. Marie, Ontario, where, for a while, the author lived and worked and watched freighters pass through the Soo Locks many years ago. PHOTO BY CRIS KOHL

LAKE SUPERIOR

ST. MARYS RIVER

Sault Ste. Marie

ONTARIO

-N-

Sault Ste. Marie

MICHIGAN

Bruce Mines

Thessalon

ST. JOSEPH ISLAND

De Tour

DRUMMOND ISLAND

1. Pointe aux Pins
2. *L. J. Farwell* and memorial
3. Beechcraft airplane
4. Garden River drift dive
5. Squirrel Island

6. *B. F. Bruce*
7. St. Joseph Island
8. *Premier*
9. *Oregon*

1. POINTE AUX PINS

DEPTH: To 45 feet   LEVEL: Intermediate-Advanced

LOCATION: A few miles west of Sault Ste. Marie, Ontario.

Pointe aux Pins is famous for being the first shipyard on Lake Superior, used by early explorers and settlers from 1730 to 1836. One can drift dive from Pointe Louise to Furkey's Marina searching for old bottles. The diver should have some experience in current diving. Since boating traffic is heavy, use of a dive flag is strongly recommended.

2. *L. J. FARWELL* AND PEER MEMORIAL

LORAN: 31030.4/47820.5   GPS:
DEPTH: To 43 feet   LEVEL: Intermediate-Advanced

LOCATION: This wreck lies west of Sault Ste. Marie, Ontario, off Pointe aux Pins, downstream from the dock and the navigation buoy.

The *L.J. Farwell.* CRIS KOHL COLLECTION

The oak-hulled, two-masted schooner, *L. J. Farwell* (136' x 26' x 10'), built in 1856 at Black River, Ohio, worked mainly in the lumber trade until 1903 when she was abandoned due to her age and poor hull condition. Once thought to be a wreck named the *Russell* (which was the previous name of the *Checotah,* which lies in Lake Huron and is also in this book), the *L. J. Farwell* sits upright with her hull intact, but her deck has collapsed.

Positioned just off this schooner's photogenic bow is a concrete and brass plaque memorial to David Eric Peer, a Master Scuba Instructor who had been in the business in the Canadian Sault for many years, and who had passed away from illness on August 28, 1990. The 2,400-pound memorial, provided by the Lake Superior Tridents Dive Club, was placed on August 28, 1991. Among many other things he did for diving, David Peer had served on the Executive Board of the Ontario Underwater Council at the same time as the author.

This site can be done as a shore or a boat dive.

The memorial to David Peer just prior to its placement by (left to right) Hugh Wyatt, Mark Iskrowicz, Ken Wyatt, and Norm McLaren. PHOTO BY BONNIE SHELLY

3. BEECHCRAFT AIRPLANE

DEPTH: 42 feet   LEVEL: Intermediate-Advanced

LOCATION: About 1,100' downstream from the *L. J. Farwell* (see site #2).

Local scuba divers purposely planted this vintage Beechcraft 18 airplane in the St. Marys River on June 5, 1982, about 75' upstream of the schooner, *L. J. Farwell,* but a huge "seiche" (an inland lake tidal-like wave) swept the plane downstream on July 15, 1988, leaving a trail of scattered wreckage. The plane finally came to rest upside-down more than 1,000' away. This can be done as a shore or a boat dive.

4. GARDEN RIVER DRIFT DIVE

DEPTH: To 30 feet   LEVEL: Novice-Intermediate

LOCATION: The community of Garden River is east of Sault Ste. Marie, Ontario.
This drift dive is usually done along the steep underwater clay bank, or the "drop-off."
Old bottles have been seen here. Near the former site of a late 19th century cookhouse is the underwater area known as the "boneyard" where cattle bones and horns lie in abundance. Divers can also appreciate seeing discarded cooking utensils, axes, saws and other broken garbage. There is current and boating traffic here. Fly a dive flag.

5. SQUIRREL ISLAND

Squirrel Island, just east of Garden River (see site #4), is a good bottle site. A boat is required to reach the island, but once there, virtually any area is good to dive.

6. *B. F. BRUCE*

DEPTH: 30 feet   LEVEL: Advanced

LOCATION: This wreck lies off Sailor's Encampment in the lower St. Marys River, at channel marker C "15." The schooner, *B. F. Bruce,* sank in October, 1895. It was located on August 8, 1969 by five scuba divers from the Sault area, including Tom Farnquist. The usually poor visibility and the fast speed of the river's current make this site an advanced dive for experienced divers. Beware of boating traffic, too.

7. ST. JOSEPH ISLAND

DEPTH: To 30 feet LEVEL: Novice-Intermediate

St. Joseph Island is rich with history, commencing with the strategic fort at Old Fort St. Joe Point on the southern portion of the island during the War of 1812. Most waterfront communities on this large island have (or had) their own docks, and exploring around those areas can be rewarding. Beware of boating traffic and fly a dive flag.

The schooner, *B. F. Bruce.*
CRIS KOHL COLLECTION

8. *PREMIER*

DEPTH: 10 to 20 feet   LEVEL: Novice

LOCATION: This wreck lies at the old government dock just east of Bruce Mines, ON.
The wooden combination passenger and package freight steamer, *Premier* (139'3" x 35' x 9'), launched as the *Greyhound* at Hamilton, Ontario, in 1888, and renamed *Lincoln* in 1899 before being given her final name in 1906 (didn't anyone tell these people that it's bad luck to change a ship's name?) was destroyed by fire on Nov. 13, 1920. No lives were lost. The engine and boiler were salvaged, but the hull with charred timbers inside remains quite intact, bow nestled into a crib pointing towards open water, rudder lying off the port side. Access is from shore or boat. Identification of this mystery wreck was made by Hugh and Glenna Wyatt in 1996.

The steamer, *Premier.* CRIS KOHL COLLECTION

573

9. OREGON

LORAN:	GPS: 46° 14.765'/083° 31.838'
DEPTH: 15 to 45 feet	LEVEL: Novice

LOCATION: This wreck lies just west of Dyment Rock, east of Thessalon, Ontario.

The wooden steam barge, *Oregon* (197' x 33' x 13'9"), launched on September 20, 1882, at West Bay City, MI, grounded with a pulpwood cargo on Dyment Shoals on August 22, 1908, caught fire and burned to a complete loss, with no lives lost.

Divers are impressed by the large, 4-bladed propeller and the anchor wedged between a rock and the ship. So large is the boiler that divers can swim through it. Massive hull portions, wood with iron

The steamer, *Oregon*. CRIS KOHL COLLECTION

bracing, bollards, cleats, a windlass and a winch remain at this site. A hardhat diver explored it long ago, but Hugh Wyatt of Sault Ste. Marie, Ontario, rediscovered the *Oregon* on August 12, 1993.

NEW SHIPWRECK AND DIVE SITE INFORMATION WELCOMED!

In a consuming effort to keep up-to-date with Great Lakes dive sites and shipwrecks, I am inviting any new or overlooked information which you may be willing to share. This includes sites in all five of the Great Lakes, plus the St. Lawrence River and the other interconnecting waterways, plus any inland sites. Usable shipwreck information would be acknowledged in our "Shipwrecks!" newsletter, as well as in any future editions of *The Great Lakes Diving Guide*. Please email any information to SeawolfRex@aol.com, and I thank you in advance.

50. Sites near Lake Superior

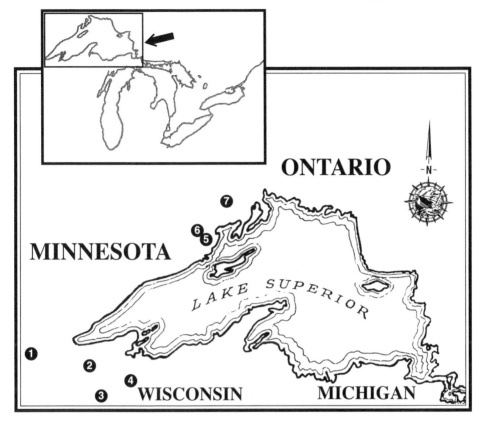

1. Cayuna Range Mine Pit Lakes, MN
2. Bond Lake, WI
3. Red Cedar Lake, WI
4. Lake Owen, WI

5. Oliver Lake, ON
6. Lake Shebandewan, ON
7. Silver Lake, ON

There are literally thousands of unmentioned places (anywhere where there is water!) to go scuba diving around the Great Lakes. The following sites are located near Lake Superior in Minnesota, Wisconsin, and Ontario:

1. CAYUNA RANGE MINE PIT LAKES, MINNESOTA

The city of Brainerd, MN, 125 miles north of Minnesota's Twin Cities, is the jumping off point for exciting explorations of mines, including fish (mostly trout, sunfish, bass, northern pike, and walleye) and flooded forests. You could spend an entire summer exploring the string of 27 lakes from about 50 dive sites. The iron ore mines operated from 1904 until the early 1960's when competition from overseas as well as the nearby Mesabi Range closed these mines. When their pumps stopped working, water filled the pits. Even the forests which once ringed the mine pits are now underwater. Mining remnants remain, such as submerged building foundations, pipes, shafts, roads and railroad tracks. The average depth is 40′, with the reputed maximum depth being 450′. Water visibility in the summer ranges from 25′ to 50′. Mine owners stopped chasing out scuba divers in the mid-1980's, and this area recently became the Cuyuna County State Recreation Area. The Crosby Mines, near the town of Crosby, MN, are part of this range. When the mines closed in the 1960's, any mine shafts were supposed to be dynamited closed, but a few were missed; however, penetration diving is not recommended because of the unstable nature of the ore. Besides seeing a wide variety of fish, divers have also reported giant snapping turtles, diving loons, and skittish beaver swimming through the trees.

2. BOND LAKE, WISCONSIN

LOCATION: About 60 miles south of Duluth, off County Road "T," which runs west off Highway 53 in Douglas County, about 10 miles north of Minong, Wisconsin.

This lake, with a maximum depth of about 80', offers views of several types of freshwater fish among the thick aquatic vegetation (avoid entanglement!).

3. RED CEDAR LAKE, WISCONSIN

LOCATION: Two miles south of Birchwood, Wisconsin, on Highway 48.

This long, narrow lake with a maximum depth of 60' features a sunken boathouse and old bottles. Ice diving is popular here.

4. LAKE OWEN, WISCONSIN

LOCATION: About 20 miles east of the community of Hayward in Bayfield County and about three miles south of Drummond. Access to the lake is via Highway 63 and county roads. Long, narrow Lake Owen covers 2,250 acres and reaches a maximum depth of 95'. The lake bottom is a mixture of sand and gravel, plus large boulders. The 24 miles of shoreline offer two boat launches at the north end. Divers here will encounter fish, such as bass, bluegills, crappies, walleye and pike, and an underwater railroad station at the north end.

5. OLIVER LAKE, ONTARIO

LOCATION: About 16 miles southwest of Thunder Bay, Ontario (the largest city on Lake Superior). This northern Ontario lake is reputed to be the clearest of the many inland lakes in this area. Visibility of 20' to 30' can be expected, with views of bass, pickerel, northern pike and lake trout. Depths can exceed 100' in this lake, so be cautious of your depth and bottom time.

6. LAKE SHEBANDEWAN, ONTARIO

LOCATION: West of the city of Thunder Bay, Ontario.

This deep lake demands that divers use lights if they venture deeper than 50' because of the darkness. Bass, pickerel (walleye), and northern pike are the main features at this site.

7. SILVER LAKE, ONTARIO

LOCATION: About 35 miles northeast of Thunder Bay, Ontario, this lake is about 1.5 miles long and 0.5 mile wide. Near the eastern shore, a reef runs the entire length of the lake at a depth of 20'. At the base of this reef, the depth is 60', with the middle of the lake dropping to the deepest point at over 100'. This lake abounds with lake trout and bass.

The Hunt for Great Lakes Shipwrecks

The Great Lakes are gifted with a rich endowment of maritime history, one that easily rivals the saltwater heritage of the East Coast or any other parts of the world. With the voluminous shipping traffic covering our freshwater seas in the past two centuries, it is little wonder that we have over 6,000 shipwrecks in the Great Lakes, with fewer than a third located.

A century ago, shipwrecks in the Great Lakes were sought for their commercial value in recovery. The old profession of "wrecking" has changed considerably since then, primarily because they're not making shipwrecks like they used to. In 1987, one Great Lakes historian and commercial fishing expert, Frank Prothero of St. Thomas, Ontario, said, "I can't think of a quicker way to go bankrupt than to become a commercial salvager in the Great Lakes today." The very few who have pursued Great Lakes shipwrecks with a goal of financial gain have found it to be a costly experience in this more heritage-conscious modern age.

But the hunt for Great Lakes shipwrecks continues, mainly for the satisfaction of locating another "needle in the haystack" which will add one more piece to that enormous patchwork quilt of Great Lakes Maritime History: the tapestry of lost ships and the intertwining stories behind them. Up until the Second World War, hardhat divers still pursued commercial shipwreck salvage utilizing the equipment which was prohibitively expensive for mere weekend aquatic warriors. However, since the advent of scuba (self-contained underwater breathing apparatus) after World War II, the barrier of costly and cumbersome equipment was eliminated. Also available in the 1950's were surplus "pingers," or electronic submarine detectors. Crude by comparison to today's sophisticated sidescan sonar units which offer color, high resolution digitized printouts of precisely what the shipwreck looks like so far underwater, these early machines nonetheless worked. Great Lakes explorers in search of shipwrecks, men like John Steele and Dick Race, were on their way by the late 1950's to locating long-lost history at the bottom of our inland seas.

The stern deck of the Great Lakes Shipwreck Society's research ship, *David Boyd,* from Whitefish Point, shows only some of its sophisticated shipwreck-hunting equipment. This high-tech vessel located the wreck of the *A.A. Parker* in June, 2001. PHOTO BY CRIS KOHL

The list is long, the adventures are many, and the hunters' research and discoveries have made us all richer with dramatic tales and material history from our maritime past. We go in quest of shipwrecks, to paraphrase Sir Edmund Hillary, who was the first person to reach the summit of Mount Everest, "because they are there." Just as technology had reached the point where it could be used for man to climb successfully to the highest point on earth in the 1950's, so too has technology developed in leaps and bounds in the last two decades to allow man to plumb the lowest depths on the planet, including our Lakes.

With sensitive sidescan sonar, the global positioning system, remote-operated vehicles equipped with strong lights and sensitive cameras, and exotic mixed gases which let divers go deeper and stay longer than ever before, technology has come a long way in a scant 20 years. Goverments set controls; in Canada, a permit is required to do a sidescan search. Despite such controls, we ourselves are reaching the point where we can responsibly manage that which technology is allowing us to discover.

Today's shipwreck hunters are adventurers who were born a couple of centuries too late. But even in modern times, those who are first to find shipwrecks, like the first people to climb Mt. Everest, are making history. The hunt for Great Lakes shipwrecks continues....

◆ ◆ ◆ ◆ ◆ ◆ ◆ ◆ ◆

The Most Hunted Great Lakes Shipwrecks

Here is the top twenty-five countdown of the most hunted Great Lakes shipwrecks:

25 *Moira* **(Lake Ontario, 1862)**

The wooden steamer, *Moira* (123' x 25'), built in 1855 at Belleville, Canada West (Ontario was at that time called "Canada West"), leaked and sank south of Main Duck Island on Oct. 9, 1862, reportedly in 50' to 70' of water, with its cargo of general merchandise and coal. All on board were saved in the lifeboats, but for one unfortunate horse. CRIS KOHL COLLECTION

24 *Lambton* **(Lake Superior, 1922)**

The steel steamer, *Lambton* (108' x 25'1" x 12'7"), disappeared with all 22 hands, mostly lighthouse keepers being taken out to their places of employment for another shipping season, on April 19, 1922, somewhere between Caribou Island and Whitefish Bay.   CRIS KOHL COLLECTION

23 *Wilkins Expedition* **(Lake Erie, 1763)**

Major John Wilkins' naval expedition to relieve the troops at Fort Detroit met with natural disaster off Pointe Aux Pins (today called Rondeau Provincial Park, Ontario) in Nov., 1763, when a gale sank 20 of his lake boats and killed about 70 of his men. His lake boats carried small cannons like the one at the right which was found by a diver off Cleveland and is from the similar Bradstreet Expedition of 1764.   PHOTO BY CRIS KOHL

22 *Zealand* **(Lake Ontario, 1880)**

The steamer, *Zealand* (132' x 24' x 12') foundered with all 16 hands in eastern Lake Ontario on November 7, 1880.   CRIS KOHL COLLECTION

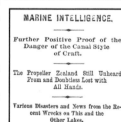

MARINE INTELLIGENCE.

Further Positive Proof of the Danger of the Canal Style of Craft.

The Propeller Zealand Still Unheard From and Doubtless Lost with All Hands.

Various Disasters and News from the Recent Wrecks on This and the Other Lakes.

21 *Lodner Phillips Submarine* **(Lake Erie, 1853)**

Lodner Phillips, amateur inventor from Michigan City, Indiana, built an experimental submarine which sank during on-site testing for a deep dive to the wreck of the *Atlantic* (sunk in 1852; see p. 154). No lives were lost, but this historic submarine, about 20' in length, remains on the bottom.

PHILIPS' SUBMARINE, 1851.
By favour of the *Illustrated London News.*
CRIS KOHL COLLECTION

578

20 *Andaste* (Lake Michigan, 1929)

The steel, semi-whaleback freighter, *Andaste* (246'9" x 38'1" x 17'9"), built in 1892 at Cleveland, foundered somewhere southwest of Grand Haven, Michigan, on September 9, 1929, with the loss of all 25 lives. CRIS KOHL COLLECTION

19 *R. G. Coburn* (Lake Huron, 1871)

The one-year-old wooden steamer, *R. G. Coburn* (193'4" x 30'8" x 8'5"), built in 1870 at Marine City, Michigan, foundered about 25 miles off Point Aux Barques on Oct. 15, 1871, with the loss of 31 of the 49 lives on board. CRIS KOHL COLLECTION

18 *J. H. Jones* (Lake Huron, 1906)

The small, wooden steamer, *J. H. Jones* (107' x 21'4" x 9'5"), bound from Owen Sound, Ontario, to Lion's Head and Tobermory, sank in a storm with all 26 hands off Cape Croker, in Lake Huron's Georgian Bay, on November 22, 1906. Wreckage washed ashore on nearby Christian Island. The ship was built in 1888 at Goderich, Ontario.
CRIS KOHL COLLECTION

17 *Barge 129* (Lake Superior, 1902)

The steel whaleback barge, *129* (292' x 36' x 22'), built as hull number 129 at Superior, Wisconsin, in 1893, sank in a collision with her towing steamer, the *Maunaloa*, on October 13, 1902, off Vermilion Point, Michigan. No lives were lost.
CRIS KOHL COLLECTION

16 *Clifton* (Lake Huron, 1924)

One of the few whalebacks in our Great Lakes, the steamer, *Clifton* (308' x 38' x 24'), built at Superior, Wisconsin, in 1892 as the *Samuel Mather*, foundered with all 24 hands about 25 miles off Thunder Bay, Michigan, on September 22, 1924.
CRIS KOHL COLLECTION

15 *F. J. King* (Lake Michigan, 1886)

The schooner, *F. J. King* (144' x 26'2" x 12'), built in 1867 at Toledo, Ohio, foundered off Cana Island, Wisconsin, on Sept. 15, 1886, with no lives lost. One dive club, the Neptune's Nimrods of Green Bay, WI, has offered a $1,000 reward for the location of this shipwreck (what a great idea for a club activity, complete with wild-west-type "wanted" posters!) CRIS KOHL COLLECTION; POSTER COURTESY OF THE NEPTUNE'S NIMRODS DIVE CLUB, GREEN BAY, WI

14 *W. H. Gilcher* (Lake Michigan, 1892)

One of the first steel steamers on the Great Lakes, the *W. H. Gilcher* (301'5" x 41'2" x 21'1"), foundered in a storm off High Island on Oct. 28, 1892, with all hands (17). Rumors started that the *Gilcher* had collided with the schooner, *Ostrich*, which also sank in that storm. Unsubstantiated discovery claims have been made, e.g. by Chicago hardhat diver, Frank Blair, on July 12, 1935. CRIS KOHL COLLECTION

13 *Western Reserve* (Lake Superior, 1892)

An early steel steamer on the Great Lakes, the *Western Reserve* (300'7" x 41'2" x 21'), built in 1890 at Cleveland, broke in half during a storm and sank off Deer Park, Michigan, on August 30, 1892, with 26 of her 27 lives lost. This created suspicion of steel ships. CRIS KOHL COLLECTION

12 *City of New York* (Lake Ontario, 1921)

Launched at Cleveland, Ohio, in August, 1863, the Civil War-era wooden steamer, *City of New York* (136' x 27'6" x 11'6"), worked until the beginning of the "Roaring '20's." The ship foundered with the loss of all eight hands during a snowstorm on November 25, 1921, between Main Duck Island and Galloo Island. The victims included the captain, his wife, and their two children. Five bodies were found in a lifeboat on the open waters. CRIS KOHL COLLECTION

11 *Alpena* (Lake Michigan, 1880)

The wooden sidewheel passenger steamer, *Alpena* (175' x 35' x 12'), built at Marine City, Michigan, in 1867, foundered with all 73 people on board, reportedly about 20 miles off Kenosha, Wisconsin, on Oct. 16, 1880, in fierce gales. Wreckage washed ashore near Holland, Michigan.
CRIS KOHL COLLECTION

10 *Hydrus* (Lake Huron, 1913)

One of the many victims of the Great Storm of November 9-10, 1913, the steel steamer, *Hydrus* (416' x 50' x 28'), foundered with all 24 hands somewhere off Southampton, Ontario, where bodies and wreckage washed ashore. The ship was built in 1903 at Lorain, Ohio. She will be one of the last two to be discovered of the 8 steel freighters lost with all hands in lower Lake Huron in that overwhelmingly tragic 1913 storm. CRIS KOHL COLLECTION

9 *James Carruthers* (Lake Huron, 1913)

The youngest and the largest victim of the Great Storm of November 9-10, 1913, the *James Carruthers* (550' x 58'2" x 26'7"), built at Collingwood, Ontario, earlier that year, foundered with all hands (about 24) and her wheat cargo off Kincardine, Ontario. CRIS KOHL COLLECTION

8 *Kent* (Lake Erie, 1845)

The much-sought 122-ton paddlewheel steamer, *Kent* (122' x 20' x 7'), built at Chatham, Canada West (now called Ontario) in 1841, sank in about 67' of water after a collision with the steamer, *London,* somewhere to the east of Point Pelee on August 12, 1845, with the loss of about 10 lives and most of the personal effects of the 75 passengers. This wreck may be embedded in mud. PUBLIC ARCHIVES OF CANADA

7 *Bannockburn* (Lake Superior, 1902)

Only a lifeboat oar was recovered 18 months after the steel steamer, *Bannockburn* (245' x 40'1" x 18'4"), foundered with all 22 hands on November 22, 1902. Built in England in 1893, this ship has become the Great Lakes' "Flying Dutchman," reportedly seen afloat several times since she disappeared. CRIS KOHL COLLECTION

6 *Asia* (Lake Huron, 1882)

The wooden steamer, *Asia* (136' x 23'4" x 11'), built at St. Catharines, ON, in 1873, foundered in one of the worst losses in Great Lakes history in Georgian Bay off Byng Inlet, ON, on Sept. 14, 1882, with 123 lives lost and only two survivors. Several parties have been searching for this wreck, with a tip that some of it lies in 83'. CRIS KOHL COLLECTION

5 *Chicora* (Lake Michigan, 1895)

A long-sought shipwreck, the wooden steamer, *Chicora* (208'5" x 35' x 13'6"), built at Detroit in 1892, disappeared with all 26 hands on January 21, 1895, while on a run from Milwaukee to St. Joseph, Michigan. A 2001 claim of discovery was premature, the found wreck eventually proving to be a different vessel. CRIS KOHL COLLECTION

4 *Cerisoles* and *Inkerman* (Lake Superior, 1918)

The cannon-mounted warships, *Cerisoles* and *Inkerman* (each 135'6" x 26'2" x 12'7"), built at the end of World War I at Fort William (today Thunder Bay), Ontario, foundered with all 76 people on them in a storm on Nov. 24, 1918, on their maiden voyages to France. CRIS KOHL COLLECTION

3 *Marquette & Bessemer #2* (Lake Erie, 1909)

Long-elusive, much-hyped, and prematurely claimed as found, this steel railroad car ferry (338' x 54' x 19'5"), built at Cleveland in 1905, disappeared with all hands (31 to 38) between Port Stanley, ON, and Conneaut, OH, in a severe blizzard on Dec. 8, 1909. I told wreckhunter Roy Pickering where I think it is, but he hasn't found it yet (so he says). CRIS KOHL COLLECTION

2 *Frontenac* (Lake Ontario, 1679)

The two-masted barque, *Frontenac*, about 40' in length, the largest of four small ships built by LaSalle on Lake Ontario before 1679, carried men and supplies to Niagara for the construction of the *Griffon*, but sank in bad weather near New York's Thirty Mile Point on Jan. 8, 1679, making it officially the very first shipwreck in the Great Lakes. Very little might remain of it by now.

The *Frontenac* being outfitted on Lake Ontario, 1678. ART BY GEORGE CUTHBERTSON, COURTESY OF THE CANADA STEAMSHIP LINES

1 *Griffon*
(Lake Michigan? Lake Huron? 1679)

The fabled, elusive 45-ton brig, *Griffon* (about 55' x 16' x 8'), the dream of marine archaeologists, disappeared with all 5 hands, 5 cannons and cargo of furs on her return maiden voyage in Sept., 1679, to become the first shipwreck in the *upper* Great Lakes (but the second Great Lakes shipwreck overall). The waters off western Manitoulin Island offer the most credible of the 16+ claims in the quest for this holy grail of freshwater shipwrecks.

The *Griffon* being built at Niagara, 1679. CRIS KOHL COLLECTION

◆　　◆　　◆　　◆　　◆　　◆　　◆　　◆　　◆

Great Lakes Shipwreck Hunters

Numerous people have searched for Great Lakes shipwrecks in the modern era.

Between 1987 and 2003, I interviewed most of the following principal shipwreck hunters in the Great Lakes. Some interviews lasted one hour, some went on for three; all were audiotaped and/or videotaped. During the winter of 1995-1996, I put together a multimedia presentation called "Great Lakes Explorers: In Search of Shipwrecks" which I presented at major shows in 1996, and which I recently updated and have been re-presenting as "Great Lakes Shipwreck Hunters." It contains most of the following information.

Over the next few pages, roughly in chronological order, you will meet some of the best-known Great Lakes shipwreck hunters of the modern era. There are others. Jerry Guyer has been locating numerous shipwrecks off Milwaukee in recent years. Darryl Ertel has been finding eastern Lake Superior shipwrecks. Ken Merryman, Jerry Eliason, Kraig Smith, Randy Beebe, sometimes teaming up with others, have located magnificent shipwrecks in western Lake Superior. Sam Mareci has found shipwrecks in Lake Michigan and Lake Huron. Dan Johnson located wrecks off Racine, Wisconsin. Richard Hammond has found many shipwrecks around Manitoulin Island. Lake Erie shipwrecks are surrendering their hiding spots regularly to Mike and Georgann Wachter, and Kevin Magee and CLUE -- the Cleveland Underwater Explorers. It is an exciting time to be a Great Lakes scuba diver, because we are now in the golden age of shipwreck discovery and identification!

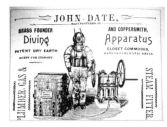

Ships sank with alarming frequency 100-150 years ago, and hardhat divers were hired to find and raise shipwrecks, or at least recover the cargo and rigging. Some famous Great Lakes hardhat divers were Johnny Green, Elliot Harrington, William Baker, James Quinn, Peter Falcon, and the Reid family of salvagers. CRIS KOHL COLLECTION

Above, left: Called the "King of the Great Lakes Wreck Hunters" because he succeeded at Great Lakes shipwreck hunting longer than anybody else (from 1959 until 1997), in spite of initially using primitive electronics left over from World War II, the dynamic John Steele was the subject of numerous newspaper and magazine articles in the 1970's and 1980's.   PHOTO SUBMITTED BY JOHN STEELE
Above, center: In July of 1997, John Steele (on his boat, center, standing tallest), gathered some of his longtime wreck hunting buddies, George West, Kent Bellrichard, Steve Radovan, and Jim Brotz, at Grand Marais, MI, for a reunion and a search (unsuccessful, as it turned out, for Lake Superior's *A.A. Parker*). The author was honored to have been invited to join this group. The "reunion" part, with its many reminiscences, on lake and on land, far outweighed the finding of any shipwreck during those days. John Steele ended his wreck hunting career with this event. PHOTO BY CRIS KOHL
Above, right: John Steele at the author's home in 2002, examining maritime furnishings. John, who shot underwater 16mm movies (expensive and very difficult to shoot) of many of his wreck discoveries for presentations to divers and history buffs, often said, "If you dive with a crowbar, you dive alone. But if you dive with a camera, you can take a thousand people with you." PHOTO BY CRIS KOHL

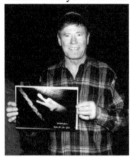

Milwaukee's Kent Bellrichard found wrecks independently and as a team searcher since the late 1960's. He located Lake Huron's *Dunderberg*, and appreciated receiving a photo of its unique figurehead from Cris Kohl. *Center:* Kent watches the sidescan sonar on John Steele's boat. Kent found the *Rouse Simmons*, the famous Christmas Tree Ship, in 1971 while using John's boat and equipment. *Right:* Steve Radovan, part of the Steele team since 1973, also worked independently finding wrecks. *Below:* Gene Turner found most of the known wrecks in lower Lake Michigan, searching since the early 1960's (*left:* PHOTO SUBMITTED BY GENE TURNER). *Below:* Gene and his scrapbook at his winter home in Florida. PHOTO BY CRIS KOHL. *Right:* Paul Ehorn has found numerous shipwrecks, both independently

and with others, including perhaps the best preserved one of them all -- the schooner *Cornelia B. Windiate* (see p. 340-341) while he was wreckhunting with John Steele on May 11, 1986.   PHOTO BY CRIS KOHL

584

Since 1969, Tom Farnquist (*left,* at the helm of the search vessel, *David Boyd*) has been locating shipwrecks in the southeastern end of Lake Superior. Over the years, he has also teamed up with other notable wreck hunters like John Steele, Kent Bellrichard, and Dave Trotter, to find wrecks such as (respectively) the *John Mitchell* in 1972, the *Vienna* in 1974, and the *Sadie Thompson* in 1992. Tom, instrumental in establishing the Great Lakes Shipwreck Historical Society and the popular Great Lakes shipwreck museum at Whitefish Point in the mid-1980's, most recently found the wreck of the *Cyprus*.   PHOTO BY CRIS KOHL

Between the 1950's and the 1980's, these two divers, Bill Patterson and Fred Dufty, from the Port Huron-Mt. Clemens area of Michigan, located approximately 75% of all the shipwrecks in the St. Clair River.   PHOTO BY CRIS KOHL

Canadian hardhat diver Mike Schoger found Lake Erie wrecks like the *Willis* and the *F. A. Meyer*.   PHOTO BY CRIS KOHL

Lloyd Shales of Kingston, Ontario, along with his cousin, Barbara Carson, led dive teams in the 1960's which located such notable wrecks as the *Aloha*, the *City of Sheboygan*, the *William Jamieson,* and the *George A. Marsh*.   PHOTO BY CRIS KOHL

Please turn to page 435 to see our ad for Love's Park Scuba

Paul LaPointe ran the first scuba dive shop that author Cris Kohl ever walked into in Canada. He also operated a charter boat business at Tobermory. In his spare time, Paul found shipwrecks, such as the *Explorer* in 1975 and the *San Jacinto* in 1990, often using a remote-operated video camera from his boat. PHOTOS BY CRIS KOHL

Doug Pettingill, from Picton, Ontario, has found or co-found many eastern Lake Ontario shipwrecks, such as the beautiful schooner, the *Annie Falconer*, in 1975, the tragic *Manola* in 1976, and many others since then. PHOTOS BY CRIS KOHL

Left: In the early 1980's, commercial diver Mike Fletcher, from Port Dover, ON, found Lake Erie wrecks, most notably the controversial *Atlantic*, before working full time on author Clive Cussler's TV series. PHOTO BY CRIS KOHL

Left: Since the late 1970's, Ryan Le-Blanc has found north shore Lake Superior shipwrecks such as the *Ontario* and whaleback barge *115*. *Right*: Ryan, an early trimix experimenter, fills scuba tanks at his home in Canada for visitor Joyce Hayward in the 1980's. PHOTOS BY CRIS KOHL

Diver's Guide to the Kitchen

Jim Kennard *(left)* has been locating ship-wrecks, mostly in Lake Ontario and smaller nearby lakes, for 30+ years. Teamed up with tech diver Dan Scoville, they were recently interviewed by the Discovery Channel *(right)*. PHOTOS SUBMITTED BY JIM KENNARD

Dave Trotter is probably the most active wreck hunter on the Great Lakes today. Known equally for his ship-wreck presentations and his confront-ations with bureaucracy, he has found many Great Lakes wrecks since 1978. His handpicked team of deep divers are able to keep secrets. Fiercely independent, Dave has occasionally hired out his services to groups such as Save Ontario Shipwrecks and the Michigan Shipwreck Research Associates, and he has succeeded in finding numerous wrecks for them. Dave's long list of impressive finds include the *Hunter Savidge*, the *Minnedosa* and the *Frank H. Goodyear*. PHOTOS BY CRIS KOHL

The Book--

Shipwreck Hunter chronicles **David Trotter's** discoveries along with those of some other pioneers of Great Lakes deep-water diving. Through the pages of this book, the stories of divers making history and long-lost ships come to life.

"This is a complex story about motivation and determi-nation. It is also about sacrifice and hope. These guys are the real deal and you won't be able to put this book down. If you like *Shadow Divers* or *The Last Dive*, then this book is for you." -- **John Chatterton**.

"Few can compare to the tenacity that Dave Trotter has in locating and identifying many of the most signifi-cant shipwrecks in the Great Lakes, *Shipwreck Hunter* details those successes, and the terrible cost explorers sometimes pay to be the first...." -- **Richie Kohler**. John and Richie are subjects of the bestselling book, *Shadow Divers*, and co-host of The History Channel's *Deep Sea Detectives*.

"A page-turning, thrilling and informative look into the often dangerous, competitive world of the legendary Great Lakes wreck hunters, and the maritime history behind their dives." -- **Bernie Chowdhury**, author, *The Last Dive*.

Thousands of people have seen and enjoyed David's "in-person" tales and DVD's of discovery and exploration. The programs are designed for people of all ages with each program tailored to the audience...children to grandparents.

Contact David for program information and to purchase an autographed copy of *Shipwreck Hunter* at:

DLTrotter@msn.com<mailto:DLTrotter@msn.com>

www.shipwreck1.com<http://www.shipwreck1.com/> (URA Website) **(734) 455-7585**

Garry Kozak spent 8 summers in the late 1970's-early 1980's searching for the legendary wreck of the *Dean Richmond* in Lake Erie. By the time he found it, he had amassed a fleet of 31 shipwreck discoveries. A Windsor, Ontario, native (like the author), Garry has lived in New Hampshire and worked for a major side-scan sonar company for 30+ years. He continues to find shipwrecks today. *Left:* Reading his log book at his home. *Right:* At a major scuba show in 2006.

PHOTOS BY CRIS KOHL

Chuck and Jeri Feltner located many of the popular shipwrecks in the Straits of Mackinac in the late 1970's-early 1980's, including the *Sandusky* and the *Eber Ward*. Because they were well-known shipwreck discoverers, divers sometimes followed them out of the harbor in hopes of being led to their newest wreck site. To avoid this, Chuck and Jeri did their underwater photography at night. Chuck would drop Jeri off in the dark above their submerged buoy marker to the *Eber Ward*, for example, and speed away while she would descend to the wreck, shoot a roll of film, then come up and bob patiently in the dark until Chuck picked her up again. In recent years, they have turned their attention to lighthouse conservation, an activity fraught with slightly less peril.   PHOTO BY CRIS KOHL

Left: Stan Stock, of Gaylord, MI, found wrecks with the Felt-ners in 1979-1981, then located wrecks himself, mainly in NW Lake Huron, like the *L. Van Valkenburg* in 1981 and the *W. P. Thew* in 1982. He still finds wrecks today. PHOTO BY CRIS KOHL

Right: Roy Pickering, of Erieau, Ontario, has been known to find ship-wrecks the old-fashioned way: by towing a diver behind his boat. This is how he located Lake Erie's *Colonial* in 1991. Since then, he has moved up to more high-tech equipment and continues searching.

PHOTO BY CRIS KOHL

Lake Huron wreck hunters, Wayne Brusate and Gary Biniecki *(lower left)* led a team which found the *Regina* in 1986, but it split their relationship. Gary joined Jim and Pat Stayer and Tim Juhl *(above, left)* for a while in finding wrecks like the *New York* and the *Mary Alice B. Middle:* Pat patiently watches the sidescan monitor. PHOTOS BY CRIS KOHL. *Right:* Cris Kohl joined Jim, Pat and Tim in finding and identifying the "Ghost Fleet of the St. Clair River" in 1993 (see p. 223). PHOTO BY PAT STAYER

Dr. Robert Ballard, the man who found the *Titanic* in 1985, moved his high-tech equipment to the inland seas in 2001 and 2002 and located shipwrecks in the NOAA Thunder Bay Sanctuary and Preserve off Alpena, Michigan.
PHOTOS BY CRIS KOHL

Right: Several new shipwreck discoveries were discussed at a recent annual conference of the Association for Great Lakes Maritime History. *Left to right,* Valerie Olson van Heest did a presentation about her group (Michigan Shipwreck Research Associates, which she founded in 2001) finding the historic *Hennepin* in Lake Michigan; David VanZandt of CLUE -- Cleveland Underwater Explorers -- told of their Lake Erie *Cortland* and *General Anthony Wayne* discoveries; Tom Farnquist showed incredibly detailed sidescan sonar images of his group's (Great Lakes Shipwreck Historical Society) discovery of the *Cyprus* in Lake Superior two weeks earlier. PHOTO BY CRIS KOHL

The Great Lakes World of Cris Kohl

BACKGROUND PHOTO BY JOAN FORSBERG
SEAWOLF COMMUNICATIONS: (630) 293-8996
AVAILABILITY OF BOOKS VARIES AND COULD CHANGE

SHIPWRECKS AT DEATH'S DOOR — CRIS KOHL AND JOAN FORSBERG — 2006

SHIPWRECK TALES OF THE GREAT LAKES — CRIS KOHL — 2004

The Great Lakes Diving Guide — Cris Kohl — 2001

Treacherous Waters: Kingston's Shipwrecks — Cris Kohl — 1997

THE 100 BEST GREAT LAKES SHIPWRECKS — VOLUME I — LAKE ONTARIO • LAKE ERIE • LAKE HURON — SECOND EDITION — CRIS KOHL — 1998

THE 100 BEST GREAT LAKES SHIPWRECKS — VOLUME II — LAKE MICHIGAN • LAKE SUPERIOR — SECOND EDITION — CRIS KOHL — 1998

TITANIC: THE GREAT LAKES CONNECTIONS — CRIS KOHL — 2000

Dive Ontario Two! MORE ONTARIO SHIPWRECK STORIES — Cris Kohl — 1994

Dive Ontario! Cris Kohl — THE COMPLETE GUIDE TO SHIPWRECKS AND SCUBA DIVING IN ONTARIO — 1990

Cris Kohl — Shipwreck Tales: The St. Clair River (to 1900) — 1987

DIVE SOUTHWESTERN ONTARIO! by CRIS KOHL — 1985

590

BIBLIOGRAPHY

Books

Amos, Art, and Patrick Folkes. *A Diver's Guide to Georgian Bay.* Toronto, Ontario: Ontario Underwater Council, 1979.

Amos, Art, and Dan Lindsay. *The Discovery of the Schooner* St. James. Ontario Marine Heritage Committee, April, 2001.

Arlov, Gary. *Divers Guide to the Shipwrecks of Lake Michigan.* Milwaukee, Wisconsin: The Arlov Company, 1987.

Baillod, Brendon. *Ghosts of the Ozaukee Coast, A Survey of Historical Port Washington Marine Accidents.* Wauwatosa, WI: Great Lakes Shipwreck Research Foundation, Inc., 2002.

Barkhausen, Henry N. *The Riddle of the Naubinway Sands.* Association for Great Lakes Maritime History, Publication B-5, 1991.

Barry, James P. *Ships of the Great Lakes, 300 Years of Navigation.* Berkeley, California: Howell-North Books, 1973.

Bennett, Dale. *The Captain's Shipwreck Book of South-West Lake Michigan.* Wheeling, Illinois: Captain Dale's, Inc., 2000.

Berent, John. *Diving the Lake Erie Island Wrecks.* Marblehead, Ohio: John Berent, 1992.

Bors, Brian J., ed. *New York State Dive Site Directory.* Niagara Falls, New York: The New York State Divers Association, 1993 and 2000 editions.

Club Poseidon. *The St. Clair River...a sport diver's guide.* Port Huron, Michigan, June, 1983.

Cooper, David J. ed., *By Fire, Storm, and Ice: Underwater Archaeological Investigations in the Apostle Islands.* Madison, WI: State Historical Society of Wisconsin, 1991, revised 1996.

.... with John O. Jensen. *Davidson's Goliaths, Underwater Archaeological Investigations of the Steamer Frank O'Connor and the Schooner-Barge Pretoria.* Madison, WI: State Historical Society of Wisconsin, 1995.

.... *Survey of Submerged Cultural Resources in Northern Door County, 1988 Field Season Report.* Madison, WI: State Historical Society of Wisconsin, 1989.

Creviere, Paul J., Jr. *Wild Gales and Tattered Sails.* Paul John Creviere, Jr., 1997.

Curtis, Andrea. *Into the Blue, Family Secrets and the Search for a Great Lakes Shipwreck.* Toronto: Random House Canada, 2003.

Engman, Elmer. *In the Belly of a Whale, Duluth's Shipwreck Tragedy.* Duluth, Minnesota: Innerspace, 1976; revised 1988.

.... *Shipwreck Guide to the Western Half of Lake Superior.* Duluth, Minnesota: Innerspace, 1976.

Feltner, Dr. Charles E., and Jeri Baron. *Shipwrecks of the Straits of Mackinac.* Dearborn, Michigan: Seajay Publications, 1991.

Forsberg, Joan. *Diver's Guide to the Kitchen.* West Chicago, Illinois: Seawolf Communications, Inc., 2003.

Frederickson, Arthur C. and Lucy F. *Ships and Shipwrecks in Door County, Wisconsin, Volume One.* Frankfort, Michigan: Arthur C. and Lucy F. Frederickson, 1961.

.... *Ships and Shipwrecks in Door County, Wisconsin, Volume Two.* Frankfort, Michigan: Arthur C. and Lucy F. Frederickson, 1963.

Frimodig, Mac. *Shipwrecks off Keweenaw.* The Fort Wilkins Natural History Association in cooperation with the Michigan Department of Natural Resources.

Gibbs, Barry L. *Quarry Quest, The Diver's Guide to the Midwest.* Crawfordsville, IN: Palmer Publishing, 1987.

Greenwood, John O. *Namesakes 1900-1909.* Cleveland, Ohio: Freshwater Press, Inc., 1987.

.... *Namesakes 1910-1919.* Cleveland, Ohio: Freshwater Press, Inc., 1986.

.... *Namesakes 1920-1929.* Cleveland, Ohio: Freshwater Press, Inc., 1984.

.... *Namesakes 1930-1955.* Cleveland, Ohio: Freshwater Press, Inc., 1978.

.... *Namesakes 1956-1980.* Cleveland, Ohio: Freshwater Press, Inc., 1981.

Guyer, Jerry. *Jerry's Shipwreck Charts,* 9th edition. Milwaukee, WI: Jerry Guyer, 2006.

Halsey, John R. *Beneath the Inland Seas: Michigan's Underwater Archaeological Heritage.* Lansing: Bureau of History, Michigan Department of State, 1990.

Hammer, Patrick. *Lake Michigan Shipwrecks.* Alsip, Illinois: Scuba Emporium, 1996 (5th edition).

Harold, Steve. *Shipwrecks of the Sleeping Bear.* Traverse City, Michigan: Pioneer Study Center, 1984.

Harrington, Steve. *Divers Guide to Michigan,* Mason, Michigan: Maritime Press, 1990; rev. ed., 1998.

.... *Shipwreck in the Sands, The Story of the Discovery and Exploration of Lake Michigan's Oldest Shipwreck.* Michigan: Maritime Press, 2002.

Harrington, Steve, with David J. Cooper. *Divers Guide to Wisconsin, including Minnesota's North Shore.* Mason, Michigan: Maritime Press, 1991.

Heyl, Eric. *Early American Steamers, Volumes I-VI.* Buffalo, New York: Eric Heyl, 1953-1969.

Hirthe, Walter M. and Mary K. *Schooner Days in Door County.* Minneapolis: Voyageur Press, 1986.

Holden, Thom. *Above and Below, A History of Lighthouses and Shipwrecks of Isle Royale.* Houghton, Michigan: Isle Royale Natural History Association. 1985.

Keatts, Henry C., and G. C. Farr. *Dive Into History, Volume 3: U-Boats.* Houston: Pisces Books, 1994.

Keller, James M. *The "Unholy" Apostles, Tales of Chequamegon Shipwrecks.* Bayfield, Wisconsin: Apostle Island Press, 1984.

Kohl, Cris. *The 100 Best Great Lakes Shipwrecks, Volume I.* West Chicago, Illinois: Seawolf Communications, Inc., 1998, revised edition 2005.

.... *The 100 Best Great Lakes Shipwrecks, Volume II.* West Chicago, Illinois: Seawolf Communications, Inc., 1998, revised edition 2005.

.... *Dive Ontario! The Guide to Shipwrecks and Scuba.* Chatham, Ontario: Cris Kohl, 1990, revised 1995.

.... *Dive Ontario Two! More Ontario Shipwrecks Stories.* Chatham, Ontario: Cris Kohl, 1994.

.... *Dive Southwestern Ontario!* Chatham, Ontario: Cris Kohl, 1985.

.... *Shipwreck Tales: The St. Clair River (to 1900).* Chatham, Ontario: Cris Kohl, 1987.

.... *Shipwreck Tales of the Great Lakes.* West Chicago, Illinois: Seawolf Communications, Inc., 2004.

.... *Titanic, The Great Lakes Connections.* West Chicago, Illinois: Seawolf Communications, Inc., 2000

.... *Treacherous Waters: Kingston's Shipwrecks.* Chatham, Ontario: Cris Kohl, 1997.

Kohl, Cris, and Joan Forsberg. *Shipwrecks at Death's Door.* West Chicago, Illinois: Seawolf Communications, Inc., 2007.

Lane, Kit. *Chicora, Lost on Lake Michigan.* Douglas, Michigan: Pavilion Press, 1996.

.... *Shipwrecks of the Saugatuck Area.* Saugatuck, MI: Saugatuck Commercial Record, 1974.

Lauer, Richard, compiler. *Freshwater Vision, A Guide to Diving in Ohio, Pennsylvania, and West Virginia.* Reynoldsburg, Ohio: Sub-Aquatics, Inc., 1989.

Lenihan, Daniel. *Shipwrecks of Isle Royale National Park.* Duluth, Minnesota: Lake Superior Port Cities, Inc., 1996.

Mansfield, J. B., ed. *History of the Great Lakes, Volumes I and II,* Chicago, IL: J. H. Beers & Co, 1899

Marshall, James R. *Shipwrecks of Lake Superior.* Duluth, MN: Lake Superior Port Cities, Inc., 1988

McKenney, Jack. *Dive to Adventure.* Vancouver: Panorama Publications, Inc., 1983.

Metcalfe, Willis. *Canvas & Steam on Quinte Waters.* South Bay, Ontario: the South Marysburgh Marine Society, 1979.

Neel, Robert, ed. *Diving in Ohio.* Ohio Council of Skin and Scuba Divers, Inc., 1979.

O'Keefe, Jack V. *The Dean Richmond Story.* Annapolis, MD: Jack V. O'Keefe, 1995.

Pittelkow, Tom. *Wreck of the Sebastopol, A Unique Perspective of an Early Milwaukee Shipwreck.* Milwaukee, WI: Tom Pittelkow, 1994.

Roberts, Mark and Kathy. *An Underwater Guide to Lake Superior's Keweenaw Peninsula.* Houghton, Michigan: Mark and Kathy Roberts, 1991.

Salen, Rick. *The Tobermory Shipwrecks.* Tobermory, Ontario: The Mariner Chart Shop, 1996 edition.

Smith, Arthur Britton. *Legend of the Lake, The 22-Gun Brig-Sloop* Ontario, *1780.* Kingston, ON: Quarry Press, 1997.

Stabelfeldt, Kimm A. *Explore Great Lakes Shipwrecks, Volume I Covering Wrecks on Part of the Lower Lake Michigan.* Wauwatosa, WI: Stabelfeldt & Associates, Inc., 1992 (6th ed., 1996).

.... *Explore Great Lakes Shiwprecks, Volume II Covering Wrecks on the Upper Part of Lake Michigan and Green Bay off the Coasts of Wisconsin and Michigan.* Wauwatosa, Wisconsin: Stabelfeldt & Associates, Inc., 1993 (fourth edition, 1996).

.... *Explore Great Lakes Shipwrecks, Volume III, Known Wrecks around Whitefish Point and the Surrounding Area*. Wauwatosa, Wisconsin: Adventure Diving, Inc., 1998.

Stanton, Samuel Ward. *American Steam Vessels*. New York: Smith & Stanton, 1895.

Stayer, Pat and Jim. *Shipwrecks of Sanilac*. Lexington, Michigan: Out of the Blue Productions, 1989, revised edition 1995.

.... and Tim Juhl, as told to. *Sole Survivor, Dennis Hale's Own Story*. Lexington, Michigan: Out of the Blue Productions, 1996.

.... and Tim Juhl, as told to. *If We Make It 'til Daylight, The Story of Frank Mays*. Lexington, Michigan: Out of the Blue Productions, 2003.

Stone, David. *Long Point, Last Port of Call*. Erin, Ontario: Boston Mills Press, 1988.

Stonehouse, Frederick. *Isle Royale Shipwrecks*. Au Train, Michigan: Avery Color Studios, 1983.

.... *Keweenaw Shipwrecks*. Au Train, Michigan, Avery Color Studios, 1988.

.... *Lake Superior's Shipwreck Coast*. Au Train, Michigan: Avery Color Studios, 1985.

.... *Marquette Shipwrecks*. Au Train, Michigan: Avery Color Studioes, 1974.

.... *Munising Shipwrecks*. Au Train, Michigan: Avery Color Studios, 1983.

.... *Shipwreck of the Mesquite*. Duluth, Minnesota: Lake Superior Port Cities, Inc., 1991.

.... *Short Guide to the Shipwrecks of Thunder Bay, A*. Alpena, MI: B&L Watery World, 1986.

.... with Daniel R. Fountain. *Dangerous Coast: Pictured Rocks Shipwrecks*. Marquette, Michigan: Avery Color Studios, 1997.

Van der Linden, Rev. Peter J., ed. and the Marine Historical Society of Detroit. *Great Lakes Ships We Remember*. Cleveland, Ohio: Freshwater Press, 1979; revised 1984.

.... *Great Lakes Ships We Remember II*. Cleveland, Ohio: Freshwater Press, 1984.

.... *Great Lakes Ships We Remember III*. Cleveland, Ohio: Freshwater Press, 1994.

Van Harpen, Jon Paul. *Door Peninsula Shipwrecks*. Charleston SC, Chicago IL, Portsmouth NH, San Francisco CA: Arcadia Publishing, 2006.

Wachter, Georgann and Michael. *Erie Wrecks East, A Guide to Shipwrecks of Eastern Lake Erie*. Avon Lake, Ohio: Corporate*Impact*, 2000.

.... *Erie Wrecks West, A Guide to Shipwrecks of Western Lake Erie*. Avon Lake, Ohio: Corporate*Impact,* 2001 (second edition; originally published in 1997).

Wolff, Julius F., Jr., *Lake Superior Shipwrecks*. Duluth, MN: Lake Superior Port Cities, Inc., 1990.

Wrigley, Ronald. *Shipwrecked, Vessels That Met Tragedy on Northern Lake Superior*. Cobalt, Ontario: Highway Book Shop, 1985.

Periodicals

Alford, Terry. "Kingston's Newest Wreck Dive (*Wolfe Islander II*)." *Diver Magazine*. Vol. 12, No. 1 (March, 1986), 18-21.

.... "Time Capsule in Kingston, Queen of Kingston's Wrecks (*Wolfe Islander II*)." *Diver Magazine*. Vol. 14, No. 1 (March, 1988), 19-20.

Armbruster, Peter. "*Verano* Found After 48 Years." *Great Lakes Diving Magazine* (Oct/Nov,1994), 26

Arnberg, Doug. "Mystery Wrecks off Point Traverse." *Wreck Diving Magazine*. Issue 4 (2004), 28-34

.... "Schooner *Katie Eccles*, The." *Wreck Diving Magazine*. Issue 6 (2005), 18-22.

.... "Three-Masted Schooner, *City of Sheboygan*." *Wreck Diving Mag*. Issue 10 (2006), 70-75.

.... "Wrecks of the 1000 Islands, Part I: Canadian Side." *Wreck Diving Magazine*. Issue 7 (2005), 10-15.

.... "Wrecks of the 1000 Islands, Part II: American Side." *Wreck Diving Magazine*. Issue 8 (2005), 34-39.

.... "Wrecks of the 1000 Islands, Part III: Deep Wrecks." *Wreck Diving Magazine*. Issue 9 (2006), 66-69.

Bailey, Dan Holden. "Mackinac Straits." *Diver Magazine*. Vol. 25, No. 6 (September, 1999), 18-19.

.... "Time in Tobermory." *Diver Magazine*. Vol 24, No. 2 (April, 1998), 20-22.

.... "Wrecks of the St. Lawrence." *Diver Magazine*. Vol. 23, No. 1 (April, 1997), 36-37.

Bellefeuille, Monique and Mike. "*Lillie Parsons*." *Diver Magazine*. Vol. 16, No. 7 (Nov., 1990) 18-19

Bennett, Capt Dale. "Diving S.S. *Wisconsin*." *Midwest Scuba Diving*. Vol. 1, No. 1 (Summer, 2006), 14-15.

.... "Diving Steamer *Lady Elgin*." *Midwest Scuba Diving*. Vol. 1, No. 2 (Fall, 2006), 16-17.

.... "Diving Schooner, *St. Mary*." *Midwest Scuba Diving*. Vol. 2, No. 1 (Spring, 2007), 20-21.

Blake, Erica, with photographs by Andy Morrison. "Great Lakes Wreck Diving." *Wreck Diving*

Magazine. Issue 11 (2006), 8-15.

Bowen, Curt. *"Vienna, 1873-1892."* *Advanced Diver Magazine.* Issue 1 (Spring, 1999), 44-46.

Boyd, Ellsworth. "The *Regina.*" *Skin Diver.* Vol. 37, No. 10 (October, 1988), 78. 150-152.

Coplin, Larry, and Bruce McLaughlan. "A Shipwreck Shrouded in Mystery (*Kamloops*)." *Diver Magazine.* Vol. 10, No. 9 (December, 1984), 15-19.

Dekina, Vlada. "Midnight Chase." (*Dunderberg*). *Wreck Diving Magazine.* Issue 7 (2005), 54-61.

.... "Two Lives of *Northwind* (sic), The." *Wreck Diving Magazine.* Issue 5 (2005), 67-73.

Drew, Richard C. "Chicago's Most Popular Dive (*Material Service*)." *Skin Diver.* Vol. 39, No. 1 (January, 1990), 12, 146-150.

Emering, Ed. "The Fated Lady (*Wisconsin*)." *Scuba Times.* Vol. 14, No. 3 (May-June 1993), 48-49.

Feltner, Charles. "*Cedarville* Tragedy." *Diving Times* (June/July, 1981).

.... "*Eber Ward.*" *Diver Magazine.* Vol. 7, No. 6 (September, 1981), 18-22. Reprinted from the November/December, 1980, issue of *Diving Times* of Royal Oak, Michigan.

.... "Raise the *Cayuga.*" *Diving Times* (April/May, 1981).

.... "Strange Tale of Two Ships (*Maitland* and *Northwest*). *Diving Times* (Feb./March, 1981).

.... "Wreck of the *Col. Ellsworth.*" *Diving Times* (June/July, 1980).

.... "Wreck of the Brig *Sandusky.*" *Diving Times* (October/November, 1981).

.... "Wreck of the *William H. Barnum.*" *Diving Times* (August/September, 1980).

Forsberg, Joan. "Sea Storyteller, Cris Kohl." *Immersed.* Vol. 5, No. 3 (Fall, 2000), 20-25.

Garn, Myk. "Return to the *Emperor,* The Pride of Canada." *Skin Diver.* Vol. 35, No. 4 (Apr., 1986), 30

Gilchrist, David. "Diving Weekend at Port Colborne, Ontario (the Wreck of the Steamer, *Raleigh*)." *Diver Magazine.* Vol. 20, No. 5 (August, 1994), 14-15.

.... "Lake Erie Wreck Dive (*Carlingford*)." *Diver Magazine.* Vol. 20, No. 1 (Mar., 1994) 22-23

.... "Shipwreck Discovery in Lake Ontario (*Henry Clay?*)." *Diver Magazine.* Vol. 25, No. 5 (July/August, 1999), 25.

.... "Wrecks of Lower Georgian Bay." *Diver Magazine.* Vol. 26, No. 3 (May, 2000), 17-19.

Golding, Peter. "Fathom Five Park." *Diver Magazine.* Vol. 5, No. 6 (August/September, 1979), 24-27.

.... "Inner Space Adventure, *Comet* in Lake Ontario." *Diver Magazine.* Vol. 5, No. 4 (June, 1979), 21 -24.

.... "Innerkip Quarry, An Unusual Experience." *Diver Magazine.* Vol. 5, No. 2 (February/March, 1979), 22-23, 44, 45.

.... "Lady of Muskoka, The *Waome.*" *Diver Magazine.* Vol. 6, No. 4 (June, 1980), 20-21.

.... "*Maple Dawn* (sic)." *Diver Magazine.* Vol. 6, No. 4 (April-May, 1980), 36-37.

.... "*Michigan's* Muscle Machines." *Diver Magazine.* Vol. 5, No. 4 (June, 1979), 20-21.

.... "The *Price* Adventure." *Diver Magazine.* Vol. 4, No. 8 (Nov.-Dec., 1978), 34-38.

.... "Tale of Two Wrecks, *Sweepstakes--City of Grand Rapids.*" *Diver Magazine.* Vol. 6, No. 1 (January/February, 1980), 24-25.

.... "Tobermory Tug." *Diver Magazine.* Vol. 7, No. 2 (March, 1981), 38-39.

.... "Tobermory's Limestone Grottos." *Diver Magazine.* Vol. 5, No. 3 (April/May, 1979) 28-31

.... "Wreck of the *George A. Marsh.*" *Diver Magazine.* Vol. 5, No. 8. (Nov.-Dec., 1979), 38-40

Halsey, John R., and Scott M. Peters. "Resurrection of a Great Lakes Steamer (*Three Brothers*)." *Michigan History Magazine.* (November-December, 1996), 22-25.

Hector, Bruce. "Kingston Wrecks." *Diver Magazine.* Vol. 17, No. 1 (March, 1991), 32-33.

Holland, Sean. "A Deep Freshwater Adventure, *Roy A. Jodrey.*" *Immersed.* Vol. 5, No. 3 (Fall, 2000), 46-52.

Jalbert, Andrew. "Wreck of the *Niagara.*" *Diver Magazine.* Vol. 26, No. 9 (Jan.-Feb., 2001), 24-25.

Jarvey, Michele. (Photos by Kim Brungraber). "The *Vernon* - Chicago." *Midwest Scuba Diving.* Vol. 2, No. 2 (Summer, 2007), 16-19, plus cover.

Jensen, John Odin. "The History and Archaeology of the Great Lakes Steamboat, *Niagara.*" *Wisconsin Magazine of History.* Vol. 82, No. 3 (Spring, 1999), 198-230.

Johnson, Ken. "Graveyard of Lake Superior, Whitefish Point and Whitefish Bay." *Diver Magazine.* Vol. 11, No. 1 (January-February, 1985), 16-19.

.... "Strange Story of the Steamer, *Myron.*" *Diver Magazine.* Vol. 10, No. 6 (Sept., 1984) 20-21

.... "The Controversial Loss of the Motorship *Material Service.*" *Diver Magazine.* Vol. 11, No. 8 (December, 1985), 16-19.

Kemp, Bruce. "Lake Huron Mystery (The *Charles S. Price*)." *Diver Magazine.* Vol. 8, No. 2 (March, 1981), 7-20.

.... "Shipwrecks of the St. Clair River." *Diver Magazine.* Vol. 9, No. 8 (Dec., 1983), 18-20.

594

Kohl, Cris. "10 Great Wrecks of the Great Lakes." *Rodale's Scuba Diving Magazine*. Vol. 13, No. 3, Issue 115 (April, 2004), 43-50, 105.

.... "12-Fathom Maiden: Lake Erie's *Willis*." *Diver Magazine*. Vol. 25, No. 5 (July-August, 1999), 26-27.

.... "*America*, the Beautiful---Shipwreck." *Diver Magazine*. Vol. 23, No. 8 (December, 1997), 25-28

.... "Backwoods Secret (*Columbus*)." *Diver Magazine*. Vol. 17, No. 5 (August, 1991), 33-35.

.... "*Barge 115*--Last Shipwreck of the 1800's." *Diver Magazine*. Vol. 25, No. 8 (December, 1999), 6-8.

.... "Battle for the *Atlantic*." *Diver Magazine*. Vol. 19, No. 3 (May, 1993), 36-37.

.... "Beautiful, Tragic *Myron*, The." *Diver Magazine*. Vol. 24, No. 8 (December, 1998), 25-27.

.... "Broken Lady of Driftwood Cove, the *Caroline Rose*." *Diver Magazine*. Vol. 24, No. 2 (April, 1998), 26-27.

.... "Chicago's Tragic Schooner, The *Wells Burt*." *Wreck Diving Magazine*. Issue 2 (2004), 56-63.

.... "Christmas Tree Wreck, The" (The *Rouse Simmons*). *Wreck Diving Magazine*. Issue 4 (2004), 8-15.

.... "Current Diving on the *Conestoga*." *Diver Magazine*. Vol. 24, No. 1 (March, 1998), 26-27.

.... "Dead Captain's Secrets, The." (The *George A. Marsh*). *Wreck Diving Magazine*. Premiere Issue (2004), 40-47.

.... "Deep Dive in Superior (*Samuel Mather*)." *Diver Magazine*. Vol. 25, No. 1 (March, 1999), 26-28.

.... "Dredge *Munson*." *Diver Magazine*. Vol. 23, No. 6 (September, 1997), 26-27.

.... "Elusive Little Lady of Lake Huron, The." (The *Mary Alice B*.) *Wreck Diving Magazine*. Issue 10 (2006), 28-37.

.... "Flames on Lake Michigan (the *Frank O'Connor*)," *Wreck Diving Magazine*, Issue 5 (2005), 30-35.

.... "*Fleur Marie*." *Diver Magazine*. Vol. 23, No. 7 (October-November, 1997), 26-27.

.... "Gargantua Harbor: Lake Superior's Secret." *Great Lakes Diving Magazine*. (December, 1994/January, 1995), 16-19.

.... "*George A. Marsh* Mystery, The." *Diver Magazine*. Vol. 24, No. 5 (July-August, 1998), 26-28.

.... "Georgian Bay's *Jane McLeod*." *Diver Magazine*. Vol. 22, No. 5 (July/August, 1996), 24-25.

.... "Georgian Bay's *Mapledawn*." *Diver Magazine*. Vol. 24, No. 9 (January-February, 1999), 16-17.

.... "Ghost Fleet of the St. Clair River." *Diver Magazine*. Vol. 22, No. 3 (May, 1996), 24-25.

.... "Great Lakes! Great Wrecks!" *Skin Diver*. Vo. 51, No. 6 (June, 2002), 52-55.

.... "Great Lakes Queen Turned Widow Maker, A." (The *Merida*). *Wreck Diving Magazine*. Issue 6 (2005), 32-38.

.... "Great Lakes Report Card." *Diver Magazine*. Vol. 24, No. 7 (October-November, 1998), 26-28.

.... "Great Lakes Schooners." *Scuba Diving Magazine*. Vol. 14, No. 9, Issue 132 (October, 2005), 33-38, 96.

.... "Great Lakes Shipwrecks." *Sport Diver*. (July, 2004), 63, 94-96.

.... "Great Lakes' *Sandusky*, The. A Gem of the Great Lakes." *Dive Chronicles*. Vol. 3, Issue 2. (undated), 57-60.

.... "Honeymoon Wreck: Lake Huron's *Joyland*." *Diver Magazine*. Vol. 22, No. 2 (April, 1996), 30-31.

.... "Kingston's Newest Shipwreck: the Tug, *Frontenac*." *Diver Magazine*. Vol. 23, No. 3 (May, 1997), 18-19.

.... "Lake Erie Shipwreck Discovery." *Diver Magazine*. Vol. 15, No. 8 (December, 1989), 18-22.

.... "Lake Erie's Lost Steamer, *Colonial*." *Diver Magazine*. Vol. 20, Vol. 4 (June, 1994), 22-23; modified and printed in *Great Lakes Diving Magazine* (April/May, 1995), 19-21.

.... "Lake Huron Gem: *Emma E. Thompson*." *Diver Magazine*. Vol. 23, No. 4 (June, 1997), 18-19.

.... "Lake Huron's Narrow Island Shipwreck: *B. B. Buckhout*." *Diver Magazine*. Vol. 22, No.

8 (December, 1996), 14-15.

.... "Lake Huron's *Sport*." *Diver Magazine*. Vol. 25, No. 2 (April, 1999), 24-25.

.... "Lake Huron's Tobermory." *Discover Diving*. Vol. 17, No. 2 (April, 1999), 68-72.

.... "Lake Ontario's Lost Team: *Condor* and *Atlasco*." *Diver Magazine*. Vol. 22, No. 7 (November, 1996), 24-25.

.... "Lake Superior's Wreck of the *Batchawana*." *Diver Magazine*. Vol. 22, No. 1 (March, 1996), 26.

.... "Lost with All Hands--the *Olive Branch*." *Diver Magazine*. Vol. 25, No. 3 (May, 1999), 24-25.

.... "*Manola*--Half a Shipwreck." *Diver Magazine*. Vol. 21, No. 9 (February, 1996), 28.

.... "Mystery of the Murray Bay Wreck, The." (The *Bermuda*). *Wreck Diving Magazine*. Issue 7 (2005), 36-41.

.... "*Ocean Wave,* Old Shipwreck, New Controversy, The." *Wreck Diving Magazine*. Issue 8 (2005), 46-53.

.... "Once-Mighty *Metamora,* The." *Diver Magazine*. Vol. 23, No. 5. (July/August, 1997), 18-19.

.... "Power of a Simple Schooner, The" (The *Annie Falconer*). *Wreck Diving Magazine*. Issue 13 (2007), 64-73.

.... "Shipwreck Which Lies in Two Lakes, The" (The *Manola/Mapledawn*). *Wreck Diving Magazine*. Issue 9 (2006), 52-57.

.... "Shipwrecks Threatened by Freshwater Barnacles." *Diving Times*. Vol. 12, No. 2 (Summer, 1989).

.... "Sleepless on the *Seattle*." *Diver Magazine*. Vol. 23, No. 2 (April, 1997), 18-19.

.... "Steamer *Canisteo*." *Diver Magazine*. Vol. 24, No. 6. (September, 1998), 26-28.

.... "Steamer *Myron*, The: Ironies & Tragedies." *Wreck Diving Magazine*. Issue 11 (2006), 48-55.

.... "Steamer *Northern Indiana*, Lake Erie Tragedy." *Diver Magazine*. Vol. 22, No. 9 (February, 1997), 20-22.

.... "Steamer *Philip Minch*." *Diver Magazine*. Vol. 23, No. 9 (February, 1998), 24, 26.

.... "Tale of Two Lake Erie Steamships, A." (The *Lycoming* and the *Colonial*). *Wreck Diving Magazine*. Issue 12 (2007), 38-47.

.... "Tobermory: Shipwreck Waters!" *Great Lakes Cruiser Magazine*. (November, 1995), 6-8.

.... "Tobermory's Forgotten Shipwrecks." *Diver Magazine*. Vol. 22, No. 4 (June, 1996), 24-26

.... "Tragic Wreck on Lake Erie (*Merida*)." *Diver Magazine*. Vol. 24, No. 3 (May, 1998), 26-27.

.... "Three Strikes Against the *Burlington*." *Diver Magazine*. Vol. 21, No. 8 (December, 1995), 26.

.... "...Unless Some Diver Discovers Her." (The *Cornelia B. Windiate*). *Wreck Diving Magazine*. Issue 3. (2004), 30-39, plus cover photo.

.... "Whitefish Point." *Diver Magazine*. Vol. 23, No. 1 (March, 1997), 18-19, 26.

.... "Wreck of the *William H. Wolf*." *Ontario Diver's Digest*. August, 1990.

.... and Joan Forsberg. "Lake Michigan's Showcase Shipwrecks." *Northeast Dive News*. Vol. 3, No. 2 (February, 2007), 22-23.

.... and Sharon Hamilton. "*City of Genoa*." *Diving Times*. Vol. 10, No. 4 (Winter, 1987-88), 14

.... (Photos by Cris Kohl) Pierce Hoover, "Shipwreck City" (Kingston, Ontario). *Sport Diver*. Vol. 9, No. 3 (April, 2001), 56-61.

.... (Photos by Cris Kohl) Kathy Andrews, "Underwater Museums." *Outdoor Illinois*. Vol. 14, No. 6 (June, 2006), 10-13.

Kozmik, Jim. "*Arabia*. Fathom Five's Deep Lady." *Diver Magazine*. Vol. 7, No. 2 (March, 1981), 28-29.

.... "Diving the Flowerpots of Georgian Bay. *Diver Magazine*. Vol. 8, No. 3 (April/May, 1982), 34-35

.... "Stokes Bay for Wreck Diving Enthusiasts." *Diver Magazine*. Vol. 6, No. 2 (March, 1980) 14-15

Kuss, Dan. "Wreck of the *Rappahannock*." *Diver Magazine*. Vol. 16, No. 8 (December, 1990), 19-21.

.... "Lake Superior's Storm to Remember." *Diver Magazine*. Vol. 10, No. 7 (October-November, 1984), 12-14.

Labadie, C. Patrick. "Lake Superior's *Bermuda*." *Skin Diver*. Vol. 39, No. 10 (October, 1990), 12-13, 154-155.

Laughrey, Chris. "Great Lakes Freighter, *Dean Richmond*." *Immersed*. Vol.3, No.3 (Fall, 1998) 46-50

.... "Lake Erie's Mystery Schooner X, *Saint James*." *Advanced Diver Magazine*. Issue 3 (Fall, 1999), 43-46.

Lewis, Steve. "Discovery of Lake Huron's Elusive *Wexford?*" *Advanced Diver Magazine*. Issue 7 (Fall, 2000), 30-31.

Mack, Robert. "Ten Dives in Eastern Ontario." *Diver Magazine*. Vol. 16, No. 3 (May, 1990), 14-15.

Marshall, James R. "Isle Royale's Most Unusual Tragedy, The *George M. Cox*." *Lake Superior Magazine*. (March-April, 1988), 62-64.

.... "Farewell *Mesquite*." *Lake Superior Magazine*. (December-January, 1991), 24-28.

McDaniel, Neil. "Fathom Five's Deep Treasure, the Barque *Arabia*." *Diver Magazine*. Vol. 13, No. 3 (May, 1987), 22-23.

.... Tobermory, Ontario's Wreck Diving Capital." *Diver Mag*. Vol. 12, No. 8 (December,1986), 24-31

.... "Tobermory's Wreck of the Steam Barge, *Wetmore*." *Diver Magazine*. Vol. 13, No. 5 (July/August, 1987), 14-15.

.... "Wreck Diving at the Tip of the Bruce in Canada's First National Marine Park: Fathom Five." *Diver Magazine*. Vol. 15, No. 5 (July/August, 1989), 26-29.

McLaughlin, Bruce. "Lake Huron's Five-Mile-Long Shipwreck (*Daniel J. Morrell*)." *Diver Magazine*. Vol. 10, No. 4 (June, 1984), 32-34.

Moore, Jeff, and David and Mickey Trotter. "Discovery and Exploration of the Steamer, *City of Detroit*." *Wreck Diving Magazine*. Issue 3 (2004), 70-76.

.... "URA Team Discovers the *Frank H. Goodyear*." *Wreck Diving Magazine*. Issue 2 (2004), 8-13.

Mullings, Ken. "The Fate of the *Falconer*." *Diver Magazine*. Vol. 18, No. 6 (September, 1992), 18-19.

Neilsen, Rick. "Hat Trick at Kingston, *George T. Davie*." *Diver Magazine*. Vol. 27, No. 1 (March, 2001), 18-19.

.... "*R. H. Rae,* Lake Ontario." *Diver Magazine*. Vol. 24, No. 1 (March, 1998), 28-29.

.... "Sidewheeler, *Cornwall*." *Diver Magazine*. Vol. 17, No. 4 (June, 1991), 32-33.

Orr, Dan. "The Barque *Arabia:* 1853-1884." *Diver Magazine*. Vol. 11, No. 6 (September, 1985), 30-32.

Orth, Darryl, and Rick Skoryk. "Flagship of the Muskokas." *Diver Magazine*. Vol. 19, No. 9 (February, 1994), 30-32.

Petkovic, Erik. "Deep Survival: Adventure and Terror While Diving the *J. Boland, Jr.*" *Wreck Diving Magazine*. Issue 6 (2005), 68-76.

Remick, Teddy. "Wreck of the *S. S. Wisconsin*." *Skin Diver*. Vol. 14, No. 9 (September, 1965), 55, 66.

Schmitt, Paul J. "Lake Huron's *Sport*." *Skin Diver*. Vol. 38, No. 10 (October, 1989), 16, 58.

Soegtrop, Michael. "Bruce Peninsula National Park." *Diver Magazine*. Vol. 14, No. 2 (April, 1988), 14-17

.... "Deep or Shallow, Tobermory Has It All." *Diver Magazine*. Vol. 19, No. 1 (March, 1993), 26-29

.... "Killarney, Ontario." *Diver Magazine*. Vol. 14, No. 3 (May, 1988), 28-31.

.... "Killarney, Diving Georgian Bay's N. Shore." *Diver Magazine*. Vol. 11, No. 4 (June,1985)20-21

.... "Killarney Wrecks." *Diver Magazine*. Vol. 17, No. 1 (March, 1991), 25-27.

.... "*Mapledawn,* Wreck in Southern Georgian Bay." *Diver Magazine*. Vol. 18, No. 4 (June, 1992), 20-21.

.... "The *Mayflower*." *Diver Magazine*. Vol. 17, No. 3 (May, 1991), 36-37.

.... "Tobermory's Classic Shipwreck, *City of Cleveland*." *Diver Magazine*. Vol. 13, No. 1 (March, 1987), 24-29.

.... "Twice Lost by Fire (*Atlantic*)." *Diver Magazine,* Vol. 7, No. 3 (April-May, 1981), 27-29.

.... with Eva Woloszciuk. "Kingston." *Diver Magazine*. Vol. 7, No. 1 (January/February, 1981), 23-24.

Steinborn, Bill. "Lake Michigan's *Milwaukee*." *Skin Diver*. Vol. 40, No. 5 (May, 1991), 30, 66.

.... "Lake Michigan's *Norland* (sic)." *Skin Diver*. Vol. 39, No. 3 (March, 1990), 8, 56-57.

.... "Lake Superior's *Smith Moore*." *Skin Diver*. Vol. 40, No. 7 (July, 1991), 188-190.

.... "Milwaukee's *Prins Willem V.*" *Skin Diver*. Vol. 39, No. 7 (July, 1990), 16, 18-19.

.... "Wisconsin's *S. S. Wisconsin*." *Skin Diver*. Vol. 40, No. 4 (April, 1991), 24, 182-183.

Swierczewski, John. "Isle Royale, Lake Superior's Shipwreck Mecca." *Diver Magazine*. Vol. 10, No. 2 (March, 1984), 34-35.

Tomasi, Bettey. "Sinking of the *Wisconsin*." *Diver Magazine*. Vol. 7, No. 8 (December, 1981), 26-27, 38-39

Triebe, Richard. "*Milwaukee* Car Ferry." *Skin Diver*. Vol. 36, No. 1 (January, 1987), 110, 113-114, 120.

.... "*S. S. Wisconsin*." *Skin Diver*. Vol. 36, No. 5 (May, 1987), pp. 142-147.

.... "The Burning of the *Niagara,* Gold & Goodies, Sizzle & Sink." *Skin Diver*. Vol. 37, No. 5 (May, 1988), 184-188.

Trotter, David. "The Discovery of the *John McGean*." *Diver Magazine*. Vol. 13, No. 6 (September, 1987), 30-33.

.... with Mickey Trotter. "*Morrell* Encounter, The." (The *Daniel J. Morrell*). *Wreck Diving Magazine*. Issue 11 (2006), 66-76.

Van Heest, Valerie. "The *Hennepin*." *Great Laker*. Vol. 36, No. 1 (July-September, 2007), 76-77.

VandenHazel, Besel. "Lake Nipissing Shipwreck, the Story of the *John Fraser*." *Diver Magazine*. Vol. 8, No. 7 (October/November, 1982), 26-27.

Wachter, Mike, and Darin Cowhardt and Mike King. "*Oxford,* Lake Erie." *Advanced Diver Magazine*. Issue 8 (Winter, 2000), 16-17, 48.

Wachter, Mike and Georgann. "Lake Erie's Schooner *C. B. Benson*." *Advanced Diver Magazine*. Issue 8 (Winter, 2000), 60-61.

Weir, Stephen. "Bottle Mania, The Bottle Collecting Story: Ten Tips for Beginners." *Diver Magazine*. Vol. 16, No. 3 (May, 1990), 30-32.

.... "*City of Sheboygan,* The." *Diver Magazine*. Vol. 26, No. 2 (April, 2000), 18-19.

.... "Double Dip Kingston's *Marsh* and *Comet*." *Diver Magazine*. Vol. 26, No. 7 (October-November, 2000), 8-9.

.... "Dyer Bay." *Diver Magazine*. Vol. 9, No. 2 (March, 1983), 20-22.

.... "Hunting for Bottles." *Diver Magazine*. Vol. 7, No. 6 (September, 1981), 35-39.

Miscellaneous

Ackerman, Paul. Chicago, Illinois: Midwest Explorers League. "Lake Erie Dive Chart" (1998 edition), "Lake Huron Dive Chart" (1999 edition), "Lake Michigan Dive Chart" (1992 edition), "Lake Michigan Shipwrecks, South Shores" (1988 edition), "Lake Ontario Dive Chart" (1990 edition), "Lake Superior Dive Chart" (1990 edition). Updated versions of these popular, large, yellow charts are available from Loves Park Scuba and Snorkel, Loves Park, Illinois.

Collections of Archival Materials available at: Center for Archival Collections, Bowling Green State University, Bowling Green, Ohio (formerly named the Institute for Great Lakes Research): Great Lakes Historical Society, Vermilion, Ohio; Cris Kohl Collection, Great Lakes Shipwrecks and Maritime History; Marine Historical Collection of the Milwaukee Public Library, Milwaukee, Wisconsin; Wisconsin Marine Historical Society, Milwaukee, Wisconsin.

Dive Portal DVD Magazine #2 (November, 2006), John Chatterton and Richie Kohler, subjects of the best-selling book, *Shadow Divers* by Robert Kurson, and hosts of the "Deep Sea Detectives" series on the History Channel; video interview with Cris Kohl.

Explore Michigan's Underwater Preserves 2001. (Booklet) Lexington, Michigan: Out of the Blue Productions, for the Michigan Underwater Preserve Council, Inc., 2001.

Newspapers: 79 different Great Lakes newspapers on microfilm were accessed at 35 different locations, such as state historical libraries and municipal libraries, with dates ranging from 1834 to the present.

Olson, Valerie, ed. *The Goshawk Project, A Reconnaissance Survey of the Great Lake's Oldest Schooner*. February, 1995.

S. S. Regina, 1987 Report to the State of Michigan. Marysville, Michigan: Commercial Diving and Marine Service, 1987.

INDEX

Ships' names are in *italics*

604

ADVERTISERS' INDEX

We thank the following advertisers for their support of, and faith in, this project. Please contact them for all your dive equipment, training, and scuba travel needs, and please mention that you saw their ad in this book:

606

ABOUT THE AUTHOR

CRIS KOHL has spent his life around water, whether crossing the Atlantic Ocean by ship several times, or exploring his beloved Great Lakes in his sailboat or powerboat. After his initial exposure to the underwater world in Bermuda and the Florida Keys in 1974, he became fascinated by the mysteries of the sea, especially with shipwrecks and the stories behind them.

An intrepid explorer, he has studied hundreds of shipwrecks underwater in three oceans and all five of the Great Lakes for more than thirty years. He has a Master's degree in History, specializing in Great Lakes Maritime History, plus a degree in English, important elements which have helped him research, locate, identify and write effectively about Great Lakes shipwrecks. He is also a certified Divemaster and Full Cave Diver, and he has taught Power Squadron courses for safer and more knowledgeable boating.

PHOTO BY CINDY BURNHAM

A prolific writer and prize-winning underwater photographer, Cris Kohl's work has appeared in numerous newspapers such as the *Washington Post* and the Toronto *Globe and Mail,* and he has written hundreds of articles for newsletters and magazines including *Skin Diver, Immersed, Sport Diver, (Rodale's) Scuba Diving, Discover Diving, Cottage Life, Chicago, Outdoor Illinois, Great Lakes Cruiser, Inland Seas* and many others. Canada's *Diver* magazine has published several dozen of his articles, along with many of his photographs, and a Cris Kohl article with photos has appeared in every issue of *Wreck Diving Magazine* since it commenced publication several years ago.

Cris Kohl is a popular speaker who has given over 1,200 shipwreck presentations, most in a multimedia format, to a variety of audiences, from grade school classes and boy scout groups to dive clubs, history conferences, and scuba shows. Large annual shows have included Our World--Underwater (Chicago), Beneath the Sea (New York City), the Sea Rovers Clinic (Boston), Seaspace (Houston), and Underwater Canada (Toronto). He has often been interviewed on radio and television (most recently in "Shipwrecked: Rage of the Great Lakes" on the Discovery Channel, and several episodes of the History Channel's "Deep Sea Detectives") where he is able to promote both the maritime history of the inland seas, and the scuba diving on the best-preserved shipwrecks in the world, which, understandably, are the mainstay of sport scuba diving in the Great Lakes.

He is a Past President of the Underwater Archaeological Soc-iety of Chicago, having served on their Executive Board for several

Cris Kohl, *right,* and Jim Stayer after a deep dive. PHOTO BY PAT STAYER

years. He has also served in the capacity of scuba club President (three years), Executive Board member of the Ontario Underwater Council (nine years), and Executive Board member (six years) of the Windsor branch of Save Ontario Shipwrecks, which he co-founded.

His eleven published books include the popular two-volume *The 100 Best Great Lakes Shipwrecks,* the *Dive Ontario!* books, *Shipwreck Tales of the Great Lakes, TITANIC The Great Lakes Connections,* and *The Great Lakes Diving Guide,* which is the most comprehensive reference work ever published on Great Lakes scuba diving. His Great Lakes shipwreck resources, collected over the past 30 years, are vast.

In 2004, Cris Kohl was inducted into the prestigious Boston Sea Rovers organization, whose list of 127 inductees reads like a *Who's Who* of the diving world.

Raised in Windsor, Ontario, he now resides with his wife, writer, diver, and historian Joan Forsberg, at High Lake, Illinois, just outside Chicago. Besides doing shipwreck presentations together, they recently co-authored the book, *Shipwrecks at Death's Door,* and they produce a quarterly newsletter called "Shipwrecks! ...The Great Lakes and Beyond."